Market, State, and Society in Contemporary Latin America

Edited
by

William C. Smith and Laura Gómez-Mera

WILEY-BLACKWELL

Blackwell Publishing was acquired by John Wiley & Sons in February 2007. Blackwell's publishing program has been merged with Wiley's global Scientific, Technical, and Medical business to form Wiley-Blackwell.

Registered Office
John Wiley & Sons Ltd, The Atrium, Southern Gate, Chichester, West Sussex, PO19 8SQ, United Kingdom

Editorial Offices
350 Main Street, Malden, MA 02148-5020, USA
9600 Garsington Road, Oxford, OX4 2DQ, UK
The Atrium, Southern Gate, Chichester, West Sussex, PO19 8SQ, UK

For details of our global editorial offices, for customer services, and for information about how to apply for permission to reuse the copyright material in this book please see our website at www.wiley.com/wiley-blackwell.

Library of Congress Cataloging-in-Publication Data has been applied for.

A catalogue record for this book is available from the British Library.

Set in 10 on 12 pt Garamond Light by Toppan Best-set Premedia Limited
Printed in the U.S.A. by The Sheridan Press

01—2010

For Enrique José Souto, Isabel Johnson, and Juan V. Gómez Mera

MARKET, STATE, AND SOCIETY IN CONTEMPORARY LATIN AMERICA

Edited
by

William C. Smith and Laura Gómez-Mera
University of Miami

About the Editors and Contributors

Editors

William C. Smith, Professor of International Studies at the University of Miami, received his Ph.D. from Stanford University. He is the author of *Authoritarianism and the Crisis of the Argentine Political Economy* (1991) and the editor of numerous volumes, including *Latin American Democratic Transformations* (2009), *Politics, Social change, and Economic Restructuring in Latin America* (1997), *Latin America and the World-Economy* (1996), *Latin American Political Economy in the Age of Neoliberal Reform* (1994); and *Democracy, Markets and Structural Reform in Contemporary Latin America* (1994). His articles have appeared in *Studies in Comparative International Development, Revista Mexicana de Sociología, Dados, Desarrollo Económico, Political Power and Social Theory, Contexto Internacional, Fuerzas Armadas y Sociedad, Nueva Sociedad, América Latina Hoy,* and the *Latin American Research Review.* Smith is the editor of *Latin American Politics and Society.*

Laura Gómez-Mera, Assistant Professor of International Studies at the University of Miami, received her D.Phil from Oxford University. Her research interests focus on the political economy of conflict and cooperation in regional trade agreements, with particular emphasis on the MERCOSUR. Gómez-Mera's articles have been published in a number of scholarly journals, including *Review of International Political Economy, Latin American Politics and Society, Journal of Latin American Studies,* and *Journal of International Relations and Development.* Gómez-Mera is a member of the editorial board of *Latin American Politics and Society.*

Contributors

Mark Anner, Assistant Professor of Labor Studies and Employment Relations, and Political Science at Penn State University, received his Ph.D. from Cornell University. His research examines labor law enforcement in Latin America, industrial restructuring in the auto and apparel industries, and labor responses to globalization. His scholarly articles have been published in *International Studies Quarterly, Latin American Politics and Society, The European Journal of Industrial Relations, The Latin American Research Review,* and *International Labor and Working-Class History.* He is currently working on a book manuscript that examines new forms of labor solidarity in the global economy.

Moises Arce, Associate Professor of Political Science at the University of Missouri, received his Ph.D. from the University of New Mexico. A native of Peru, he previously taught at Louisiana State University. Arce's primary research interests are in the areas of the politics of market transitions, public opinion, and contentious politics. He is the author of *Market Reform in Society: Post-Crisis Politics and Economic Change in Authoritarian Peru* (2005) and several articles in leading journals of political science. In Peru, he has served as visiting Fulbright lecturer at the Pontificia Universidad Católica del Perú. His current research examines the changing basis of antigovernment mobilizations against economic liberalization in Latin America.

Leslie Elliott Armijo, currently a Visiting Scholar at Portland State University, Oregon, received her Ph.D. from the University of California, Berkeley. She is the editor of several volumes, including *Debating the Global Financial Architecture* (2002) and *Financial Globalization and Democracy in Emerging Markets* (1999). Armijo's articles have been published in *Polity, Democratization, Latin American Research Review, Global Governance, International Studies Review, Comparative Political Studies, World Development, Asian Perspectives, Journal of Democracy, Dados, Revue Tiers Monde, Asian Perspective,* and *Revista de Economia Política,* among others. Her current research focuses on the politics of financial statecraft, regional integration, and emerging market economies.

Sarah Brooks, Associate Professor of Political Science at Ohio State University, received her Ph.D. from Duke University. Her research interests center on the relationship between the state and market in social and economic relations, risk protection and income security. She is the author of *Social Protection and the Market in Latin America: The Transformation of Social Security Institutions* (2009). Her scholarly articles have appeared in *The American Journal of Political Science, The Journal of Politics, World Politics, International Studies Quarterly,* and *Comparative Political Studies.* Her current research includes analyses of sovereign risk and government policy autonomy, path dependence in policy diffusion and the politics of risk protection.

Michelle Dion, Assistant Professor of Political Science at McMaster University in Canada, received her Ph.D. from the University of North Carolina, Chapel Hill. She previously taught at the Sam Nunn School of International Affairs at Georgia Tech. She is the author of *Workers and Welfare: Comparative Institutional Change in Twentieth Century Mexico* (2010). Her scholarly articles have appeared in *PS: Political Science and Politics, International Studies Quarterly, Social Policy and Administration, Social Politics, Política y Gobierno, Mexican Studies, Latin American Politics and Society,* and *Estudios Sociológicos.*

Sebastián Etchemendy, Assistant Professor of Political Science at Torcuato Di Tella University, Argentina, received his Ph D. from the University of California at Berkeley. He has published articles on the political economy of Argentina, Spain and Chile in the journals *Comparative Politics, Comparative Political Studies, Politics and Society, Latin American Politics and Society,* and *Desarrollo Económico.* His current research focuses on alternative modes of economic liberalization and capitalist organization in Ibero-America.

Philippe Faucher, Professor of Political Science at the Université de Montréal, received his Ph.D. from the Ecole des Haustes Éstudes en Sciences Sociales. Faucher has been a visiting professor at the Universidade de Brasília, the École des Hautes Études en Sciences Sociales, and the Université de Lille II. His books include *Le Brésil des militaires* (1981), *Authoritarian Capitalism: Brazil's Contemporary Economic and Political Development* (1981), *Hydro-Québec, la société de l'heure de pointe* (1986), and *Grands projets et innovations technologiques au Canada* (1999). His current research focuses on political institutions in Latin America and the economic integration of North America.

Kathryn Hochstetler, CIGI Chair of Governance in the Americas at the Balsillie School of International Affairs and Professor of Political Science at the University of Waterloo, received her Ph.D. from the University of Minnesota. Previously, she taught in the Political Science departments of the University of New Mexico and Colorado State University. Hochstetler has published widely on topics such as civil society and social movements, environmental politics, and presidentialism. Her books include *Greening Brazil: Environmental Activism in State and Society* (2007), *Advances in International Environmental Politics* (2006), and *Sovereignty, Democracy and Global Civil Society* (2005). Her current research projects examine the role of protest and civil society organizations in South America and Brazilian development choices in the 21st century. Hochstetler is a member of the editorial board of *Latin American Politics and Society*.

Evelyne Huber, Morehead Alumni Professor of Political Science, received her Ph.D. from Yale University. She is the author of *The Politics of Workers' Participation: The Peruvian Approach in Comparative Perspective* (1980), co-author of *Democratic Socialism in Jamaica* (with John D. Stephens, 1986); co-author of *Capitalist Development and Democracy* (with Dietrich Rueschemeyer and John D. Stephens, 1992), co-author of *Development and Crisis of the Welfare State* (with John D. Stephens, 2001). She has also contributed articles to, among others, World Politics, *Latin American Research Review, Comparative Politics, Politics and Society, Comparative Political Studies, Studies in Comparative International Development, American Journal of Sociology*, and *American Sociological Review*. She is currently doing research on comparative social policy.

Fernando Leiva, is currently Associate Professor of Latin American, Caribbean, and U.S. Latino Studies at the University at Albany (SUNY). His most recent book is *Latin American Neostructuralism: The Contradictions of Post-Neoliberal Development* (2008). He is the co-author of several other books, including *Democracy in Chile: The Legacy of September 11, 1973* (2005) and *Democracy and Poverty in Chile: The Limits to Electoral Politics* (1994). His research focuses on how the economic, political, and social restructuring of the past three decades has transformed how power is exercised and contested in the region. His current research focuses on flexible accumulation, inequality and social cohesion, and the Chilean Left after 1990.

Raúl L. Madrid, Associate Professor in the Department of Government at the University of Texas at Austin, received his Ph.D. from Stanford University. He is the author of *Retiring the State: The Politics of Pension Privatization in Latin America and Beyond* (2003). His articles on economic and social policy reform, elections and party systems, and ethnic politics in Latin America have appeared in *Comparative Politics, Electoral Studies, Journal of Latin American Studies, Latin American Politics and Society, Latin American Research Review*, and *World Politics*. He is currently working on a book on the rise of ethnic politics in Latin America, and a co-edited volume on the policies and performance of leftist governments in Latin America. Madrid has served as associate editor of the *Latin American Research Review* and is a member of the editorial board of *Latin American Politics and Society*.

Juliana Martínez Franzoni, Professor at the School of Political Science and researcher at the Institute of Social Research, University of Costa Rica, received her Ph.D. from the University of Pittsburgh. She is currently conducting United Nations-sponsored research projects on Nicaragua and Costa Rica as part of her broader research agenda focusing on labor markets, social policies, families and inequality in Latin America. Martínez Franzoni is the author of *Domesticar la incertidumbre en América Latina: mercado laboral, política social y familias* (2008). Among other journals, her scholarly articles have appeared in *Latin American Politics and Society, Social Policy and Administration, Revista Centroamericana de Ciencias Sociales,* and *Revista Política y Gestión.* Martínez Franzoni is the coauthor (with Diego Sánchez-Ancochea and Maxine Molyneux) of the lead article in a 2009 special issue of *Economy and Society* on "Latin American Capitalism: Economic and Social Policy in Transition."

Marcus André Melo, Professor of Political Science at the Federal University of Pernambuco, received his Ph.D. from Sussex University. He is the author of *Reformas constitucionais no Brasil: instituições políticas e processo decisório* (2002). His articles have appeared in several scholarly journals, including *Political Research Quarterly* and *International Political Science Review.* He has contributed chapters to numerous edited volumes, including *Reinventing Leviathan: The Politics of Administrative Reform in Developing Countries* (2003), edited by Ben Ross Schneider (2003); *Political Institutions, Policy-Making Processes, and Economic Policy* (2007), edited by Mariano Tommasi and Ernesto Stein; and *Democratic Brazil Revisited* (2009), edited by Timothy J. Power and Peter J. Kingstone.

Nicola Phillips is Professor of Political Economy and Director of the Political Economy Institute at the University of Manchester in the UK. Her research interests lie broadly in the political economy of development, and she has published widely in this field. Her present projects focus on questions of migration and development, on the one hand, and on labor in contemporary global production networks, on the other. Phillips has published widely in a variety of scholarly journals, including *Review of International Political Economy, Government and Opposition,* and *Latin American Politics and Society.* Her most recent books are *Development* (co-authored with Anthony Payne, 2009), *The Southern Cone Model: The Political Economy of Regional Capitalist Development in Latin America* (2004) and, as editor, *Globalizing International Political Economy* (2005). Phillips is editor-in-chief of the journal *New Political Economy* and the co-editor of the Lynne Rienner International Political Economy Yearbook series.

Lucio R. Renno, Associate Professor at the Center for the Study of the Americas at the Universidade de Brasília, received his Ph.D. from the University of Pittsburgh. He is co-editor (with Gláucio Ary Dillon Soares) of *Reforma política: lições da história recente* (2006) and is co-editor (with Magna Inácio) of *Legislativo Brasileiro em Perspectiva Comparada* (2009). His articles have been published in the *Journal of Latin American Studies, Revista de Sociologia e Política, Journal of Legislative Studies, Dados-Revista de Ciências Sociais, Electoral Studies, Legislative Studies Quarterly, Revista de Economia Política, American Journal of Political Science, Journal of Politics* and *Comparative Political Studies.*

Anthony P. Spanakos, Assistant Professor of Political Science and Law at Montclair State University, received his Ph.D. from the University of Massachusetts Amherst. Spanakos recently was a Fulbright scholar at Institute for Advanced Studies in Administration (IESA) in Caracas, Venezuela. His research focuses on the politics of economic reforms, democratization, and security. Recent articles have appeared in *Latin American Research Review, Dados-Revista de Ciências Sociais, New Political Science, Comparative Political Studies, Latin American Research Review,* and *Latin American Politics and Society.* He is also the co-editor (with Mauricio A. Font) of *Reforming Brazil* (2004).

Judith Teichman, Professor of Political Science at the University of Toronto, where she received her Ph.D. She is co-author of *Social Democracy in the Global Periphery* (2007), and the author of *The Politics of Freeing Markets in Latin America, Chile, Argentina and Mexico* (2001), *Privatization and Political Change in Mexico* (1995), and *Policymaking in Mexico: From Boom to Crisis* (1988). She has published numerous articles on Latin American politics and policy in scholarly journals such as *Studies in Comparative International Development, Third World Quarterly, Comparative Politics, Mexican Studies, World Development, Global Governance, Latin American Politics and Society*, and *International Political Science Review*. Her current research interests include a comparative study of poverty, inequality and welfare regimes in Mexico, Chile and South Korea and the relationship between inequality, poverty and violence in Mexico.

Marisa von Bülow, Professor of Political Science and Assistant Director of the Instituto de Ciência Política at the Universidade de Brasília, received her Ph.D. from The Johns Hopkins University She is the author of *Pathways to Transnationality: Civil Society Networks and Trade Debates in the Americas* (2010). In addition to contributions to several edited volumes, von Bülow's scholarly articles have appeared in *Latin American Politics and Society, Perfiles Latinoamericanos*, and *Estudios Sociológicos*.

Preface and Acknowledgements

Market, State, and Society in Contemporary Latin America is the second volume in a series making available to a broader public some of the articles originally featured in *Latin American Politics and Society* (LAPS), a peer reviewed journal published under the auspices of the Center for Latin American Studies at the University of Miami. The idea for this project originated during a pleasant lunch with Augusto Varas in Miami accompanied by bottle of Argentine Malbec. At the time with the Ford Foundation in Santiago, Chile, Varas praised the transformation of LAPS into one of the leading venues for research on contemporary Latin America by political scientists, sociologists, historians and scholars from allied disciplines.

Varas suggested publishing a series of volumes on major themes such as democracy, political economy of market reforms, social movements and contentious politics, as well as volumes on countries, including Argentina, Brazil, Chile and Mexico, regularly analyzed in contributions to our journal. We are grateful to Augusto Varas for the inspiration and to the Ford Foundation for it support in launching this project.

We would also like to express our appreciation to Ana Morgenstern, our graduate research assistant, for her invaluable help in preparing the manuscripts, and to Eleanor T. Lahn, the journal's Managing Editor, for her tireless work in preparing the original articles published in LAPSs. Our gratitude goes to the colleagues whose work is collected in this volume who collaborated enthusiastically in revising and updating their chapters. Finally, we want to mention Michael Streeter and Teresa Huang, at Wiley-Blackwell in Boston, for their constant support for LAPS and for this the publication of this volume.

William C. Smith
Editor, *Latin American Politics and Society*
Department of International Studies
Center for Latin American Studies
University of Miami

Laura Gómez-Mera
Editorial Board Member
Department of International Studies
Center for Latin American Studies
University of Miami

Chapter 1

Market, State, and Society in Contemporary Latin American Political Economy

William C. Smith
Laura Gómez-Mera

In the past three decades, the Latin American countries have experienced profound transformations in their strategies of economic development, transformations that have significantly altered the nature and stability of the relationships among states, markets, and societies. The 1982 debt crisis resulted in a dramatic break with the state-centered economic model that had prevailed throughout the region during the post–World War II period. The unprecedented embrace of controversial and contested market-oriented economic reforms (e.g., privatization, trade liberalization, financial deregulation, labor market flexibilization, and so on) coincided in several countries with the equally traumatic and conflictive processes of democratic transition. Important shifts in the international economic and political contexts following the end of the Cold War further conditioned the complex relationship between economic and political liberalization in Latin American countries. In particular, the increasing pace of globalization and the greater magnitude of international economic interdependence posed unexpected challenges to the democratizing governments in Latin America.[1]

Toward the end of the 1990s, the disappointing economic, social, and political consequences of the Washington Consensus policies led to a new reassessment of the balance between states and markets. The actual implications of the recent, so-called shift to the left in several countries in the region, for the nature and quality of democratic governance, remain unclear (Roberts 2007 and forthcoming). Yet as several of the chapters in this volume illustrate, the first decade of the twenty-first century has witnessed greater efforts by social groups at the domestic and transnational levels to play a more central role in restructuring their countries' political economy. Beyond its likely detrimental economic implications, the current global financial crisis will surely have significant impact on social structures while concomitantly redefining the market-state balance.

The shifting nature of relations among markets, states, and social forces has generated significant interest among scholars in several of the social sciences. As one of the leading social science journals in Latin American studies, *Latin American Politics and Society* has served as a forum for this innovative theoretical and empirical research. In an attempt to contribute further to this literature, *Market, State, and Society in Contemporary Latin America* brings together 15 articles originally published in the journal. These studies form a coherent yet diverse body of theoretically and methodologically rigorous work on the political economy of Latin America in the early twenty-first century. Because they address a number of broader debates in comparative politics and international relations, the contributions to this volume will interest not only Latin American specialists but also scholars working on other regions.

The volume is organized in five sections. The chapters in the first section address central theoretical and methodological issues, offering critical assessments of competing approaches to the study of Latin American political economy and alternative perspectives on development policy in the region. The remaining chapters are organized around four central debates in the international and comparative political economy literatures. The second section focuses on the politics of market-oriented reform. The four chapters in this section shed light on the role that international and domestic political factors play in the initiation, design, and sustainability of the neoliberal policy packages introduced in Latin American countries in the 1980s and 1990s. The findings of these studies challenge state-centric political insulation explanations, emphasizing the centrality of state-society bargaining in the introduction and implementation of the reforms.

The chapters in the third section are concerned with another central debate in the field; namely, the extent to which pervasive global economic forces have eroded the autonomy and protective role of the state. These contributions challenge simplistic state declinist arguments, demonstrating the crucial role of varied configurations of domestic political actors and institutions in mediating the effects of globalization on welfare, labor, and pension policy choices. The empirical studies also highlight the various mechanisms through which external constraints interact with domestic material and ideational factors to shape national outcomes. The importance of considering the interaction of external and domestic forces when studying the politics of policymaking in Latin America is further confirmed by the chapters in the fourth section, which focus on macroeconomic policies. The two empirical studies in this section illustrate how domestic interests and institutions condition the nature and shape of macroeconomic policy choices.

The fifth and final section examines issues related to the domestic and international politics of trade, including social movements, distributional interests, and interstate power asymmetries surrounding trade negotiations in the Western Hemisphere.

THEORETICAL DEBATES

In chapter 2, Evelyne Huber and Michelle Dion assess the contribution of studies in the rational choice (RC) tradition to understanding Latin American politics. The authors first provide a brief overview of some of the mainstream contributions to the RC literature, emphasizing the different theoretical assumptions on which each strand of rationalist theory relies. They argue that this research has shed significant light on previously mis-understood political and political economy dynamics in Latin American countries. In their view, however, rational choice approaches do not constitute a major rethinking of established theories, and provide an incomplete and sometimes misleading picture of politics in Latin America. Given their assumptions, moreover, RC analytical frameworks may be particularly applicable to the study of advanced industrial democracies, where states and markets are more highly institutionalized and structural constraints are stable. But RC theories, they contend, are less relevant in the Latin American context. The instability and unpredictability in power relations and the often tenuous quality of formal rules in Latin American countries can render the core assumptions of rational choice models inapplicable or even misleading.

Chapter 3, by Fernando Leiva, focuses on the conceptual and theoretical underpinnings of current policy debates in the region. Building on his previous work (e.g., Leiva, 2005, 2006, 2008), Leiva offers a critical assessment of Latin American neostructuralism, the development framework that emerged in the 1990s to challenge the neoliberal market-reductionist thinking associated with the Washington Consensus. While recognizing the merits of neostructuralism and its narrative of "modernity with solidarity," the author expresses skepticism regarding its ability to present a viable and superior alternative to neoliberalism. According to Leiva, the inherent contradictions in neostructuralism derive from its attempt to distance itself from the core tenets of critical Latin American thinking, a distancing that downplays or marginalizes key power relations from the analysis of the economy and society. As a result, Leiva contends, development strategies and policies informed by neostructuralism, although intended to promote participatory democratic governance and a more robust and autonomous civil society, have paradoxically resulted in a further consolidation of the transnational capitalist model of accumulation.

THE POLITICS OF ECONOMIC REFORM

The chapters in the second section are concerned with the political dynamics surrounding the regionwide shift to market-oriented policies in Latin American countries in the late 1980s and early 1990s. In chapter 4, Leslie Elliott Armijo and Philippe Faucher seek to account for the dramatic, yet at the time unexpected, promarket reorganization of national economic governance in Latin America. Focusing on the four most industrialized countries in the region, Brazil, Mexico, Argentina, and Chile, they assess the empirical validity of a number of theoretical hypotheses regarding the role of international and domestic political factors in explaining the emergence and sustainability of neoliberal economic reforms. Using the quantitative and qualitative evidence from the case studies, the authors extend some of their previous work (Armijo 1999, 2005; Armijo, Faucher, and Dembinska 2006) to argue that economic crisis played an important role in the initiation of reforms. To account more fully for the continuity of neoliberal policies, however, Armijo and Faucher contend that it is necessary to place greater emphasis on proreform shifts in elite opinion and mass preferences that occurred in the four countries. Challenging conventional assumptions in the literature that popular resistance to reforms requires the circumvention of competitive politics, Armijo and Faucher also find that political insulation of executive actors from electoral and partisan pressures was not a necessary condition for successful introduction and sustainability of reforms.

Judith Teichman's study, presented in chapter 5, is also concerned with the international and domestic political factors driving reform in the region. This essay builds on her earlier research (Teichman 1995, 1997, 2001, 2007) that examines the role of the World Bank in promoting and facilitating the spread of market-oriented policies in Latin America. While Armijo and Faucher focus primarily on the role of on interests and institutions, Teichman emphasizes the centrality of ideational and "social learning" processes that result in the decision to enact neoliberal reforms. The cases of Argentina and Mexico are used to illustrate alternative ways that international financial institutions (IFIs) interact with domestic political arrangements to shape the process of economic policymaking. Teichman also discusses the implications of shifting patterns of external involvement for the quality of democracy in the Latin American reform processes. From Teichman's work, recent attempts by the World Bank to promote a more participatory and autonomous reform process can be seen as a positive step toward strengthening democratic governance.

In chapter 6, Sebastián Etchemendy sheds light on the intense processes of political bargaining between state and societal actors underpinning the continuity and sustainability of neoliberal economic reforms. In line with a series of empirical studies on capital, labor, and redistributive coalitions (Etchemendy and Palermo 1998; Etchemendy 2004, 2005; Etchemendy and Collier 2005), Etchemendy challenges political insulation arguments that see the marginalization of societal actors as a prerequisite for successful reform. His comparative analysis of the process of restructuring in the petroleum sector and the privatization of the steel industry in Argentina illustrates how state actors can use compensatory policies to craft reform coalitions that include old populist and interventionist groups. Etchemendy carefully traces how the Menem government in Argentina neutralized the discontent of powerful actors tied to the previous development model by offering them rents in newly created markets and limiting the extent of their exposure to deregulation and liberalization.

In chapter 7, Moisés Arce further challenges state-centric views of the process of economic liberalization. Examining patterns of popular uprising against the privatization of electric service and other revolts against foreign direct investment in Peru, Arce illuminates the changing basis of mobilization against economic liberalization in the region. He highlights the significant shift in the political opportunity structure that took place in Peru with the transition from Fujimori to Toledo, and explains how this shift facilitated societal mobilization in response to reforms. These new forms of collective action were generally geographically territorialized, and they presented concrete local demands that frequently resonated at the national level. This research challenges the heretofore received wisdom that neoliberal reforms contributed to the disarticulation of labor and the popular sectors and the concomitant erosion of their capacity for collective action. Arce's important findings are, instead, consistent with recent "repoliticization" arguments (see Arce and Bellinger 2007; Arce and Rice 2009; Arce forthcoming) that predict greater levels of mobilization in response to the adjustment costs of neoliberal policies.

GLOBALIZATION AND THE STATE: PENSION REFORM, ORGANIZED LABOR AND WELFARE REGIMES

Scholars of international and comparative political economy disagree on how much globalization has eroded the capacity of national governments to protect and provide for all their citizens. An extensive body of literature has examined the complex mechanisms through which global economic forces have influenced welfare policies throughout the region. In chapter 8, Sarah Brooks studies the complex impact of financial globalization on the decisions by Latin American governments to privatize their pension systems. Building upon her previous research (see Brooks 2002, 2005, 2009) in her analysis of the process of pension reform in Argentina and Brazil, Brooks highlights the "double-bind" of globalization. Global financial integration and pressures by IFIs have created strong incentives to privatize pension systems. Simultaneously, however, greater reliance on volatile international capital flows has heightened the risk of punishment in the short term, particularly in the most cash-poor countries.

Chapter 9, by Raúl Madrid, also seeks to illuminate the factors contributing to the recent wave of privatization. Like Brooks, Madrid underscores the role of macroeconomic considerations in the face of increasing financial integration as a key driver of pension privatization. In contrast, however, Madrid places primary emphasis on the role of economic policy ideas and the processes that diffuse these ideas at the regional and national levels (see also Madrid 2002, 2003). According to Madrid, policymakers' belief in the economic efficacy of privatization despite limited concrete evidence can best be understood by considering the mechanisms through which such economic ideas emerged and became dominant in Latin American policy circles. Two factors played a pivotal role in diffusing pension privatization: the success of the Chilean model and the increasing salience of World Bank officials in pension reform. In addition, Madrid demonstrates that there is no clear evidence that the implementation of these ideas resolved domestic financial problems or boosted savings rates, meaning that the objectives of reducing dependence on volatile flows of foreign capital and freeing resources for more productive purposes have not been achieved.

Mark Anner's research reported in Chapter 10 focuses on reforms in labor relations regimes as a central component in the larger challenge of constructing transnational and cross-sector alliances in response to neoliberal restructuring (Anner 2006a, b, 2007; Anner and Evans 2004). In chapter 10, he seeks to account for the observed decline in the power of labor unions in Latin American countries, which has occurred despite favorable legal reforms facilitating collective action. Anner argues that two related factors explain this trend. First, the "union-friendly" policy changes introduced in Latin American countries were insufficient to offset the adverse consequences of neoliberal reforms and the new challenges posed by economic restructuring and the internationalization of production. Second, reforms failed to include effective enforcement mechanisms, resulting in increased labor market flexibility in the face of increasing international competition. To illustrate these arguments, Anner uses the cases of Brazil and El Salvador. Despite extensive and seemingly favorable reforms in labor laws, both countries witnessed a weakening of unions, thus confirming that truly union-friendly labor regimes require deeper structural reforms that take into account the new challenges posed by global economic integration.

Concluding this section in chapter 11, Juliana Martínez Franzoni makes a significant contribution to the understanding of welfare regimes in Latin America (see also Martínez Franzoni 2008). She proposes a theoretical and methodological framework that considers the complex interactions among labor markets, families, and public policy (see also Martínez Franzoni, Molyneux, and Sánchez-Ancochea 2009). Using cluster analysis based on data for 18 countries, she identifies 3 different types of welfare regimes. The first 2 regimes, the protectionist (e.g., Costa Rica) and productivist (e.g., Chile), are statist in orientation. A third, familiarist regime, in contrast, is found in countries (e.g., Ecuador and Nicaragua) where the population's well-being is deeply embedded in family relations, functioning substantially at the margin of the state and the market. By paying closer attention to the interaction of social structures and public policy, Martínez Franzoni's chapter not only advances the academic debate on welfare regimes but also has important policy implications.

POLITICS AND MACROECONOMICS

The chapters in the fourth section shed light on the complex ways that political factors influence countries' macroeconomic choices and performance. These two contributions illustrate how, far from being the outcome of rational, technocratic processes of decision-making, macroeconomic policy choices in Latin American countries have been deeply shaped by domestic political calculations, as well as by the path-dependent nature of political institutions.

Chapter 12, by Anthony Spanakos and Lúcio Renno, seeks to explain macroeconomic policy in Brazil during the Cardoso and Lula administrations. The authors argue that neither political business cycles nor political capital models provide an adequate account of Brazilian macroeconomic choices and outcomes in the period from the mid-1990s to the present (see also Spanakos and McQuerry 2004). Instead, building upon extensive research on political institutions and opportunity structures in Brazil and elsewhere (Renno 2003; Pereira and Renno 2003; Pereira, Power, and Renno 2005; Spanakos and Renno 2009), the authors propose a preference congruence explanation, examining the process of negotiation among candidates, voters, and investors that takes place before elections. They find that when politicians propose policies that appeal to both voters and investors, elections may have a limited effect on economic indicators, such as inflation. But when voter and investor priorities differ significantly, economic indicators are more likely to deteriorate. Apart from illuminating the roots of the financial turbulence that surrounds presidential elections in Brazil, the model proposed by Spanakos and Renno highlights how global financial integration constrains national policymakers in the developing world, making them accountable, to different degrees under varying circumstances, to both domestic constituencies and international actors.

Shifting from monetary to fiscal policy, in chapter 12 Marcus André Melo, a specialist in Brazilian politics and institutions (Melo 2002, 2005; Melo, Pereira, and Figuieredo 2009) turns to Argentina to examine the puzzle presented by that country's very low taxation levels. Melo seeks to explain why the Argentine state has been so unsuccessful in extracting resources from society. He argues that none of the conventional explanations of taxation levels, which tend to focus on economic considerations, political regime type, or tax morale, can account for Argentina's exceptionalism. Instead, Melo advances a "transaction cost politics" explanation that emphasizes the role of political instability in Argentina as the key factor. Using the case of Brazil for comparison, Melo's study of Argentina contends that political institutions that contribute to instability, particularly federalism, reduce the discount rates of policymakers, creating incentives for them to extract resources from society through inflation rather than taxation.

TRADE AND ECONOMIC GOVERNANCE

After decades of following development strategies based on inward-oriented import substitution industrialization, many Latin American countries have vigorously embraced international trade liberalization, enthusiastically participating in multilateral and regional trade integration arrangements. The quite rapid embrace of overlapping trade regimes not only created enormous domestic economic and political conflicts, but also had important implications for the broader international security and political ties among countries in the Western Hemisphere. The chapters included in the fifth and last section of this volume explore different aspects of the international and domestic politics of trade integration in the Americas in the post—Cold War period.

In chapter 14, Nicola Phillips examines the international politics and the interstate power dynamics surrounding the emerging regional economic governance regime in the Americas (see also, among others, Phillips 2003, 2004, 2008). She argues that both the evolution of the Free Trade Area of the Americas (FTAA) and the recent proliferation of bilateral trade agreements have been driven by U.S. power and interests. In response to the deceleration and fragmentation in the process of hemispheric integration, the U.S. government has, since 2003, prioritized bilateral trade negotiations with weaker Latin American partners. In this interpretation, the asymmetrical logic of these processes of bilateral bargaining grants U.S. policymakers special influence over the shape and nature of the emerging agreements. Phillips thus emphasizes how the hegemonic power of the United States manifests itself in the substance of the hemispheric project and the shape of the governance regime associated with it.

Moving away from a focus on interstate relations and regional economic governance, chapter 15, by Marisa von Bülow, examines societal responses to the process of hemispheric trade negotiations in the Americas. Von Bülow's chapter is part of a larger project (see Von Bülow 2003, 2009, forthcoming) probing the constraints on hemispherewide collaboration among labor organizations in the context of free trade negotiations. Since the early 1990s, new national and regional political opportunity structures have made it possible for a diverse constellation of actors throughout the Americas to begin forging new forms of new labor internationalism. Based on social network data and qualitative interviews in Brazil, Mexico, Chile, and the United States, this chapter analyzes the actions taken by labor organizations and how they have changed through time.

In this regard, von Bülow identifies two main sources of contention among the groups engaged in these new forms of transborder political mobilization: frequently conflictive debates about coalition building with other civil society actors and proposals to include a social clause in trade agreements. Von Bülow's research suggests that transnational collective action occurs parallel to the continued relevance of national-level claims and targets, and that this simultaneity represents a real source of challenges, for scholars and labor organizations alike.

In the final chapter, Kathryn Hochstetler builds upon her extensive research on environmental politics and civil society activism in Brazil and throughout Latin America (see, among others, Hochstetler, Clark, and Friedman 2001; Hochstetler and Friedman 2002, 2008; Hochstetler and Keck 2007) to address the relationship between the environment and free trade agreements by focusing on the role of environmental concerns and actors in the Common Market of South America (Mercosur). Examining the process of negotiations over a regional environmental legal instrument, Hochstetler concludes that all aspects of the agreement are weak and have been downgraded in recent years. Nevertheless, her research indicates that at the same time, Mercosur members have made significant progress in national environmental protection legislation. In addition, concurring with von Bülow, Hochstetler points to the emergence of regional coalitions pushing for the inclusion of environmental provisions in hemispheric negotiations over the future of regional trade integration in the Americas.

TOWARD A NEW RESEARCH AGENDA

The chapters in this volume exemplify a variety of theoretical and methodological approaches to studying the complex and changing relations between market, state, and society. Based on careful empirical research, these studies serve to clarify and, in some cases, even challenge the conventional wisdom regarding the main trends in contemporary Latin American political economy. But apart from contributing to existing debates, the participants in this volume have in common the hope that their contributions will call attention to emerging issues and priority areas for future research on the international and comparative political economy of Latin America. Their work makes clear that while we have come quite far in our understanding of the politics of market-oriented economic reform, including the domestic political dynamics surrounding the more recent, post–Washington Consensus policies implemented in many countries in the region, much remains to be done.

For example, relatively limited attention has been paid to the emerging cleavages and distributional conflicts surrounding the "return of the state" in countries such as Argentina, Venezuela, and Bolivia. Similarly, despite growing interest in the geopolitics of oil in the Americas, there has been little research on the international and domestic political economy of alternative sources of energy. We suspect, however, that the growing international focus on climate change is already triggering a far-reaching reconfiguration of the societal landscape, with the strengthening of new business actors and social movements at the transnational and national levels. Future work must place these issues at the forefront of the research agenda.

The contributors to this volume also highlight a number of promising avenues for further research among scholars of international relations and international political economy. Of paramount importance is to analyze in greater depth the economic and political implications of the recent global financial crisis for the countries in the Western Hemisphere. In this regard, the failure of the project of hemispheric trade integration raises new questions about the nature and shape of North-South relations and governance in the post-FTAA, post-Bush era. Furthermore, a better understanding of the international relations of the Americas requires paying closer attention to the recent ascendancy of Brazil in the region. The Lula government's attempts to play a more salient role at the international and regional levels have had important, but still unclear, implications for the stability and balance of power in the Western Hemisphere.

We hope the conceptual tools and methodological techniques exemplified by the work published in *Latin American Politics and Society,* some of which is featured in the chapters of *Market, State, and Society,* will advance the study of these increasingly relevant but still underexamined issues.

NOTE

1 For one of the authors' views on this period, see Acuña and Smith 1994; Smith and Korzeniewicz 1997; and Korzeniewicz and Smith 2000.

REFERENCES

Acuña, Carlos, and William C. Smith. 1994. The Political Economy of Structural Adjustment: The Logic of Support and Opposition to Neoliberal Reform. In *Latin American Political Economy in the Age of Neoliberal Reform: Theoretical and Comparative Perspectives,* ed. Smith, Acuña, and Eduardo A. Gamarra. New Brunswick/Coral Gables: Transaction/North-South Center. 17–66.

Anner, Mark. 2006a. Labor and the Challenge of Cross-Border, Cross-Sector Alliances. In *Latin America After Neoliberalism: Turning the Tide in the 21st Century?* ed. Eric Hershberg and Fred Rosen. New York: New Press. 298–315.

——. 2006b. The Paradox of Labour Transnationalism: Trade Union Campaigns for Labor Standards in International Institutions. In *The Future of Organised Labour: Global Perspectives,* ed. Craig Phelan. Bern: Peter Lang. 63–90.

——. 2007. Forging New Labor Activism in Global Commodity Chains in Latin America. *International Labor and Working-Class History* 72, 1: 18–41.

Anner, Mark, and Peter Evans. 2004. Building Bridges Across a Double-Divide: Alliances Between U.S. and Latin American Labor and NGOs. *Development in Practice* 14, 1–2 (February): 34–47.

Arce, Moisés. Forthcoming. Parties and Social Protest in Latin America's Neoliberal Era. *Party Politics.*

Arce, Moisés, and Paul T. Bellinger, Jr. 2007. Low-Intensity Democracy Revisited: The Effects of Economic Liberalization on Political Activity in Latin America. *World Politics* 60, 1 (October): 97–121.

Arce, Moisés, and Roberta Rice. 2009. Societal Protest in Post-stabilization Bolivia. *Latin American Research Review* 44, 1: 88–101.

Armijo, Leslie Elliot. 1999. Balance Sheet or Ballot Box? Incentives to Privatize in Emerging Democracies. In *Markets and Democracy in Latin America: Conflict or Convergence?* ed. Philip Oxhorn and Pamela K. Starr. Boulder: Lynne Rienner. 161–202.

——. 2005. Who's Afraid of Economic Populism? Counter-Intuitive Observations on Democracy and Brazilian Political Economy. In *Statecrafting Monetary Reform: Democracy and Financial Order in Brazil,* ed. Lourdes Sola and Laurence Whitehead. Oxford: Centre for Brazilian Studies, Oxford University.

Armijo, Leslie Elliott, Philippe Faucher, and Magdalena Dembinska. 2006. Compared to What? Assessing Brazil's Political Institutions. *Comparative Political Studies* 39, 6 (August): 759–86.

Brooks, Sarah. 2002. Social Protection and Economic Integration: The Politics of Pension Reform in an Era of Capital Mobility. *Comparative Political Studies* 35, 5: 491–525.

———. 2005. Interdependent and Domestic Foundations of Policy Change: The Diffusion of Pension Privatization Around the World. *International Studies Quarterly* 49, 2: 273–94.

———. 2009. *Social Protection and the Market in Latin America: The Transformation of Social Security Institutions.* New York: Cambridge University Press.

Etchemendy, Sebastián. 2004. Repression, Inclusion and Exclusion: Government-Union Relations and Patterns of Labor Reform in Liberalizing Economies. *Comparative Politics* 36 (April): 273–290.

———. 2005. Old Actors in New Markets: The Transformation of the Populist/Industrial Coalition in Argentina, 1989–2000. In *Argentine Democracy: The Politics of Institutional Weakness*, ed. Victoria Murillo and Steven Levitsky. University Park: Pennsylvania State University Press: 62–87.

Etchemendy, Sebastián, and Ruth Berins Collier. 2007. Down But Not Out: Union Resurgence and Segmented Neocorporatism in Argentina: 2003–2007. *Politics and Society* 35, 3 (September): 363–401.

Etchemendy, Sebastián, and Vicente Palermo. 1998. Conflicto y concertación. Gobierno, congreso y organizaciones de interés en la reforma laboral del primer gobierno de Menem. *Desarrollo Económico* 37, 148: 559–90.

Hochstetler, Kathryn, and Elisabeth Jay Friedman. 2002. Assessing the "Third Transition" in Latin American Democratization: Civil Society in Brazil and Argentina. *Comparative Politics* 35, 1: 21–42.

———. 2008. Can Civil Society Organizations Solve the Crisis of Partisan Representation in Latin America? *Latin American Politics and Society* 50, 2 (Summer): 1–32.

Hochstetler, Kathryn, and Margaret E. Keck. 2007. *Greening Brazil: Environmental Activism in State and Society.* Durham: Duke University Press.

Hochstetler, Kathryn, Ann Marie Clark, and Elisabeth Jay Friedman. 2001. Sovereign Limits and Regional Opportunities for Global Civil Society in Latin America. *Latin American Research Review* 36, 3: 7–35.

Korzeniewicz, Roberto Patricio, and William C. Smith. 2000. Poverty, Inequality, and Growth in Latin America: Searching for the High Road to Globalization. *Latin American Research Review* 35, 3 (October): 7–54.

Leiva, Fernando Ignacio. 2005. From Pinochet's State Terrorism to the Politics of Participation. In *Democracy in Chile: The Legacy of September 11, 1973*, ed. Silvia Nagy-Zekmi and Leiva. Brighton: Sussex Academic Press.

———. 2006. Neoliberal and Neostructuralist Perspectives on Labor Flexibility, Poverty and Inequality: A Critical Appraisal. *New Political Economy* 11, 3: 337–59.

———. 2008. *Latin American Neostructuralism: The Contradictions of Post-Neoliberal Development.* Minneapolis: University of Minnesota Press.

Leoni, Eduardo, Carlos Pereira, and Lúcio Renno. 2004. Political Survival Strategies: Political Career Decisions in the Brazilian Chamber of Deputies. *Journal of Latin American Studies* 36, 1: 109–30.

Madrid, Raúl L. 2002. The Politics and Economics of Pension Privatization in Latin America. *Latin American Research Review* 37, 2: 159–82.

———. 2003. *Retiring the State: The Politics of Pension Privatization in Latin America and Beyond.* Stanford: Stanford University Press.

Martínez Franzoni, Juliana. 2008. *Domesticar la incertidumbre en América Latina: mercado laboral, política social y familias.* San José: Editorial de la Universidad de Costa Rica.

Martínez Franzoni, Juliana, Maxine Molyneux, and Diego Sánchez-Ancochea. 2009. Latin American Capitalism: Economic and Social Policy in Transition. *Economy and Society* 38, 1 (February): 1–16.

Melo, Marcus André. 2002. *Reformas constitucionais no Brasil: instituições políticas e processo decisório.* Rio de Janeiro: Editora Revan.

——. 2005. O sucesso inesperado das reformas de segunda geração: federalismo, reformas constitucionais e política social. *Dados* 48, 4: 845–90.

Melo, Marcus André, Carlos Pereira, and Carlos Maurício Figueiredo. 2009. Political and Institutional Checks on Corruption: Explaining the Performance of Brazilian Audit Institutions. *Comparative Political Studies* 42, 9: 1217–44.

Pereira, Carlos, and Lúcio Renno. 2003. Successful Re-election Strategies in Brazil: The Electoral Impact of Distinct Institutional Incentives. *Electoral Studies* 22, 3: 425–48.

Pereira, Carlos, Timothy J. Power, and Lúcio Renno. 2005. Under What Conditions Do Presidents Resort to Decree Power: Theory and Evidence from the Brazilian Case. *Journal of Politics* 67: 178–200.

Phillips, Nicola. 2003. Hemispheric Integration and Subregionalism in the Americas. *International Affairs* 79, 2: 257–79.

——. 2004. *The Southern Cone Model: The Political Economy of Regional Capitalist Development in Latin America*. London: Routledge.

——. 2008. The Politics of Trade and the Limits to U.S. Power in the Americas. In *Responding to Globalization: The Political Economy of Regional Integration in the Americas*, ed. Diego Sánchez-Ancochea and Kenneth Shadlen. London: Palgrave. 147–70.

Renno, Lúcio R. 2003. Political Opportunity Structures and Engagement in Civil Society Organizations: a Comparative Study on Latin America. *Revista de Sociologia e Politica* 21 (November): 71–82.

Roberts, Kenneth M. 2007. Repoliticizing Latin America: The Revival of Populist and Leftist Alternatives. *Woodrow Wilson Center Update on the Americas* (November): 1–11.

——. Forthcoming. *Changing Course: Parties, Populism, and Political Representation in Latin America's Neoliberal Era*. Cambridge: Cambridge University Press.

Spanakos, Anthony Peter, and Elizabeth McQuerry. 2004. Political Economy in a Time of Capital Outflows: Theory, Historical Analysis, and Prescriptions. *Latin American Research Review* 39, 2: 258–74.

Spanakos, Anthony Peter, and Lúcio R. Renno. 2009. Speak Clearly and Carry a Big Stock of Dollar Reserves: Sovereign Risk, Ideology, and Presidential Elections in Argentina, Brazil, Mexico, and Venezuela. *Comparative Political Studies* 42: 1292–1316.

Smith, William C., and Roberto Patricio Korzeniewicz. 1997. Latin America and the Second Great Transformation. In *Politics, Social Change, and Economic Restructuring in Latin America*, ed. Smith and Korzeniewicz. Boulder: Lynne Rienner. 1–20.

Teichman, Judith A. 1995. *Privatization and Political Change in Mexico*. Pittsburgh: University of Pittsburgh Press.

——. 1997. Mexico and Argentina: Economic Reform and Technocratic Decision Making. *Studies in Comparative International Development* 32, 1 (Spring): 31–55.

——. 2001. *The Politics of Freeing Markets in Latin America: Chile, Argentina, and Mexico*. Chapel Hill: University of North Carolina Press.

——. 2007. Multilateral Lending Institutions and Transnational Policy Networks in Mexico and Chile. *Global Governance* 13, 4: 557–73.

Von Bülow, Marisa. 2003. Medio ambiente y la participación de la sociedad civil. In *El ALCA y las Cumbres de las Américas: ¿una nueva relación público-privada?* Buenos Aires: Editorial Biblos/FLACSO. 77–103.

——. 2009. Atores não-estatais e os estudos internacionais na América Latina: do "casillero vacío" às redes transnacionais. In *Relaciones internacionales: los nuevos horizontes*. Quito: FLACSO. 135–67.

——. Forthcoming. *Pathways to Transnationality: Civil Society Networks and Trade Debates in the Americas*. New York: Cambridge University Press.

Chapter 2

Revolution or Contribution? Rational Choice Approaches in the Study of Latin American Politics

Evelyne Huber
Michelle Dion

The debate about the merits of the rational choice approach to the study of comparative politics relative to other theoretical approaches has been intense and at times contentious. Much of this debate has taken place at a general level, centering on the plausibility of assumptions regarding actors' utilities and the strategic nature of human behavior, and on the desirability and possibility of universal or bounded explanations of political processes. An assessment of the concrete contributions of the approach to a specific subfield of comparative politics seems useful to push the debate forward.

This article aims to assess the contributions that scholarly studies in the rational choice (RC) tradition have made to our understanding of Latin American politics, as well as their limitations. Our summary assessment, based on the application of our criteria for evaluation, is that works in the RC tradition have not forced a major rethinking of established wisdom about Latin American politics, nor have they filled major gaps in our understanding. They have, nevertheless, enriched our understanding of phenomena that before were only partially understood. We will argue that the RC approach works best for narrow questions where power relations and structural constraints are stable and taken as a given, whereas its essential assumptions become untenable in questions for which shifting power relations among social groups and the state over time are crucial.

To make this evaluation, we need first to identify what kinds of work belong to the RC approach proper or to a related category of work in the institutionalist tradition. Then we need to establish criteria for evaluating scholarly contributions that can apply to RC and other theoretical traditions alike.

It would be impossible to offer a comprehensive review of work in the RC tradition on Latin America within the scope of this article, so we have chosen a group of studies on the basis of their reputation and representativeness. We discuss some works that have attracted much attention; mostly books from the first wave of publications and a few important works published later. We group these works according to their use of RC assumptions as heuristic devices only, basic game theoretic models, and formal mathematical models. We also discuss some of the major works in the institutionalist tradition. Whereas our sample may fall short of statistical representativeness, we are confident that we have not overlooked any influential contributions that might have changed our assessment.

CLASSIFYING RATIONAL CHOICE STUDIES

In the most restricted sense, the rational choice approach is the application of microeconomic theoretical assumptions to the study of politics, or the use of economic models for the study of nonmarket phenomena. Though Ordeshook argues against the case for economic imperialism, he admits that "the paradigm's spread is a one-way street of fundamental theoretical ideas from economics to political science" (1990, 26). Supporters of this notion of RC assert that their aim is to develop universal explanations of behavior. They further declare that theirs is the most (if not the only) scientific approach to the study of politics, because RC theory is deductive and methodologically rigorous; this makes it possible to generalize results that follow from analytical propositions derived from axioms.

Fiorina, in contrast, adopts an extremely loose definition: "the only thing that all RC people would agree upon is that their explanations presume that individuals behave purposively. Beyond that, every manner of disagreement-theoretical, substantive, methodological-can be found" (1996, 87). Searching for a middle ground, three essential assumptions seem reasonable for defining the RC approach (Green and Shapiro 1994, 14–17).

- An actor's behavior is governed by utility maximization; that is, the actor will choose means that are efficient and effective for achieving goals.
- An actor's preferences are structured; that is, the preferences must be capable of being rank-ordered, and the orderings must be transitive. In standard RC language, this means that "preferences are complete, transitive, and fixed."
- The analysis of collective outcomes focuses on individuals or unitary actors; that is, individual preference orderings and strategic choices are the basic theoretical building blocks.[1]

Rational choice analysts working within these parameters disagree on further assumptions, most notably on those about human goals or motives and on the issue of the universality of RC explanations. The distinction between "thin" and "thick" rationality has gained wide currency (Ferejohn 1991). Thin rationality simply denotes the strategic pursuit of stable and ordered preferences-preferences of any kind—whether selfish or self-destructive or not. Thick rationality assumes that actors have specific preferences, in practice mostly material self-interest or the preservation or augmentation of power; for politicians, typically perpetuation in office. Whereas thin rationality clearly can be applied in the study of a much wider range of human behavior than thick rationality, it brings analyses dangerously close to being tautological, unless the analyst uses methodological tools to identify preferences independent of the behavior being explained.

The problem is that ex ante specification of preferences in this manner is extremely difficult. In practice, post hoc specification of preferences is a frequent procedure, and often the preferences and their ordering are inferred from observed behavior, in clearly circular fashion. In thick rationality, of course, the key issue is how realistic the assumptions about the specific preferences are. Psychologists as well as political scientists have taken issue with the assumption that material self-interest is an all-pervasive motive (Lewin 1991). Psychologists, moreover, have questioned the entire RC approach, whether based on thick or thin rationality, by challenging the assumption that behavior is necessarily instrumental to goal attainment (see, for example, Abelson 1996). Finally, cognitive psychologists and political scientists have shown that decision-making in complex situations takes place under bounded rationality, with decision-makers working under insurmountable limitations on information processing and thus resorting to inferential shortcuts, or cognitive heuristics (Gilovich, Griffin, and Kahneman 2002; Weyland 2006).

All three of these criticisms are supported by much evidence, and they greatly damage RC claims of superiority based on a presumed universalism. Those who insist on thick rationality certainly have to make the obvious concession that assumptions about material self-interest or the quest for power work better in some contexts than in others. As to the criticism of instrumentalism as the basic principle of behavior, Munck (2001) argues that RC defenders offer two types of responses. The purist response is to ignore evidence from cognitive psychology and to defend the RC model of behavior on the grounds that the only thing that matters is the model's capacity to generate predictions. The pragmatist response is to argue that the model works well in some contexts but maybe not in others. The defense, however, just like the concession, implies abandoning the claim that the RC approach provides universal explanations and admitting the need to specify the domain of applicability.

For the purposes of this essay, we will use inclusive criteria and take into account RC analyses based on assumptions of thin as well as thick rationality, and those claiming universality as well as those recognizing restricted domains.

Another important methodological divide in the RC camp is between those who use formal models and those who use RC assumptions as heuristic tools, generally labeled "hard" versus "soft" RC. The hard RC approach uses mathematical tools to solve the formal models and make predictions. In practice the models are based mostly on game theoretic models, but other types, such as decision theoretic models, are also used (see, for example, Gates and Humes 2000). The soft variety, by contrast, utilizes assumptions about the relevant actors, their goals, and their strategies as key tools for empirical analyses.

The formal models typically make highly restrictive assumptions about reality. But if the assumptions are transparent, the benefits of being able to derive predictions from a formal model may outweigh the costs of such abstractions. The dividing line between "hard" and "soft" is not entirely clear or universally agreed on, which is why in this analysis we use the intermediate category "application of basic game theoretic models." We include in this category two-player matrix games and game trees with simple payoffs, such as the familiar matrix games of prisoner's dilemma and chicken.

We should also clarify the relationship between RC and public choice theory, game theory, positive and modern political economy, and the new institutionalism. Again, there is no general agreement on these issues, and loose use of terminology abounds. We are in no way attempting a comprehensive survey of the multitude of ways these terms are used, but simply selecting working definitions that make it possible to include or exclude specific pieces of research in the category of the RC approach.

Public choice theory, or the public choice approach, can be usefully defined as a subset of the RC approach, characterized by the most stringent assumptions. It can be defined as the application of economic models to the study of public decisionmaking, based on assumptions of thick rationality (Friedman 1996a, 2), or "the study of nonmarket economics and the extension of the methodology of microeconomics to nonmarket settings" (Popkin 1988, 245). Bates makes a further distinction between collective choice and public choice theory, arguing that the collective choice literature is based on the application of rational choice analysis to nonmarket institutions, whereas the public choice literature remains more closely tied to conventional economics (Bates 1987, 181, n. 59). Game theory can be seen as another subset of the RC approach, defined by its focus on the interdependence of strategic actors (Collier and Norden 1992; Immergut 1998, 12; Munck 2001).

Positive political economy is defined by Alt and Shepsle as the study of rational decisions in a context of political and economic institutions (1990, 2). It treats differences among institutions as both dependent and independent variables explaining political and economic outcomes. This definition puts the emphasis on institutional characteristics rather than on individuals' strategic behavior, though the underlying assumption is that institutions have certain effects because individuals act strategically.

Frieden et al. (2000, xi) propose yet another version: modern political economy. They also assume that actors rationally pursue their interests. They propose three defining criteria: a distinction between normative and positive considerations, emphasis on microeconomic and macroeconomic constraints, and emphasis on political institutions and political power.

The new institutionalism is perhaps the least well defined of these various schools of thought. As Immergut notes, no fewer than three quite distinct branches of scholarship have adopted this label: rational choice, organization theory, and historical institutionalism (1998, 5). Yet not all research in the RC tradition of the new institutionalism fully meets the third criterion for the RC approach laid out here. Some of the research in this school does what positive political economy does: it investigates the impact of institutions on political outcomes. The analysis assumes that actors act strategically, but the focus is not necessarily on actors' behavior. Instead, actors' strategic calculations are implicit, and the analysis focuses directly on the relationship between institutional rules and political outcomes, such as the relationship between electoral rules and party systems.

Thus, public choice and game theoretic research should obviously be included in the mainstream category of actor-centered RC approaches, whereas positive political economy, modern political economy, and new institutionalist works should be included only if their analysis focuses on the strategic behavior of individuals or unitary actors.

CRITERIA FOR EVALUATION

When specific works or entire bodies of political science research are evaluated, the highest approbation generally goes to research that generates a new theoretical approach to challenge established wisdoms and forces the scientific community to see empirical regularities in a new way.[2] The second-highest ranking goes to research that generates a new theoretical approach to explain phenomena for which there is no conventional scientific explanation, either because the phenomena were not previously investigated, were not well understood, or perhaps are completely new. Third comes the elaboration, adaptation, and possibly slight modification of a new theoretical approach through its application to any kind of phenomena. All three achievements require compelling empirical evidence to demonstrate the usefulness of the new theoretical approach.

A fourth level of value is the stimulation of new research agendas, the generation of new theoretical ideas that are promising for the empirical investigation of important questions. A fifth is the confirmation of the explanatory power of a given theoretical approach through its application to empirical analyses of new cases.

The common element in these criteria is that any theoretical approach has to be judged by how well it holds up empirically. Its explanatory power has to be greater than that of other approaches; it has to help us better understand the complicated world of politics. Internal logical consistency is a necessary but not sufficient condition. Thus, the fundamental question to ask of any piece of research, and of the research accumulated within any given approach, is whether it helps us understand empirical phenomena that were previously misunderstood or simply not understood.

Expectations for Contributions of RC Approaches

Given the assumptions characterizing the RC approach, we would expect the approach to prove most useful in explaining

- Behavior in which material interests are very clearly at stake and for which the stakes are high
- The behavior of individuals or unitary actors
- Behavior in contexts where institutions are well consolidated and the actors well known

Geddes, for instance, contends that "rational choice arguments work best in situations in which actors can identify other actors and know their goals, and in which the rules that govern interactions among actors are precise and known to all" (1995, 87).[3] She further states, rational actor assumptions are likely to be plausible in regimes in which the rules governing survival and advancement are clear to both participants and observers and relatively unchanging, but not in regimes in which many decisions are made in secret by a small group of individuals and in which rules and rulers change frequently, radically, and unpredictably. (1995, 88)

There is a tension here between the assumptions of well-consolidated institutions, well-constituted and known unitary actors, and stable rules as determinants of behavior, on the one hand, and the emphasis on "possibilism" as an advantage of RC analysis (Collier and Norden 1992) and its use to analyze situations of high uncertainty in transitions from authoritarian rule (Przeworski 1991; Crescenzi 1999) on the other hand. O'Donnell and Schmitter argue that in transitions from authoritarian rule, in many cases and around many themes, it is almost impossible to specify ex ante which classes, sectors, institutions, and other groups will take what role, opt for which issues, or support what alternative. Indeed, it may be that almost all one can say is that, during crucial moments and choices of the transition, most-if not all-of those "standard" actors are likely to be divided and hesitant about their interests and ideals and, hence, incapable of coherent collective action. (1986, 4)

Accordingly, their approach is actor-centered, focusing on the interaction between hard-liners and soft-liners in the authoritarian regime and the opposition; but they do not follow the typical RC procedure of specifying the actors' preferences, constraints, and options and analyzing their strategic interactions. Instead, they attempt to map typical dilemmas, choices, and processes in an uncharted territory in an inductive way.

In contrast to O'Donnell and Schmitter's approach, Przeworski (1991) did develop a game theoretic model, which has become influential in the literature on transitions; but its explanatory power has not been assessed systematically in empirical analyses. We are skeptical about the model's explanatory power, and we side with those who argue that the RC approach generally performs best in situations of strong institutions and rule-bound behavior.

A partial exception to this general rule are attempts to make the uncertainty inherent in transitions or in other situations of poorly defined rules an explicit part of a formal model that predicts different outcomes for different choices of actors. Crescenzi (1999) does this and tests his model. Gates and Humes (2000, 113–39) expand Przeworski's model of liberalization by specifying the payoffs of civil society and incorporating conditions of incomplete information, but they do not test it. Even these attempts, however, cannot deal with changing preferences of actors and changing power relations among actors during the course of the game; that is, the transition.[4]

WORK ON LATIN AMERICA IN THE MAINSTREAM ACTOR-CENTERED RC TRADITION

The great majority of work on Latin America that takes an actor-centered, RC approach is of the soft variety. These authors make assumptions about the relevant actors, their goals, and their strategies as a heuristic device that drives their empirical analyses. For the most part they do not use any formal models or, if they do, these are only basic game theoretic models. Work with extended formal models and mathematical solutions is less frequent and more recent; it typically deals with elections and legislatures, subjects for which formal models have been widely used in studying U.S. politics.

We will discuss the model-free soft variety of RC works first, then the works with basic game theoretic models, and finally a couple of examples of the hard, mathematical variety.

Works Using RC Assumptions as Heuristic Tools

In one of the earliest applications of an actor-centered analysis in the RC tradition to Latin America, Ames (1987) examines the ways politicians manipulate public spending to maintain political office. Ames assumes thick rationality (namely, the desire to remain in office) and attempts to explain politicians' survival strategies during political crises, which he defines as the years immediately before and after elections and the year following a military coup.

By combining cross-national qualitative and statistical analyses with careful case studies of the Brazilian legislature (1947–64) and the military regime (1964–84), Ames assembles an impressive amount of empirical evidence to support the argument that legislative and executive politicians manipulate public expenditures to generate public support. Not only do politicians increase overall expenditures in times of crisis, according to Ames, but they also increase particular types of expenditures, sometimes at the expense of others, to generate support and build coalitions among particular sectoral, class, or regional interests.

While Ames does not employ formal models of strategic behavior on the part of politicians, the approach still emphasizes the behavior of individual actors to maximize their utility, which in this case is tenure in office. In contrast to actor-centered RC works of the 1990s, such as Geddes (1994), Hunter (1997), and his own later work (2001), which explicitly include institutional constraints on politicians' strategies, Ames 1987 rarely addresses the limitations that constitutional design or electoral rules place on actors' behavior. Instead, such constraints consist of contextual factors, like political rivals, public policy legacies, or the economic climate (Ames 1987, 221–24). The book's contribution is to further our understanding of the trade-offs involved when politicians spend strategically to generate political support in times of crisis, and to provide a wealth of empirical evidence to support the intuitive notion that politicians use the available resources to prolong their terms in office or political influence.

Ames 2001 is also an empirically rich study with insightful interpretations of the pathologies of Brazilian politics. Its central argument is that the immobilism of Brazil's political institutions, specifically their inability to pass major national legislation, results from the combination of majority-constraining federalism, presidentialism, and electoral rules, mainly the open PR system with candidate selection at the state level and provisions for reelection of deputies.[5] The author explicitly classifies his book as soft RC, stating that he adopts "the perspective of rational choice (RC) theorists, with a bit of historical institutionalism mixed in" (2001, 9). The bulk of the data consists of municipal election returns, budgetary amendments offered by individual deputies, ministers' distribution of grants to individual municipalities, and roll-call votes in the Chamber of Deputies. The quantitative analyses of campaign strategies and of legislative behavior rely heavily on the spatial distribution of votes and on the assumptions that deputies want to maximize their own electoral strength and that most voters want, above all, particularistic benefits.

Ames also states explicitly, however, that politicians' motivations are variable and that "simply 'assumed' preferences would be too limiting" (2001, 12), and he notes that the "primacy of reelection assumption" is not applicable to Brazil (207). He implicitly recognizes, moreover, the uncomfortable reality that deputies and voters of Brazil's PT Party, who, after all, face the same institutional constraints, seem to act differently. Indeed, Ames clearly goes beyond the confines of the RC approach by supplementing deductive theorizing with inductive analyses, and the construction of quantitative models based on RC assumptions with comparative case studies of legislative decisions and of politics in two sets of states in which historical legacies and path dependency are shown to be important. These exercises in trespassing clearly enrich the research and interpretation in this work.[6]

Hunter (1997) uses actor-centered RC analysis as a point of departure to argue that despite predictions to the contrary, Brazilian politicians after the democratic transition began to act against the interests of the Brazilian military and to limit its political pre-rogatives. They did so because the military's interests conflicted with their own oppor-tunity to gain wide electoral support; and they succeeded, particularly when they enjoyed strong popular support.

Hunter does not develop a formal model but simply builds on the reasonable assumption that civilian politicians prefer to limit the budget and the policy influence of the military to free up resources to distribute to their supporters and to satisfy popular demands to restrict the military's political influence. Through case studies of labor legisla-tion, military budget allocations, and civilian development of the Amazon, Hunter dem-onstrates that civilian politicians in both the executive and legislative branches repeatedly did act in this way. Consequently, Hunter contributes to our understanding of the cir-cumstances and the process by which civilian leaders have been able to curb the military's political role, which previous theories of democratic transition and consolidation had not explicitly addressed.

Boylan (1998) uses RC assumptions to explain why and when authoritarian regimes established autonomous central banks. She criticizes the signaling model that is supposed to explain reforms that increase the autonomy of central banks as insufficient and patently wrong for the Chilean case. This model, as developed, for example, by Maxfield (1997), is based on the presumed intention of politicians to attract foreign capital and the expected responsiveness of foreign investors. Boylan develops a competing explanation for the timing of reform and the degree of autonomy granted to the central bank by an outgoing authoritarian regime. She postulates that the preference of the authoritarian regime is to tie the hands of its democratic successors with regard to monetary policy. The greater the discrepancy between the regime's preferences and those of the demo-cratic opposition, and the greater the strength of the incoming opposition, the greater the likelihood of reform and the degree of autonomy granted to the central bank. For significant reform to take place, both threats are necessary.

Boylan applies this explanation to the Chilean case, and indeed, it explains both the timing and the depth of the reform better than the signaling model. What this example underscores is that the quality of RC explanations depends very heavily on the correct specification of the preferences of the actors in question, and that the domains for which the explanation is valid are confined to situations in which the economic and political context structure preferences in a given way.

Works Using Simple Game Theoretic Models

Geddes (1994) derives an explanation and a game theoretic model of reform from a detailed case study of reform attempts by executives and reform parties in Brazil. She argues that administrative reform is a public good seldom provided by politicians because the principal-agent problem leads politicians to pursue their own interests (reelection) instead of those of their constituents (including reform).

Political entrepreneurs, including some executives, will supply the public good only when they anticipate receiving an individual reward (Geddes 1994, 36). Politicians in legislatures will supply the public good only when the costs of reform (that is, fewer patronage resources to distribute) are about evenly distributed among parties, and when constituents exert sufficient pressure for reforms. Similarly, executives will pursue non-partisan appointment strategies only when they are confident in office, have disciplined parties behind them, and do not face an immediate threat from the military.

Geddes tests this game theoretic model of legislative behavior on the patterns of administrative reform legislation in five South American countries. In general, the game theoretic model fully explains some of the cases examined, while other cases either do not really fit the model's assumptions (that is, they were not truly democratic at the time of the reform) or they require elaborations of the original model. By focusing almost exclusively on the legislature and its behavior, furthermore, Geddes singles out one part of the process and leaves out others, such as the important role executives played in the adoption and implementation of such reforms, a point highlighted by her case study of Brazilian executive behavior before 1964. This book, then, does not offer a general explanation of reform, which would require more attention to the interaction between executives and legislatures, how reform makes its way onto the political agenda, and how reforms are implemented after being adopted.

Geddes's contribution is her analysis of an important component of an issue that had previously received little attention; one that is likely to gain greater importance in the region as state reforms rise on the political agenda, especially since international financial institutions like the World Bank have recently emphasized the need for bureau-cratic reform and efficiency (see World Bank 1998).

Gill (1998) develops an RC model to explain church-state relations in Latin America. He assumes that both church and state normally prefer cooperation and will initiate conflicts only when the opportunity costs of cooperation exceed the benefits-the benefits being legitimacy for the government and the capacity to maximize the parishioner base for the church. The analysis proper focuses on explaining the behavior of the Catholic Church, specifically the attitudes of the national episcopates toward the military regimes in the 1960s and 1970s. The model predicts that the likelihood of conflict increases with religious competition and access to external funding, and with the regime's decreasing popularity (1998, 70).

In the subsequent empirical analysis, though, in both the statistical model and the comparative-historical analysis, only one of these variables—religious competition—is systematically investigated. The decline of external funding comes up in the narrative to explain the general tendency of the Catholic Church in Latin America to soft-pedal its progressive stance, beginning in the 1980s; but it is not used to explain differences among countries, as is the religious competition variable. The statistical model includes additional variables to test alternative explanations; namely poverty, repression, and the years that bishops were appointed.

Though only religious competition appears as statistically significant, inclusion of bishops' years of appointment increases the model's explanatory power. This measure is but an inexact proxy for the influence of progressive currents within the national church. That it nonetheless improves the model lends support to previous explanations of the behavior of the Catholic Church in Latin America.

Gill's book introduces an important new variable and thereby clearly makes a major contribution by enhancing our understanding of the church's behavior. The propositions derived from the rational choice model, however, other than the impact of this one variable, are not systematically tested empirically. Thus, the rational choice analysis per se contributes relatively little to the explanation, except perhaps by having generated the idea about the importance of religious competition to begin with.

In an analysis of postauthoritarian civil-military relations in Argentina and Chile that extends her 1997 book's concluding chapter, Hunter (1998) elaborates a model that describes the strategic interaction between the military and civilian governments regarding the punishment of human rights abuses and extant military prerogatives. The model predicts that civilian leaders will abandon efforts to punish the military's past human rights abuses and instead will focus on limiting the military's power and influence in other arenas. The military will resist efforts to prosecute human rights violations but will accept other limits to its power.

The model accurately describes the strategic interaction between civilians and the military in Chile and Argentina, despite differences in the levels of cohesion, power, and political influence of the militaries after the transitions in these two countries. The model does not predict, however, just how far civilian leaders can push for the punishment of human rights abuses or limits to military prerogatives or budgets before the military defects and stands up to civilian politicians. The substantive outcomes, such as the number of convictions or the monetary reduction in the military budget, are still the result of the relative power of the two actors at the beginning of the game, which is not incorporated into the formal model of actor preferences.

Cohen (1994) develops a game theoretic explanation of the breakdown of democratic regimes in Latin America and applies it to the coups of 1964 in Brazil and 1973 in Chile. He uses a prisoner's dilemma game with moderates of the right and left as players. He postulates that neither group could break with radical allies on its own side because each player believed that the opponents would not break with their own allies; that would lead inevitably to the breakdown of democracy (1994, 74). Cohen does restrict his model's domain of applicability to situations in which left- or right-wing extremists engage in radical and intransigent behavior and moderates split into left and right, both ideologically and organizationally.

Applying this model adds little to our understanding of the two regime breakdowns, about which there is already a voluminous literature. Even though that literature offers no consensus, it does contain strong theoretical explanations that emphasize structurally induced conflicts, political institutions unfavorable for processing those conflicts, and unfortunate choices by the major political actors. All these factors made the breakdown of democracy highly likely but not inevitable. Cohen argues against deterministic explanations; but by postulating specific beliefs and preferences and a prisoner's dilemma, he ends up with just that kind.

His model, moreover, has two major problems. First, it does not clearly document the precise beliefs on both sides. How do we know that the moderates believed they just could not break with their radical allies? Pointing to moderates' legitimate and expressed fears about the other side's "real" intentions does not demonstrate that a break with the radicals was considered impossible. This is simply a post hoc inference, and it constitutes a classic illustration of the basic problem of the RC approach. Second, and more fundamental, the very essence of the prisoner's dilemma is the lack of communication between the two players. For politicians, the situation is entirely different. Not only can there be ongoing negotiations and formal and informal communication, but there is also the possibility of constant monitoring of the opponent's behavior and consequent adjustment of one's own behavior.

Przeworski's 1991 book fits squarely into the game theoretic, albeit nonmathematical, version of the RC approach, as he develops game theoretic models for the liberalization of and transition from authoritarian regimes. His models are elegant and plausible, but they are not systematically tested. To apply the models of liberalization and extrication in order to predict the outcome for a given case, for instance, would require full knowledge of the preference orderings of the four sets of actors involved (hardliners and reformers in the regime, moderates and radicals in the opposition). That these preference orderings may change as actors acquire more information about each other, as Przeworski points out, further complicates the analysis.

The models are meant to be applicable to Latin America, and indeed, Przeworski draws many examples from transitions in the region; but his aim is to develop abstract models, not to evaluate systematically their explanatory power through analyses of Latin American political dynamics. The same is true for the models of economic reforms and their political consequences developed in the second half of his book. Here again, illustrations are chosen from Latin American countries, but the explicit aim is to speculate about reforms in Eastern Europe (1991, 138–39).

Works Using Mathematical Models

Crescenzi (1999) extends Przeworski's four-player game of transition by developing a mathematical model and incorporating uncertainty into it. In his game theoretic model, the opposition does not know who controls the authoritarian regime, the hard-liners or the reformers. The initiation of liberalization is considered an ambiguous signal, whose intention could just as likely be to draw opposition into the open and facilitate repression as to invite greater opposition activity. This entails the possibility that the opposition's choice of cooperation, negotiation, or radicalization may lead to undesirable outcomes, such as unwanted violence or missed opportunities to push the process of liberalization further.

To his great credit, Crescenzi examines the explanatory power of his model for the cases of Brazil and Hungary in both a qualitative and quantitative analysis. The Hungarian case is consistent with the model in both analyses, but for Brazil the results in the two analyses differ. The qualitative analysis suggests that the opposition may have already missed an opportunity to push for a pacted transition in the late 1970s, as signs indicated that the soft-liners were in the ascendancy. The time series analysis of the impact of information about the character of the regime on peaceful opposition mobilization, in contrast, suggests that there was no such missed opportunity. Information about the character of the regime (hard-line versus soft-line control) is operationalized as a function of prior repression and liberalization, and this variable shows no significant trend toward soft-line control between 1974 and 1982. The different assessment in the qualitative analysis stems from the use of additional information, such as personnel decisions by the president, to assess the power balance between hard-liners and soft-liners.

Thus the model is very useful for elucidating the dilemmas and uncertainties faced by oppositions in authoritarian regimes that initiate liberalization. But it cannot identify effective and counterproductive strategies and thereby predict outcomes any better than other approaches can, because it is just as dependent on accurate information about the regime's intentions. What it can do better than other approaches is demonstrate that as long as uncertainty persists about the real nature of the regime, so does the probability of violence or transitions going wrong. In other words, social scientists cannot understand transitions well enough to prevent these undesirable outcomes unless they can develop reliable information about the nature of the regime and, on that basis, design appropriate opposition strategies.

Wantchekon (1999) provides another example of a mathematical model. He uses a game theoretic model to explain outcomes of first democratic elections when the parties threaten to commit political violence after the elections rather than accept defeat. He works out the model for situations of perfect information and for situations of uncertainty regarding the minimum outcome necessary to keep the party with a relatively strong military wing from rioting. He predicts that under perfect information, the least violence-prone party is likely to win, whereas under conditions of uncertainty the most aggressive party is more likely to win. He further predicts that under uncertainty, the (militarily) weaker party will participate in the elections but not compete seriously.

Wantchekon then uses the model to explain founding elections in Liberia, El Salvador, and Algeria. In the case of El Salvador, the model seems to perform well in explaining why so many peasants voted for a party that clearly opposed reforms favoring their material interests. The claim that the Democratic Convergence did not compete seriously, though, is rather controversial to many analysts of the Salvadoran transition.[7]

WORK ON LATIN AMERICA IN THE INSTITUTIONALIST TRADITION

There is a body of work in which the approach rests on assumptions of strategic action but the main focus is not on such strategic action proper.[8] Some of the authors explicitly place their work in the context of RC assumptions (for example, Shugart and Carey 1992, 14), though strategic calculations of individuals or unitary actors are not the center of their analysis; this makes their work different from that of the mainstream actor-centered RC theorists already discussed.[9] They focus instead on the relationships between the structure of institutions and economic or political outcomes. The institutional analyses of Shugart and Carey (1992), Carey (1996, 2009), and Carey and Shugart (1998), and those in the volumes edited by Lijphart and Waisman (1996), Mainwaring and Shugart (1997), Haggard and McCubbins (2001) and Morgenstern and Nacif (2002) belong in this category, as do works by Crisp on Venezuela (2000), Samuels on Brazil (2003), and Morgenstern on legislatures (2004).[10]

These authors assume that institutions shape incentives for actors to maximize their interests through some strategic actions rather than others and thereby give rise to typical patterns of behavior. Some of these authors occasionally use theoretical tools like spatial models or matrix games, but their main focus is on the impact of different institutional configurations. For instance, the bulk of Shugart and Carey's 1992 book on executives and legislatures is an analysis of system performance, based on a classification of different systems and an examination of specific electoral rules and power distributions and their impact on the propensity for breakdown, regime crisis, or cabinet durability. On rare occasions, spatial models are used to analyze interactions between presidents and assemblies with regard to the appointment of cabinet members (1992, 106–26) and the delegation of decree powers by the assembly to the president (144–47), but in general the analysis keeps to the broader level of institutions.

In similar fashion, Carey and Shugart's edited volume on executive decree authority (1998) formulates and tests a number of hypotheses regarding the effect of institutional characteristics on the extent of constitutional or delegated decree authority granted to executives. The editors conclude that the conventional view has overemphasized the extent to which executive decree powers are arrogated beyond constitutional limits and that these powers have to be understood in their institutional context, in relation to the terms under which they are granted.

Also along similar analytical lines, the contributors to Mainwaring and Shugart 1997 focus on the performance of different varieties of presidentialism in the context of the broader institutional arrangements within which these varieties function. In their synthetic analysis, the editors pay particular attention to institutional factors, such as the power distribution between presidents and assemblies, the effective number of parties in the legislature, and the degree of party discipline, which they relate to party and electoral legislation. In the same vein, Morgenstern's conclusion to an edited volume on legislatures in Latin America (2002) summarizes the contributors' findings concerning the impact of reelection rates of legislators, the electoral system, the partisan composition of the legislature, and the distribution of constitutional powers on party discipline, executive-legislative relations, and the legislature's internal organization.

The essays on the impact of the interaction of presidential systems and electoral rules on policy in the volume edited by Haggard and McCubbins (2001) extend these analyses by focusing on outcomes in terms of policymaking capacity and policy's particularistic character. As the editors explain in their introduction, the key elements under analysis are the separation of powers and the separation of purpose. The former refers to the ability of different actors to exercise a veto in the formation of public policy; the latter to different partisan control of veto positions. The book looks at presidential systems—that is, systems with separation of powers-and variations in the separation of purpose. It explains separation of purpose with electoral rules: nonconcurrent elections, staggered terms, candidate-centered campaigns, noncongruence of legislative and presidential constituencies (see Shugart and Haggard 2001).

Haggard and McCubbins posit a trade-off between decisiveness and resoluteness in policymaking—that is, between the ability to make decisions and the ability to make those decisions stick. They argue that the greater the separation of powers, the higher is state resoluteness and the lower state decisiveness. If separation of purpose is added to separation of powers, state governability is endangered by instability and stalemate.

This constellation, moreover, is highly likely to result in the privatization of public policy, because politicians will pursue particularistic benefits rather than public goods (see Cox and McCubbins 2001). The applications of these theoretical propositions to the case studies in the Haggard and McCubbins volume by and large support the editors' expectations.

Carey's 1996 comparative analysis of the effect of term limits on the behavior of legislators in Costa Rica and Venezuela-two systems with virtually identical electoral systems and other similar political institutions that shape legislative behavior, as well as similar background variables-argues that legislators are responsive to those who control their future careers.

The evidence presented to support this claim is twofold. First, party discipline is lower in Costa Rica than in Venezuela because party leaders have fewer available sanctions for noncompliance with party directives.[11] Second, legislators in Costa Rica nonetheless diligently serve their constituencies and deliver particularistic benefits, presumably because 1) this helps their party win the next presidential election; 2) a political appointment by the next president is legislators' only hope to continue their political careers after their terms end; and 3) presidents will reward legislators for contributing to the presidential election victory. The evidence, however (admittedly limited by scarcity of data), simply does not support the first and third hypothesized causal linkages. There is no relationship between the delivery of pork and electoral support for the legislator's party, or between vote gains in a legislator's bailiwick and the probability of an appointment. Carey argues that there is interview evidence-that is, that legislators believe these relationships exist-but it is purely anecdotal.

Not explored is the equally plausible hypothesis that legislators serve their constituencies and dole out particularistic favors because this is the norm. The book offers much information about how the system of bailiwicks works, how the parties assign responsibilities, and how only the party in power can provide resources for particularistic favors, but it provides no evidence that would support the assumption of legislators' strategic career-oriented action; nor does it contradict the assumption that legislators simply want to be regarded as successful in performing their duties because it brings them respect from constituents and fellow party members. This is, in other words, a very interesting comparative piece of research, but it gains its insights despite the imposition of an RC framework, not because of it.

The chapters on Latin America in Lijphart and Waisman (1996) focus on the impact of economic conditions, the design of electoral systems and executive-legislative relations, and the privatization process on economic and political outcomes; they do not focus explicitly on actors' strategic choices.[12] In their conclusion, the editors argue that explanations for the process of privatization are to be found in a combination of structural and actor-centered approaches, whereas the bargaining processes over the design of electoral and executive-legislative institutions are governed mainly by the perceived short-term interests of the parties involved. In these bargaining processes, however, the editors also find limitations to the explanatory power of strategic actions of self-interested parties, limitations stemming from constraints such as strength of institutional traditions and even from politicians' pursuit of non-self-interested goals, such as stability of the system and voter turnout (1996, 243–45).

Similarly, Crisp (2000) uses the insights from comparative studies of electoral systems and executive-legislative relations to explain the increasingly dysfunctional nature of Venezuela's highly centralized and rigid political institutions. In analyzing the impact of these institutions over time, though, he also considers their interaction with a changing economic and social context, which widens his analytical focus to include structural and policy variables.

Morgenstern and Siavelis (2008a, 2008b), in their attempt to explain patterns of political recruitment and selection, complement such standard institutionalist approaches by mapping the interactive effects of multiple institutional and party variables on the loyalties of candidates to parties, constituents, or other groups. They develop a typology of candidates and map four ideal typical paths shaped by institutional and party variables to their four types of candidates. They then formulate a set of expectations about the behavior of these types of candidates and the implications of this behavior for parties.

These works have made important contributions to our understanding of Latin American politics because most of their insights are empirically well supported. These studies elucidate previously poorly understood phenomena, but they do so predominantly by way of comparative (and often also historical) institutional analysis and not through an explicit actor-centered RC approach. To the extent that the focus is on actors, the authors have introduced new concepts (such as loyalty) that allow for more complex motivations and sets of incentives and constraints. Following the distinction drawn by Hall and Taylor (1996) between the three "new institutionalisms" (rational choice institutionalism, historical institutionalism, and sociological institutionalism), we would suggest that most of these contributions could be classified in Hall and Taylor's "historical institutionalism cum calculus approach" category.

CONTRIBUTIONS OF RATIONAL CHOICE ANALYSES AND ALTERNATIVE APPROACHES

Few, if any, RC research studies have forced a major rethinking of established tenets or have filled major lacunae in our understanding of Latin American politics. Nevertheless, some have enriched our understanding by introducing new ideas and evidence to explain phenomena that before were only partially understood.

For instance, Ames (1987) provides strong evidence for the general tendency of politicians to use public expenditures to build political support for themselves during transition periods, and in his new book (2001) paints an intricate and empirically rich picture of the functioning and consequences of the interaction of electoral, legislative, and executive institutions in Brazil. Hunter (1997) explains how civilian governments that were comparatively weak in regard to the military at the time of regime transition have reduced some of the military's influence in the process of democratic consolidation. Gill (1998) adds an important variable to our previously incomplete understanding of the behavior of the Catholic Church in Latin America-monopoly position versus competition with other religions. Geddes (1994) elucidates the conditions under which legislators are willing to pass civil service reform. Crescenzi (1999) maps the dilemmas faced by oppositions to authoritarian regimes stemming from the uncertainty regarding the regimes' true intentions.

In the related institutionalist work, Shugart and Carey (1992; and Carey and Shugart 1998) have elaborated a useful classification of relations between executives and legislatures. They have helped us understand which kinds of rules generate which types of relations, and they have successfully challenged rather widespread misunderstandings of the use of executive decree authority in Latin America. Mainwaring and Shugart (1997) draw our attention to the need to understand executive-legislative relations as they interact with the party system and thus as they function in the context of party and electoral legislation, thereby greatly enriching the debate about the strengths and weaknesses of presidential versus parliamentary systems.

The contributors to Haggard and McCubbins (2001) extend the analysis of that interaction to its impact on policymaking capacities and the tendency to privatize public policy. They also offer a useful guide to the pathologies involved when separation of powers and separation of purpose are combined. In their analysis of how new political institutions are shaped in democratizing countries, Lijphart and Waisman (1996) show that perceived short-term interests of actors participating in the design of electoral and executive-legislative institutions do provide important but only partial explanations, and that such explanations need to be complemented by reference to actors' non-self-interested motivations and to structural and historical constraints.

The RC approach as an identifiable body of research arguably has made a greater contribution to the understanding of the comparative politics of advanced industrial democracies, specifically in the areas of class relations, wage determination, and coalition formation (Przeworski and Wallerstein 1982; Lange 1984; Calmfors and Driffill 1988; Iversen 1996; Moene and Wallerstein 1999; Soskice 2000). This is not surprising, because these are areas in which material interests or access to political office are very clearly at stake and decisions carry major importance. In advanced industrial democracies, more-over, these institutions in these areas are well consolidated; their rules are largely formal, stable, known, and followed; and the actors in most cases are well organized in institutions that can speak and act authoritatively for their members.[13]

These conditions, however, are rarely encountered in Latin America. Indeed, formal rules are often a highly imperfect guide to Latin American political processes. Though the movement toward democratization over the past two decades has often led to a greater congruence between formal rules and actual behavior, that congruence remains incomplete, particularly in the relations between state and society in more peripheral social and geographical areas, but even at the centers of power (O'Donnell 1999a, 133–215, 1999b, 303–37). Informal rules would not, in principle, be a problem for RC analysis if they were stable and well known; but such they have rarely been in Latin America, and certainly not in the context of regime changes. To the extent that the explanatory power of the RC approach depends on consolidated institutions as effective guides to behavior, the approach is unlikely to perform better than others in answering the fundamental questions of politics—who gets what, when, and how—in Latin America.

To say that RC research has not forced a major rethinking of the established wisdom in Latin American politics is by no means to condemn or denigrate the RC research program in this field. After all, few theoretical traditions have done that. Three come to mind: the version of the dependency approach pioneered by Cardoso and Faletto (1979), the study of the new authoritarianism in Latin America (Collier 1979) building on O'Donnell's (1973) bureaucratic authoritarianism, and the new comparative political economy of development, building on Evans's influential study of dependent develop-ment (1979).[14]

The first of these approaches forced us to consider power relations in the interna-tional system when explaining developments in Latin America. The second put class conflict and state-class alliances at the center of attention, and the third integrated the study of class, state, state-class alliances, and the international system, specifically trans-national actors, into a coherent framework. This framework has fundamentally shaped the more recent major works on basic questions about Latin American politics, works that have added institutional or policy variables to this structural base.

Let us briefly consider some possible objections to our assessment.[15] The first is that the works by Cardoso and Faletto, O'Donnell, Evans, and other works following these approaches lack theoretical rigor and cannot be tested. This is true only if theoretical rigor is equated with deductive theorizing and testing with quantitative analysis. These theoretical approaches were generated inductively but not out of thin air; nor did they remain untested. The researchers began with expectations grounded in theoretical reflec-tions based on extant work, complemented and modified these expectations in the course of analyzing historical sequences in specific cases, developed theoretical generalizations from these cases, and then tested these generalizations in comparative historical analyses of new cases.[16]

Another objection is that the application of the RC approach to the analysis of Latin American politics is fairly new, and we cannot really judge its potential explanatory power. It is true that, with the exception of Ames's first book, all the RC works reviewed here have been published in the past two decades. No doubt, new works in this tradition will make additional valuable contributions. Given the importance of consolidated institutions or stable and known rules for RC explanations, however, we would not expect any exponential increase in the explanatory power of the RC approach for Latin American politics in the near future. Empirically well supported studies in the RC mode are likely to remain confined to subjects in which the rules are reasonably stable, such as electoral systems and legislatures in the more consolidated democracies.

Still another contention is that alternative approaches are not performing any better in helping us understand Latin American politics. The major alternative approaches to RC we would cite are structural, historical institutional, and mixed or integrative. Both RC-related institutionalist and historical institutionalist approaches have clearly enriched our understanding of the consequences of different institutional designs; of electoral systems and executive-legislature relations, for instance. But RC-related institutionalist approaches that take institutions as givens and ignore how they are shaped and reshaped along with power relations in the society contribute only a small piece of the answers to the big questions of politics—the determinants of regime forms, of stability versus breakdown in political order, of choices of development strategies, and of distributive outcomes. These big questions have more typically been addressed by structural or by integrative approaches; that is, approaches that combine social and economic structural, institutional, policy, and actor-centered variables in their explanations.

The reliance at least partly on structural explanations to answer the big questions is no accident. Typically, attempts to answer such questions involve the analysis of several cases and considerable time spans. The larger the number of cases and the longer the period analyzed, the higher the profile assumed by structural and institutional factors, because these factors contain more variation. By contrast, single-case studies over relatively short periods privilege actors and their decisions because the structural and institutional variables do not vary much-with the notable exception of political and economic transitions.

Thus, in explaining the emergence and survival of democracy in Latin America and the Caribbean over the twentieth century, Rueschemeyer et al. (1992) privilege structural factors in the form of the balance of power-in civil society, between civil society and the state, and constellations in the international system-along with an institutional factor, the nature of political parties. In their attempt to explain the formation of political coalitions, party systems, modes of political conflict, and patterns of regime change in eight Latin American countries, Collier and Collier (1991) focus on a combination of structural factors, such as strength of the oligarchy and of the emerging labor movement, with state strategies toward labor incorporation. Haggard and Kaufman (2008) follow a similar approach in their sweeping study of the formation and reform of welfare states in 21 middle income countries in Latin America, East Asia, and Eastern Europe. They emphasize changing patterns of political domination and inclusion, economic structures and policies, policy legacies, and democratization. All three of these works demonstrate that structural factors, particularly power distributions, along with institutional or policy variables, do have significant explanatory power in analyses of macropolitical change over the medium and long term.

What about the big questions over comparatively short periods of time, a decade or so? We would argue that integrative approaches have been particularly useful here. Haggard and Kaufman (1995) successfully use a combination of structural and institutional variables and policy choices to explain outcomes of the dual transition to democracies and more market-oriented economies in the last two decades of the twentieth century. They address three broad questions: the impact of economic conditions on the timing and nature of the withdrawal of authoritarian regimes, the impact of the transition's economic and institutional legacies on economic policymaking in new democratic regimes, and the conditions for reconciling market-oriented reforms and democracy and for consolidating democracy. Their main variables are economic conditions and regime change; political institutions, particularly executive authority, political parties, and the party system, and government's managerial capacity; economic management and democratic consolidation.

Linz and Stepan (1996) use an even broader array of variables to explain democratic transitions and consolidation in Southern Europe, postcommunist Europe, and the Southern Cone. They include structural variables (existence of a sovereign state), institutional variables (previous regime type), process-oriented variables (path of transition), actor-centered variables (leadership of previous regime; who controls the transition), and conjunctural factors (bases of legitimacy, international influences, and constitution making). Weyland investigates why democracy failed to bring about major equity-enhancing reforms in Brazil, and he emphasizes organizational fragmentation in state and society. Thus, he argues for the primacy of a state-centered institutionalist approach but also insists that organizational fragmentation itself needs to be explained, and that its roots lie in structural conditions (1996, 40). Mainwaring explains the development of Brazil's weakly institutionalized party system as a case of third-wave party systems with a combination of theoretical approaches: comparative macroanalysis, institutionalism, and rational choice (1999, 7). The first two of these approaches clearly dominate the analysis.

A last example to demonstrate the explanatory power of an integrative approach, in this case applied to institutional change, is Snyder's study of reregulation at the subnational level in Mexico (1999, 2001). He looks at the interaction between societal groups and political incumbents to explain institutional outcomes, and he uses the strength of societal groups (structural variables), along with the ideas and values of politicians (actor-centered variables) and institutional incentives (institutional variables) to account for their actions and the results of their interaction.

We conclude, then, that the theoretical approach one takes needs to be appropriate for the questions one asks. At the risk of oversimplification, we would argue that the larger the question and the more it concerns essential aspects of power relations among social groups and the state over a considerable time, the more useful are structural and institutional approaches. Conversely, the narrower the question, the more it is limited to the choice of policy from a given set by politicians acting under certain constraints at a given point in time, the more useful is the RC approach.

Essentially, once power relations are acknowledged as a factor in the analysis and as variable over the period in question, the crucial RC assumptions—that institutional incentives decisively shape behavior and that the rules of the game are fixed—become untenable.[17] The questions then become under what conditions actors are likely to adhere to rules or to mobilize power resources to change them, and what enables some actors to change those rules in their favor. The answers to these questions are most likely to be found in structural and institutional configurations.

NOTES

We thank Mark Crescenzi, Jonathan Hartlyn, Geraldo Munck, Richard Snyder, John Stephens, and Kurt Weyland, as well as William C. Smith, and anonymous reviewers for *Latin American Politics and Society* for very helpful comments that forced us to sharpen our arguments.

1 Green and Shapiro discuss additional assumptions that are widely shared by RC theorists but that we do not consider necessary to define the approach. For instance, though most of the more recent RC work assumes that decisions are made under uncertainty because of incomplete information available to the actors, earlier game theoretic work frequently assumed perfect information.

2 Some scholars would argue that our ordering of criteria is biased toward continuity in research questions. We agree, but we defend the ordering on the grounds that the big research questions are dictated by real problems, and that in Latin America the real problems of development, poverty, inequality, domination, and political instability are as pressing as ever.

3 Some readers see a contradiction between this statement and the successful use of game theoretic models in the analysis of international conflict. We would argue that, at least in the realist theoretical tradition out of which many of these studies have come, the actors in international conflicts can identify each other and their goals, and the rules of anarchy also are quite well understood: "might makes right."

4 Munck (2001) points to the assumptions of fixed rules (including, among other elements, the nature and ordering of the preferences of actors) as a major problem for game theory.

5 This raises the question why we classify this book in the mainstream actor-centered RC category rather than in the institutionalist category. The answer lies in the nature of the explanations. Though the functioning and consequences of institutions are the main topics, the author's explanations are based on strategic calculations of individual actors (deputies, governors, ministers), and the goals and preferences of these actors are explicitly problematized.

6 Indeed, these exercises raise the question whether this book should not be classified as using an integrative approach, along with Mainwaring's (1999) book on the Brazilian party system. Our decision is governed by the authors' own emphasis on RC compared to other theoretical approaches in their analyses.

7 Other examples of recent work on Latin American politics using formal mathematical models are Londregan (2000), Díaz-Cayeros (2006), Magaloni (2006), and Greene (2007).

8 Weyland (2002) provides an excellent review and critique of the RC institutionalist literature, coming to the same general conclusions regarding its contributions and limitations as we do. Morgenstern and Vázquez-D'Elia (2007) provide a review and critique of the literature on the effects of electoral systems on parties and party systems. The essays in Stein and Tommasi (2008) offer a useful recent survey of the institutionalist literature on Latin America, along with essays that apply an institutionalist perspective to the analysis of policymaking in eight Latin American countries.

9 Some critics might object to this distinction by pointing out that in some of the works discussed above, such as Hunter's, the arguments are based on the assumption of strategic decisions by individuals, but the empirical analysis skirts the question of information available to the actors and their cost-benefit calculations per se, and instead concentrates on the consequences of political choices. Still, we would argue that there is a difference in the degree that strategic actions of individuals are invoked as the basic explanatory variable.

10 The analyses of economic and political developments in Latin America collected in the volume by Frieden et al. (2000) belong to a more synthetic or integrative category of work, as they combine a focus on the impact of institutions with a focus on structural factors and policy patterns. A large number of the excerpts in this volume are actually surveys of arguments and discussions of methodological approaches, not empirical studies. The empirical studies in their great majority focus on structural and institutional factors and policy patterns as determinants of economic performance. Only three excerpts, those by Geddes on civil service reform, by Boylan on determinants of central bank independence, and, to some extent, the one by Maxfield on the same topic, use actor-centered RC explanatory models.

11 The relationship between party leader control over nominations for election or reelection in closed-list systems and party discipline must be one of the best-established tenets in comparative politics, and it predates the emergence of RC analyses of the subject.

12 Geddes is the only contributor to adopt an explicit RC approach, but her article is on Eastern Europe, using the Latin American cases only selectively to illustrate differences with Eastern Europe (1996, 15–41).

13 One can think of exceptions to the usual notion that rules are formal, such as the phenomenon of particular unions' leadership in wage setting. Even these informal rules or conventions, however, are generally quite stable over time, and they are certainly well known.

14 It is ironic that some scholars would like to claim O'Donnell's 1973 book for the RC tradition, pointing to chapter 4 on the impossible "game" of party competition in Argentina. Indeed, O'Donnell argues that the problem to be studied "is close to the situation dealt with by game theory," only to state later in the same paragraph, "unhappily, the real situation being studied in this chapter is too complicated in several important respects to allow for direct application of the formal tools of game theory" (p. 167). He then describes a complex situation with several players (several parties and an umpire in the form of the military), ten different rules, five different periods, and two iterations.

15 We are indebted to Geraldo Munck for suggesting that we engage these arguments.

16 See Rueschemeyer et al. (1992, 36–39) and Rueschemeyer and Stephens (1997) for further elaboration of this view of theory building and testing in comparative historical research.

17 See Munck n.d. for a more detailed discussion of the problem of power relations for RC approaches to politics.

REFERENCES

Abelson, Robert P. 1996. The Secret Existence of Expressive Behavior. In Friedman 1996b. 25–36.

Alt, James E., and Kenneth A. Shepsle. 1990. Editors' Introduction. In *Perspectives on Positive Political Economy*, ed. Alt and Shepsle. Cambridge: Cambridge University Press. 1–5.

Ames, Barry. 1987. *Political Survival: Politicians and Public Policy in Latin America*. Berkeley: University of California Press.

——. 2001. *The Deadlock of Democracy in Brazil*. Ann Arbor: University of Michigan Press.

Bates, Robert H. 1987. Agrarian Politics. In *Understanding Political Development*, ed. Samuel Huntington and Jonathan Wiener. Boston: Little, Brown.

Boylan, Delia. 1998. Preemptive Strike: Central Bank Reform in Chile's Transition from Authoritarian Rule. *Comparative Politics* 30, 4 (July): 443–62.

Calmfors, Lars, and John Driffill. 1988. Bargaining Structure, Corporatism and Macroeconomic Performance. *Economic Policy* 3 (April): 13–61.

Cardoso, Fernando Henrique, and Enzo Faletto. 1979. *Dependency and Development in Latin America*. Berkeley: University of California Press.

Carey, John M. 1996. *Term Limits and Legislative Representation*. New York: Cambridge University Press.

——. 2009. *Legislative Voting and Accountability*. New York: Cambridge.

Carey, John M., and Matthew Soberg Shugart, eds. 1998. *Executive Decree Authority*. New York: Cambridge University Press.

Cohen, Youssef. 1994. *Radicals, Reformers, and Reactionaries: The Prisoner's Dilemma and the Collapse of Democracy in Latin America*. Chicago: University of Chicago Press.

Collier, David, ed. 1979. *The New Authoritarianism in Latin America*. Princeton: Princeton University Press.

Collier, David, and Deborah L. Norden. 1992. Strategic Choice Models of Political Change in Latin America. *Comparative Politics* 24, 2 (January): 229–43.

Collier, Ruth Berins, and David Collier. 1991. *Shaping the Political Arena*. Princeton: Princeton University Press.

Cox, Gary W., and Mathew D. McCubbins. 2001. The Institutional Determinants of Economic Policy Outcomes. In Haggard and McCubbins 2001. New York: Cambridge University Press. 21–63.

Crescenzi, Mark J. C. 1999. Violence and Uncertainty in Transitions. *Journal of Conflict Resolution* 43, 2 (April): 192–212.

Crisp, Brian. 2000. *Democratic Institutional Design: The Powers and Incentives of Venezuelan Politicians and Interest Groups*. Stanford: Stanford University Press.

Díaz-Cayeros, Alberto. 2006. *Federalism, Fiscal Authority, and Centralization in Latin America.* New York: Cambridge University Press.

Evans, Peter. 1979. *Dependent Development: The Alliance of Multinational, State, and Local Capital in Brazil.* Princeton: Princeton University Press.

Ferejohn, John. 1991. Rationality and Interpretation: Parliamentary Elections in Early Stuart England. In *The Economic Approach to Politics: A Critical Reassessment of the Theory of Rational Action,* ed. Kristen Renwick Monroe. New York: Harper Collins.

Fiorina, Morris P. 1996. Rational Choice, Empirical Contributions, and the Scientific Enterprise. In Friedman 1996b. 85–94.

Frieden, Jeffry, Manuel Pastor, Jr., and Michael Tomz. 2000. *Modern Political Economy and Latin America: Theory and Policy.* Boulder: Westview Press.

Friedman, Jeffrey. 1996a. Introduction: Economic Approaches to Politics. In Friedman 1996b. 1–24.

Friedman, Jeffrey, ed. 1996b. *The Rational Choice Controversy: Economic Models of Politics Reconsidered.* New Haven: Yale University Press.

Gates, Scott, and Brian D. Humes. 2000. *Games, Information, and Politics Applying Game Theoretic Models to Political Science.* Ann Arbor: University of Michigan Press.

Geddes, Barbara. 1994. *Politician's Dilemma: Building State Capacity in Latin America.* Berkeley: University of California Press.

———. 1995. Uses and Limitations of Rational Choice. In *Latin America in Comparative Perspective: New Approaches to Methods and Analysis,* ed. Peter H. Smith. Boulder: Westview Press. 81–108.

———. 1996. Initiation of New Democratic Institutions in Eastern Europe and Latin America. In Lijphart and Waisman 1996. 15–41.

Gill, Anthony. 1998. *Rendering unto Caesar. The Catholic Church and the State in Latin America.* Chicago: University of Chicago Press.

Gilovich, Thomas, Dale Griffin, and Daniel Kahneman, eds. 2002. *Heuristics and Biases: The Psychology of Intuitive Judgment.* Cambridge University Press.

Green, Donald P., and Ian Shapiro. 1994. *Pathologies of Rational Choice Theory: A Critique of Applications in Political Science.* New Haven: Yale University Press.

Greene, Kenneth F. 2007. *Why Dominant Parties Lose: Mexico's Democratization in Comparative Perspective.* New York: Cambridge University Press.

Haggard, Stephan, and Mathew D. McCubbins, eds. 2001. *Presidents, Parliaments, and Policy.* New York: Cambridge University Press.

Haggard, Stephan, and Robert R. Kaufman. 1995. *The Political Economy of Democratic Transitions.* Princeton: Princeton University Press.

———. 2008. *Development, Democracy, and Welfare States.* Princeton, NJ: Princeton University Press.

Hall, Peter A., and Rosemary C. R. Taylor. 1996. Political Science and the Three New Institutionalisms. *Political Studies* 44, 5 (December): 936–57.

Hunter, Wendy. 1997. Eroding *Military Influence in Brazil: Politicians Against Soldiers.* Chapel Hill: University of North Carolina Press.

———. 1998. Negotiating Civil-Military Relations in Post-Authoritarian Argentina and Chile. *International Studies Quarterly* 42, 2 (June): 295–318.

Immergut, Ellen M. 1998. The Theoretical Core of the New Institutionalism. *Politics and Society* 26, 1 (March): 5–34.

Iversen, Torben. 1996. Power, Flexibility, and the Breakdown of Centralized Wage Bargaining. *Comparative Politics* 28 (July): 399–436.

Lange, Peter. 1984. Unions, Workers, and Wage Regulation: The Rational Bases of Consent. In *Order and Conflict in Contemporary Capitalism: Studies in the Political Economy of Western European Nations,* ed. John H. Goldthorpe. Oxford: Clarendon Press. 98–123.

Lewin, Leif. 1991. *Self-Interest and Public Interest in Western Politics.* New York: Oxford University Press.

Lijphart, Arend, and Carlos H. Waisman, eds. 1996. *Institutional Design in New Democracies: Eastern Europe and Latin America.* Boulder: Westview Press.

Linz, Juan J., and Alfred Stepan. 1996. Problems *of Democratic Transition and Consolidation.* Baltimore: Johns Hopkins University Press.

Londregan, John B. 2000. *Legislative Institutions and Ideology in Chile.* Cambridge: Cambridge University Press.

Magaloni, Beatriz. 2006. *Voting for Autocracy: Hegemonic Party Survival and its Demise in Mexico.* New York: Cambridge University Press.

Mainwaring, Scott. 1999. *Rethinking Party Systems in the Third Wave of Democratization: The Case of Brazil.* Stanford: Stanford University Press.

Mainwaring, Scott, and Matthew Soberg Shugart, eds. 1997. *Presidentialism and Democracy in Latin America.* Cambridge: Cambridge University Press.

Maxfield, Sylvia. 1997. *Gatekeepers of Growth: The International Political Economy of Central Banking in Developing Countries.* Princeton: Princeton University Press.

Moene, Karl Ove, and Michael Wallerstein. 1999. Social Democratic Labor Market Institutions: A Retrospective Analysis. In *Continuity and Change in Contemporary Capitalism,* ed. Herbert Kitschelt, Peter Lange, Gary Marks, and John D. Stephens. Cambridge: Cambridge University Press. 231–60.

Morgenstern, Scott. 2002. Conclusion: Explaining Legislative Politics in Latin America. In *Legislative Politics in Latin America,* ed. Scott Morgenstern and Benito Nacif. New York: Cambridge University Press. 413–45.

——. 2004. *Patterns of Legislative Politics: Roll Call Voting in the United States and Latin America's Southern Cone.* Cambridge University Press.

Morgenstern, Scott and Benito Nacif, eds. 2002. *Legislative Politics in Latin America.* New York: Cambridge University Press.

Morgenstern, Scott and Peter Siavelis, eds. 2008a. *Pathways to Power.* Pennsylvania State University Press.

Morgenstern, Scott and Peter Siavelis. 2008b. "Candidate Recruitment and Selection in Latin America: A Framework for Analysis." *Latin American Politics and Society* 50, 4 (Winter): 27–58.

Morgenstern, Scott and Javier Vázquez-D'Elia. 2007. "Electoral Laws, Parties, and Party Systems in Latin America." *Annual Review of Political Science* 10 (June): 143–68.

Munck, Gerardo. n.d. Game Theory and Comparative Politics: Theoretical and Methodological Perspectives. Unpublished mss.

——. 2001. Game Theory and Comparative Politics: New Perspectives and Old Concerns. *World Politics* 53 (January): 173–204.

O'Donnell, Guillermo. 1973. *Modernization and Bureaucratic-Authoritarianism: Studies in South American Politics.* Berkeley: Institute of International Studies, University of California.

——. 1999a. *Counterpoints: Selected Essays on Authoritarianism and Democratization.* Notre Dame: University of Notre Dame Press.

——. 1999b. Polyarchies and the (Un)Rule of Law in Latin America: A Partial Conclusion. In *The (Un)Rule of Law and the Underprivileged in Latin America,* ed. Juan E. Mendez, Guillermo O'Donnell, and Paulo Sérgio Pinheiro. Notre Dame: University of Notre Dame Press. 303–37.

O'Donnell, Guillermo, and Philippe C. Schmitter. 1986. *Transitions from Authoritarian Rule: Tentative Conclusions About Uncertain Democracies.* Baltimore: Johns Hopkins University Press.

Ordeshook, Peter C. 1990. *The Emerging Discipline of Political Economy.* In Alt and Shepsle 1990. 9–30.

Popkin, Samuel L. 1988. *Public Choice and Peasant Organization.* In *Toward a Political Economy of Development,* ed. Robert H. Bates. Berkeley: University of California Press. 245–71.

Przeworski, Adam. 1991. *Democracy and the Market: Political and Economic Reforms in Eastern Europe and Latin America.* Cambridge: Cambridge University Press.

Przeworski, Adam, and Michael Wallerstein. 1982. The Structure of Class Conflict in Democratic Capitalist Societies. *American Political Science Review* 76: 215–38.

Rueschemeyer, Dietrich, and John D. Stephens. 1997. Comparing Historical Sequences—A Powerful Tool for Causal Analysis. *Comparative Social Research* 16: 55–72.

Rueschemeyer, Dietrich, Evelyne Huber Stephens, and John D. Stephens. 1992. *Capitalist Development and Democracy.* Chicago: University of Chicago Press.

Samuels, David. 2003. *Ambition, Federalism, and Legislative Politics in Brazil*. New York: Cambridge University Press.

Shugart, Matthew Soberg, and John M. Carey. 1992. *Presidents and Assemblies: Constitutional Design and Electoral Dynamics*. Cambridge: Cambridge University Press.

Shugart, Matthew Soberg, and Stephan Haggard. 2001. Institutions and Public Policy in Presidential Systems. In Haggard and McCubbins 2001. 64–102.

Snyder, Richard. 1999. After Neoliberalism: The Politics of Reregulation in Mexico. *World Politics* 51, 2 (January): 173–204.

——. 2001. *Politics After Neoliberalism: Reregulation in Mexico*. Cambridge: Cambridge University Press.

Soskice, David. 2000. Macroeconomic Analysis and the Political Economy of Unemployment. In *Unions, Employers, and Central Banks: Macroeconomic Coordination and Institutional Change in Social Market Economies*, ed. Torben Iversen, Jonas Pontusson, and David Soskice. Cambridge: Cambridge University Press. 38–74.

Stein, Ernesto and Mariano Tommasi, eds. 2008. *Policymaking in Latin America: How Politics Shapes Policies*. Washington, DC: Inter-American Development Bank.

Wantchekon, Leonard. 1999. On the Nature of First Democratic Elections. *Journal of Conflict Resolution* 43, 2 (April): 245–58.

Weyland, Kurt. 1996. *Democracy Without Equity: Failures of Reform in Brazil*. Pittsburgh: University of Pittsburgh Press.

——. 2002. Limitations of Rational-Choice Institutionalism for the Study of Latin American Politics. *Studies in Comparative International Development*, 37, 1 (Spring): 57–85.

——. 2006. *Bounded Rationality and Policy Diffusion: Social Sector Reform in Latin America*. Princeton: Princeton University Press.

World Bank. 1998. *Beyond the Washington Consensus: Institutions Matter*. Washington, DC: World Bank.

Chapter 3

Toward a Critique of Latin American Neostructuralism

Fernando Ignacio Leiva

A new development approach has gained ascendancy among policymakers in Latin America. Officially launched in 1990 with the publication of *Changing Production Patterns with Social Equity* by the United Nations Economic Commission for Latin America and the Caribbean (ECLAC), Latin American neostructuralism has gradually replaced neoliberal market fundamentalism as the prevailing economic development perspective in the region.[1]

Almost twenty years after its 1990 debut and six decades since the founding of ECLAC, neostructuralism has garnered widespread intellectual and political influence, successfully moving from the margins to the very center of economic development policy formulation. The failure of neoliberalism to deliver high rates of economic growth and its role in causing widespread popular discontent and massive mobilizations, along with electoral victories by center-left coalitions, point to the decline in the hegemony of neoliberal economic ideas in the region. The election of progressive candidates like Ricardo Lagos (2000) and Michelle Bachelet (2006) in Chile, Luiz Inácio Lula ad Silva in Brazil (2002), Nestor Kirchner (2003) and Cristina Fernández de Kirchner (2007) in Argentina, and Tabaré Vasquez in Uruguay (2005) raises hopes that an alternative development path shaped by Latin American neostructuralism can successfully deal with the unresolved socioeconomic problems faced by the majority of almost six hundred million Latin Americans. As a 2005 *Wall Street Journal* article acknowledged, a "new breed of pragmatic leftists" dedicated to combining "the left's traditional warm-hearted social goals with a newfound appreciation for cold economic calculus" now occupies key economic posts in Latin America (Luhnow 2005). In academia, such shifts have been seen either as a welcome quest for the "high road" to globalization (Korzeniewicz and Smith 2000) or as a more problematic "revival of structuralism" among economists (Weyland 2007).

Whether one agrees with such interpretations or not, it is indisputable that since 2000, the election of progressive governments in Chile, Brazil, Argentina, Uruguay, Bolivia, Venezuela, Ecuador, Nicaragua, and more recently Guatemala, Paraguay and El Salvador, along with the continued presence of powerful social movements, suggests that a historically significant political and intellectual realignment is under way.

The emergence and rise to predominance of a new, more pragmatic approach to economic development, known as Latin American neostructuralism, is an important factor, though clearly not the only one, behind Latin America's "postneoliberal" turn. Yet despite growing intellectual influence, no systematic and comprehensive critical appraisal of the new postneoliberal development approach is currently available.[2] Major questions posed by Latin American neostructuralism's displacement of neoliberalism remain unaddressed: What are the key strengths and weaknesses of this new development discourse? What scope of transformations can Latin American neostructuralism really enact? How are we to assay the internal consistency and overall impact of the emergent Latin American neostructuralist framework? How can a critical evaluation of Latin American neostructuralism proceed at a time when it enjoys widespread intellectual and political support and its lines of defense seem impregnable?[3] Using Terry Eagleton's apt metaphor, this essay attempts to look behind neostructuralism's "imposing tapestry" to "expose in all its unglamorously disheveled tangle the threads constituting the well-heeled image it presents to the world" (Eagleton 1986, 80).[4]

THE MANY FACES OF LATIN AMERICAN NEOSTRUCTURALISM

Latin American neostructuralism is the first fully articulated development discourse to challenge directly the hegemony of neoliberal ideas. While calling Latin American neo-structuralism a new paradigm might seem to some an overreach, just calling it a package of economic policies is misleading.[5] Even before Anthony Giddens, Britain's New Labor, or European Social Democracy had formulated the Third Way, Latin American neostruc-turalists working at ECLAC had laid the intellectual foundations for contesting neoliberal-ism's supremacy (Giddens 1998).[6] Over the course of its ascent, neostructuralism recast conceptions about the relationship among economy, state, and society; it introduced a new development lexicon that was increasingly embraced by international development institutions, such as the World Bank and the Inter-American Development Bank; and it advanced a program of action for establishing a new relationship among institutional reform, modernity, social cohesion, and globalization in the twenty-first century.

What is Latin American neostructuralism, then? Its discursive potency derives from being simultaneously an alternative vision to neoliberal dogmatism, a comprehensive development strategy, an integrated policy framework, and a grand narrative about the path toward modernity that the twenty-first century allegedly offers to Latin American and Caribbean societies. To reduce it to just one of these dimensions is to misrepresent and underestimate it. Precisely because it is more than just an economic policy approach, Latin American neostructuralism has been able to influence policy planners and interna-tional development agencies and to suffuse the discourse of center-left political coalitions, such as those presently governing in Chile, Brazil, and Uruguay.

An Alternative Vision to Neoliberal Market Dogmatism

Latin American neostructuralism is the first counterdiscourse to confront neoliberal dog-matism and to surface in the wake of the profound processes of capitalist restructuring experienced over the past decades. It is the response by thinkers at ECLAC to the intel-lectual offensive of neoliberalism, and to the perceived deficiencies of structuralism and state-led industrialization development strategy that neoliberalism supported from the late 1940s to the 1960s. Whereas during the second half of the 1970s and 1980s, neolib-erals insisted that market and price signals alone remained the fundamental tools for reforming Latin American economies and achieving international competitiveness, neo-structuralists countered that though market forces continued to be primary, politics and government intervention were imperative for constructing the society-wide "systemic competitiveness" necessary to compete successfully in world markets (ECLAC 1990). Political and institutional intervention, they argued, were essential for generating the synergy, coordination, and social harmony indispensable for fluid and speedy integration into the globalization process (Bielschowsky 2009).

By replacing the market dogmatism of the 1970s and 1980s with a more holistic approach that restores the political, institutional, and cultural dimensions to economic development, Latin American neostructuralism promises to transform Latin America. To recouple economic growth with social equity in the new historical context, ECLAC argues, intellectual and political leadership, not just laissez-faire policies, are needed (see table 1).

Table 1. Structuralism, Neoliberalism, and Latin American Neostructuralism

Paradigm	Structuralism (1950–1970)	Neoliberalism (1973–present)	Latin American Neostructuralism (1990–present)
Motto	Structural change	Structural adjustment	Productive transformation with social equity
Purpose	Modernization via industrialization	Modernization via privatization	Modernization via globalization
View of development	Requires explicit development political will and state intervention rationalized through planning process	Spontaneous outcome of market forces and free operation of prices as allocative mechanism	Deliberate process in which social and political energies are focused in support of export drive and achieving dynamic entry into world economic flows
Key agent of development	State	Market	Technical change resulting from dynamic insertion in world economy
Obstacles	Legacy of historic power relations and institutions that erode efficiency of price system International market that reproduces center-periphery asymmetries	Mistaken domestic policies that hobble market allocation: inward-looking growth strategies, overvalued currency, protectionist policies; state role that suffocates private initiative	Pattern of external insertion: uncoordinated productive apparatus that traps countries in "low" road (competing via cheap labor and currency devaluations) rather than through productivity increases and innovation
Role of the state	Structural reforms Steer capital accumulation Develop key industrial sectors Protect economy from external fluctuations	Provide minimum conditions for market to function: private property; enforce contracts; maintain order, collect data, provide limited safety net	Generate social and political consensus Increase competitiveness of exports (clusters, public-private partnerships) Facilitate adaptability and upgrading of labor force Produce social cohesion
Social Conflict	State absorbs pressure from conflicting social groups politically to regulate economic variables	Repression to disarticulate collective social actors "Trickle down" effect Targeted subsidies	Channel/subordinate social conflict to "common goal" of competitive insertion in world economy Tap social capital Link civil society to export drive
Outcome	Economy is subordinate to politics	Politics is subordinate to economy	Political, cultural and emotional space needs to be shaped to meet requirements of globalization

Source: Adapted from Petras and Leiva 1994.

In contrast to the trauma and suffering brought by laissez-faire economics and dictatorial rule during the "lost decade" of the 1980s, Latin American neostructuralism hoists the highly seductive notion that international competitiveness, social integration, and political legitimacy can synergistically be attained by swimming along with, not against, the swift currents unleashed by globalization. Through a conceptual and policy framework wherein economic growth, equity, and democracy mutually reinforce one another, it offers the region a new path through which to remake the countenance of globalization and Latin American countries' economic insertion into it (Ocampo 2000; Ocampo and Martín 2002). Without challenging the power of transnational corporate capital, but by relying on a lucid policy and political intervention, neostructuralism makes it possible to fashion a new "globalization with a human face."

Neostructuralists argue that if Latin America and the Caribbean are to travel down this more desirable path toward globalization, a broader vision of economic development is required; governments, institutions, and political systems must prepare themselves to play a qualitatively different leadership role in ensuring international competitiveness. Productive development policies, in addition to social pacts and explicit initiatives to sustain social cohesion, must become part of an integrated menu of development policies. Through this more holistic approach, individual export enterprises, as well as entire economies, can be transformed into radiating hubs propagating globalization's economic, technological, and social benefits. Chile since 1990 has been the launching site, testing ground, and, arguably, showcase for this new postneoliberal development approach.

An Integrated Policy Framework That Supports a "Post-Washington Consensus"

Latin American neostructuralism has also been called a package of economic measures that will help remedy the crises spawned by neoliberalism through policies that "will prove viable politically and socioeconomically but also promote democratic regimes and greater social justice" (Meller 1991, 1). Neostructuralism's main premise is that through a different set of economic policies, more attentive to institutional, political, and cultural factors too long excluded by free market reductionism, countries can attain the high road to globalization.

This requires a shift toward exports with higher value-added and an international competitiveness based on increased productivity and innovation. If Latin America is to gain the economic, social, and political benefits offered by globalization, it must abandon its current export profile, based mainly on the export of natural resources with low levels of processing and produced by low-wage workers. Switching from the current, unfavorable low road to the promising high road to globalization requires exporting ketchup instead of tomatoes; modular, ready-to-assemble furniture rather than sawn wood; frozen and packaged food instead of fresh fish and produce.

Instead of radical reforms, Latin America's massive problems of poverty, inequality, and disappointing economic growth rates can therefore be better addressed by ensuring a more dynamic entry into world markets. On the basis of "reforming the reforms" and improving policy design, international competitiveness, economic growth, social equity, political democracy, and legitimacy can be made to mutually reinforce one another in an ever-expanding virtuous circle.

Latin American neostructuralism therefore represents an explicit awareness that if market forces are to operate effectively, they need to be complemented by non-market-based forms of coordination. Economic policies must be conceived with an eye to the role that institutions, culture, and social capital play in economic coordination. Economic growth, social equity, democratic governance, and governability consequently require a much expanded policy mindset and palette. The main characteristic of the neostructuralist policy framework, then, is the active promotion of new forms of social coordination beyond those offered by market forces alone. Neostructuralist policies acknowledge the importance of institutional intervention, civic-state alliances, and trust-based networking to overcome market imperfections, asymmetrical information, and transaction costs, and most important, to win the race of international competitiveness.

In terms of economic policies, neostructuralists believe that without active export promotion policies, exports would tend to concentrate on a few firms and a few products vulnerable to fluctuations in international demand, trapping a country's exports in a tranche of raw materials with low levels of processing. Among policies considered in this area, neostructuralists call for supporting technical innovation through partial subsidies and the promotion of strategic alliances between local and transnational firms, along with programs aimed at training the labor force and improving its skills through firm-specific training programs (ECLAC 1994). Such a framework represents a significant departure from neoliberalism's market-reductionist, laissez-faire approach.

A Narrative about "Progressive Modernity" in the Twenty-first Century

It is, however, as a grand narrative about how to reach that perennially elusive goal of modernity that Latin American neostructuralism displays its greatest discursive potency and enacts its most relevant political practices. Latin American neostructuralists and ECLAC have constructed a discourse and operational guidelines aimed at promoting modernization (the means) to achieve modernity (the goal) at a time when other paths, those offered by socialist revolution in the 1960s and neoliberalism in the 1980s, have shown themselves to be seriously flawed, particularly in light of the technological and cultural transformations and challenges brought about by globalizing capital.

The thrust of neostructuralism's discourse and policy efforts is to midwife the region's transition to a "progressive modernity," one in which "macroeconomic equilibrium, and productive modernization, coincide also with macrosocial and macroenvironmental equilibria" (Rosales 1995, 99). To achieve it, one needs to understand that

> A solidarity-based modernization will be possible only insofar as it emanates from solid social accords, supported by institutions that promote informed debate among those social actors who are most representative and have a greater technical component in their proposals, engaged not only in the diagnosis, but also in the solution, with a culture of shared compromises and of negotiated solution to conflicts (Rosales 1995, 98–99).

ECLAC argues that such a progressive or solidarity-based modernity requires a new pragmatism that places social cohesion at the essential core of international competitiveness, and ergo, as the beacon guiding the design of social policy (ECLAC 2007). Instead of focusing on redrawing property rights or redistributing the economic surplus, this framework displaces the center of gravity in policy intervention from economics to the realm of subjectivity, symbolic politics, and the cultural dimension. The actions of the state and political institutions must serve to create a new type of expectations, new citizens, and ways of understanding citizenship congruent with this new master narrative. Policies are thus increasingly displaced to operate at the symbolic, socioemotional, and subjective levels, and to produce identities, behaviors, and modes of regulation in tune with the region's transnationalized, export-oriented regime of accumulation.

THE PASSAGE FROM STRUCTURALISM TO NEOSTRUCTURALISM

Throughout the 1970s and 1980s, in the face of the neoliberal onslaught, ECLAC policy-makers were on the defensive, unable to articulate a coherent counterproposal as neo-liberal policies supported by the World Bank, the International Monetary Fund, and the repressive power of much of Latin America's military imposed far-reaching programs of structural reform inspired by neoliberalism. As Gert Rosenthal, then secretary-general of ECLAC, recalls, "the institution was frankly on the defensive, both in terms of the collective imaginary as well as in the academic world" (Rosenthal 2000, 74).

Caught between neoliberal orthodoxy and the exhausted import substitution industrialization pattern of accumulation, the ECLAC leadership confronted the daunting task of providing the answer to a key question: what development paradigm could be offered to the region? Facing increasing pressure, ECLAC found itself intellectually disoriented and theoretically unarmed to respond to the new challenges and the new conditions. Rosenthal describes the intellectual climate among the staff he directed: "Some staff members leaned toward defending the cepalino message of yore, while others were finding some merits to the theoretical winds that were starting to blow, especially in the Southern Cone" (Rosenthal 2000, 74). Buffeted by these crosswinds, ECLAC found itself without a theoretical rudder for a good part of the 1980s. "For many years, there was no synthesis of the internal debate into a renovated and coherent message, but it led to different proposals that offered ambiguous and even contradictory signals regarding the institutional stance" (Rosenthal 2000, 75).

It was not until ECLAC stole neoliberalism's thunder, thanks to the intellectual leadership of Fernando Fajnzylber in the 1990 publication, that the defensiveness, perplexity, and internal disarray could be overcome. During its subsequent upward trajectory, Latin American neostructuralism challenged neoliberal market-reductionist thinking; reconceptualized the relationship between economy, state, and society; and introduced a new development discourse that, over the coming years, would be increasingly embraced by governments and international development institutions.

In its metamorphosis from structuralist to neostructuralist policies, however, ECLAC jettisoned the "core-periphery" paradigm, which, despite its shortcomings (emphasis on circulation and not social relations of production), had the merit of conceptualizing that "the process of development and underdevelopment is a single process: that the center and periphery are closely interrelated, forming part of one world economy" (Kay 1989, 26).

Thus, although it is a step forward in relation to dogmatic neoliberalism, Latin American neostructuralism represents a significant theoretical and political retreat in comparison to the best traditions of Latin American critical thinking (see table 1).

SEVEN CRITICAL PROPOSITIONS ON LATIN AMERICAN NEOSTRUCTURALLISM

Since its 1990 debut, Latin American neostructuralism has gained intellectual and political influence in the region at an impressive speed.[7] Its discursive innovations, its ability to nourish the political discourse of center-left electoral coalitions intent on channeling rising popular discontent with neoliberal dogmatism, and the absence of fully formed, more radical alternatives have shielded Latin American neostructuralism from a critical evaluation. Such a critique is long overdue. It can provide greater insight into the nature of the emerging economic development approach, the current narrative about globalization and Latin America's path to modernity, and the progressive project for recasting the relationship between the state, society, and subjectivity.

A comprehensive assessment of Latin American neostructuralism is undoubtedly a vast and multidimensional endeavor. As a contribution to a necessary debate, this essay presents the following insights in the form of theses on Latin American neostructuralism.

Proposition 1. Latin American neostructuralism differentiates itself from neoliberalism through five foundational core ideas that operate as foundational myths

Latin American neostructuralism makes five central assertions about the prospects of Latin American countries. These assertions, and the assumptions behind them, act as the five "foundational myths" that enable Latin American neostructuralism to differentiate itself from neoliberalism and to construct a discourse that has seduced policymakers and voters. These five "myths" allow neostructuralists to frame the problem of Latin American development, in the context of the current globalizing processes, fundamentally as one of deciding and applying more holistic policies, so that the region may reap the fruits of a more dynamic and equitable development. The five core assertions are the following:

- The prospect of a relatively easy on-ramp to the high road to globalization
- The promotion of open regionalism, which makes the global economic rules of the World Trade Organization compatible with the aspirations for regional integration
- The possibility of delinking distribution from accumulation, so that "productive transformation with social equity" can be achieved within the confines of (and on account of) the current export-oriented regime of accumulation
- The purported dichotomy between "spurious" (cheap labor-based) and "genuine" (productivity-and innovation-based) competitiveness at the firm and country level
- The desirability of building a national consensus behind the export drive and the effectiveness of political interventions and "new social contracts" in the context of the region's open economies

Each one of these fundamental assertions starkly highlights major differences from neoliberalism. Instead of a dismal economic future determined by an export-oriented economy that competes via super-exploited workers and unprocessed natural resources, neostructuralism raises the prospect of reversing the deindustrialization of Latin American economies produced by neoliberal policies by achieving a different export profile, one based more on manufactures, productivity increases, and technical innovation. Instead of betraying Bolivar's dream and deepening neocolonial subordination to U.S. geopolitics and U.S.-based transnational capital, economic globalization, as promoted by the WTO, NAFTA, and the FTAA, when seen through the lens of open regionalism, is transformed into an adjutant to the dream of Latin American integration. Instead of the neoliberal "trickle-down" theory, in which equity and the well-being of entire generations have to be sacrificed at the altar of market-centric policies, neostructuralists promise that sensible economic and social policies can offset the exclusionary and wealth-concentrating dynamics of markets and export-oriented growth.

Under neoliberalism, participation in global markets became socially destructive because international competition was achieved through "spurious" means—lowering of wages, artificial devaluations. Neostructuralists offer an alternative path, one that can engender virtuous circles. Instead of authoritarian regimes, which imposed the laws of the market through state terrorism and the threat of imprisonment, neostructuralists propose an alternative form of participatory and democratic governance of the economy and the efforts to make a country more competitive. Increased public-private sector partnerships, state-civil society alliances, and taking advantage of existing social capital are all new forms of coordination that increase a society's capacity to innovate and participate in the race to achieve international competitiveness.

In sum, each of these five assertions is highly attractive not only for political reasons, but because each is presented as also responding to sound economic theory and to a more comprehensive understanding of the economy than what prevailed when neoliberalism predominated.

Deeply embedded in each of these five notions, however, are profound contradictions, which stem precisely from the acts of omission and marginalization of power relations from economic analysis. Such acts of exclusion should be understood not as responding to "sound economic analysis" but as stemming from the trauma-induced commitment to "social harmony" after the "Greek tragedy" of the 1970s.[8] One economist who suffered, in the flesh, the experience of Pinochet's concentration camps explains the neostructuralists' mindset and their hypersensitivity to conflict.

> The experience of the Southern Cone countries led a number of social scientists and political leaders to explain the crumbling of democratic systems at least partially in terms of the rupture of certain minimum social agreements and the unleashing of a struggle over the appropriation of state surplus. . . . These experiences have influenced the neostructuralist paradigm, promoting the search for a modality of consensuses, concerted action and participation that make it possible either to reduce conflicts, or at least subordinate them to the attainment of a common goal (Bitar 1988, 60).

Like the effects of fetal alcohol syndrome, the traumas of the 1970s suffuse the theorizing of neostructuralists, impairing their ability to question their founding myths. Although in Chile, such pragmatism allowed them successfully to negotiate a political transition from military to civilian regimes, it is not proving as effective in navigating the challenges of twenty-first-century capitalist globalization. How will the high road be achieved when Latin American states have become even more subordinated to domestic conglomerates and transnational capital than in the 1960s, losing all political and administrative capacity to "discipline capital"? To what extent does open regionalism legitimate foreign capital control of assets and WTO rules that gut the possibilities for activist industrial, trade, and technology policies essential for achieving the high road? Do a transnationalized economy and a capitalist class constrain fiscal social policies from counterbalancing the poverty and inequalities intensified in global economies? Given the nature of the labor process and large firms' competitive strategies, does a dichotomy really exist between "spurious" and "genuine" competitiveness? Have consensus and participatory governance become a way of building capitalist hegemony instead of popular sovereignty (Schild 2000; Greaves 2004; Leiva 2005)? Answering each of these questions requires a theoretical perspective that explicitly incorporates power relations into economic, social, and political analysis, a step that Latin American neostructuralism so far has refused to take.

Proposition 2. Latin American neostructuralism's mode of theorizing marginalizes key power relations from the analysis of the economy and society

A critical assessment of the emergent approach must focus not only on those concepts that differentiate it from its neoliberal predecessor—systemic competitiveness, open regionalism, technical progress, proactive labor flexibility, virtuous circles—but must also account for Latin American neostructuralism's own "inconsistency syndromes" (Stallings and Peres 2000).[9] These inconsistencies are rooted in two linked processes intrinsic to Latin American neostructuralism's formulation. First, neostructuralist theorizing commits critical acts of omission, marginalizing key dimensions of social reality from careful analytic consideration.[10] In the construction of systemic competitiveness, proactive labor flexibility, and the high road to globalization—the foundations for the virtuous circle—neostructuralism excludes critical aspects of Latin American social reality from theorization.

Specifically, neostructuralism excises fundamental analytical categories dealing with power and those power relations that constitute the realm of labor-capital relations, the increasingly transnationalized circuits of accumulation of capital, and the capital accumulation-social reproduction nexus (Leiva 2006). It excludes categories such as class and labor process from discussions about productivity and technical change. It ignores the gendered nature of the economy and social reproduction in countries that have undergone drastic, many times violent, transformations of social arrangements at the level of the household, workplace, and community. Latin American neostructuralism fails to delve deeply into the nature of power relations that characterize the current dynamics of the international political economy, where transnational productive and finance capital exercise ever-increasing control over the region's resources, economies, and societies, deepening the asymmetries in today's global economy.

Second, neostructuralist theorizing engages in more than just acts of exclusion; it explicitly characterizes key economic relations as essentially nonantagonistic. More than an "attempt to come to terms with a new reality" (Kay and Gwynne 2000, 62), neostructuralism radically breaks with its structuralist intellectual origins by postulating, a priori, a mutually beneficial relationship between global flows, the export-oriented regime of accumulation established by neoliberalism, the growth of Latin American economies, and equity and social development of Latin American societies.

It is this marginalization of power relations from production, the sphere of social reproduction, and international economic relations, along with a utopian, sanitized vision of corporate-led globalization that emphasizes management over explanation, which lies at the base of neostructuralist conceptualization. If the intellectual roots of neoliberalism's "practical set of recommendations" can be traced to the economic liberalism of previous centuries, the forefathers of neostructuralism and neostructuralist policies are of a much more recent origin: the 1950s and the work of Raul Prebisch and ECLAC, which came to be known as structuralism.[11] Whereas neoliberals resuscitate their ancestors' conceptions, however, neostructuralists forswear the ideas of their progenitors.

Proposition 3. Latin American neostructuralism's capacity for seduction (its discursive and policy formulation strengths) and its inherent contradictions (its weakness) have the same root: an analysis of Latin American economy and society sanitized of conflict and asymmetrical power relations, an approach that abjures core tenets of critical Latin American thought

By accepting the status quo (the export-oriented regime of accumulation) and by rejecting core ideas from its structuralist past—the main one being that transnational corporations and the internationalization of productive structures helped to reproduce Latin America's under development—neostructuralism proceeds to hyperbolize the purported harmonious nature of Latin America's actually existing capitalism.[12] Both neoliberalism and neostructuralism have sought thoroughly to reshape the region's economic and social structures, at the same time that they have actively marginalized key dimensions of economic and social life from theorizing and policy formulation. Deeply embedded in neostructuralist conceptualization and practice, such a contradiction offers a crevice through which both its strengths and weaknesses can be deconstructed. Raul Prebisch, the intellectual father of structuralism, in his mature years pointed out,

> The root cause of the incapacity of neoclassical thinking to interpret peripheral capitalism lies above all in its failure to take into consideration the economic surplus, which is the hub of this system's basic characteristics. It disregards the structural heterogeneity which makes possible the existence of a surplus; it bypasses the structure and dynamics of power which explain how the surplus is appropriated and shared out; it shuts its eyes to the monetary mechanism of production which allows the surplus to be retained by the upper strata; and it underestimates the waste involved in the ways in which the surplus is currently used (Prebisch 1981, 153; also cited by Kay 1989, 214).

By placing international competitiveness as the ultimate goal of both economics and politics, Latin American neostructuralists not only fail to take account of economic surplus but also tend to ignore the far-reaching set of power relations that are embedded in its production, distribution, and consumption.

Instead of being the root and propagating mechanism for economic backwardness, internationalization of productive and commercial structures is now welcomed as the only route to modernization. Foreign capital and multinational corporations, previously considered mechanisms for deepening technological underdevelopment, become now the indispensable promoters of productive modernization and technological innovation.[13]

Therefore, neostructuralists do not disagree in principle with the "outward-oriented" development strategy defended by their erstwhile opponents, but criticize neoliberals' tendency to "attribute export and output success to a fairly narrow set of policy instruments being manipulated in a tightly defined way. Their analysis takes account of very little else" (Colclough 1991, 11). In the words of Sergio Bitar, neoliberals "emphasize fiscal, monetary, tariff, and tax instruments but neglect structural, institutional and political factors" (Bitar 1988, emphasis added).

Proposition 4. Despite its claim of deploying a more holistic methodological approach than that of neoliberalism, Latin American neostructuralism remains incapable of fully understanding the strategic transformations Latin American capitalism has experienced over the past decade

Its omission of power and power relations from economic analysis—and its tendency to mollify conflicts—render Latin American neostructuralism incapable of adequately explaining the transnationalization and financialization of the region's economy and the growing informalization of labor-capital relations. Moreover, in the context of increasing transnationalization of capital, social classes, and social reproduction practices, neostructuralism tends to rely on describing the situation and to emphasize short-term policies, instead of formulating explanations that attempt to reveal the deep structure of Latin American economics (Osorio 2002; Robinson 2003, 2004). Consequently, its promises of virtuous circles and productive transformation with social equity, grounded more in ideological motives than in observed material dynamics in the political economy, dull neostructuralism's intellectual edge.

This impairment is especially evident when it confronts the task of explaining different phenomena, such as the continuous reorganization of the social and technical basis of production brought about by the rising transnationalization of Latin American capitalism, the financialization of the economy, the increasing informalization of labor-capital relations and precariousness of employment that accompany the expansion of globally integrated systems of production, and the transnationalization of the capitalist class, capitalist productive structures, and arrangements for the social reproduction of the population. Each one of these understudied trends undermines the possibilities of productive transformation with social equity as originally conceived by ECLAC. Moreover, they seriously undermine and condition the chances of deploying policies to produce social cohesion and effective, not just backroom, social accords negotiated among elites.

Each one of these processes is qualitatively changing the economic and social struc-ture and dynamics of the region, yet they remain outside the scope of neostructuralist concerns. Although they are partially and tangentially reflected in ECLAC studies, the neostructuralist approach has so far failed to place these processes at the center of analysis, much less to explain how each of these three qualitative transformations—transnationalization, precarization, and financialization—is inextricably linked to one another, and how they all increasingly undermine the possibility of achieving economic development and social equity in the region. The weight of these ignored dynamics also undermines the consistency of the key claims of neostructuralism and the possibility of achieving the high road to globalization under the current status quo and in the current constellation of power.

To reverse such a situation would mean returning to the critical spirit and not the specifics of the discarded center-periphery paradigm; namely, the notion that Latin American development can be intelligible only when it is inscribed within the expansion of a single world capitalist system as a whole. In other words, it is not just in the ups and downs of the external sector of a particular Latin American country where fruitful explanations are to be found. Instead, it is in understanding the development of capital-ism as a whole, and in elucidating how this process shapes the production, appropriation, and distribution of economic surplus in Latin America in a concrete historical moment, where the key insights about Latin American development are to be found.

Proposition 5. Latin American neostructuralism is not an alternative to neoliberalism; instead, it completes the historical task initiated by neo-liberalism, the consolidation and legitimation of a new, export-oriented regime of accumulation

Neoliberalism and neostructuralism are not wholly conflicting economic models or eco-nomic development strategies; thanks to their differences, they have played complemen-tary roles at different stages in the process of capitalist restructuring in the region. Armed with the concept of comparative advantage and zealously defending the free market, neoliberals helped to topple and destroy those institutional and societal mechanisms that, under ISI, provided individuals and social groups important levels of autonomy from the iron laws of the market. Neostructuralists, on the other hand, wield the concept of sys-temic competitiveness. They emphasize social harmony and political interventions to generate consensus, participatory governance, and nonmarket-based forms of coordina-tion, and to constitute individualistic risk-assuming subjectivities. They contribute later on to the consolidation of the new order and the establishment of an appropriate mode of regulation. Instead of protecting individuals, communities, and firms from the market, neostructuralists deploy a vast palette of policies to ensure the adaptability of those people to the laws of an increasingly asymmetrical, concentrated, and transnationalized system of capital valorization. Neoliberals and neostructuralists can be seen as a tag team rather than as antagonists; they deploy policies that radically transform the class and gender correlation of forces in society, making it possible to complete the transition from ISI to an export-oriented (EO) regime of capital accumulation.

By situating Latin American neostructuralism in a concrete historical context in the process of capitalist restructuring and transition from one regime of accumulation to another, and by examining the impact neostructuralism has had on existing social power, it is possible to state that it is not a genuine alternative to neoliberalism. Neostructuralism does not "cave in" to neoliberalism, but neither does it bring about a sharp rupture with the existing economic model or regime of accumulation; nor does it radically redefine its international insertion. Due to its theoretical and policy innovations, it contributes to consolidating and legitimating the export-oriented regime of accumulation. As the recent experiences of Chile and Brazil demonstrate, such a political project can be supported by a wide array of social actors, even those previously marginalized from shaping public policies. By opening up the management of the state apparatus to a new set of actors, by deploying policies that draw on the social capital and social energy of the excluded while leaving unquestioned the main constellation of class power and the bloc in power, Latin American neostructuralism contributes to consolidating and legitimating the new regime of accumulation.

Thanks to its political imaginary and more holistic approach, neostructuralism is better equipped to construct and shape the new set of institutions, behaviors, and expectations that the new regime of accumulation demands. Therefore it can be situated in the realm of politics more than strictly that of economics, where neostructuralist conceptualizations currently seem to be having their greatest impact. It is in the political realm that we find the most politically and ideologically potent of Latin American neostructuralism's core foundational ideas: namely, that concerted action, effective leadership, and promotion of participatory governance can best ensure society's adaptability to the requirements of international competitiveness, while at the same time deepening equity and social cohesion.

It is here that neostructuralism fully assumes its role in providing a grand narrative for Latin America's path toward modernity in the twenty-first century. This grand vision promotes the active though carefully circumscribed agency of a broad spectrum of social actors, ranging from state managers, capitalist exporters, and unionized workers to leaders of political parties, nongovernmental organizations, and communities. Neostructuralism sees participation and concerted action as the most effective means of marshaling the forces of cooperation in a society thrust into the raging fires of competition, constantly fanned by globalization, Leadership, provided by a restructured state and supported by the concerted action of a political system, is essential for orchestrating and guiding the cultural transformations required; such state intervention constitutes the linchpin guaranteeing that the virtuous circle of international competitiveness, social cohesion, and political stability can take root and prosper.

To achieve these goals, public policies formulated by Latin American neostructuralism include the promotion of different modalities of consensus building, participatory governance, public-private sector partnerships, taking advantage of and nurturing social capital, and constructing new forms of citizenship that rely on state-civil society alliances. Although these policies are not uniquely ECLAC creations, the merit of Latin American neostructuralism lies in using these to formulate a seemingly coherent framework for strengthening the political and ideological role of the state and for establishing action-oriented guidelines through which politically to direct the state's contribution to the long-term stabilization of the export-oriented regime of accumulation.

History has had a way of ironically twisting the pretensions of the economic development paradigms that have prevailed in the region over the past three decades. In this sense, neoliberalism gave rise to the "orthodox paradox"; namely, that "economic policy reforms aimed at expanding the role of markets appear to strengthen the power of the core of the state, the executive branch, and to enhance its control over key economic policy variables which affect the outcome of key economic activity" (Bates and Krueger 1993, 463). Latin American neostructuralism, in turn, gives rise to what may be called the heterodox paradox; namely, that economic and social policies aimed at expanding the role of participatory governance and civil society result in reinforcing the subordination of the public sphere and the noneconomic realm to the logic of transnational capital.[14] The outcome is the weakening of popular sovereignty and citizenship and the consolidation of transnational capitalist hegemony.

Proposition 6. Latin American neostructuralism should not be seen as fixed or unchanging but instead as being in a constant fluid state, given that it must constantly strive to negotiate and overcome the gaps between its rhetoric and socioeconomic reality

Just like many perishable commodities stamped with a clearly visible "sell by" date, economic discourses also possess a comparable "shelf life," a span of time after which their ability to perform appears to decline. Alas, unlike yogurt or sour cream, economic discourses do not come to us with a previously embossed expiration date. No public service regulatory agency performs such a beneficial task. The shelf life of economic discourses is the outcome of a complex set of conflicting factors, not the least of which is each discourse's ability to negotiate its own internal inconsistencies and adapt to changing circumstances. Latin American neostructuralism has deployed many strategies to extend its own shelf life since its 1990 debut. It has evolved as it confronts the recalcitrant realities of Latin American capitalism.

Although its headquarters are in Santiago, ECLAC has offices throughout Latin America and the Caribbean and employs scores of economists and social scientists, who regularly produce an impressive amount of research and data on the economy and societies of the region. Like any large bureaucracy and international organization, it has its internal currents and cliques, and its discourse is highly sensitive to political pressures and realities. All of this further underlines the necessity of understanding Latin American neostructuralism as being in a constant state of change and adaptation (Hoffman and Torres 2008). Divergent voices continue to speak, and new research problematizing Latin American neostructuralism's initial assumptions and different aspects of its foundational myths is constantly being produced (see, e.g., Bouzas 2005).

Instead of moving in a more status quo-transforming direction, however, Latin American neostructuralism's official discourse is moving backward. With the publication of ECLAC's *Productive Development in Open Economies* in 2004, Latin American neostructuralism attempted to plug the gaping holes in its analytical apparatus. It finally discarded the exuberant optimism supporting "productive transformation with social equity" that had prevailed during much of the 1990s. This shift took the form of dusting off and updating the old structuralist notion of structural heterogeneity through a new characterization of Latin America as a "three-speed" economy.

This three-speed model sought better to capture the diversity of Latin America's productive structure. Using a classification based on the size and legal status of enterprises, it identified three sectors: informal enterprises, which, "because of their structure and capacity, are of lower productivity and operate in an environment that offers them little opportunity for development and learning" (ECLAC 2004, 21); formal small and medium-sized enterprises, which face difficulties "accessing resources (particularly financial) and gaining access to certain markets"; and large national and foreign enterprises, with "productivity that often rivals businesses operating on the global scale, but with few links to the rest of the economy, and in some cases, with poor capacity for innovation" (ECLAC 2004, 21). Besides sharing a common space bounded by the nation-state, nothing structurally or dynamically connects these three sectors—not the underlying process of capitalist accumulation or its unfolding on a world scale. All pretense of situating the existence, structure, and reproduction of these three sectors as rooted in the overarching logic of capitalist accumulation on a world scale has been discarded.

After 2004, neostructuralists further acknowledged that equity would not easily flow from productivity-led export growth and globalizing processes, as originally thought. A more focused set of differentiated policies was necessary as neostructuralism shifted emphasis toward "society-creating" and social cohesion-enhancing policy interventions.

In "Elusive Equity in Latin American Development: A Structural Vision, A Multidimensional Approach," a document originally presented to the Fourth Meeting of Former Presidents of Latin America in June 2005, José Luis Machinea, the current executive secretary of ECLAC, and Martín Hopenhayn, from ECLAC's Social Division, identify the "strategic lines of action for a pro-equity agenda" conceived according to ECLAC's new three-speed model. This document is of interest because the authors identify those specific key policies "whose effects can be more encompassing over society, such as policies toward the productive sector, employment, education, and conditional transfers" (Machinea and Hopenhayn 2005, 35). The root explanation for persistent inequality is the refurbished notion of structural heterogeneity, which tended to intensify during the 1990s, not because of transnationalization per se, but as a result of "segmented transnationalization," defined as the "segmented incorporation of the productive sector into the information and knowledge economy" (Machinea and Hopenhayn 2005, 8). In other words, unequal and differentiated development is the product not of capitalist globalization but of not enough capitalist globalization.

ECLAC's publication *Social Cohesion: Inclusion and a Sense of Belonging in Latin America and the Caribbean*, prepared for the November 2007 Ibero-American Summit of Heads of State and Government, illustrates the current directions of Latin American neostructuralist thinking (Ottone and Sojo 2007). This document seeks to relink economics, politics, and culture by showing that "in terms of economic rationality, societies with higher levels of social cohesion provide a better institutional framework for economic growth that constitutes an attractive factor for investment by offering an environment of confidence and clear rules" (ECLAC 2007). From an analytical point of view, such policy design reveals that Prebisch's key question—how the economic surplus is being captured, distributed, and used by enterprises owned by the domestic conglomerates, transnational corporations, and banks making up the "high speed" sector—has not even been imagined, much less raised as a possible component of ECLAC's "forward-looking" new policies.

Proposition 7. The only effective antidote to the cycle of illusion, disenchantment, and crisis accompanying Latin American neostructuralism is a revitalization of a theoretically self-conscious and critical political economy

As the neostructuralist paradigm gains predominance and the center-left gains electoral support, strong incentives come into play to foster and prolong a climate of intellectual complacency and pragmatism. In the aftermath of the massive poverty and persistent inequality left by neoliberal policies, the promises of Latin American neostructuralism, its broader perspective and intellectual sophistication, make it sound soothingly seductive; it is able to tap into broadly based unrealized expectations and desires for inclusion and change. On an individual level, intellectuals and economists who have been marginalized for decades have seen in Latin American neostructuralism the possibility of leaving behind their condition as outcasts and actually administering key levers of power. The silver coin demanded acceptance of the "existing realities" of the global economy and a commitment to envision only policies that do not undermine the present structures constituting the current status quo.

The subordination of intellectual activity and economic analysis to the parameters permitted by "social consensus," or subordination to a "common goal," is a recipe for analytical mediocrity and obscurantism. Such a climate can be altered only by engaging in creative and rigorous analysis of the region's political economy and increased theoretical self-awareness about how we construct our meanings; in other words, a revitalization of critical political economy that does not avoid the analysis of power relations, conflict or the role of subjectivity but that locates these at the center of analysis is the pressing intellectual challenge of the moment.

CONCLUSIONS

The meteoric rise of Latin American neostructuralism, its expanding influence in shaping public discourse, its capacity to advance debates on economic policy and development strategy merit acknowledgment and careful study (Kirby 2009). The delay in critically engaging the new paradigm is partly based on the misplaced belief that Latin American neostructuralism indeed offers an alternative to neoliberalism, or at least retains the power to realize the hope that the dramatic social and economic costs of neoliberal policies can be assuaged within the parameters of the current status quo. It is also rooted in the persistent, weak theoretical self-awareness on the part of economics in general, and development economics in particular.

Given the dearth of critical assessments, this essay has outlined one possible approach for exploring the nature of Latin American neostructuralism, its conceptual and policy innovations, and the role it is currently playing in the development of Latin American capitalism. Subjecting Latin American neostructuralism to a critical and comprehensive assessment remains a pressing task in the study of the history of economic ideas and of development models in Latin America and elsewhere. Such an approach seems possible only once social scientists, policymakers, and particularly economists become more self-aware as to how they construct their claims to knowledge and truth.

This self-awareness, however, does not seem enough. It is also necessary that in the process they strive to become conscious of the role of economic ideas and theories in the reproduction or transformation of the existing constellation of power. Until such awareness becomes predominant in economics and especially development economics, neoliberalism, and the allegedly more benevolent Latin American neostructuralism, will remain instruments at the service of dominant social power, despite their repeated claims to objectivity, scientific rigor, and more recently, a promised capacity to deliver modernity without immiseration or social dislocation.

NOTES

I would like to thank the anonymous reviewers for their insightful comments and suggestions. The usual disclaimers apply. All translations are mine.

1 Neoliberalism has become an omnipresent term, employed with vastly different meanings in the literature to denote alternatively a set of economic ideas, a policy regime, an economic model, and the all-encompassing mode of experiencing economic, political, and cultural existence under the current era of globalization. This study uses neoliberalism in a tightly restricted sense of indicating a particular set of economic ideas and policies. It employs the term transnationalized export-oriented regime of accumulation when referring to the "new economic model" that replaced import substitution industrialization (ISI) in most countries of the region. Ergo, declining influence of neoliberal economic ideas or election of center-leftists does not necessarily mean that the export-oriented regime of accumulation (erroneously called the neoliberal model) that neoliberals helped implant is being questioned. Clarity on this difference is key for understanding the historical political-economic and ideological role of Latin American neostructuralism.

2 The literature on Latin American neostructuralism is woefully outdated. Most authors (e.g., Meller 1991; Colclough 1991; Sunkel 1993; Green 2003) have focused on comparing the policy bundles endorsed by each of these two schools of thought. For the most part, these authors are wholly partial to and uncritical of the neostructuralist approach, and acknowledge it as an "alternative" to neoliberalism. More recent works, such as Gwynne and Kay (2004) and Kirby (2003), offer useful descriptive treatments of Latin American neostructuralism but avoid critically probing its origins, conceptual underpinnings, or societal outcomes.

3 This essay draws on a broader research project. See Leiva 2008.

4 See Leiva 2008 for detail on how the study combines political economy with elements from literary theory, and specifically the work of Terry Eagleton (1986, 1991, and 1996). The method deployed consists of a series of connected analytical steps, which can be described as identifying its core concepts, historicizing Latin American neostructuralist economic discourse, revealing acts of omission, studying how economic discourse interacts with existing power relations, and tracing efforts to prolong the "shelf life" of neostructuralist concepts.

5 Calling Latin American neostructuralism a paradigm is justified if we follow Thomas Kuhn's (1962) definition. Ben Fine's work (2000) highlights the notion that a paradigm has three components: an exemplar, a world vision, and a body of professionals. Even though it is not an academic creation but has emerged as a collection of policy orientations and proposals to deal with concrete problems, in my opinion, Latin American neostructuralism meets all of these criteria.

6 Though neostructuralism pioneered the formulation of an alternative development discourse, it later incorporated many of the Third Way's recommendations on how the role of the state and public policies needed to be reconceptualized and reconfigured.

7 For expository purposes, this essay treats Latin American neostructuralism as a monolithic entity. The analysis presented here is based on those writings that have received ECLAC's institutional nibil obstat or that have been published by key staff members. These publications appear in the list of institutional publications on the ECLAC website. This assumed uniformity, however, is far from the truth. Latin American neostructuralism has experienced significant modifications since its launching in 1990, as evidenced in various ECLAC publications (1992, 1994, 2004) and the impressive amount of research and policy papers produced. At the same time, a number of ECLAC authors have attempted to address some of the omitted issues, but have done so mostly indirectly, without challenging neostructuralism's core tenets.

8 Rosales argues that their structuralist past was to blame for the "Greek tragedy of social change" (Rosales 1991, 5).

9 Stallings and Peres identify three inconsistency syndromes (policies that operate at cross-purposes) that were embedded in Latin America's neoliberal reform process. These syndromes revolved around capital account liberalization and the short- and long-term effects of reversible capital inflows; financial liberalization and monetary policy that resulted in higher interest rates; and reducing fiscal deficits at the same time that tax reform lowered fiscal revenues by lowering tax rates on corporations and individuals.

10 Every discourse inevitably commits certain acts of omission and exclusion in the process of its formulation; what becomes relevant is identifying these and determining their impact on the discourse's internal coherence and, more important (following Eagleton), the impact that such omissions have on the maintenance or challenge of social power and the status quo.

11 For an excellent discussion of structuralism, see Kay 1989, chap. 2.

12 The rupture with the structuralist past is evident in four dimensions. Internationalization of productive structures is now welcomed and no longer seen as helping to reproduce international asymmetries. Foreign capital and multinational corporations are envisioned as a key positive force in economic development. Private capitalists and the market, not the state, are celebrated as the key actors in development; and distribution is now conceived of as autonomous from accumulation. For a discussion of the transition from structuralism to neostructuralism see Petras and Leiva 1994, chap. 4.

13 Other key tenets of structuralism renounced by neostructuralism are that the logic of distribution is now theorized as independent from the logic of capitalist accumulation, and that private capitalists and the market, not the state, are today the key and most efficient actors in economic development. See Leiva 2008, esp. chap. 2.

14 For an analysis of the Chilean case, see Leiva 2005.

REFERENCES

Bates, Robert, and Anne Krueger. 1993. *Political and Economic Interactions in Economic Policy Reform: Evidence from Eight Countries*. Oxford: Blackwell.

Bielschowsky, Ricardo. 2009. Sesenta años de estructuralismo y neoestructuralismo. *Revista de la CEPAL* 97 (abril): 173–194.

Bitar, Sergio. 1988. Neoliberalismo versus neoestructuralismo en América Latina. *Revista de la CEPAL* 34 (April).

Bouzas, Roberto. 2005. El nuevo regionalismo y el área de libre comercio de las Américas: un enfoque menos indulgente. *Revista de la CEPAL* 85 (April): 7–12.

Colclough, Christopher. 1991. Structuralism versus Neoliberalism: An Introduction. In *States and Markets: Neoliberalism and the Development Policy Debate*, ed. Colclough and J. Manor. Oxford: Clarendon Press.

Eagleton, Terry. 1986. *Against the Grain: Essays 1975–1985*. London: Verso.

——. 1991. *On Ideology: An Introduction*. London: Verso.

——. 1996. *The Illusions of Postmodernism*. Oxford: Blackwell.

ECLAC. (Economic Commission for Latin America and the Caribbean). 1990. *Changing Production Patterns with Social Equity*. Santiago: United Nations.

——. 1992. *Social Equity and Changing Production Patterns: An Integrated Approach*. Santiago: United Nations.

——. 1994. *Latin America and the Caribbean: Policies to Improve Linkages with the Global Economy*. Santiago: United Nations.

——. 2004. *Productive Development in Open Economies*. Santiago: United Nations.

——. 2007. *Social Cohesion: Inclusion and a Sense of Belonging in Latin America and the Caribbean*. Press release. February 16. <www.eclac.org>

Fine, Ben. 2000. Economic Imperialism and the New Development Economics as Kuhnian Paradigm Shift? *World Development* 30, 12: 2057–70.

Giddens, Anthony. 1998. *The Third Way and the Renewal of Social Democracy*. Cambridge: Polity Press.

Greaves, Edward F. 2004. Municipality and Community in Chile: Building Imagined Civic Communities and Its Impact on the Political. *Politics and Society* 34, 2: 203–30.

Green, Duncan. 2003. *Silent Revolution: The Rise and Fall of Market Economics in Latin America*. New York: Monthly Review Press.

Gwynne, Robert, and Cristobal Kay. 2004. *Latin America Transformed: Globalization and Modernity*. New York: Oxford University Press.

Hoffman, André, and Miguel Torres. 2008. ECLAC Thinking in the CEPAL Review, 1976–2008. *CEPAL Review* 96: 9–26.

Kay, Cristobal. 1989. *Latin American Theories of Development and Underdevelopment*. London: Routledge.

Kay, Cristobal, and Robert Gwynne. 2002. Relevance of Structuralist and Dependency Theories in the Neoliberal Period: A Latin American Perspective. In *Critical Perspectives on Globalization and Neoliberalism in Developing Countries*, ed. Richard L. Harris and Melinda J. Seid. Leiden: Brill Academic.

Kirby, Peadar. 2003. *Introduction to Latin America: Twenty-First Century Challenges*. Thousand Oaks: Sage.

——. 2009. Neo-structuralism and Reforming the Latin American State: Lessons from the Irish Case. *Economy and Society*. 38, 1: 132–53.

Korzeniewicz, Roberto P., and William C. Smith. 2000. Poverty, Inequality, and Growth in Latin America: Searching for the High Road to Globalization. *Latin American Research Review* 35, 3: 7–54.

Kuhn, Thomas. 1962. *The Structure of Scientific Revolutions*. Chicago: University of Chicago Press.

Leiva, Fernando Ignacio. 2005. From Pinochet's State Terrorism to the Politics of Participation. In *Democracy in Chile: The Legacy of September 11, 1973*, ed. Silvia Nagy-Zekmi and Leiva. Brighton: Sussex Academic Press.

——. 2006. Neoliberal and Neostructuralist Perspectives on Labor Flexibility, Poverty and Inequality: A Critical Appraisal. *New Political Economy*. 11, 3: 337–59.

——. 2008. *Latin American Neostructuralism: The Contradictions of Post-Neoliberal Development*. Minneapolis: University of Minnesota Press.

Luhnow, David. 2005. Latin America's Left Takes Pragmatic Tack. *Wall Street Journal*, March 2: A15.

Machinea, José Luis, and Martín Hopenhayn. 2005. La esquiva equidad en el desarrollo latino-americano: una visión estructural, una aproximación multifacética. Informe y Estudio Especial no. 14. Santiago: United Nations. June.

Meller, Patricio, ed. 1991. *The Latin American Development Debate: Neostructuralism, Neomonetarism, and Adjustment Processes*. Boulder: Westview Press.

Ocampo, José A., ed. 2000. Equidad, desarrollo y ciudadanía: visión global. Vol. 1, Visión global; vol. 2., Agenda social; vol. 3, Agenda económica. Santiago/Bogotá: CEPAL/Alfaomega.

Ocampo José A., and Juan Martín, eds. 2002. *Globalization and Development*. Santiago: United Nations.

Osorio, Jaime. 2002. Sobre las recetas para salir del subdesarrollo. *Política y Cultura* 17: 69–98.

Ottone, Ernesto, and Ana Sojo. 2007. *Cohesión social: inclusión y sentido de pertenencia en América Latina y el Caribe*. Santiago: United Nations.

Petras, James, and Fernando I. Leiva. 1994. *Democracy and Poverty in Chile: The Limits to Electoral Politics*. Boulder: Westview Press.

Prebisch, Raúl. 1981. *Dialogue on Friedman and Hayek from the Standpoint of the Periphery*. CEPAL Review 15: 153–74.

Robinson, William I. 2003. *Transnational Conflicts: Central America, Social Change, and Globalization*. London: Verso.

——. 2004. *A Theory of Global Capitalism: Production, Class, and State in a Transnational World*. Baltimore: Johns Hopkins University Press.

Rosales, Osvaldo. 1991. Posibilidades y desafíos de una estrategia de desarrollo alternativo. In *Chile: problemas y perspectivas del actual modelo de desarrollo*, vol. 2. Santiago: Sociedad Chilena de Economía Política.

——. 1995. Hacia una modernización solidaria: el debate entre progresismo y neoliberalismo. *Debates y Propuestas* (Revista. del Instituto Fernando Otorgues) 3: 98–126.

Rosenthal, Gert. 2000. *Los años ochenta y noventa. In La CEPAL en sus 50 años: notas de un seminario conmemorativo*. Santiago: United Nations. 73–80.

Schild, Verónica. 2000. Neoliberalism's New Gendered Market Citizens: The "Civilizing" Dimensions of Social Programmes in Chile. *Citizenship Studies* 4, 3: 275–305.

Stallings, Barbara, and Wilson Peres. 2000. *Growth, Employment, and Equity: The Impact of the Economic Reforms in Latin America and the Caribbean*. Washington, DC: Brookings Institution/ECLAC.

Sunkel, Osvaldo, ed. 1993. *Development from Within: Toward a Neostructuralist Approach in Latin America*. Boulder: Lynne Rienner.

Weyland, Kurt. 2007. The Political Economy of Market Reform and a Revival of Structuralism. *Latin American Research Review* 42, 3: 235:50.

Chapter 4

"We Have a Consensus": Explaining Political Support for Market Reforms in Latin America

Leslie Elliott Armijo
Phillippe Faucher

What accounts for the widespread adoption and maintenance of market-oriented reforms in Latin America in recent years? This essay examines the course of market reforms—more polemically known as neoliberalism—in the four most industrialized countries in the region during the final decades of the twentieth century. It finds that economic crisis has been important in initiating reform, but that proreform shifts in both elite and mass preferences account for much of the demonstrable staying power of market-oriented reforms in all the country cases. Moreover, and contrary to much academic and policy opinion, political insulation of the executive is not an essential prerequisite of successful economic reform.

THE BERLIN WALL OF DEVELOPMENT STUDIES

The reorganization of the national model of economic governance in Latin America in the final two decades of the twentieth century was profound. Yet there were convincing reasons why most development analysts, not excluding the authors of this essay, even as late as the very early 1990s, predicted that such sweeping changes would not easily occur (Armijo et al. 1994).

The pre-reform model of national economic governance was known as import-substituting industrialization (ISI) and was strongly associated with a type of political system termed urban populism.[1] ISI involved a process of state-led resource allocation, using high tariff walls, to stimulate local manufacturing. Policymakers combined industrial promotion with programs of limited redistribution, creating a market accessible to urban workers and to a burgeoning middle class, a large proportion of which worked for the state. Local private firms benefited from cheap inputs, such as energy, steel, transportation, and communication services, provided at below-cost prices by subsidized, over-staffed state-owned enterprises. Few among business, organized labor, or the political elite had any interest in changing this arrangement.[2]

Profound distortions in resource allocations, inefficiencies, and lost opportunities notwithstanding, ISI caused a radical transformation of the economic structure that amounted, in many countries, to a political and social revolution (Thorp 1998, 197). Traditional landowning oligarchs and primary goods exporters lost influence relative to urban-based entrepreneurs and a new class of technically skilled bureaucrats and managers of public enterprises, often called the "state-bourgeoisie."[3] This state-led industrialization process lasted just under 40 years in most countries.

Market-oriented reforms represented a shift in policies at the core of the national political process. This shift involved all major actors—the state and its bureaucracy, the political elite, business and other economic interest groups, the international financial community—and most political, economic, and social institutions. Market-oriented reforms bundle together a large number of policies, which aim, among other things, to accomplish the following:

- Reduce state economic intervention.
- Increase competition, and thus the probability that efficiency will be rewarded and inefficiency punished.
- Create incentives for economic agents to comply with market forces, rather than, for example, seeking political protections from them.
- Integrate domestic and international markets.
- Shift responsibility over investment and growth to the private sector.
- Create pressures for public agencies better to enforce rules and regulations without discrimination (Lindblom 1977; Przeworski 1991).

Among the most significant specific measures applied in Latin America were stabilization and fiscal reform, trade liberalization and adoption of an export-oriented bias in commercial strategy, reduction of subsidized pricing of strategic and basic goods, privatization of state-owned enterprises, social security reform (often implying full or partial privatization), financial market liberalization, and withdrawal of restrictions on foreign investment. These policies represented a dramatic shift away from the status quo.

Two lines of argument had purported to explain why market reform in Latin America would not work. First, it would be opposed by all those who had benefited from the previous model of national economic governance. Economic elites, business, and organized labor—including both blue-collar industrial labor in private industries and, crucially, the mostly white-collar unions of public sector firms—could be expected to denounce and oppose market-oriented reforms because such reforms were likely to mean job losses or benefit reduction. Even if neoliberal economists could convince policymakers that aggregate national income would increase as a consequence of market opening, incumbent leaders could be expected to find a shift to the proposed new economic model politically unviable, as politicians found their support bases in the groups that had benefited from ISI. The impeccable logic of collective action thus predicted considerably less reform than would be optimal, from the viewpoint of society as a whole. Organizations would demand "protection" while politicians, by exchanging policies for political support, would supply "rents" to their constituencies (see, for example, Schamis 1999, 239). The conclusion was that serious economic restructuring would be opposed at every turn, leading rational political incumbents to desist.

Second, many analysts also considered progressive political change in the region inconsistent with market reform. Earlier in the twentieth century, the transition from a landlord-dominated, primary product export model of development to ISI had benefited urban industrial labor and the urban middle class, which consisted of middle-income groups rather than economic elites.[4] Somewhat unwittingly, perhaps, many Latin American intellectuals and scholars consequently assumed that ISI policies of state-led development had a permanently redistributive and politically progressive bias. Many worried that economic liberalization carried an inevitably conservative bias that favored capital at the expense of industrial labor, multinational business at the expense of local firms, and stability instead of growth (Foxley 1983; Pastor 1992). By this logic, the redemocratization that occurred throughout the region in the 1980s should have given political voice to those deemed most likely to oppose market-oriented reforms: the poor majority of the population. What, then, accounts for the dramatic promarket reorganizations of Latin America's patterns of national economic governance?

RESEARCH DESIGN

This study aimed to investigate the surprising depth and staying power of market-oriented reforms in Latin America. As cases, we chose Brazil, Mexico, and Argentina, the three largest countries in population and gross national product (GDP), plus Chile, a midsized country most often cited as the archetype of ISI through the early 1970s and the leading edge of market reform thereafter. These also are the four most industrialized countries in the region, and collectively their trajectories encompass the main variations in "Latin American" patterns of national economic governance (see Sheahan 1987; Haggard 1990; Skidmore and Smith 1992). We initially assumed that our task would be to explain variation in economic reform across the cases: Chile is almost universally typed as a rapid, wholesale reformer (Piñera 2000), while Brazil has a long reputation as a laggard. Our first surprise, consequently, was the empirical discovery that all four countries, by the late 1990s, had to be understood as substantial and successful market reformers.

We constructed the inquiry so that we could investigate, in four moderately detailed and intrinsically pivotal case studies, some of the main findings of the current literature on the political economy of reform in Latin America. In particular, and for the sake of cumulative social science, we intended the independent variables in our five hypotheses to be somewhat parallel to those used by Karen Remmer (1998) in her recent quantitative study of the correlates of economic stabilization. Remmer hypothesizes that frequent economic crises, high levels of foreign aid, a strong electoral mandate for the incumbent, and a large or increasing share of exports in the economy would predict reform, while a high vote share for candidates representing historically leftist political parties would bring less neoliberal reform. She finds support for all her hypotheses except the one linking a stronger electoral mandate to more reform.

Our loosely parallel hypotheses suggest that market reforms are more likely to be initiated and sustained in countries with a recent experience of economic crisis, external material support for economic reform, political insulation of executive branch policymakers, promarket shifts in elite preferences, and promarket shifts in mass preferences. We find that economic crisis probably is necessary but not sufficient for the initiation of reform. Both external support and political insulation are sometimes helpful, but were neither necessary nor sufficient for reform initiation or consolidation in our four pivotal cases. Also, consolidation of the new, market-oriented pattern of national economic governance requires both a proreform shift in elite preferences and mass popular support.

THE DEPENDENT VARIABLE: PROGRESS IN MARKET-ORIENTED REFORM

A brief analysis of the objective economic reform experiences of Chile, Mexico, Argentina, and Brazil leads us to conclude, unlike much other scholarship on contemporary Latin America, that the reform performance of these four countries was much more similar than it was different.

Although we intend our independent variables to be somewhat similar to Remmer's, there is a larger gap between her specified dependent variable and our own. Remmer measures the initiation of reform by the adoption of a stabilization program involving an agreement with the International Monetary Fund, and considers a given reform effort to have been maintained if annual inflation is either below 35 percent or less than that of the previous year. Given the comparative case study methodology of our investigation, we can employ a more complex understanding. We consider market-oriented reform to be an ongoing process that cumulatively results in a dramatic reorientation of the regulatory and institutional framework in which economic activity occurs. In evaluating the "reform effort" of our four country cases, we combine a quantitative and a qualitative assessment.

Measuring the Reform Effort: The Morley Index

Morley et al. (1999) designed an index to make comparisons of the degree of reform across countries over time (see figure 1). This index combines measures of five structural reforms: trade reform, domestic financial reform, international financial liberalization, tax reform, and privatization. Each individual reform index includes components that reflect the degree of government intervention (or non-neutrality, in the cases of tariffs and taxes). The index measures relative change in that it assesses each country's performance relative to that of the most liberalized country in the region during the entire time period of the study (Morley et al. 1999, 7). Morley and his colleagues conclude that by 1995 there was widespread agreement and policy convergence among countries on most areas of reform.

At the beginning of the survey period, the early 1970s, Morley and his colleagues assigned values to the four countries in our sample for their overall levels of economic liberalization. These scores differed among themselves by about 20 percent, with Chile being the least open economy in that period. Twenty-five years later—and this in our

Figure 1. General Reform Index

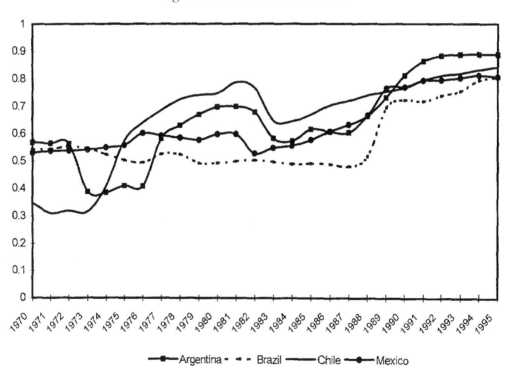

———Argentina - ◆ - Brazil ———Chile —◆—Mexico

view is the most remarkable conclusion of the Morley study—that difference was reduced to only 8 percent using the same index. This means that although the timing of the introduction of reforms differed significantly among countries, the difference in degrees of liberalization had practically disappeared by 1995. Each country index, moreover, "climbed" by at least 30 percent, which more than compensates for the remaining differences among countries.[5]

Differences in the timing and pace of reform can justify the distinctions analysts often make among "vigorous" and "cautious" reformers (see Stallings and Peres 2000). Yet the comparative outcome, as the index reveals, also allows us to stress the commonalities among our four countries. Another counterintuitive result is that Chile, considered a model early reformer, ranks only seventh by 1995 in a comparison of 17 Latin American countries, having been passed by Argentina (in second rank), among others. Morley and his colleagues rank the reform effort in Mexico and Brazil as slightly below the Latin American average, but by less than 2 percent.

A Qualitative Assessment of Four Crucial Reforms

We have independently constructed a mostly qualitative description of progress in each country in four substantive policy arenas: inflation stabilization, trade liberalization, privatization of state-owned enterprises (SOEs), and reform of social security. Each of these policy arenas is one in which we could have expected that entrenched interests receiving "rents" from the existing ISI pattern of national economic governance would have resisted market reforms.

Inflation stabilization implies breaking the characteristic ISI cycle of economic actors with market power, each trying to enlist the government's help to increase its relative returns, often cast as a classic problem of collective action (Hirschman 1968). Trade liberalization means ending the protections for domestic industry and lowering prices of tradables for domestic consumers, but at the possible cost of domestic bankruptcies, job losses, and deindustrialization. Privatization of SOEs not only involves increasing the efficiency of service provision for public utilities and intermediate industrial goods such as steel, but also implies job losses for the middle class and a labor elite of formal sector workers, as well as fewer subsidized inputs for local industry. Social security reform means reducing the generous retirement entitlements of the privileged middle sector of formal sector workers, especially those in public employment, and returning funds to government, ostensibly to free up monies for new social spending targeted more redistributively. Most Latin American governments attempted versions of these four broad types of reforms during the final quarter of the twentieth century.

Chile began market-oriented reforms in the mid-1970s, well before its neighbors. By the early 1980s, the Pinochet government had stabilized inflation, although at the cost of high unemployment (Foxley 1983). In trade, the average tariff fell from 94 percent in 1977 to only 11 percent in 1999 (Edwards and Lederman 1998). Most state-owned enterprises were sold, with the very significant exception of the system's crown jewels: public firms in petroleum and copper production and in marketing. In 1974, employers' contributions to social security payments represented 49 percent of their total wage bills, while social security spending, at 17 percent of GDP, was the highest in the region (Mesa-Lago 1994; Arenas de Mesa and Bertranou 1997). By 1981, however, Chile had leveled benefits—eliminating, in particular, the privileged treatment granted to civil servants—and had replaced its defined-benefit, pay-as-you-go (PAYG) social security system with a defined-contribution system, in which workers fund their own retirements through contributions to individual accounts (Borzutzky 1991; Albuquerque 1997; Ruiz-Tagle 1997).

Mexico's policy stance since the mid-1980s has been remarkably orthodox and pro-market (Lustig 1992). Stabilization became a high priority following the 1982 debt crisis, although the government did not finally control inflation until the 1990s. Mexico's comparatively early and unilateral shift to free trade was extremely rapid—it was initiated and completed between 1985 and 1988—and overall quite uniform across sectors (Ros 1993).[6] Mexico formally entered into the North American Free Trade Agreement (NAFTA) only in January 1994, but it made the decision to do so in 1989. Average tariffs were 100 percent in 1983 but only 12.5 percent in 1994 (GATT 1993b). Privatization was slow to begin but ultimately very extensive. Only firms in petroleum, petrochemicals, and electricity remained under state control by the end of 1999. In 1978, SOE investment accounted for 26 percent of gross domestic investment; but by 1996, this share had dropped to only 10 percent (World Bank 2000). Mexico's social security reform in the 1990s initially created private pension funds that complemented the public system. Then it shifted from a public PAYG system to a fully privatized one, with pension contributions channeled to individually owned accounts that private administrators invest in financial markets (OECD 1999).

After numerous failed attempts at inflation stabilization, and facing genuine hyperinflation, Argentina in 1991 imposed on itself a currency board, effectively tying its currency to the U.S. dollar to stabilize its value (Starr 1997). In 1985, Argentina began bilateral market integration with Brazil, a process that culminated in Mercosur (Southern Cone Common Market). Between 1987 and the early 1990s, average tariffs fell from 43 percent to only 7 percent, although temporary tariffs and quantitative restrictions, particularly in relation to Brazilian products, have been introduced on various occasions (Veganzones and Winograd 1997). Privatization in the early 1990s was swift, comprehensive, and controversial, in that most large firms were sold to foreigners. The result of extensive negotiations over social security reform in the 1990s was a mixed system, with the pre-existing public sector pension system still in place, though with contributions now equalized among different categories of workers, along with a new private system in which workers invest their own funds. In January 2002, as this article went to press, Argentina's rigidly fixed exchange rate system, increasingly overvalued for some years, exploded in a financial and political crisis. We cannot predict the future, yet we expect that the core of the promarket restructuring of the 1990s will endure.

Brazil experienced serious economic difficulties in the decade following the late-1982 onset of Latin America's debt crisis. Brazil managed nevertheless—through export revenues, through external capital flows attracted by high interest rates and debt refinancing, and at the cost of a long period of low growth with high inflation—to weather the 1980s with neither adjustment nor economic collapse. After multiple attempts, the nation finally achieved stabilization with the introduction of the Real Plan in mid-1994.

Cautious trade opening began only in 1988. Brazil reduced the number of goods subject to the "similarity test"—by which any company could block potential imports by showing that it produced similar goods domestically—in the early 1990s (GATT 1993a). By forming Mercosur along with Argentina, Paraguay, and Uruguay, Brazil chose to abolish trade barriers with its neighbors to the south. Brazil remains both less dependent on trade and less open to it than the other countries in this study, which are comparatively smaller. Yet its increases in trade openness have been nonetheless substantial. Brazilian privatization has been deliberate, even slow in its pace. Unlike those of Argentina, Brazil's privatization rules through the 1990s discriminated against foreign buyers. The extent of privatization, however, is large. For example, SOE investment hit

Table 1. Market Reforms, 1970–1999

	Inflation Stabilization	Trade Liberalization	Privatization	Social Security Refrom	Country Total
Chile	2	2	1	2	7/8 = 0.875
Mexico	2	2	1	2	7/8 = 0.875
Argentina	2	2	2	1	7/8 = 0.875
Brazil	2	2	2	0	6/8 = 0.750

Note: Authors' subjective, but not uninformed, assessment. Each country has been given a score of 0 (little or no reform), 1 (some reform), or 2 (intended reforms largely complete) for progress through 1999 in each of the four policy arenas, for a total possible score of 8.

a high of 53 percent of gross domestic investment (GDI) in 1979, but fell to only 6 percent in 1995 (World Bank 2000). Social security reform, in contrast, was on the national agenda throughout the 1990s, but relatively little had changed as of late 1999.

Allowing the various governments in each country to define the exact extent of their own reform goals in each of these arenas (unlike Morley et al., who evaluated country convergence with an externally derived and comparatively objective standard), we evaluate the reform effort in each country in each arena, cumulatively over the entire period 1970–99, as being "unsuccessful to date," "moderately successful," or "largely complete" for scores of 0, 1, and 2, respectively (see table 1). (For reasons of space, we simply summarize our results.) Each of the countries began the period with a score of 0 across the board.[7] Possible cumulative scores range from 0 (0/8) to 1 (8/8). Our evaluation suggests that Brazil is a relative laggard in the group, but also that even in Brazil, the shape of national economic governance had been dramatically reoriented by the late 1990s.

Our assessment leads us to three main conclusions. First and most important, all four of these countries have implemented significant market-oriented economic reforms. The distance between any of the cases in the 1970s and any of the cases in the late 1990s is much greater than the distance among the four in either period, using either of two independently developed methods of assessment. Second, there is some chronological difference in the onset of reform among the cases, which can be ordered as Chile, Mexico, Argentina, and finally Brazil. Third, there is some (though a relatively small) difference in the degree to which the four countries had embraced the full panoply of market-oriented reforms as of late 1999. Here the ordering, from fullest to shallowest reform, is probably Argentina, Chile, then Mexico, and finally Brazil.[8]

HYPOTHESES ASSUMING THAT MARKET REFORMS CANNOT BE POPULAR

A common theme in each of our first three hypotheses is the assumption that market-oriented economic reforms are intrinsically and inevitably unpopular. Successful reform efforts therefore are those in which the citizenry is either prevented from complaining or induced by special circumstances not to complain. Citizen intolerance of the transitional pain of neoliberal economic reform, except under limited and very unusual circumstances, is assumed as an underlying truth. This is, of course, the dominant theme of much of the literature on the political economy of economic reform (Przeworski 1991; Haggard and Kaufman 1992b; Bates and Krueger 1993; Pinheiro and Schneider 1995; Armijo et al. 1994).

Hypothesis 1. Economic Crisis Helps to Introduce and Sustain Economic Reform

The logic of this argument is that economic crisis stimulates reform efforts by political leaders, who recognize that something must be done to end the crisis. The experience of economic crisis, moreover, makes ordinary citizens more willing to endure the transitional pain of neoliberal economic reforms. Paradoxically, therefore, deep, frequent, or sustained crises improve the chances for subsequent reform by galvanizing leaders and inducing ordinary citizens to put up with macroeconomic outcomes that they ordinarily would not willingly accept. This hypothesis comes with a believable story: when conditions grew bad enough, both leaders and followers are willing to risk change (Weyland 1996).

One problem arises in the choice of how to operationalize "economic crisis." We have chosen to follow precedent here: like Remmer (1998), we consider a contemporary Latin American economy to be "in crisis" whenever inflation is equal to or greater than 35 percent in a year, or wherever official nongold reserves drop below a level that would pay for seven months of imports. These are both dichotomous measures; the country is either in crisis in a given year or it is not. Defined this way, all four countries were quite crisis-prone during the 1970s and 1980s, as table 2 shows. They all did better during the reform years of the 1990s, especially Chile and Argentina. Chile looks slightly less crisis-prone overall than the remaining three, in that slightly less than half of all the years in the study were in crisis by either measure. This comparatively good outcome, however, results from Chile's status as an early reformer, because outcomes improved following market-oriented reforms. We may conclude that economic crisis was endemic to the ISI economic model by the 1970s, and that policymakers and publics in all four countries had good reasons to seek reforms.

The advent of economic crisis, however, does not appear to have a close relationship to the timing of market-oriented reforms within our set of four countries. If we assume that Mexico had close to ten years of low foreign exchange reserves in the 1970s

Table 2. Prevalence of Economic Crises 1970–1999 (number of years)

	Crisis Indicator	1970–79	1980–89	1990–96[a] 1990–99[b]	Total (%)
Chile	Inflation	7	1	0	31
	Forex reserves	10	4	0	48
Mexico	Inflation	0	7	0	27
	Forex reserves	NA	10	9	at least 65
Argentina	Inflation	8	10	2	77
	Forex reserves	7	6	0	45
Brazil	Inflation	5	10	5	77
	Forex reserves	7	8	2	59

[a]Inflation.
[b]Foreign exchange.
Note: *Crisis* is defined as inflation greater than or equal to 35 percent or official foreign exchange reserves equivalent to less than seven months' import cover.
Sources: Inflation: CPI from World Bank 1998, except Brazil in 1970s: GDP deflator, from Fundação Getúlio Vargas (FGV). Foreign exchange reserves and imports: IMF 2000.

(a period during which the government refused to release this data), then it is not at all obvious that early reformer Chile was significantly worse off during the 1970s than any of the other three countries.

We surmise that the saving grace from the 1950s through the 1970s, in the minds of both Latin American governments and those portions of the population that enjoyed political rights, was probably high growth. When growth crashed in all four countries in the 1980s, then these long-standing flaws of the ISI economic model appeared as genuine crises, needing serious solutions. Overall, the presence of "economic crisis" thus looks like a helpful, possibly even a necessary, condition for the initiation of far-reaching structural economic reform. It is not, however, on its own a sufficient condition for either the early initiation or the continuation of serious reform (see also Armijo 1999).

Hypothesis 2. The Greater the Level of External Assistance, the Greater the Probability of Sustained Reform

Like the first hypothesis, this one begins with the premise that market-oriented structural reform typically is painful and therefore unpopular with citizens. The basic idea is that governments that receive large amounts of external assistance from international financial institutions and other official agencies can use these funds to help ease the pain of the transition period, providing resources that eventually can be used to compensate losers.

Remmer (1998, 16) finds a fairly consequential relationship between international aid (excluding use of IMF credit) and the initiation of neoliberal reform programs approved by the IMF. Stephan Haggard and Steven B. Webb, however, summarizing the experience of eight countries with inflation stabilization and trade liberalization, are more skeptical, concluding, "There is no evidence from the country studies that external actors tipped the political scales in favor of reform when the domestic institutional and coalitional environment was unfavorable; there is evidence that lending in such settings postponed adjustment" (1994, 5).

Because we have measured our dependent variable by achievement during the period as a whole and by progress in a number of reform arenas, we do not have the data set to look for a direct link between the initiation of economic reform in a specific year and levels of external assistance in or near that year, as Remmer does. We do note that each of the four countries has received well below the mean level of aid when compared with Latin America and the Caribbean as a whole or with all developing countries. The common observation that small countries tend to receive more aid than large countries, whether measured on a per capita basis or as a share of GDP, holds true in our case; Chile has received relatively more than the other three countries. On the straightforward quantitative measure, foreign assistance does not seem to have been crucial to the reform efforts of these four relatively large Latin American countries.

Defined more broadly, direct assistance by foreign governments and the main international financial institutions has been important as an emergency backstop for countries threatened with an acute external crisis, as in the "Latin American" debt crisis of 1982–83, the Mexican peso and regional "tequila" crises of 1994–95, or the "Asian" financial crisis of 1997–99. Quite possibly, assistance at these critical times prevented total economic collapse, thus allowing economic reform to begin (as in Chile in the mid-1970s or Mexico in the early 1980s) or to continue (as in Mexico, Argentina, and Brazil in the 1990s). Still, we do not see evidence that foreign governments have successfully imposed "conditionality," or specific reforms as a quid pro quo for aid (Stallings 1992; Kahler 1992). Our subjective judgment is that relatively large and regionally significant developing countries (all of the four, but especially Brazil) or countries with special bargaining levers in regard to major advanced industrial countries (especially Mexico, because of the long border with the United States) are relatively immune from foreign pressure to reform—unless and until domestic political leaders and other relevant political actors decide that serious economic restructuring is in their own best interests.

Our qualitative assessment of these countries thus confirms Remmer's fascinating quantitative finding (1998, 22–23) that the more successful market-oriented reforms were those that were designed and initiated locally and that had somewhat looser formal ties to the IMF and other outside agencies and experts. With respect to our cases, then, we can drop this hypothesis without much loss.

Hypothesis 3. Political Insulation of the President and Senior Technocrats, Regardless of Their Ideology, Helps to Introduce and Maintain Market-oriented Reforms

The third hypothesis builds on Remmer's (1998) hypothesized link between a president with a strong mandate and successful neoliberal reform, irrespective of the president's presumed political ideology or party base. Although Remmer's results disconfirm the hypothesis, we think it is worth further investigation. Her example of a president with a strong electoral mandate, moreover, is but one special case of a much larger class of arguments united by the theme that reformist policymaking will be enhanced if the political executive is insulated from the day-to-day demands of other political actors, including legislators of the same political party or coalition, opposition politicians, special interest groups, and even ordinary voters.

The logic of this hypothesis is that market-oriented economic reforms, even if they promise to improve aggregate economic outcomes, hurt politically influential special interests that previously had benefited from ISI policies. Structural reforms, moreover, inflict transitional pain on ordinary citizens. This problem of collective action can be solved or eased if circumstances allow the chief executive and his team of technocrats to innovate aggressively while being somewhat insulated from the constant importuning of other politically relevant actors. This hypothesis has a great deal of support in the literature (Bates and Krueger 1993, 462; Evans 1992; Haggard and Kaufman 1992a, 23–25; Callaghy 1993, 239–44; Gasiorowski 2000, 345–46; Geddes 1994).

The literature suggests three main ways political executives can be insulated, either temporarily or permanently: authoritarianism, a strong electoral mandate, and national political institutions that provide comparatively centralized decisionmaking authority. The notion of insulation by authoritarian political rules comes from the old—and partly but never fully discredited—hypothesis that benevolent dictators enable superior economic progress in developing countries. It was a particularly potent viewpoint in the 1970s and early 1980s, when developing nations in East Asia under more or less authoritarian regimes, including South Korea, Taiwan, Singapore, and Thailand, were lauded as "tigers" or "dragons." Throughout the 1970s and 1980s, moreover, most conservative and many mainstream economists perceived authoritarian Chile as clearly the star performer in Latin America.

Alternatively, a strong and decisive electoral victory can provide a democratic leader a honeymoon during which normally fractious politicians and special interests are willing to follow his or her lead (Remmer 1998, 11–12). The "strong executive" hypothesis does not imply that all incumbents able to pursue a reform will do so, but only that "the higher the anticipated capacity to pursue a reformist program, the more the political calculus will be tipped in the direction of reform" (Remmer 1998, 12).

In yet a third version of this hypothesis, a political leader can achieve de facto insulation by inheriting a particular set of political institutions, including electoral rules, parliamentary as compared to presidential systems, procedures for passing constitutional amendments and ordinary legislation, or rules delimiting the authority of various branches and levels of government. If one begins with the assumption that most of a society's influential special interests, as well as the majority of the general public, will oppose market-oriented restructuring, then it seems reasonable to value political institutions that centralize policymaking, and policy implementation, minimize disruptive "checks and balances," and allow technocratic and expert leadership to emanate from the political executive.

Our sense, however, is that none of these forms of the political insulation hypothesis helps very much in understanding the core of the economic reform process in Chile, Mexico, Argentina, or Brazil. The first version suggests that authoritarian leaders, as long as they are "developmentalist" rather than merely rapacious and corrupt, have an advantage in implementing tough reforms. Just as Singapore under Lee Kwan Yew is the usual East Asian exemplar, Chile under Augusto Pinochet (1973–89) is the Latin American case most often cited in support of this proposition. All four of our country cases, however, had authoritarian rulers in the 1970s, all of whom arguably were "developmentalist," or motivated more by an ideological commitment to national grandeur and economic growth than a desire for personal profit. Explaining Chile's early and sustained reform as a direct consequence of its chief executive's iron hand therefore seems quite problematic (compare Remmer 1986; Maravall 1995). The logic here is same input (that is, developmentalist authoritarianism in the 1970s), different reform outcomes, so perhaps the input is not so crucial.

Perhaps the second version of the hypothesis works better. After all, the tragedy of Chile's first democratically elected president from the left, Salvador Allende (1970–73), is often said to have unfolded precisely because Chile's electoral rules permitted Allende to win with only a plurality, saddling him with a weak mandate (Skidmore and Smith 1992, 133–40). It is interesting that Remmer (1998) finds the opposite relationship: electorally strong presidents, whether measured in terms of their own vote share or the percentage of seats controlled by their party or coalition, were less vigorous reformers than their supposedly weaker counterparts.

We also did a quick test, examining the vote share for each of the (more or less) democratically elected chief executives in our sample, coding those who won with 48 percent or less of the total popular vote as having a weak mandate, those with 49 to 51 percent as having a moderate mandate, and those with 52 percent or more as entering office with a strong mandate. We found a wide variation in our sample, as shown in table 3.

Although we did not evaluate the dependent variable, progress in market-oriented reform, on the basis of presidential administrations, there is a consensus among most observers that the most active reforms took place under Presidents Pinochet in Chile (who was never elected, so does not appear in our table), Menem in Argentina, Salinas in Mexico, and both Collor and Cardoso in Brazil (see Armijo 1999).[9] Yet according to the strength of their electoral mandate, among these presidents only Cardoso, in both 1994 and 1998, came into office in a strong position. Salinas in 1998 had a moderate mandate by the numbers. Many Mexicans believed, however, that the PRI stole the election, which profoundly undermined Salinas's perceived mandate. Menem in both 1989

Table 3. Presidents' Electoral Mandates, 1985–2000 (by percent of vote)

	Strong Mandate	Moderate Mandate	Weak Mandate
Chile	1989 Aylwin (55%) 1993 Frei (58%)		1999 Lagos, first round (48%)
Mexico		1988 Salinas (51%) 1994 Zedillo (50%)	2000 Fox (43%)
Argentian	1983 Alfonsín (52%)	1995 Menem (49%) 1999 De la Rua (50%)	1989 Menem (48%)
Brazil	1985 Neves/Sarney (70% of electoral college) 1994 Cardoso (54%) 1998 Cardoso (53%)		1989 Collor, first round (29%)

and 1995 and Collor in 1989 had relatively weak electoral mandates. This measure, taken in isolation, clearly does not predict reform success among our cases.

The most sophisticated incarnation of the political insulation hypothesis recommends political institutions that tend to protect the chief executive from having to make excessive compromises with other political power centers. Useful language comes from George Tsebelis's 1995 work on "veto points." Tsebelis focuses on the number of political actors with formal authority to withhold consent for the passage of new policies and legislation: the greater the number of veto points, all other things being equal, the more difficult it will be for a society to enact new policies.[10] Many institutional analyses of Latin American politics can be understood as arguments of the general form that greater political insulation—that is, political systems with fewer veto points—will increase political "capacity" and thereby allow faster and deeper economic reforms (compare Geddes 1994). It should be emphasized that centralized or insulated policymaking is not necessarily undemocratic, although it can be.

Table 4 evaluates the four countries in terms of some of the major recent institutional arguments about Latin America. Linz and Valenzuela (1994), among others, have argued that policy reform will be easier in parliamentary systems, because the chief executive is a prime minister who usually can count on the support of a party or coalition in the legislature (see row 1). All four countries here, however, are presidential systems.

If the country is a unitary rather than a federal polity, then more decisions will be made by the central government, which is less likely to be opposed by regional politicians with independent power bases (row 2). Chile is a unitary state, with regional and provincial officials appointed by the center. Mexico is a formally federal polity in which state governors and regional leaders have been, until recently, de facto chosen by and beholden to the central government. Argentina and Brazil have long histories of provincial independence (Skidmore and Smith 1992).

An independent central bank, not responsible to the legislature and only intermittently beholden to the political executive, can depoliticize monetary policymaking, insulating the executive from demands for deficit spending (row 3). Chile's central bank became independent in 1989, and Argentina's achieved independence through the radical step of creating its currency board in 1991 (Boylan 1998; Starr 1997). The Brazilian and Mexican central banks enjoy some autonomy but yield to the political authorities on major issues (Maxfield 1997).

Table 4. Index of Insulated Policymaking

Insulating Dimension	Chile	Mexico	Argentina	Brazil
Parliamentary, not presidential	No	No	No	No
Unitary, not federal	Yes	No, but docile states	No	No
Independent monetary authority	No thru 1989; Yes from 1990	No	No thru 1990; Yes from 1991	No
Cohesive, disciplined parties	Yes	Yes	Yes	No
Monopolistic corporatism	Yes	Yes	No	No
Legislation easily emended	Yes	Yes	No	No
High business concentration	Yes	Yes	Yes	Yes, but less than others
Total	5, then 6 (71%, then 86%)	4 (57%)	2, then 3 (29%, then 43%)	1 (14%)

Coherent, disciplined political parties aggregate interests and give the political executive societal counterparts with whom to negotiate policy reform. Coherent parties thus protect the political executive from having to respond to multiple and conflicting citizen demands, and reduce the need for wasteful resource expenditure via patronage (row 4). Although their party systems and degrees of democratic representativeness have been very different, Mexico, Chile, and Argentina all have had historically strong parties, capable of negotiating and voting as a bloc in the legislature (Skidmore and Smith 1992; Manzetti 1994). Brazil's parties have been notoriously weak; the weakness may result from another set of inherited perverse institutions: Brazil's specific electoral rules (Ames 1995; Mainwaring 1999).

Corporatist peak associations representing business and labor can aggregate interests, give the executive someone with whom to negotiate, and reduce the need for multiple, expensive, and conflicting side payments (row 5). Mexico and Chile have had strong and monopolistic peak associations. In Argentina they have been active but frequently mutually competitive. By all accounts, Brazilian corporatist institutions are unremittingly weak (Hagopian 1998; Murillo 2000; Schneider 2000).

The number of checks and balances (loosely, veto points) built into the process for amending legislation also should affect the ease of policy reform (row 6). Chilean and Mexican presidents have had a relatively straightforward route to amending economic legislation, partly because of strong parties whose leaders could speak on behalf of the membership, but also because the legislative amendment rules are comparatively straightforward. Given the onerous procedural requirements of their legislatures, Argentine and especially Brazilian presidents have had a comparatively harder time getting bills passed. For example, detailed laws on such topics as the minimum wage and retirement benefits for various categories of civil servants were written into the 1988 Brazilian Constitution. Changing these highly specific directives, many of which run directly counter to the program of market-oriented reform, requires not just the simple majority vote of ordinary legislation but also a "supermajority" of three-fifths.

Finally, a private business sector highly concentrated by ownership insulates policy-makers from having to respond to a myriad of demands (row 7). In this case, even without strong corporatist institutions, a few individuals can informally negotiate with the government on behalf of the most important private investors (Schneider 2000). All four of these countries have had highly concentrated business sectors, although Brazil, mainly because of its larger economy, is somewhat less oligopolized than the other three.

We have thus constructed a "quick and dirty" but perhaps not unreasonable measure for estimating the degree of "political insulation of the executive" provided by a country's institutional framework (row 8). Our scale runs from a minimum of 0 to a maximum of 7. The rankings from most to least politically insulated are therefore Chile (5 to 1989, and 6 thereafter), Mexico (4), Argentina (2 before 1991, 3 thereafter), and Brazil (1), which accords nicely with most of the monographic literature on these countries. Once again, we find a large variation in the independent variable, which has not translated into a large variation in economic reform. Nevertheless, the various institutional arguments do help explain why Brazil has been a relative laggard among this group of four countries that have implemented market reforms—which no doubt accounts for the particular popularity of such arguments among Brazil specialists (Geddes 1994; Ames 1995; Mainwaring 1999).

With respect to the implementation of market-oriented reforms in these four important Latin American countries, therefore, we conclude that the occurrence of economic crisis probably was a necessary, but in itself insufficient, stimulus to serious economic reform and that foreign aid played a marginal role. Our most startling conclusion in this regard is that rather large differences among the countries in the amount of political insulation enjoyed by presidents resulted in fairly small differences in economic reform outcomes, at least over the medium-term time frame adopted in this study.

HYPOTHESES ASSUMING THAT SUCCESSFUL MARKET REFORMS HAVE POLITICAL SUPPORT

Each of the first three hypotheses implicitly assumes that market-oriented economic reform cannot be popular, either with established economic interests or with the masses. Reform thus will occur only when something—economic crisis, money from foreign governments, or insulated political institutions—allows leaders to leap over popular resistance to changes in the pattern of national economic governance. An alternative way of thinking about the question is to posit that the president's political leadership is necessary but that reforming presidents, particularly in full or partial democracies, are unlikely to ignore constituent preferences. Our final two hypotheses suggest that the adoption of market-oriented reforms moves in tandem with the evolution of both elite and mass preferences.

Hypothesis 4. A Proreform Shift in Elites' Net Preferences Is Necessary to Maintain Market-oriented Economic Reform

Our fourth hypothesis states that insulated political leaders, even under conditions of economic crisis and with ample foreign assistance, cannot sustain market opening unless key interest groups come to support it. This hypothesis is grounded in the proposition that rational political incumbents, in all types of political systems, depend for their survival in office on support from a set of relevant political actors, the identity of which will vary among different types of political regimes (Przeworski 1991).

This hypothesis therefore posits that sustained market reform implies some mechanism or process through which the previous regime support coalition (the phrase comes from Cardoso 1979) for ISI policies becomes a support coalition for market-oriented policies. This may happen via a shift in elites, as new groups with promarket preferences displace the older, pro-ISI groups. Remmer (1998), for example, finds that successful economic stabilization (which she evaluates annually) correlates with a larger share of exports to GDP, the logic being that exporters will be more pro-liberalization than industrialists oriented toward domestic sales.

In our cases, structural economic change plausibly contributed to a shift in elites. From 1970 to 1996, Chile's trade integration (the absolute value of imports plus the absolute value of exports, divided by the GDP) doubled from an already high 29 to more than 58 percent; Mexico's quadrupled, from about 15 to 62 percent. Argentina and Brazil each became somewhat more integrated, moving from the low to the high teens during the period. Financial integration with the international economy also increased markedly in all four countries between 1970 and the late 1990s, suggesting greater political influence for foreign investors and domestic financial capital, presumably at the expense of traditional industrialists. Moreover, the recessions associated with the debt crisis of the 1980s weakened organized labor. Businesses tied to international integration become more economically and thus more politically important, and interests associated with production for the domestic market less so.

A consensus for reform also could come about through a shift in preferences among existing elites, including individuals, business associations, political parties, and trade unions. There are several mechanisms through which ISI elites might come to support market reforms. They may become convinced that their losses from remaining in the old framework exceed their transitional losses in switching to the new, market-oriented framework. The pain of economic crisis may inspire defection—but so also may negotiation, perhaps sweetened by side payments, with a reforming government (Hagopian 1998; Kingstone 1999; Murillo 2000; Schneider 2000; Thacker 2000).

Established elites may also realize that the regulatory reforms are going ahead whether they approve or not. So at some point, the sole rational response is to climb on the bandwagon. Of course, excessive inducements may eviscerate the reforms, becoming Faustian bargains for chief executives. In this view, reformist presidents (often technopols themselves), in an effort to conjure up political support from key societal interests, sell their souls and undermine democracy, equity, and future fiscal responsibility (see Schamis 1999; Hagopian 1998; Weyland 1996; on technopols, see Williamson 1994; Dominguez 1997).

There is also a more optimistic version of the coalition-building change mechanism. Although new interests and political coalitions have fairly quickly formed to take advantage of the new regulatory framework, optimists like Jorge Dominguez (1998) predict that dysfunctional "rent seeking" will be significantly less likely in the future than under the previous ISI framework. The regulatory state, simply because it is smaller and it distributes fewer discretionary resources, is less apt to be "colonized" by special interests than the more interventionist ISI state (Bates 1988). Open, competitive mass democracy, moreover, makes public criticism of crony capitalism and other abuses much more likely than it was under past authoritarianism.

The bargaining process between elites and reformers within the government can be illustrated with examples from the components of our qualitative reform index: stabilization, trade opening, privatization, and social security reform. In Chile, elite preferences were somewhat unusual to start with: the generic story of business elites who had prospered under ISI regimes resisting market liberalization does not completely apply. In the early 1970s, the business community, which had seen its assets socialized by Allende, openly supported a return to market principles. It did not need neoliberal economists and generals to tell it where its interests lay (Kurtz 1999, 408). Jeffry Frieden (1991) has argued persuasively that the high degree of class conflict in Chile in the early 1970s encouraged even entrepreneurs who ultimately lost from neoliberal reforms to stick with Pinochet, including industrialists ruined by import competition in the late 1970s and early 1980s. Gradualism was nonetheless a part of the strategy adopted by the ruling Chilean armed forces (Silva 1996; Kurtz 1999).

Inflation stabilization implied very tight monetary policy, yet business was to some degree compensated by active state involvement in promoting new investment. The Chilean state used CORFO (the Chilean Development Corporation) to provide financial incentives to nontraditional exporters (Schurman 1996). During trade liberalization between 1975 and 1980, business owners received a number of rebates on taxes and import duties, as well as some export subsidies. The specific design of privatization also stimulated private sector support: during the 1980s, CORFO provided subsidized credit for small investors and individuals who bought shares on the open market, in an explicit effort to use "popular capitalism" to rally political allies (Piñera 1991).

The case of Chilean social security reform is particularly interesting. Typically, social security reform provides a classic problem of collective action, in which the losers (those receiving outsized benefits under the previous system) are few but concentrated, while the post-reform winners (that is, taxpayers and the general public) gain more, in the aggregate, but are dispersed and thus disinclined to dedicate time and resources to promote reform (Olson 1971). In Chile, however, social security reform was responsible for a transfer of assets equivalent to 25 percent of GDP to privately managed funds, which helped the government to gain support from financial conglomerates, known as *grupos* (Kurtz 1999, 418). Businesses, moreover, reduced their contributions to their workers' pension funds just as tariffs were coming down. Finally, military officers' pensions were exempted from a reform that ultimately reduced the benefits of other civil servants.

What can we conclude about the market reform process in Chile? On the one hand, it frequently was not fair or just. Among pre-reform economic interests, business clearly gained, though not equally across sectors, while organized labor lost (Winn n.d.). Some analysis have hinted that the side payments made by the state of further the privatization process seriously have undermined the economic as well as the political integrity of the entire process of neoliberal reform (Schamis 1999).

Our own best judgment, however, is that it was precisely the authoritarian auspices under which radical economic reforms were implemented that made Chile vulnerable to charges of having created new groups of "neoliberal rent seekers" by 1990. Authoritarianism, and the political insulation that it provided to the state, stimulated the main part of the problem, not the necessity of coalition building, political horse trading, and side payments per se. Once Chilean politics was redemocratized in 1989, the economic reforms were widely seen as having been so successful that the majority of politicians and other leaders, of all ideologies, had become converts.

In Mexico, the government tried political coalition building. In December 1987, the central government explicitly linked the acceleration of trade opening to price stabilization through the introduction of the Pacto de Solidaridad Económico (PSE). The PSE reduced the salience of distributional cleavages over trade reform by portraying liberalization as part of a strategy aimed at increasing aggregate gains in the form of reduced inflation. This and subsequent government-business-labor pacts also proved pivotal in mobilizing support for market liberalization in general among large business groups, sometimes by the hypocritical expedient of exempting the most powerful business groups from trade opening in particular sectors (Heredia 1996, 273). As in Chile, the strongest support came from exporters and from private financial actors, particularly brokerage houses that stood to benefit from privatization.

Still, it is hard to deny the relatively large role of insulated policymaking and the imposition of reforms from above in the specifics of the Mexican reform story. For the most part, Mexican government authorities prohibited labor and business leaders from negotiating specific aspects of economic reform (Hagopian 1998; Teichman 1995, 2000), except, significantly, during the negotiation of NAFTA, when Salinas administration officials actively solicited specific business input at the sectoral level (Thacker 2000). Thus the pact of 1987, and subsequent direct consultation with key industrial and commercial firms, proved sufficient for the Salinas administration to bypass encompassing business organizations dominated by import substituting firms. The unchallenged political hegemony of the PRI was such that legislative support for reform was never an issue.

In mid-2000 Mexico remained, despite the election of the PAN's Vicente Fox to the presidency, the most authoritarian of the four country cases. The legislature has been tame in its criticism of government economic policies, even though the 1997 congressional elections brought a majority of opposition deputies to the lower house for the first time in modern Mexican history. Technocratic reformers in the executive branch extended assorted side payments and favors to selected elements of the business community and the PRI apparatus in order to build a viable coalition for economic policy reform (Teichman 1995, 2000). In contrast to the other three cases during the 1990s, Mexico missed much of the countervailing pressure of political openness, which would have allowed the losers in neoliberal reform to denounce corruption in the press, for example.

The important conclusion we draw from these specifics, however, is that political insulation and technocratic imposition from above were not necessary to Mexico's reasonably successful market reform process, merely convenient and expedient. As the political system becomes more open in the future, any market reforms around which political support has not grown up become vulnerable to reversal.

Argentina's market reform process was remarkable for its speed (Acuña 1994).[11] At first glance, the process also appears quite insulated and centralized, or perhaps even authoritarian. In 1988 Carlos Menem ran a traditional Peronist campaign, promising increased salaries to workers and a moratorium on the foreign debt. After his inauguration, he became a radical neoliberal reformer. The emergency associated with the economic crisis allowed the newly elected president to negotiate with the Radical Party, the major opposition party, and to obtain congressional support for significant reforms in 1989. The State Reform Law provided the legal framework that gave the government wide leeway to privatize through presidential decree. The Economic Emergency Law gave the government full power to modify legislation without the intervention of Congress, and provided for the suspension of subsidies, preference for local capital in privatization, and obligatory government procurement of domestically manufactured goods (Teichman 1997, 45–46; Manzetti 1999). These circumstances sound suspiciously like insulated policymaking, and some observers have interpreted them as such.

Yet the specifics of Argentina's privatization and social security reform reveal considerable evidence of executive bargaining with economic elites. Despite the immediate costs to their members in terms of job security, powerful unions found privatization worth supporting, in the hope that their long-term affiliation with the incumbent party would facilitate future collaboration with the government (Murillo 2000). Because the grupos did not have the financial capacity or managerial know-how to take over local industry, majority control of most previously public firms would have to be sold to foreign investors. The Menem team, however, added sweeteners for local business elites.

For example, many members of the lobbying group known as the *patria contratista* (formed from a dozen of the largest holding groups that had made their fortunes through public works contracts), which was notoriously opposed to privatization, joined the proprivatization coalition after Menem's administration reordered property rights to allow local capital to participate on advantageous terms. As a result, the group's cohesion collapsed as members "that were left without a deal, did everything possible to try to secure one" (Corrales 1998, 39). The speed of Argentina's privatization process was subsequently criticized for leading to undeserved windfalls for several local business groups (Hagopian 1998). It may be, however, that these side payments were politically necessary.

Similar bargaining led to the passage of social security reform in 1994. The process began around 1991, when the Menem administration began to court the support of private bankers by dangling future lucrative contracts to administer privatized pension funds. Unions relatively disadvantaged under the former piecemeal system of coverage were lured on board by promises of greater equity among contributor-beneficiaries. Once again, after the government had gained a critical mass of supporters, the holdouts felt compelled to go along, so as not to be politically marginalized in the future. The process was messy, inequitable in its details, but—and this is the point—not especially politically insulated, either from private economic interests or from the Argentine Congress; its members often served as political intermediaries between the political executive and societal interest groups, just as in every other contemporary industrial democracy.

The clearest evidence that political bargaining is a viable market reform strategy, however, comes from Brazil, the country in our sample whose chief executives have enjoyed the least insulation from societal and political pressures (Armijo, Faucher, and Dembinska 2006). The process of ending triple- and then quadruple-digit inflation took multiple, continuous tries from the early 1980s through the mid-1990s. The plan that ultimately worked, the Real Plan, did not rely on a clever "shock treatment" design like so many of its predecessors, but was instead a very straightforward project (Amann and Baer 2000). Its main innovation was that all its specifics were known, and publicly negotiated, well in advance of its implementation in mid-1994. Trade liberalization was also a distinctly political process. Sector-specific rounds of tariff reductions allowed the larger domestic firms, foreign investors, and exporters to use their market power (as the mostly foreign-owned car industry in 1995 had done) to obtain partial exemptions and delays on tariff reductions, along with substantial tax rebates. The quid pro quo was a formal agreement by automobile multinationals to make further investments (Shapiro 1993, 1996).

Brazil's privatization process reveals much about the character of its reforms. The nation's state-owned enterprises were sold at a relatively slow pace. New "privatization monies," moreover, were created from devalued domestic government securities. These processes were important in creating successive pools of domestic buyers, which generated the necessary political support for privatization (Montero 1998; Turcotte and Faucher 2000). The order in which firms were offered partly depended on the expected political opposition. No specific individual buyer was preselected, unlike what happened occasionally in Mexico; and sales were formally performed through auctions. Nevertheless, the conditions for acquiring state-owned enterprises effectively limited bidders to a handful of large domestic firms, in partnership with banks and foreign multinationals (Montero 1998; Manzetti 1999). The National Bank for Social and Economic Development (BNDES) also made subsidized credit available for local purchasers.

Like Argentina's Menem, Brazilian presidents have used decrees to launch economic reforms. It would be wrong, however, to view provisional decrees simply as a means to impose the executive agenda against the will of Congress. Congress later rejected less than 3 percent of provisional decrees (Figueiredo and Limongi 2000, 155). It has even been suggested that many legislators endorse the president's use of decrees as a way to deflect the anger of rent-seeking special interests hurt by specific changes, and that executive decrees may be a low-cost means of evaluating the initial impact of reforms and then adjusting the details as necessary (Amorim Neto and Tafner 1999). At crucial points in the process, moreover, the Cardoso administration successfully cobbled together the three-fifths congressional majority needed to amend the 1988 Constitution to allow privatization in certain "strategic" sectors.

Thus our fourth hypothesis, that reforming governments need the support of societal elites, is supported by diverse quantitative and qualitative evidence. Granted, this is a hard proposition to falsify; short of an all-out capital strike or mobilization of other elite-controlled resources, such as campaign contributions or the media, it is hard to distinguish among different degrees of support or resistance from key interest groups. Still, two summary propositions may be valid.

First, changes in the sectoral composition of the economy and in the organizational strength of unions occurred in all four countries and helped increase the political weight of presumably proliberalization interests. Yet the considerable divergence among the four countries in the extent of their international integration in the 1990s suggests that those were not the sole factors influencing changes in elite preferences.

Second, in all four countries, an apparently durable elite consensus now exists in support of market reforms. In our understanding, consensus does not mean unanimity; instead, it is the result of a bargaining process, after concessions have been made to accommodate conflicting interests. All influential parties eventually sign on, though perhaps with the assistance of some horse-trading or arm-twisting, both widespread democratic political phenomena.

In Chile and Mexico, where the major reforms occurred under authoritarian governments, political insulation of the reformist executive and imposition played an important, perhaps crucial, role in initiating reforms. Yet even in these countries, reforms were consolidated by political negotiations with economic interests, including organized workers (Murillo 2000), and political opening has not seen them repudiated. In Argentina and Brazil, where reforms occurred under democratic rules and executive branch policymakers were much less insulated, the bargaining was more overt and more likely to involve elected legislators (as well as governors and other elected officials, although space precludes their consideration here) and representatives of economic interests. Whether these bargains struck by political incumbents with already relatively privileged groups ultimately undermine democracy itself is a matter of opinion. We tend to think they do not.

Hypothesis 5. When the Political Regime Is Mass Democracy, a Proreform Shift in Ordinary Voters' Net Preferences Is Necessary to Maintain Market-oriented Economic Reform

Our fifth hypothesis asserts that public policy choice, at least in countries that minimally qualify as procedural democracies, is a fundamentally democratic process—not in its details, and not without significant distortion, but in its broad lines. That is, public policies that work against the core interests of the majority of citizens will not endure, because sooner or later the public will recognize that it is being cheated and will vote to "throw the bums out." Of course, these links are imperfect; public opinion can be manipulated, citizens en masse are poorly informed, politicians always have incentives to pander to elites whose support is crucial for funding campaigns, oddities in national electoral rules may distort representation, and so on. Yet a major reorganization of the national economic regulatory framework will not escape the notice of ordinary citizens (see Baker 2000, 5–6).

Remmer (1998) found that a significant vote for leftist and anticapitalist candidates and parties boded ill for both the initiation and sustainability of orthodox economic reforms. We turned Remmer's test around and inquired into the popularity of candidates clearly associated with the neoliberal agenda of market opening, fiscal belt tightening, and structural adjustment.[12] We divide the 14 recent elections into 3 categories: elections won by candidates who explicitly promised either to initiate or to continue market-oriented reforms; elections won by candidates who explicitly opposed the initiation or continuation of market-oriented reforms; and elections in which the main contentious issues were non-economic and in which the winning candidate expressed no clear opinion about market-oriented reforms before the voting (table 5).

We find ten elections, or an overwhelming 71 percent, in which the winning candidate took an explicit position in favor of the initiation or continuation of neoliberal reforms. Our coding of these elections, as far as we know, is not controversial.[13] In only one election (7 percent of our sample) did the winning candidate take a clear pre-election stand against policies closely identified with neoliberal economic reform: candidate Carlos Menem in 1989 railed against privatization and "unfair" treatment of loyal state workers and promised generous increases in traditional Peronist party patronage-oriented spending. Whatever the reasons for his post-election conversion (see Acuña 1994; Armijo 1999), in office Menem soon promoted wide-reaching market-oriented reforms. Reforms turned out to be popular, and Menem was able to get the Constitution amended to allow his reelection in 1995.

The final category is elections in which economic issues were not supremely important and in which the winning candidate did not express clear opinions about market reforms in advance. We place three elections (21 percent) in this category: those of

Table 5. Electoral Popularity of Proreform Candidates, 1983–2000

	Elections Won by Clearly Proreform Candidates	Elections Won by Clearly Antireform Candidates	Elections in which Market Reforms Not a Major Issue
Chile	1989 Aylwin 1993 Frei 1999 Lagos		
Argentina	1995 Menem 1999 De la Rua	1989 Menem	1983 Alfonsín
Mexico	1994 Zedillo 2000 Fox		1988 Salinas
Brazil	1989 Collor 1994 Cardoso 1998 Cardoso		1985 Neves/Sarney
Total	10	1	3
Percent	71%	7%	21%

Argentina's Raúl Alfonsín in 1983, Brazil's Tancredo Neves (who died before assuming office and was succeeded by his running mate, José Sarney) in 1985, and Mexico's Carlos Salinas de Gortari in 1988. In all three cases, the major issues were related to the democratic transition. In Chile's similar "foundational" democratic election in 1989, the pro-democracy consensus candidate, Patricio Aylwin, explicitly promised to continue the market reforms implemented under his authoritarian predecessor. Indisputably, market reformers have been overwhelmingly electorally successful in these four large Latin American countries.[14]

The question of why the citizenry as a whole in the four most industrialized Latin American countries apparently supports the broad agenda of market-oriented reforms is more of a puzzle. Many political scientists are distressed by the popularity of market-oriented reform, decrying conservative "neopopulist" leaders, such as Brazil's Collor, Argentina's Menem, and Peru's Alberto Fujimori, who undermine established channels of interest aggregation and political intermediation (such as political parties and national legislatures) to pass legislation without the approval of Congress, employing a program of populist speeches and patronage gestures to gain wide support among unsophisticated voters (see especially Weyland 1996). In this view, the undoubted electoral support for neoliberal chief executives appears manipulated and fundamentally illegitimate. Because neoliberal policies are increasing inequality and poverty, the argument continues, the masses are being misled (see Ducatenzeiler and Oxhorn 1999).

Once again, our view is more optimistic.[15] First, there are good reasons to believe that lower-income groups have a greater political voice today in these countries than they did before the late 1980s. Political voice has multiple dimensions. A more democratic set of national political rules allows for freer, fairer, and more competitive elections, as well as greater respect for civil rights and liberties. Expansion of suffrage is also very important in Latin America. The region's characteristic extreme inequalities of income and wealth have been perpetuated, even in previous periods of relatively competitive politics, by de facto and de jure exclusion of large percentages of the population from voting.

In all four of our sample countries, suffrage has expanded greatly since the mid-1940s. In Chile and Brazil, moreover, the percentage of the adult population that votes has increased dramatically even recently, rising in Chile from 46 percent in the 1960s to 82 percent during the most recent election for which turnout figures are available (1997), and in Brazil from 35 percent in the in 1960s to 77 percent in 1994 (IDEA 2000). It seems reasonable to assume that the newly included voters come overwhelmingly from lower-income groups. For instance, only in 1986 did Brazil's newly elected democratic Congress remove the "exemption" for illiterates from compulsory voting, a loophole that had operated quite effectively as a bar to lower-class political participation (except when landowners trucked peasants to the polls).

That relatively low-income persons are today participating in national politics in greater numbers than before, and that many of the most politically visible policy reforms differentially benefit those citizens, may help explain the political popularity of market-oriented reforms in Latin America. The poor have reasons to "vote for reform," as Haggard and Webb (1994) put it, beyond the perception that there is no alternative.

The most obvious specific reform that aids the humble is inflation stabilization. The authors of a recent 80-country study have labeled this policy change "super pro-poor," particularly when inflation is high, because of stabilization's highly positive implications for income redistribution (Dollar and Kraay 2000, 5, 26–27, 43; see also Easterly and Fischer 1999). We suspect that the single biggest reason for popular support of reformist politicians in our four countries is that market reforms have ended inflation. Inflation remained above our earlier cutoff of 35 percent a year for many years, or even decades, ending only in 1980 in Chile, 1989 in Mexico, 1992 in Argentina, and 1995 in Brazil.

The experience of high and hyperinflation was sufficiently painful and sufficiently recent, even in Chile, for voters to recall it, fear it, and support those whom they trusted to protect them from it (Gervasoni 1999). Ordinary voters quite correctly associated the ISI policy framework with recurring and persistent inflation. Some upper-income groups even managed to extract net profits from the highly inflationary environment (Armijo 1996). In sharp contrast, the poor gain from what is usually one of the earliest and most durable results of neoliberal economic reforms: the ending of inflation. In this context, it is not irrational that "neoliberal" inflation stabilization and fiscal reforms should be popular, even populist (Armijo 2005).

Dollar and Kraay (2000, 5, 43) also note that cutting overall government spending in developing countries often has positive implications for income distribution, simply because so many developing countries spend more on middle- and even upper-class citizens than on the poor. Government spending that is, in the aggregate, regressive in its implications for income distribution long has characterized Latin America. Since market-oriented reforms began, not only has overall government spending been cut, but purely social spending has risen as a share of both total government spending and of GDP (Stallings and Peres 2000, 16).

In Argentina, Brazil, and Chile, the three countries in our sample that clearly were democratic throughout the 1990s, the overall effect of all government social spending in that decade was to redistribute income toward the poorest 40 percent of the population (Stallings and Peres 2000, 36). Many of the reforms that political analysts most expected rent-seeking special interests to resist, including privatization, social security reform, and salary and benefit reductions for civil servants, are precisely those the "silent majority" rationally should support.

Ultimately, our expectation is that, as long as democracy endures—and we have every reason to believe it will endure in each of these countries—the days of wild swings in macroeconomic outcomes are probably over, or at least curtailed. Mass publics will demand (and get) reasonably stable macroeconomic outcomes. Publics in contemporary mass liberal democracies in the advanced industrial countries have proved unwilling to tolerate either hyperinflation or long periods of negative growth. Why should mass publics in democratic Latin America be any different? We therefore expect that market-oriented reforms will, on the whole, continue to be implemented, because their broad and obvious consequences so far have often made life better for the majority.

At the same time, the need for democratic legitimacy imposes national variations on the precise reform packages implemented in each country. For example, certain policies often identified as essential reforms, particularly external financial liberalization, increase a country's vulnerability to imported macroeconomic instability, which is particularly onerous for the poor. A country with a democratic as opposed to an authoritarian government, however, is in a better position to bargain with external actors, such as the IMF, on controversial matters, such as capital controls or higher social spending. (In game theory terms, an elected and generally proreform government can "credibly threaten" to lose the subsequent election to economic populists of the old ISI type, whom the international financial institutions and foreign investors will like much less.)

We anticipate that the coming of mass procedural political democracy to Argentina, Brazil, Chile, and now Mexico should itself provide the best possible reason (that is, winning votes) for incumbent political leaders to keep inflation low—and also to do whatever else it takes to restart growth and decrease Latin America's scandalous and globally unmatched levels of inequality.

CONCLUSIONS

The persistence of market discipline as the main orientation of the economic policies applied in most of Latin America for the past 25 years is a puzzle, given that these reforms significantly changed the regulatory environment of the previous 40 years. The earlier system benefited local business, the urban middle class, and organized workers, a coalition of interests difficult to defeat in any society. The implementation of market-oriented reforms, furthermore, coincided with democratization, which, many analysts claimed, would liberate massive expressions of opposition from "losers" in all social sectors and would put an end to neoliberalism.

Instead, a remarkable policy convergence around market liberalization has occurred throughout the region. The remaining differences in degrees of economic openness among the four countries in our sample are negligible by comparison. This finding, which contradicts a significant number of works that discriminate between "vigorous" and "cautious" reformers, has been somewhat overlooked.

We propose that market reforms could not be consolidated until a substantial shift occurred in both elite preferences and the opinions of ordinary voters. Evidence of both types of political support for economic reform suggests that the process has not simply been imposed from above. The significant growth of foreign trade in these economies has increased the likelihood that business preferences in support of commercial opening and exchange rate stability will be voiced with renewed emphasis. The sharp increase in foreign investment integration in all four countries is both an expression of confidence from foreign investors and a reminder to political leaders that a change of course could prove costly.

This lock-in dimension of market deregulation probably accounts for a part of the observed empirical shift in elite preferences. When opposition has failed, and when the course of market liberalization is set and unlikely to be altered, then those businesses that stand to lose from the change have little choice but to adapt to the new environment, reinforcing by their own actions the trend they initially opposed. Frances Hagopian (1998) has astutely observed that once reformers achieved some preliminary victories, usually in stabilization and commercial opening, negotiations among interested parties increased. It is important to recognize the extent to which old economic elites, unions, prereform parties, and other interest groups have accommodated themselves to the new realities. In a region where military dictators have regularly changed clothes to return to power as elected presidents, perhaps this should come as no surprise.

This argument departs from the many analyses that seriously overestimated the capacity of the so-called ISI coalition of interests to oppose market deregulation. Reformist political leaders undoubtedly recognized the potential opposition they were facing and developed reform strategies accordingly. This is where negotiation intervened, as proreform political executives and their teams both actively promoted supporting coalitions and created programs to compensate losers or neutralize their opposition through exemption. These complex and, at times, contradictory measures may have slowed or postponed the introduction of reform; but liberalization, once well launched, has not been derailed.

This notable shift in elite preferences also confirms that, as Bresser Pereira (1977) correctly announced, the postwar class alliance in Latin America has collapsed. What, then, is the nature of the new political arrangement? There is always the possibility that a new set of clientelistic politicians will operate to serve the old elites, now reinvented as market entrepreneurs seeking to appropriate the side payments that governments make in order to achieve lasting results in market liberalization. Many of our colleagues clearly fear that something like this is happening. As evidence, they point to irregularities in the privatization process in Argentina, sharply increased foreign penetration in Chile and Mexico, and the extraordinary staying power of the most traditional and clientelistic politicians in Brazil.

Our argument about shifts in mass preferences, however, points in another direction, allowing for cautious optimism. Political exclusion is not a necessary condition for the regulatory changes required by market liberalization. Democracy does not run contrary to market reforms, as the evidence of recent electoral contests has shown. Chile, and more recently Mexico, have demonstrated that a transition to democracy is likely to be associated with the persistence of prior economic liberalization or even, as is probable in the case of Mexico, its further deepening.

One can always question the quality of democratic expressions of mass preferences, claiming that masses are bedazzled by charismatic neoliberal leaders who have created neopopulist coalitions. The pessimists legitimately note that in the last years of the twentieth century, growth was slow in the region, with inequality and poverty on the increase. In our four sample countries, the overall effects of all policies plus all exogenous shocks was that the income share of the poorest 40 percent improved (albeit from very unequal levels) between the mid-1980s and 2000 in two countries, Brazil and Chile, but worsened in the other two, Argentina and Mexico (Mostajo 2000, 21–24). More recent research suggests that institutional reforms that tend to widen democratic participation—such as electoral rules that make voting compulsory, on pain of being assessed a small fine—have been associated with improved income distribution (Chong and Oliveira 2008).

We believe that recent expansions in the franchise and in other forms of meaningful political participation are not illusory. Just as the weight of mass public opinion has helped comparatively uninsulated reformist leaders, such as Argentina's Menem and Brazil's Cardoso, overcome elite resistance to the changes necessary to achieve genuine control over inflation, so the public's demands for growth and jobs can help national leaders take some policy stands that are at odds with the demands of international investors and neoliberal orthodoxy itself. This has perhaps been demonstrated by Chile's courageous insistence in the 1990s on broad market openness iconoclastically combined with the maintenance of some capital controls and state ownership of the copper mines.

As the initial version of this chapter went to press, Argentina was in crisis. We predicted then that its leaders would maintain a broadly promarket regulatory framework while nonetheless accepting the democratic political imperative that the pain of economic adjustment should be shared among various stakeholders, including both citizens and foreign direct investors. Mass preferences, we argued, could act as a strong and useful reality check for political incumbents, as ordinary voters, particularly after the experience of high inflation, recognize that their interests are best served not by extraordinary subsidies, but instead by stable, noninflationary growth. In the seven plus years since this chapter was first published, much attention has been given to the election of a number of left-wing presidents in Latin America (in Brazil, Argentina, Ecuador, Uruguay, Bolivia, Nicaragua, Paraguay, and El Salvador) and to the resurgence of populist policies in some countries. These events do not negate the gist of our analysis.

First, there has been no dramatic shift in economic policy orientation in the four countries we analyze, despite important changes in the expressed ideological inclinations of the majority coalitions in power. Chile has stayed the course, the stability of its macroeconomic policy being mirrored by the stability of the ruling coalition. Mexico, under President Felipe Calderón, the only one of our four countries to have an explicit position supporting market-oriented policies, has been the hardest hit by the 2008–2009 global economic and financial crisis that began in the United States. This could well bring a leftward political shift, arguably a much needed one, but will not undo the promarket regulatory framework. Brazil's Lula has surprised his followers and many analysts by repeatedly endorsing the strict adherence of his government to fiscal responsibility. Meanwhile, Brazil's highly regressive income distribution has continued to improve slowly. Finally, and despite their inflammatory rhetoric, friendship with Venezuela's Hugo Chávez, and various contentious initiatives recalling the colorful years of Perón, Argentina's Kirchners (Néstor, succeeded in the presidency by his wife, Cristina Fernández) have maintained most of Argentina's significant promarket policies.

Second, and more importantly, it is an indication of *normal democratic politics* that after a period of relatively conservative but necessary economic reforms, there should be a widespread electoral shift toward incoming leaders with an explicit commitment to prioritizing policies aimed at closing Latin America's "social deficit." With the November 2008 election of Barak Obama, voters in the United States manifested the same impulse. True, some other Latin American countries besides the four profiled here have implemented policies that closely replicate some aspects of the classical economic populist model. Hugo Chávez' crusading influence has been felt throughout the region. Bolivia's Evo Morales and Ecuador's Rafael Corréa have introduced controversial policy shifts, including Morales' nationalization of the natural gas holdings of both neighbors and foreign powers, and similar conflicts with transnational firms in Ecuador. In both cases the revolutionary accents have been used as much to mobilize domestic support in favor of additional rounds of constitutional reform favoring the incumbent as for the stated purpose of renegotiating contracts with foreign firms over rents and export revenues. Argentina, Ecuador and Bolivia, as well as several smaller Central American and Caribbean countries, recently have accepted Venezuela's financial help.

Yet Chávez has faced opposition from Colombia, Peru, and Brazil and has not been able to convince any of the larger countries of the region to embark on his Bolivarian revolution as an alternative to market-led economic development. Although the U.S.-led Summit of the Americas process has been moribund since Argentina, Brazil and Venezuela joined in rejecting the plans for the Free Trade Area of the Americas (FTAA) in late 2005, the likely winner is not radical populism. It is instead a network of bilateral links coupled with an eminently moderate regional integration project spearheaded by Brazil, which builds on existing institutional links between the Common Market of the South (MERCOSUR) and the Andean Community (CAN). Mass democratic politics typically trend toward centrist politics, even when they may not look moderate to outsiders unfamiliar with the particular national and regional context. In the end we have a consensus—and it is one with which most citizens of the Americas can live.

NOTES

The authors thank Delia Boylan, Luis Carlos Bresser Pereira, Ruth Collier, Carlos Gervasoni, Luigi Manzetti, Wayne Moyer, Pablo Silva, William C. Smith, Lourdes Sola, Erik Wibbels, John Williamson, Eliza Willis, and three anonymous reviewers of *Latin American Politics and Society* for their helpful comments and suggestions. Remaining errors are entirely ours.

1 We refer to populism in its political sense, defined by Kurt Weyland (2001, 5) as "a political strategy through which a personalistic leader seeks or exercises government power based on direct, unmediated, uninstitutionalized support from a large number of followers." See also Castro Rea et al. 1992; Kessler 1998.

2 In countries such as Brazil and Argentina, the military regimes that overthrew populist politicians nonetheless continued most of the ISI economic institutions and regulatory framework.

3 The term was introduced by Latin American scholars, such as Cardoso and Faletto (1979) and Bresser Pereira (1977, 1978, and 1984). Peter Evans (1979) popularized the label among North American scholars.

4 Several of the region's smaller and less-industrialized countries, including Honduras, Guatemala, and Ecuador, displayed the classic patterns of the earlier oligarchic, agroexport model throughout the twentieth century.

5 Admittedly, the absolute level of the reform effort is not well measured by the Morley scale, which takes as its upper limit the most economically liberal regulatory framework actually achieved by any country in the study. We subjectively assert that the overall extent of the changes was "large."

6 The most important exception was the auto industry; see Shapiro 1993.

7 In Mexico, unlike the other three countries, inflation per se was not a large problem in the 1970s. It quickly became one, however, when other economic problems arose after 1982, which suggests that the basic institutional framework in Mexico also needed revising.

8 Thus, Stallings and Peres (2000), who rely on the Morley et al. (1999) data, label Argentina and Chile "vigorous" reformers and Mexico and Brazil "cautious" ones.

9 In these fine distinctions of which presidential administration should be credited with the greatest reforms, we rely more heavily on our qualitative analysis than on Morley et al., which we find not credible in certain cases, particularly with respect to the Sarney (1985–89) administration in Brazil.

10 It is interesting that Tsebelis himself is explicitly neutral as to whether ease of policy innovation (facilitated by fewer veto points) is or is not a desirable attribute of a political system.

11 Argentina's military leaders in the late 1970s instituted some market-oriented reforms that were overturned well before the military relinquished power to civilians in 1983. These reforms never achieved the minimum elite political support (even among senior officers themselves) and institutional infrastructure necessary for them to endure (Lewis 1990; Manzetti 1994).

12 Our choice of electoral, rather than polling, evidence of popular support for market reforms was guided by both pragmatism (comparative polls begin in the mid-1990s, while our study reaches back to the 1970s) and our sense that votes were ultimately a superior indicator. Polls give voters more options but do not exact any costs. In contrast, the choice of a candidate in an election is a complex calculation that requires voters to balance a number of factors—and then make only one selection.

13 One reviewer questioned our identification of Collor as proreform. Even in the first round, candidate Collor clearly advocated trade liberalization, privatization, and firing overpaid and under-worked government bureaucrats, whom he derided as "maharajahs."

14 In a careful quantitative evaluation of 15 Latin American countries from 1982 to 1995, Carlos Gervasoni (1999) also found no support for the proposition that voters punished market reformers.

 15 In an excellent review article, Korzeniewicz and Smith (2000) observe that the overwhelming consensus of economists is that market reforms are, on balance, absolutely necessary for Latin America to return to a path of sustainable growth, clearly a requisite for poverty reduction. They find that the results for income distribution from 1980 to the late 1990s are ambiguous to bad, however, an outcome partially but perhaps not wholly attributable to the series of external shocks and consequent low growth that hit the region in the 1990s.

REFERENCES

Acuña, Carlos H. 1994. Politics and Economics in the Argentina of the Nineties (Or, Why the Future No Longer Is What It Used to Be). In *Democracy, Markets, and Structural Reform in Latin America*, ed. William C. Smith, Carlos H. Acuña, and Eduardo A. Gamarra. New Brunswick: Transaction. 31–73.

Albuquerque, Mario. 1997. El sistema privado de pensiones: el caso chileno. In *La seguridad social en America Latina: ¿reforma o liquidación?* ed. Jaime Insignia and Rolando Díaz. Caracas: Nueva Sociedad.

Ames, Barry. 1995. Electoral Rules, Constituency Pressures, and Pork Barrel: Bases of Voting in the Brazilian Congress. *Journal of Politics* 39, 2 (May): 324–43.

Amann, Edmund, and Werner Baer. 2000. The Illusion of Stability: The Brazilian Economy Under Cardoso. *World Development* 28, 10 (October): 1805-1819.

Amorim Neto, Octavio, and Paulo Tafner. 1999. O congresso e as edidas provisórias: delegação, coordenação, e conflito. Mimeograph. Rio de Janeiro: IUPERJ.

Arenas de Mesa, Alberto, and Fabio Bertranou. 1997. Learning from Social Security Reform: Two Different Cases, Chile and Argentina. *World Development* 25, 3 (March): 329–48.

Armijo, Leslie Elliott. 1996. Inflation and Insouciance: The Peculiar Brazilian Game. *Latin American Research Review* 31, 3: 7–46.

——. 1999. Balance Sheet or Ballot Box? Incentives to Privatize inn Emerging Democracies. In *Markets and Democracy in Latin America: Conflict or Convergence?* ed. Philip Oxhorn and Pamela K. Starr. Boulder: Lynne Rienner. 161–202.

——. 2005. Who's Afraid of Economic Populism? Counter-Intuitive Observations on Democracy and Brazilian Political Economy. In Lourdes Sola and Laurence Whitehead, eds., *Statecrafting Monetary Reform: Democracy and Financial Order in Brazil,* Oxford: Centre for Brazilian Studies, Oxford University, Fall.

Armijo, Leslie Elliott, Thomas J. Biersteker, and Abraham F. Lowenthal. 1994. The Problems of Simultaneous Transitions. *Journal of Democracy* 5, 4 (October): 161–75.

Armijo, Leslie Elliott, Philippe Faucher, and Magdalena Dembinska. 2006. Compared to What? Assessing Brazil's Political Institutions. *Comparative Political Studies* 39, 6 (August): 759–786.

Baker, Andy. 2000. Mass Support for Free Market Reforms: Self-Interest and Elite Influence in Brazil. Paper presented at the Annual Meeting of the American Political Science Association, Washington, DC, August 31–September 3.

Bates, Robert H., ed. 1988. *Toward a Political Economy of Development: A Rational Choice Perspective.* Berkeley: University of California Press.

Bates, Robert H., and Anne O. Krueger. 1993. Generalizations Arising from the Country Studies. In *Political and Economic Interactions in Economic Policy Reform,* ed. Bates and Krueger. Cambridge: Basil Blackwell. 444–72.

Borzutzky, Silvia, 1991. The Chicago Boys: Social Security and Welfare in Chile. In *The Radical Right and the Welfare State*, ed. Howard Glennester and James Midgley. Savage, MD: Barnes and Noble. 79–99.

Boylan, Delia M. 1998. Preemptive Strike: Central Bank Reform in Chile's Transition from Authoritarian Rule. *Comparative Politics* 30, 4 (July): 443–62.

Bresser Pereira, Luiz Carlos. 1977. *O colapso de uma aliança de classes.* São Paulo: Brasiliense.

——. 1978. *Estado e subdesenvolvimento industrializado.* São Paulo: Brasiliense.

——. 1984 (1968). *Economic Crisis and State Reform in Brazil.* Boulder: Lynne Rienner.

Callaghy, Thomas M. 1993. Vision and Politics in the Transformation of the Global Political Economy: Lessons from the Second and Third Worlds. In *Global Transformation and the Third World*, eds. Robert O. Slater, Barry M. Schutz, and Steven R. Dorr. Boulder: Lynne Rienner. 161–258.

Cardoso, Fernando Henrique. 1979. On the Characterization of Authoritarian Regimes in Latin America. In *The New Authoritarianism in Latin America*, ed. David Collier. Princeton: Princeton University Press. 33–57.

Cardoso, Fernando Henrique, and Enzo Faletto. 1979. *Dependency and Development in Latin America.* Berkeley: University of California Press.

Castro Rea, Julián, Graciela Ducatenzeiler, and Philippe Faucher. 1992. Back to Populism: Latin America's Alternative to Democracy. In *Latin America to the Year 2000*, eds. Archibald R. M. Ritter, Maxwell A. Cameron, and David H. Pollock. New York: Praeger. 125–46.

Chong, Alberto and Maurício Oliveira. 2008. Does Compulsory Voting Help Equalize Incomes? *Economics and Politics* 20, 3 (November): 391–415.

Corrales, Javier. 1998. Coalitions and Corporate Choices in Argentina, 1976–1994: The Recent Private Sector Support of Privatization. *Studies in Comparative International Development* 32, 4 (Winter): 24–51.

Dollar, David, and Aart Kraay. 2000. Growth Is Good for the Poor. Working Paper. Washington,
    DC: Development Research Group, World Bank. <www.worldbank.org/research>
Domínguez, Jorge I. 1997. *Technopols: Freeing Politics and Markets in Latin America in the 1990s.*
    University Park: Pennsylvania State University Press.
——. 1998. Free Politics and Free Markets in Latin America. *Journal of Democracy* 9, 4 (October):
    70–84.
Ducatenzeiler, Graciela, and Philip Oxhorn. 1999. The Problematic Relationship Between Economic
    and Political Liberalization: Some Theoretical Considerations. In *Markets and Democracy in
    Latin America: Conflict or Convergence?* ed. Philip Oxhorn and Pamela K. Starr. Boulder:
    Lynne Rienner. 13–42.
Easterly, William, and Stanley Fischer. 1999. Inflation and the Poor. Paper presented at the Annual
    World Bank Conference on Development and the Poor, April.
Edwards, Sebastián, and Daniel Lederman. 1998. The Political Economy of Unilateral Trade Liber-
    alization: The Case of Chile. Working Paper 6510. Cambridge, MA: National Bureau of Eco-
    nomic Research.
Evans, Peter. 1979. *Dependent Development: The Alliance of Multinational, State, and Local Capital
    in Brazil.* Princeton: Princeton University Press.
——. 1992. The State as Problem and Solution: Predation, Embedded Autonomy, and Structural
    Change. In Haggard and Kaufman 1992. Princeton: Princeton University Press. 139–80.
Figueiredo, Argelina Cheibub, and Fernando Limongi. 2000. Presidential Power, Legislative Orga-
    nization, and Party Behavior in Brazil. *Comparative Politics* 32, 2 (January): 151–69.
Foxley, Alejandro. 1983. *Latin American Experiments in Neo-Conservative Economics.* Berkeley:
    University of California Press.
Frieden, Jeffry A. 1991. *Debt, Development, and Democracy: Modern Political Economy and Latin
    America, 1965–1982.* Princeton: Princeton University Press.
Gasiorowski, Mark J. 2000. Democracy and Macroeconomic Performance in Underdeveloped
    Countries: An Empirical Analysis. *Comparative Political Studies* 33, 3 (April): 319–49.
Geddes, Barbara. 1994. *The Politicians' Dilemma: Reforming the State in Latin America.* Berkeley:
    University of California Press.
General Agreement on Tariffs and Trade (GATT). 1993a. Examen des politiques commerciales:
    Bresil. Geneva: GATT.
——. 1993b. Examen des politiques commerciales: Mexique. Geneva: GATT.
Gervasoni, Carlos. 1999. El impacto electoral de las reformas económicas en America Latina
    (1982–1995). Mimeograph. Buenos Aires: Universidad Torcuato Di Tella.
Haggard, Stephan. 1990. *Pathways from the Periphery: The Politics of Growth in the Newly Indus-
    trializing Countries.* Ithaca: Cornell University Press.
Haggard, Stephan, and Robert R. Kaufman. 1992a. Institutions and Economic Adjustment. In
    Haggard and Kaufman 1992b. 3–39.
Haggard, Stephan, and Robert R. Kaufman, eds. 1992b. *The Politics of Economic Adjustment.*
    Princeton: Princeton University Press.
Haggard, Stephan, and Steven B. Webb, eds. 1994. *Voting for Reform: Democracy, Political
    Liberalization, and Economic Adjustment.* New York: World Bank.
Hagopian, Frances. 1998. Negotiating Economic Transitions in Liberalizing Polities: Political Rep-
    resentation and Economic Reform in Latin America. Working Paper. Weatherhead Center for
    International Affairs, Harvard University.
Heredia, Blanca. 1996. *Contested State: The Politics of Trade Reform in Mexico.* Ph.D. diss., Columbia
    University.
Hirschman, Albert O. 1968. The Political Economy of Import-Substituting Industrialization in Latin
    America. *Quarterly Journal of Economics* 82 (February). 1–32.
IDEA (Institute for Democracy and Electoral Assistance). 2000. Voter Turnout: A Global Survey.
    Stockholm: IDEA. <www.idea.int>
International Monetary Fund (IMF). 2000. International Financial Statistics. CDROM. Washington,
    DC: IMF.
Kahler, Miles. 1992. External Influence, Conditionality, and the Politics of Adjustment. In Haggard
    and Kaufman 1992. 89–136.

Kessler, Timothy. 1998. Political Capital: Mexican Financial Policy Under Salinas. *World Politics* 51, 1 (October): 36–66.

Kingstone, Peter. 1999. *Crafting Coalitions for Reform: Business Strategies, Political Institutions, and Neoliberal Reforms in Brazil.* University Park: Pennsylvania State University Press.

Korzeniewicz, Roberto Patricio, and William C. Smith. 2000. Poverty, Inequality, and Growth in Latin America: Searching for the High Road to Globalization. *Latin American Research Review* 35, 3 (October): 7–54.

Kurtz, Marcus J. 1999. Chile's Neo-liberal Revolution: Incremental Decisions and Structural Transformation, 1973–89. *Journal of Latin American Studies* 31, 2: 399–427.

Lewis, Paul H. 1990. *The Crisis of Argentine Capitalism.* Chapel Hill: University of North Carolina Press.

Lindblom, Charles. 1977. *Politics and Markets: The World's Political-Economic Systems.* New York: Basic Books.

Linz, Juan J., and Arturo Valenzuela, eds. 1994. *The Failure of Presidential Democracy.* Vol. 1: Comparative Perspectives. Baltimore: Johns Hopkins University Press.

Lustig, Nora. 1992. *Mexico: The Remaking of an Economy.* Washington, DC: Brookings Institution Press.

Mainwaring, Scott. 1999. *Rethinking Political Systems in the Third Wave of Democratization: The Case of Brazil.* Stanford: Stanford University Press.

Manzetti, Luigi. 1994. *Institutions, Parties, and Coalitions in Argentine Politics.* Pittsburgh: University of Pittsburgh Press.

———. 1999. *Privatization South American Style.* New York: Oxford University Press.

Maravall, José María. 1995. The Myth of the Authoritarian Advantage. In *Economic Reform and Democracy,* ed. Larry Diamond and Mark F. Plattner. Baltimore: Johns Hopkins University Press. 13–27.

Maxfield, Sylvia. 1997. *Gatekeepers of Growth: The International Political Economy of Central Banking in Developing Countries.* Princeton: Princeton University Press.

Mesa-Lago, Carmelo. 1994. *Changing Social Security in Latin America: Toward Alleviating the Costs of Economic Reform.* Boulder: Lynne Rienner.

Montero, Alfred P. 1998. State Interests and the New Industrial Policy in Brazil: The Privatization of Steel, 1990–1994. *Journal of Interamerican Studies and World Affairs* 40, 3 (Fall): 27–62.

Morley, Samuel A., Roberto Machado, and Stefano Pettinato. 1999. Indexes of Structural Reform in Latin America. ECLAC serie reformas económicas 12. Santiago: United Nations Economic Commission on Latin America and the Caribbean (ECLAC).

Mostajo, Rossana. 2000. Gasto social y distribución de ingreso: caracterización e impacto redistributivo en países seleccionados de America Latina y el Caribe. ECLAC serie reformas económicas 69. Santiago: ECLAC.

Murillo, M. Victoria. 2000. From Populism to Neoliberalism: Labor Unions and Market Reforms in Latin America. *World Politics* 52, 2 (January): 135–74.

OECD (Organization for Economic Cooperation and Development). 1999. OECD Economic Survey: Mexico. Paris: OECD.

Olson, Mancur. 1971. *The Logic of Collective Action.* Cambridge: Harvard University Press.

Pastor, Manuel, Jr. 1992. *Inflation, Stabilization, and Debt: Macroeconomic Experiments in Peru and Bolivia.* Boulder: Westview Press.

Piñera, Jose. 1991. The Path to Privatization in Chile. In *Privatization of Public Enterprises in Latin America,* ed. William Glade. San Diego: University of California Center for U.S.-Mexican Studies.

———. 2000. A Chilean Model for Russia. *Foreign Affairs* 79, 5 (September-October): 62–73.

Pinheiro, Armando Castelar, and Ben Ross Schneider. 1995. The Fiscal Impact of Privatization in Latin America. *Journal of Development Studies* 31, 5:751–76.

Przeworski, Adam. 1991. *Democracy and the Market: Political and Economic Reforms in Eastern Europe and Latin America.* Cambridge: Cambridge University Press.

Remmer, Karen L. 1986. The Politics of Economic Stabilization: IMF Standby Programs in Latin America, 1954–1984. *Comparative Politics* 19, 1 (October): 1–24.

———. 1998. The Politics of Neo-liberal Economic Reform in South America, 1980–1994. *Studies in Comparative International Development* 33, 2: 3–29.

Ros, Jaime. 1993. La reforma del régimen comercial en México durante los años ochenta: sus efectos económicos y dimensiones políticas. ECLAC serie reformas de política pública 4. Santiago: ECLAC.

Ruiz-Tagle, Jaime. 1997. El nuevo sistema de pensiones en Chile: una evaluación provisoria (1981–1995). In *La seguridad social en América Latina: ¿reforma o liquidación?* ed. Jaime Insignia and Rolando Díaz. Caracas: Nueva Sociedad.

Schamis, Héctor E. 1999. Distributional Coalitions and the Politics of Economic Reform in Latin America. *World Politics* 51, 2 (January): 236–68.

Schneider, Ben Ross. 2000. The State and Collective Action: The Politics of Organizing Business in Latin America. Paper presented at the Annual Meeting of the International Political Science Association, August 1–5, Quebec.

Schurman, Rachel A. 1996. Chile's New Entrepreneurs and the Economic Miracle: The Invisible Hand or a Hand from the State? *Studies in Comparative International Development* 31, 2: 83–109.

Shapiro, Helen. 1993. Automobiles: From Import Substitution to Export Promotion in Brazil and Mexico. In *Beyond Free Trade: Firms, Governments, and Global Competition*, ed. David B. Yoffie. Boston: Harvard Business School Press, 193–248.

———. 1996. The Mechanics of Brazil's Auto Industry. *NACLA Report on the Americas* 29, 4 (November-December): 28–33.

Sheahan, John. 1987. *Patterns of Development in Latin America: Poverty, Repression, and Economic Strategy.* Princeton: Princeton University Press.

Silva, Eduardo. 1996. From Dictatorship to Democracy: The Business-State Nexus in Chile's Economic Transformation, 1975–1994. *Comparative Politics* 28, 3 (April): 299–320.

Skidmore, Thomas, and Peter Smith. 1992. *Modern Latin America.* 3d edition. New York: Oxford University Press.

Stallings, Barbara. 1992. International Influence on Economic Policy: Debt, Stabilization, and Structural Reform. In Haggard and Kaufman 1992. 41–88.

Stallings, Barbara, and Wilson Peres. 2000. *Growth, Employment, and Equity: The Impact of the Economic Reforms in Latin America and the Caribbean.* Washington DC: Brookings Institution Press.

Starr, Pamela K. 1997. Government Coalitions and the Viability of Currency Boards: Argentina under the Cavallo Plan. *Journal of Interamerican Studies and World Affairs* 39, 2 (Summer): 83–133.

Teichman, Judith. 1995. *Privatization and Political Change in Mexico.* Pittsburgh: University of Pittsburgh Press.

———. 1997. Mexico and Argentina: Economic Reform and Technocratic Decision Making. *Studies in Comparative International Development* 32, 1: 31–55.

———. 2000. Consensus and Economic Policy Reform in Mexico: Before and After the 1997 Mid-term Elections. Paper presented at the 18th World Congress of the International Political Science Association, Quebec City, August 1–5.

Thacker, Strom C. 2000. *Big Business, the State, and Free Trade: Constructing Coalitions in Mexico.* Cambridge: Cambridge University Press.

Thorp, Rosemary. 1998. *Progress, Poverty, and Exclusion: An Economic History of Latin America in the 20th Century.* New York: Inter-American Development Bank.

Tsebelis, George. 1995. Decision-Making in Political Systems: Veto Players in Presidentialism, Parlamentarism, Multicameralism and Multipartyism. *British Journal of Political Science* 25: 289–325.

Turcotte, Sylvain, and Philippe Faucher. 2000. How Markets and Business Power Influenced Privatization in Latin America. Paper presented at the 22d International Congress of the Latin American Studies Association, Miami, March.

Veganzones, Marie-Ange, and Carlos Winograd. 1997. *Argentina in the 20th Century: An Account of Long-Awaited Growth.* Paris: OECD.

Weyland, Kurt. 1996. Neo-Populism and Neo-Liberalism in Latin America: Unexpected Affinities. *Studies in Comparative International Development* 31, 3 (Fall): 3–31.

——. 2001. Clarifying a Contested Concept: Populism in the Study of Latin American Politics. Comparative Politics 34, 1: 1–23.

Williamson, John. 1994. Search of a Manual for Technopols. In *The Political Economy of Policy Reform*, ed. Williamson. Washington, DC: Institute for International Economics. 9–28.

Winn, Peter, ed. n.d. Victims of the Miracle: Chilean Workers in the Age of Pinochet. Unpublished mss.

World Bank. 1998. World Development Indicators. CD-ROM. Washington, DC: World Bank.

——. 2000. World Development Indicators. CD-ROM. Washington, DC: World Bank.

Chapter 5

The World Bank and Policy Reform in Mexico and Argentina

Judith Teichman

Two themes that have occupied scholars on Latin America since the mid-1980s are democratization and market reform. Work on Latin American democracy has shifted from an earlier interest in transitions from military rule to a consideration of the quality of Latin American democracy—which has involved such features as public accountability and the independence and strength of civil society.[1] (1) The struggle for democracy has been enormously complicated by the parallel process of market reform, which mainly involves trade liberalization, privatization, and deregulation. It is through these policy changes that Latin American countries have tried to find a place in the new global order. Generally, these reforms were carried out in the context of tough negotiations with major multilateral lending institutions, the International Monetary Fund (IMF) and the World Bank; and loans were made conditional on market-liberalizing (structural adjustment) policy reforms.

The issues of market reform and democracy became linked in scholarly debates in a number of ways. Those who saw market reform as favorable to democracy argued that market reform contributes to democracy by reducing rent seeking and corrupt behavior by bureaucratic agencies and trade unions (Williamson 1994, 13; Hausman 1994, 174) and by setting the stage for future economic growth (Remmer 1995, 115). But market reform has come to be increasingly perceived as having aggravated ongoing social problems, particularly inequality. Hence, a number of observers have noted an erosion in public support for democracy linked to citizens' belief that their voices are not being heard particularly with regard to social rights and demands for greater equality (Hagopian, 2005: 319, 325, 343; Diamond and Morlino; 2005, xi; Rueschmeyer, 2004, 76).

Much of the market reform literature, emphasized the role of highly trained technocrats, individuals with graduate degrees in such subjects as economics and public administration from prestigious U.S. universities, as the major driving force behind these policy changes. It is widely agreed that technocrats were involved in a policy reform process that was highly exclusionary, often overriding democratic institutions such as national congresses (Haggard and Webb 1994; Haggard and Kaufman 1995; Conaghan and Malloy 1994). Concern also arose about the democratic implications of the secretive way that first-generation reforms (trade liberalization, privatization, and deregulation) were negotiated with multilateral lending institutions and, more recently, about the impact on democratic practices of multilateral consultation of civil society organizations over reforms affecting social issues (Casaburi, et al. 2000; Teichman 2007).

While there is a broad consensus that policy reform could not go forward unless domestic political and economic conditions were ripe, the role of multilateral lending institutions in the Latin American reform process is also widely recognized. In some cases, direct supervision was an essential part of propelling reform forward (Morales 1996, 11). Considering, however, that explicit policy conditionality generally failed to induce countries to carry out policies they opposed (Killick 1995, 121; Remmer 1986), the imposition of reforms through policy-based loans may not have been the most important way multilaterals contributed to policy reforms. Policy "influence," although acknowledged as a concept that is slippery and hard to measure, may have been important nonetheless (Nelson 1990, 27). Some observers suggest that ongoing discussions and negotiations over many years may have been an important avenue for these international organizations to influence policy change (Ikenberry 1990, 103; Kahler 1991, 123; Nelson 1992, 314). One observer sees an interplay between the direct pressure coming from international financial institutions and a more subtle form of knowledge transfer (Babb 2002, 188). In the era of second-generation reforms, changes requiring even more intrusive conditionality, such as anti corruption measures, have involved ongoing involvement and negotiation with local actors (Riggirozzi 2009).

Hence, the professional staffs of multilateral lending agencies can be seen as participants in "epistemic communities," international networks of professionals who either advise or staff such organizations. These individuals share a "common causal model" and are committed to translating that truth into public policy by persuading political decisionmakers (Haas 1990, 41–42).

The truth to be conveyed has been, in this case, the efficacy of state streamlining and greater reliance on the market. Those who see policy reform as involving a process of policy persuasion (involving ideas rather than interests) use the term social learning to describe the enterprise by which experts in a particular policy field transfer new policy ideas (Heclo 1974, 312; Hall 1993). Defined as "a deliberate attempt to adjust goals and techniques of policy in response to past experiences and new information," social learning is "social" because it involves learning by policymakers doing it on society's behalf (Hall 1993, 276, 278). In its most radical form, it can represent the transfer of an entirely new interpretative framework, or a new policy paradigm. We see this process occurring in Latin American policy reform.

The notion of social learning as a stimulus or support for policy change, however, cannot be considered separately from client country domestic political conditions and arrangements. New information is assimilated in response to past experiences and in particular contexts. Domestic conditions, power relations, and institutional structures are absolutely key in patterning the nature and extent of such influence. Moreover, multilateral lending institutions and Latin American countries operate in a larger international political context: they have distinct relations with the hegemonic political power, the United States, a country that has also played a determinant role in the policies and practices of multilateral lending institutions.

This article examines the role of the World Bank in the market policy reform experiences of Mexico and Argentina. It argues that while reform was driven by domestic elites, the World Bank played an important role in policy reform, providing technical advice and financial support and contributing in important ways to the spread of the new market reform policy paradigm.[2] The bank's role differed substantially in the two cases, however, a consequence of the distinct economic conditions and political and social structures of the two countries and of their different geopolitical importance to the United States. While the Mexican technocratic elite used the bank to drive forward market reform in accordance with its policy preferences, the bank was much more intimately involved in the reform process in Argentina and was able to exercise considerably greater direct influence, especially during the initial years of reform. In both cases, domestic and multilateral deliberations took place in highly personalistic policy networks, which excluded democratic deliberative institutions (congresses) and precluded public accountability.

As Mexico and Argentina have moved into what has been referred to as the second generation of market reforms, bank involvement continues to be considerably more intense in Argentina than in Mexico, largely a consequence of the distinct political histories and circumstances of the two countries.[3] The bank's current commitment to involve civil society in its lending policies has important implications for the democratic development of these two countries and others in the region.

THE INTERNATIONAL CONTEXT AND POLICY-BASED LENDING

The 1982 international debt crisis was instrumental in setting the stage for the policy changes to come over the next two decades. It immediately thrust the top finance officials of highly indebted Latin American countries into negotiations with the IMF for loans based on standby and extended fund facility agreements, and with the World Bank for structural adjustment loans and sectoral adjustment loans (SALs and SECALs). The Baker Plan, announced by the U.S. Secretary of the Treasury James Baker in 1985, gave impetus to those negotiations and to structural adjustment lending, as it set aside US$20 billion for the highest debtors over the following three years in exchange for economic reforms, including trade liberalization, the liberalization of investment regimes, and privatization. In 1986, the bank's adjustment lending to Latin America tripled, to US$2 billion, representing about 40 percent of the bank's loan commitments to the region that year (Kapur, et al. 1997, 630).

Mexico cut a deal under Baker, as did Argentina. But in a few short years, as a consequence of the commercial banks' reluctance to engage in new lending, the Baker Plan had run out of steam. In 1989, the Brady Plan, announced by the new U.S. Treasury Secretary, Nicolas Brady, called for debt relief in exchange for market reforms and coincided with an upsurge in reform in the region. In providing for debt relief, Brady offered an enormous incentive to policy reform by insisting that such reform be well under way before an agreement could be reached. Indeed, the Brady conception of structural adjustment and the commitment of its designers to market reform had become, by the late 1980s, far deeper than ever. In the area of privatization, for example, Brady moved into the promotion of privatization in core areas, such as petroleum and minerals (Ramamurti 1992, 164).

The Brady Plan's insistence on prior commitment to a market reform agenda signaled the recognition that success in policy reform would only be possible with government "ownership" of reform; that is, governments would themselves have to be fully committed to a reform agenda for it to take hold. For the IMF and the World Bank, "policy dialogue" with the officials of client countries was the means by which commitment to reform could be engendered and sustained. But the bank had considerably greater leeway in the development of the sort of ongoing dialogue that could push client countries toward reform than did the fund. Bank officials deal with a much wider array of government officials, and therefore often have the opportunity to gain access to a broader range of channels through which they can influence the direction of policy. While IMF negotiations occur in situations of extreme crisis, when agreements must be arrived at quickly and confrontation is more likely, the bank's negotiations are lower-profile and less intense, because partial agreement can be arrived at and the consequences of not reaching any agreement are less severe. Hence, bank officials are in a much better position to develop close and collaborative relationships with client country officials (Interviews, two senior LAC officials, one middle-ranking official; Stern 1983, 100–4).

Important changes within the bank, however, and particularly within the Latin American and Caribbean Section (LAC), were necessary before market reform in Latin America would be carried forward with a new style of "policy dialogue." In general, the bank, through the 1960s and into the early 1970s, was characterized by a fairly prostatist attitude: it supported protection for infant industries and economic planning and lent heavily to state-owned enterprises (Kapur et al. 1997, 450–51; Babai 1988, 259). But while the energy crisis of 1973–74 triggered a firmer commitment to trade liberalization and a growing abandonment of support for public enterprises in the bank generally (Fortin 1988, 310; Kapur, et al. 1997, 483), prostatist attitudes lingered in the LAC section. It was not until the 1982 economic crisis and consequent attitudinal and organizational changes in the LAC section that an important role for the bank in Latin American policy reform became possible.

The LAC's failure to foresee correctly the Mexican crisis of 1982 led to a major shake-up of the section, which resulted in a clearing out of prostatists and the emergence of a consensus on the importance and necessity of policy reform in Latin America (Interviews, two senior LAC officials). Change in the leadership of the LAC section further altered its traditional modus operandi and set the stage for a highly successful form of "policy dialogue." In 1985, the replacement of David Knox by Shahid Husain as vice president of LAC resulted in a move away from an arm's-length formalism in the relationship between LAC officials and officials of its client countries to one in which senior and middle-level LAC officials would cultivate relationships of trust, even friendship, between themselves and the officials of Latin American countries.[4] As a consequence, from the mid-1980s on, LAC officials were probably unique even for the bank's freewheeling culture: not only were they committed to policy reform, but they spoke the language of their client countries, had a strong esprit de corps, and developed strong attachments to the personalities and countries they were dealing with.

The years following the shake-up of the LAC section, moreover, saw considerable continuity in officials working there. A number of participants held positions throughout the 1985–95 period: Vice President Shahid Husain, Rainer B. Steckhan, Paul M. Meo, Pieter P. Bottlelier, Peter R. Scherer, Myrna Alexander, Hans Binswanger, Ricardo Halperin (World Bank Group 1995). This continuity gave LAC officials both the time and the opportunity to develop relationships of trust with the officials of client countries.

The rapid expansion of negotiations from 1985 on and the pursuit by LAC bank officials of "policy dialogue" established the conditions for the emergence of international policy networks, policy development groups composed of domestic and World Bank officials whose discussions became a crucial component of the market reform process.[5] During first-stage market reform, usually the nucleus of the international policy network was composed of anywhere from 3 or 4 to 15 people. Latin American-LAC policy networks were informal and fluid; they were often (though not necessarily) composed of individuals with similar educational backgrounds, particularly individuals with graduate degrees in economics; and members of the network generally agreed on a particular policy goal, if not a market reform agenda. By far the most important feature of these networks, however, was that they were bound by personal relationships of trust and sometimes friendship. Face-to-face contact, in a context of developing personal trust, was the process by which market reform policy ideas and the language of market reform were transferred, strengthened, and sustained.[6]

At the same time, however, these networks contained an inherent tension, because although officials shared a common policy commitment (market reform), they answered to distinct institutional and contextual pressures. While client country officials had to answer to political pressures at home, World Bank officials did not, and were therefore more inclined to press on with politically risky reforms. Bank officials did have career concerns, however, and as a consequence, avoided directions that might raise criticism from senior levels of the bank, a concern that would have implications for how hard they would press for reform. But in general, bank LAC region officials wanted to keep conflict to a minimum, because this would ensure that dialogue and access would be ongoing. Their strategy was to have policy proposals ready should political or other obstacles diminish and to push on with those reforms where there was the least resistance. While senior LAC officials were the key bank actors in this process, especially at the beginning, over time, middle-level officials became very actively involved as well.

International policy networks during the first phase of reform were generally closed and resistant to outside penetration and influence. Indeed, networks resisted penetration even from important intrastate actors, such as senior officials in those ministries wishing a more gradual process of policy reform. By the mid-1990s, however, pressure was growing for greater public participation in international lending programs. Throughout the 1980s, nongovernmental organizations proliferated in Latin American countries in response to the dislocation occasioned by mega-infrastructural projects and the decline in state and trade union involvement in social welfare activities. While criticism of the bank's lending practices came from many quarters, NGOs were especially critical of what they viewed to be the negative social impact of structural adjustment, and demanded that the bank involve civil society in its lending programs (Nelson 1997, 24).

This pressure was key in the bank's move to a more participatory policy process, a process that was under way by the mid-1990s. The bank's 2000 World Development Report, World Bank Development Report, 2000/2001, *Attacking Poverty*, sets forth its major ideas on the subject. It identifies poverty reduction as the bank's major concern and civil society involvement in the design and monitoring of reforms as an essential part of the process (World Bank 2000a, 8–9).

It is important to note, however, the limitations of the bank's new thrust toward public involvement in policy development. While consultation is most prevalent in projects involving population resettlement and indigenous lands and is increasingly sought after in social sector programs (Nelson 1997, 43), openness and public scrutiny of structural adjustment programs has not occurred. At the same time, the closed nature of international policy networks has also been challenged on the domestic political front. In 1997, in both Mexico and Argentina, midterm elections saw governments that had carried out market-liberalizing reforms lose control of their respective congresses. These reversals were followed by the electoral defeats of the governments themselves (Carlos Menem and the Peronist Party in Argentina and the PRI's presidential candidate, Francisco Labastida, in Mexico). In each case, resistance to further market reform measures has grown, along with public concern for social issues (Starr 1999, 50; Teichman 2001, 154, 122).

From 1982 on, circumstances forced Mexico and Argentina, along with other countries of the region, to avail themselves of the various lending facilities provided by the IMF and the World Bank. Both countries' ongoing negotiations with the World Bank from the early 1980s on set the stage for the emergence of international policy networks. The bank provided a Special Action Program loan to Mexico in 1983 for export development and, between 1984 and 1991, provided a variety of SECALs in such areas as agriculture, trade, export promotion, and privatization, in addition to numerous project loans.

From 1992 on, the pace of lending continued but moved more heavily into lending for environmental projects, health, education, social protection, poverty alleviation and agriculture, particularly projects dealing with marginal areas and indigenous peoples. Similarly, between 1983 and 1988, the bank increased its structural adjustment lending to Argentina for export promotion and for state reform while continuing to make a variety of project loans. Indeed, by 1988, the bank had stepped in to replace the IMF in Argentina. After withdrawing from Argentina briefly, the bank resumed lending in 1990, and has been closely and intensely involved in Argentina ever since. Here, too, while lending for public sector restructuring during the initial years of market reform dominated, the bank has moved increasingly into lending for health, education, and social protection.

The facility with which the bank could influence and guide the process of reform was closely linked to domestic political factors and processes. Institutions, defined broadly as the entire framework—informal, formal, written, and unwritten—in which human activity occurs, determine human choices and economic outcomes. As such, institutions play a major role in determining the extent and manner in which ideas will affect policy change (North 1990, 4, 111). A voluminous literature has explored the links between the adoption of market reform policies and domestic institutional arrangements. One-party-dominant regimes, for example, have been identified as being in one of the best positions to insulate technocratic decision-makers and to manage (control) the political fallout of market reform; while new democracies, facing fierce redistributive pressures, are in the worst position to carry through such reforms (Haggard and Kaufman 1995, 14, 152; Cavarozzi et al. 1994; 18; Bresser Pereira 1993, 52–55).

The key impact of a profound economic crisis in discrediting the old economic model and in engendering public support for reforms has also been broadly acknowledged (Haggard and Kaufman 1995, 159; Morales 1996, 18; Bresser Pereira, 57). In addition, party systems appear to be relevant: a highly fragmented system is not conducive to reform, while a two-party system is more likely to make change possible (Haggard and Kaufman 1992; Nelson 1992, 123). The relative power of organized interest groups may also be key in determining what aspects of reform go forward and how quickly (Nelson 1990, 21). In the two countries analyzed here, such political circumstances and institutional arrangements would prove crucial in patterning the nature, extent, success, and reach of international policy networks.

MEXICO: USING THE BANK TO DRIVE REFORM

Mexico's first phase of reform (1985–94) occurred in the authoritarian context of a one-party-dominant regime, a regime that was firmly in the hands of a tightly knit group of technocratic market reformers (Centeno 1997; Teichman 1995; Babb 2002). For more than 70 years, until its defeat in 2000, Mexico was ruled by the Institutional Revolutionary Party (PRI). Highly effective mechanisms of corporatist control involved the incorporation of national worker, peasant, and popular organizations in the PRI, while clientelist networks ensured the loyalty of a wide spectrum of sectoral leaders, politicians, government officials, and party activists.

While the breakdown of this system can be traced to the student strike and massacre of 1968, a rapid acceleration of the process began with the administration of President Carlos Salinas de Gortari (1989–94), who, faced with rising political opposition to his policy reforms, implemented a variety of political reforms geared to making the electoral system fairer and more competitive. But PRI dominance and the corporatist-clientelist system of political control remained, until the mid-1990s, effective in containing opposition to market reform measures. Through its control of the PRI, the technocratic elite retained full control of the policymaking process, and was able to carry through trade liberalization and privatization without substantial interference from the congress.[7]

Clientelism, in the form of social investment funds, associated through the media directly with the person of the president, was key in dissuading worker and peasant organizations from blocking reforms the way they would in Argentina between 1985 and 1989. At the same time, Mexico's long years of political stability had produced a large and relatively stable state bureaucracy, with large enclaves (especially in the Finance Ministry and Central Bank) of highly trained officials. It was only with the 1995 peso crisis that the unraveling of the traditional political system became readily apparent; under President Ernesto Zedillo (1995–2000), trade unions and Congress blocked privatization in the energy sector and demanded greater emphasis on social policy.

Mexico's technocratic policy elite (the president and his closest cabinet collaborators) became the interlocutors between their country and bank officials. Their exclusionary form of decisionmaking was reflected in the nature of Mexican-World Bank discussions and in the kind of influence the bank would be allowed to exert on the Mexican reform process. Their control of the Mexican state and politics determined whom the bank would dialogue with. At least initially, their control of Mexican politics also controlled what issues would be open to dialogue. Mexico's enormous geopolitical importance to the United States, moreover, gave Mexican technocrats the clout to resist reforms they opposed and to recruit the bank to help them drive forward those reforms they favored. Within the limitations defined by Mexico's policymakers, however, the bank's role was not a passive one. Bank officials sought out and strengthened the hand of the radical market reformers and contributed to the spread of market reform policy ideas in the Mexican bureaucracy. The bank provided funding and technical support, which was especially important in the privatization process.

Although market reform was initiated under President Miguel de la Madrid (1983–88), the leading figure among Mexico's radical reformers was his successor, Carlos Salinas. Salinas's closest collaborators included Francisco Gil Díaz, Ernesto Zedillo, Pedro Aspe, Jaime Serra Puche, and José Córdoba (Heredia 1996; Teichman 1995). When Salinas assumed the presidency, these individuals, forming a homogeneous super-elite and sharing educational and career experiences, took over the most important administrative positions and propelled the market reform process forward in an exclusionary and authoritarian manner.[8] Although trade liberalization was virtually complete by 1988 (Banco de México 1993, 202), once Salinas became president, privatization moved into the politically sensitive areas of telecommunications, airlines, mining and steel, and banks. Foreign investment was deregulated, and initial steps were taken to liberalize the agricultural sector.

By far the most important and controversial agricultural reform involved the reform of Article 27 of the Constitution. With the objective of stimulating investment and export competitiveness in agriculture, this reform declared the end of land redistribution and gave communal farmers (*ejiditarios*) the legal right to hold title to land and therefore the right to sell or rent it or to form joint ventures with agribusiness, whether foreign or domestic. Finally, the North American Free Trade Agreement (NAFTA) required that foreign capital be allowed into the electricity sector and stipulated the gradual opening up of the finance and agricultural sectors.

The World Bank was involved in almost all aspects of this reform agenda. Indeed, the full extent of the bank's involvement cannot be gleaned by just a perusal of its loans to Mexico because discussions with Mexican officials occurred in all policy areas, including many in which the bank had no intention of making loans. This broadening of policy discussion was a major achievement for the bank because, before the mid-1980s, Mexico had sought to confine the bank's involvement to certain sectors (mainly infrastructure) and had rebuffed bank policy advice (Interview, senior LAC official; World Bank 1994). The 1982 debt crisis opened an opportunity for more extensive policy discussions. Then-senior vice president of operations for the bank, Ernest Stern, a strong advocate of market reform, offered bank support for Mexico's economic recovery with a reform package that included trade liberalization, measures to bring about greater efficiency in public enterprises, and improved transparency in the financial sector (Interview, senior LAC official). Meanwhile, LAC officials, who by this time had reached a consensus on the need for reform, especially trade liberalization, began to seek out like-minded Mexican officials and quickly made contact with and cultivated leading radical technocratic reformers (Interviews, two senior LAC officials).[9]

Although the Mexican government had not reached a consensus on trade liberalization, the radical reformers were able to extend an invitation to the bank to send a trade policy mission. Discussions over trade liberalization between bank and Mexican government officials during 1983–84 were acrimonious, however, because at this time trade liberalization resisters in SECOFI, the Ministry of Trade and Industrial Development, had not yet been defeated. The 1983 export development loan therefore did not, much to the bank's disappointment, call for a generalized trade liberalization program. But it did help to place the discussion of policy reform on the Mexican government agenda and set the stage for the emergence of the first Mexican LAC policy network on trade liberalization (Interviews, two senior LAC officials).

Economic deterioration, in the form of a drop in petroleum prices in 1985, further increased the bank's opportunity to become involved Mexico's policy reform. As the deteriorating economic scenario demonstrated that drastic policy changes were in order, resisters to trade liberalization within the Mexican state lost influence, and the radical reform group gained ground. The first World Bank-Mexican policy network, on trade liberalization, emerged as the bank took on the role of supporting and strengthening the arguments of the radical reform group. A bank-financed trade policy seminar, held to coincide with the government's announcement of trade liberalization measures in July 1985, supported the spread of market liberalizing ideas, helping to secure adherents in the state and the private sector. At the same time, Mexican technocrats used bank studies on trade reform to help defeat those resisting reform in the state (Interviews, two senior bank officials and a senior Mexican government official).

Over the following five years, LAC officials strove to build loyalty and trust with Mexican officials. The bank's role in the debt issue was probably the most important factor in engendering those ties. Mexican officials were grateful for the bank's contribution to debt negotiations and restructuring, especially for the cofinancing and guarantees it provided, which stimulated international financial flows (World Bank 1994, 51; interview, senior LAC official). The bank not only played an important role in providing advice to Mexico in its negotiations with the commercial banks but also intervened to strengthen Mexico's negotiating hand.[10] The bank provided advice on the design and formulation of options for debt and debt service reduction for Mexico's Brady deal, and its projections of Mexico's financial needs lent decisive support to Mexico's case in negotiations with the commercial banks (World Bank 1994, xv). The policy network on the debt issue involved high-level officials of the bank and the Mexican government and the top technical advisers of each, with one particularly trusted bank official on call to the Mexican government. Most of the analytical work was carried out jointly by World Bank and Mexican officials (Interview, senior LAC official).

Despite this success in building trust, however, LAC officials learned to operate with considerable caution when dealing with Mexican officials. The Mexicans, moreover, maintained the upper hand in determining where the bank would be allowed to exercise influence. Particularly during the Salinas years, features of Mexican policy networks reflected the concentration of power in the Mexican state and the country's geopolitical importance to the United States. Generally, dialogue with bank officials involved, especially in the first instance, the highest level of Mexican government and LAC bank officials. Bank officials did not have access to public enterprise officials or, for a number of years, to sectoral or middle-level Mexican officials, and were explicitly prohibited from initiating contacts with Mexican officials without authorization from the Finance Ministry.[11] Only when policy reform was well under way, after the early 1990s, did discussions go forward in such policy areas as petroleum, the financial sector, and social issues such as health and poverty reduction.

Mexico's geopolitical importance was reflected in the way Mexican officials used their country's relationship with the United States to pressure high-level World Bank authorities to censor opinion and pressures coming from LAC that they saw as inimical to their goals. This reality was reinforced early in the market reform process and was key in determining LAC officials' behavior thereafter. Angered at what they viewed to be too much pressure on the trade liberalization issue, Mexican authorities complained to the chairman of the Federal Reserve Board, Paul Volcker, who took the matter up with the U.S. treasury secretary and top World Bank officials. The consequence: the LAC division was reprimanded for pushing too hard (Interviews, senior LAC official).[12] But there had been earlier evidence of Mexico's clout. In 1980, a junior official in the bank wrote a minority report critical of Mexico's rapid petroleum export strategy—a strategy the Mexicans were loath to abandon at the time—predicting that the public expenditure expansion, financed by debt and money creation, would almost inevitably lead to crisis. The report was attacked by the Mexican official who was, at the time, a director-general in the Ministry of Budget and Planning, Carlos Salinas; and the Mexicans used their influence with the United States and upper levels of the bank to attempt to have the bank official fired (Urzua 1997, 74; interview, two middle-level LAC officials).

The consequence of such experiences was that bank officials were unlikely to make policy demands that they feared might antagonize Mexican officials (Interviews, three senior LAC officials). This had implications for Mexico's ability to resist reforms its policy elite opposed. Bank officials also had to tread carefully on the issue of policy conditionality. Mexican officials were, initially at least, strongly averse to the attachment of explicit conditionality to loans. LAC officials developed a strategy for dealing with Mexico that involved ongoing dialogue and informal understandings (World Bank 1994, xiii; interview, senior LAC official). It is therefore particularly difficult to measure the extent of bank involvement in the country's policy reforms.

Nevertheless, similar educational backgrounds (graduate degrees in economics) and personal ties (the same universities) between some bank officials and the Mexican technocrats helped facilitate the ongoing dialogue and the eventually close working relationship (Interviews, two LAC officials). Hence, once Salinas, the principal figure among the radical reform technocrats, was designated PRI presidential candidate in 1987, relations between Mexico and the bank became closer, and policy networks proliferated. In 1988, as Salinas campaigned for the presidency, Finance Minister Pedro Aspe, his technical team, and top-level bank LAC officials worked out the general lines of the program for the rapidly accelerating reform process that would characterize the Salinas years. The Ministry of Finance was the principal point of contact for both bank lending and policy dialogue during most of the Salinas administration, although networks also developed with officials in the Central Bank, the Office of the Presidency, the Ministry of Trade, and occasionally with sectoral ministries, such as the Ministry of Agriculture. Once reform was well under way, Mexican authorities began to request the inclusion of conditions in loan agreements in order to consolidate policy reforms—to ensure that groups in the government that opposed such changes could not tamper with them (Interviews, two senior LAC officials).

While much of the policy dialogue that occurred between the World Bank and Mexico would result in loans, discussion also took place in a wide array of policy areas.

Indeed, most bank informants believed that informal discussions on policy areas not leading to bank loans nonetheless offered opportunities to influence policy. Joint bank-Mexican government studies were produced on such topics as public sector investment, deregulation of foreign investment, the financial sector, the industrial sector, transportation, public enterprise reform, privatization (telephone, fertilizers, steel, electricity), and agriculture. These reports were frequently used to bolster arguments against intrastate reform resisters, who argued for a slower, more gradual reform process (Interviews, senior Mexican and LAC officials).

In the area of privatizations, technical support was widely acknowledged by both Mexican and World Bank officials as particularly important. The bank provided studies on the international experience of public enterprise restructuring and privatization (Interviews, senior Mexican and LAC officials). Bank studies and joint bank-Mexican studies formed the basis for further dialogue with the bank and propelled the process forward as reforms were evaluated and new areas for reform identified. The bank tended not to lend for reforms, such as for the tool road program (World Bank 2001b, 7), in which it perceived extensive corruption; but it nevertheless continued dialogue.

Bank-Mexican discussion on agricultural reform is an example of the role of an international policy network (and the role of the bank side of such a network) in helping to build consensus for reform. In 1985–86, the bank began tentative discussions with Mexican technocrats (those in the Finance Ministry) on the need for reform in agriculture. Initial, more formal discussions, however, which involved the key radical reformers, Zedillo, Serra Puche, and Aspe, did not really get under way until Salinas took over the presidency (Interview, senior bank official).

Mexican government officials saw the ejido system as the most important obstacle to greater agricultural productivity. Although eager to get reform off the ground, they faced resistance from their own agricultural bureaucracy; that is, from bureaucrats in the ministry below the subsecretary level. While the radical reform technocrats wanted the ejido eliminated, many in the agricultural bureaucracy resisted any attempt to tamper with the institution, fearing that even lifting the restrictions on the transfer of ejido land or allowing ejido members to decide on the tenure regime under which they would operate would trigger the widespread sell-off of lands and the pauperization of ejido members.

Bank experts, on the other hand, focused less on reform of this communal form of land tenure (indeed, there is evidence of support for it from some bank officials; see, for example, Heath 1992).[13] The official bank position favored owner-operated family farms as the best means to ensure equity and efficiency; property titling would increase owners' incentives while providing collateral for further investment (Deininger and Binswanger 1999, 249). At the same time, the bank had come to recognize that efficiency losses under communal landholding arrangements were more modest than originally assumed (Deininger and Binswanger 1999, 258). While bank officials did favor alterations in ejido arrangements in order to make private titling possible, they preferred that Mexican policymakers focus on improvements in areas such as health, education, and technical support, and on removing state interference in the agricultural pricing system. They also wanted inefficient public enterprises and marketing boards eliminated (Interview, senior bank and middle-level officials).

It was in this context that discussions between the bank and Mexican finance and agriculture officials got under way in 1989–90. Over the next three or four years, the Mexican government sent about ten groups of Agriculture Ministry officials (with about ten people per group) to Washington for discussions with the bank's agricultural specialists. One of the most important purposes of this dialogue, from the perspective of

Mexico's radical reformers, was for the bank's agricultural specialists to help them convince these Mexican agricultural bureaucrats that altering the ejido regime would not actually lead to increased poverty and outmigration.[14] At the same time, however, bank dialogue with the radical reform technocrats involved pressure to place policy priorities elsewhere and to move away from their strong anti-ejidal position.

The bank weighed in on the side of ejido reform, although not the drastic type espoused by the radical reformers. Admittedly, it is difficult to measure the extent of the bank's impact on this issue. It was certainly integrally involved in this intrastate debate and, through helping to moderate the radical reformers while assuaging the fears of the skeptics, it probably contributed to the buildup of sufficient intrastate consensus to allow reform of the ejido to go forward. The Mexicans, according to bank officials, insisted on the insertion of agricultural reforms as conditions in loan agreements, a measure they believed would consolidate the changes.[15] But even in agriculture, where bank and Mexican officials had different policy concerns, informants spoke of the development of a relationship of "trust" between bank officials and Mexican officials.

Mexican officials' selective use of bank policy advice and their ability to force LAC officials to back off from policy reforms continued to be an important feature of bank-Mexico relations despite the close working relationships that developed. The Mexicans resisted bank officials' advice that the financial sector be opened up to foreign investment (Interviews, senior Mexican official, two senior LAC officials). Their resistance to bank policy recommendations was particularly evident in their reaction to the bank's assessment of the Mexican economic situation just before the peso crisis. A 1993 World Bank report argued that unless Mexico continued on the road of structural reform, including opening the energy and finance sectors to foreign capital investment, and unless it changed its exchange rate policy, it would face an economic crisis. Mexican officials strongly disagreed with the report, and succeeded in suppressing its wider dissemination in the bank (Interview, LAC official).[16]

Mexican officials did not move on these bank policy recommendations, and the 1995 peso crisis was, as a consequence, probably more devastating than it might otherwise have been. The immediate impact of the 1995 crisis was a lessening of bank policy influence as the United States became the key external actor in Mexico's economic recovery. Discussions on the Mexican rescue package between Mexican officials and the U.S. Treasury reportedly involved pressure for a variety of policy reforms in areas such as illegal immigration and foreign capital participation in the state petroleum company (Ramírez de la O. 1996).

The World Bank lent heavily to support the failed Mexican banking system through funding for FOBAPROA (Bank Fund for the Protection of Savings) (Urzua 1997, 103, 109). FOBAPROA was a private bank rescue effort established by the government and supported by the Mexican policy elite in which the World Bank had little policy input and about which it maintained a considerable degree of skepticism (Interview, senior LAC official). Disagreement between Mexican and World Bank officials over this issue was an important factor in the erosion of trust between Mexican officials and their bank counterparts between 1995 and 1997, as was bank staff turnover in some sectors (OED 2001, 12, 24). By 1997, however, once bank personnel working on Mexico had stabilized, good working relationships apparently resumed in such areas as pension reform, decentralization, health, education, support for small and medium-sized businesses and farmers, environment, and poverty alleviation.

Policy dialogue on poverty, which had traditionally been closed to the bank, began to open up under Salinas but continued more fully under his successor. Santiago Levy, the architect of the most important antipoverty program under Zedillo, had worked on a contract basis for the World Bank before joining the Zedillo administration in the Ministry of Finance. While at the bank, he had produced a report titled *Poverty Alleviation in Mexico* (World Bank 1991), which became the basis for the PROGRESA program. This program, which called for the targeting of extreme poverty, was opposed by the then-Mexican minister of social development, Francisco Rojas, and criticized by career bureaucrats in the Ministry of Social Development who favored a more generalized approach. President Zedillo, however, was reportedly impressed by the report, eventually choosing it over other proposals (Interviews, one senior-level and two middle-level officials). The bank funded a pilot project for PROGRESA in 1992. But while informal discussions between the bank and Mexican officials continued on this program, the bank did not lend explicitly for it.[17]

The decentralization dialogue, begun in the 1990s, went more slowly, partly because domestic pressure for decentralization had also been coming from opposition state governments, which the PRI regime did not wish to see strengthened. By the end of 1999, however, there was movement on the issue (Interview, senior government official; OED 2001, 13). Until then, decentralization had been problematic: increased funding was allocated to state governments for distribution to municipalities, but funds were earmarked for specific purposes, giving municipalities little latitude to establish their own priorities or programs.

Meanwhile, the bank began to take an active role in building up support for decentralization, so as to have key interlocutors in place. In the last years of the Zedillo administration, the bank provided contracts to disaffected government technocrats, some of whom became involved in bank-supported decentralization projects, such as the improvement of state-level administrative capacity.[18] But the bank also kept discussions going on privatization in the energy sector, especially electricity, an area where political opposition effectively blocked reform; and it kept the country's fiscal situation in the forefront of dialogue, providing analytical and advisory services and pressing for tax reform (Interview, senior LAC official).

Although the number of policy areas discussed by the bank and Mexican officials continued to expand under President Zedillo and the bank was interacting with a larger number of government officials and even former officials, policy network discussions excluded members of Congress, opposition parties, opponents in the state bureaucracy, and most civil society organizations. Although civil society organizations have had an impact on bank policy since the mid-1990s in Mexico, that impact has been largely uninvited—a consequence of fierce resistance to specific bank projects (Fernandez de Villegas and Adelson 2000, 476). In the realm of policy reform, the first significant participation occurred in health policy, involving a bank loan in 1998; but that participation, too, was largely uninvited, and important pertinent documents still were not made available to Congress and civil society organizations. Despite the move to electoral democracy, moreover, old corporatist-clientelist arrangements continued to survive in rural areas, civil society organizations participated little in bank programs, and the government continued to use programs in a clientelistic way (Fernández de Villegas and Adelson 2000, 483, 488).

The bank continued its involvement with the Mexican administration of President Vicente Fox, providing a set of "Policy Notes" for the incoming Fox administration, later published as Mexico: A Comprehensive Development Agenda (World Bank 2001b). Today the bank's priority for Mexico is poverty reduction, to be achieved through the maintenance of macroeconomic indicators; and productivity increases, along with a variety of targeted programs and expanded coverage of basic ones. In Mexico, as elsewhere, the bank claims to be seeking to abandon the closed policy networks of the past. But openness is confined to compensatory programs, particularly poverty alleviation. According to the bank, moreover, many in the Mexican government still oppose bringing nongovernmental actors into the bank-Mexican dialogue, while civil societal and political groups are suspicious or hostile toward the bank (OED 2001, 26).[19]

ARGENTINA: THE WORLD BANK DRIVES REFORM

The World Bank's greater involvement in Argentina's reform experience was the product of a number of intersecting factors, including the timing of economic reform, closely following a transition from authoritarian rule; the depth of Argentina's economic crisis; and the changing position of U.S. administrations concerning how much pressure should be brought to bear on Argentine policymakers to carry out reform. In sharp contrast to the Mexican case, Argentina's political history was one of instability; persistent cycles of democracy and military rule culminated in the brutally repressive military dictatorship of 1976–82. Unlike the Mexican case, moreover, Argentina's labor movement was not historically contained by corporatist-clientelist mechanisms of political control, and it reemerged as an independent and powerful actor with the transition to democracy. Labor's demands for improvements in wages reflected the more general rapid rise in public expectations characteristic of new democracies.

Market reform therefore made little headway during the first civilian government of Raúl Alfonsín (1983–89). This delay in adjustment, combined with the sharp increase in government expenditure occasioned by attempts to meet public expectations, led to the onset of extreme crisis in the form of two hyperinflationary episodes in 1989 and 1990 (Bresser Pereira 1993, 52–53). It was the depth of that economic crisis, however, that neutralized opposition to reform (Gerchunoff and Torre 1996, 749). It also gave the regime the ability to concentrate political power and liberally to open channels of discussion with the bank. In addition, the country's history of chronic political instability had left it with a much weaker state bureaucracy and no cadre of highly trained technocrats, as Mexico had (Teichman 1997, 33–34). This situation created greater reliance on World Bank technical support once market reform was begun in 1989. The bank's proactive role in Argentine policy reform was reflected in the greater incursion of international policy networks into the Argentine state and society. Lacking the tight authoritarian control of Mexican market reformers and their geopolitical clout with the United States, Argentine policymakers lacked the ability to confine bank officials to specific policy areas, or to strongly resist policy advice—nor did they want to after 1989. They usually enthusiastically accepted (and even recruited) the bank's help in bringing recalcitrant resisters to support reform. Resistance to market reform came from powerful private sector interests some of whom had to be brought onside by means of rent-seeking opportunities (Etchemendy, chapter 6). Bank officials were certainly aware of this aspect of the process but claim to have been powerless to effectively discourage it (Teichman 2001, 116, 125).

Probably no other country carried out market reform as rapidly as did Argentina under President Carlos Menem (1989–99). It was during this period that international policy networks proliferated rapidly. Yet those networks originated in the Alfonsín regime; ongoing policy discussion with bank officials during those years played an important part in convincing Argentine policymakers that market reform was efficacious. It was during that period that policy reform was placed on the policy agenda. In the face of mounting inflation and sharp resistance from creditors, by 1985 the administration had developed the Austral Plan, a heterodox stabilization plan involving wage and price freezes and reduction of the fiscal deficit. The Austral Plan called for the restructuring of public enterprises and trade liberalization. When this economic plan failed, however, further proposals for trade liberalization and public sector restructuring were put forward, culminating in the announcement of the sale of 40 percent of the shares of the state telephone company (ENTEL) and the airline, Aerolíneas Argentinas.[20] None of the various economic programs implemented by President Alfonsín, ending with the Primavera Plan in late 1988 (calling for, among other things, privatization and a revised fiscal deficit target), managed to reform or stabilize the Argentine economy. They all crumbled in the face of trade union and business opposition (Peralta-Ramos 1992, 114–16; Smith 1992, 25–38).

Once Carlos Menem took power, policy reform proceeded rapidly. Two omnibus laws passed in 1989, the Law for the Reform of the State and the Economic Emergency Law, provided the legal framework for the radical reform to come, allowing the president to bypass Congress and institute many of the early reform measures through presidential decree. Unlike Mexico's, the Argentine privatization drive did not shy away from sacrosanct public companies: the state-owned telephone, electric, airline, railway, petroleum, steel, and military defense companies were all privatized by 1994. Tariff rates were consistently reduced; and by 1991, most quantitative controls on imports had been removed. The Convertibility Plan, introduced by Economy Minister Domingo Cavallo in 1991, tied the peso to the dollar, backed fully by Central Bank reserves. In 1996, the executive obtained additional emergency powers for its "second reform of the state," a proposal that foresaw the elimination and merging of government departments and agencies, accelerated privatization, and a tax increase in order to remedy the fiscal deficit. The social security system was reformed and, by 1998, three pieces of legislation had taken some steps toward labor flexibilization.[21] Labor was kept on side by means of selective inducements such as subsidies to union welfare funds and the opportunity to buy the shares of privatized companies (Murillo 2003, 151–162). Measures were initiated to improve the fiscal situation of the provinces and to privatize provincially owned banks and services.

The key actors among the domestic policy elite who propelled first-stage policy reform were Menem himself and two of his closest collaborators (who, at different times, became his minister of economy), Erman González and Domingo Cavallo. Unlike the Mexican case, here important nontechnocratic actors steered the market reform process, particularly at the beginning. In its initial and most difficult period, 1989–91, the most important figure was Gonzalez, a politico who served as minister of economy from 1990 to 1991, minister of defense from 1991 to 1993, and later minister of labor.[22] As minister of defense, Gonzalez led the very difficult negotiations with the military, thereby playing an essential role in securing the privatization of the various military equipment and material companies.[23]

Although Cavallo had played an important role in developing official policy behind the scenes, it was only with his appointment as economy minister in early 1991 that the Argentine reform process began to include the substantial participation of domestic technocrats. Cavallo, who held a doctorate in economics from Harvard, brought with him a highly qualified economic team, many from the Fundación Mediterránea, a think tank with a history of close and friendly relations with the World Bank.[24] Cavallo himself had a long history with the bank, having acted in a consulting capacity on many occasions. This personal relationship, combined with Argentina's relatively smaller technocratic capacity compared to that of Mexico, contributed to the depth of the bank's role.

Despite the formal concentration of power in the hands of the minister of economy and the use (and threatened use) of presidential decree power (Teichman 1997, 46–47), Argentina's radical reformers never achieved the policy isolation and authoritarian decisionmaking capacity obtained by Mexican technocrats during the Salinas years. Once the trauma of hyperinflation began to wear off (after about 1991), the legislature and the trade unions were able to alter government bills on privatization, health care reform, and social security reforms (Llanos 2001; Acuña and Tuozzo 2000, 446). The Peronist Party lacked the control of the labor movement that characterized the PRI during the Salinas years; and while deeply divided, labor resistance was continuous and effective in blocking reforms to the labor code (Acuña and Tuozzo 2000, 438).

In addition, there was stiff resistance to reform in the Argentine cabinet. The minister of social action, the defense minister, and the secretary-general of the presidency challenged accelerated reform of the state, demanding a more gradual process and an end to continued cutbacks in government expenditures, especially because of their negative social implications. The labor minister opposed the economic minister on the issue of imposing labor reform on the labor movement (Etchemendy and Palermo 1998, 585). Indeed, Cavallo's departure from the Economy Ministry in 1996 was no doubt linked to these conflicts.[25]

The World Bank's policy role in Argentina began with its involvement with the Austral Plan and continued throughout the Alfonsín years. During this time, bank officials made a strong pitch for trade liberalization and public enterprise reform. It was with the bank's participation in the formulation of the Primavera Plan, however, that the relationship between Argentina and the bank solidified, and a very intense and close relationship developed into the 1990s. The key event propelling this involvement occurred in 1988 with the IMF's refusal to grant a standby loan to Argentina because of the nation's repeated failure to meet performance criteria. The World Bank stepped in and lent Argentina US$1.25 billion. Interviews overwhelmingly revealed the key role of the United States in the bank's decision to lend.[26] Facing an election year in 1988, senior U.S. officials were anxious to avoid a confrontation with a major debtor, and therefore were eager to prop up Argentina, and pressed the bank to lend. The result was to stimulate an ongoing relationship with the bank that would become even closer in the years to come. In the words of one senior LAC official, "the World Bank was never as involved so closely in policy as it was in the Argentine case, particularly in trade policy, public sector reform, and privatization."

Indeed, the Primavera Plan, the final economic program of the Alfonsín administration, was largely a bank initiative, and was developed over several months of detailed and intense discussions between high-level bank officials and Argentine officials. This first international policy network was a fairly loose and often conflictive one, lacking the high degree of trust and the close personal relations of later networks. Bank officials used this opportunity to push for full-scale reform, including public enterprise restructuring, privatization, labor flexibilization, and tariff policy reform (Interviews, Argentine and LAC senior officials). Given the country's dire economic situation at the time and its desperate need for funds, Argentine officials were warming to the idea of radical reforms, especially privatization. By strongly backing reform, the bank encouraged Argentine officials to initiate reforms they saw as necessary but feared to try because of the anticipated political fallout (Interviews, two senior Argentine government officials). Bank demands, moreover, became a useful political tool: in their defense of reforms such as trade liberalization to the private sector, Argentine officials diverted blame from themselves by claiming that Argentina had no choice but to implement the bank's policy demands (Interviews, senior Argentine and LAC officials).

By 1989, however, the pressure on Argentina from multilateral lending institutions and the United States became much more direct—a situation that never developed in the Mexican case. By this time, U.S. willingness to support Argentine recalcitrance had worn thin, while the bank's position had hardened. In April 1988, Argentina ceased to make interest payments to foreign banks, and arrears built up throughout that year. The incoming Bush administration no longer felt any need to support Argentina in its conflicts with the IMF. By early 1989, the bank had suspended disbursements on its loans, and the IMF said it would consider a new standby loan only after the Argentine national election, scheduled for May 1989.

The Argentine economic situation spiraled downward. As dollars were massively withdrawn from the banking system, the country's reserves plummeted, and the inflation rate exceeded 4,000 percent, reaching its highest point in June 1989. Public order disintegrated as mobs rioted and the government declared a state of emergency (Smith 1992, 39). The trauma of hyperinflation opened the door to more intensive World Bank participation in policy reform. Throughout 1989, the bank's continued efforts to press its case for reform included a meeting with Carlos Menem's brother Eduardo to gage Menem's receptiveness to reform and an offer to brief Menem's team should he win the election (Interview, senior LAC official).

The depth of the economic and fiscal crisis also opened the way for direct and explicit pressure by the bank for policy reform. Now the bank called on Argentina to demonstrate a firm commitment to structural reform in order to gain the confidence of international creditors, which was especially important given Argentina's less-than-glowing record in policy reform. All government officials interviewed stressed that the first privatizations Menem carried out (ENTEL and Aerolíneas Argentinas) were explicitly in response to this pressure.[27] Bank officials demanded that Argentina make this gesture. The IMF conditioned the conclusion of the 1989 standby agreement on a public deficit target of 1 percent of GDP, a monumental task and one that Argentine officials believed could be met only by divesting loss-prone public companies (Interviews, two senior Argentine officials).[28]

At the end of 1989, the new Menem administration invited the bank to become involved in a thorough reform program.[29] A top-level discussion involving senior LAC officials, President Menem, soon-to-be-appointed economy minister Gonzalez, and then-foreign minister Cavallo took place, and a reform program involving trade liberalization, the privatization of all public companies, and the establishment of currency board was worked out. As in the Mexican case, in the following years, international policy networks developed in a wide variety of areas, including those where loans were not forthcoming.[30]

Policy networks ran the gamut, from top-level macropolicy formulation to trade policy, labor reform, social security, and public sector restructuring and privatization. Two of the key features of this process were the fluidity and informality with which officials in the bank and the Argentine state maintained ongoing contacts, generally without a great deal of regard to formal rank—very much unlike the Mexican case. Middle-rank bank officers, for example, appear to have had easy access to the Argentine economy minister, and even to the president. Another distinguishing feature of these networks is that they were not initially technocratic. Indeed, it was precisely the relative absence of highly trained technocrats that made the bank's role in providing technical support so important (Interviews, senior LAC and Argentine officials).

Relationships of trust between LAC officials, including desk officers and sectoral specialists, and Argentine officials developed in the context of ongoing policy dialogue, often in the form of informal discussions on a broad range of reform issues. The extent to which the bank could actually affect policy change, however, depended mightily on the strength of domestic political opposition, particularly opposition from labor. In those areas where labor had a strong vested interest, reforms occurred slowly or were blocked.

International policy networks engaged in public enterprise reform contributed in important ways to the spread and acceptance of market reform ideas, especially the necessity of restructuring public enterprises and, later, the need for privatization. By 1987, intense discussions on public enterprise reform were already under way. Bank officials took a much more activist approach in pushing for reform than in the Mexican case, often encouraged to do so by higher-level Argentine officials (Interviews, LAC middle-level official, senior Argentine official). Bank officials moved freely within the Argentine state, lobbying public enterprise managers and trade union leaders. The bank funded studies on public enterprise price policies, restructuring, and privatization. Bank officials organized conferences to bring both state enterprise managers and trade union leaders into contact with outside experts on public enterprise reform.

The bank also brought in and paid for outside consultants to help carry out restructuring in specific public firms. These consultants, along with bank officials, played an important role in convincing public enterprise managers of the need for substantial change. While many of these reformist collaborators were forced out in the face of bureaucratic and trade union resistance in the public enterprise, the legacy was a positive attitude toward public sector reform among the senior executives of many public enterprises (Interviews, two middle-level LAC officers, one senior LAC official).

Initially, bank officials focused on public enterprise restructuring. But with the repeated failure to reform public enterprises sufficiently, both bank and Argentine officials came to the conclusion that only drastic action, in the form of privatization, would solve the problem (Interviews, two middle-level LAC officials; senior Argentine official). In politically difficult privatization cases, restructuring was pursued until political resistance could be overcome. Restructuring of public enterprises, then, was an essential part of the spread of the ideas favoring state streamlining and, eventually, privatization; as such, it helped strengthen policy resolve and break down political resistance to privatization, sometimes in very practical ways. In one case, a bank official's promise to a trade union that the bank would provide funding for severance pay was important in inducing trade union support for restructuring and eventually for privatization.[31]

With Domingo Cavallo heading the Economy Ministry between 1991 and 1996, international policy networks assumed the more technocratic character of the Mexican experience, with members sharing both educational experience and policy goals. The relationship between the World Bank and Argentina prospered, partly as a consequence of Domingo Cavallo's long relationship with the bank. Cavallo had worked as a consultant for the bank for many years, and had developed a close and cordial relationship with senior bank and LAC officials (Interviews, senior Argentine official; two senior LAC officials).[32]

Cavallo's successor as economy minister was Roque Fernández, with a doctorate in economics from the University of Chicago. He drew his technocratic team of advisers, many also with Chicago graduate degrees, from another of Argentina's think tanks, the Center for Macroeconomic Studies (CEMA).[33] Bank informants stressed the trust that existed between Argentine Economy Ministry officials, particularly Cavallo and Fernandez, and them because of their similar educational training and work experience with the bank and the IMF. In the words of one bank official, "Argentine Economy officials are well known to us; we speak the same language, and there are no basic differences in our views." International technocratic networks did not maintain an exclusive hold on the policy process, however; they faced stiff challenges from within the cabinet, from Congress, and from labor.

Although consultation of civil society in other Latin American client countries is gaining ground, the bank claims that the process has gone farther in Argentina than in any other country (World Bank 2000b). There, civil society participation in bank programs first occurred in 1993 with PROMIN, the Mother and Infant Nutrition Program. NGOs were involved only in implementing the program, however (Acuña and Tuozzo 2000, 450). NGO involvement in bank programs can be problematic; for example, the representative credentials of those NGOs that do participate in bank-funded Argentine social programs have been questioned (Tussie et al. 1997, 77). As in Mexico, civil society participation was largely uninvited, viewed as destructive rather than positive; and it occurred in compensatory rather than structural adjustment programs.

Recently, the bank has attempted to involve civil society groups in its compensatory, especially poverty, programs. In 1999, the bank carried out a survey of 1,200 poor households in 29 cities, based on a series of open-ended questions that attempted to identify how society defined poverty, the perceived changes in the last five years, and the roles of institutions in reducing poverty. It also used focus group discussions to add further depth. In March 2000, the bank met with more than 400 civil society leaders of NGOs, trade unions, community-based organizations, academia, research centers, and religious groups in five forums held across the country.[34] In addition, it surveyed the views of some 70 government officials. The International Finance Corporation, the bank's private sector lending affiliate, consulted with the Argentine private sector (World Bank 2000c, 20). The bank, moreover, has promised to respond to civil society participants about how, or whether, it incorporated their suggestions (World Bank 2000c, 29).

While the bank's primary concern remained Argentina's fiscal situation, as in the Mexican case, it has decided to focus more selectively on other policy areas. As in Mexico, it has selected poverty, particularly policies to aid the most vulnerable, as the key focus area (World Bank 2000c, 36–38).

The World Bank's involvement in policy reform in Argentina has been, and continues to be, considerably greater than it has been in Mexico. Operating in a less authoritarian, more plural political environment, LAC officials had considerably greater leeway in penetrating the state and spreading market reform ideas. The extreme nature of Argentine economic difficulties from late 1988 on opened the way for direct policy pressure, while the lack of technical capacity encouraged the incoming Menem administration to rely heavily on the bank. Unlike their Mexican counterparts, Argentine reformers generally did not stop the bank from dialoguing with intra- and extrastate groups, and they sometimes used the bank as a handy excuse for their pursuit of unpopular measures (Interviews, three senior Argentine officials).[35] At the same time, Argentina's lesser geopolitical importance meant that LAC officials would not be inhibited from pressing reform by the threats or potential threat of reprimand by senior bank officials. The United States, while initially sympathetic to Argentine resistance to reform, had changed its tune by 1989 and could not be enlisted to slow down LAC's drive for reform in particular policy areas, as had occurred in the Mexican case. But there were clear limits to the bank's influence, largely revolving around domestic political opposition.

CONCLUSIONS

This article has argued that the market reformers of Latin America have not acted alone in carrying out the momentous policy reform changes of the past decade or more. They have had important support from World Bank officials operating in international policy networks. Networks of bank and client country officials, bound by personal relations of trust and even friendship and with shared policy goals, have helped to spread market reform ideas, guided the development of most of the major reform programs, and provided essential technical and financial support. The bank, in providing this support, played a key role in strengthening the hand of market reformers in relation to their detractors both inside and outside the state.

The two cases analyzed here, however, reveal important differences in the nature of their policy networks. Distinct institutional arrangements and different geopolitical positions determined how international policy networks would operate. In a liberalizing, single-party-dominant regime, Mexico's technocratic policy elite controlled bank officials' access to the Mexican state and defined the policy areas in which the bank could become involved. Mexican policymakers used the World Bank to build support for the reforms they wished to realize, and tried to use bank conditionality to thwart future attempts to dismantle those reforms. Because of Mexico's special geopolitical situation, Mexican officials were able to force LAC officials to back off from reforms they did not favor, such as in the energy and finance sectors. Mexico's special relationship with the United States gave Mexican officials special weight with the bank, mitigating the pressure for change and allowing the Mexicans to pursue a slower-paced program.

The bank's influence on the Argentine reform process, on the other hand, was much more pervasive. Bank officials had access to virtually all areas of the Argentine state and to organized groups, such as trade unions. Unlike Mexico, where authoritarian structures remained largely intact during the heyday of market reform, Argentina's policy reform was carried out after the transition to electoral democracy had been completed. That transition, following a period of brutal military rule, raised public expectations and delayed policy reform. The delay rendered the economic crisis, when it hit, much deeper than it would otherwise have been. But the trauma of hyperinflation swept away support for the old economic model and ensured the implantation of the new market reform policy ideas, opening the way for the bank to play an integral and essential role in Argentina's market reform experience. Because Argentina's importance to the United States was less than Mexico's, in the end the U.S. attitude toward Argentina helped to propel reform forward.

The discussion and development of policy that occurred in international policy networks was not subject to domestic public scrutiny; nor could the bank officials involved in such policy development be held accountable. While bank involvement in policy development has not been directly coercive, it has unquestionably increased the strength of market reformers in the state by providing them with intellectual and technical support, financial resources, and help in spreading market reform ideas. Meanwhile, opposing intra- and extrastate actors have lacked a voice in the process. Opponents to PROGRESA in Mexico's Social Development Ministry, for example, were not given the opportunity to enter policy development discussions; and certainly, peasant organizations in southern Mexico were not given the opportunity to enter discussions of agricultural reforms, including reform of the ejido.[36] The bank resisted the involvement of the Argentine labor movement in changes directly affecting its interests (Acuña and Tuozzo 2000, 445). It is likely that involvement of congresses and interest groups in policy reforms would have slowed down the process of change or made the reforms different in important respects. Such reforms certainly would have had a higher degree of public "ownership."

The process of structural adjustment with which international policy networks have been so intimately involved was corrosive to democratic practices insofar as bank positions, policies, and the debates that occurred in international policy networks were not shared with congresses and the civil society of client countries. With the failure of market reforms to bring sustained prosperity to all, opposition groups in client countries have gained ground, and voices critical of past policies and practices now have more weight. The World Bank's recent commitment to civil society consultations appears to recognize

the importance of public involvement in policy development, but has some serious limitations; consultation is confined largely to compensatory policies (social policies) and to
infrastructural projects that affect populations and the environment. The bank does not
proffer public involvement in structural adjustment programs. Indeed, it does not view
public involvement in policy development as an important end in itself; instead, its move
in this direction is motivated largely by a desire to improve the efficacy of policy outcome
(Nelson 1997, 47). This is apparent in its support for civil society consultation on conditional cash transfer programs (Teichman 2007, 567–568).

The Argentine case points to other difficulties. The bank is selective in the social
groups it deems appropriate to consult. Clearly, NGOs are strongly favored, while participation by trade unions, perhaps the strongest adversary of bank programs, is regarded
as detrimental. More important, democratizing the policy process means the involvement
of elected representatives in public policy decisions. The bank's public consultation
initiatives do not address this issue. Indeed, it could be argued that the bank, in directly
consulting civil society, is assuming the rightful place of democratic government, the
function of which is to attempt fairly to aggregate competing societal interests and to be
held accountable for its performance. This is a role that most Latin American governments
have not performed well (as evidenced by the process by which first-stage reforms were
carried out). It is one that must first be learned and then practiced for democracy to
prosper.

INTERVIEWS

Much of the data for this paper comes from in-depth, open-ended interviews with World
Bank and country officials. Because interview subjects were guaranteed confidentiality
to encourage candor, informants are not identified by name; and identifying features,
such as official position, have been disguised or excluded.

World Bank

Washington, April 1998. Total 15 interviews.
    Senior Latin American and Caribbean Section (LAC) officials: vice presidents, division
chiefs, senior and lead economists, and lead sectoral specialists.
    Middle-ranking LAC officials.
    Country economists (desk officers), resident representatives.

Argentina

Buenos Aires, March 1995. Total 17. Ministers and senior and middle-level officials, Peronist and Radical governments. Government agencies included the Ministry of Economy,
Central Bank, Ministry of Interior, and Ministry of Labor.

Mexico

Mexico City, February–April 1991, December 1999. Total 27.
    Cabinet ministers (secretaries), senior and middle-level officials, Salinas and Zedillo
governments.
    Agencies included the Ministry of Finance; Ministry of Industry, Mines, and Public
Enterprises; Ministry of Commerce and Industrial Development; Ministry of Social Development; and the state petroleum company, PEMEX.

NOTES

The author gratefully acknowledges financial support from the Social Sciences and Humanities Research Council of Canada.

1 Examples of the former include O'Donnell and Schmitter 1986; and Seligson 1989. See, for the latter Peruzzotti and Smulovitz 2006; Arvitzer 2002; Stahler-Sholk, et al., 2008.

2 The analysis presented in this chapter departs from those who do not accord any appreciable role to the multilateral lending institutions in explaining market reform outcomes (Weyland 2001; Corrales 2002).

3 Generally, second-stage reform is seen as including such policies as the privatization of companies remaining in state hands; regulatory reforms, especially those governing monopolies; and measures to combat poverty and improve governance, including the reduction and elimination of corruption and decentralization (Pastor and Wise 1999; Naim 1994).

4 Virtually all LAC officials interviewed stressed this important change in LAC strategy, which came with the change in leadership. Interviews, Mexico City, 1999.

5 The term policy network, originating in work on British and U.S. politics, does not include international actors, as the present study does (see Marsh and Rhodes 1992). While technocrats are important, often predominant actors in these networks, the involvement of nontechnocrats distinguishes this study's use of the concept of a policy network from an "epistemic community" (Haas 1990) or an "economic knowledge network" ("living social communities of likeminded professionals"; Hira 1998, 13).

6 This argument that personal relationships, particularly of trust, were key aspects of market reform policy networks springs from repeated assertions that this was the case, as well as from often-repeated references to interaction at social gatherings outside the office environment (including the development of social relationships among wives). In addition, the relationships between bank officials and Mexican and Argentine officials were, it was widely admitted, qualitatively different from those between bank officials and Chilean government officials, with whom there was policy dialogue but little personal trust or admiration—a consequence of the bank's participation in structural adjustment during the Pinochet years (Teichman 2001, 87).

7 Under Salinas, the PRI held a clear majority in the lower house, ending up with 260 seats out of 500 in the Chamber of Deputies after the 1988 national election and 290 seats in the 1991 midterm elections. It maintained overwhelming dominance in the Senate, with 31 of 32 seats. With the notable exception of the bank privatization, divestitures of state companies had only to receive a simple majority in Congress. In addition, Salinas appointed loyal supporters to head the PRI, who purged the party of dissident elements.

8 The career backgrounds of this technocratic elite were in the finance sector; they were young (in their early forties) and had graduate degrees from major U.S. universities. Serra Puche and Zedillo hold graduate degrees in economics from Yale; Aspe holds the Ph.D. in economics from MIT, while Salinas earned a Ph.D. in public administration from Harvard and Cordoba an incomplete Ph.D. from Stanford.

9 During the de la Madrid years, most radical technocratic reformers were serving in a variety of influential, although initially not cabinet-level positions. Gil Diaz was deputy director of economic research in the Central Bank; Zedillo worked with him and later replaced Aspe as subsecretary of planning and budget (one level below ministerial rank) when Aspe moved on to take over the Planning and Budget Ministry. Serra Puche was subsecretary of revenue in the Finance Ministry. Cordoba was director of economic and social policy in the Ministry of Budget and Planning. Salinas was minister of budget and planning from 1985 to 1987.

10 During the negotiations for Mexico's Brady deal, President Salinas complained to a senior World Bank official about the difficulties his administration was having with the commercial banks. The bank official took up the problem with top officials of the bank, who went to President George H. W. Bush. Bush, in turn, put pressure on the commercial banks to soften their position (Interview, senior LAC official, Mexico City, 1999).

11 One LAC official who had failed to obtain Finance Ministry authorization related that he had been forced to cancel an appointment with an official in the state petroleum company, PEMEX, when a Finance Ministry official found out.

12 The official who reported this event claims he was close to losing his job.

13 Although Heath was a World Bank official, this article expresses his personal views on the topic, not the official bank position.

14 Bank officials believed that granting ejido members the opportunity for private ownership would give them a strong incentive to stay on the land. Not only did the ejido reform not result in the large-scale sale of ejido lands, but land titling has been slow. Ejido members, moreover, even if they proceed with titling, are likely to continue working their land as usual (Cornelius and Mhyre 1998, 12; Cornelius 1998, 237). Bank officials saw this as a vindication of their position. Interview, senior LAC official.

15 According to one bank informant, the Mexicans wanted the reform of the ejido included as a condition in a bank agricultural loan. The bank refused, apparently because the enormous political sensitivity of the issue and because it did not see the ejido as the root of the country's agricultural difficulties.

16 Indeed, the bank official who wrote the report was told by Mexican officials (some of whom were friends from university days) to burn it. Interview, senior LAC official.

17 According to the bank, Mexican government officials rejected bank lending for PROGRESA for fear of the negative political repercussions of high-profile bank involvement in such a politically sensitive area (OED 2001, 26). This seems to be a reasonable explanation, given past Mexican predisposition to keep the bank out of what are considered politically sensitive policy areas. It should be noted that because funding for PROGRESA came from the Social, Health, and Education ministries, the bank's funding of other health and educational programs meant that it contributed indirectly to PROGRESA by freeing up ministry funds for that program.

18 In late 1999, senior government levels were taking a greater interest in decentralization. The Ministry of Finance brought back one official who had ceased consulting for it a few years earlier and had gone to work for the World Bank out of frustration at the government's failure to move substantively on the issue. Another frustrated technocrat had set up his own consulting company, which was receiving World Bank funds to prepare state governments for decentralization (Interview, two middle-level Mexican officials).

19 The Mexican government, on the other hand, asserts that the bank fails to recognize that government openness to NGOs has made major advances in recent years (OED 2001, 55).

20 Considerable progress was made in trade liberalization under Alfonsín: by late 1988 the number of products subject to prohibition or quantitative restrictions had been reduced from 4,000 to 3,000, and the average tariff rate reduced from 51 percent to 36 percent (de la Baize 1995, 115).

21 Labor flexibilization refers to changes in the norms governing labor relations, with the objective of increasing investment and international competitiveness. In practice, it involves reduction in the cost of labor.

22 Gonzalez was part of what has been described as the "anti-elite," politicians who constituted the majority of Menem's cabinet when market reform got under way. These were politicians with roots in the interior provinces and without links to established interests in Buenos Aires, who were accustomed to a patrimonial leadership heavily dependent on personal loyalty (Sidicaro 1995, 125).

23 Agreement from the military was achieved through negotiations carried out by commissions composed of government officials, military representatives, and private consultants, set up to oversee the privatizations (Interview, senior Argentine official).

24 The bank sent some of its most distinguished market reform proponents to Fundación meetings, while Fundación economists presented papers to World Bank officials (N'haux 1993, 248, 267).

25 The precise reason for his departure is not clear. Congress deeply resented Cavallo's attempt to get a tax reform passed by presidential decree, followed by his failure to make himself available for questioning. One version suggests that Cavallo's departure was the price Menem agreed to pay to get legislators to pass a backlog of bills.

26 It is also true that some World Bank officials believed that Argentina could not possibly meet the IMF's rigid targets and were therefore not predisposed to tie bank programs to such requirements (Interviews, two senior LAC officials).

27 Another interpretation points to inflation and fiscal reduction as the motives behind these privatizations (Gerchunoff and Torre 2000, 739).

28 In 1989, the public deficit as a percentage of GDP stood at 16.1 percent (World Bank 1993, 7).

29 There has been considerable speculation as to why Menem adopted a rapid market reform program following an electoral campaign that had been critical of such reforms. One explanation maintains that Menem's policy conversion came as a consequence of conversations with government officials during a trip to Europe with Cavallo just a few days after entering the race for his party's presidential candidacy. Others claim that Menem could not be described as having "converted" to market reform because he lacked political principles in the first place. Interviews, three senior government officials.

30 The World Bank refused to lend if it felt that Argentine officials were unlikely to take measures to ensure a modicum of transparency in reform. The Aerolíneas Argentinas and the highway privatizations were two such cases (Interview, two senior LAC officials).

31 Actually, the bank official in question was not authorized to make such a specific promise. But given that bank loans are fungible, he went ahead, knowing that this promise was necessary to bring the trade union on side and trusting that Argentine officials would honor the deal.

32 Differences of opinion and tough discussions did, however, occur. World Bank officials, for example, strongly disagreed with Cavallo's establishment of a currency board to stabilize the peso (Interviews, two senior LAC officials).

33 Despite the growing tension between President Menem and Cavallo, the latter's economic policies were never in question. When Cavallo left the Economy Ministry, Menem steadfastly defended Cavallo's economic policies and underlined that his new appointee, Fernandez, would continue them.

34 The bank notes that those exchanges revealed "some deep differences in perception and approach between the bank and some participants" (World Bank 2000b).

35 At the same time, a few bank officials suggested that there were important "cultural" differences in the two countries that help account for the degree of penetration in the Argentine case as opposed to the more restricted access of the bank in Mexico; the Mexicans were viewed as being more predisposed to hierarchy. Interviews, two senior LAC officials.

36 Although many ejiditarios apparently welcomed or were not adverse to reform, the reform of Article 27 of the constitution had an adverse psychological impact in southern Mexico, especially Chiapas. It has been suggested that reform of the ejido had a critical psychological impact in that it ended hope for further land redistribution and destroyed the image of the state as protector of peasant rights, thereby contributing to support for insurgent movements (Bailón 1994, 19; Serrano 1997, 80).

REFERENCES

Acuña, Carlos H., and María Fernanda Tuozzo. 2000. Civil Society Participation in World Bank and Inter-American Development Bank Programs: The Case of Argentina. *Global Governance* 6, 4: 433–55.

Avritzer, Leonardo. 2002. *Democracy and the Public Space in Latin America*. Princeton: Princeton University Press.

Babai, Don. 1988. The World Bank and the IMF: Rolling Back the State or Backing Its Role? In *The Promise of Privatization: A Challenge for U.S. Policy*, ed. Raymond Vernon. New York: Council on Foreign Affairs. 254–78.

Babb, Sarah. 2002. *Managing Mexico. Economists from Nationalism to Neoliberalism*. Princeton: Princeton University Press.

Bailón, Moisés J. 1994. *Semejanzas y diferencias en dos regiones in indígenas del sur de México*. Paper presented at the 28th International Congress of the Latin American Studies Association. Atlanta, March 10–13.

Banco de México. 1993. *The Mexican Economy 1992*. Mexico City.

Bresser Pereira, Luiz Carlos. 1993. Economic Reforms and Economic Growth: Efficiency and Politics in Latin America. In *Economic Reforms in New Democracies: A Social-Democratic Approach*, ed. Bresser Pereira, José María Maravall, and Adam Przeworski. Cambridge: Cambridge University Press. 15–76.

Casaburi, Gabriel, María Pía Riggirozzi, María Fernanda Tuozzo, and Diana Tussie. 2000. Multilateral Development Banks, Governments, and Civil Society: Chiaroscuros in a Triangular Relationship. *Global Governance* 6, 4: 493–517.

Cavarozzi, Marcelo, Joan Nelson, and Miguel Urrutia. 1994. Economic and Political Transitions in Latin America: The Interplay Between Democratization and Market Reforms. In *Precarious Balance: Democracy and Economic Reforms in Latin America*, ed. Nelson. vol. 11. San Francisco: Institute for Contemporary Studies. 1–98.

Centeno, Miguel Angel. 1997. *Democracy Within Reason*. University Park: Pennsylvania State University Press.

Conaghan, Catherine M., and James M. Malloy. 1994. *Unsettling Statecraft: Democracy and Neoliberalism in the Central Andes*. Pittsburgh: University of Pittsburgh Press.

Cornelius, Wayne A. 1998. Ejido Reform: Stimulus or Alternative to Migration? In *The Transformation of Rural Mexico: Reforming the Ejido Sector*, ed. Cornelius and David Myhre. La Jolla: Center for U.S.-Mexican Studies, University of California. 229–46.

Cornelius, Wayne A., and David Myhre. 1998. Introduction. In *The Transformation of Rural Mexico: Reforming the Ejido Sector*, ed. Cornelius and Myhre. La Jolla: Center for U.S.-Mexican Studies, University of California. 1–21.

Corrales, Javier. 2002. *The Politics of Economic Reform in Argentina and Venezuela in the 1990s*. University Park: The Pennsylvania State University Press.

De la Baize, Felipe A. M. 1995. *Remaking the Argentine Economy*. New York: Council on Foreign Relations Press.

Deininger, Klaus, and Hans Binswanger. 1999. The Evolution of the World Bank's Land Policy: Principles, Experiences, and Future Challenges. *World Research Observer* 14, 2: 249–75.

Diamond, Larry and Leonardo Molino. 2005. Introduction. In *Assessing the Quality of Democracy*, ed. Larry Diamond and Leonardo Molino. Baltimore: The Johns Hopkins University Press: ix–xviii.

Etchemendy, Sebastián, and Vicente Palermo. 1998. Conflicto y concertación. Gobierno, congreso y organizaciones de interés en la reforma laboral del primer gobierno de Menem (1989–1995*). Desarrollo Económico* 37, 148: 559–90.

Fernández de Villegas, Manuel, and Naomi Adelson. 2000. Civil Society Participation in World Bank and Inter-American Development Bank Programs: The Case of Mexico. *Global Governance* 6, 4: 473–91.

Fortín, Carlos. 1988. Power, Bargaining and the Latin American Debt Negotiations. In *Managing World Debt*, ed. Stephany Griffith-Jones. New York: St. Martin's Press.

Gerchunoff, Pablo, and Juan Carlos Torre. 1996. La política de liberalización económica en la administración de Menem. *Desarrollo Económico* 36, 143: 733–457.

Haas, Ernst B. 1990. *When Knowledge Is Power: Three Models of Change in International Organizations*. Berkeley: University of California Press.

Haggard, Stephan, and Robert R. Kaufman. 1992. The Political Economy of Inflation and Stabilization in Middle-Income Countries. In *The Politics of Economic Adjustment*, ed. Haggard and Kaufman. Princeton: Princeton University Press. 270–315.

——. 1995. *The Political Economy of Democratic Transitions*. Princeton: Princeton University Press.

Haggard, Stephan, and Steven B. Webb. 1994. Introduction. In *Voting for Reform: Democracy, Political Liberalization, and Economic Adjustment*, ed. Haggard and Webb. Washington, DC: World Bank. 1–32.

Hagopian, Frances. 2005. Conclusions: Government Performance, Political Representation and Public Perceptions of Contemporary Democracy in Latin America. In *The Third Wave of Democratization in Latin America, Advances and Setbacks*. ed. Frances Hagopian and Scott P. Mainwaring. Cambridge: Cambridge University Press:

Hall, Peter H. 1993. Policy Paradigms, Social Learning, and the State. *Comparative Politics* 25, 3: 275–96.

Hausman, Ricardo. 1994. Sustaining Reform: What Role for Social Policy? In *Redefining the State in Latin America*, ed. Colin I. Bradford. Paris: Organization for Economic Cooperation and Development. 173–90.

Heath, John R. 1992. Evaluating the Impact of Mexico's Land Reform on Agricultural Productivity. *World Development* 20: 695–711.

Heclo, Hugh. 1974. *Social Politics in Britain and Sweden.* New Haven: Yale University Press.

Heredia, Blanca. 1996. *Contested State: The Politics of Trade Liberalization in Mexico.* Ph.D. diss., Columbia University.

Hira, Anil. 1998. *Ideas and Economic Policy in Latin America: Regional, National, and Organizational Case Studies.* Westport: Praeger.

Ikenberry, John G. 1990. The International Spread of Privatization Policies: Inducements, Learning, and "Policy Bandwagoning." In *The Political Economy of Public Sector Reform,* ed. Ezra N. Suleimen and John Waterbury. Boulder: Westview Press. 88–109.

Kahler, Miles. 1991. External Influence, Conditionality, and the Politics of Adjustment. In *The Politics of Economic Adjustment,* ed. Stephan Haggard and Robert R. Kaufman. Princeton: Princeton University Press. 149–450.

Kapur, Devish, John P. Lewis, and Richard Webb. 1997. *The World Bank: Its First Half-Century.* Vol. 1, History. Washington, DC: Brookings Institution Press.

Killick, Tony. 1995. *IMF Programmes in Developing Countries.* London: Routledge. Latin American Weekly Report. 1991. November 19: 2.

———. 1996. August 8: 350.

Llanos, Mariana. 2001. Understanding Presidential Power in Argentina: A Study of the Policy of Privatization in the 1990s. *Journal of Latin American Studies* 33, 1: 67–99.

Marsh, David, and R. A. W. Rhodes. 1992. Policy Communities and Issue Networks: Beyond Typology. In *Policy Networks in British Government,* ed. Marsh and Rhodes. Oxford: Clarendon Press. 249–68.

Morales, Juan Antonio. 1996. Economic Policy After the Transition to Democracy: A Synthesis. In *Economic Policy and the Transition to Democracy,* ed. Morales and Gary McMahon. New York: St. Martin's Press. 1–29

Murillo, Victoria. 2003. *Labor Unions, Partisan Coalitions and Market Reforms in Latin America.* Cambridge: Cambridge Unversity Press.

Naim, Moíses. 1994. Latin America: The Second Stage of Reform. *Journal of Democracy* 5 (October): 32–48.

Nelson, Joan M. 1990. Introduction. In Economic *Crisis and Policy Choice: The Politics of Adjustment in the Third World,* ed. Nelson. Princeton: Princeton University Press.

———. 1992. Good Governance, Democracy, and Conditional Economic Aid. In *Development Finance and Policy Reform: Essays on the Theory and Practice of Conditionality,* ed. Paul Mosely. New York: St. Martin's Press. 309–20.

Nelson, Paul J. 1997. *Transparencia, fiscalización y participación.* In *El BID, el Banco Mundial y la sociedad civil: nuevas formas de financiamiento internacional,* ed. Diana Tussie. Buenos Aires: FLACSO/Oficina de Publicaciones del CBC, Universidad de Buenos Aires. 21–58.

N'haux, Enrique. 1993. Menem-Cavallo: *El Poder Mediterráneo.* Buenos Aires: Ediciones Corregidor.

North, Douglas C. 1990. *Institutions, Institutional Change and Economic Performance.* Cambridge: Cambridge University Press.

O'Donnell, Guillermo, and Philippe C. Schmitter. 1986. *Transitions from Authoritarian Rule: Tentative Conclusions About Uncertain Democracies.* Baltimore: Johns Hopkins University Press.

Pastor, Manuel, Jr., and Carol Wise. 1999. The Politics of Second-Generation Reform. *Journal of Democracy* 10, 3 (July): 3–48.

Peralta-Ramos, Mónica. 1992. *The Political Economy of Argentina: Power and Class Since 1930.* Boulder: Westview Press.

Peruzzotti, Enrique and Catalina Smulovitz, eds. 2006. *Enforcing the Rule of Law: Social Accountability in the New Latin American Democracies.* Pittsburgh: University of Pittsburgh Press.

Ramamurti, Ravi. 1992. Privatization and the Latin American Debt Problem. In *Private Sector Solutions to the Latin American Debt Problem, ed. Robert Grosse.* New Brunswick: Transaction. 153–75.

Ramírez de la O., Rogelio. 1996. The Mexican Peso Crisis and Recession of 1994–1995: Preventable Then, Avoidable in the Future. In *The Mexican Peso Crisis: International Perspectives,* ed. Riordan Roett. Boulder: Lynne Rienner. 11–32.

Remmer, Karen. 1986. The Politics of Economic Stabilization: IMF Standby Programs in Latin America, 1954–1984. *Comparative Politics* 19 (October): 77–800.

———. 1995. New Theoretical Perspectives on Democratization. *Comparative Politics* 28 (October): 103–22.

Riggirozzi, Pía. 2009. *Advancing Governance in the South. What Role for International Financial Institutions in Developing States?* New York: Palgrave Macmillan.

Rueschemeyer, Dietrich. 2004. The Quality of Democracy: Addressing Inequality. *Journal of Democracy* 15, 4: 76–90.

Seligson, Mitchell A. 1989. Introduction: From Uncertainty to Uncertainty: The Institutionalization of Elections in Central America. In *Elections and Democracy in Central America,* ed. John A. Booth and Seligson. Chapel Hill: University of North Carolina Press. 1–39.

Serrano, Mónica. 1997. Civil Violence in Chiapas: The Origins and Causes of the Revolt. In *Mexico: Assessing Neoliberal Reform,* ed. Serrano. London: Institute of Latin American Studies, University of London. 75–93.

Sidicaro, Ricardo. 1995. Poder político, liberalismo económico y sectores populares en la Argentina, 1989–1995. In *Peronismo y menemismo: avatares del populismo en la Argentina,* ed. Atilio Borón, Manuel Moray Araujo, José Nun, Juan Carlos Portantiero, and Sidicaro. Buenos Aires: Ediciones El Cielo por Asalto. 121–58.

Smith, William C. 1992. Hyperinflation, Macroeconomic Instability, and Neoliberal Restructuring in Democratic Argentina. In *The New Argentine Democracy: The Search for a Successful Formula,* ed. Edward C. Epstein. Westport: Praeger. 20–58.

Stahler-Sholk, Harry E. Vanden and Glen Kuecker, eds. 2008. *Latin American Social Movements in the 21st Century: Resistance, Power and Democracy.* Lanham: Rowman and Littlefield.

Starr, Pamela K. 1999. Monetary Mismanagement and Inadvertent Democratization in Technocratic Mexico. *Studies in Comparative International Development* 33 (Winter): 33–68.

Stern, Ernest. 1983. World Bank Financing of Structural Adjustment. In *IMF Conditionality,* ed. John Williamson. Washington, DC: Institute for International Economics.

Teichman, Judith A. 1995. *Privatization and Political Change in Mexico.* Pittsburgh: University of Pittsburgh Press.

———. 1997. Mexico and Argentina: Economic Reform and Technocratic Decision Making. *Studies in Comparative International Development* 32, 1 (Spring): 31–55.

———. 2001. *The Politics of Freeing Markets in Latin America: Chile, Argentina, and Mexico.* Chapel Hill: University of North Carolina Press.

———. 2007. Multilateral Lending Institutions and Transnational Policy Networks in Mexico and Chile. *Global Governance,* 13, 4: 557–573.

Tussie, Diana (ed.), Marcos Mendiburu, and Patricia I. Vásquez. 1997. Los nuevos mandatos de los bancos multilaterales desarrollo: su aplicación en el caso de Argentina. In *El BID, el Banco Mundial y la sociedad civil: nuevas formas de financiamiento internacional,* ed. Tussie. Buenos Aires: FLACSO/Oficina de Publicaciones del CBC, Universidad de Buenos Aires. 63–98.

Urzua, Carlos M. 1997. Five Decades of Relations Between the World Bank and Mexico. In *The World Bank: Its First Half-Century, vol. 2: Perspectives,* ed. Devesh Kapur, John P. Lewis, and Richard Webb. Washington, DC: Brookings Institution Press. 49–108.

Weyland, Kurt. 2001. *The Politics of Market Reform in Fragile Democracies: Argentina, Brazil, Peru and Venezuela.* Princeton: Princeton University Press.

Williamson, John. 1994. In Search of a Manual for Technopolis. In *The Political Economy of Policy Reform,* ed. Williamson. Washington, DC: Institute for International Economics. 11–28.

World Bank. 1991. *Poverty Alleviation in Mexico.* Washington, DC: World Bank.

———. 1993. Argentina: *From Insolvency to Growth.* Washington, DC: World Bank.

———. 1994. *Operations Evaluation Department (OED)*. Study of Bank/Mexico Relations, 1948–1992. Washington, DC: World Bank.

———. 2000a. *World Bank Development Report, 2000/01: Attacking Poverty*. Washington, DC: World Bank.

———. 2000b. *Bank Consults Civil Society Extensively on Argentina Strategy*. May 12. <http://wbln0018.worldbank.org/external/lac>

———. 2000c. *Country Assistance Strategy of the World Bank Group for the Argentine Republic*. Report No. 20354. Washington, DC: World Bank.

———. 2001a. *Mexico: A Comprehensive Development Agenda*. Washington, DC: World Bank.

———. 2001b. *Mexico Country Assistance Evaluation*. Washington, DC: World Bank.

World Bank Group. 1985–95. Directory. Annual publication. Washington, DC: World Bank.

Chapter 6

Constructing Reform Coalitions: The Politics of Compensations in Argentina's Economic Liberalization

Sebastián Etchemendy

During the 1990s, Argentina underwent one of the most sweeping market transformations among developing countries. In less than five years, the country witnessed a fundamental restructuring of state-society relations. President Carlos Menem's rush to implement market reforms was praised by local elites, international financial institutions, and think tanks. Sebastian Edwards, formerly the World Bank's chief economist for Latin America, situated Argentina as a front-runner in the intensity and scope of market reforms among what he called "second and third wave reformers" (Edwards 1995, 8–9). By 1996 the conservative publication *Economic Freedom of the World* ranked Argentina well above established reformers such as Chile, Spain, and Mexico in its Index of Economic Freedom, and located the country in second place, behind only New Zealand, in the index of Most Improved Economic Freedom in the world during the decade 1985–1995 (Gwartney, et al. 1996, xxi, 79).

This chapter argues that what is often viewed as an orthodox and unilaterally imposed market transformation was, to a considerable extent, founded on coalitions cemented in more or less formal bargains with a variety of sectoral interests anchored in the old model. This perspective aims to highlight how the state could shape the interests of social actors and create promarket constituencies out of old populist and interventionist actors. This process of coalition building was achieved by constructing reform policies oriented to compensate, through payoffs in alternative areas of policy reform, what these actors were losing in other areas. The government crafted these policies of compensation by granting rents in newly created markets to business and organized labor and by avoiding sweeping and unilateral deregulation in some sectors; specifically, those where reform would hurt traditional powerful actors of the inward-oriented model.

It is frequently argued that radical economic liberalization in "successful" cases of implementation, such as the Argentine, depends on undermining or marginalizing traditional interest groups that profit from interventionist regulatory regimes. In the Argentine case, an exchange-rate based stabilization process, i.e., the imposition of a currency board that tied the peso to the dollar, and the consequent overvaluation of the currency in the context of increasing capital inflows, burdened protected economic actors even more. The hardest test for this thesis would be, then, in those areas where the costs of marketization are said to be unavoidable for the established actors in the context of an inward-oriented model: trade unions and protected firms in industrial tradable sectors.

This chapter analyzes five areas of policy reform in Argentina: administrative reform, labor deregulation, and economic restructuring in the steel, petroleum, and auto sectors. Argentina had developed, since the 1940s, a system of institutional inducements that greatly favored labor in general and public unions in particular. The country's steel, petroleum, and auto sectors, moreover, were a paradigm of what the neoclassical view denominates as rent seekers: protected by tariffs, holding privileged contracts with the state, enjoying subsidized inputs; in short, shielded from any external competition.

Despite the abundant literature on the politics of economic adjustment in Argentina and Latin America, the crucial role that vested interests of the old order can perform in carving out the new one has not been assessed adequately, neither in theoretical terms nor in an empirical and systematic way. The idea of a coalition-building process in which the negotiated allocation of sectoral payoffs is an essential component of the general process of market transformation represents an alternative to the three dominant approaches to economic reform in Latin America: the institutionalist, the public choice or neoclassical, and the classist perspective. The institutionalist approach stresses how economic crises weakened traditional actors and empowered states with renewed capacity. It tends to focus on state insulation and to ignore institutional and interest group mediations. The public choice approach considers the role of vested interests (when they enter the picture) as, by definition, inimical to market transformation, and the whole process as generally reducing officials' discretion to distribute benefits to sectoral economic groups. The third approach accounts for the process of economic liberalization merely as the result of the pressure exerted by the most concentrated or internationalized sectors of the capitalist class. This view understates both how market reform threatens powerful actors in the tradable sectors and how organized labor figures in the dominant coalition in the Argentine case.

The literature in the field generally conceives of compensations, in successful cases of reform, in terms of extending welfare benefits or subsidies to the poor, unemployed, or weak and backward industrial sectors; that is, to individual losers in the market. Yet the Argentine experience in certain tradable sectors and in labor reveals the significance of payoffs targeted to the powerful collective actors entrenched in the old state-centered system. Among the potential losers, compensations were oriented not to the weak but to the strong interests.

Many analysts of the politics of reform in Argentina, moreover, have emphasized how a few national holdings were awarded with rents through the privatization process, generally focusing on the services and utilities sectors. The argument here, by contrast, stresses the capacity of some domestic groups to protect their market share in their traditional base of tradables, even displacing international capital within their specific sector. This chapter will suggest that, with the advent of deregulation, it was in their historical base of tradables—probably more than in the privatization process in nontradables—that the main battle for these actors was waged.

THE POLITICAL ECONOMY OF MARKET REFORMS: THE ROLE OF FUNCTIONAL ECONOMIC INTERESTS

The institutionalist perspective was heavily influenced by the combination of neoliberal policies and strong presidential leadership that was unfolding mostly in Argentina, Peru, and Mexico. Initial comparative volumes on the politics of adjustment, such as Haggard and Kaufman (1992, 1995) and Nelson (1990), emphatically stressed the idea of state capacity and the advantages of autonomy for sustaining the liberalization path.[1] Although economic liberalization was not always formally treated as a dependent variable, the implications of the analysis were straightforward: many times, in an environment of deep economic crises and social dislocation, reformist executives profited from the social demand for "authority" in order to bypass, and even openly challenge, the power of representative institutions, such as Congress, parties, and traditional interest organizations.[2]

The public choice or neoclassical approach rests mainly on the idea that economic liberalization is a public good, and therefore that the dynamics of reform are essentially governed by a collective action problem: losers from reform are concentrated, whereas beneficiaries are diffused. Consequently, the former deploy their powerful resources to block any possibility of change (Bates 1992; Krueger 1993; Bates and Krueger 1993). The core actor in this view is the "rent seeker." Once a statist economic intervention is developed, a powerful set of incentives to preserve the "artificial" benefits is created, actors will tend to devote their resources more to preserving protection than to productive use.[3]

Although this literature is not always clear about when reform is possible, given this set of vested interests entrenched in the status quo, the logical implication is the need for a strong authority that can solve the collective action problem. Overall, this approach takes the behavior of interventionist rent seekers as a given and focuses on the incentives for politicians to create "new institutions" and overcome the demands that originate in the old network of interests (see especially Geddes 1994a, b; Sturzenegger and Tommasi 1998). Reform seems to be feasible when the state compels interests to give up their rent-seeking behavior. A central assumption is that "market-extending policy changes reduce officials' discretion over the distribution of individual benefits and thus cost officials political resources" (Geddes 1994b, 210). More recent works by Weyland (2002) and Stokes (2001), while not fully adopting a public choice framework, focus primarily on the type of incentives (most prominently the eruption of economic crises) that would compel politicians to adopt market policies in the face of presumably hostile electorates and economic interest groups.

Héctor Schamis (1999), however, has pointed out the need to go beyond the common view that a proreform government must neutralize the losers. Schamis convincingly argues that vested interests may not oppose reform, because economic liberalization can generate opportunities for rent-seeking behavior, a point the public choice approach generally overlooks. In this view, reform is basically driven by the power of a concentrated and internationalized economic elite, which, in countries such as Argentina, Mexico, and Chile, has colonized the state and relentlessly imposed the neoliberal agenda since the 1970s.[4]

In sum, both the institutionalist and the public choice perspectives posit an elective affinity between neoliberal economics and unilateral decisionmaking. (Indeed, both approaches tend to view economic reform as a public good that triggers collective action dilemmas. See Haggard and Kaufman 1995, 154–59.) The main asset of the institutionalist approach is that it tries to go beyond the neoclassical perennial undertheorization of the state. Because of its focus on the logic of price stabilization and its emphasis on state isolation from civil society, however, this perspective downplays the role of special interests in shaping the policy outcome. The public choice literature carries forward the assumption that interest groups, by definition, gain sectoral rents by pursuing interventionist policies, and that liberalization forcefully reduces the ability of the executive to allocate sectoral payoffs or compensations. In short, a trade-off or contradictory relationship is posed between rent seeking and economic liberalization.

Against the background of the public choice and institutionalist approaches, Schamis insightfully advocates putting "societal interests at the forefront in our theorization in political economy" and warns that rents can also be generated as economies become more open (1999, 239). Still, to conceptualize economic liberalization exclusively as a result of Olsonian distributional coalitions driven by the capitalist class, or a fraction of it, can also be problematic. Rents and market niches for protected business in the tradable sector are threatened by deregulation and import liberalization. Some actors in tradables were able to avoid those costs nevertheless, and they managed to influence the reform trend in order to protect their market share. In the case of Argentina, more-over, this approach cannot account for the role of organized labor as part of the dominant reformist coalition, and it overlooks the importance of payoffs targeted to the union structure. In other words, interests, particularly in labor and tradable sectors, can be losing and winning at the same time.

BUILDING CONSTITUENCIES FOR REFORM

A more recent group of studies has focused in the capacity of executives to control the timing of implementation and the scope of specific policy reforms in order to forge coalitions that can achieve some degree of governability. This approach grants the state more leeway to accommodate the interests of some sectors that are likely to lose when economies become more open, such as the protected domestic bourgeoisie, traditionally corporatist unions, the official party in Congress, or constituencies in the peripheral provinces. Unlike the classist approach, these studies portray the state as having some autonomy as a coordinating agent in the process of market transformation.[5] The new emphasis is on how officials may buy off stakeholders in order to get their acquiescence to the marketization project. For instance, Kessler (1998) and Pérez (1997) showed how the liberalization process in Mexico and Spain involved the allocation of market reserves to the local financial sector. Murillo (2001, 2002), Teichman (2001) and Corrales (1998) have argued that concessions funneled to unions and heavily protected industrial groups in the form of state assets, partial labor law deregulation or market reserves were inher-ent to the process of market transformation in Argentina, Mexico and Chile. Gibson (1997), Gibson and Calvo (2001), Eaton (2004), and Kurtz (2004) have underlined that the courting of provincial governors and regional constituencies, often through spending or market-inhibiting mechanisms, has helped consolidate the general stabilization and marketization trend in Argentina, Mexico, and Chile. Building on his earlier work on Russia, Treisman (2003: 104) insightfully notes that market reformers in Argentina and Brazil essentially offered stakeholders in the privatization process "three co-optation cur-rencies: money, property or rents."

Overall, these studies have shown that governments who have undertaken extensive market reforms in semi-closed economies engage in complicated bargains with certain established interests in order to make the reform path sustainable. In effect, in this per-spective, an active state builds its reform constituencies by providing rents and usually limiting its orthodox zeal in some policy reforms, such as federal spending, sectoral deregulation, or a specific privatization, while it pushes sweeping adjustment in some other sectors.[6] Thus our task is to formulate a systematic assessment of what type of compensations were bestowed on formerly protected sectors in labor and tradables, and to identify the mechanisms through which the Argentine government shaped its liberal-ization policies in order to appease powerful constituencies entrenched in the old state-centered model.

ADMINISTRATIVE REFORM: ALLIANCE WITH THE STATE EMPLYEES UNION

For Menem's government, administrative reform meant, first and foremost, an important reduction of employment in the public administration and the reform and flexibilization of labor regulations in the civil service.[7] In a second phase, the administration decentral-ized the school and hospital systems from control by the national administration to the jurisdiction of the provincial public sector.[8]

This reform potentially affected three main unions. The UPCN (Union of Civil Personnel of the Nation) was the oldest and most traditionally Peronist union in the sector. Its members were employed mainly in the national public administration. The ATE (Association of State Workers) had grown more recently, and most of its members came from the provincial public sector. The ATE was, from the outset, anti-Menemist and frontally opposed to the policies of state adjustment. Finally, the teachers' unions, most important the CTERA (Confederation of Education Workers of Argentina) and UDA (Union of Argentine Teachers), opposed decentralization for its lack of provision for adequate financing at the provincial level. The government ended up building an alliance with UPCN that protected the union's ranks to a great extent from the downsizing, and even managed to enhance its organizational structure.

In 1990 the Menem administration issued a series of decrees that reduced the number of undersecretaries, induced the retirement of state employees, and suspended all collective bargaining agreements at the level of the national public administration. Decree 1750/90 advanced the downsizing and created the Executive Committee for the Coordination of the Administrative Reform (CECRA) under the direct supervision of the Ministry of Economy. The CECRA was spared from the political pressure of Congress and even from pressures originating in other state agencies. As one of the main public officials on the Committee declared, "The Committee was a true 'funnel' for all decisions concerning administrative reforms, we were only five officials implementing the program and we worked in total confidentiality" (quoted in Ghio and Etchemendy 1997, 21).

Although granted substantial power and autonomy, the CECRA was the arena of interaction and exchange with another important actor: the leadership of the Peronist (and Menemist) UPCN. The UPCN's participation in the CECRA was legally recognized in decree 1750, whereas opposing union ATE was excluded. As one member of the CECRA reported, UPCN representatives had considerable voice in redesigning the structure of state agencies, trying to protect the union's ranks.

In addition, the union bargained with state officials for a new labor code that would regulate collective bargaining for state employees in the national administration. Law 24.185 established that each union would have representation at the bargaining table proportional to its share of members at the national level, a feature that directly benefited UPCN. It also established workers' quotas for the labor union that were mandatory even for workers not affiliated with the union. The new code, which took effect in 1998, preserved the institutional power of UPCN and sketched a model of centralized collective bargaining for the public sector (see Law 24.185, November 11, 1992, especially articles 4, 12, and 13; on the collective agreement see Orlansky and Gómez 2000).[9]

A second additional compensation was that UPGN received state recognition to administer the welfare system (*obras sociales*) for workers in the entire national public sector, displacing ATE in this function. Thus, as a result of a government decision, UPCN came to control Union Personal, the monopoly health insurance administration for state workers, meaning a huge increase in the financial power of the Menemist state union.

Table 1 shows the results and final design of the administrative reform concerning the downsizing of public employment. Considerable downsizing took place at the level of the national public administration (NPA). The presidency and the eight ministries shrank by 118,173 employees (28.4 percent) between 1989 and 1995. It can be argued, however, that much of that downsizing corresponded to the transfer of education and health services to provincial jurisdiction, which was implemented mostly in 1992–93 (see numbers for the Education and Health Ministries).

Outside the Education and Health Ministries, the degree of downsizing is much less impressive, even through the period of the adjustment decrees, 1989–91. During that period, employment (excluding the Health and Education Ministries) declined from

Table 1. Number of Employees in the Argentine Public Sector, 1989–1995

	1989	1990	1991	1992	1993	1994	1995	Employment Evolution[a]	
								Absolute	%
Presidency	18,573	19,501	17,301	17,370	20,289	19,248	19,714	+1,141	+6,1
Ministry of Interior	42,233	38,220	40,612	40,746	41,510	42,578	39,063	−3,170	−7.5
Ministry of Foreign Affairs	1,128	1,108	1,664	1,664	1,607	1,664	1,673	+545	+48.3
Ministry of Justice	9,553	9,593	10,100	10,326	10,144	10,075	9,777	+224	+2.3
Ministry of Defense	154,214	147,257	140,710	135,691	131,545	129,099	156,091	+1,877	+1.2
Ministry of Economy	57,007	50,210	39,495	50,308	49,632	49,794	46,777	−10,230	−17.9
Ministry of Labor	10,888	10,515	9,879	9,296	11,474	9,060	9,456	−1,432	−13.1
Ministry of Health	29,473	41,755	27,145	12,480	11,823	12,742	10,544	−18,929	−64.2
Ministry of Education	92,983	92,940	91,052	44,793	11,603	5,036	4,784	−88,129	−94.8
Total NPA	416,052	411,099	377,958	322,674	289,727	279,341	297,879	−118,173	−28.4
Total minus Health and Education	293,596	276,404	259,761	265,401	266,301	261,563	282,551	−11,045	−3.7
Public enterprises[b]		236,694			41,102			−195,592	−82.6
Provincial public sector	923,619	929,443	929,443	1,238,874				+315,255	+34.1

[a]For national administration 1989–95, for public enterprises 1990–93, for provincial public sector 1989–92.
[b]Numbers do not include the official bank system.
Notes: Total National public administration (NPA) includes centralized and decentralized national administration and excludes judicial and legislative powers. Does not include Jefatura de Gabinete y Ministerio Público created by the 1994 constitutional reform. Interior includes security agencies; Defense includes military personnel.
Sources: [a]Ministry of Economy, National Office of Employment and Salaries in the public sector, unpublished data, 1997; [b]FIDE 1997; World Bank 1993.

293,596 to 259,761, an 11.5 percent reduction; overall, in the period 1989–95, the employ-ment reduction was only 3.7 percent. It is worth noting that only this attenuated decline of 3.7 percent in employment affected the UPCN. The data show that the bulk of the adjustment in public employment at the federal level during the Menem administration came from the decentralization of the educational and health systems (64.2 percent and 94.8 percent of downsizing, respectively) and from the privatization of public enterprises (82.6 percent), where other unions (for example teachers, health services) and not UPCN were hurt more. The last row of the table shows that the levels of public employment in the provinces increased with the path of adjustment.[10]

LABOR DEREGULATION: THE POLITICS OF PARTIAL REFORM

Labor deregulation was on the government's agenda from the outset. Institutional frame-works fostered initially by Peronism in the 1940s helped shape what was probably the strongest labor movement in the region. The corporatist structure of labor market regula-tions combined institutional inducements, which tended to strengthen the position of organized labor, and constraints, which gave the state considerable control over the union leadership. Still, the Argentine case evinced a greater emphasis on inducements compared to constraints, and labor regulations that bestowed great power to the unions survived the Peronist government and even subsequent dictatorships (Collier and Collier 1979, 1972).

Labor market regulations had not changed for decades in their main features: the predominance of permanent contracts of indefinite duration, a state-sanctioned monopoly of a single union by sector, centralized collective bargaining in which only the union legally recognized by the state could participate, and trade-union control of the health system (*obras sociales*) for union and nonunion members through their appropriation of the social security taxes paid by both business and workers."[11]

The Menem administration was, it could be argued, not very successful in passing legislative modifications that would hurt the economic and political power of the trade unions, a traditional constituency of the governing party. Among 20 labor reform bills sent to Congress between 1989 and 1995, only 8 (40 percent) were sanctioned as laws, whereas, for example, 9 out of 10 privatization bills where passed (Etchemendy and Palermo 1998, 564). Until 1994, furthermore, the government had obtained from Congress only minor reforms. Its broader attempts at labor reform, which included a decentralized framework for collective bargaining, the repeal of prereform sectoral collective agree-ments, and a major flexibilization of labor contracts, had been consistently blocked by the Peronist party and the union representatives in the Committee on Labor Legislation of the Chamber of Deputies. Nor were reforms passed by decree.[12] The Ministry of Economy's attempt to introduce competition in the health insurance system cont rolled by the unions was also consistently blocked.

In view of this situation, the government changed its strategy. In 1994, under a new labor minister, Armando Caro Figueroa, the state organized a broad concertation—the so-called Pact for Productivity and Social Equity—with the peak workers' association, the CGT (General Confederation of Workers), and the UIA (Argentine Industrial Union), jointly to formulate and design the bills before sending them to Congress.[13] This step was the key to the government's main achievements in the domain of labor reform. The union-controlled Labor Legislation Committee did not block the bills, and Congress now passed the reforms drafted through the corporatist concertation virtually without modifications.

The CGT accepted the imposed greater flexibility of contracts and the reduction of severance payments in some categories of workers (such as those in small firms, young workers, women, workers in bankrupt firms), and a structural modification of the system of compensations for workers' accidents. In exchange, the unionists obtained monetary subsidies for the union-run health system. Meanwhile, legislation concerning collective bargaining, union monopoly, and the system of severance payments for the workers already employed remained untouched.[14]

The unions, moreover, were allowed to enter the business of private insurance for workers' accidents that the reform had created—and, as a result of union leaders' pressure, private companies were not allowed to provide workers' health insurance. Healthcare deregulation was thus essentially restricted to competition within the union-run system. This mechanism of partial deregulation tended to benefit the most powerful or efficient unions, which were in a better position to receive the contributions of workers in smaller unions or unions with financial problems.

In addition to the degree of institutional change, reform should have affected the degree of labor flexibilization in the market. Admittedly, unemployment (Argentina reached 18 percent after 4 years of reform, and then it subsided slightly) and the spread of unregistered workers imply a huge flexibilization in the labor market. The issue here is, though, whether the government was able to push deregulation in the formal sector of the work force. Two good measures to check the scope of reform in the labor market are the percentage of workers under flexible contracts and the number of workers under collective bargaining agreements signed before the reform process.

Menem's first government did poorly in its attempts to deregulate labor. Until 1995, six years after market-friendly policies were inaugurated, the unions successfully prevented a major move to fixed-term contracts, which constituted 6.3 percent of the labor force in the formal sector (only 0.4 percent more than in 1993). Only after the negotiated reform of 1994 did the percentage of the labor population under flexible contracts start to increase steadily, reaching 12 percent in 1997 (Ministry of Labor and Social Security 1998). Fixed-term contracts passed in the 1994 concertation, however, were repealed in a new labor reform that the government negotiated with unions in 1998.

By 1995, moreover, workers in the formal sector were overwhelmingly covered by collective agreements or contracts signed before the reform, which generally involved a higher level of regulation and prerogatives to the unions, particularly to the leadership and to the structure of the organization. Only a minor part of the labor force in the formal sector was under new agreements, which were almost always more flexible and less favorable to unions.[15] These "old" collective agreements were still enforced due to automatic renewal clause stipulated in Act 14,250 (the collective bargaining law passed under Peron's second presidency), which the government was unable to overturn. The Peronist government's 1998 labor reform, moreover, preserved the automatic renewal clause and strengthened the union leaders' role in the centralized pattern of collective bargaining, two elements that would persist until questioned by the Alianza government in 2000.

RESTRUCTURING IN THE PETROLEUM SECTOR

Since the first oil reserves in Argentina were discovered at the beginning of the twentieth century, the petroleum industry had been dominated by the state enterprise Yacimientos Petrolíferos Fiscales (YPF). The state regulated the three major segments in which petroleum activity can be subdivided: extraction, refinement, and distribution. In petroleum

industry jargon, exploration and production (or extraction) are called "upstream" activities, whereas refining and distribution are often referred to as "downstream." This analysis
will concentrate on the segment of production or extraction of crude oil, a subsector
that was greatly protected before the reform period.

Except for some minor concessions of oil fields before 1935, most private capital
was integrated into the subsector through extraction contracts with the state. These were
signed in different periods after the 1950s, particularly during the Frondizi government
(1958–62) and the military dictatorships of 1966–73 and 1976–83. Up to the 1990s, private
subcontractors at the level of extraction (*contratistas*) did not own the oil but had to
deliver it to YPF for a fixed price. YPF would refine part of it and sell the rest of the
crude to private refining companies. Actually, all prices in the sector were regulated by
YPF; the state company also set the prices from refiner to the distributor and from the
latter to the consumer.

The Menem administration included the oil sector in its initial plans for deregulation
and privatization. Overall, the deregulation of the petroleum industry evolved in three
stages:

- Removal of state intervention in price setting, tariffs, and production levels. The
  government ruled that refining companies were free to purchase crude and deriva-
  tives, removing YPF's domestic monopoly on the sale of crude. The government
  also eliminated import and export oil duties. Decree 1212/89 established "freedom
  of prices" both for crude oil and oil products beginning January 1, 1991.
- Privatization of oil fields and awarding of new areas for exploration. The government followed three main strategies for the privatization of oil fields. It organized
  an international bidding for the so-called "marginal areas," oil fields with lower
  productivity. It promoted new contracts of association (joint ventures) with private
  capital for the exploitation of low-risk, high-return reserves, also called "central
  areas." Finally, it also renegotiated old contracts of extraction with private
  producers.
- Privatization of some of YPF's assets and, later, the company itself. In June 1993,
  through a public auction of shares for domestic and international investors, YPF—
  the biggest Argentine company ($3.9 billion in net sales for 1992), the public
  enterprise symbol of the state-led development period—passed into private hands.
  For the first time, an Argentine company was offering stocks on Wall Street.

Arguably, the petroleum sector in Argentina had developed according to a paradigm
of what public choice theories in political economy would characterize as rent-seeking
activities of economic interests. Since YPF was founded in 1922, the goals of the Argentine state had been the appropriation of a resource considered strategic, self-sufficiency
in oil, and the distribution of oil profits to the rest of society through YPF surpluses
and taxation of the company, oil products (mainly gasoline), and private producers.
Whatever the initial success in fulfilling those objectives, it was clear, particularly when
the Argentine economy slid into the long night of recession at the end of the 1960s, that
in practice those distribution goals had been compromised.

YPF had been transformed into a weak monopoly, incapable of resisting the pressures of private producers, the union, and the government itself, as its profit goals were
subordinated to the political goals of state officials at the Department of Energy. For
example, the price that YPF paid to contractors in the upstream segment was many times
higher than international prices. The regulations of the Department of Energy resulted
in prices for private refiners that were lower than the price YPF was paying for the

extracted oil. The (mostly) national companies at the upstream level of production, and the international refining companies downstream, were clear beneficiaries of a weak monopoly in a protected sector.

Deregulation, consequently, posed a severe threat to private producers upstream. Their old contracts for extraction could become uncertain in a general restructuring of the sector. Refiners would be allowed to buy crude oil in the international market, and obviously, a reconverted and private YPF would stop buying crude from private producers at subsidized prices.

Any assessment of the new morphology of the petroleum sector in Argentina, nevertheless, should begin with the analysis of the governmental strategies for deregulation mentioned above. The privatization of low-return areas was performed through a bidding process that analysts view as considerably open and competitive. The method of awarding new concessions in high-return areas, however, appears less clear and competitive. Initially, there was a period of prequalifications, in which bidders negotiated their investment plans with the state enterprise (see Gerchunoff 1992, 348–449; Gadano and Sturzenegger 1998, 85–88; see also Kozulj and Bravo 1993, 142–58). As a result, the normative framework changed repeatedly, often as a consequence of the pressure of private producers. Finally, in the reconversion of old contracts there was no competition at all. The majority of private producers had to return their oil fields to the state within the next few years. In view of this situation, the government could have waited for the expiration of the contracts or could have canceled them, appealing to legal emergency powers, as it did with other state contracts at the time. Yet the administration chose to transform the old contracts into concessions in which the private producers were free owners of the oil extracted for the next 25 years, with an option for 10 more. Consequently, the administration failed to capture the oil rent: it converted contracts of private producers (in which they had to deliver the oil to YPF) into concessions (in which they owned the oil) without receiving a single dollar.[16]

Given this diverse and complex strategy of negotiating privatization, what form did the market take after deregulation? Table 2 compares both periods. Supply at the level of production diversified to a certain degree after the Peronist attempt at deregulation. The power of the old private domestic producers to preserve their positions in the new market structure should be emphasized, however. This capacity was ostensibly a consequence of the governmental strategies for privatization, especially the two we have depicted as noncompetitive bidding for central areas and reconversion of old contracts in concessions. By 1993, Pérez Companc, a national company and a private contractor of YPF since the Onganía dictatorship, had almost doubled its market share and displaced the U.S. company Amoco as the largest private producer of petroleum in Argentina after YPF. In times of economic internationalization, it was, paradoxically, the national bourgeoisie traditionally protected by the state, the actor that obtained the best market positions in the subsector, displacing international capital.

Another way to assess how much traditional actors protected their market share is to check the petroleum extraction by legal regime; that is, the type of normative framework (contract or concession) under which the private agent extracted the oil. The larger the share of petroleum extracted under regimes instituted (without any competitive bidding) before the reform period, the less diversified has been supply after deregulation, and the less the threat to traditional producers.

The legal regimes instituted before reform include YPF's own areas; the contracts of extraction signed under Frondizi and the military regimes in the period 1958–83, which were reconverted in concessions after 1990; the Houston Plan (a project launched under the Alfonsín administration that would include YPF and private producers with defined

Table 2. Total Petroleum Production by Company (in thousands of cubic meters)

| | Before Reform | | | | After Reform | | | |
| | 1987 | | 1988 | | 1993 | | 1994 | |
	No.	%	No.	%	No.	%	No.	%
Domestic								
YPF	15,967	64.2	17,036	65.2	13,270	38.4	16,502	42.6
Pérez Companc S.A.[a]	2,218	8.9	2,094	8.0	5,404	15.6	5,279	13.6
P.San Jorge S.A.	129	0.5	124	0.5	1,290	3.7	2,251	5.8
ASTRA CAPSA	456	1.8	745	2.9	1,647	4.8	2,026	5.2
BRIDAS P.I.C.S.R.L.	686	2.8	804	3.1	1,717	5.0	1,659	4.3
PLUSPETROL	412	1.7	444	1.7	1,084	3.1	1,096	2.8
TECPETROL S.A.	0	0.0	0	0.0	1,089	3.2	1,047	2.7
Foreign AMOCO Argentina Oil	2,486	10.0	2,341	9.0	2,656	7.7	2,721	7.0
Cities Service S.A.	1,544	6.2	1,435	5.5	0	0.0	0	0.0
Total Austral S.A.[b]	—	—	—	—	2,249	6.5	2,325	6.0
Remainder (50 companies)	968	3.9	1,099	4.2	4,161	12.0	3,861	10.0
Total	24,867	100.0	26,123	100.0	34,569	100.0	38,767	100.0

[a]Includes Company S.A. and Petrolera Company S.A.
[b]Production before reform included in Remainder.
Source: Instituto Argentino del Petróleo, unpublished data, 1997.

rights over the extracted oil), a few contracts that were not reconverted into concessions, and the concessions from before 1958. After reform, a series of new legal regimes was instituted, which, theoretically, made possible competitive bids on areas and regulated different rights and obligations for private producers.

Overall, table 3 shows that in 1996, after 6 years of deregulation, 70.8 percent of the petroleum produced in Argentina was extracted under regimes established *before* the deregulation process and only 29.2 percent was the result of areas awarded after the 1990 process of liberalization, under the new regimes of extraction. Furthermore, it is clear that the roughly 30 percent of the petroleum extracted in areas awarded after 1990 is more a consequence of production given up by YPF in the bidding of its own fields than the result of what old producers might have lost.

Put differently, YPF's administration lost about 22 percent of share, but the private producers with its reconverted contracts—who, it is worth noting, before reform were extracting YPF's crude but did not own it—lost only around five points in market share, depending on the year. In short, the notable increase in the share of Pérez Companc and other national producers is a consequence both of maintaining the old regimes of extraction and participating in the new awarding of areas after 1990.

The situation of the other main actor in the sector, the trade union, presents more nuances. The national oil union, SUPE, chose a strategy of negotiation rather than one of increasing militancy. Was this alternative successful for the union? In terms of

Table 3. Percent of Total Petroleum Production by Legal Regime

	Before Reform		After Reform		
	1987	1988	1992	1994	1996
Regimes Instituted Before Reform					
Houston Plan	0.0	0.0	0.1	0.0	0.1
Contracts 1958–83	33.3	32.5	28.7	28.1	26.3
Without reconversion	0.1	0.1	0.1	0.1	0.1
Old concessions	2.3	2.2	1.7	1.2	1.2
YPF administration	64.2	65.2	40.8	42.6	43.1
Total	100.0	100.0	71.4	72.0	70.8
Regimes Instituted After Reform					
Central area	0.0	0.0	16.3	13.2	11.3
Marginal area	0.0	0.0	4.7	4.0	4.0
Provincial area	0.0	0.0	0.0	0.2	0.2
Risk contracts	0.0	0.0	5.5	3.2	2.7
New association	0.0	0.0	2.1	7.4	10.9
Argentine Plan	0.0	0.0	0.0	0.0	0.2
Total	0.0	0.0	28.6	28.0	29.2

Source: Instituto Argentino del Petróleo 1997.

membership, SUPE was decimated, probably more than any trade union in the reform period: YPF went from 36,935 to 9,350 employees (FIDE 1997). The Economic Emergency Act and subsequent decrees repealed SUPE's collective bargaining contract, which guaranteed job stability, and bestowed strong institutional prerogatives to the union.

SUPE, however, adopted a strategy that Murillo (1997) has called "organizational survival." Unable to maintain its political and industrial resources, the union profited from some selective incentives that the privatization process provided in order to protect its organizational resources. The union organized small firms, which hired former YPF workers and that operate as YPF suppliers. It also bought part of the YPF fleet (Murillo 1997, 42). After privatization, SUPE negotiated with the government to maintain the monopoly on representation of former YPF workers, who were claimed by the Federation of Private Workers of Oil and Gas. In addition, the workers held 10 percent of the stock after YPF privatization. Even though the legal framework that regulates workers' participation in privatization, State Reform Act 23.696, does not mention the unions, in practice the government allowed unions to be the exclusive administrator of the workers' shares, which meant that the workers' organizations would earn a part of the share's profits.

PRIVATIZATION AND RESTRUCTURING IN THE STEEL SECTOR

Like their counterparts in the petroleum industry, Argentina's private steel producers developed a strong association with and dependence on the state. Economic holding companies Acindar and Techint (the latter through its controlled firms Siderca and Propulsora Siderúrgica) were the only private companies integrated into the three main segments of the production chain: processing and reduction of iron, production of crude steel, and hot or cold steel rolling. Propulsora Siderúrgica concentrated its activities in cold-rolling sheets. Acindar traditionally concentrated in the market of nonflat rolled products, such as raw material for wires and steel bars. Siderca specialized in seamless tubes. Both Acindar and Siderca were (and are) among the most important industrial firms in Argentina in terms of sales volume. Siderca was the only producer of seamless tubes in the country and, under the National Purchase Regime, YPF and other domestic petroleum producers could purchase oil pipes only from Techint's company. Not surprisingly, prices for the sector in the domestic market were set well above international prices.

Deregulation policies undertaken by Menem's administration posed important challenges to the main actors in the sector. Since 1989, the government had repealed almost all the regulations that bestowed special privileges on the steel sector in the domain of tariffs, quotas, and industrial promotion laws. The Economic Emergency Act revoked the National Purchase Regime, for example, a move that seriously affected Siderca, the exclusive supplier of oil pipes in the domestic market. The removal of tariff exemptions for imported inputs particularly hurt Propulsora Siderúrgica, which based its production both in inputs supplied by the state steel mill, SOMISA, and those imported with a zero tariff.

It should be noted, however, that the steel sector was one of the most dynamic in Argentine industry, and that it had already responded to the domestic depression of the late 1980s with an important increase in exports. Nevertheless, the macroeconomic situation in the early 1990s also hampered the "export solution" because of a considerable overvaluation of the fixed exchange rate after the stabilization plan launched in 1991. In sum, the steel industry was severely hit by the successive rounds of liberalization. Prices went down, overall production shrank during the first three years of adjustment, and, unlike its experience in the 1980s, the sector showed a pronounced trade deficit (see Bisang and Chidiak 1995, 53).

Still, any assessment of the restructuring of the steel industry should take into account the privatization of SOMISA in 1992. The government sold it to the holding company Techint, the only holding company that participated in the bidding. Before 1992, some other alternatives were considered; for instance, the state would hold 40 percent of the shares and would negotiate the company's future with the new owners, trying to avoid any further reduction of the firm activities. But the government finally decided to sell the firm in one block to one major company, precluding any diffusion of property. In addition, the Menem administration ruled that it would accept bonds of the internal debt as part of the installment payments, a financial mechanism that directly benefited domestic holders of internal debt such as Techint.

Arguing that the conditions under which the privatization was carried out were unclear, the Italian steelmaker Iretecnia and the German Thyssen did not participate in the final bidding, although they had bought the bidding forms and evaluated the company for purchase. They withdrew, denouncing a bias in favor of domestic producers (Lozano 1992, 11; see also Bisang and Chidiak 1995, 17). SOMISA was renamed Siderar and was fused with Techint's own Propulsora Siderúrgica.

After deregulation, the position of the traditional private producers of steel in the domestic market was notably stronger. In 1989, Techint held 13.3 percent of the output in the segment of reduction; six years later, in 1995, its participation soared to 72.4 percent. In the subsector of solid crude, the pattern was similar: 11.9 percent to 63.7 percent (CIS 1998). Techint also began to control 100 percent of the market of cold-rolled sheets compared to 46.8 percent in 1989. Table 4 depicts the trends in the subsector of steel transformation.

Techint, furthermore, expanded not only horizontally in each segment, but also vertically in the chain of production. SOMISA was the only national supplier of the main

Table 4. Change in Steel Industry Operating Capacity (in thousands of tons per year)

| | Before Reform | | After Reform | |
| | 1989 | | 1994 | |
	No.	%	No.	%
Hot-Rolled Flat Products				
SOMISA (state)	1,400	93.3	—	—
Acindar	100	6.7	190	10.1
Techint (Siderar)	—	—	1,700	89.9
Total	1,500	100.0	1,890	100
Nonflat Products (excluding tubes)				
SOMISA/SIDERAR	110	5.1	—	—
La Cantab	1,245	57.7	855	64.8
Aceros Brag	170	7.9	—	—
A. Zapla	120	5.6	80	6.1
Others[a]	99	4.6	99	7.5
Total	413	19.1	286	21.7
	2,157	100.0	1,320	100.0
Cold-Rolled Products				
SOMISA (state)	810	51.6	—	—
Total Techint	735	46.8	1,270	100.0
Propulsora	735	—	—	—
Siderar	—	—	1,270	—
Adabor	25	1.6	—	—
Total	1,570	100.0	1,270	100.0

[a]1989 = 26 firms; 1994 = 8 firms.
Source: La Siderúrgica Argentina 1992, 1995.

input for the production of cold-rolled steel—hot-rolled coils—by Techint's owned Propulsora Siderurgica. Furthermore, Siderar (formerly SOMISA) decided to eliminate its production in nonflat rolled steel, and thus Acindar consolidated as the head of the oligopoly in that subsector (see table 4). Thus, after privatization, each firm was absolutely dominant in a segment of the market: Acindar in nonflat steel products; Techint in both flat-rolled products and in cold-rolling steel (through its controlled Siderar); and, through Siderca, continued to be the only producer of seamless industrial tubes.

The restructuring process had a huge impact on the labor force, which was reduced by almost half. In 1989 the steel sector in Argentina employed 32,148 workers, and in 1994 it employed 16,220 (CIS 1996). Despite some strikes in the regional branches (particularly in response to Acindar's layoffs), the metalworkers' union UOM was unable to restrain the pace of restructuring. Still, the union managed to obtain a greater share in the stocks of Siderar than in most cases of privatization: 20 percent.

As in the case of petroleum production, the domestic bourgeoisie's old linkages with the state allowed some Argentine companies to absorb the reformist spurt, economic internationalization notwithstanding. The main steel companies compensated for the end of subsidies and promotional regimes, and the lowering of tariffs by tightening their control of the (already greatly concentrated) domestic market. Even if the overvalued exchange rate made it more difficult to increase the level of exports, this newly enlarged control allowed them to profit from the domestic consumption boom that the same fixed exchange rate and the "cheap dollar" was triggering. As Gerchunoff et al. (1994, 10) point out, moreover, the government also started to enact antidumping measures. These measures seriously undermined the opening of the sector and consolidated the old producers' hegemony in the domestic market. Techint reoriented former SOMISA mostly to production for the domestic market and concentrated its export activities in Siderca. Acindar sold almost 50 percent of its production in international markets in 1988 and almost 100 percent in domestic markets in the first part of the 1990s (Bisang and Chidiak 1995, 18). In this way, a defined governmental privatization strategy significantly abetted national private producers' reliance on the domestic market to soften the storm of liberalization.

THE MOTOR VEHICLE COALITION

The "motor vehicle regime" crystallized in a series of decrees issued between 1990 and 1992. Its structure was negotiated in the Concertation Committee for the Reconversion of the Auto Industry, created by the Menem administration in 1990. The committee comprised representatives from the government, labor, and business (for background, see Villalón 1999). The regime's main features were

- A wage agreement between capital and labor designed to moderate wages and reduce the prices of vehicles
- An agreement among the automobile firms to invest in technology to cover the technological gap with international markets
- A tariff barrier of 30 percent (the average tariff for the whole economy after trade reform was about 10 percent), combined with the possibility for the terminal industry to import units with a tariff of only 2 percent
- Import quotas on commercial vehicles of 10 percent of the local production per year. Companies also had to compensate with a vehicle exported for each one imported at a preferential tariff

The parts and components industry, on the other hand, was initially not included in the special regime. In effect, the terminal plants could import parts and components at a 2 percent tariff, whereas the tariff was 18 percent for auto companies not established in the country. This aspect of the regime conferred great bargaining power to the assembly plants that were already established, both in regard to foreign competitors and to the parts and components domestic industry. During the first years of regime, the output of the parts sector grew at a considerably lower rate than that of the terminal plants (see Llach et al. 1997, 152–54; Vispo 1999, 302). Only in 1996 was the special tariff regime for the terminal plants extended to the parts and components industry, but without the need to compensate imports with exports.[17]

The motor vehicle regime, coupled with the consumption boom triggered by economic stabilization and by an increasingly overvalued exchange rate, fostered a thriving domestic-oriented motor vehicle industry during the adjustment years in Argentina. The industrial GDP annual growth rate for the auto industry increased almost 50 percent in the period 1991–95, 20 percent above the second-best industrial performer (IDI 1996). Table 5 depicts the main trends in the sector after deregulation.

The table shows the huge internationalization of the sector measured by imports and exports. It reveals the important increase in production after 1990, which, for the most part, was poured into the domestic market. Exports also increased, but at a much lesser

Table 5. Sales and Production of Automobiles in the Argentine Market,
1988–1997 (in units)

	Apparent National Consumption	Domestic Market Sales		National Production		
		Produced in Argentina	Imported	As % of ANC	Total	Exports
Before Reform						
1988	163,896	162,517	1,379	99.2	164,160	1,634
1989	133,563	132,921	642	99.5	127,823	1,841
1990	95,960	94,787	1,173	98.8	99,639	1,126
After Reform						
1991	165,806	137,175	28,631	82.7	138,958	5,205
1994	508,152	360,721	147,431	71.0	408,777	38,657
1997	426,326	228,297	198,029	53.5	446,045	210,386

Source: ADEFA, Anuario Estadístico 1992, 1997.

Table 6. Domestic Market Share, General Commercial and
Family Automobiles (unit sales)

	Before Reform				After Reform			
	1987		1988		1994		1996	
	No.	%	No.	%	No.	%	No.	%
Sevel[a]	69,912	42.7	62,289	40.4	166,307	37.5	79,542	24.8
Autolatina[b]	39,424	24.1	45,831	29.8	96,517	21.8	—	0.0
Renault Arg. (Ciadea)	54,251	33.2	45,886	29.8	96,695	21.8	64,898	20.3
Ford Argentina							45,886	14.3
Volkswagen Arg.							63,858	19.9
Fiat Auto							21,443	6.7
General Motors					3,661	0.8	21,100	6.6
Mercedes Benz							553	0.2
Imported by others					79,850	18.0	23,159	7.2
Total	163,587	100.0	154,006	100.0	443,030	100.0	320,439	100.0

[a]Sevel gave up its Fiat license. FIAT returned to Argentina after 1994.
[b]Ford and Volkswagen separated and ended their association with Autolatina after 1994.
Note: Includes local production and imports.
Source: ADEFA 1997.

rate, and the terminal industry actually did not comply with the export goals established
by the regime (see Llach et al. 1997). The important increase in imports can be appreci-
ated by noting that in 1990, domestic production provided 98.8 percent of national
consumption, and that the percentage decreased to 71 percent in 1994 and 53 percent
in 1997. Older producers, meanwhile, protected their interests in the midst of the general
deregulation process. Their capacity to do this can be seen in table 6, which describes
market share in the main category of vehicles, general commercial and family vehicles.

Even if the share of automobiles produced in Argentina as part of the total national
consumption shrank by almost 30 points, in 1994 the market share of the main domestic
producer, Sevel (part of an Argentine group, SOGMA, that held the license of Fiat and
Peugeot), decreased only 3 points. The same can be shown for Ciadea (Renault license,
also controlled by Argentine capital since 1992) and Autolatina (the merger of the trans-

nationals Ford and Volkswagen in Argentina), although here the loss in market share is greater. This outcome is undoubtedly associated with the specific features of the motor vehicle regime. In addition to their market reserve through tariffs and quotas, the terminal plants' authority to import at a 2 percent tariff enabled them to supply imported cars to fuel the increase in domestic consumption.

Not surprisingly, ADEFA (the terminal plants business association) and unions in the auto sector, especially SMATA, were actively involved in the lobbying for and formulation of the series of decrees that regulated the sector. SMATA leader Jose Rodriguez in particular became an outspoken lobbyist for the motor vehicle regime. When the regime was being negotiated with Brazil in the context of Mercosur, SMATA organized a massive street demonstration in its defense. Autos were, further-more, the only industrial sector that created employment amid an adjustment that was expelling labor force from the market.[18] Still, SMATA's informal alliance with the government extended beyond the framing of the regime. When new transnational corporations reestablished themselves in Argentina, attracted by the new prospects opened by Mercosur, SMATA obtained the government's backing to recruit the new workers for its membership. In exchange, SMATA accepted collective agreements that included labor flexibilization mechanisms in the new plants established after 1991.

In summary, a specific and negotiated pattern of deregulation meant that some actors—basically the old private producers, two of them Argentine, and the main union in the terminal plant sector, SMATA—could largely attenuate the costs of adjustment and deregulation. At the same time, the auto sector underwent an impressive transformation during Menem's administration. The opening was important, and the domestic production share of national consumption of vehicles fell abruptly. In the subsector of commercial vehicles, for example, the number of domestic manufacturers tripled: three companies were producing cars in Argentina in 1990, seven accounted for the total production six years later, and nine in 1997 (including Chrysler and Toyota).

WINNERS AND LOSERS: TRADE-OFFS ACROSS REFORMS

Considering the policy areas analyzed in this chapter, it is in the politics of negotiated rent allocations and partial deregulation that we find the coalitional foundations of what is often viewed, paradoxically, as an orthodox and unilaterally imposed process of economic liberalization (see, for example, Kvaternik 1998, 454–57).[19] The government shaped specific coalitions for each policy and chose to push reform to different degrees in different areas, according to the strength of different power contenders.

Table 7 depicts the main costs entailed by the liberalization process for each actor and the specific patterns of compensations in the Argentine case. In some areas of reform, such as state downsizing, labor deregulation, and trade liberalization in the auto sector, the government did not go as far as it initially intended. Instead, it resorted to a strategy of formal concertation with key actors—the public sector union, UPCN; the trade union leadership; auto manufacturers; and the autoworkers' union, SMATA—to control the pace of liberalization.[20] In the other areas analyzed, the bargain was less formal, though it was also oriented to a pattern of rent allocations and partial reforms granted by the state in the newly created market structure. In the case of petroleum restructuring, the administration shaped a coalition with the domestic bourgeoisie, traditionally linked to the state, and the established international refiners in the downstream subsectors, with the minor participation of the union SUPE. Likewise, in steel, the coalition partners were the largest domestic producers.

Table 7. Compensations to the Winners: Organized Labor and Industrial
Tradable Sectors

Sector/Actor	Main Costs Entailed by Reform	Compensations: Negotiated/Partial Deregulation	Compensations: Direct Rent Allocations
Labor (State) State Union (UPCN)	• Flexibilization contracts/end of collective agreements in the state • Employment downsizing	• Downsizing limited to privatization/ transfer of services • New labor code preserves UPCN's institutional power	• Control of healthcare system for state workers
Labor (private sector) Trade Unions	• Wages increases tied to productivity • Unemployment • New, more "flexible" collective companies	• Union monopoly and, centralized bargaining preserved, automatic renovation prereform collective agreements (except privatized firms) • Flexibilization in Individual contracts limited to categories of workers • Partial deregulation of health system	• Participation in private pension funds • Participation in insurance firms for workers' accidents • 10% shares in privatized companies • Other state assets (electric generators, YPF fleet, rail lines, etc.)
Petroleum (upstream) Domestic Producers	• Trade liberalization and formal opening to new players • End of YPF price subsidies	• Conversion of old contracts (1958–83) in concessions	• Awarding of former VPF areas. • Participation in the stock share of privatized YPF
SUPE (Union)	• Downsizing • End of prereform collective agreement	• Monopoly in former YPF workers	• Former VPF Assets (mainly YPF's fleet) • 100Al shares in YPF
Steel Domestic Producers	• Trade liberalization • Exchange rate overvaluation • End of industrial promotion subsidies	• Strong antidumping measures	• Awarding of SOMISA
Automobiles Terminal Industry	• Trade liberalization • Exchange rate overvaluation • End of industrial promotion subsidies	• Motor Vehicle Regime: special tariff for autos. Imports of autos and components by terminals at lower tariffs	
SMATA (union)	• Wages tied to productivity • Flexible contracts in new plants	• Motor Vehicle Regime: growth in sector's employment	• Affiliation of workers of new TNC's established in the country

The intention to compensate these actors was neither obvious nor inherent in the liberalization process. These benefits were, instead, the result of deliberate government policy decisions targeted to those groups: low levels of competition in the bidding for high-return areas and the conversion of old contracts into concessions in the case of oil extraction; facilities offered to domestic producers in the case of steel. It is significant that a third mechanism of compensation in tradables was that of rent allocations in non-tradables: holding companies Pérez Companc, Techint, and SOCMA (based in autos) all obtained (sometimes minor) participation in the privatization of services such as telecommunications and electricity. Nevertheless, this chapter has concentrated on the patterns of compensations in the sectors threatened by deregulation.

Although the focus here has been the political bargain with the winners, there were obviously losers in the sectors studied (Table 8). Arguably, ATE and the teachers' unions benefited much less than UPCN did. Smaller private producers of rolling steel were seriously hit by the pattern of deregulation, and the number of firms declined from 26 to 8, almost a 70 percent decrease in five years (see table 4). Likewise, in the same period the number of workers in the steel sector was reduced by half, and the metal-workers' union, UOM, did not get payoffs comparable to what UPCN, SMATA, or, to lesser extent, SUPE were able to obtain in their sectors. UOM, moreover, is heavily represented in the parts and components subsector, which was badly hit by deregulation. Unlike the assembly plants, the parts and components industry could not get comparable side payments within the initial framework of the motor vehicle regime. Consequently, from about 350 parts and components firms in 1990, about 150 remained in 1995 (Llach et al. 1997, 154).

In the upstream subsector of the petroleum industry, foreign producers, such as Amoco, Cities Service, and Shell were relative losers after deregulation. Amoco's market share stagnated from the bias in favor of old national companies in the subsector, and Shell was relegated to the few bids on areas where it participated. By the same logic, after adjustment, the unemployed in Argentina hardly got analogous compensations compared to the important side payments targeted to the union structure and, arguably, workers in segments of the formal sector.[21]

This chapter's main concerns are the political sustainability of reform in Argentina and how Menem's government managed to buy off the "winners" in formerly protected industry and labor. Yet a second important question remains: what distinguishes the losers from the winners? The answer would require a more developed theory of the politics of compensations in cases of extensive liberalization, and a comparative approach to check if analogous actors in labor and tradables were compensated in the same way in other cases of reform.

This chapter, therefore, can offer only a preliminary answer: the winners in tradables and labor were those actors that had grown more powerful in economic and organizational terms in the years prior to reform. For example, UPCN, with its centralized leadership and consolidated financial structure, was the most traditional, the biggest, and the most hegemonic union in the national administration. In steel, petroleum, and autos, national producers had grown consistently in the years before reform, especially because they were privileged by state contracts, tariffs, and the like during the 1976–83 dictatorship. The bigger steel producers are grouped in the CIS (Center of Steel Industrialists), which wields great influence in the UIA (Argentine Industrial Union); and the national and foreign assembly plants are grouped in a single and powerful organization ADEFA (Association of Automakers). SMATA had been growing steadily before the early 1990s, especially because of its capacity to regain the affiliation of workers in the main assembly plants after 1976 and to its efficient management of the workers' welfare system.

Table 8. Economic Liberalization in Labor and Selected Tradable Sectors:
Winners and Losers

Area of Reform	Winners (Compensated)	Losers
Administrative Reform	UPCN (union)	ATE (union), teacher/health unions
Labor	Trade union leadership, segments of the formal sector	Unemployed
Petroleum (upstream)	Domestic producers SUPE (union)	U.S. producers–foreign refiners Laid-off workers
Steel	Domestic integrated producers (Techint—Acindar)	Small producers of rolling steel Laid-off Workers UOM (union)
Autos	Terminal industry SMATA (union)	Parts and component firms Laid-offs in parts and components industry UOM

Conversely, the losers were economically less powerful and generally more fragmented in organizational terms when the reform program was launched. ATE had developed more recently, and based its strength in the ranks of the discontented in the provincial public sector. The teachers' labor unions had been historically fragmented. Smaller producers in the steel sector, and the parts and components industry in the auto sector, are not only economically less powerful (that is, they generate less output value and employment), but are divided into many different interest organizations. In the same way, U.S. petroleum producers in the upstream subsectors had been losing ground in Argentina since the last two military dictatorships regularly privileged national capital in the awarding of contracts. Finally, UOM was already in decline, both in level of affiliation relative to SMATA in the assembly plants and in financial terms, even before the reform process started.

Thus it can be argued that the winners were more powerful in economic terms, and sometimes in organizational terms, at the onset of reform, and therefore represented a bigger threat to the political sustainability of the whole process. Pérez Companc, Techint, and SOCMA, with their base in tradables, and certain union bosses in the CGT leadership constituted a much more powerful challenge for the reformist government than, say, the unemployed, the textile or the parts and components industries

ECONOMIC LIBERALIZATION AS A MULTIDIMENSIONAL PHENOMENON AND LEGACIES FOR THE NEW MARKET SETTING

The present study contradicts some common knowledge regarding countries that are taken as "successful" cases of market reform implementation: that reform is unilaterally imposed by an "autonomous state," that it attacks the interests of traditional "rent seekers," that it tends almost exclusively to benefit international and financial capital and holders of liquid assets. The idea of liberalization as a task of political construction, in which the state acts as a coordinating agent attacking vested interests in some policy areas but at the same time opens windows to administer compensations in others, is, to a great extent, overlooked by traditional approaches.[22]

The approach here attempts to capture, the dynamics of state/society relations in the midst of the reform process, stressing the capacity of the state to shape the preferences of societal actors. In this more complex picture, and against the logic of the public choice approach to economic reforms, in a "successful" case of reform implementation, traditional rent seekers are able to protect their rents in the new market setting. Moreover, it is not merely that the state regains capacity to neutralize or "defeat" the interests from above, as the institutionalist perspective would suggest. More than autonomy and unilateral imposition, we see complicated bargains and concertation, often as a result of the pressure "from below"; that is, from societal interests. Finally, even though liberalization involves a redistribution of benefits to the capitalist class, reform alignments in Argentina are probably better read vertically than horizontally. Certain sectors of business and labor were much more capable of protecting their interests in the new market structure compared with other actors both at the level of capital and of the working class.

As the literature widely acknowledges, it is by no means obvious that tradable sectors that are protected and generally not internationally competitive would join a reformist coalition. Indeed, the business sectors analyzed in this chapter were among the same actors that helped to block liberalization attempts under both the 1976–83 dictatorship and the 1983–89 UCR government (see Corrales 1998, 27–32). The initial studies of the politics of reform in Argentina generally pointed out how national economic holdings won rents through their participation in the privatization in nontradables, such as telecommunications and electricity (Corrales 1998, 39). This analysis has shown, by contrast, the importance of compensations designed to protect these actors from competition in their historical economic base of tradables. Indeed, the move by some of these groups (such as Techint and Pérez Companc) to sell some of their assets in utilities and concentrate on their traditional activities might suggest that the compensations analyzed here, and not the former, were the more crucial for these groups.

The multidimensional logic of economic liberalization must therefore be restated. Academics and financial analysts frequently draw a teleological view of liberalization, in which one country advances from a statist economy to a liberalized or market economy along a one dimensional path (for a critique of this view see Torre 1998, 84–86; Stark and Bruszt 1998, 80–84; see also Corrales 1998, 44). This view is generally restricted to inflation and fiscal and trade indicators. As it suggests, a sector protected by tariffs, subsides, monopoly in state contracts, or corporatist labor law at time A will surely lose compared to time B, when the subsidies and privileges have been repealed and the sector is harshly exposed to international and domestic market forces. In reality, however, liberalization is a game played in various arenas. This multidimensional logic is essentially what models based in the "rent-seeking actor" seem to overlook.

As the Argentine example reveals, the situation is hardly one of abrupt and one-dimensional change from A to B. It is instead full of midpoints, partial reforms, and economic privileges politically bestowed, be they the awarding of dominant firms in economic sectors, the negotiation of special tariff regimes, incomplete deregulation of the health system or the labor law, or and interest participation in the pension funds and other newly created markets. This analytical perspective is not merely intended to show that reform is more thorough in some sectors than in others. Instead, such reform and liberalization can be radical, politically viable, and unilaterally imposed in some areas, such as trade (see Viguera 1997), financial deregulation, monetary and exchange rate policy, and the wide scope of the privatization program *because*, with the goal of bringing about a coalition, reform was negotiated or incomplete in others, such as the provincial public sector, labor and health regulations, specific trade regimes, or the model of privatization implemented.

Finally, the compensations described in this chapter entailed important legacies for the more liberalized Argentine political economy, both in the medium- and long-run. Initially, compensations served Menem to forge a broad coalition by rewarding the losers from the exchange rate regime (unions in the tradable sector and domestic industry). Therefore, these actors, although subordinated, were included in an interest coalition led by financiers, privatized companies mostly in the service sector and international investors. However, by buying off the losers from an increasingly overvalued exchange rate during the 1990s, compensations underpinned the staunch maintenance of an exchange rate policy that would eventually undermine Argentina's economic competitiveness.

In addition, no governmental strategy of industrial policy for global competition was developed beyond side-payments such as targeted privatization or the granting of market reserves. In times of international liberalization, the compensations found in the Argentine case were, paradoxically, based on control of *domestic* markets, i.e., the preservation of market share in the case of business and the maintenance of the monopolies in the labor and health markets for unions. Consequently, when those payoffs were "consumed" in the boom of the first half of the 1990s (i.e., no more domestic market share could be gained and the privatization process was over and it was not possible to offer additional rewards to either firms or unions), and in view of the continuous overvaluation of the Argentine currency, even the most powerful players in industrial business or labor were caught with very disadvantageous relative prices. By the end of 2001 industrial business and arguably significant portions of the labor movement had defected to the devaluation camp, which contributed to the financial meltdown and the collapse of the Alianza government (1999–2001).

The compensatory arrangements also had important consequences in the long run for both labor and domestic industry. In the case of labor, the preservation of the corporatist labor legislation and the associational power of unions implied that those resources could be available in less hostile times. In effect, after the 2001 crises when the economy rebounded and labor markets tightened, unions used their representation monopoly, the centralized collective bargaining framework, and the control of workers' health services (all benefits secured in the compensatory bargains of the 1990s) to increase their capacity for mobilization to press for real wage gains. Therefore, a considerably powerful, if downsized, labor movement emerged as one of the main coalitional supporters of the Néstor and Cristina Kirchner leftist-populitst governments in the period 2003–09.

The fate of the large domestic industrial groups involved in the compensatory arrangements was less positive in the long run. In the three sectors analyzed in this study—autos, steel and petroleum—only in steel could an Argentine group use compensation as a platform to expand in global markets. In effect, after the purchase of SOMISA, and building upon its enhanced control of the domestic market for flat steel, the domestic group Techint bought Hysalmex in Mexico and Sidor in Venezuela—the latter recently nationalized by the government of Hugo Chávez. These three companies formed the backbone of the subsidiary Ternium, which meant the consolidation of Techint as a regional producer of flat steel in addition to its traditional business in tubes. But Techint was an efficient producer of steel pipes and had internationalized to some extent before neoliberal reform. Aluar, the domestic aluminum-based group, also compensated through privatization is the other example of a large industrial group that could keep up international expansion after the end of the 1990s (see Finchelstein 2008).

Most of other compensated industrial groups, however, were not able to cope with open markets in the long run. In the auto sector, local producers under foreign licenses were not viable in a global market dominated by a group of multinational firms, and were soon taken over by foreign companies. In petroleum, by the end of the 1990s Pérez Companc, the largest local group compensated, had become the most important private energy company in South America. Pérez Companc deployed oil drilling operations throughout the region and had ventures in energy transmission and generation. However, it could not weather the storm of the 2001 financial crises in Argentina and ended up selling its energy division to the Brazilian state company Petrobras.[23] In short, left to the vagaries of the market and without the support of the state or a public development bank—unlike, for example, the largest Brazilian companies—it seems that only those domestic groups that had internationalized to some extent before neoliberal reform, and concentrated in a specific industrial commodity (such as steel or aluminum) were able to profit from the compensatory arrangements to thrive in global markets.

ACRONYMS

ADEFA: Asociación de Fabricas de Automotores
ATE: Asociación de Trabajadores del Estado
CECRA: Comité Ejecutivo para la Coordinación de la Reforma Administrativa
CGT: Confederación General del Trabajo
CIS: Centro de Industriales Siderúrgicos
CTERA: Confederación de Trabajadores de la Educación de la República Argentina
SMATA: Sindicato de Mecánicos y Afines del Transporte Automotor
SOMISA: Sociedad Mixta Siderúrgica Argentina
SUPE: Sindicato Unido de Petroleros del Estado
UDA: Unión Docentes Argentina
UIA: Unión Industrial Argentina
UOM: Unión Obrera Metalúrgica
UPCN: Unión de Personal Civil de la Nación
YPF: Yacimientos Petrolíferos Fiscales

NOTES

The author acknowledges the comments of David Collier, Ruth B. Collier, Barbara Geddes, Marcus Kurtz, Steven Levitsky, Germán Lodola, M. Victoria Murillo, Mariano Tommasi, and three anonymous reviewers for *Latin American Politics and Society*.

1 For example, Nelson (1990, 342) states that the governments that have launched state reforms but were less successful in following through were also the "less autonomous" from interest groups.

2 A now-classic, though still unpublished, piece in Argentine social science that echoes the institutionalist preoccupation with state capacity is Palermo and Torre 1992. Acuña and Smith (1994, 26) also point to the restored state strength when they see Menem as a "Hobbesian solution," which deepened the exclusionary character of the policy process.

3 So the group activity is rent seeking in the sense that the resources devoted to obtaining the item of value do not themselves create value in economic terms and constitute a deadweight cost (see Krueger 1993, 58, 1974, 301–2).

4 The work of Argentine economists Notcheff and Azpiazu, although from a different methodological perspective than Schamis, depicts the market transformation as a result of the pressure

of the most concentrated segments of capital over the state. See Azpiazu and Notcheff (1994). Margheritis's 1999 study also views the reform process as essentially driven by a few concentrated winners in the capitalist sector.

5 From a more general perspective (studies that do not focus on specific reforms), arguments for the Argentine case that point out the shift toward a pattern of moderation and negotiation with interests after the initial stage of stabilization can be found in Gerchunoff and Torre 1996; Palermo and Novaro 1996, Llanos 1998, Etchemendy and Palermo 1998, and Hagopian 1998.

6 Of course, some authors who have emphasized the Menem administration's ability to regain autonomy and "neutralize" interest groups have nonetheless also pointed out the government's concessions to the domestic economic groups. Carlos Acuña (1994, 52–55) points to the use of a carrot-and-stick policy with unions and writes that the government allowed some groups "to appropriate, through privatization, public sector firms that have ended up as monopolies or oligopolies. This helped to mitigate the loss of profits from retraction of state contracts" (1994, 53).

7 Cook defines flexibilization of the labor law as those changes in individual and collective labor relations that "lower employers' costs, and generally grant employers greater maneuverability in contracting and deploying their labor force" (1998, 317).

8 The following account of administrative reform under Menem is based on Ghio and Etchemendy (1997) and Orlansky (1994). For the official view see Domeniconi, et al. (1992).

9 The Ministry of Labor established that UPGN represented 72.30 percent of affiliation, compared to 27.69 percent of ATE, a measure ATE questioned. ATE contested the agreement in the courts.

10 For a convincing argument about the political importance of the absence of reform in the provincial public sector in the context of market reforms in Argentina, see Gibson and Calvo (1997).

11 The assessment of labor reform is based on Etchemendy and Palermo (1998) and Giordano and Torres (1997). A very interesting account of the process based on interviews with Menem's labor ministers is found in Senén González and Bosoer (1999). For a more general assessment in which labor policy is part of the broader social reform agenda, see Cortes and Marshall (1999).

12 With one important exception: the government ruled by decree that, since 1991, every salary increase should be negotiated according to the levels of productivity.

13 David Collier defines concertation as a mechanism of policy formation that entails "the overarching process of forming social pacts and shaping public policy at the pinnacle of organized labor, organized business, and the state" (1995, 143).

14 Business was demanding not only the decentralization of collective bargaining but an end to the union monopoly of representation. Its goal was to negotiate with an independent union at the level of the firm, and not necessarily with one affiliated with the sectoral trade union organization.

15 According unpublished data from the Technical Commission for Wages and Productivity of the Ministry of Labor, by 1995, 89.6 percent of the labor force in the formal sector was covered by collective agreements signed between 1975 and 1990. Only 10.4 percent was under new and more flexible collective agreements signed between 1991 and 1995. Of course, many unions covered by prereform collective contracts negotiated informal and more flexible agreements at the level of the plant. For an excellent analysis of this tendency in the metallurgic and steel sectors, see Freytes Rey (1999).

16 Analyzing only four of the 25 contracts, Gadano and Sturzenegger (1998, 97) estimate that the reconversion of contracts in concessions cost the state $120 million. For a comparison of the returns of the reconverted contracts with what the old contracts with the state would have yielded see the illuminating analysis in Gadano and Sturzenegger (1998, 89–98).

17 The Ouro Preto agreements that formalized the common market Mercosur in 1994 accepted the Argentine Motor Vehicle Regime until the year 2000, when the special regime would be renegotiated with Brazil and the other Mercosur partners.

18 The automotive industry in Argentina was employing 17,430 workers in 1990 and 26,286 in 1996 (ADEFA 1997).

19 The idea of partial reform as a distributional strategy of the reformer is analyzed by Hellman 1998 in the context of economic liberalization in Eastern Europe.

20 Of course, this is not intended to suggest that the unions were "winners" at the same level as economic holding companies such as Techint and Pérez Companc. Rather, among those potentially affected by adjustment, the government chose to benefit the unions (particularly the union leadership, but also workers who remained in the formal sector) and not the unemployed or the informal sector.

21 Unemployment subsidies are negligible in Argentina, even though unemployment peaked at 18 percent in 1995. According to data from the Ministry of Labor (1998), only 7.1 percent of the unemployed were receiving compensations in that year.

22 Paradoxically, the role of established actors of the prereform period in carving out the new policies of liberalization has been more systematically assessed in the cases of Eastern Europe and Russia, where societies were more controlled by the state, than in Latin America, were economies were mixed and civil societies arguably stronger. See the seminal books of Stark and Bruszt (1998) and Shleifer and Treisman (2000).

23 Many compensated industrial groups would follow this course, especially in the petrochemical, autos and oil sectors. Among others, Astra, Sevel, Ciadea, Ipako and Indupa were sold to foreign investors. In the case of Pérez Companc the sale was triggered by the 2001 crises and the firm's large dollar-denominated debt. It should be noted that these were not, however, "defensive" sales as a result of liberalization pressures but occurred in the post-adjustment period in which these companies had expanded market share and significantly increased their asset value. For a broader view on the group's post-adjustment performance see Finchelstein (2008).

REFERENCES

Acuña, Carlos H. 1994. Politics and Economics in the Argentina of the Nineties (Or Why the Future No Longer Is What It Used to Be). In *Democracy, Markets, and Structural Reform in Latin America*, ed. William C. Smith, Carlos H. Acuña, and Eduardo Gamarra. Coral Gables: North-South Center.

Acuña, Carlos, and William C. Smith. 1994. The Political Economy of Structural Adjustment: The Logic of Support and Opposition to Neoliberal Reform. In *Latin American Political Economy in The Age of Neoliberal Reform: Theoretical and Comparative Perspectives*, ed. Smith, Acuña, and Eduardo Gamarra. New Brunswick: Transaction. 17–66.

Asociación de Fábricas de Automotores (ADEFA). 1997. Anuario Estadístico. Buenos Aires: ADEFA.

Azpiazu, Daniel, and Notcheff, Hugo. 1994. *El desarrollo ausente*. Buenos Aires: FLACSO.

Bates, Robert. 1992. Macropolitical Economy in the Field of Development. In *Perspectives on Positive Political Economy*, ed. James Alt and Kenneth A. Shepsle. Cambridge: Cambridge University Press. 31–54.

Bates, Robert, and Anne Krueger, eds. 1993. *Political and Economic Interactions in Policy Reforms*. Oxford: Basil Blackwell.

Bisang, Roberto, and Martina Chidiak. 1995. Apertura económica, reestructuración y medio ambiente. La siderurgia Argentina en los 90. Working Paper 19. Buenos Aires: CENIT (Centro de Investigaciones Para la Transformación).

Centro de Industriales Siderúrgicos (CIS). 1996. *Estadísticas siderúrgicas, 1960–1995*. Buenos Aires: CIS.

——. 1998. La siderurgia argentina, 1993–1997 Buenos Aires: CIS. Collier, David. 1995. Trajectory of a Concept: "Corporatism" in the Study of Latin American Politics. In *Latin America in Comparative Perspective: New Approaches to Methods and Analysis*, ed. Peter Smith. Boulder: Westview Press.

Collier, David. 1995. Trajectory of a Concept: "Corporatism" in the Study of Latin American Politics. In *Latin America in Comparative Perspective: New Approaches to Methods and Analysis*, ed. Peter Smith. Boulder: Westview Press.

Collier, Ruth, and David Collier. 1979. Inducements versus Constraints: Disaggregating Corporatism. *American Political Science Review* 73, 4: 967–86.

Cook, María Lorena. 1998. Toward Flexible Industrial Relations? Neo-Liberalism, Democracy and Labor Reform in Latin America. *Industrial Relations* 37, 3: 311–35.

Corrales, Javier. 1998. Coalitions and Corporate Choices in Argentina, 1976–1994: The Recent Private Sector Support of Privatization. *Studies in Comparative International Development* 32, 4: 24–51.

Cortes, Rosalía, and Adriana Marshall. 1999. Estrategia económica, instituciones y negociación política de la reforma social de los 90. *Desarrollo Económico* 36, 154: 195–212.

Domeniconi, Héctor, Ricardo Gaudio, and Armando Guibert. 1992. La reforma administrativa en Argentina. *Boletín Informativo Techint* no. 2. Buenos Aires: Techint.

Eaton, Kent. 2004. *Politics beyond the Capital: The Design of Subnational Institutions in South America*. Stanford: Stanford University Press.

Edwards, Sebastian. 1995. *Crisis and Reform in Latin America: From Despair to Hope*. New York: World Bank/Oxford University Press.

Etchemendy, Sebastián, and Vicente Palermo. 1998. Conflicto y concertación. Gobierno, congreso y organizaciones de interés en la reforma laboral del primer gobierno de Menem. *Desarrollo Económico* 37, 148: 559–90.

Evans, Peter. 1995. *Embedded Autonomy*. Princeton: Princeton University Press.

Finchelstein, Diego. 2008. Corporate Governance in Argentina: Business Group Adaptation During Post Market Reform Period. Paper submitted to the Sloan Industry Annual Conference, Boston, May 1–2 2008.

Freytes Rey, Ada Cora. 1999. Las relaciones laborales en la actividad siderometalúrgica: informalidad y fragmentación. In *Política y relaciones laborales en la transición democrática Argentina*, ed. A. Fernández y Raúl Bisio. Buenos Aires: Lumen-Humanitas.

Fundación de Investigaciones Para el Desarrollo (FIDE). 1997. *Coyuntura y Desarrollo* no. 225 (July).

Gadano, Nicolás, and Federico Sturzenegger. 1998. La privatización de las reservas en el sector hidrocarburífero. El caso de Argentina. *Revista de Análisis Económico* 13, 1: 75–115.

Geddes, Barbara. 1994a. How Politicians Decide Who Bears the Costs of Liberalization. In *Transition to a Market Economy at the End of the Twentieth Century: 11th International Economic History Congress*, Milan, Italy, Session A-3, September 12–17, 1994.

——. 1994b. *Politician's Dilemma: Building State Capacity in Latin America*. Berkeley: University of California Press.

Gerchunoff, Pablo. 1992. Petróleo. In *Las privatizaciones en Argentina*, ed. Gerchunoff. Buenos Aires: Instituto Torcuato Di Tella. 348–449.

Gerchunoff, Pablo, Carlos Bozzalla, and Julio Sanguinetti. 1994. *Privatización, apertura y concentración. El caso del sector siderúrgico argentino*. Series Reforma Política Pública. Santiago de Chile: CEPAL.

Gerchunoff, Pablo, and Juan Carlos Torre. 1996. La política de liberalización económica en la administración de Menem. *Desarrollo Económico* 36 (October–December): 733–768.

Ghio, Jose, and Etchemendy, Sebastián. 1997. "Escaping From the Flames": The Politics of Administrative Reform in Menem's Argentina. Paper presented to the conference "The Political Economy of Administrative Reform in Developing Countries." Northwestern University, Chicago, May 30–31.

Gibson, Edward. 1997. The Populist Road to Market Reform: Policy and Electoral Coalitions in Mexico and Argentina. *World Politics* 49: 339–70.

Gibson, Edward, and Ernesto Calvo. 1997. *Electoral Coalitions and Market Reforms: Evidence from Argentina*. Working Paper 35. Buenos Aires: Universidad Torcuato Di Tella.

——. 2001. Federalism and Low-Maintenance Constituencies: Territorial Dimensions of Economic Reform in Argentina. *Studies in Comparative International Development* 35, 3 (Winter 2001): 32–55.

Giordano, Osvaldo, and Alejandra Torres. 1997. *Las instituciones laborales en el contexto de las reformas estructurales en el empleo en la Argentina*. Buenos Aires: FIEL.

Gwartney, James D., Robert Lawson, and Walter Block. 1996. *Economic Freedom of the World, 1975–1995*. Vancouver, BC: Fraser Institute.

Haggard, Stephen, and Robert R. Kaufman. 1992. Introduction. In *The Politics of Economic Adjustment*, ed. Haggard and Kaufman. Princeton: Princeton University Press.

——. 1995. *The Political Economy of Democratic Transitions*. Princeton: Princeton University Press.

Haggard, Stephen, and Steven Webb. 1994. Introduction. In *Voting for Reform*, ed. Haggard and Webb. New York: Oxford University Press.

Hellman, Joel. 1998. Winners Take All: The Politics of Partial Reform in Post-communist Transitions. *World Politics* 50: 203–34.

Instituto para el Desarrollo Industrial (IDI). 1996. Evolución reciente y situación actual de la industria argentina. *Boletín Informativo Techint* no. 287: 4 1–55.

Kessler, Timothy. 1998. Political Capital: Mexican Financial Policy Under Salinas. *World Politics* 51: 36–66.

Kozulj, Roberto, and Víctor Bravo. 1993. *La Política de Desregulación Petrolera Argentina*. Buenos Aires: Centro Editor de América Latina.

Krueger, Anne O. 1974. The Political Economy of the Rent-Seeking Society. *American Economic Review* 64: 291–303.

——. 1993. *Economic Policies At Cross Purposes: The United States And Developing Countries*. Washington, DC: The Brookings Institution.

Kurtz, Marcus. 2004. *Free Market Democracy and the Chilean and Mexican Countryside*. Cambridge: Cambridge University Press.

Kvaternik, Eugenio. 1998. Ciclos Políticos en Argentina. In *Elementos para el análisis Político,* ed. E. Kvaternik. Buenos Aires: Paidós.

Llach, Juan, Pablo Sierra, and Gustavo Lugones. 1997. *La industria automotriz argentina.* Unpublished mss. Buenos Aires.

Llanos, Mariana. 1998, *President–Congress Relationships in Argentina: The Case of Privatization Under Alfonsín and Menem.* Ph.D. diss., Oxford University.

Lozano, Claudio. 1992. *La privatización de SOMISA.* Buenos Aires: Cuadernos IDEP (Instituto de Estado y Participación).

Margheritis, Ana. 1999. *Ajuste y reforma en Argentina (1989–1995)*. Buenos Aires: GEL (Grupo Editor Latinoamericano).

Murillo, M. Victoria. 1997. Union Responses to Economic Reform in Argentina: Organizational Autonomy and the Marketization of Corporatism. In *The New Politics of Inequality In Latin America: Rethinking Participation and Representation*, ed. Douglas Chalmers et al. Oxford: Oxford University Press, 1997.

——. 2001. *Labor Unions, Partisan Coalitions and Market Reforms in Latin America*. Cambridge: Cambridge University Press.

——. 2002. Political Bias in Policy Convergence. Privatization Choices in Latin America. *World Politics* 54: 462–93.

Nelson, Joan. 1990. Conclusions. In *Economic Crises and Policy Choice: The Politics of Adjustment In the Third World*, ed. Nelson. Princeton: Princeton University Press.

——. 1994. Labor and Business Roles in Dual Transitions: Building Blocks or Stumbling Blocks? In *Intricate Links: Democratization and Market Reforms in Latin America and Eastern Europe*, ed. Nelson. New Brunswick: Transaction.

Orlansky, Dora. 1994. Crisis y transformación del estado en Argentina. *Ciclos* 4: 3–27.

Orlansky, Dora, and Diana Gómez. 2000. *Negociación colectiva estatal en las postrimerías del gobierno de Menem*. Paper presented to the seminar "Labor Market and Union Intervention," Instituto de Desarrollo Económico y Social, Buenos Aires, October 4–5.

Palermo, Vicente, and Marcos Novaro. 1996. *Política y poder en el primer gobierno de Menem*. Buenos Aires: Grupo Editorial Norma and FLACO.

Palermo, Vicente, and Juan Carlos Torre. 1992. A la sombra de la hiperinflación. La política de las reformas estructurales en Argentina. Unpublished mss. Buenos Aires: Instituto Torcuato Di Tella.

Pérez, Sofía. 1997. *Banking on Privilege: The Politics of Spanish Financial Reform*. Ithaca: Cornell University Press.

Republic of Argentina. Ministry of Labor and Social Security. 1998. *Boletín de Estadísticas Laborales*. Buenos Aires.

Schamis, Héctor. 1999. Distributional Coalitions and the Politics of Market Reforms in Latin America. *World Politics* 51: 236–68.

Senén González Santiago, and Fabián Bosoer. 1999. *El sindicalismo en tiempos de Menem.* Buenos Aires: Corregidor.

Shleifer Andrei, and Daniel Treisman. 2000. *Without a Map: Political Tactics and Economic Reform in Russia.* Cambridge: MIT Press.

Stark, David, and Laszlo Bruszt. 1998. *Postsocialist Pathways.* Cambridge: Cambridge University Press.

Stokes, Susan. 2001. *Mandates and Democracy.* Cambridge: Cambridge University Press.

Sturzenegger, Federico, and Mariano Tommasi, eds. 1998. *The Political Economy of Reform.* Cambridge: MIT Press.

Teichman, Judith. 2001. *The Politics of Freeing Markets in Latin America.* Chapel Hill: The University of North Carolina Press.

Torre, Juan Carlos. 1998. *El proceso político de las reformas en América Latina.* Buenos Aires: Paidós.

Treisman, Daniel. 2003. Cardoso, Menem, and Machiavelli: Political Tactics and Privatization in Latin America. *Studies in Comparative and International Development* 38: 93–109.

Viguera, Aníbal. 1997. *La política de la reforma económica en la Argentina. Estado y empresarios en torno a la apertura comercial, 1987–1996.* Ph.D. diss., FLACSO, Mexico City.

Villalón, Roberta. 1999. *Proteccionismo y política industrial en la Argentina de los 90.* Senior Thesis, Universidad Torcuato Di Tella.

Vispo, Adolfo. 1999. Reservas de mercado, cuasi-rentas de privilegio y deficiencias regulatorias: el régimen automotriz argentino. In *La desregulación de los mercados,* ed., Daniel Azpiazu, G. Gutman, and Vispo. Buenos Aires: Grupo Editorial Norma. 270–374.

Waterbury, John. 1989. The Political Management of Economic Adjustment and Reform. in *Fragile Coalitions: The Politics of Economic Adjustment,* ed. Joan Nelson. Washington, DC: Overseas Development Council.

Weyland, Kurt. 2002. *The Politics of Reform in Fragile Democracies.* Princeton: Princeton University

World Bank. 1993. *Argentina from Insolvency to Growth.* Washington, DC: World Bank.

Chapter 7

The Repoliticization of Collective Action After Neoliberalism in Peru

Moisés Arce

In mid-June 2002, the residents and local government of the city of Arequipa, Peru, fiercely opposed the sale of two state-owned electric companies, Egasa and Egasur. The popular protest turned violent, and the central government responded by imposing a state of emergency and a curfew. The popular uprising successfully derailed the privatization program, not least by triggering a cabinet shake-up and thus weakening the newly installed democratic regime of Alejandro Toledo. Arequipa's local officials and residents dreaded higher electricity prices and worker layoffs. They objected to the sale of electric companies that were profitable under state management.

A similar anti-market backlash has ensued in other impoverished provinces of Peru and beyond. For instance, in April 2000, residents of Cochabamba, Bolivia, managed to expel the private, foreign-led consortium that had taken over the city's water system. Outraged at the exorbitant increases in water prices and convinced that access to clean water was a basic human right, Cochabamba residents violently opposed the plans to "lease the rain" (Finnegan 2002). What explains this wave of localized protests against market policies?[1]

In the literature on how economic liberalization affects collective political activity, two main currents can be distinguished. The dominant perspective frames economic liberalization as the cause and consequence of widespread social depoliticization and demobilization (e.g., Kurtz 2004; Wolff 2005, 2007) and does not expect political liberalization to regenerate collective political activity. This atomization literature emphasizes the "intolerable consequences" of chronic economic crises and their drastic neoliberal resolution, such as increased poverty and inequality, higher levels of unemployment, and lower standards of living. These economic conditions hurt the collective capacity of popular subjects and produce, among other things, anomie, disorder, and societal disorganization (e.g., Zermeño 1990). Given that these economic conditions have arguably not changed much in recent years, however, the atomization literature remains ill prepared to explain the most recent surge in collective protest across the region.

Recently a second school of thought has emerged, which emphasizes the repoliticization of collective actors in the wake of economic liberalization, especially in the context of political liberalization. Existing research has shown an increase in the level of political protest in Latin America and has sought to understand the effects of these mobilizations on important political processes. Hochstetler (2006), for instance, examines the role of collective protests in forcing challenged presidents to leave office early. Other studies document the changing basis of anti-government mobilizations against economic liberalization, including the emergence of alternative forms of collective action (Garay 2007; Arce and Rice 2009) and the geographic segmentation of protest activity in peripheral provinces (Kohl 2002; Murillo and Ronconi 2004). The unemployed in Argentina, rural villagers in Peru, and indigenous movements in Ecuador and Bolivia, among other examples, have been the most important social forces opposing the continuation of neoliberal policies.

Recent cross-national empirical studies (e.g., Arce and Bellinger 2007) have also shown that economic liberalization leads to higher levels of protest in the presence of open and democratic politics. However, as is widely known, large-N analyses often obscure the mechanisms that cause societal actors to react to economic liberalization polices. Large-N analyses also suffer from an analytical bias in favor of national-level processes of economic and political change, thereby overlooking important changes at the subnational level. Widespread decentralizing reforms in Latin America have shifted important decisionmaking downward in the political system, so that the appropriate locus of protest activity is likely to have changed in recent decades. The existing literature continues to overlook these important changes at the subnational level. At times, these mobilizations have been far more violent than hitherto anticipated by the literature that associates economic liberalization with societal exclusion and anomie.

Understanding the interrelationship between economic and political liberalization has become a core question in comparative politics in Latin America and beyond as research has sought to understand how these two phenomena contradict or complement each other (e.g., Przeworski 1991; Haggard and Kaufman 1995). The atomization approach suggests that economic and political liberalization have been on a collision course over the last two decades, and that political democracy has taken the brunt of this impact while the forces of economic liberalization reign uncontested in the political arena. The implication is that democracy has been reduced to a mere procedure, and thus it has made no difference to the social actors affected by economic liberalization. In contrast, the repoliticization perspective portrays political democracy as a firewall that can help correct the excesses of economic liberalization policies, through either the ballot box or extra institutional forms of protest.

This chapter focuses on the latter approach. The implication in this case is that open and democratic politics, however imperfect, matter, and have influenced societal responses to economic liberalization. Thus, it is theoretically and substantively important to know how political liberalization conditions societal responses to economic liberalization.

Analyzing the Arequipazo, as the antiprivatization revolt came to be known, and several local mobilizations against foreign direct investment in other regions of Peru, this chapter seeks to explain the changing basis of collective political activity that has resulted from economic liberalization. Instead of the complete erosion of collective action from civil society, as the atomization literature suggests, other forms of protest have come to replace collective action in the labor sphere as the most important societal reaction to continued neoliberal restructuring. By extension, the focal points where significant protests take place have moved beyond large metropolitan areas. By considering these alternative patterns of collective action, including types of protest and their location, we can begin to discern how economic liberalization has transformed the societal landscape in contemporary Latin America. Existing studies do not capture these important changes in the repertoire of societal protest; or they are simply too aggregated to serve as the basis for meaningful comparative research.

Provincial revolts like those in Arequipa and Cochabamba resemble the so-called provincial outbursts (estallidos provinciales) of Argentina, which began in the early 1990s (Auyero 2002). These geographically segmented or territorialized uprisings represent "eventful protests," given their size, length, intensity, resonance, and symbolism (McAdam et al. 2001). They have had politically destabilizing effects. In the Peruvian case, as many observers would agree, Toledo's apparent failures in government began with the Arequipazo, which "immediately resonated at the national level" (IDB 2005, 116) and subsequently spread to other areas.[2]

Against this background, this study traces changes in the repertoire of societal protest. It explains how the transition from the regime of Alberto Fujimori to that of Alejandro Toledo led to more liberalized politics, a change that, as political opportunity theories emphasize, creates a more conducive environment for greater levels of mobilization. Toledo's decentralization efforts not only expanded political opportunities but also helped to territorialize a number of societal conflicts. The cycle of contentious activity in Peru is exemplified by the Arequipa uprising and other geographically segmented conflicts against foreign direct investment. Many scholars (e.g., Maxfield 1997) have identified foreign direct investment as the hallmark of globalization and economic liberalization policies; therefore these conflicts can be seen as reactions to neoliberal or market policies.

THE CHANGING REPERTOIRE OF SOCIETAL PROTEST

Much of the discussion of how economic liberalization has weakened the collective capacity of traditional organizations—labor unions in particular—focuses on the declining trend of strike activity. Reviewing strike rates in five Latin American countries (México, Chile, Ecuador, Bolivia, and Peru), Kurtz (2004, 292) concludes, "the level of labor protest has declined to near nonexistence, where it has remained." The strike figures, however, do not fully capture the new, rich diversity of mobilizations, led by a variety of new actors, that are shaping the pattern of social protest in Argentina, Bolivia, Peru, Venezuela, and beyond (Auyero 2002; Delamata 2002; López-Maya 2002; Lucero 2001; Garay 2007). Societal mobilizations have also become geographically segmented or territorialized in peripheral regions or interior provinces. These two phenomena are interrelated. The alternative patterns of collective political activity approximate Polanyi's 1944 description of the "double movement" of the market: an increase in economic liberalization imposes high social costs, and is countered by societal responses that seek to shelter the poor from the devastating effects of an untamed market.

A preliminary review of patterns of collective political activity in a number of Latin American countries reveals a shift in the pattern of social protest from institutionalized to noninstitutionalized forms of collective action.[3] By shifting important decisionmaking downward in the political system, administrative and political decentralization to subnational units is one of the main forces contributing to the geographical segmentation of protest activity (Murillo and Roncoci 2004; Kohl 2002). Decentralization has indeed changed the targets of protests, yet it cannot account for the underlying sources of collective protest.

In Argentina, Auyero (2002, 190) writes, "factory strikes have ceased to be the predominant form of protest but rather have been replaced by road blockades of national and provincial routes." Road blockades increased from 514 in 2000 to 2,336 in 2002. There were 5,608 road blockades in 2008, representing the highest number of blockades recorded since January 1997 (*Nueva Mayoría* 2009). Writing about teachers' strikes, Murillo and Roncoci (2004, 78) note how the decentralization of social services in Argentina has resulted in an "uneven pattern of provincialization of protest." Similarly, in contemporary Venezuela, Lopez-Maya and Lander (2004, 215–17) note a "dramatic rise in the number of violent or confrontational street protests." Based on news reports for the period 1985–99, their figures "reveal the prevalence of riots over the more conventional, peaceful forms of protest employed frequently in the history of Venezuelan democracy"; at the same time, they note a high amount of "illegal protest activity," such as highway blockades, land invasions, and occupations.

In Bolivia, Laserna and Ortego (2003) observe that road blockades, seizures of public buildings, and marches are dominating the current pattern of social conflict more than labor strikes. Similar to the Argentine case, according to Kohl (2002, 449), decentralization in Bolivia has "served to territorialize opposition to privatization and neoliberal economic policies and, in some areas, reinforce regional social movements." Localized revolts in the provinces of the interior have also surfaced in Peru, where decentralization initiatives have just begun to take place. Similar to the Arequipazo, pre-"water war" Cochabamba was the Bolivian province with the highest percentage of conflicts after La Paz, the capital (Calderón and Szmukler 2000, 335–46). Both Arequipa and Cochabamba had a high incidence of mobilizations compared to other provinces in Peru and Bolivia, respectively.

Recent rounds of protest have joined together numerous civil society groups, including indigenous peoples, students, women's organizations, workers, artists, neighborhood associations, religious groups, and sectors of the middle class. Building on preexisting social networks, mobilization sometimes occurs virtually spontaneously, without instruction or a general coordinating body. In keeping with the cyclical nature of popular mobilization (Tarrow 1998), resistance movements and protest coalitions often prove to be only transitory, disappearing shortly after a conflict is resolved or political opportunities close (Wolff 2007). Nevertheless, they have, at times, been highly effective at bringing their respective political and economic systems to a grinding halt until their demands were met or specific reform measures were reversed.

Figure 1 reports data on social protests in Peru from news reports for the period 1995–2004. The available data show that these mobilizations outnumber the traditional labor-based strikes. Rather than depicting social atomization or political apathy, as argued by the conventional wisdom about the effects of market reform, these figures capture the fallout from the continuation of neoliberal policies, where collective action simply changes, rather than disappears. Figure 1 helps us to visualize the paradoxical effect of neoliberalism: it simultaneously debilitates certain types of popular resistance while activating others. A recent article in *The Economist* (2008) characterized these mobilization events in Peru as the "the politics of non-stop protest."

Figure 1. Number of Social Protests and Strikes in Peru, 1995–2004

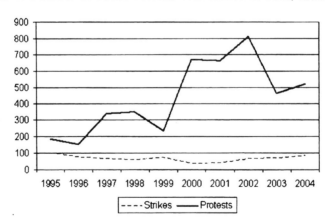

Source: Data on strikes from INEl (2005). Data on protests is based on information from the Peruvian Social Protest Dataset constructed by the author.

In particular, the most recent report from Peru's Defensoría del Pueblo (Ombudsman Office) places mobilizations against foreign direct investment as the most common type of social conflict in Peru today. These protests represent 50 percent of all conflicts (Defensoría del Pueblo 2009, 4). The mobilizations pit local communities against large- and medium-sized transnational mining firms, which seek to extract natural resources from the surrounding area. These localized conflicts are driven by mineral extraction and the environmental contamination that comes with it (Defensoría del Pueblo 2009, 47). Similar to the Arequipazo, these conflicts are territorially grounded, and emerge from a specific issue, yet they have a high profile and economic impact.

FUJIMORI FALLING

Political opportunity theories emphasize changes in the immediate political environment as facilitating or constraining collective action. These changes might include an opening of access to political power, a polity's crackdown on collective behavior, political alignments that shift or become unstable, or the appearance of new key allies or support groups. Sources of economic discontent, in contrast, are thought to be constant and inherent in all societies; yet grievances play a vital role in framing and mounting successful collective action (see, e.g., Tarrow 1998; McAdam et al. 2001).

The transition from Fujimori (1990–2000) to Toledo (2001–6) signaled a major shift in the structure of political opportunity that allowed for the greater use of protest. This central idea is consistent with existing research that suggests that political liberalization creates a more conducive environment for greater levels of mobilization while increasing the leverage of challengers, as well as their chances to achieve their goals (see, e.g., Yashar 1998, 31–32; Arce and Bellinger 2007). Following the 1992 autogolpe, Fujimori recentralized political authority and effectively created a system with few or no veto points, which, in turn, allowed for dramatic policy change. During this period, Fujimori enjoyed majority support in Congress and was able to minimize political dissension within his own party, thereby expediting legislative approval for policy initiatives drafted by the executive. This rigid discipline made Congress more isolated and less engaged with society, allowing Fujimori's majority to override any type of political opposition.

Fujimori also reversed the decentralization initiative that had created 13 regional governments in 1989. In so doing, he closed off any political space to potential challengers. Fujimori, moreover, was less willing to respond to societal grievances, particularly those wrought by the implementation of market policy reforms. Besides supporting his authoritarian tendencies, which have been widely documented (e.g., Carrión 2006; Conaghan 2005), these circumstances created a closed political system that muted the opposition from challengers.

The period of the Fujimori regime, indeed, was characterized by a general decline in strike activity, largely because the political environment delegitimated the use of protest and the economic conditions eroded and weakened collective action (Roberts 1996, 81; Tanaka 2002, 7). To be sure, a number of strikes and provincial revolts took place, albeit with limited success. In the early 1990s, for instance, unionized teachers organized a major strike. It lasted almost four months, and it ended largely from fatigue, as the government offered only minimal concessions (*Caretas* 2003). At the regional level, in 1997 the mayor of Huancavelica, Federico Salas, captured the national spotlight by making a weeklong horseback ride to Lima. He hoped to meet with Fujimori to discuss the problems of his city. But Fujimori refused to greet him, and Salas returned empty-handed (*Debate* 1997).[4]

In contrast to Fujimori's authoritarian regime, the democratic government of Toledo provided an environment that facilitated greater levels of mobilization. Unlike Fujimori after his autogolpe, Toledo did not have majority support in Congress, and disagreements within his party were customary. Indeed, many observers have noted that Toledo's strongest political opposition came from his own party, Perú Posible.

In 2002, Toledo restarted the decentralization process that the Fujimori regime had abruptly interrupted. The decentralization dispersed considerable political power from the central government to regional governments and created new opportunities for opposition parties to hold positions in those governments, outlets that Perú Posible ultimately failed to secure. Toledo also sought to relieve the dislocations associated with neoliberal reforms, thereby increasing the likelihood of success for mobilizations against those types of policies. In all, the more open access to political power—from Congress to Toledo's party to the newly created regional governments—enabled challengers to mobilize opposition and effectively resist further policy reforms.

Not surprisingly, Toledo's democratic government faced many mobilizations. According to the weekly magazine *Caretas*, in 2002 the city of Lima lived through at least 800 different protests, a statistic not seen in the previous decade (*Caretas* 2002a, reporting data from Ministerio del Interior 2002). On November 11 of that year, there were 24 demonstrations in Lima, or one protest for each hour of the day.

Outside the capital, in September 2001, peasants in Cuzco seized the city's airport, demanding the construction of an access road to Quillabamba (*Semana Económica* 2001). Later that month, residents of Puno arrived in Lima requesting that the government build through Puno, instead of Cuzco, the so-called intercoastal highway (carretera interoceanica) between Peru and Brazil (see Llosa 2003). The following month, 15 different mayors from 3 poverty-stricken regions, Junín, Huancavelica, and Ayacucho, arrived in Lima demanding more public works (*Caretas* 2001). In August 2002, rice producers in Tarapoto went on strike demanding a financial bailout from falling rice prices (*Caretas* 2002c). At least 13 different departments, mostly in the poorer regions of the country, harbor several active and latent conflicts involving local communities and transnational mining corporations over the extraction of natural resources. Perhaps no other protest was as powerful as the one that rocked Arequipa in June 2002, when citizens violently resisted the sale of the city's electric companies. Overall, this upsurge in localized protests was unprecedented (Ballón 2002).

Compared to the authoritarian regime of Fujimori, moreover, the Toledo government showed a willingness to accommodate societal and regional demands. In May 2003, nearly three hundred thousand unionized teachers sought higher wages and threatened to strike again. Government officials initially stated that fiscal constraints made it impossible to accommodate the teachers' demands (Gestión 2003b). The teachers decided to strike, and after almost four weeks of negotiations, the government offered a wage increase in the amount of one hundred Peruvian soles (Gestión 2003a).

The wage increase has not prevented teachers from organizing more strikes since then. Similarly, in Arequipa, the weeklong popular uprising successfully derailed the privatization of the city's electricity generators and triggered the resignations of various cabinet members. In 2006, weeks of protests and roadblocks by villagers in Cajamarca successfully halted the operations of Newmont, the largest gold-mining company in the world.

It is interesting that since 2000, Peruvians have held favorable attitudes toward these mobilizations: 84 percent of respondents to a poll approved of the teachers' strike (Apoyo 2003), and 58 percent approved of protest mobilizations in general (Apoyo 2002b). Moreover, 72 percent of respondents said that the antiprivatization revolt in Arequipa was justifiable, while 68 percent disapproved of the government's initial handling of the situation (Apoyo 2002a).[5] In contrast, business owners have decried the effects of these mobilizations on private property and the country's investment climate and demanded a firmer stance from the Toledo government (*El Comercio* 2007).

DECENTRALIZATION AND THE GEOGRAPHIC SEGMENTATION OF PROTEST

As noted by Tarrow (1998, 8), "periods of generalized disorder sometimes result in immediate repression, sometimes in reform, often in both." Seeking to placate the economic problems of peripheral provinces and to decentralize the state, in November 2002 Toledo called for the election of 25 regional governments. Each of these regions elected a president. The regional authorities were set up to complement the preexisting government structure, which involved 24 departments, 195 provinces, and 1,828 districts. Among the provinces, the port city of Callao enjoyed special status because of its economic importance. The regionalization project thus provided for political representation at the departmental level and also in Callao.

Decentralization in Peru is not new (Slater 1991; Contreras 2000). In the late 1980s, the government of Alan Garcia provided for the creation of 13 regions, but these subnational units were dismantled by the Fujimori regime following the 1992 autogolpe. Before the November 2002 regional elections, departments were considered administrative units of the central government, which appointed governors (prefectos) for each department. Since the early 1980s, in contrast, provincial and district-level mayors have been chosen at municipal elections every three years.[6]

Many observers agree that Toledo's decentralization initiative was highly disorganized and poorly improvised (Tanaka 2002, 25). In the view of economist Gonzales de Olarte (2002, 18), the hastiness of the decentralization process signaled "the impatience of a government eager to fight the problems of unemployment and development among an anxious population." Neither voters nor those seeking regional office knew what these subnational governments were originally supposed to do (*Perú Económico* 2002b). In reality, the laws that structure these new institutional openings for representation were approved months after the November election and continue to be revised. Moreover, less than a third of the population believed that regionalization would slow down the rise of social protests (Apoyo 2002c).[7]

Although many people welcomed the decentralization drive, it also dispersed considerable political power from the central government, creating veto points for challengers to mobilize opposition against the government in some cases, or to fight over the allocation of central government revenues in others. In other words, decentralization expanded political opportunities while adding to the geographic segmentation of societal conflicts. Neither the Toledo government, which started the decentralization process, nor the second Garcia government, which continues to support it, has been able to rein in the subnational governments, and thus the potential for conflict between central and regional authorities has increased. In the regional elections of 2002, for instance, Toledo's party, Perú Posible, won only one regional government, Callao. The bulk of the regional presidencies were won by APRA (12 regions) and independent movements (8 regions).[8] Yet APRA's electoral gains were also short-lived, and this underscores the continuing fragmentation of Peru's party system. In the regional elections of 2006, APRA's control was reduced to two regions, La Libertad and Piura. What's more, 23 different independent parties or movements gained control of the rest of the country's 25 regional governments.

This proliferation of regional parties and movements with no ties to national parties suggests that regional politicians generally are "loose cannons" and likely to exacerbate coordination problems with the central government.[9] Indeed, weak political parties and a poorly institutionalized party system like those in Peru are unable to channel popular sector demands to the state, much less respond to them effectively (Mainwaring and Scully 1995; Arce forthcoming). The lack of responsiveness may fuel social protest as groups pressure the formal political system from outside.

Decentralization in Peru has also served to territorialize a number of political conflicts. Based on the most recent report from Peru's Defensoría del Pueblo (2009, 4), the second-largest type of conflict in Peru today pits local residents against corrupt or inefficient local authorities. These conflicts represent 14 percent of all conflicts. Consistent with this information, in less than a year since the creation of these regions, 9 of the 25 regional governments have faced fraud and corruption investigations (*Correo* 2003; *El Comercio* 2003a). Regional authorities in Ancash, for instance, were charged with misappropriation of public funds. The charges related to the disappearance of emergency funds allocated by the Ministry of Finance (*El Comercio* 2003b). The regional president of Lima, Miguel Angel Mufarech, also faced a congressional inquiry because of electoral promises made to his creditors (*El Comercio* 2003c). In a taped telephone conversation, Mufarech stated that his election as president of the Lima region was a foregone conclusion and offered his creditors "thousands of business opportunities" to erase his US$240,000 debt. In the region of Apurimac, more than one thousand bags of cement donated by Cementos Lima to the regional government disappeared and were later found at the house of the regional president's mother. The regional president of Arequipa, Daniel Vera Ballón, faced a judicial investigation for diverting funds earmarked for investment to hiring personnel on the basis of patronage and nepotism. The regions of Ancash, Lima, Apurimac, and Arequipa were controlled by APRA. Given the absence of an effective framework of accountability, it appears that regionalization in Peru has also served to "decentralize corruption," similar to Kohl's observations in the Bolivian case (2002, 462).

Comparing the decentralization experience in countries such as Bolivia reveals that the recovery of provincial economies, which served as an impetus to promote decentralization in Peru, requires much more than fiscal transfers from the national government. Since the mid-1990s, Bolivia's central government has transferred 20 percent of government revenues to municipalities, many of them newly created. The central government has also devolved responsibilities in the areas of health, education, infrastructure, and culture (Grindle 2000). Since 1999, however, the country has been paralyzed by a wave of sectoral strikes and localized protests; the "water war" in Cochabamba was perhaps the most visible (Nickson and Vargas 2002; Assies 2003).

While teachers and the national police demanded higher wages, coca leaf farmers protested U.S.-sponsored eradication programs. In most cases, the government of Hugo Banzer gave in: the national police gained pay raises, indigenous groups obtained farming concessions, and the Cochabamba water privatization was rolled back. Faced with large-scale protests, Banzer "showed great restraint," largely to "overcome his old reputation for brutality garnered when he ruled as a military dictator in the 1970s" (*New York Times* 2000). The government of Gonzalo Sánchez de Lozada (2002–3) encountered nothing but organized discontent by people fed up with neoliberal reforms (Barr 2005; *New York Times* 2003). In October 2003, a month of continuous social protests that left a death toll of more than 70 people forced President Sánchez de Lozada to resign from office.

Referring to the current cycle of protest in Bolivia, Barr (2005, 70) notes, "The demands of farmers, teachers, miners, police, retirees, and other protesters have not been of an ideological or esoteric sort, but have reflected very concrete concerns about economic issues and living conditions." As in Peru, the diversity of groups taking to the streets in Bolivia points to changes in the repertoire of social protest, in which traditional, class-based collective action has steadily declined. In its place, diverse new social actors and new forms of protest have emerged to take the lead in popular resistance efforts. Geographically segmented conflicts are thus part and parcel of a widespread rejection of neoliberal policies and their lingering effects. The top-down manner in which neoliberal economic policies have been designed and implemented has exacerbated the sense of exclusion, which has undoubtedly contributed to a resurgence of protest behavior. In some cases, governments appear to have little room to maneuver.

While the transition from Fujimori to Toledo made the political context more prone to mobilization, the economy of the region of Arequipa stagnated and declined, with an outmigration of businesses and jobs beginning in the mid-1990s. These economic losses were important in mobilizing citizens across different sectors of society.

THE AREQUIPAZO

By the end of the 1990s, the province of Arequipa had the highest rate of unemployment in the country, averaging 15 percent (*Perú Económico* 2001). On average, the province's GDP as a share of the country's GDP declined from 6 percent in the 1991–95 period to 5 percent in the 1996–2000 period. Specifically, Arequipa's Human Development Index dropped from a 0.695 score in 1997 to 0.635 in 2000; the latter figure was only slightly better than the 0.633 score registered in 1993 (PNUD 2002).[10]

In the 1990s, during the heyday of neoliberalism, important local industries in search of bigger markets and profits gradually began to move their production facilities to the capital city, Lima, and the shift contributed to Arequipa's high unemployment rate. Companies that moved to the capital included Aceros Arequipa S.A. (steel manufacturer), Cervesur (brewer), and Leche Gloria (milk-processing plant). These companies were icons of a distinct local identity, so their exodus to Lima was an indication of, as well as a contributor to, the weakening of the provincial economy. The provincial mayor at the time of the Arequipazo, Juan Manuel Guillén, later remarked, "Like the great majority of Peruvians, we were only witnesses to this process" (2003). Other economic and political forces also contributed to the eventual mobilization.

Economic Conditions

Credit allocation was another indicator of the contraction of productive activities in Arequipa. In an action it considered necessary to sustain macroeconomic discipline, in the early 1990s the Fujimori government liquidated a number of decentralized state development banks in agriculture, manufacturing, and mining, thereby leaving credit allocation decisions to revolve entirely around the private sector. Arequipa's share of total private lending in the country during this period was approximately 5 percent. By the early 2000s, credit allocation in the region had shrunk to 2.5 percent. In contrast, Lima's share of private lending increased from 83 percent in 1990 to 87 percent in 2002 (Superintendencia de Banca y Seguros 2004). Arequipa is the region with the second-highest percentage of private credit allocation after Lima.

While Lima has historically received much of the stock of private lending (Caravedo Molinari 1988, 24), this pattern was augmented considerably by the fusion of various provincial banks, such as Banco del Sur and Banco Regional del Norte, with larger banks from the capital. Even though new and larger banks now operate in the regions, moreover, credit decisions for cities like Arequipa are actually made in Lima (*Perú Económico* 2001).

The sheer size of Lima's economy may well explain the mass departure of local companies and the further concentration of private lending in the capital. Compared to the rest of the country, Lima clearly provides better infrastructure facilities, services, and human capital, among other factors.[11] However, it is also evident that provincial politicians like Arequipa's Guillén lacked the policy tools to counteract this recentralization of productive activities. The economic recession of the late 1990s further exacerbated these conditions.

Historical Legacies

The 2002 revolt shares a number of similarities with an earlier uprising that took place in the mid-1950s, suggesting the importance not only of economic conditions but also of historical continuities. In the mid-1950s, a broad array of actors, including merchants from the local chamber of commerce, members of the local lawyers' guild, university students, and railroad workers, coalesced under the Frente Unico de Defensa (FUD) and fought collectively against the policies of the regime of Manuel A. Odría (1948–56). Caravedo Molinari (1978, 105–25) notes that Odría's "liberal policies," such as export-led growth, led to serious economic dislocations in the region of Arequipa and further concentration of industrial activities in Lima.

Arequipa's local bourgeoisie played an important role during that uprising. They helped identify and define collective grievances (for example, centralization), ascribe responsibility (e.g., to the Odría regime), and prescribe a solution (e.g., collective resistance).[12] Local chamber of commerce members even agreed to pay the wages and salaries of employees and workers who participated in the protest (Caravedo Molinari 1978, 139).

The provincial revolt of 2002 was also a response to the implementation of market policies and to some of the same economic problems that surfaced in the aftermath of Odría's "liberal policies." However, whereas the 2002 uprising was also popularly widespread, the popular appeal of the city's local bourgeoisie of the 1950s had clearly disappeared by the late 1990s. Residents of Arequipa quickly rejected the last-minute proprivatization endorsement made by the local chamber of commerce (Ballón 2003). More important, it was local politicians, rather than the local business elite, who helped rearticulate the shared regional identity against neoliberalism in 2002.

Political Context

Before discussing the popular revolt in Arequipa, a few words are in order on the political context preceding Toledo's rise to power. Born in the impoverished region of Ancash, President Toledo raised hopes for the possibility of lessening the economic problems of peripheral provinces. Toledo's political campaign pledged to create jobs to relieve the unemployment wrought by neoliberalism.

During the Fujimori regime, furthermore, Arequipa's economic deterioration had already taken a toll on the relationship between the capital and the province. Mayor Guillén was a staunch critic of neoliberalism and Fujimorismo. To name but one example, in 1997, when Fujimori came to Arequipa to inaugurate a new 60,000-seat stadium, the president could say only a few words, as he was widely booed by local residents. Not surprisingly, Arequipa's residents welcomed the collapse of the Fujimori regime in 2000 and endorsed Toledo. In Arequipa, Toledo defeated Fujimori in the first round of the presidential election of 2000, and Garcia in the first and second rounds of the presidential election of 2001.

On the campaign trail, Toledo told residents of Arequipa that the city's electric companies would not be sold to outsiders. Toledo subsequently signed a document indicating just that (Vargas Gutiérrez 2002). According to Guillén, Toledo's gesture led to the expectation that the relationship between Lima and Arequipa would improve and that the centralized, autocratic imposition of market reforms that had damaged the provincial economy was a thing of the past (Guillén 2003).

The Uprising

These expectations proved to be short-lived when Toledo, once elected president, decided to privatize these companies, offering no explanation for the course change. Resistance to the sale began to build as early as April 2002, and local authorities initiated a judicial process seeking to prevent the privatization from taking place. By early June, more than a dozen city mayors, led by Guillén, went on a hunger strike. Further complicating the political scenario, in the days before the bidding (June 14), Toledo announced that the privatization would take place despite the popular discontent.

The interior minister, Fernando Rospigliosi, reportedly said that only a small minority of "beggars" opposed the privatization initiative.[13] The minister of justice, Fernando Olivera, threatened to open an internal administrative process against the judges who had blocked the government's plan. In many ways, the Toledo government reproduced the authoritarian ways of the Fujimori regime, but in a context where politics became more liberalized and with a livelier and freer press than in the 1990s. The remarks made by various government officials simply added to the popular sentiment against the privatization decision. In the streets, thousands of local residents chanted, "Now let them say that we are a minority" (Abora que digan que somos minoría).

More important, Mayor Guillén questioned the alleged benefits of privatization. As he put it later, "privatizations have not reduced poverty; instead they have increased unemployment, utility prices, and corruption" (2003). Certainly, unlike the privatizations of the early 1990s, the divestitures of Arequipa's Egasa and Egasur did not enjoy a "favorable public mood" (Manzetti 1999, 18), thus complicating state goals.

In the judicial process that blocked the privatization, local authorities questioned the legality of the sale itself, claiming that the central government did not actually own the electric companies. Guillén also noted that many of the existing electric connections had been either paid for by beneficiaries themselves or partly subsidized by the municipality of Arequipa, which oversaw those companies. In other words, the proposed privatization did not distinguish the generation of electricity from its distribution. The Belgian company Tractebel, the only bidder in the auction, would have gained exclusive rights to all of the city's electricity. The granting of the distribution rights to outsiders like Tractebel thus denoted a form of expropriation, and this expropriation would have been similar to the one from the aborted privatization of water in Bolivia's Cochabamba. The residents of Cochabamba had also built wells and water networks through cooperatives. If the privatization process had gone forward, it would have given the U.S.-based Bechtel Corporation, the sole bidder in that process, exclusive rights to all the city's water (Finnegan 2002).

Having overwhelmingly supported Toledo, residents of Arequipa now vowed to overthrow him with demonstrations. As in the cacerolazos in Argentina, when people took to the streets banging pots and pans in protest, residents of Arequipa did the same. Recalling an old custom, others urged the ringing of church bells from the city's main cathedral, calling people to take action. Throughout the city, the Peruvian flag appeared above many houses as a sign of solidarity with the protest.

The demonstration succeeded. Arequipans rolled back the state of emergency imposed, not least by tumbling Toledo's 11-month-old cabinet. In late 2002, a judicial ruling declared that the electric companies were owned by the province of Arequipa (Paredes 2002, 46), effectively ending any central government plan to auction off these companies.

Arequipans simply felt betrayed by Toledo, who had promised a more participatory, decentralizing approach (Tanaka 2002, 24). The government's failure to take into account the provincial social discontent simply replicated the centralized, autocratic imposition of economic reforms, which, by the end of the 1990s, were already widely discredited. Yet the Arequipazo was not an isolated protest event. Other significant mobilizations against neoliberalism were equally visible and had a comparable economic impact.

OTHER MOBILIZATIONS AGAINST FOREIGN DIRECT INVESTMENT

One area of contention developed around the mining industry. As a consequence of Fujimori's liberalization and privatization schemes, mining investment in Peru increased fivefold during the 1990s. In 1992 alone, mining companies sought more land claims than they had in the previous 15 years (Bury 2002). Mining, furthermore, represents approximately 15 percent of all the foreign direct investment that has flooded Peru since Fujimori (INEI 2005, 847). The strong emphasis placed on foreign direct investment in Peru's economic restructuring made mining a very attractive industry.

Transnational mining companies responded very favorably to this change in economic policies; 11 of the world's top 20 mining corporations now have operations in Peru (Bury 2002, 6). Due to the geographic location of mining, which takes place in the highlands, this booming industry has had a dramatic impact on the rural population, some of Peru's poorest citizens. Given the detrimental environmental effects of mining, it is no wonder that the transnational mining companies operating in Peru's highlands have repeatedly come under siege by rural, national, and transnational protesters. Indeed, this is the most common type of social conflict in Peru today (Defensoría del Pueblo 2009).

While these conflicts are geographically segmented, they have a high profile and economic impact. Furthermore, the link between foreign direct investment—a clear indicator of the trend toward globalization and economic liberalization—and protest is indisputable. Several of these conflicts, led by local villagers, have halted a number of mining activities. Most of them have taken place since Fujimori left office in 2000.

Reports from the Fraser Institute (2001–7) confirm the impact of these mobilizations. The Fraser Institute conducts an annual survey of metal mining and exploration companies to assess how mineral endowments and public policy factors, such as taxation and regulation, affect exploration investment. The survey provides a couple of indexes: the Policy Potential Index (PPI) and the Mineral Potential Index (MPI). These indexes serve as a report card to governments on how attractive their policies are from the point of view of an exploration manager. In the 2005–6 survey, for instance, the MPI index placed Peru at the top of the sample of 64 countries, suggesting that the sheer potential of the country's mineral resources was extremely high. In contrast, the PPI index—which takes into account, among other things, the presence of political stability and societal conflicts—has consistently dropped since 2003 (see figure 2).[14]

In almost all cases, protests have been sparked by mining accidents that have fueled longstanding fears of environmental degradation, or by mining companies' failure to live

Figure 2. Peru's Policy Potential Index for Mining

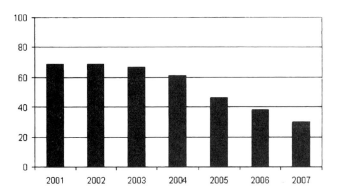

Source: Frasier Institute 2001–7. The policy potential index reports a ranking score of policy attractiveness from the perspective of mineral exploration managers. The measure is normalized ranking score ranging from 0 to 100, where 100 is the best score.

up to their social investment commitments. Some of the larger protests have been orchestrated by local and transnational social networks, ranging from peasants and community groups to international NGOs, such as Oxfam. Each of the following examples shows how local resistance to large transnational mining companies has been at least partly successful at reducing the impact of mining on local communities.[15]

The most noteworthy protest events against mining have taken place in Cajamarca Province in northwest Peru. The Denver-based Newmont Mining Company, the world's largest mining company, saw a number of protests at its Yanacocha mine between 1999 and 2006, some of which turned violent.[16] Conflict broke out at Yanacocha in December 1999 when more than six thousand local residents blocked the entrance to the mine, protesting against the environmental and social costs of mining activity (Bury 2002, 10). According to survey data gathered by Bury (2002, 13), locals were most concerned about water pollution, reduced water flow, and social ills that came with mining boom communities, such as prostitution, crime, and debt problems.

In Bury's survey, respondents who said that their water resources were affected were more than twice as likely to engage in protest activity as other respondents (Bury 2002, 12). Local fears of water pollution appear to be validated by international NGOs. In 1999 alone, Newmont was charged more than 159 times by the World Health Organization for violating clean water practices (Bury 2002). Negative perceptions were further fueled in June 2000, when a transportation company contracted by Newmont spilled poisonous mercury along 25 miles of road. Contention came to a head once again in September 2004, when Newmont began prospecting on the Cerro Quilish mountain. For a full month, thousands of protesters blocked the mine entrance, forcing Newmont to use helicopters to continue operations. Reports indicate that protests continued despite the presence of more than 150 special operations officers, who used tear gas, arrested a number of protesters, and even shot one in the leg (Perlez and Bergman 2005).

The same month, a regionwide strike was carried out, organized by antimining protesters and Father Marco Arana and his Grufides organization, which receives international support from Oxfam. Ultimately, protest efforts succeeded at preventing Newmont from mining on Cerro Quilish mountain, and the company's license to do so was revoked. In December 2004, three provinces in the region were brought to a stand-still by another regionwide protest against mining. In late August 2006, Newmont was forced to shut down production for a full day due to a blockade led by farmers. Contentious activity has continued at Yanacocha to this day.

Violent protests began at the Tambo Grande mine in the northern province of Piura in February 2001 (Muradian et al. 2003) when about five thousand people "stormed the company's offices, burning machinery and destroying models of houses for relocating people" (Muradian et al. 2003, 780). A protest leader was killed by gunshot one month later. A number of groups opposed the mining project there, including the archbishop of the diocese of Piura and the Front for Defense of Tambo Grande (Muradian et al. 2003, 780). In 2002, a straw poll funded by Oxfam UK showed that 94 percent of voters from Tambo Grande were against the project. International NGOs involved in the conflict included Oxfam America, Oxfam UK, the Mineral Policy Center, the Environmental Mining Council of British Columbia, and the Friends of the Earth from Costa Rica and Ecuador (Muradian et al. 2003, 780).

A survey conducted by Muradian et al. (2003, 783) found local residents fearful of the environmental impact of the proposed project; 85 percent were against the project, 46 percent did not trust the government to enforce environmental laws, and 47 percent believed that pollution levels would be very high. Protests continued in June 2002, when more than one thousand villagers from all over Peru mobilized in Lima against the Tambo Grande project. Another three-day protest took place in November 2003 at Tambo Grande. Protests continued until the project was finally abandoned in 2005. Operated by Canada's Manhattan Minerals Company, Tambo Grande was permanently shut down in February of that year; Manhattan Minerals cited a lack of funding due to ongoing protests.

In late May 2005, one of the most respectable multinational mining companies operating in Peru, BHP Billiton (an Anglo-Australian company and the world's third-largest mining company) was forced to halt operations at its Tintaya copper mine for a month due to continuous peasant protests and raids on the site. About two thousand protesters actually took over the world's third-largest copper mine for a brief period. At least three thousand demonstrators opposed BHP Billiton's plan to open a new tailings operation, which, villagers believed, would poison water supplies. Protesters were also unhappy with the amount of community investment BHP Billiton was putting into the region; they charged that BHP Billiton had not lived up to its promises. BHP Billiton tried to settle with protesters by offering an investment package worth US$330,000 per year, but the effort failed. Repeated protests apparently forced BHP Billiton to sell its Tintaya mine in May 2006 to another mining company, the Swiss-based Xstrata.

These conflicts over mining illustrate the paradoxical effect of neoliberalism to simultaneously debilitate certain types of popular resistance while activating others. They also challenge the conventional wisdom that protest is so difficult to organize in rural areas that it should not be expected. Ultimately, these conflicts suggest that the locus of protest activity has changed.

CONCLUSIONS

Since the early 1990s, Peru has been experimenting with market-oriented economic reforms. These reforms succeeded in restoring macroeconomic stability and reigniting growth. The atomization literature associates marketization with depoliticization, whereby societal actors are presumed to be passive recipients of painful economic reforms. Consistent with recent cross-national empirical studies (e.g., Arce and Bellinger 2007), this case study challenges these assumptions. Economic liberalization has repoliticized collective political activity by altering the traditional pattern of class-based organizing. Diverse new social actors have emerged to take the lead in popular resistance efforts. As this chapter has documented, market policies have sparked a number of geographically segmented mobilizations against Peru's market-oriented policies and programs, often having an impact on national policies. Future research ought to explore the implications of this new pattern of organizing and mobilizing for meeting the pressing needs of the region's poor.

Contrary to the state-centric literature on the politics of economic reform, moreover (e.g., Haggard and Kaufman 1995), the central lesson of the current round of societal mobilization in Peru is that national policy decisions can no longer be made exclusively by the legislative and executive branches of government, but must be conducted in consultation with civil society. The societal protests constitute an explicit rejection of the decisions being made by democratic actors and institutions. All together, these localized protests represent society's "protective countermovement" (Polanyi 1944) in response to the efforts to create a market society.

Future research should also examine the spatial distributional consequences of economic liberalization, a topic that cross-national studies continue to ignore. In the Peruvian case, growing disparities among regions apparently were important in framing and mounting successful collective political activity. The Toledo government reinstituted a decentralized structure in an effort to revamp peripheral economies. The decentralization process has indeed changed the locus where protest takes place; and at least until very recently, has encouraged an increase in mobilizations and protests. As this chapter has shown, the rise in mobilizations signals a major shift in the structure of political opportunity that has allowed for greater use of protest. If the decentralization drive stagnates, these subnational governments could also serve to further "territorialize" discontent with neoliberal economic policies, as recently seen in Bolivia.

NOTES

1 In this study the terms market reform and neoliberal reform are used interchangeably, implying policies that seek to reduce state intervention in the economy. Examples include trade liberalization, privatization of state enterprises, and domestic and international financial liberalization.

2 According to Toledo's former vice president, David Waisman, the government lost much of its authority when former prime minister Roberto Daniño, anticipating the potential conflict in Arequipa, decided to go to Washington in the days immediately preceding the announcement of the privatizations (*El Comercio* 2004). The government appeared to be divided, and subsequently, the blame for the privatization process was directed at President Toledo.

3 For a strong distinction between institutionalized and noninstitutionalized forms of political activity, see Huntington 1968, 196.

4 Fujimori subsequently co-opted Salas, making him prime minister in 2000.

5 The questions read as follows: ¿Aprueba o desaprueba usted la huelga del SUTEP? ¿Diría usted que aprueba o desaprueba los movimientos de protesta en general? ¿Usted diría que las protestas en Arequipa con la privatización de Egasa y Egesur estaban justificadas o no estaban justificadas? ¿Aprueba o desaprueba la manera cómo el gobierno enfrentó inicialmente la crisis en Arequipa?

6 Historically, provinces and districts were fiscally dependent on the central government. These subnational units accounted for 6 percent of the country's revenue base and 12 percent of its spending. For further discussion, see World Bank 2003; *Perú Económico* 2002a.

7 The question read, ¿Cree que las protestas sociales aumentaran, seguirán igual o disminuirán a partir de la regionalización? In the responses, 31 percent said that social protests would increase, 34 percent that they would be about the same, and 25 that they would decrease.

8 As Toledo put it, "in the regional elections [APRA] ate us alive" (en las elecciones regionales [el APRA] nos han comido con zapatos y todo) (*La República* 2003).

9 I thank an anonymous reviewer for this suggestion.

10 The Human Development Index is a summary composite index that measures a country's average achievements in three basic aspects of human development: longevity (life expectancy), knowledge (literacy), and a decent standard of living (GDP per capita).

11 Lima's GDP as a share of the country's GDP is approximately 50 percent. Gonzales de Olarte (2000) discusses economic recentralization during Fujimori's wave of neoliberal reforms.

12 On Arequipa's business elite, see Hammergren 1974; Durand 1982.

13 At the time of the protests, Rospigliosi was reported to have said, "Solo unos mil muertos de hambre se oponen a las privatizaciones en Arequipa." Later it was reported that Rospigliosi did not utter those words (see *Caretas* 2002b).

14 The Policy Potential Index is a composite index that measures the effects on exploration of government policies, including uncertainty concerning the administration, interpretation, and enforcement of existing regulations; environmental regulations; regulatory duplication and inconsistencies; taxation; uncertainty concerning native land claims and protected areas; infrastructure; socioeconomic agreements; political stability; labor issues; geological database; and security.

15 The information about these mining protests was taken from *The Economist* 2005; Griffin 2006a, b; Perlez and Bergman 2005; Weitzman 2005, 2006; and Teh-White 2005.

16 Minera Yanacocha's stakeholders include Denver-based Newmont Gold Co. (51 percent); Compañía de Minas Buenaventura, a Peruvian company (44 percent); and the International Finance Corporation, a member of the World Bank Group (5 percent). The IFC's stake in Yanacocha was also an important point of contention for global activists. I thank an anonymous reviewer for raising this point.

REFERENCES

Apoyo S.A. 2002a. Informe de opinión. July.
——. 2002b. Informe de opinión. August.
——. 2002c. Informe de opinión. December.
——. 2003. Informe de opinión. May.
Arce, Moisés. Forthcoming. Parties and Social Protest in Latin America's Neoliberal Era, *Party Politics.*
Arce, Moisés, and Paul T. Bellinger, Jr. 2007. Low-Intensity Democracy Revisited: The Effects of Economic Liberalization on Political Activity in Latin America. *World Politics* 60, 1 (October): 97–121.
Arce, Moisés, and Roberta Rice. 2009. Societal Protest in Post-stabilization Bolivia. *Latin American Research Review* 44, 1: 88–101.
Assies, Willem. 2003. David versus Goliath in Cochabamba: Water Rights, Neoliberalism, and the Revival of Social Protest in Bolivia. *Latin American Perspectives* 30, 3 (May): 14–36.
Auyero, Javier. 2002. Los cambios en el repertorio de la protesta social en la Argentina. *Desarrollo Económico* 42, 166 (July–September): 187–210.
Ballón, Eduardo. 2002. El toledismo y el movimiento social. In *Perú hoy, Toledo: a un año de gobierno*, ed. Eduardo Ballón. Lima: Centro de Estudios y Promoción del Desarrollo DESCO.
——. 2003. DESCO investigator. Author interview. Lima, November 7.
Barr, Robert. 2005. Bolivia: Another Uncompleted Revolution. *Latin American Politics and Society* 47, 3 (Fall): 69–90.
Bury, Jeffrey. 2002. Livelihoods, Mining, and Peasant Protests in the Peruvian Andes. *Journal of Latin American Geography* 1, 1: 3–19.
Calderón, Fernando, and Alicia Szmukler. 2000. *La política en las calles: política, urbanización y desarrollo.* La Paz: CERES/Universidad Andina.
Caravedo Molinari, Baltasar. 1978. *Desarrollo desigual y lucha política en el Perú 1948–1956: la burguesía arequipeña y el estado peruano.* Lima: Instituto de Estudios Peruanos.

——. 1988. *Ciudad y región: los límites del nuevo descentralismo*. Lima: M. J. Bustamante de la Fuente.

Caretas (Lima). 2001. *En octubre no hay milagros*. October 4.

——. 2002a. *¿El que no llora no mama?* December 5.

——. 2002b. *El volcán Characato*. June 27.

——. 2002c. *!Qué calor hace en Tarapoto!* August 2.

——. 2003. *Huelgan comentarios*. May 22.

Carrión, Julio F., ed. 2006. *The Fujimori Legacy: The Rise of Electoral Authoritarianism in Peru*. University Park: Pennsylvania State University Press.

Conaghan, Catherine M. 2005. *Fujimori's Perú: Deception in the Public Sphere*. Pittsburgh: University of Pittsburgh Press.

Contreras, Carlos. 2000. Centralismo y descentralismo en la historia del Perú independiente. Working Paper no. 127. Lima: Instituto de Estudios Peruanos.

Correo (Lima). 2003. Nueve presidentes regionales involucrados en actos irregulares. November 10.

Debate (Lima). 1997. Obtener poder para resolver problemas. October-November: 6–10.

Defensoría del Pueblo. 2009. *Conflictos sociales conocidos por la Defensoría del Pueblo al 30 de abril del 2009*. Informe No. 62. Lima: Defensoría del Pueblo, Dirección de la Unidad de Conflictos Sociales.

Delamata, Gabriela. 2002. De los "estallidos" provinciales a la generalización de las protestas en Argentina. *Nueva Sociedad* 182 (November-December): 121–38.

Durand, Francisco. 1982. Arequipa: clases sociales, regionalismo e industrialización. Working Paper. Lima: Pontificia Universidad Católica del Perú.

The Economist. 2005. Halting the Rush Against Gold. February 5.

——. 2008. To the Barricades: The Politics of Non-stop Protest. December 4.

El Comercio. (Lima). 2003a. Involucran a 6 presidentes de región en hechos irregulares. July 14.

——. 2003b. Juzgado cita a ex gerente Unzueta. July 9.

——. 2003c. Mufarech ofreció "favores" antes de ganar elección. July 10.

——. 2004. Imputan a Dañino la pérdida de autoridad. May 10.

——. 2007. Las protestas ocasionan al país 200 millones de soles diarios en perdidas. July 12.

Finnegan, William. 2002. Leasing the Rain. *The New Yorker*, April 8.

Fraser Institute. 2001–2007. *Annual Survey of Mining Companies*. Vancouver, BC: Fraser Institute.

Garay, Candelaria. 2007. Social Policy and Collective Action: Unemployed Workers, Community Associations, and Protest in Argentina. *Politics and Society* 35, 2 (June): 301–28.

Gestión (Lima). 2003a. Mandatario: se duplicará sueldos de maestros al término de mi gobierno. May 14.

——. 2003b. Silva Ruete reitera: "no hay dinero" para aumento de sueldos a maestros. May 16.

Gonzáles de Olarte, Efraín. 2000. *Neocentralismo y neoliberalismo en el Perú*. Lima: Instituto de Estudios Peruanos-Consorcio de Investigación Económica.

——. 2002. Descentralización a la peruana. *Debate* 118 (December): 16–20.

Griffin, Greg. 2006a. Newmont Mining Begins to Close Perú Site over Protests. *Denver Post*, August 29.

——. 2006b. Newmont Mine in Peru Set to Reopen. *Denver Post*, August 30.

Grindle, Merilee S. 2000. *Audacious Reforms: Institutional Invention and Democracy in Latin America*. Baltimore: John Hopkins University Press.

Guillén, Juan Manuel. 2003. Former provincial mayor, Arequipa. Author interview. Arequipa, June 4.

Haggard, Stephan, and Robert Kaufman. 1995. *The Political Economy of Democratic Transitions*. Princeton: Princeton University Press.

Hammergren, Linn. 1974. *Politics in the Periphery: A Study of National Integration and the Development of Local Political Organization*. Ph.D. diss., University of Wisconsin, Madison.

Hochstetler, Kathryn. 2006. Rethinking Presidentialism: Challenges and Presidential Falls in South America. *Comparative Politics* 38, 4: 401–18.

Huntington, Samuel P. 1968. *Political Order in Changing Societies*. New Haven: Yale University Press.

INEI (Instituto Nacional de Estadística e Informática). 2005. *Perú: compendio estadístico 2005*. Lima: INEI.

Inter-American Development Bank (IDB). 2005. *The Politics of Policies: Economic and Social Progress in Latin America, 2006 Report*. Washington, DC: IDB.

Kohl, Benjamin. 2002. Stabilizing Neoliberalism in Bolivia: Popular Participation and Privatization. *Political Geography* 21: 449–72.

Kurtz, Marcus J. 2004. The Dilemmas of Democracy in the Open Economy: Lessons from Latin America. *World Politics* 56, 2 (January): 262–302.

La República (Lima). 2003. Ustedes no van a dejar que el APRA tenga el poder. June 26.

Laserna, Roberto, and Jesús Ortega. 2003. Reflexiones sobre violencia, conflicto y dialogo social en Bolivia. Boletín 8. Cochabamba: Centro de Estudios de la Realidad Económica y Social (CERES).

Llosa, Eleana. 2003. La batalla por la carretera interoceánica en el sur peruano: ¿localismo o descentralismo? Working Paper no. 129. Lima: Instituto de Estudios Peruanos.

López-Maya, Margarita. 2002. Venezuela After the Caracazo: Forms of Protest in a Deinstitutionalized Context. *Bulletin of Latin American Research* 21, 2: 199–218.

López-Maya, Margarita, and Luis E. Lander. 2004. The Struggle for Hegemony in Venezuela: Poverty, Protest, and the Future of Democracy. In *Politics in the Andes: Identity, Conflict, Reform*, eds. Jo-Marie Burt and Philip Mauceri. Pittsburgh: University of Pittsburgh Press. 207–27.

Lucero, José Antonio. 2001. Crisis and Contention in Ecuador. *Journal of Democracy* 12, 2 (April): 59–73.

Mainwaring, Scott, and Timothy R. Scully. 1995. Introduction: Party Systems in Latin America. In *Building Democratic Institutions: Party Systems in Latin America*, ed. Mainwaring and Scully. Stanford: Stanford University Press. 1–34.

Manzetti, Luigi. 1999. *Privatization South American Style*. Oxford: Oxford University Press.

Maxfield, Sylvia. 1997. *Gatekeepers of Growth: The International Political Economy of Central Banking in Developing Countries*. Princeton: Princeton University Press.

McAdam, Doug, Sidney Tarrow, and Charles Tilly. 2001. *Dynamics of Contention*. New York: Cambridge University Press.

Ministerio del Interior. 2002. Memoria del Servicio Nacional de Inteligencia del Ministerio del Interior. Lima: Ministerio del Interior.

Muradian, Roldan, Joan Martínez-Alier, and Humberto Correa. 2003. International Capital versus Local Population: The Environmental Conflict of the Tambo-grande Mining Project, Peru. *Society and Natural Resources* 16: 775–92.

Murillo, María Victoria, and Lucas Ronconi. 2004. Teachers' Strikes in Argentina: Partisan Alignments and Public-sector Labor Relations. *Studies in Comparative International Development* 39, 1 (Spring): 77–98.

New York Times. 2000. Bolivia Makes Key Concessions to Indians. October 7: A8.

———. 2003. Unrest Clouds Bolivian Leader's Future. March 10: A6.

Nickson, Andrew, and Claudia Vargas. 2002. The Limitations of Water Regulation: The Failure of the Cochabamba Concession in Bolivia. *Bulletin of Latin American Research* 21, 1: 99–120.

Nueva Mayoría. 2009. "Con 5608 cortes de ruta y vías públicas, el 2008 registró la mayor cantidad de cortes desde 1997." ⟨http://www.nuevamayoria.com/⟩ Accessed May 2009.

Paredes, Fernando. 2002. Gobernabilidad regional: preguntas desde Arequipa. *Economía y Sociedad* 46 (October): 44–48.

Perlez, Jane, and Lowell Bergman. 2005. Tangled Strands in Fight over Perú Gold Mine. *New York Times*, October 25.

Perú Económico. 2001. La "nevada" arequipeña. June. 19–20, 23.

———. 2002a. Lima = Perú. April. 7–8.

———. 2002b. Regionalización: un circo de múltiples pistas. November.

Polanyi, Karl. 1944. *The Great Transformation*. New York: Farrar and Rinehart.

Programa de las Naciones Unidas para el Desarrollo (PNUD, United Nations Development Program). 2002. *Informe sobre el desarrollo humano Perú 2002: aprovechando las potencialidades*. Lima: PNUD.

Przeworski, Adam. 1991. *Democracy and the Market: Political and Economic Reforms in Eastern Europe and Latin America*. Cambridge: Cambridge University Press.

Roberts, Kenneth M. 1996. Economic Crisis and the Demise of the Legal Left in Perú. *Comparative Politics* 29, 1 (October): 69–92.

Semana Económica (Lima). 2001. ¿El que no llora no mama? September 30: 3–4.

Slater, David. 1991. Regionalización en una época de crisis social: Perú, 1985–1990. *Revista Latinomericana de Estudios Urbano-Regionales* 17, 51: 33–41.

Superintendencia de Banca y Seguros. 2004. Data on regional credit allocation. ⟨www.sbs.gob.pe⟩ Accessed September 2004.

Tanaka, Martín. 2002. La dinámica de los actores regionales y el proceso de decentralización: ¿el despertar del letargo? Working Paper no. 125. Lima: Instituto de Estudios Peruanos.

Tarrow, Sidney. 1998. *Power in Movement: Social Movements and Contentious Politics*. Cambridge: Cambridge University Press.

Teh-White, Katherine. 2005. A Tale of Two Mines. *The Age,* July 14: 3.

Vargas Gutiérrez, José Luis. 2002. ¡Erupcionó Arequipa! *Quehacer* 136 (May–June): 72–77.

Weitzman, Hal. 2005. Mining Groups Struggle to Obtain "Social License" for Their Operations in Perú. *Financial Times* (London), June 4: 10.

——. 2006. Roof Caves in for Mining Groups in Perú. *Financial Times*, August 31: 21.

Wolff, Jonas. 2005. Ambivalent Consequences of Social Exclusion for Real-Existing Democracy in Latin America. *Journal of International Relations and Development* 8, 1: 58–87.

——. 2007. (De-)Mobilising the Marginalised: A Comparison of the Argentine Piqueteros and Ecuador's Indigenous Movement. *Journal of Latin American Studies* 39, 1 (February): 1–29.

World Bank. 2003. *Restoring Fiscal Discipline for Poverty Reduction in Perú: A Public Expenditure Review*. Washington, DC: World Bank.

Yashar, Deborah J. 1998. Contesting Citizenship: Indigenous Movements and Democracy in Latin America. *Comparative Politics* 31, 1 (October): 23–42.

Zermeño, Sergio. 1990. Crisis, Neoliberalism, and Disorder. In *Popular Movements and Political Change in Mexico*, ed. Joe Foweraker and Ann L. Craig. Boulder: Lynne Rienner.

Chapter 8

Globalization and Pension Reform in Latin America

Sarah M. Brooks

Since 1980, more than 29 governments around the world have implemented some form of market-oriented pension reform, or "privatization." Nearly a third of these reforms have been conducted in Latin America, where 10 governments had implemented some form of pension privatization by 2009. Although the specific design of pension privatizations has varied considerably across the region, this trend is striking as much for its geographic and temporal clustering as it is for the deeply transformative implications of the privatization measure, which fundamentally rewrites the basic social bargain of old age income protection in privatizing countries.

Pension privatization, moreover, is costly to implement, both in financial and political terms. Not only must governments impose new risks and costs on beneficiaries of traditional social insurance pension systems while offering only long-term and uncertain benefits, but they also must continue to finance current benefits owed to retirees, even as workers divert payroll contributions to their private pension accounts. Pension privatization is therefore far from a quick fix for ailing state pension systems; instead, it is a costly and perilous measure for any government, and particularly for the young democracies in Latin America.

A rich body of scholarly research has emerged to address the puzzle of why and how so many Latin American governments have privatized their national pension systems. For some scholars, the answer rests heavily on international financial pressures, which buffeted Latin American governments in the 1990s. This view holds, first, that global economic forces, such as trade competition and capital mobility, generate strong pressures on governments to lower domestic production costs and diminish inflation risks as a means to enhance trade competitiveness and attract foreign investment. It also underscores the financial rewards and punishments wielded as critical power resources by international financial institutions (IFIs). In both dimensions, globalization emerges as a powerful force pushing inexorably toward the adoption of more market-oriented reform, especially in the most capital-scarce nations.

This study affirms the importance of international economic forces in domestic political decisions about pension reform, but offers an alternative conceptualization of their role and ultimate impact on privatization decisions in Latin America. It argues that the most significant effects of global economic forces and IFIs have not been wielded through coercion; nor have they conduced strictly toward greater privatization in the most cash-poor nations. Instead, while global financial integration and IFI promotion of structural pension reform have combined most powerfully to enhance the attractiveness of private pension reform models, exposure to increasingly volatile international capital markets has created powerful obstacles to the adoption of this costly structural reform in the most cash-strapped nations.

Comparative analysis of the technocratic process of pension reform in Argentina and Brazil brings evidence to this argument. In the technocratic arena, state actors weigh the long-term goals of state action against short-term constraints on their proposed solutions. By focusing the analysis on just the technocratic component of the reform process, this study sets aside the broader social and political processes associated with institutional reform in order to isolate the arena in which global financial influences are likely to be most clearly defined. These countries also were selected in order to control for important factors shaping the influence of global economic forces, including country wealth and democratic status, while providing broad variation in the key factors expected to shape the intensity of global incentives and constraints on globalization.

In both Argentina and Brazil, government actors counted on extensive financial support from IFIs, such as the World Bank, while also facing strong pressures to attract and maintain the confidence of owners of increasingly footloose international capital. In both cases, however, it was the threat of punishment by private market actors that more powerfully influenced decisions on the final reform design. Paradoxically, by attending to the short-term concerns of global capital, reformers in both countries wound up limiting the extent of market orientation in proposed pension reform designs.

GLOBAL PRESSURES AND PENSION REFORM

The profound social and economic crises of the 1980s provide an important backdrop for understanding the ascent of pension reform to the top of political agendas in the 1990s. After decades of postwar expansion in coverage and generosity, Latin American pension systems fell on hard times following the 1980s debt crisis. Just as hyperinflation eroded any reserves that remained in ailing state pension funds, high unemployment, rising poverty, and social dislocation narrowed the contributory base for these systems while sharply raising demands for social services (Mesa-Lago 1989). At the same time, the ability of governments to respond to these needs was constrained by spending limits stipulated by orthodox stabilization plans. These plans, along with an array of market-based structural reforms, such as privatization, trade and financial liberalization, and deregulation, were prescribed by Washington-based international financial institutions as remedies to the macroeconomic problems gripping Latin America, catalyzing a region-wide shift toward integration with the global economy.

As liberalization proceeded, the once heavily protected Latin American economies confronted powerful market forces demanding greater efficiency and competitiveness, including cuts in labor costs through social policy reform (Dion 2006, 53–54; Kay 2000, 186). The enhanced factor mobility that attended trade and capital account liberalization also created new incentives for governments to cut social spending in order to diminish the risk of inflation, and thus to attract foreign investment (Dion 2006; Kaufman and Segura-Ubiergo 2001; Wibbels 2006). Indeed, the most radical pension privatizations in Latin America were enacted in precisely the countries that also adopted the deepest macroeconomic liberalization programs (Mesa-Lago 1997, 503). In light of these trends, global economic forces came to be seen by many analysts as an important catalyst behind the adoption of market-oriented pension reforms.

The financial leverage borne by IFIs also came to be viewed as a powerful catalyst of pension privatization in Latin America (Cruz-Saco and Mesa-Lago 1998; Huber and Stephens 2000, 19; Madrid 2005, 23–50). Chief among these was the World Bank, which provided financial, technical, and political support for pension privatization throughout the world (Kay 2000; Müller 2001, 69). For Huber and Stephens (2000, 19), IFIs, along with private business interests, "pushed and supported" capital-scarce governments to adopt pension privatization through the exercise of financial leverage—specifically, loan conditionality. Even where loans were not explicitly conditioned on pension privatization, scholars maintain, policymakers anticipated that IFI financial support depended on the adoption of a market-oriented pension reform (Kay 1999; Mesa-Lago and Müller 2002, 710). The ability to provide or withhold financial resources was said to have magnified the influence of IFIs in domestic policy debates over pension reform (Madrid 2005, 29). Huber and Stephens (2000, 19–20) sum up this view by stating, "It is essentially correct to argue, then, that globalization has been a major force behind the privatization of pension funds in Latin America."

Assessing International Pressures

There is good reason to take seriously the influence of economic integration and IFIs in the rapid ascent of pension privatization on reform agendas in Latin America. Not only did IFIs use policy-based conditions to advance the "first generation" of macroeconomic reforms, but policy-based lending in Latin America also rose considerably during the late 1980s and 1990s, just as the issue of pension privatization came to the fore (Mesa-Lago and Müller 2002, 710). Can we take this, however, as evidence either that Latin American governments were pressured or coerced to privatize, or that globalization has conducted strictly toward privatization? These claims are unsatisfying. For one thing, closer examination of lending patterns by the World Bank casts doubt on the notion that resource power became the institution's most effective instrument for promoting privatization. Not only has the bank been more active to support pension reform in countries that did not privatize than in countries that did—offering a greater number and more generous loans (Holzmann and Hinz 2005; World Bank 2005a), but in many cases, loan conditions associated with pension reform related more directly to the creation of legal infrastructure and social assistance benefits than to the creation of private systems (Deacon and Hulse 1997, 53).

Even where World Bank loans were granted to support pension privatization, we cannot be sure that domestic politicians did not desire such a reform for independent reasons, whether ideological or instrumental. Indeed, there is evidence that domestic coalitions of financial elites and government technocrats—even broad public opinion in some cases—turned against state pension systems as declining performance in the late 1980s eroded confidence in state institutions and in the broader state-led development model (Arce 2001; Kay 1999; Margheritis 2002; Müller 1999). Whereas Mesa-Lago and Müller (2002, 708) identify the main sponsors of pension privatization as domestic actors (mainly neoliberal technocrats, rather than international actors), other scholars suggest that governments sometimes sought policy conditions on IFI loans in order to gain leverage over domestic political opposition (Vreeland 2003, 321–43; Nelson 1996, 1551, 2004). Several Latin American governments, moreover, such as Argentina, Mexico, and Peru, embraced this reform well before the World Bank began actively to promote it in the mid-1990s (Nelson 2004; Queisser 2000).

Emphasis on the leverage exerted by the World Bank through its extension of loans and development assistance also may overstate the significance of these resources as a source of finance for Latin American governments. World Bank loans as a share of GDP in most Latin American countries are dwarfed by the vastly greater size and significance of private capital flows in Latin America, as illustrated in figures 1 and 2. If government actors were swayed by the resources or ideas proffered by powerful financial actors, then the punishing force of international financial markets in domestic politics must be taken seriously. Indeed, the liberalization of capital markets in the 1990s vastly magnified this punishing capacity, generating an ever-present threat of swift and massive capital

Figure 1. Brazil: External Debt to Private Market and World Bank (Current US$)

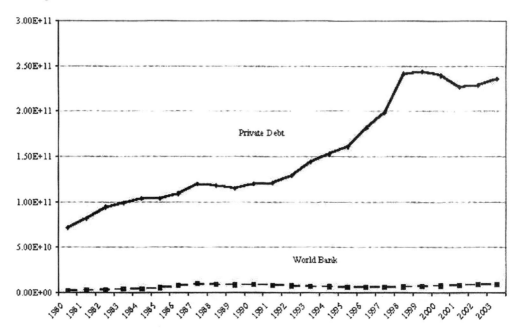

Figure 2. Argentina: External Debt to Private Market and World Bank (Current US$)

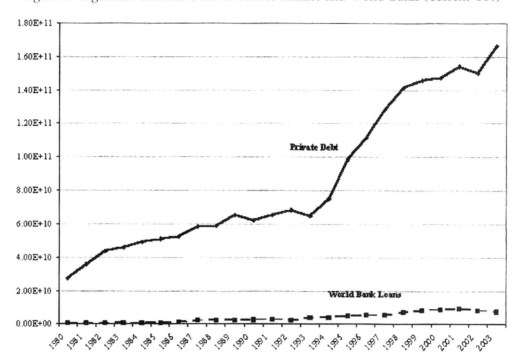

flight. This sanctioning capacity was demonstrated with devastating consequences in the 1995 Mexican peso crisis, which reverberated with capital flight throughout Latin America.

Close examination of capital market dynamics, however, suggests that financial integration has not just been a source of strict pressure for market-oriented pension reform; it has also generated powerful constraints on pension privatization efforts. Such constraints relate to the heavy financial toll imposed by this reform and the consequence of this cost for investor confidence in an economy. Indeed, pension privatization exacerbates rather than alleviates financial pressures created by deficitary pension systems in the short- to medium-term. This financial toll—the "transition cost" of privatization—arises as workers begin to divert payroll contributions from the state social insurance system to private pension funds, forcing the government to surrender its principal source of revenue with which to finance ongoing state pension liabilities.

In no case, moreover, have social sector loans from IFIs come close to covering the annual cost of transition to a private pension system, which in Chile exceeded 4 percent of GDP in the first decade after the reform. For owners of highly liquid assets, whose investment decisions in an economy may be revised daily or even hourly, it is precisely the short-term effects of pension privatization—including the widening of fiscal deficits or swelling of government debt—to which they will respond most forcefully. When the time horizon over which investors—and therefore government actors—weigh the merits of policy change is short, privatization's putative long-term benefits (such as raising domestic savings) may be heavily discounted.

Globalization thus entails much more than pressures for reform; it also carries the threat of swift punishment for governments that lose the confidence of external creditors. The critical question in regard to globalization's effect on decisions to enact pension privatization, then, is at what point this reform raises the risk of market punishment such that the near-term possibility of capital flight would outweigh the positive inducements associated with the measure's purported long-term benefits.

GLOBALIZATION'S DOUBLE BIND

A theoretical alternative to the view of global capital as a strict source of pressure for pension privatization might be based on the argument that IFIs were most influential in privatization processes through the exercise of "soft power" or attraction (Keohane and Nye 1998). By packaging and disseminating pension privatization as a policy tool to raise domestic savings and deepen capital markets, the World Bank, in particular, helped to make this reform attractive to governments in capital-scarce nations, such as many in Latin America, which suffered under the increasing cost of exposure to highly volatile capital flows. Attraction alone, however, cannot explain the adoption of this reform. For economic integration also generated powerful constraints on the ability of cash-strapped governments to privatize old age pension systems, the force of which varies with the domestic financial conditions of the government and with the impact of the pension reform on key indicators of sovereign creditworthiness, such as debt and deficit levels.

Attraction to Pension Privatization in Latin America

To understand how a common policy innovation came to be enacted in some countries but not others, we must look closely at the domestic processes through which such policy models are taken up, evaluated, or adopted. Technocratic processes serve as a critical gateway to structural reforms, and in this process, policy specialists play a pivotal role in shaping the political agenda. Before institutional reforms may be adopted, a new policy model must come to the attention of technocrats and must be perceived as an attractive option for reform. Once an attractive policy model is chosen for further consideration, issues of viability come to the fore. At this stage, short-term costs and constraints are weighed against the expected long-term gains of policy change.

The technocratic process is neither a one-shot decision nor simply a gradual win-nowing of alternatives; rather, discrete choices are made in this realm, and they often involve considerations weighed over very different time horizons. Whereas attraction to pension privatization may rest heavily on the measure's expected long-term implications, such as lowering the government financial role in pension provision and possibly raising domestic savings, consideration of the viability of this reform often revolves more closely around concerns about the model's near-term political and economic feasibility, particu-larly when market feedback to these reforms may be immediate. As Santiso (2003) has demonstrated, as the time horizons governing investor decisions in the 1990s narrowed, they imposed a similarly constricted temporality on government decision-making. For Latin American technocrats weighing alternative policy models, this meant anticipating the near-term effect of reform on investor confidence in their economy.

Two factors combined to make pension privatization highly attractive to many gov-ernment technocrats in Latin America. The first was the embedding of this model in a coherent set of ideas—indeed, a new paradigm—that provided intellectual and economic justifications for the reform. These ideas rested on claims of inherent failure of the state-centric model and associated privatization with macroeconomic ends, such as increased savings, growth, and capital market deepening. The packaging and dissemination of these ideas was spearheaded globally by the World Bank (Orenstein 2005), although other IFIs, along with Chilean economists and liberal think tanks, participated actively in its promotion. But the market-oriented paradigm in social protection did not hold the same allure for all governments. Rather, attraction was reinforced by the particular macroeco-nomic circumstances of many countries in the region, which combined chronically low growth and capital shortages with institutional crises that undermined the performance of, and political support for, traditional state pension systems.

Indeed, in the late 1980s, low levels of domestic savings and heavy reliance on foreign capital came to be seen by government technocrats as powerful constraints on domestic investment, and hence on growth, as well as a major source of the region's vulnerability to capital flight. Many Latin American technocrats therefore embraced the goal of diminishing their country's reliance on foreign savings as a means to achieve sustained growth (Solis Soberón and Villagómez 1997, 107–26). As these ideas began to gain ground, the 1981 pension privatization in Chile captured the international spotlight. That reform, decreed by the authoritarian regime of Augusto Pinochet, replaced the nation's traditional state-run pension system with a fully individualized private savings scheme in which the state would provide only a minimum pension guarantee to "top up" the accounts of workers whose lifetime savings failed to reach a minimal level. For most workers, however, pensions would derive solely from individual savings accumu-lated in privately managed retirement accounts.

International fanfare surrounded Chile's pension reform in the late 1980s as the nation's positive macroeconomic performance set it apart from its neighbors. As other Latin American economies endured prolonged contractions and outflows of savings, Chile's growth surged and domestic savings boomed. When prominent economists linked Chile's pension privatization to these positive macroeconomic outcomes, policymakers throughout the region took notice. Interest in Chile's pension reform therefore surged on the perceived links to the nation's strong macroeconomic performance, even though academic research questioned those links, and privatization was just one element of the country's broad move toward free-market reform (Kurtz 1999).

Nevertheless, when pension privatization was endorsed by the World Bank (1994) as a means to deepen local capital markets and increase private savings and growth, pension privatization secured a place in the new market-based "orthodoxy" (LoVuolo 1996; Müller 1999). In this sense, IFIs such as the World Bank played a critical role in the process of pension reform by shifting the terms of debate toward macroeconomic concerns (Müller 2001; see also Orenstein 2005). They did so, according to Müller, not through coercion or by threatening to withhold financial support but by offering "conceptual, technical and strategic knowhow" (Müller 2001, 69) to privatization's supporters. Peer diffusion reinforced the attraction to this model in Latin America. For Weyland (2005), it was the more "available" example provided by regional peers that accounted for the broad regional diffusion, superseding the influence of IFIs. Peer decisions also may have assured reformers that the very general set of ideas promoted by IFIs were both relevant and feasible in a country like their own (Brooks 2005).

Attraction to private pension reform models was also reinforced by the imperative of attracting and retaining inflows of savings to remonitize domestic financial sectors and spur growth. Indeed, while many economies of the region were long burdened by chronic capital shortages and low growth, the 1990s brought a new problem: the increasingly costly exposure to volatile international capital markets. As investment flows to emerging markets became ever more unstable in the 1990s, vulnerability to capital flight led many Latin American governments to prioritize structural reforms that were expected to raise domestic savings and thus diminish their exposure to precarious global capital flows (Brooks 2002; Madrid 2003; Mesa-Lago and Müller 2002).

Sending policy signals to maintain the confidence of those investors thus became a crucial policy priority. On this level, pension privatization had both positive and negative implications. On the positive side, this reform came to be seen as a costly, and therefore credible, signal of the government's commitment to playing by the market rules (Kay 2000). But privatization could also compromise government performance on key indicators of sovereign risk, such as debt and deficit ratios, and thus could also send negative signals to international markets, threatening punishment of reforming states.

Market-Based Constraints on Pension Privatization

Indeed, as capital mobility increased in the 1990s, market actors' loss of confidence in an investment decision could evoke swift and massive capital flight from an economy. Confidence in the creditworthiness of a capital-importing government could be lost, for example, if the government debt (as a share of GDP) ratio rose above commonly accepted levels, raising the perceived risk of default; or if the fiscal deficit ballooned, raising the specter of inflation, which would erode the value of an investment in the local currency. In such instances, a government's sovereign risk rating could be lowered, spurring concerns of default or devaluation and therefore a sell-off of assets in the economy. In addition to raising the cost of access to international credit for the government, the loss of investor confidence could potentially destabilize the entire financial sector of developing nations, dampening economic activity and causing deep and prolonged social dislocations. Thus, while financial liberalization in the early 1990s brought the benefits of access to credit and higher growth, it also rendered Latin American countries vulnerable to the punishment of swift and massive capital flight. Coping with financial openness in the 1990s therefore obliged governments in capital-importing nations to pay close attention to the signals of creditworthiness that even the smallest policy change would transmit.

Whether pension privatization is likely to invoke a market punishment in the near term depends on a variety of factors, including the potential cost of the reform, the financial leeway that governments enjoy to finance the transition, and the economy's vulnerability to capital flight. The cost of transition from a public, pay-as-you-go pension system to a fully funded private scheme has been widely acknowledged as a key obstacle to structural reform (Kay 1999; Brooks 2002; Madrid 2003; Müller 1999). The magnitude of this financing gap varies with the inherited pension cost, the "implicit pension debt" (IPD), and the explicit debt and deficit in the old pension system. Transition costs also depend on the extent of privatization that government actors propose. When state pension liabilities are large, the financing gap created by a deep or radical privatization can be enormous. Governments may cover this financial breach in a variety of ways, although most use some combination of spending cuts, tax increases, and borrowing. Because the imposition of a "double payment" burden on working generations is often politically unpopular, however, the most common means of financing the transition to a private pension system are the use of general budget revenue and the issuance of new sovereign debt.

A government's ability to expand its budget deficit or debt burden is not unlimited, however, for these are key indicators of sovereign risk; and a significant rise in debt and deficit ratios may threaten to spark a loss of investor confidence, and with it, capital flight. It is critical to note, however, that the likelihood that privatization would invoke such punishment varies across nations and over time. For one thing, the importance of the signals that a government sends to international market actors varies with the extent to which a government relies on foreign investment to finance its balance of payments (Maxfield 1997). Not only are capital-importing governments vulnerable to the reversal of those flows, but in the particular circumstances of a persistent current account deficit (which is financed through foreign capital inflows), the loss of confidence and attendant reversal of capital inflows may spark a potentially devastating balance of payments crisis.

Countries with large and persistent current account deficits thus become more vulnerable to the sentiments and confidence of international capital markets, and enjoy less domestic policy autonomy (Mosley 2003). When international capital flows are in short supply—where international liquidity is low, moreover, such as when international interest rates are high—investors become more discriminating with regard to risk, rationing credit to developing countries and paying closer attention to signals of investment risk from state action (Maxfield 1997).

Taking on the fiscal cost of pension privatization depends, further, on the government's debt and deficit levels before the reform. If a government is in a tenuous financial position when considering privatization, the added cost of financing such a reform may push government debt or deficit beyond the levels that international markets will tolerate. Because governments carrying higher levels of sovereign debt (relative to the country's GDP) generally present a greater risk of default, and a large fiscal deficit is a signal of inflation risk (Eichengreen and Mody 1998), the ability to finance pension privatization through these means is tightly constrained when debt and deficit ratios are already high. By contrast, governments with access to strong cash flows (a fiscal surplus or revenue from the privatization of state-owned enterprises) or a low debt-to-GDP ratio enjoy greater leeway to finance this reform without the risk of losing investor confidence.

Importantly, it is not true that investors respond negatively to privatization per se or directly to its costs, for the "cost" of transition is largely a relabeling of implicit pension liabilities as explicit debt; these are equivalent from an intertemporal budget perspective.

Still, to the extent that investors do not take the long view when evaluating investment decisions—which occurs with "risky" emerging market nations—they may respond vertiginously to short-term changes in explicit government debt and deficit levels, rather than weighing the potential long-term consequences of a reform. Capital-importing countries that carry high sovereign debt and deficit levels before initiating a pension privatization thus may be forced to trade off some or all of their long-term privatization objectives to diminish the risk of short-term capital flight. Globalization thus generates a time inconsistency problem for capital-importing governments: to avoid punishment in the short term, they must divert from a longer-term strategy of expanding the market orientation of the economy, limiting the extent of the pension privatization they propose.

GLOBAL CAPITAL AND TECHNOCRATIC DECISIONS

Evidence for this argument is found by examining the technocratic process of pension reform in Argentina and Brazil. As figure 3 illustrates, both governments recorded steep current account deficits at the time of their reforms, and thus were highly vulnerable to reversals in capital flows as they considered their options for reform. As figure 4 shows, furthermore, both nations relied on volatile international capital inflows in the 1990s.

Their circumstances also differed in critical ways, however. International liquidity was high when Argentina's pension reform came to the top of the political agenda in the early 1990s; U.S. interest rates had fallen from 10 percent in 1990 to 6 percent in 1993. But the supply of global capital was much more restrictive later in the decade, when pension reform became the policy priority in Brazil: U.S. interest rates rose to 8.35 percent in 1998 (World Bank 2005b). The Argentine government also enjoyed a positive,

Figure 3. Current Account Balance in Argentina and Brazil

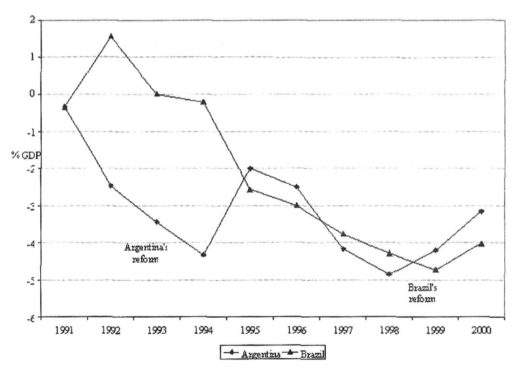

Figure 4. Annual Change in Gross Private Capital Flows: Argentina and Brazil

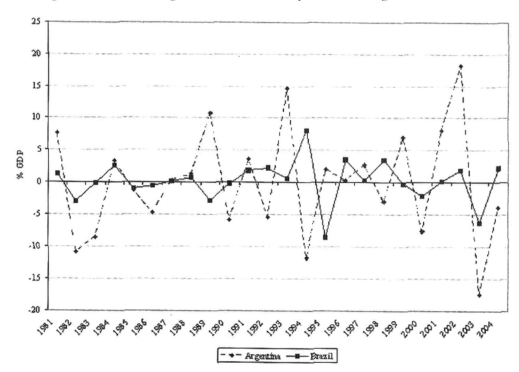

Table 1. Primary Fiscal Balance: Argentina and Brazil

	Primary Budget Balance
Argentina	
1992	1.4
1993	1.4
Brazil	
1998	−0.01
1999	−3.13

Sources: Argentina: IMF 2004; Brazil: Rocha and Pichetti 2003.

although fragile, fiscal position at the time of its reform, while the Brazilian government struggled with fiscal deficits.

Table 1 compares the primary balance for the two countries in the years when structural pension reform was examined. Both the Argentine and Brazilian technocrats enjoyed considerable autonomy during the design phase of pension reforms. The two governments received extensive support from the World Bank and the International Monetary Fund, with multilateral debt service equaling 23.4 percent of public debt in Argentina and 16.7 percent in Brazil at the time of each country's reform (World Bank 2005b). Yet while Argentina enacted a deep pension privatization in 1993, Brazil did not privatize.

ARGENTINA

In September 1993, the Argentine National Congress sanctioned law 24,241, creating a "mixed" public and private pension system. Under the new pension system, all qualified workers would receive a flat public "universal" pension, and could choose whether to participate in a private pension system based on individual retirement accounts or remain in the reformed public social insurance system for their earnings-related benefit. For workers choosing to participate in the new mixed system, more than half of the average retirement benefit was expected to derive from individual savings. The reform, which took effect in 1994, brought a significant shift in the structure and logic of old age income provision in Argentina.

For President Carlos Menem, who oversaw the enactment of the reform, privatization was attractive mainly for the signal it would send to international market actors of his credibility and commitment to market-oriented reform. Government technocrats, for their part, were drawn to the private pension model by its putative long-term fiscal and macro-economic ends, including the prospect of lowering state pension costs, raising domestic capital accumulation, and deepening local capital markets.

Privatization thus was expected to help end the cycle of Argentina's reliance on unstable foreign investment while curtailing the rapid rise in pension costs since the late 1980s. Yet while Argentina's vulnerability to capital flight enhanced the appeal of this model, the ever more urgent need to signal the government's commitment to maintaining economic stability (i.e., the currency peg) shortened the time horizon for making key decisions on the pension system's design. While key concessions in the proposed reform made democratic approval of the new pension system viable in the short term, they traded off key long-term objectives that had originally drawn reformers to this reform model. In order to understand how these design choices were made, we must examine how the powerful pressures and opportunities emerging from short-term economic circumstances weighed on technocratic decisions.

Globalization and Attraction

President Menem came to office in July 1989, five months earlier than scheduled, due to a grave economic crisis gripping Argentina. As an outsider in the Peronist party, and as one who had campaigned on a populist and protectionist platform, Menem enjoyed very little support or confidence from market actors either in Argentina or internationally (Palermo and Collins 1998). On taking office, Menem radically reversed his campaign pledges by embracing an orthodox market-oriented stabilization and structural reform plan (Stokes 2001, 46–47).

After several false starts and failed stabilization efforts, in 1991 Menem shifted to the extremes of neoliberalism in order to make himself credible to the international community (Palermo and Collins 1998, 45). He did so first by placing authority for economic policy in the hands of an insulated economic team led by his newly appointed economic minister, Domingo Cavallo. Widely regarded as a close friend of the investment community in Argentina, Cavallo was "a man of the City," the Argentine stock market, and was associated with the Argentine free market think tank Fundación Mediterránea (Torre 1997; Gerchunoff and Machinea 1995). Cavallo brought with him a group of free market economists, who designed and launched a series of deep, market-oriented structural reforms. The cornerstone of these measures was the inflation-quelling Convertibility Plan, which pegged the new currency, the peso, directly to the U.S. dollar (Gerchunoff and Machinea 1995, 43).

With price stability came an immediate surge in consumption and inflows of capital, stimulating a swift economic recovery. Although the Argentine government did not embrace all market-oriented reforms across the social and economic policy spectrum (Murillo and Schrank 2005), Cavallo turned his attention to the nation's social security system. In 1991, he appointed Walter Schulthess, a macroeconomist, as secretary of social security and charged him with the goal of crafting a structural pension reform. Schulthess assembled a highly insulated team of technocrats that answered directly to Cavallo, rather than to the social security bureaucrats on whom they were formally dependent. The group enjoyed financial support from a World Bank program administered by the United Nations (Programa Nacional de Asistencia Técnica para la Administración de los Servicios Sociales, PRONATASS), which financed a series of consultations by international pension experts, including economists from Chile and Washington (Demarco 1998, 2004; Diaz 1998).

Although the World Bank had been active in policy lending in Argentina, and offered some early technical advice to reformers in the early 1990s, participants and close observers of the PRONATASS team argue that the bank did not define Argentina's pension reform objectives or contribute to the specific design of the country's pension reform proposal (Demarco 1998; Nelson 2004, 46; Rofman 1998; Schulthess 1998). Nor were domestic political interests influential in the early stages of the reform, as members of the reform team worked in what they describe as "laboratory conditions," tightly insulated from the pressure of traditional social security interests (Schulthess 1998). Argentine technocrats thus enjoyed considerable latitude to define the scope and objectives of their pension reform. Far from imposing privatization as a condition for the receipt of financial aid, the IFIs provided resources for Argentina's pension reform that allowed technocrats to seek advice from an array of international experts.

When the Argentine reform team began its work, the country's economy was in the midst of a boom in private consumption and growth that followed its successful stabilization. Consequently, strong inflows of capital and tax receipts created a situation of relative "fiscal plentitude" that temporarily slackened important financial constraints on government action (Torre and Gerchunoff 1998). Although this positive fiscal balance only thinly veiled the deep structural imbalances in government finances, reformers took advantage of the broadened financial leeway to move forward with the structural pension reform. This decision was also catalyzed by a secondary and paradoxical effect of heavy inflows of capital; namely, the deepening of Argentina's vulnerability to capital flight. Such vulnerability heightened the urgency of passing the pension privatization in order to signal the government's resolve to maintain the stable currency while also diminishing the country's reliance on precarious foreign capital flows.

Macroeconomic Context

Argentina's enhanced vulnerability to capital flight arose from both the radical liberalization of the country's capital account and the appreciation of the national currency that followed stabilization. The latter further aggravated this vulnerability by causing Argentina's trade surplus of $3.7 billion in 1991 to become a deficit of $5.9 billion by 1994 (Bustos 1995, 27). Given Argentina's low levels of domestic capital accumulation, this deficit was financed almost completely through foreign capital inflows, resulting in a wide current account deficit. Because capital could freely enter and leave the country, such foreign inflows became a highly precarious source of financing for the current account deficit, rendering it vulnerable to sudden shifts in market sentiment. This sense of vulnerability was unprecedented in Argentina (Torre 1998), and lent urgency to the technocrats' goal of enacting a private pension reform; indeed, it placed them in a race against time to enact the reform before international sentiments or market conditions changed.

For Argentine politicians, gaining the confidence of market actors meant "playing by the market rules" (Santín 1998); specifically, adopting market-oriented structural reforms and sustaining low fiscal deficits and government debt levels (Diaz 1998). The goal of reducing the cost of social security was particularly important, as the old pension system in Argentina had suffered grave financial and institutional troubles in the late 1980s and early 1990s. Not only was the system running a wide deficit, which in 1993 equaled 45 percent of its promised benefits, but after defaulting on its pension promises in the 1980s, the government faced a proliferation of lawsuits from pensioners demanding payment of these arrears (Isuani, et al. 1996, 95; Rofman 1997). Technocrats therefore perceived that keeping the status quo public pension system would be simply "too expensive," given the precarious international economic context (Gaviola 1998; Rofman 1998; Etala 1998; Cetrangolo 1998; Schulthess 1998). As one analyst put it, the new pension system would have to be less costly because "the mobility of capital simply does not support high public deficits" (Facal 1998).

The sense of vulnerability to capital flight thus fueled the belief among technocrats that Argentina should adopt a deep structural pension reform, rather than simply adjusting the existing public system, in order to send a credible signal of its commitment to macroeconomic stability (Rofman 1998; Schulthess 1998; Demarco 1998; Gaviola 1998; Etala 1998; Caro Figueroa 1998). In the longer term, they expected this system to build more stable sources of domestic savings and thereby to provide a critical "buffer" for the domestic economy against exposure to volatile international capital flows (Bustos 1998; Gaviola 1998; Isuani et al. 1996. 94; Torre 1997; Torre and Gerchunoff 1998; Gerchunoff and Machinea 1995; Rofman 1998; Schulthess 1998).

Despite this strong attraction, however, Argentine technocrats perceived that wholesale replication of the Chilean archetype of pension privatization was neither politically nor financially viable (Demarco 1998). Even partial privatization faced an uphill political battle, given Argentina's longer-term welfare state legacy. Lowering political obstacles to privatization would be costly, however, and would compromise important fiscal goals that had originally animated the reform, such as reducing the long-term cost of social security.

The Argentine government could make these compromises, however, because of economic circumstances that broadened its short-term financial scope for maneuver. These included strong foreign capital inflows spurred by the high global liquidity and economic stability, which, in turn, brought a surge in growth and tax revenues for the federal government. Argentina's fiscal situation was improved further by windfall revenue from extensive privatization efforts in the early 1990s. These factors temporarily opened a window of opportunity for the government to make key political compromises that lowered political obstacles to privatization (Cetrangolo 1998) and allowed the pension program to advance in the legislature.

Short-Term Imperatives

In early 1992, before sending the first structural pension reform proposal to the congress, the technocratic reform team convoked a roundtable for "political dialogue" with the main social and political actors in the reform process. This dialogue was intended to provide the technocrats with a preview of the counterarguments that the pension reform would encounter and to establish consensus on the reform's main provisions. Social and political actors made clear to members of the reform team that a private pension reform would not gain legitimacy in Argentina if it lacked a substantial "solidarity" pillar; that is, a public and redistributive component (Demarco 1998).

On the basis of this feedback, the reform team designed and sent the first pension reform proposal to the National Congress in June 1992. The proposal envisioned a "mixed" pension system with a small public universal basic pension and a mandatory private pension system for all new entrants in the labor market and all current workers under the age of 45. In order to limit the short-term transition cost, this proposal did not recognize or compensate workers for pension benefits earned from contributions to the old pension system.

The short-term political context in Argentina was highly favorable to the advance of a deep structural pension reform. The poor performance of the state pension system in Argentina in the 1980s, along with the striking success of the market-based Convertibility Plan in the early 1990s, provided fertile ground to justify the reform as a necessary and effective alternative to the old "failed" model. Indeed, the state had been blamed for the country's deep economic crisis in the late 1980s and had become the target of broad criticism. Powerful political and business leaders also backed Menem's broad plans to remove the state from major allocative functions in the economy (Margheritis 2002, 889–90).

Nevertheless, the first draft of the pension reform met with strong resistance from members of the president's own Peronist party, as well as from the legislative opposition. Politicians' misgivings centered on the plan's failure to recognize contributions made to the old pension system, the lack of macroeconomic infrastructure to develop a private pension fund market, and the weak administrative capacity to support a private pension industry (Isuani and San Martino 1995). Government technocrats accordingly withdrew that first reform proposal before it was even discussed in committee. The message that government technocrats took from these discussions was that pension privatization would not advance unless benefit rights acquired in the old system were recognized for the transitional generation.

At this point, the weight of long-term macroeconomic and fiscal goals diminished significantly in comparison to the more pressing short-term objective of quickly enacting the reform. This task, in turn, brought attention to the immediate concern with making privatization politically viable, revealing the narrowed time horizon over which crucial reform decisions were made. The shift to short-term thinking was permitted by the slackening of fiscal constraints in the context of heavy foreign capital inflows, and by the rising sense of vulnerability to a cessation or reversal of capital flows (and thus a balance of payments crisis), which lent urgency to the enactment of the reform.

The critical task for reformers was therefore to redesign their proposal in such a way that it would acknowledge acquired pension rights while still moving the reform toward passage, allowing the government to send positive short-term signals to international markets. While fiscal constraints were loosened in the short term, permitting these costly compromises, they were not removed altogether. Indeed, Argentine technocrats were aware that acknowledging contributions to the old system in the way that the Chilean government had—through the issuance of a "recognition bond"—would cause a sharp elevation of the government's debt-to-GDP ratio, which would lower the country's sovereign risk rating and threaten the loss of investor confidence.

The technocrats therefore devised an alternative method of recognizing pension contributions in the old system: a "compensatory pension." Payable on retirement, this benefit acknowledged workers' contributions to the old public pension system as a function of income and years of contribution. Not only did this design fulfill a key political condition for the reform's advance, it also allowed the government to spread the transition cost over a long time horizon, keeping most unfunded pension liabilities implicit, or out of sight of international investors, in the short term.

While sidestepping the market limits on Argentina's debt-to-GDP ratio, the new compensatory benefit expanded the government's medium-term fiscal obligations beyond what reformers originally anticipated. While macroeconomic and fiscal circumstances permitted this added financial cost in the short term, not only were the medium- to long-term goals of lowering the cost of pension provision compromised, but the government became even more vulnerable to shifts in international and domestic economic conditions. In responding to short-term market constraints on the government's explicit debt ratios, therefore, the Argentine technocrats traded off the longer-term goal of reducing the fiscal impact of the pension system.

Paradoxically, analysts have noted that the principal cost-cutting goals of the reform were advanced primarily in the parametric reforms to the "pay-as-you-go" component of the pension system, such as the increase in the minimum retirement age and expansion of the number of years of contribution required to earn a pension, among other changes (Isuani et al. 1996, 95). Furthermore, Argentina's privatization did little to reduce the administrative burden on weak state institutions, which was blamed for the failures of the old system. Instead, the new pension system added to the administrative demands on state social security institutions by creating new responsibilities for collecting pension contributions and establishing, regulating, and supervising the new private pension industry (Kay 2003). At the same time, Menem's decision to slash employer contributions to social security exacerbated further the decline in social security revenue, and thus the reform's fiscal toll. Consequently, the share of social security finances derived from payroll contributions fell from 74.8 percent in 1991 to just 30.4 percent in 2000 (Kay 2003: 9). The result was a yawning fiscal gap that had to be filled from other revenue sources.

By the late 1990s, the financial toll of Argentina's pension reform collided forcefully with the constraints imposed by tightening international liquidity and the decreasing market tolerance for risk. This time, however, it was the pension reform that was compromised in order to maintain credibility the eyes of global market actors as the government of Fernando de la Rúa looked to the private pension industry to obtain the foreign exchange needed to meet its external debt service obligations. At first, the government simply "encouraged" the private pension fund industry to make a "patriotic investment" of US$30 billion in government bonds (at below-market interest rates) with dollar-denominated assets that had been invested in domestic banks. When this proved insufficient to hold off international creditors, the Argentine government seized $42 billion more in dollar-denominated assets in domestic banks, much of which was held by the private pension fund industry; these were replaced with government bonds that carried a lower interest rate and had no secondary market. These moves were followed in early 2002 by the announcement of the largest sovereign debt default in history and conversion of all dollar-denominated government bonds to pesos. The result was to immediately slash the dollar value of pension fund holdings by more than 40 percent (Bertranou, Rofman and Grushka 2003).

To the surprise of many, these interventions failed to generate a broad public outcry; instead, they were greeted largely with apathy outside the financial community (Brooks 2009). Not only had Argentine citizens lost more than $12 billion in the dollar value of pension fund savings as a result of the government interventions during the crisis, but coverage of the pension system had declined dramatically as unemployment and informality widened (Rofman 2003). Later, President Néstor Kirchner took advantage of souring public sentiment toward the pension system to pass Law 26,222 in March 2007, which expanded the role of the state in the reformed pension system. And as a final blow to the private pension system, his successor, President Cristina Fernández de Kirchner, proposed the nationalization of the Argentine pension system in October 2008. That decision was approved by the Peronist-dominated Congress in November 2008, transferring to government coffers nearly US$30 billion in pension fund assets that had been invested in the Argentine pension fund industry (Partlow and Byrnes 2009) and bringing to an end the 15-year experiment of pension privatization in Argentina.

BRAZIL

Between 1992 and 2003, the Brazilian government made nearly unceasing efforts to reform the country's public and private pension systems. These efforts yielded two constitutional amendments (in 1998 and 2003) and a structural reform of the "pay-as-you-go" private sector pension system (in 1999), which was passed through ordinary law.

The pension reforms in Brazil brought substantial changes in the design and generosity of old age pension provision but did not privatize the system. This is not because Brazil did not rely on highly mobile international capital flows; nor is it due to a lack of financial involvement from international financial institutions. Instead—besides the effect of powerful political obstacles—it is partly a result of Brazilian technocrats' weak attraction to the model, and partly a function of the powerful short-term financial restrictions on the government. These mechanisms are evident in the technocratic processes surrounding the 1999 private sector pension reform. This measure brought a shift toward a system of individualized "notional" (i.e., not private) pension accounts, which transferred a greater share of income and demographic risks to individuals while maintaining a pay-as-you-go financing structure. The new pension formula represented a balance between the long-term institutional and fiscal objectives of reform and the powerful short-term political and financial constraints.

Tenuous Attraction

Unlike policymakers in neighboring countries, technocrats in Brazil were not drawn to the Chilean archetype of private pension reform. This is not for the absence of macro-economic crisis, which has been viewed as a critical catalyst for the embrace of such models throughout the region. Indeed, Brazil endured severe bouts of hyperinflation and repeated failures of heterodox stabilization plans before finally achieving macroeconomic stability in 1994. In contrast to Argentina, however, the Brazilian government did not go to the extremes of neoliberal reform to quell inflation and liberalize the economy. Government consumption continued to claim a larger share of GDP in Brazil than in its peer countries, averaging 18.4 percent of GDP in the 1990s, compared to the regional average of 10.5 percent (World Bank 2005b). At the same time, capital account liberalization in Brazil was undertaken with greater moderation than elsewhere in Latin America (Morley et al. 1999).

Nor was state intervention in the economy broadly discredited in Brazil to the extent that it was in Argentina. In contrast to the Convertibility Plan, Brazil's inflation-ending Real Plan did not identify the state-led economic model as the root cause of hyperinflation; instead, it diagnosed inflation as a remediable fiscal "disorder" with many symptoms, including the lack of sufficient resources to finance development, distributional conflicts, and excess indebtedness (Ministério da Fazenda 2004). Unlike what occurred in Argentina, therefore, hyperinflationary crisis in Brazil did not cultivate a widespread view among political or technocratic elites that the state must be removed from its allocative role in the economy.

In addition to a greater political diffidence toward neoliberal economic models, Brazil enjoyed a privileged capacity to attract foreign capital without radical liberalization. Unlike other emerging markets, where the dismantling of capital controls and financial regulations became a fundamental condition for the receipt of foreign investment, capital flows to Brazil were not conditioned on radical neoliberal policy signals. Instead, strong capital inflows depended heavily on signals of Brazil's fiscal and macroeconomic performance. With market actors closely following the Brazilian government's debt and deficit ratios, technocrats came to evaluate policy changes according to their likely effects on these key sovereign risk indicators (Bier 1999). Technocrats in Brazil therefore did not see pension privatization as an opportunity to signal credibility through market-oriented reform, but rather as a means to restore financial balance to the pension system, and thus to the state budget more broadly.

Macroeconomic Conditions

As in other countries that used an exchange rate-based stabilization, the quelling of inflation in Brazil brought an appreciation of the national currency, the real, and with it a widening current account deficit, which reached 4.7 percent of GDP by 1998 (Savitsky and Burki 2003, 19). As in Argentina, this deficit heightened Brazil's vulnerability to sudden shifts in investor confidence, and thereby to the risk of destabilizing capital flight. Because the success of Brazil's stabilization plan depended heavily on the government's ability to carry out a fiscal adjustment, market actors attended closely to the evolution of policy reforms that were perceived to have a significant impact on the fiscal deficit. Chief among these was the pension reform.

As Brazil's pension system deficit reached 4.6 percent of GDP by 1998, President Fernando Henrique Cardoso's effort to reform the public and private pension systems attracted considerable attention from market actors. Again, however, the signal that market actors sought from the Brazilian reform was fiscal rather than institutional. That is, unlike Argentina, where technocrats perceived that only a privatization would adequately signal the government's commitment to the currency peg, Brazilian technocrats felt pressure simply to diminish the fiscal cost of the pension system rather than to privatize it (Bier 1999; Oliveira 1999). Accordingly, Brazilian government priorities for reform centered on cost-cutting measures, rather than privatization, as a means to win investor confidence.

Brazil's macroeconomic situation similarly dampened attraction to pension privatization. Whereas in much of Latin America, privatization appealed to technocrats as a long-term tool to develop national capital markets, local financial markets had been created in Brazil in the 1960s and deepened considerably between 1970 and the late 1990s (Loureiro, et al. 2003). Although domestic bond markets in Brazil were dominated by public debt instruments and therefore had considerable room for development, the near-term compulsion to use pension privatization as a means to cultivate a domestic source of financing for the public and private sectors was far less pressing. Indeed, this deep local capital market allowed the Brazilian government to place most of its sovereign debt in domestic markets in the late 1990s (Bevilaqua, et al. 2001).

Brazil also had an established private pension industry. With more than $86 billion invested in private pension funds in 1998, the voluntary pension market in Brazil was twice the size of the Chilean industry (ABRAPP 1999). Government technocrats anticipated, moreover, that very little real savings could be gained through the creation of mandatory individual pension accounts because approximately 80 percent of the labor force earned less than twice the minimum wage in the late 1990s, or less than $200 per month (Bier 1999). Overall, these factors combined to dampen the allure of pension privatization as a tool to build domestic capital markets and as a signal of the government's commitment to market reform.

Brazilian technocrats actively consulted with IFIs such as the World Bank, which provided substantial financial support during the 1990s. They evaluated closely the ideas and models proffered by the World Bank, including its 1994 report, Averting the Old Age Crisis, as they began to design the private sector pension reform (Najberg 1998). Yet these ideas held little sway; nor was the Chilean experience considered relevant to the Brazilian political and economic context (Beltrão 1999; Oliveira 1999). Instead, technocratic objectives remained centered on the goal of correcting long-term financial imbalances in the state pension system.

Many of these problems were rooted in the 1988 Constitution, which vastly expanded state social protection obligations and elevated the minutiae of pension benefit rules to the status of constitutional right (Weyland 1996). Although new progressive forms of redistribution were established, including the expansion of the rural pension system, the 1988 Constitution upheld a set of highly regressive benefit rules. These included a "time-of-service" pension, which used only the last 36 months of contributions as the basis for calculating pension benefits while requiring no minimum age for retirement (Pinheiro and Viera 2000, 9). More than half of the pension benefits offered in the private sector pension scheme (INSS) were time-of-service pensions; and these were disproportionately claimed by higher-income workers, while low-wage earners who could not establish a full labor history were obliged to work a longer number of years in order to receive the less-generous "age" pension.

It is significant that the expansion of old age benefits enshrined in the 1988 Constitution was not matched by the creation of equivalent sources of new revenue. While pension outlays more than doubled between 1988 and 1996, tax receipts rose by only one-third, generating a wide gap in the system's finances (Ministério da Previdência Social 1997, 5). The objective of closing the financial imbalance in Brazil's social security system therefore was the most urgent reform priority.

Constitutional Reform and Pension System Restructuring

The first step in the reform process was a constitutional amendment project (PEC-33), which President Cardoso launched in 1995. This proposal sought to remove from Brazil's constitution the detailed terms of pension provision for public and private sector workers while adding provisions for a minimum retirement age. The amendment faced stiff opposition both in public opinion, where it was incorrectly tarred as a "privatizing project," and in the legislature, where the powerful civil servants lobbied forcefully against it, calling its supporters traitors. After three arduous years of legislative struggle, the pension reform amendment was largely dismantled.

Facing the possibility that his principal reform objectives were not likely to be fully achieved through that project, Cardoso in early 1997 began the "second phase" of pension reform, which focused on reforming the private sector pension system. He created a special technocratic reform team under the leadership of André Lara Resende, the architect of the inflation-ending Real Plan. The group was tightly insulated from state actors that typically controlled the reform process, particularly the Social Security Ministry, but also from legislative and partisan pressures. Technocrats thus enjoyed considerable latitude to define the primary objectives of reform and new policy instruments to achieve them (Oliveira 1999).

The reformers, however, faced powerful political and economic constraints. The first of these arose from the defeat of a provision in the constitutional amendment project to create a minimum retirement age for private sector workers. Workers could retire at any age, as long as they fulfilled the rule of 35 years of contributions to the pension system (30 for women). With many workers joining the labor force in their teens, retirement at age 50 was not unusual under this system, resulting in a heavy financial burden on the government. A second constraint on the reform options emerged from the high payroll taxes in Brazil. Given the growing pressures of international trade competition, the option of raising employer or employee contributions to increase revenue to the pension system was foreclosed (Beltrão 1999; Oliveira 1999).

There was also little public support for the concept of privatization. As one deputy put it, "the society here still is strongly of the belief that the state should play the primary role in the payment of pensions; that [social security] should be from the purse of the state, not the private sector" (Madeira 1999). Reformers therefore looked for ways to alter the long-term structure and financial balance of Brazil's private sector pension system without privatizing or raising the retirement age or payroll taxes.

The Lara Resende group worked intensively throughout 1997 to design a reform that would restore financial balance to the system while conforming to their distinctive political and financial constraints (Pinheiro 1998; Najberg 1998). They chose a reform design that would alter the structure of risk sharing in the pension system by separating the insurance and redistributive functions. In a way similar to the market-oriented model, the proposed reform would link the expected value of old age benefits closely to each worker's lifetime contributions while shifting the principal redistributive function to means-tested programs (Oliveira et al. 1999).

The proposal anticipated a considerable reduction in state pension liabilities. By lowering the ceiling on contributions and benefits, however, this proposal would create a short-term financing gap in the state pension system as higher-income workers would be encouraged to divert payroll contributions to a private pension fund. This gap in finances, the technocrats anticipated, could be covered through the issuance of new government debt. The prospective impact of this proposal on the government's debt-to-GDP ratio, however, would ultimately prove fatal for the proposal.

The basic outline of the technocrats' initial reform plan was approved by President Cardoso and his close financial advisers in late 1997 and presented to other executive branch actors in early 1998. Among the first groups consulted were technocrats in the Central Bank and the Finance Ministry, whose input in Brazil's reform process had been amplified in recent months by rising international financial pressure after the 1997 Asian financial crisis. Increasing risk aversion among international investors was magnified further by tightening international liquidity, which brought a restriction of credit to developing countries. Further narrowing this space for maneuver was Brazil's fragile fiscal position, particularly the government's rising debt burden, which reached 45 percent of GDP (net) in 1998. The consequence of these factors was to shorten policymakers' time horizon considerably and to shift policy goals overwhelmingly toward that of avoiding any erosion of government debt or deficit ratios in the short term (Bier 1999).

The reduction in pension contributions resulting from the lower ceiling on taxable wages in the Lara Resende group's proposal, however, would have significantly strained government finances, even before considering the government's poor fiscal situation.

Consequently, Central Bank officials vetoed the measure on the grounds that it would spur a loss of investor confidence and thereby threaten capital flight (Beltrão 1999; see also Melo 2004; Nassif and Caldas 1999). The bankers explained that "it would look bad internationally" if they did anything "that would require additional indebtedness of the public sector to finance it" (Oliveira 1999). Due to the risks of market punishment, therefore, the first reform proposal was blocked by precisely the government ministries that are typically considered the most ardent supporters of pension privatization.

International financial pressures continued to worsen over the course of 1998. Following the Russian default in August, capital began to pour rapidly out of Brazil on fears that the country would be next. To stem the tide of capital outflows, the Brazilian government signed a S41.5 billion loan from the International Monetary Fund and agreed to a series of quarterly fiscal targets, which required a sharp curtailment of government spending. After a series of political alterations in the government in mid-1998 that changed the composition of the pension reform team, the group began anew to draft a private sector pension reform.

With a grant from the World Bank, two members of the reform group attended a World Bank summer pension workshop held at Harvard University, where they learned of a new model of structural pension reform based on systems of notional accounts, which had recently been adopted in Sweden (Najberg 1998; Pinheiro 1998). This model incorporates key features of privatization, such as the transfer of cost and risk of old age pension savings from the state to individuals through the creation of individual retirement accounts; but it maintains the pay-as-you-go financing and public management of old age pensions. Most important for the Brazilian technocrats, notional account reforms do not create significant medium-term transition costs. This feature proved highly attractive to Brazil's reform team, given the narrow financial leeway with which the government could operate. Reformers therefore drafted a second reform proposal in late 1998 that drew heavily on the Swedish notional account model, although with important adjustments for the Brazilian context.

The first and most significant modification responded to the impracticality of attaching an explicit interest rate to workers' contributions to the notional accounts. Given Brazil's very high short-term interest rates, which ranged in 1999 from 45 percent on liquid bank deposits to 21.12 percent real average return on certificates of deposit, any effort to match these rates would be financially untenable for the government, while using a lower interest rate would prove politically unpopular (Pinheiro and Viera 2000, 11). The government also had to adjust the proposed reform to account for the absence of a minimum retirement age for the private sector. It did so by lowering the pension benefits for individuals choosing to retire at a young age. As one member of the reform team explained, "The key is that the constitution gives people some rights. It does not say, however, what kind of price you are going to have to pay for those rights" (Oliveira 1999). The centerpiece of the proposal thus was a new pension formula called the fator previdenciário, or social security factor, which incorporated each worker's life expectancy into the benefit formula so that workers who retired early would receive lower pensions, while late retirement was rewarded by a higher annual pension benefit.

This reform proposal was finalized shortly after the promulgation of the 1998 constitutional amendment; it was sent to the Brazilian Congress in mid-1999 and was sanctioned in December. Together, the 1988 constitutional amendment and the 1999 private sector pension reform were projected to cut the long-term pension system deficit in half (World Bank 2005c, 8). Although Brazil's 1999 pension reform brought a significant change in the structure of the risk sharing in old age pension provision and a reduction in pension costs, it did so without privatizing the system, and thereby departed sharply from the broader Latin American trend.

CONCLUSIONS

Globalization has often been viewed as a principal source of pressure for market-oriented reform and social policy retrenchment in the developing world. Less often, however, is economic integration treated as a factor that may limit how governments, particularly those in capital-scarce countries, expand the role of market forces in social protection. The principal thesis advanced in this study is that rather than simply generating pressures on governments to enact more extensive market reform, globalization creates a double bind for capital-scarce governments, simultaneously generating powerful incentives to privatize as a long-term means to raise domestic capital accumulation and as a signal to win or maintain the confidence of international investors, and creating powerful short-term constraints on this reform.

Capital mobility has exposed developing-country governments to a virtual daily or even hourly referendum by capital market actors, obliging them to make critical, long-term reform decisions on the basis of short-term pressures and constraints. While it is widely noted that Latin American governments have embraced pension privatization for its putative long-term macroeconomic implications, the implication of this study is that we cannot assume that such ends were ultimately decisive in the process of designing and advancing structural pension reform. Instead, government technocrats faced a critical time inconsistency problem: they could be punished with capital flight in the short term for enacting a reform for which market actors would otherwise reward them in the long term. Consequently, governments have responded to these short-term pressures and constraints of globalization by curtailing the long-term goals of structural reform by curtailing or forgoing pension privatization altogether.

How generalizable are the cases of Argentina and Brazil? While the two countries vary in their openness to international capital flows, they are among the largest and therefore most powerful Latin American economies. In one sense, this makes these countries more difficult cases in which to observe the punishing force of globalization's double bind in government decisions. Yet as we have seen, both the Argentine and Brazilian governments were ultimately constrained in their reform goals by the threat of short-term capital flight.

It could be the case that market actors pay less attention to smaller economies, given the more restricted investment opportunities in such nations. Other research, however, suggests that a similar dynamic obtained in Uruguay: there, technocrats explicitly designed their pension reform so as to avoid the use of a recognition bond, instead maintaining a larger public pension component in order to avoid any increase in the government debt ratio and, thereby, short-term market punishment (Brooks 2009). In Nicaragua, moreover, the government approved a pension privatization in 2000 but did not implement it because the transition cost would have been prohibitive, given the country's large fiscal debt and heavy debt burden.

In large and small developing countries alike, global forces have powerfully transformed the criteria and time horizons of policymaking. By taking account of these temporal shifts, we might better understand how globalization has shaped the process and outcome of the dramatic renegotiation of the state and market balance in Latin America since the early 1990s.

REFERENCES

Arce, Moisés. 2001. The Politics of Pension Reform in Peru. *Studies in Comparative International Development* 36, 3: 90–115.

Associação Brasileira de Entidades de Previdência Privada (ABRAPP). 1999. *Consolidado Estatístico* 7, 11. São Paulo, Brazil: ABRAPP.

Beltrão, Kaizô. 1999. Demographer; Member, Lara Resende group, Instituto Brasileiro de Geografia e Estatística. Author interview. Rio de Janeiro, June 23.

Bertranou, Fábio, Rafael Rofman, and Carlos O. Grushka. 2003. From Reform to Crisis: Argentina's Pension System. *International Social Security Review* 56, 2: 103–114.

Bevilaqua, Afonso Sant'anna, et al. 2001. The Structure of Public Sector Debt in Brazil. *Research Network Working Paper* R-424. Washington, DC: Inter-American Development Bank.

Bier, Amaury. 1999. Executive Secretary, Ministério da Fazenda. Author interview. Brasília, June 9.

Brasil. Ministério da Fazenda. Immediate Action Program. <www.fazenda.gov.br> Accessed June 2004.

Brasil. Ministério da Previdência e Assistência Social. 1997. *INFORME da Previdência Social* 9, 12.

Brooks, Sarah. 2002. Social Protection and Economic Integration: The Politics of Pension Reform in an Era of Capital Mobility. *Comparative Political Studies* 35, 5: 491–525.

——. 2005. Interdependent and Domestic Foundations of Policy Change: The Diffusion of Pension Privatization around the World. *International Studies Quarterly* 49, 2: 273–94.

——. 2009. *Social Protection and the Market in Latin America: The Transformation of Social Security Institutions.* New York: Cambridge University Press.

Bustos, Pablo. 1995. Argentina: ¿un capitalismo emergente? In *Más allá de la estabilidad: Argentina en la época de la globalización y la regionalización*, ed. Bustos. Buenos Aires: Fundación Friedrich Ebert. 11–38.

——. 1998. Economist, Fundación Ebert. Author interview. Buenos Aires, July 26.

Caro Figueroa, Armando. 1998. Former Minister of Labor and Social Security, Argentina. Author interview. Buenos Aires, July 27.

Cetrangolo, Oscar. 1998. Pension analyst, Centro de Estudios para el Cambio Estructural. Author interview. Buenos Aires, June 9.

Cruz-Saco, María Amparo, and Carmelo Mesa-Lago, eds. 1998. *Do Options Exist? The Reform of Pension and Health Care Systems in Latin America.* Pittsburgh: University of Pittsburgh Press.

Deacon, Bob, and Michelle Hulse. 1997. The Making of Post-Communist Social Policy: The Role of International Agencies. *Journal of Social Policy* 26, 1: 43–62.

Demarco, Gustavo. 2004. The Argentine Pension System Reform and International Lessons. In *Learning From Foreign Models in Latin American Policy Reform*, ed. Kurt Weyland. Baltimore: Johns Hopkins University Press. 81–109.

——. 1998. General Manager, Superintendencia de Administradoras de Fondos de Jubilaciones y Pensiones. Author interview. Buenos Aires, June 16.

Díaz, Rodolfo. 1998. Former Minister of Labor and Social Security, Argentina. Author interview. Buenos Aires, June 25.

Dion, Michelle. 2006. Globalización, democratización y reforma del sistema de seguridad social en México, 1988–2005. *Foro Internacional* 183, 1: 51–80.

Eichengreen, Barry, and Ashoka Mody. 1998. What Explains Changing Spreads on Emerging-Market Debt: Fundamentals or Market Sentiment? *NBER* Working Paper 6408. Cambridge, MA: National Bureau of Economic Research.

Etala, Carlos. 1998. Lawyer and pension reform analyst, Yomho, Antuñez & Etala. Author interview. Buenos Aires, July 20.

Facal, Carlos. 1998. Insurance executive, Berkley International ART. Author interview. Buenos Aires, July 6.

Gaviola, Juan González. 1998. Peronist Deputy, National Congress. Author interview. Buenos Aires, June 17.

Gerchunoff, Pablo, and José Luis Machinea. 1995. Un ensayo sobre la política económica después de la estabilización. In *Mas allá de la estabilidad: Argentina en la época de la globalización y la regionalización*, ed. Pablo Bustos. Buenos Aires: Fundación Friedrich Ebert. 39–92.

Holzmann, Robert, and Richard Hinz. 2005. *Old Age Income Support in the 21st Century*. Washington, DC: World Bank.

Huber, Evelyne, and John D. Stephens. 2000. The Political Economy of Pension Reform: Latin America in Comparative Perspective. United Nations Research Institute for Social Development Occasional Paper 7. Geneva: UNRISD. May.

Isuani, Ernesto A., and Jorge San Martino. 1995. El nuevo sistema previsional argentino. ¿Punto final a una larga crisis? *Boletín Informativo Techint* 286 (April–June): 281–82.

Isuani, Ernesto A., Rafael Rofman, and Jorge San Martino. 1996. Las jubilaciones del siglo XXI, ¿podemos gastar la cuenta? *Boletín Informativo Techint* 286 April–June: 79–104.

International Monetary Fund (IMF). 2004. Appendix 3: A Retrospective on Argentina's Fiscal Policy, 1991–2001. In *The IMF and Argentina: 1991–2001*. Washington, DC: IMF. 80–82.

Kaufman, Robert, and Alex Segura-Ubiergo. 2001. Globalization, Domestic Politics and Social Spending in Latin America, 1973–1997. *World Politics* 53, 4: 553–87.

Kay, Stephen. 1999. Unexpected Privatizations: Politics and Social Security Reform in the Southern Cone. *Comparative Politics* 31, 1: 403–22.

——. 2000. Recent Changes in Latin American Welfare States: Is There Social Dumping? *Journal of European Social Policy* 10, 2: 185–203.

——. 2003. State Capacity and Pensions. Paper prepared for the 24th International Congress of the Latin American Studies Association, Dallas, March 27–29.

Keohane, Robert O., and Joseph Nye. 1998. Power and Interdependence in the Information Age. *Foreign Affairs* 77, 5. 81–94.

Kurtz, Marcus J. 1999. Chile's Neo-Liberal Revolution: Incremental Decisions and Structural Transformation, 1973–89. *Journal of Latin American Studies* 31, 2 (May): 399–427.

Loureiro, André Soares, and Fernando de Holanda Barbosa. 2003. Public Debt and Risk Premium of Public Securities in Brazil. Technical Notes 42. Brasília: Banco Central do Brasil.

LoVuolo, Rubén. 1996. Reformas previsionales en América Latina: una visión crítica en base al caso argentino. *Comercio Exterior* 46, 9 (September): 692–702.

Madeira, Arnaldo. 1999. PSDB Party leader and National Deputy, National Congress. Author interview. Brasilia, May 27.

Madrid, Raúl. 2003. *Retiring the State: The Politics of Pension Privatization in Latin America and Beyond*. Stanford: Stanford University Press.

——. 2005. Ideas, Economic Pressures, and Pension Privatization. *Latin American Politics and Society* 47, 2 (Summer): 23–50.

Margheritis, Ana. 2002. Policy Innovation and Leaders' Perceptions: Building a Reformist Consensus in Argentina. *Journal of Latin American Studies* 34, 4 (November): 881–914.

Maxfield, Sylvia. 1997. *Gatekeepers of Growth: Central Banking in Developing Countries*. Princeton: Princeton University Press.

Melo, Marcus André. 2004. Institutional Choice and the Diffusion of Policy Paradigms: Brazil and the Second Wave of Pension Reform. *International Political Science Review* 25, 3: 320–41.

Mesa-Lago, Carmelo. 1989. *Ascent to Bankruptcy: Financing Social Security in Latin America*. Pittsburgh: University of Pittsburgh Press.

——. 1997. Social Welfare Reform in the Context of Economic-Political Liberalization: Latin American Cases. *World Development* 25, 1: 497–517.

Mesa-Lago, Carmelo, and Katharina Müller. 2002. The Politics of Pension Reform in Latin America. *Journal of Latin American Studies* 34, 3 (August): 687–715.

Morley, Samuel A., Roberto Machado, and Stefano Pettinato. 1999. Indexes of Structural Reform in Latin America. *Serie Reformas Económicas* No. 12. Santiago: ECLAC.

Mosley, Layna. 2003. *Global Capital and National Governments*. New York: Cambridge University Press.

Müller, Katharina. 1999. *The Political Economy of Pension Reform in Central-Eastern Europe*. Cheltenham: Edward Elgar Press.

——. 2001. The Political Economy of Pension Reform in Eastern Europe. *International Social Security Review* 54, 2–3: 57–79.

Murillo, María Victoria, and Andrew Schrank. 2005. With a Little Help from My Friends: Partisan Politics, Transnational Alliances, and Labor Rights in Latin America. *Comparative Political Studies*. 38, 8: 971–99.

Najberg, Sheila. 1998. Special Adviser, Cabinet of the President, Banco Nacional de Desenvolvimento Econômico e Social. Author interview. Rio de Janeiro, December 13.

Nassif, Maria Inés, and Sueli Caldas. 1999. Para economista, situação da previdência piorou. *Estado de São Paulo*, May 20.

Nelson, Joan. 1996. Promoting Policy Reforms: The Twilight of Conditionality. *World Development* 24, 9: 1551–59.

——. 2004. External Models, International Influence, and the Politics of Social Sector Reforms. In *Learning from Foreign Models in Latin American Policy Reform*, ed. Kurt Weyland. Baltimore: Johns Hopkins University Press. 273–94.

Oliveira, Francisco. 1999. Pension expert, Instituto de Pesquisa Econômica Aplicada. Author interview. Rio de Janeiro, June 25.

Oliveira, Francisco, Eduardo Barreto, Kaizô Iwakami Beltrão, and Maria Tereza de Marsillac Pasinato. 1999. Reforma estrutural da previdência: uma proposta para assegurar proteção social e equidade. *IPEA Discussion Text* 690. Rio de Janeiro: Instituto de Pesquisa Econômica Aplicada.

Orenstein, Mitchell. 2005. The New Pension Reform as Global Policy. *Global Social Policy* 5, 2: 175–202.

Palermo, Vicente, and John Collins. 1998. Moderate Populism: A Political Approach to Argentina's 1991 Convertibility Plan. *Latin American Perspectives* 25, 1: 36–62.

Partlow, Joshua, and Brian Byrnes. 2008. Argentina to Nationalize Pension Funds. *Washington Post.* November 21, 2008; Page A17.

Pinheiro, Vinicius. 1998. Secretary of Social Security, Ministério da Previdência e Assistência Social. Author interview. Brasília, November 18.

Pinheiro, Vinicius, and Solange Viera. 2000. Reforma previsional en Brasil: la nueva regla para el cálculo de los beneficios. Serie *Financiamiento del Desarrollo* No. 97. Santiago de Chile: CEPAL.

Queisser, Monika. 2000. Pension Reform and International Organizations: From Conflict to Convergence. *International Social Security Review* 53, 2: 31–46.

Rocha, Fabiana, and Paulo Picchetti. 2003. Fiscal adjustment in Brazil. *Revista Brasileira de Economia* 57, 1: 239–52.

Rofman, Rafael. 1997. Pension Reform in Argentina: The Political Process and Transition Costs. Unpublished mss. Buenos Aires: Superintendencia de Administradoras de Fondos de Jubilaciones y Pensiones.

——. 1998. Economist, AFJP La Nación. Author interview. Buenos Aires, June 10.

——. 2003. El sistema previsional ly la crisis de la Argentina. Buenos Aires: Banco Mundial. Documento de Trabajo N.7/03 (July).

Santín, Eduardo. 1998. National Deputy, Unión Cívica Radical, National Congress. Author interview. Buenos Aires, June 15.

Santiso, Javier. 2003. *The Political Economy of Emerging Markets: Actors, Institutions and Crisis in Latin America.* New York: Palgrave.

Savitsky, Joseph, and Shavid Burki. 2003. Capital Flows to Emerging Markets and Policy Implications: The Experience of Latin America and the Caribbean. Japan Program Working Paper Series on Globalization No. 5. Washington, DC: Inter-American Development Bank.

Schulthess, Walter. 1998. Former Secretary of Social Security, Argentina; Economist, AJFP Provincia. Author interview. Buenos Aires, June 11.

Solis Soberón, Fernando, and Alejandro Villagómez. 1997. Domestic Savings in Mexico and Pension Reform. In *Mexico: Assessing Neo-Liberal Reform*, ed. Mónica Serrano. London: Institute of Latin American Studies. 106–26.

Stokes, Susan. 2001. *Mandates and Democracy: Neoliberalism by Surprise in Latin America.* New York: Cambridge University Press.

Torre, Juan Carlos. 1997. El lanzamiento político de las reformas estructurales en América Latina. *Política y Gobierno* 4, 2: 471–98.

——. 1998. Professor, Universidad Torcuato di Tella. Author interview. Buenos Aires, June 20.

Torre, Juan Carlos, and Pablo Gerchunoff. 1998. La economía política de las reformas institucionales en Argentina. Los casos de la política de privatización de Entel, la reforma de la seguridad social y la reforma laboral. Unpublished mss. Buenos Aires: Instituto Torcuato di Tella.

Vreeland, James. 2003. Why Do Governments and the IMF Enter into Agreements? Statistically Selected Cases. *International Political Science Review* 24, 3: 159–83.

Weyland, Kurt. 1996. *Democracy Without Equity: The Failure of Reform in Brazil.* Pittsburgh: University of Pittsburgh Press.

——. 2005. Theories of Policy Diffusion: Lessons from Latin American Pension Reform. *World Politics* 57, 2 (October): 262–95.

Wibbels, Erik. 2006. Dependency Revisited: International Markets, Business Cycles, and Social Spending in the Developing World. *International Organization* 60, 2: 433–68.

World Bank. 1994. *Averting the Old Age Crisis: Policies to Protect the Old and Promote Growth.* Washington, DC: World Bank.

——. 2005a. Projects Database. <www.worldbank.org> Accessed July 2005.

——. 2005b. *World Development Indicators.* CD-ROM. Washington, DC: World Bank.

——. 2005c. Program Document for a Proposed Fiscal Reform Loan—Social Security Reform in the Amount Equivalent to US$658.3 million to the Federative Republic of Brazil. Report No. 32226-Br. May 6.

Chapter 9

Ideas, Economic Pressures, and Pension Privatization

Raúl L. Madrid

A vast wave of pension privatization has swept much of the world in recent decades. Nowhere has this wave been more powerful than in Latin America. Since 1992, ten Latin American countries have privatized their pension systems, and a handful of other countries in the region have considered or are considering similar measures. The privatization schemes allow (or oblige) members of the existing public pension system to deposit some or all of their mandatory social security contributions in individual retirement accounts managed (principally) by private pension fund administrators, instead of paying these contributions to the state-run pension system.[1] To varying degrees, the privatization schemes thus transfer the responsibility for the provision of retirement pensions away from the state and toward the private sector.

It is not clear whether the new private pension systems will generate higher pensions on average than the old public systems. Nor is it clear whether the private pension systems will generate economic benefits. It is certain, however, that the privatization measures will increase the financial risks faced by workers and create substantial funding deficits for the state in the medium term.

Why, then, have so many countries opted to privatize their pension systems? One potential explanation would focus on the role of economic crisis, which much of the existing literature on economic reform has identified as the principal cause of market-oriented reform (Haggard and Kaufman 1995; Tommasi and Sturzenegger 1998; Weyland 2002b; for a skeptical view, see Corrales 1997–98). Economic crises have indeed facilitated pension privatization in a number of ways. First, economic crisis undermined support for the existing state-led development model in many countries, which paved the way for market-oriented reforms, such as pension privatization. Second, economic crises weakened some groups that opposed pension privatization, such as organized labor, and strengthened some actors that supported it, such as the World Bank. Third, in many countries, economic crises helped create domestic capital shortages and wreaked havoc on the finances of public pension systems, both of which helped foster pension privatization.

Nevertheless, economic crisis is only one of the many factors that determine the degree of public support for market reform, the strength of organized interest groups, or the level of public pension spending or domestic savings in a given country. Moreover, it seems unlikely that a government would respond to an economic crisis by privatizing its pension system, because such a move could worsen the crisis by dramatically increasing the size of the government's fiscal deficit. We might, indeed, reasonably expect governments facing economic crises to be quite reluctant to privatize their pension systems, at least in the short run. Economic crises may discourage pension privatization by undermining confidence in the stock market and the ability of the private sector to manage the retirement funds effectively. These offsetting effects of economic crisis mean that any relationship between crisis and pension privatization is likely to be weak, distant, and indirect.

This article maintains that the recent wave of pension privatization has been spurred not by economic crisis in general, but by a more specific set of economic problems. Policymakers have sought to privatize their pension systems largely because of concerns about domestic capital shortages and the economic burden of public pension spending, which are only indirectly related to economic crisis. Many policymakers have believed that privatizing their public pension systems would boost their domestic savings rate and cut their long-term public pension expenditures, thereby reducing their dependence on unstable foreign capital and freeing up resources for other, more productive uses. To understand why many policymakers believed that pension privatization would yield these benefits, however, it is necessary to explore how ideas about pension privatization and its effects have taken hold.

This study argues that two factors have played a particularly important role in spreading beliefs about the economic efficacy of pension privatization: the emergence and diffusion of the Chilean model and the growing influence of the World Bank in the area of pension policy.[2] The findings of this article suggest that ideas need to be taken more seriously in studies of policy reform, but they also imply that the influence of ideas may depend less on the intrinsic value of an idea than on the regional salience of an idea and the strength of its advocates.

The article develops this argument first with a review of the economic pressures that have placed pension reform on the policy agenda in many countries. There follows a discussion of how the Chilean model and the World Bank have shaped beliefs about how pension privatization might address these economic problems. The analysis presents a simple statistical test of the preceding arguments, and the conclusion discusses the implications of the findings for theories of ideas and policy reform.

ECONOMIC PRESSURES AND PENSION REFORM

Public pension systems have become an increasing economic burden around the world. This is the case not only in the industrialized world, but also in Eastern Europe and some Latin American countries, such as Argentina, Brazil, Chile, Costa Rica, and Uruguay. Over the last several decades, public pension expenditures have skyrocketed, partly because of demographic trends, which have caused the population to age rapidly in many countries. The maturation of pension systems has also led pension expenditures to grow by making an increasing number of people eligible for pension benefits. Some countries, including a large number of Latin American countries, have inadvertently accelerated the maturation of their pension systems by imposing loose requirements for gaining pensions. Economic difficulties, such as rising unemployment and the growth of the informal sector, have also worsened the financial problems of public pension systems in many countries.

The growth in public pension expenditures has put pressure on countries to reform their systems, especially those countries in which public pension expenditures (as a percentage of GDP) are high (Kay 1999; World Bank 1994). Governments with large and growing public pension expenditures have feared that their public pension programs would hinder economic growth and absorb scarce resources that would be better devoted to other programs. Governments have become increasingly reluctant to pay for growing pension expenditures by boosting payroll taxes because they have feared that such measures would increase unemployment and reduce their ability to compete in the global economy.

Some policymakers have advocated pension privatization as a solution to these problems. As advocates of privatization point out, private pension systems, unlike most of the public systems, are fully funded. Therefore they are not undermined by the aging of the population to the same extent as are the public pay-as-you-go systems. Proponents of privatization also maintain that the private systems can generate better rates of return than the public systems, which means that they can make do with lower payroll taxes. The assumption underlying this contention is that the long-term rate of return to capital, on which private fully funded schemes depend, will be higher than the annual percentage growth in total real wages, on which public pay-as-you-go systems depend. In addition, advocates of privatization maintain that it will improve the financial health of the pension system by reducing payment evasion. They point out that workers will have greater incentives to contribute to a system based on individual capitalization because pensions in such systems are tied more directly to contributions. Proponents of privatization also contend that private pension systems will not be so easily manipulated for political purposes, which will help ensure their financial health.

Rising public pension spending was not the only economic factor to put pension privatization on the policy agenda of many nations, however. Concerns about capital shortages did so as well (Madrid 2002). In many countries, domestic savings rates have declined in recent decades, limiting the supply of local capital. As a result, many countries have become increasingly dependent on unstable foreign capital. The global rise in capital mobility has caused cross-border financing to mushroom as firms, countries, and individual investors have sought attractive opportunities to borrow, lend, and invest abroad. At the same time, the increasing mobility of international capital has made it easier for investors to pull money out of a country in the event of a crisis. In the last two decades, numerous countries have experienced massive capital outflows when investors have suddenly lost confidence in their economies.

Their rising vulnerability to capital outflows has led many countries to try to boost their domestic savings rates as a means to reduce their dependence on skittish foreign sources of capital. Many policymakers have viewed pension privatization as one of the most effective ways to boost their countries' savings rates. According to pension privatization advocates, mandatory private pension schemes would boost private savings by requiring people to save above the level that they would voluntarily save. Some economists have long argued that pay-as-you-go systems reduce national savings by discouraging private savings, because individual workers know that the government will provide them with a pension in their old age. Privatizing the pension system, they argue, would reverse this negative effect.

The authors of an important World Bank study of pension reform acknowledge that a mandatory private pension system would probably reduce voluntary savings to some degree, but they suggest that "this crowd-out effect may be only partial because people are shortsighted and would not have saved as much voluntarily for old age" (World Bank 1994, 209). Advocates of pension privatization also argue that it will promote savings by reducing "the probability that governments will have to borrow to cover escalating pension costs as populations age" (James 1997, 20). They maintain, furthermore, that pension privatization will reduce payroll taxes and other labor market distortions that impede growth and improve the efficiency of the local capital markets. Higher growth will boost savings, which, in turn, will promote further growth.

Those countries with low domestic savings rates have found pension privatization particularly attractive. In both Argentina and Mexico, the architects of the reforms proclaimed that raising their sagging domestic savings was one of the main goals of the reforms, and they carried out analyses that estimated the effects of the reforms on the savings rate (Schulthess 1996; Demarco 1996; Martinez 1997; Davila 1997; see also Cottani and Demarco 1998; Cámara de Diputados 1995). In their expositions of the motives for their reforms, the Nicaraguan and Salvadoran governments justified the privatization plans on similar grounds, arguing that the privatization schemes would generate domestic savings and stimulate the local capital markets (INSS n.d.; Instituto Salvadoreño del Seguro Social 1997). Colombian President Álvaro Uribe Vélez, who was one of the key backers of the reform when he served in the Colombian Senate, has written, "the pension reform seduces me because of its macroeconomic effects—its impact on savings. Colombia is a country with a very low savings rate. I do not see a sufficiently valid reason to sacrifice the opportunity to improve [the savings rate] substantially" (Uribe Vélez 1993, 19).

A desire to raise the domestic savings rate and bolster the local capital markets also reportedly motivated the reforms in Hungary, Poland, and Kazakhstan (Nelson 2001; Muller 1999; Orenstein 1999). Indeed, the Hungarian government sought to finance the transition costs of its privatization plan through taxes and expenditure reduction rather than debt, specifically in order to boost the domestic savings rate (Palacios and Rocha 1998, 27).

IDEATIONAL INFLUENCES

An explanation for pension reform choices that focuses solely on economic factors is insufficient, however. Economic factors alone cannot explain reform choices or even the decision to reform. As Adler has pointed out, the "environment does not 'instruct' policymakers, it challenges them" (1991, 53). How policymakers respond to those challenges depends partly on what sort of beliefs the policymakers and other actors hold.

Investigating the beliefs that frame the policymakers' choices is particularly important in this case because of the controversy surrounding the economic effects of pension privatization. It is not clear that pension privatization is an effective solution to the problem of rising public pension spending. Indeed, social security privatization worsens rather than improves the financial situation of the public pension system in the medium term. Pension privatization schemes are costly in the medium term because they allow (or oblige) members of the social security system to transfer some portion of their social security contributions to private pension fund accounts instead of paying them to the state. The state, however, continues to pay the pensions of existing retirees and, in most cases, also compensates members who transfer to the private system for the contributions they previously made to the public system. The state therefore loses a substantial portion of its social security revenue, with no corresponding drop in expenditures in the medium term.

It is not even certain that pension privatization will resolve the pension systems' financial problems in the long run. Political interference may wreak havoc on the finances of the private pension systems, just as with public pension systems, given that the government decides who may operate private pension funds and in what entities they can invest. Moreover, the government can opt to interfere or take over the private system at any time. Indeed, the Argentine government first forced the Argentine private pension funds to lend it billions of dollars at low interest rates and then in late 2008 enacted legislation nationalizing the private pension system. Private fully funded pension systems, like public pay-as-you-go systems, may also be affected by demographic transitions, because the return on their investments may decline once large cohorts of workers retire and begin to sell their assets.[3] Private systems are also vulnerable to inflation, bankruptcy, and fraud. Should a private pension system run into serious financial problems, the state would almost certainly be obliged to cover some of its debts, which could prove extremely costly.

The link between pension privatization and higher savings rates is even more controversial. Some strong theoretical arguments have been made as to why pension privatization might generate increased domestic savings. Nevertheless, as proponents of privatization acknowledge, privatizing the pension system is unlikely to generate any increase in savings if the costs of the transition are financed by borrowing rather than through taxation or fiscal cutbacks (Corsetti and Schmidt-Hebbel 1995; James 1997; Orszag and Stiglitz 2001). Where the transition is debt-financed, the increase in private savings generated by the pension privatization plan will be offset by an increase in public dissaving. Skeptics also point out that the empirical evidence linking pension privatization to higher savings is tenuous. Indeed, in a noteworthy paper, the Nobel Prize-winning economist Joseph Stiglitz and a collaborator declared the idea that pension privatization boosts national savings to be "myth number 1" in the debate on social security (Orszag and Stiglitz 1997, 9–12).

Most of the studies of the macroeconomic effects of pension privatization have examined a single country, Chile, and have yielded contradictory results (Corsetti and Schmidt-Hebbel 1995; Haindl 1997; Holzmann 1997). The sizable literature on the macroeconomic effects of pay-as-you-go systems, meanwhile, has yet to find conclusive evidence that these systems lower domestic savings (World Bank 1994; Thompson 1998). This ambiguity is partly a result of the thorny nature of the problem. It is difficult to isolate the impact of the pension system on savings rates, partly because savings rates depend on numerous factors.

These controversies raise several key questions. Why have so many policymakers assumed that privatizing their pension systems would boost their savings rates and ease their fiscal burdens? Why have some policymakers reached this conclusion more readily than others? Where do ideas about the effects of pension privatization come from, and what determines whether they take hold?

Regional Salience

The literature on ideas and policy reform suggests that two factors often play a key role in shaping how policy ideas are received: the regional salience of the idea and the influence of its advocates. As numerous studies have noted, policy innovations often diffuse in regional clusters (Walker 1969; Berry and Berry 1992; Mooney 2001). This occurs because policymakers are more likely to be aware of innovations that take place in their region, and they are more likely to view such innovations as relevant to their own situation.

Regional policy networks typically play a key role in facilitating regional diffusion because they bring policymakers in frequent contact with each other and create standards about what are appropriate policies (Mintrom and Vergari 1998; Teichman 2001). Other types of cultural, institutional, and economic ties, such as shared media, mutual trade and investment, and common values, may also facilitate regional diffusion by increasing the awareness and acceptability of policies that originate in neighboring areas. Weyland (2002a), moreover, suggests that psychological factors can help explain the geographic pattern of policy diffusion. Policymakers will tend to draw on information that is immediately available to them rather than gathering information from a variety of sources and areas.

Influence of the Advocates

The power of the promoters of ideas, meanwhile, matters because the ideas of the powerful tend to carry more weight (Hall 1989; Sikkink 1991; Goldstein and Keohane 1993; Hira 1998). Actors that control substantial resources may not be able to compel policymakers to adopt certain reforms, but their influence tends to grant privileged access to their ideas and often makes them more persuasive. Policymakers who hear conflicting claims about the effectiveness of a particular policy will often give greater credence to the views of the more powerful actor. Indeed, powerful actors often get their way because they have greater technical expertise in a given area, making it more difficult for opponents of their ideas to refute their claims.

The influence of the powerful, however, also stems from their ability to make available or take away the resources they control. DiMaggio and Powell (1983) and Babb (2001) argue that policy convergence frequently results from the pressures of resource dependence, because powerful actors, such as international financial institutions, will often provide significant material incentives for governments to adopt certain policies.

Evaluations of the costs and benefits of reforms are thus profoundly shaped not only by the regional salience of an idea, which tends to make certain policy ideas more prominent than others, but also by the distribution of power, which helps policymakers assign weight to different information and evaluate conflicting claims. The achievements of the Chilean model helped pension privatization gain a high degree of salience in Latin America beginning in the late 1980s. The World Bank, meanwhile, used its substantial influence to help persuade many policymakers that privatizing their pension systems would yield substantial benefits.

REGIONAL DIFFUSION OF THE CHILEAN MODEL

During the military regime of General Augusto Pinochet (1973–90), the government of Chile carried out an unprecedented number of market-oriented reforms. After some initial difficulties, these reforms succeeded in generating impressive economic growth, prompting widespread interest in the Chilean economic model throughout Latin America.

Chile's pension privatization scheme attracted especially great attention because it represented a bold new policy approach. Although the possibility of pension privatization had long been discussed in academic circles, before the 1980s it was an untested idea with unclear implementation guidelines and unknown consequences. As a result, it was rarely considered as a serious policy option. The 1981 Chilean social security reform changed all that, providing a model that policymakers from other countries could use to craft similar reforms.

The Chilean reform persuaded many observers that pension privatization would bring numerous macroeconomic benefits. Policymakers and the media commonly attributed the rapid rise of the Chilean savings rate in the late 1980s and 1990s to the pension privatization scheme, although the evidence for this is mixed at best.[4] A 1994 *New York Times* article was typically effusive, arguing that "private pension funds have almost doubled [Chile's] savings rate in a decade" (Brooke 1994, 27). Gustavo Demarco, one of the main architects of pension privatization in Argentina, acknowledges,

> the arguments based on the effects of private pensions on savings and the capital markets were probably overweighed by some of the sectors promoting the reform in Argentina and other Latin American countries. . . . In most cases the conclusions [about the economic benefits of pension privatization] were only supported by "common

sense" arguments, or [by] diffusion material with simple correlations of variables from the Chilean experience. . . . (Demarco 2000, 4–5).

The Chilean reform also convinced many people that a private pension system would function more efficiently than a public system, which would reduce the amount of resources devoted to pensions. From the outset, the Chilean private pension system generated very high returns on the funds that workers deposited in their individual retirement accounts. Between 1982 and 2000, the pension funds generated returns averaging 10.9 percent annually above inflation (AIOS 2001, 24). As a result of these strong returns, pensions have so far been substantially higher in the Chilean private system than in the public system, in spite of the lower level of contributions (and the relatively high administrative costs) in the private system.

The Chilean pension privatization model has been especially influential in Latin America because of the cultural, economic, and institutional ties that bind the countries of that region to Chile. Policymakers, along with interest groups in Latin America, became acquainted with the Chilean reform before their counterparts outside of the region did, and the Chilean model continues to be much more salient in Latin America than elsewhere. Indeed, pension privatization has been widely discussed in almost every Latin American country.

Latin American policymakers not only have become more familiar with the Chilean model than their counterparts outside the region, but they have also been more inclined to view the Chilean experience as relevant to their own countries because of their countries' numerous cultural and economic similarities to Chile. In addition, Chile has represented an especially compelling model for many Latin American policymakers because it is the only country in the region that has enjoyed strong and sustained economic growth since the mid-1980s. Policymakers from other regions, in contrast, have typically held up other countries as models; in their view, their own countries have little in common with the South American nation. In Hungary and Poland, for example, many participants in the reform debate criticized social security privatization as a Latin American import, arguing that these countries should opt for the European model of reform (Palacios and Rocha 1998; Muller 1999). As one former World Bank pension expert put it, "It's easier for Peru and Argentina to accept the reform of a relatively small and poor country like Chile . . . it has little relevance for Germany, France, the United States, and so on that a reform has been successful [in Chile]" (Schmidt-Hebbel 1997).

Regional policy networks have played a key role in diffusing the Chilean model throughout Latin America. Regionally based institutions, such as the Inter-American Development Bank, the Inter-American Conference on Social Security, and the United Nations Economic Commission for Latin America, have brought Latin American policymakers in contact with one another and have served as forums where the Chilean model is widely discussed. Numerous Chilean firms, research institutions, and government agencies, meanwhile, have actively sought to spread the Chilean model in the region. The Superintendency of Private Pension Funds in Chile, for example, has advised numerous Latin American countries on pension reform. PrimAmerica, a consulting firm founded by two former directors of a Chilean pension fund, has also been quite active in the region, carrying out consulting missions in El Salvador, Honduras, Bolivia, Ecuador, Mexico, Panama, Paraguay, and Guatemala, among other countries (Iglesias 1996).

Perhaps the most influential Latin American advocate of pension reform has been the architect of the Chilean reform, José Piñera. A former Chilean minister of labor, Piñera has traveled throughout Latin America, meeting with ministers and presidents in his effort to promote pension privatization (Piñera 1997). According to well-placed Peruvian officials, Piñera played a key role in persuading President Alberto Fujimori to privatize the Peruvian pension system (Boloña 1997; Roggero 1997). Indeed, Fujimori approved the project at the end of a three-hour meeting with Piñera (Roggero 1997, 41). Carlos Boloña, a former minister of economy in Peru, recalls,

> At the time of the reform, the president of Peru was very concerned. He wasn't convinced that we should privatize the pension system. So we brought José [Piñera] to talk to him, to discuss what privatization had done for Chile. And, of course, José was able to convince him that privatization was in Peru's best interest. The reform might not have been signed into law without José's assistance. (Boloña 1997, 1)

Piñera also reportedly helped convince Colombian president-elect César Gaviria and his economic advisers of the merits of pension privatization during a 1990 visit to that country (Santos 1997; Nelson 1998, 3). According to Juan Manuel Santos, a former Colombian minister of trade,

> The arguments and results presented by Piñera [at a presentation on pension reform] made a deep impression on those who knew about the problem and on Colombian public opinion. That day Piñera met with the president-elect and with his team of economic advisers. It was an intense meeting of five hours, after which Gaviria's economic team was convinced of the necessity of pushing the pension reform and of working on the basis of the Chilean scheme of private pensions. (Santos 1997, 42)

The influence of the Chilean model is particularly noticeable in the details of the pension reform legislation in Latin American countries, which tend to resemble closely the Chilean legislation. The original Colombian reform proposal, for example, was so close to the Chilean model that one World Bank adviser joked that they had taken the Chilean legislation and used a computer search-and-replace function to substitute the word Colombia for Chile (von Gersdorff 1998). Many Latin American policymakers freely acknowledge their debt to the Chilean reform, although they also highlight the adaptations that they have made to the Chilean model. Bolivian president Gonzalo Sánchez de Losada, for example, acknowledged that the Bolivian pension reform "is something that we have received and copied from Chile," although he noted, "obviously, we have made changes, taking advantage of the Chilean experience" (*Presencia* 1996). The main architect of the reform in Argentina, Walter Schulthess, said, "We used a lot from Chile; we saw what functioned well. We made some changes—a different way of presenting the problem—but we used their experience a lot" (Schulthess 1996). One key Argentine policymaker went so far as to say that "if the Chilean case had not existed, it is probable that we still wouldn't have the reform [in Argentina]" (Barassi 1996). The Chilean model has thus profoundly shaped the content of pension reform in Latin America, but it is only beginning to exercise the same sort of influence outside the region.

THE ROLE OF THE WORLD BANK

The World Bank has also helped convince policymakers of the merits of pension privatization. In recent years, the World Bank has sought to recast itself as a "knowledge bank," arguing that it may foster development more efficiently by serving as a conduit of ideas rather than by simply distributing resources (World Bank 1999).

In no policy area has the bank's effort to influence thinking been more noticeable than in pension reform. Since 1990, the World Bank has carried out a vast amount of research; held numerous courses, workshops, and conferences; and disseminated a wide variety of publications detailing the problems with the existing public pension systems and extolling the benefits of pension privatization. Its landmark 1994 study of pension systems around the world, *Averting the Old Age Crisis*, has been especially influential. A subsequent publication asserts that "partly as a result of this report, the bank has witnessed an upsurge in pension reform efforts among client countries, and its support to such efforts has increased dramatically" (World Bank 1996, 2). A later report states,

> Averting the Old Age Crisis showed how a low-cost form of international assistance can stimulate reform of pension policy. In the wake of that report, donors have helped a wide range of countries—among them Argentina, China, Hungary, Mexico, Poland, and Uruguay—study the long-term fiscal and distributional consequences of their old age security systems. These countries were able to draw on the lessons of, for example, the successful Chilean pension reform. (World Bank 1999, 136)

The World Bank has played a particularly important role in persuading policymakers that pension privatization would bring major macroeconomic benefits, including an increase in the domestic savings rate. *Averting the Old Age Crisis*, for example, trumpeted the economic benefits of pension privatization—indeed, its subtitle is "Policies to Protect the Old and Promote Growth" (emphasis added). Estelle James, the lead author of *Averting the Old Age Crisis* and one of the principal architects of the new World Bank pension reform strategy, has written elsewhere that "the chief theoretical argument for the recommended multipillar system is that it will have a positive effect on efficiency and growth" (1997, 16).

The World Bank has also provided loans that have reduced some of the financial obstacles to pension privatization. Indeed, in the late 1980s and 1990s, the World Bank granted a total of $3.4 billion in loans to 36 countries to finance pension reform, including loans to cover the transition costs of pension privatization in Argentina, Mexico, Uruguay, Hungary, and Kazakhstan (Holzmann 2000; Queisser 2000, 39). These financial incentives were nevertheless relatively minor, typically amounting to less than 1 percent of the total transition costs of the privatization schemes. On the whole, the influence of the World Bank has been more ideational than material in nature, although both types of influence have mattered. As a former secretary of social security in Brazil noted in one paper, the World Bank has promoted pension privatization through the diffusion of ideas and the construction of a pro-privatization rhetoric, rather than by making financing conditional on pension privatization (Pinheiro 2004, 111).

The World Bank has been particularly influential in those countries where it has carried out pension reform missions. Such missions have enabled World Bank representatives to maintain extended contacts with host country social security policymakers, which have provided them greater policy influence. The pension reform missions have also provided access to the demographic and financial data necessary to carry out sophisticated analyses of the problems facing the countries' public pension systems, as well as analyses of the economic consequences of privatization. The technical and financial assistance provided by the World Bank has strengthened domestic advocates of pension privatization in their struggles with opponents of privatization.

The World Bank had numerous pension reform missions in Latin America during the late 1980s and early 1990s, including programs in Argentina and Mexico that gave impetus to the pension privatization efforts in those countries. The pension reform missions financed preliminary studies of the problems facing the countries' public pension systems, which ultimately led to the formulation of pension privatization proposals. World Bank officials in both countries also used their formal and informal contacts with policymakers to encourage them to privatize their pension systems, and the bank provided some financing to ease the implementation costs of the reforms.

In El Salvador and Bolivia, the World Bank's pension reform mission brought in Chilean pension experts to study the countries' pension systems. These experts encouraged the countries to privatize their pension systems and formulated privatization proposals that were eventually implemented, albeit with some changes. The pension reform mission in Costa Rica similarly enabled the bank to lobby hard for pension privatization in that country. A 1995 World Bank report on Costa Rica argued that privatization would reduce evasion, produce higher returns, and "generate savings for the economy," whereas limited reform "simply delays problems rather than solving them once and for all" (Demiruc-Kunt and Schwarz 1995, 29).

The World Bank has also carried out a large number of pension reform missions in the postcommunist world, promoting pension privatization in that region. It established a pension reform mission in Hungary in the early 1990s, for example, and in 1995 published a study that described the main problems of the existing Hungarian pension system and proposed partial privatization. That same year, the World Bank began to fund a working group of the Hungarian Ministry of Finance that was developing a privatization proposal. The World Bank's financial and technical assistance helped strengthen the Ministry of Finance in negotiations with other governmental and societal actors. Subsequently, the bank became heavily involved in funding and participating directly in an interministerial working group on pension reform that worked out differences within the government with regard to the reform. The World Bank also brought in international pension experts from various countries to serve as consultants on the reform, and it helped finance the transition costs of the reform after the privatization plan was implemented.

In both Poland and Croatia, a World Bank official (on leave) headed the government's pension reform team, which provided the bank with considerable policymaking influence (Muller 2002). In Poland, the bank assisted in the creation and funding of the Plenipotentiary for Social Security Reform, which planned and implemented the pension privatization scheme in that country. In Croatia, the bank sponsored a 1995 conference that brought in foreign pension experts and led the incoming prime minister to endorse partial pension privatization (Muller 2002, 85). The World Bank also provided technical assistance to the Croatian government and helped finance the transition costs of the reform.

In Kazakhstan, the World Bank did not become involved until the reform was well under way (Andrews 1998; Orenstein 1999). Nevertheless, the reform's principal architect, Grigori Marchenko, read World Bank publications on pension reform and attended World Bank conferences on the topic, both of which, he acknowledges, influenced his thinking about pension reform (Orenstein 1999, 24).

The World Bank has thus helped shape policymaking on pension reform around the world. In some instances, the bank has had to overcome countries' initial reluctance to privatize. As one bank pension expert said, "some countries initially have said that they don't want [to privatize their pension systems], but we have sometimes been able to convince them to do so" (Schwarz 1998). In other instances, governments have been divided over what type of pension reform to carry out; the World Bank's recommendations, along with its technical and financial resources, have helped tip the balance in favor of pension privatization.

EXECUTIVE CONTROL OF THE LEGISLATURE

Pension privatization proposals have typically met staunch opposition from a variety of sources, including pensioners' associations, labor unions, and opposition political parties. Because pension privatization measures usually require congressional approval, the legislature has often been the setting for major battles over the reform proposals.[5]

Legislators have come under intense pressure from opponents of pension privatization to vote against the reform proposals, making it difficult for the executive to obtain votes for such legislation. Even legislators who are ideologically sympathetic to privatization have often been loath to assume the political costs of voting for the unpopular reforms. To gain approval for pension privatization bills, executives have therefore typically needed to wield a good deal of control over their legislatures.

The degree of control that the executive has over the legislature depends largely on the percentage of seats the ruling party holds. The executive typically has much more influence over the votes of members of its own party than those of other parties, particularly when it comes to unpopular measures like social security reform. The degree of internal unity or discipline of the ruling party varies considerably from country to country, however. Where the ruling party has been relatively unified and has held a majority or near-majority of the seats in the legislature, the executive has typically been able to enact pension privatization legislation.

The ruling party, for example, used its majority or near-majority and strong party discipline to push through pension privatization plans in Mexico, Argentina, Bolivia, El Salvador, Nicaragua, Hungary, and Croatia despite resistance from the main opposition parties. Presidents have had a much more difficult time gaining legislative approval for pension reforms in instances where the ruling party has held a small minority of seats in the legislature or where the ruling party has been split. Repeated efforts to enact major pension reforms in Brazil and Ecuador, for example, were undermined by the president's low degree of control of the legislature. A lack of internal party unity, meanwhile, hindered efforts to privatize the pension system in Colombia, Paraguay, and Venezuela, although the Colombian government eventually managed to enact a watered-down version of its original pension privatization bill. The executive's degree of control of the legislature has thus shaped the political feasibility of pension privatization.

A QUANTITATIVE ANALYSIS

To test these arguments, a probit analysis was conducted on the determinants of pension privatization worldwide.[6] The dependent variable was coded as 1 if a country enacted legislation privatizing its pension system between the years 1990 and 2000, and 0 if it did not enact any sort of privatization legislation during that period. The sample was limited to middle- and upper-income countries with populations above one million, partly because of the difficulty of finding reliable data for low-income countries and nations with tiny populations.[7] Many low-income countries, moreover, lack the financial infrastructure necessary to privatize their pension systems or have no pension systems at all. The sample comprised a total of 82 countries, including 17 that privatized their pension systems to some degree.[8]

The independent variables were measured in the following manner. Public pension expenditures as a percent of gross domestic product were used to measure the economic burden of public pension spending. These data represent various years in the 1990s or, in a few cases, estimates based on regional averages.[9] The average domestic savings rate between 1990 and 1998 was used to measure the sufficiency of local capital sources.[10] To minimize problems of endogeneity, only the years before a nation privatized its pension system were used for those countries that enacted pension privatization schemes during this period. The extent of World Bank influence over local pension policy was measured by whether a country had hosted a World Bank pension reform mission.[11] An additional, dummy variable was created for Latin American countries, to accommodate the argument that these countries were particularly likely to privatize their pension systems because of regional diffusion of the Chilean model. The executive's degree of control of the legislature was gauged by the average share of seats held by the ruling party in the lower chamber during the 1990s.[12] Unfortunately, cross-national data on party discipline were not available.

The results of the statistical analysis provide broad support for the arguments made in this article. The first column of table 1, labeled Model 1, displays the results of the initial probit analysis. The model correctly predicts 91.5 percent of the cases, including 13 of the 17 cases of privatization and 62 of the 65 cases of non-privatization.

As the table makes evident, the variables in the initial analysis all had the expected signs, and most of them were statistically significant at the 0.05 level or better. The coefficient of public pension expenditures had a positive sign, as expected, and was statistically significant at the 0.01 level. This indicates that the likelihood that a nation will privatize its pension system does indeed increase as its public pension spending rises. The substantive effect of this variable is powerful. The probability that a nation will privatize its pension system is less than 2 percent if all variables are held at their means. However, a one-standard-deviation increase in public pension expenditures from 5.1 percent of GDP to 9.5 percent of GDP (holding all other variables at their means) boosts the probability that a nation will privatize its pension system from less than 2 percent to 39 percent.

The variable that measures the ruling party's share of seats in the legislature was also positive and statistically significant at the 0.05 level. This suggests that, as expected, the probability of pension privatization rises as the ruling party's control of the legislature increases. The substantive effect of this variable is somewhat weaker than the public pension spending variable. If the ruling party's share of legislative seats is increased by one standard deviation from its mean (from 49 percent to 71 percent) and all other variables are held at their means, the probability that a nation will privatize its pension system rises from 2 to 12 percent.

The regional dummy variable for Latin America was also positive and statistically significant at the 0.01 level, indicating that, other things being equal, Latin American nations are more likely to privatize their pension systems. This study has argued that the Latin American bias toward pension privatization is largely a result of regional diffusion of the Chilean model, but other factors that are unaccounted for in this analysis might also lead Latin American nations to want to privatize their pension systems. The Latin America dummy variable had a strong substantive effect on the likelihood of pension privatization. If we increase this variable by one standard deviation from its mean and hold all other variables at their means, the probability that a nation will privatize its pension system rises from less than 2 to 21 percent. Other things being equal, Latin American nations have a 69 percent probability of privatizing their systems.

The World Bank pension reform mission variable also had a positive sign, and its coefficient was statistically significant at the 0.01 level, which indicates that countries that host World Bank missions are more likely to privatize their pension systems. Its substantive effect was also relatively large. Ceteris paribus, nations that host World Bank pension reform missions have an approximately 20 percent likelihood of privatizing their pension systems, as opposed to a minimal likelihood for those countries that do not host pension reform missions.

The relationship between World Bank pension reform missions and pension privatization is at least partly endogenous—that is, some governments request World Bank missions because they intend to privatize their pension systems. Interviews with World

Table 1. Determinants of Pension Privatization Around the World

	Model 1 (binary probit)	Model 2 (binary probit)	Model 3 (binary probit)	Model 4 (binary probit)	Model 5 (binary probit)
Constant	−7.749** (−3.154)[a]	−7.550** (−2.972)	−3.015* (−2.416)	−7.715** (−3.038)	−3.413** (−2.999)
Public pension spending (as percent of GDP)	0.423** (3.030)	0.481** (3.109)	0.243** (3.248)	0.482** (3.159)	0.162** (2.822)
Gross domestic savings (as percent of GDP)	−0.036 (−1.448)	−0.102* (−2.241)	−0.079* (−2.271)	−0.101* (−2.184)	−0.072** (−2.591)
Ruling party's share of seats in legislature	0.045* (2.453)	0.053** (2.622)	0.030* (2.152)	0.055** (2.661)	−0.295* (2.370)
Latin America	3.359** (3.213)	3.600** (3.254)	2.600** (3.580)	3.774** (3.237)	1.847** (3.387)
World Bank pension reform mission	2.621** (2.932)	3.006** (2.973)		2.700* (2.432)	1.631** (2.997)
World Bank loans/GDP			2.241 (0.408)		
Economic recession				0.383 (0.549)	
Number of observations	82	81	81	81	81
Percent correctly predicted	91.5	96.3	83.9	95.0	82.7
Log likelihood (at convergence)	−18.061	−15.453	−24.516	−15.303	−29.734
Log likelihood (initial)	−56.838	−56.145	−56.145	−56.145	−69.366

*<.05; **<.01 (two-tailed t-tests).
[a]t-statistics in parentheses.

Bank staff members and Latin American policymakers, however, suggest that the causal relationship also runs in the other direction—the World Bank pension reform missions are at times able to persuade reluctant policymakers to privatize their systems. For example, neither the Argentine government, the Costa Rican government, nor the Mexican government was fully committed to privatizing its pension system when it invited the World Bank to establish pension reform missions in the country. In all three cases, the World Bank missions put pension privatization at the forefront of the policy agenda and helped pave the way for subsequent administrations to carry out the privatization schemes.

The one variable that did not perform as well as expected was the domestic savings rate variable. The coefficient of this variable had a negative sign, as predicted, but it was not statistically significant at conventional levels. The lack of statistical significance of this variable, however, is because of a single outlier, Albania—and there are strong theoretical reasons for excluding Albania from the analysis. Albania suffered from a great deal of political and economic instability during the 1990s, which made it difficult to privatize the nation's pension system. This may explain why the country did not do so even though it presumably had substantial economic incentives, given its extraordinarily low domestic savings rate (−16.3 percent) during that period.

As model 2 of the table shows, if we exclude Albania from the analysis, the domestic savings rate variable achieves statistical significance at the 0.05 level. (Excluding Albania has only a minimal effect on the other variables.) Even excluding the Albanian case, the substantive effect of the domestic savings rate is modest. If we decrease the domestic savings rate by one standard deviation from its mean (from 21.4 percent to 12.4 percent) while holding all other variables at their means, the likelihood that a nation will privatize its pension system rises from less than 1 percent to 6 percent.

To test alternative explanations of pension privatization, the statistical model was reestimated with a number of additional variables. The first of these was a variable that measured the value of World Bank loans (as a percentage of GDP) to each country between 1990 and 1998, so as to test whether the World Bank's influence was based on the financial inducements it could offer instead of the bank's ability to persuade policymakers of the merits of pension privatization.[13] The assumption was that if the World Bank had influence principally because of the financing it provided, the likelihood that a country would privatize its pension system would rise as the amount of World Bank loans increased. As model 3 indicates, a statistical analysis provides little support for this alternative hypothesis.[14] Although the World Bank loan variable had the expected sign, it did not approach statistical significance. Moreover, the explanatory power of the model declined significantly when this variable, instead of the World Bank pension mission variable, was included in the analysis. This finding provides support for the hypothesis that World Bank influence is more ideational than material in nature.

Second, a statistical test was conducted to see whether economic crisis, either in the 1980s or the 1990s, had a significant effect on the likelihood of pension privatization. Economic crisis was initially measured by whether a country had experienced hyperinflation (measured as an annual inflation rate of more than 100 percent) or a serious economic recession (measured as a downturn of more than 5 percent of GDP in a single year) at any point between 1980 and 1998.[15] Additional tests examined whether pension privatization was correlated with the average inflation rate or the average growth in GDP between 1990 and 1998. All these variables had the expected sign, but none of them proved to be statistically significant at conventional levels. (Model 4 of the table presents the economic crisis dummy variable.) These findings suggest that economic crisis has, at best, a weak relationship with the likelihood of pension privatization. Nevertheless, economic crisis may affect the probability of pension privatization indirectly through its effect on some of the other variables.

DETERMINING THE SCOPE OF PRIVATIZATION

The preceding analyses suggest that the aforementioned variables affect the likelihood of pension privatization, but do they also increase the scope of privatization? To examine this question, the dependent variable was reformulated, assigning a score of 2 to countries that fully privatized their pension systems between 1990 and 2000, 1 to countries that partially privatized their pension systems, and 0 to countries that did not enact any type of pension privatization scheme during this period. Model 5 of the table presents the results of an ordered probit analysis with the reformulated dependent variable.

All the variables remain statistically significant, but only the Latin America and domestic savings rate variables achieve higher levels of statistical significance in the ordered probit model. (The coefficients from the binomial probit and the ordered probit models are not strictly comparable, however.) More important, only the Latin America variable significantly increased the likelihood of full-scale pension privatization in the ordered probit model, and even then the impact was modest. According to a simulation based on the ordered probit results, Latin American countries are 10 percent more likely to privatize fully their pension systems than non-Latin American countries (holding all other variables at their means), presumably because the influence of the Chilean full privatization model is greater in the region.

The other variables included in the analysis do not appear to increase the scope of pension privatization. It can be argued that one of these variables, the level of public pension spending, will actually tend to reduce the scope of pension privatization, largely because the medium-term costs of pension privatization are quite high for countries with high public pension expenditures. The transition costs are particularly large for such countries because they tend to have a greater number of retirees whose pensions must continue to come from the state after the pension system is privatized. They also tend to have more elderly workers who may need to be compensated for their past contributions to the public pension system. Countries with high levels of public pension expenditures are therefore much more likely to opt for partial privatization.[16] By only partially privatizing the pension system, the government may continue to collect a portion of the contributions that were traditionally paid to the public system. (Under full privatization, the state typically forgoes these revenues entirely.) The payroll taxes that the state collects can be used to finance partially the pensions of current retirees, which makes the fiscal burden of such reforms more manageable.[17]

Whereas the transition costs of pension privatization are quite large for countries with high current public pension expenditures, they are considerably smaller for countries with low public pension expenditures. Countries with low pension expenditures thus enjoy what Pei (1995) has termed an "advantage of backwardness": sweeping reform is easier in these countries because their pension systems are still relatively undeveloped. These countries are therefore much more likely to opt for full privatization if they choose to privatize their pension systems at all.

Another variable that has constrained the scope of pension privatization is the degree of democracy (Mesa-Lago 1997; Mesa-Lago and Muller 2002). Authoritarian regimes are no more likely to choose to privatize their pension systems than democratic regimes. Indeed, if a variable measuring the level of democracy is included in the probit model, it does not achieve statistical significance. Authoritarian regimes nevertheless are more likely to carry out full-scale pension privatization when they do choose to privatize their pension systems.

In a democracy, by contrast, privatizing the pension system typically requires the consent of numerous political actors, from legislators to particular powerful interest groups. Sweeping pension privatization plans are therefore likely to get watered down in democratic regimes, which is exactly what occurred in Argentina, Colombia, and Costa Rica, among other countries. In authoritarian regimes, interest groups often have little ability to affect public policy, and authoritarian legislatures are typically "rubber stamp" institutions, if they exist at all. As a result, authoritarian or semiauthoritarian regimes that have sought to implement full-scale pension privatization measures have typically been

Table 2. Determinants of Degree of Pension Privatization

	Degree of Democracy[a]	Public Pension Spending (as percent of GDP)
Partial Privatizers		
Argentina	2.5	6.2
Bulgaria	2.5	7.3
Colombia	3.0	1.1
Costa Rica	1.5	3.8
Croatia	4.0	11.6
Estonia	1.5	7.0
Hungary	1.5	9.7
Latvia	1.5	10.2
Macedonia	3.0	8.7
Poland	1.5	14.4
Sweden	1.0	11.4
United Kingdom	1.5	8.3
Uruguay	2.0	15.0
Average	2.1	8.2
Broad Privatizers		
Bolivia	3.0	2.5
Chile	6.0	5.6
Dominican Republic	2.5	0.4
El Salvador	3.0	1.3
Kazakhstan	5.5	5.0
Mexico	4.0	0.4
Nicaragua	3.0	4.3
Peru	5.5	1.2
Average	4.1	2.4

[a]Scale based on the Freedom House index of civil and political rights, ranging from 1 (most free or democratic) to 7 (least free or democratic).
Note: Scores correspond to the year the pension system was privatized or the nearest year for which data are available.
Source: Palacios and Pallarès-Miralles 2000; Gastil 1985–2000.

able to do so with relatively little difficulty. Such was the case in Chile, Kazakhstan, and, to a lesser extent, Peru and Mexico.

Table 2 presents some evidence in support of the aforementioned hypotheses. As the table indicates, the countries that opted for sweeping privatization measures had an average score of 4.1 on the Freedom House index of civil and political rights while the countries that only partially privatized their systems had an average score of 2.1, which suggests that broad privatization measures may be more likely to take place under regimes that restrict civil and political liberties (Gastil various years).

The difference between the two groups of countries is even more glaring with regard to public pension expenditures. Public pension expenditures represent, on average, only 2.4 percent of the gross domestic product of those countries that fully privatized their pension systems, but they average 8.2 percent of gross domestic product in those countries that have opted for partial privatization. This suggests that sweeping privatization measures may also be more likely to take place in countries with relatively low public pension expenditures.

CONCLUSIONS

This article has argued that a specific set of economic concerns, rather than economic crisis in general, has contributed to the wave of pension spending in Latin America and around the world. The specific concerns include limited access to capital and the growing economic burden of public pension expenditures. Many countries have opted to privatize their pension systems in the belief that such measures would boost their sagging domestic savings rates and solve the long-term financial problems of their public pension systems. There is no clear-cut evidence, however, that pension privatization will resolve either of these economic problems. Why, then, did so many policymakers believe that pension privatization would yield major economic benefits?

This study maintains that the Chilean model and the World Bank have been particularly influential in forming beliefs about the economic efficacy of pension privatization. The sharp rise in Chile's domestic savings rate in the late 1980s and the strong financial performance of the country's private pension system helped persuade many policymakers that pension privatization would boost their domestic savings rates and resolve the long-term financial problems of their pension systems. The Chilean model was particularly influential in Latin America because Latin American policymakers were more familiar with the Chilean model and more likely to think it relevant to their own countries. The World Bank, meanwhile, constantly championed the economic benefits of pension privatization and used its considerable financial and technical resources to help persuade policymakers to privatize their systems. The World Bank has been particularly influential in those countries where it has had pension reform missions because the missions have granted the bank extensive access to key policymakers and technical data.

The article thus shows that ideas play a crucial role in policy choice. For any given economic problem, a variety of possible policy solutions typically exist. Ideas not only determine the range of possible policy solutions but also suggest, correctly or incorrectly, the costs and benefits associated with each type of policy solution. Ideas thus suggest to policymakers what they ought to do to maximize their interests in an uncertain world. The challenge for theorists of ideas is to show how and where ideas matter. This article has suggested that the local salience of an idea and the power of its promoters often play a crucial role in determining whether an idea takes hold. Where policy ideas have high visibility and influential advocates, they are likely to be enacted, regardless of the merits of the ideas themselves.

NOTES

I would like to thank Evelyne Huber, Robert R. Kaufman, and Kurt Weyland for their useful comments on an earlier version of this article. This article also benefited from the review process of *Latin American Politics and Society* and, in particular, from the helpful suggestions of the journal's editors and four anonymous reviewers. The author is solely responsible for any remaining errors or omissions. The article is adapted from *Retiring the State: The Politics of Pension Privatization in Latin America and Beyond*, copyright [c] 2003 by the Board of Trustees of the Leland Stanford Jr. University, by permission of the publisher.

1 Pension privatization is defined here as the partial or complete replacement of a publicly managed pension system with a privately managed system. By definition, this excludes add-on schemes that create new private pension schemes without reducing the scope of the existing public pension systems.

2 For an expanded version of this argument, see Madrid 2003.

3 This risk is reduced to the extent that the pension funds invest abroad. Most of the countries that have privatized their pension systems, however, have placed low limits on the funds that can be invested in other countries.

4 The Chilean model did not become the object of envy until the end of the 1980s, largely because the dramatic increase in Chile's savings rate did not occur until the late 1980s. By this time, the Chilean private pension system had also been achieving high returns for a long time.

5 To date, no democratic government has privatized its pension system by decree. Even democratic leaders who enjoy decree powers have preferred to seek legislative approval for the reform measures, so as to give the private pension systems a solid legal foundation.

6 Unfortunately, the absence of annual data for many of the variables under study precluded a cross-sectional time series analysis.

7 This includes all countries that the World Bank publication World Development Indicators lists as having a gross domestic product per capita of more than two thousand dollars in 1995. See World Bank 2000.

8 The countries that enacted privatization schemes during this period were Argentina, Bolivia, Bulgaria, Colombia, Costa Rica, Croatia, El Salvador, Hungary, Kazakhstan, Latvia, Macedonia, Mexico, Nicaragua, Peru, Poland, Sweden, and Uruguay. Including in the sample the countries that privatized their pension systems during the 1980s does not significantly change the results. Nor do the findings change significantly by including the countries that added private pension schemes to their existing public pension schemes.

9 The public pension spending data come from Palacios and Pallares-Miralles 2000 and World Bank 1994.

10 The domestic savings rate data were culled from World Bank 2000.

11 Data on World Bank pension reform missions come from Schwarz and Demirguc-Kunt 1999.

12 These data come from the *Europa World Year Book* 1985–2000.

13 Data on World Bank loans come from World Bank 2000.

14 Using data from World Bank 2000, two alternative measures of World Bank influence were tried: debt service payments as a proportion of total exports in 1995, and external debt as a proportion of gross domestic product in 1995. Neither of these variables achieved statistical significance. Debt service payments/GDP had a coefficient of .039 and a standard error of .033, and external debt/GDP had a coefficient of −.037 and a standard error of 1.222. Inclusion of these variables did not qualitatively change the overall results.

15 These data come from World Bank 2000. Data were not available before 1990 for a number of countries in the sample.

16 Countries with high pension expenditures may also try to reduce the costs of privatization by declining to compensate workers for the past contributions to the public pension system or reneging on other pension commitments.

17 In mixed systems, the social security contributions that the state collects will also eventually be used to pay a basic pension to future retirees, but in the near term these payments will be minor, which makes the transition from a public system to a mixed system considerably easier.

REFERENCES

Adler, Emanuel. 1991. Cognitive Evolution: A Dynamic Approach for the Study of International Relations and Their Progress. In *Progress in Postwar International Relations*, ed. Adler and Beverly Crawford. New York: Columbia University Press. 43–88.

AIOS (Asociación Internacional de Organismos de Supervisión de Fondos de Pensiones. 2001. Boletín Estadístico AIOS 5 (June).

Andrews, Emily. 1998. Staff Economist, World Bank. Author interview. Washington, DC, May 15.

Babb, Sarah. 2001. *Managing Mexico: Economists from Nationalism to Neoliberalism*. Princeton: Princeton University Press.

Barassi, Mauricio. 1996. Former adviser to the Secretary for Social Security, Argentina. Author interview. Buenos Aires, October 15.

Berry, Frances Stokes, and William D. Berry, 1992. Tax Innovation in the States. American *Journal of Political Science* 36, 3 (August): 715–42.

Boloña, Carlos. 1997. Testimony: Pension Reform in Peru. Paper delivered at the conference "The Global Pension Crisis," sponsored by the Cato Institute and *The Economist*, London, December 8–9.

Brooke, James. 1994. Quiet Revolution in Latin Pensions. *New York Times*, September 10: 37.

Cámara de Diputados de los Estados Unidos Mexicanos. 1995. *Diario de los Debates*, año 2, no. 18 (November 9): 2360–68.

Corrales, Javier. 1997–98. Do Economic Crises Contribute to Economic Reform? Argentina and Venezuela in the 1990s. *Political Science Quarterly* 112, 4: 617–44.

Corsetti, Giancarlo, and Klaus Schmidt-Hebbel. 1995. Pension Reform and Growth. World Bank Policy Research Working Paper 1471. Washington, DC: World Bank.

Cottani, Joaquín, and Gustavo Demarco. 1998. The Shift to a Funded Social Security System: The Case of Argentina. In *Privatizing Social Security*, ed. Martin Feldstein. Chicago: University of Chicago Press. 177–212.

Dávila, Enrique. 1997. Coordinator of Advisers, Secretariat of Finance and Public Credit, Mexico. Author interview. Mexico City, June 13.

Demarco, Gustavo. 1996. Adviser to the Secretary of Social Security, Argentina. Author interview. Buenos Aires, October 25.

——. 2000. The Argentine Pension System Reform and the International Experience. Paper delivered at the Woodrow Wilson Center conference "Learning from Foreign Models in Latin American Policy Reform." Washington, DC, September.

Demirguc-Kunt, Asli, and Anita Schwarz. 1995. The Costa Rican Pension System: Options for Reform. World Bank Policy Research Working Paper 1483. Washington, DC: World Bank.

DiMaggio, Paul, and Walter Powell. 1983. The Iron Cage Revisited. *American Sociological Review* 48, 2: 147–60.

Europa World Year Book. 1985–2000. London: Europa Publications.

Gastil, Raymond. 1985–2000. *Freedom in the World: Political Rights and Civil Liberties*. New York: Freedom House.

Goldstein, Judith, and Robert O. Keohane, eds. 1993. *Ideas and Foreign Policy: Beliefs, Institutions, and Political Change*. Ithaca: Cornell University Press.

Haggard, Stephan, and Robert R. Kaufman. 1995. *The Political Economy of Democratic Transitions*. Princeton: Princeton University Press.

Haindl, Erik. 1997. The Chilean Pension Fund Reform and Its Impact on Saving. In *Generating Savings for Latin American Development*, ed. Robert Grosse. Coral Gables: North-South Center Press. 113–34.

Hall, Peter, ed. 1989. *The Political Power of Economic Ideas: Keynesianism Across Nations*. Princeton: Princeton University Press.

Hira, Anil. 1998. Ideas *and Economic Policy in Latin America*. Westport: Praeger.

Holzmann, Robert. 1997. Pension Reform, Financial Market Development, and Economic Growth: Preliminary Evidence from Chile. International Monetary Fund Staff Papers 44. Washington, DC: International Monetary Fund.

——. 2000. The World Bank Approach to Pension Reform. *International Social Security Review* 53, 1: 11–34.

Iglesias, Augusto. 1996. Director of PrimAmerica Consultores. Author interview. Santiago, December 23.

Instituto Nicaragüense de Seguridad Social (INSS). n.d. Sobre la reforma de pensiones: las razones que la justifican. <www.inss.org.ni/CREPEN.htm> Accessed July 2001.

Instituto Salvadoreño del Seguro Social. 1997. Exposición de motivos: ley del sistema de ahorro para pensiones. <www.spensiones.gob.sv/Documentos/Motivos.html> Accessed March 7, 2001.

James, Estelle. 1997. New Systems for Old Age Security: Theory, Practice, and Empirical Evidence. World Bank Policy Research Working Paper 1766. Washington, DC: World Bank.

Kay, Stephen. 1999. Unexpected Privatizations: Politics and Social Security Reform in the Southern Cone. *Comparative Politics* 31,4 (July): 403–22.

Madrid, Raúl L. 2002. The Politics and Economics of Pension Privatization in Latin America. *Latin American Research Review* 37, 2: 159–82.

———. 2003. *Retiring the State: The Politics of Pension Privatization in Latin America and Beyond.* Stanford: Stanford University Press.

Martínez, Gabriel. 1997. Director of Planning, Mexican Social Security Institute. Author interview. México City, June 10.

Mesa-Lago, Carmelo. 1997. Social Welfare Reform in the Context of Economic-Political Liberalization: Latin American Cases. *World Development* 24, 4: 497–517.

Mesa-Lago, Carmelo, and Katharina Muller. 2002. The Politics of Pension Reform in Latin America. *Journal of Latin American Studies* 34, 3 (August): 687–715.

Mintrom, Michael, and Sandra Vergari. 1998. Policy Networks and Innovation Diffusion: The Case of State Education Reforms. *The Journal of Politics* 60, 1 (February): 126–48.

Mooney, Christopher. 2001. Modeling Regional Effects on State Policy Diffusion. *Political Research Quarterly* 54, 1 (March): 103–24.

Muller, Katharina. 1999. *The Political Economy of Pension Reform in Central-Eastern Europe.* Northampton, U.K.: Edward Elgar.

———. 2002. Privatising Old-Age Security: Latin America and Eastern Europe Compared. Discussion paper. Frankfurt: Frankfurt Institute for Transformation Studies. March.

Nelson, Joan M. 1998. The Political Economy of Colombia's Health Reforms of 1993. Mimeograph. Washington, DC: Overseas Development Council, June.

———. 2001. The Politics of Pension and Health-Care Reforms in Hungary and Poland. In *Reforming the State: Fiscal and Welfare Reform in Post-Socialist Countries*, ed. Janos Kornai, Stephan Haggard, and Robert R. Kaufman. New York: Cambridge University Press. 235–66.

Orenstein, Mitchell A. 1999. How Politics and Institutions Affect Pension Reform in Three Post-Communist Countries. World Bank Policy Research Working Paper 2310. Washington, DC: World Bank.

Orszag, Peter R., and Joseph E. Stiglitz. 2001. Rethinking Pension Reform: Ten Myths About Social Security Systems. In *New Ideas About Old Age Security*, ed. Robert Holzmann and Stiglitz. Washington, DC: World Bank. 17–56.

Palacios, Robert, and Montserrat Pallares-Miralles. 2000. *International Patterns of Pension Provision.* Mimeograph. Washington, DC: World Bank. <www.worldbank.org/pensions> Accessed July 2000.

Palacios, Robert, and Robert Rocha. 1998. The Hungarian Pension System in Transition. World Bank Social Protection Discussion Paper 9805. Washington, DC: World Bank. March.

Pei, Minxin. 1995. The Puzzle of East Asian Exceptionalism. In *Economic Reform and Democracy*, ed. Larry Diamond and Marc F. Plattner. Baltimore: Johns Hopkins University Press. 112–25.

Piñera, José. 1997. Former Minister of Labor, Chile. Author interview. Santiago, January 15.

Pinheiro, Vinícius C. 2004. The Politics of Social Security Reform in Brazil. In *Learning from Foreign Models in Latin American Policy Reform*, ed. Kurt Weyland. Baltimore: Johns Hopkins University Press. 110–38.

Presencia (La Paz). 1996. Goni: ley de pensiones fue copiada de Chile. November 13: Sección de Economía, 9.

Queisser, Monika. 2000. Pension Reform and International Organizations: From Conflict to Convergence. *International Social Security Review* 53, 2: 31–45.

Roggero, Mario. 1997. Peru. In La revolución latinoamericano de las pensiones, ed. José Piñera. Santiago: *International Center for Pension Privatization.* Mimeograph. 39–41.

Santos, Juan Manuel. 1997. Colombia. In *La revolución latinoamericano de las pensiones*, ed. José Pinera Santiago: International Center for Pension Privatization. Mimeograph. 41–43.

Schmidt-Hebbel, Klaus. 1997. Former Staff Economist, World Bank. Author interview. Santiago, January 17.

Schulthess, Walter. 1996. Secretary of Social Security, Argentina. Author interview. Buenos Aires, November 6.

Schwarz, Anita. 1998. World Bank Economist. Author interview. Washington, DC, May 14.

Schwarz, Anita, and Asli Demirguc-Kunt. 1999. *Taking Stock of Pension Reforms Around the World—An Update.* Mimeograph. Washington, DC: World Bank. <www.worldbank.org/pensions> Accessed July 2000.

Sikkink, Kathryn. 1991. *Ideas and Institutions: Developmentalism in Brazil and Argentina.* Ithaca: Cornell University Press.

Teichman, Judith. 2001. *The Politics of Freeing Markets in Latin America: Chile, Argentina, and Mexico.* Chapel Hill: University of North Carolina Press.

Thompson, Lawrence. 1998. *Older and Wiser: The Economics of Public Pensions.* Washington: Urban Institute.

Tommasi, Mariano, and Federico Sturzenegger, eds. 1998. *The Political Economy of Reform.* Cambridge: MIT Press.

Uribe Vélez, Álvaro. 1993. Solidaridad . . . es seguridad. *Estrategia* (August): 19.

Von Gersdorff, Hermann. 1998. Staff Economist, World Bank. Author interview. Washington, DC, May 15.

Walker, Jack L. 1969. The Diffusion of Innovations Among the American States. *American Political Science Review* 63 (September): 880–99.

Weyland, Kurt. 2002a. The Diffusion of Innovations: A Theoretical Analysis. Paper presented at the 97th annual meeting of the American Political Science Association, Boston, August 29–September 1.

——. 2002b. *The Politics of Market Reform in Fragile Democracies.* Princeton: Princeton University Press.

World Bank. 1994. *Averting the Old Age Crisis: Policies to Protect the Old and Promote Growth.* New York: Oxford University Press.

——. 1996. World Bank Research in the Marketplace of Ideas. *World Bank Policy and Research Bulletin* 7, 1 (January–March): 2.

——. 1999. World Development Report 1998/1999: *Knowledge for Development.* New York: Oxford University Press.

——. 2000. *World Development Indicators on CD-ROM.* Washington, DC: World Bank.

Chapter 10

The Challenge of Economic Restructuring and the Limits of Labor Reform in Latin America

Mark Anner

Most scholars concur that globalization has not engendered an unambiguous decline in the protective role of the state. Notably, scholars of Latin American politics have argued that the state did not abandon its legal protections of organized labor; most collective labor law reforms in Latin America have been "union-friendly" (Bronstein 1995; Cook 1998; Córdova 1996; Murillo and Schrank 2005). This is partly because neoliberal economic reforms often coincided with processes of democratization that restored or deepened labor rights. It also is the result of international activist pressure and domestic coalitions between labor unions and labor-based political parties (Murillo and Schrank 2005).

The aforementioned literature has made a valuable contribution to our understanding of the transformation of employment relations in Latin America. It has rectified the misperception that labor law reform was a one-way affair in which employers and neo-liberal governments pushed through their free market agenda unopposed. This literature highlights the role of national and international labor actors and their allies and reveals their capacity to influence reform processes. Yet now, well over a decade since the initial round of labor reforms, labor unions continue to lose power in the region. This is especially true in the manufacturing sector, where unionization rates have declined and real wages have been unable to keep up with productivity gains.[1]

This chapter argues that two related factors can explain this trend. First, favorable labor law reforms were insufficient to counterbalance the adverse effects of market-oriented reforms because they did not fully take into account the new economic context (outsourcing, internationalization, informalization, and so on). While these reforms can be classified as "favorable" in relation to the previous law, they are not necessarily favorable in relation to the current economic context.

Second, trade liberalization and competition for foreign direct investment created intense cost-reduction pressure on producers. Avoidance of a "race to the bottom" through labor rights violations required effective mechanisms of labor law enforcement. Yet many Latin American governments in the 1990s either maintained or reduced state resources dedicated to enforcement. The result was a de facto form of labor market flexibility that contributed to the decline of union power. This provoked a backlash in the first decade of the 2000s to increase resources dedicated to enforcement.

This chapter reviews the debate on globalization and labor rights and provides an explanation for why unions lost power following favorable collective labor law reforms. The arguments presented here are illustrated through an overview of several Latin American cases, followed by in-depth analyses of Brazil and El Salvador, two countries in the region that represent different means for achieving union-friendly labor law reforms. Reforms in Brazil were the result of the internal dynamics of democratization and labor protests. Reforms in El Salvador were largely the result of international pressure and International Labor Organization (ILO) recommendations. In both cases, the reforms were steps in the right direction—particularly in Brazil, where reforms were influenced by strong domestic labor activism. Yet in both cases, the reforms could not adequately respond to the challenges presented by economic restructuring, and unions continued to lose power. Recent political trends in the region are starting to address some of the limitations of the first round of reforms.

GLOBALIZATION AND COLLECTIVE LABOR LAW REFORM

In response to early proclamations of state decline (Ohmae 1995), scholars have found that under conditions of globalization, the role of the state in the regulation of economic relations may actually be increasing. For example, Peter Evans argues that international integration requires greater state action to regulate economic activity (Evans 1997, 72). Dani Rodrik finds that exposure to risk correlates with greater government consumption, because the vulnerability caused by risk exposure creates a need for more social protection (Rodrik 1997, 52–53).

The changing role of the state extends to labor relations. While some scholars argue that globalization creates pressure for more flexible labor relations regimes with weaker collective rights (Cingranelli 2003), long-time Latin American labor scholar and practitioner Efrén Córdova contends

> The fears expressed by some Latin American labor law experts about the rapid spread of flexibility seem today somewhat exaggerated. The progress of the flexibility trend has been neither linear nor overwhelming. Latin America is still largely a protectionist region in terms of labor standards. (Córdova 1996, 331–32)

Indeed, most Latin American labor specialists concur that national labor legislation, on average, has become more protective of collective labor rights.

Eduardo Lora finds that over the course of the 1990s, while the average cost to employers of layoffs declined (indicating greater flexibility), business contributions to employee social security increased, a sign of more worker protection (Lora 2001). Maria Lorena Cook's research indicates that not all labor law reforms entailed flexibility in order to facilitate market dynamics (Cook 1998, 2007). Cook writes, "Some countries made their laws more flexible. Others responded by strengthening employment protection for workers and retaining a strong role for the state in industrial relations" (Cook 1998, 311–12). Victoria Murillo and Andrew Schrank focus exclusively on collective labor law reforms and find that "13 of the 18 collective labor reforms approved in Latin America between 1985 and 1998 have enhanced rather than undercut labor's ability to organize and bargain collectively" (Murillo and Schrank 2005, 972).

Many favorable reforms, particularly in terms of collective rights, can be linked to democratization in the region, which often included constitutional reforms that restored rights removed under military rule. These constitutional reforms were later followed by labor law reform. Since democratization coincided with a shift toward market-oriented economic policies, some reforms—particularly those regarding individual labor law—weakened worker protections, with the goal of making labor markets more flexible. Yet other reforms were more protective of labor. Arturo Bronstein, an ILO expert, observes, "the most important legislative changes addressed the exercise of trade union rights, and almost always brought far-reaching change to the benefit of workers and their trade unions" (Bronstein 1995, 172).

Data on unionization, however, indicate a continued decline throughout Latin America. Moreover, there appears to be no dramatic difference in the average rate of decline between countries with union-friendly and union-averse reforms (see table 1).[2] Thus, while collective labor rights have become stronger, unions have become weaker. What explains this apparent paradox?

To understand this trend, it is necessary to situate labor law reform in the broader labor relations context. Labor relations regimes include the institutions and practices that govern labor, capital, and state relations (Dunlop 1993 [1958]). Labor relations regimes also encompass "the overt and latent mechanisms which connect the workplace to broader social, political and economic dynamics at national and indeed transnational levels" (Hyman 1995, 19). For example, to understand fully the impact on labor of an employment relations regime, it is necessary to go beyond the legal context and situate the labor reforms in the context of larger economic transformations. Are mild reforms of old corporatist labor laws the best way to address the problems in an export-oriented economy? Do union structures that proved adequate in protected industries work as effectively in trade-sensitive industries?

ECONOMIC RESTRUCTURING IN LATIN AMERICA

Unions in Latin America gained strength during a period of import substitution industrialization (ISI) and populist labor laws that facilitated union formation and incorporated labor into the political process (Collier and Collier 1991; Drake 1996). Since the 1980s, Latin American economies have shifted away from ISI in two directions. First, ISI policies have been replaced by trade liberalization and export promotion. Second, declining employment opportunities—most notably in the public sector and in agriculture—have led to an increase in the private service sector and the informal sector (Portes and Hoffman 2003). On average, 53 percent of Latin Americans work in informal activities (ILO 2005).

Both private services and the informal sector are notoriously difficult to organize. Jobs in restaurants, hotels, and retail stores have much higher turnover rates and smaller workforces than traditional manufacturing, which contributes to weaker worker identity and lower unionization. Many informal sector jobs—street vendors, shoeshine boys, and so on—do not entail a traditional employment relationship (work at a wage rate for an employer), and thus preclude unionization. Where an employment relationship does exist, workers in small, informal enterprises often are prohibited from unionizing by laws that require a minimum of 30 workers to form a union. Thus, much of the decline in national unionization in Latin America can be linked to the shift in employment to formal services and especially the informal sector.

What is curious is the declining percentage of manufacturing workers represented by labor unions. Not only have unions often lost power in the manufacturing sector, but in many cases the rate of decline is greater than that of national unionization rates. This trend stands at odds with the view of many scholars of labor relations that industry is a crucial source of union strength; the coming together of large groups of workers for long-term employment provides the collective identities and financial means for strong unions (Sabel 1982). Thus, where industry develops, strong unions are expected to follow (Kerr et al. 1960; Sabel 1982). The recent decline in industry (deindustrialization) in developed economies is therefore seen as a principal cause of declining union power in those countries (Lee 2005).

In Brazil and the Southern Cone, deindustrialization has been a strong trend. In Chile, deindustrialization entailed a shift away from highly unionized sectors and contributed to a weakening and fragmentation of the labor movement (Etchemendy and Collier 2007).[3] In Brazil between 1988 and 1998, 1.7 million industry jobs were lost (Cardoso

Table 1. Labor Law Reform and Unionization Trends in Latin America

	Main Direction of Reforms	Percent of Workforce Unionized	Change in Unionization Rate (%)
Argentina	Union-averse (1990s)	28.7 (1995); 25.6 (1999)	−10.80
Bolivia	Union-friendly (1995)	30.9 (90/95); 16.4 (96/00)	−46.93
Brazil	Union-friendly (Const. '88)	24.88 (1990); 23.58 (2001)	−5.22
Chile	Union-friendly (1990)	13.6 (1990); 11.3 (1998)	−16.91
Colombia	Union-friendly (1990)	11.2 (1985); 7.0 (1995)	−37.50
Costa Rica	Union-friendly (1990)	21.4 (1993) 13.8 (2003)	−35.46
Dom. Rep.	Union-friendly (1992)	17.3 (1995); 10 (2006)	−42.20
Ecuador	Union-averse (1991)	14.3 (86/90); 13.5 (91/95)	−5.59
El Salvad.	Union-friendly (1994)	5.58 (1994); 4.80 (1999)	−13.78
Guatemala	Mixed (1992, 1995)	2.92 (1990); 1.55 (2004)	−46.91
Honduras	No changes	30.2 (1990); 14 (2003)	−53.64
Mexico	No changes	35.3 (86/90); 22.4 (91/95)	−36.29
Nicaragua	Mixed (1990, 1996)	32 (86/90); 23.4 (90/95)	−26.88
Panama	Union-friendly (1995)	17 (86/90); 14.2 (90/95)	−16.71
Paraguay	Union-friendly (1993)	7.7 (1992); 2.8 (2002)	−63.64
Peru	Union-averse (1991)	30.0 (1991); 10.0 (1998)	−66.67
Venezuela	Union-friendly (1990)	25.9 (1988); 14.9 (1995)	−42.47

Note: Data on unionization in Latin America are notoriously lacking. As result, the data presented here are collected from a range of sources and should be considered approximations and thus indications of trends. Starting unionization data points were selected as the closest available data point to the reforms. Ending data points were selected as the most up-to-date available figures. When available, data from official government sources were favored other sources.

Sources: Data on labor law reform (mid-1980s through 1990s) based on Bronstein 1995: Cook 1998, 2007; Murillo and Schrank 2005; Murillo 2005. Unionization data for Bolivia, Ecuador, Mexico, Nicaragua, Panama, and Peru from IDB 2003; for Brazil, IBGE 2002; for Chile, Buchanan and Nicholls 2003; for Colombia, Costa Rica, and Venezuela, ILO 1997; for Argentina, El Salvador, and Guatemala, data are from the respective Ministries of Labor. Data for Honduras from the ILO (http://web.oit.or.cr/) and the ICFTU, Country Reports: WTO & Labour Standards (http://www.icftu.org/). For Paraguay, see Villalba 1996; Pilz 2005. For the Dominican Republic, data are from the ILO (http://web.oit.or.cr/) and the ICFTU, Country Reports: WTO & Labour Standards (http://www.icftu.org/), and U.S. Department of State, Country Reports on Human Rights Practices (http://www.state.gov/g/drl/rls/hrrpt/).

2001). Not only did unions lose members in the industrial sector; the rate of unionization in industry declined by almost twice the national rate of decline (Cardoso 2001). The deindustrialization argument can explain a drop in the national unionization rate, but it cannot explain why, for the remaining workers in the industrial sector, the percentage of workers who are union members dropped.[4]

Moreover, deindustrialization cannot be the cause of union decline in many Latin American countries. In Mexico, Honduras, El Salvador, Nicaragua, Panama, Guatemala, and the Dominican Republic, the percent of the workforce employed in industry actually increased slightly from 1990 to 2005 (ECLAC 2006). This trend can be attributed primarily to the outsourcing of manufacturing jobs from developed countries to these countries. Union decline in the midst of industrial growth is a puzzle that needs to be explained, especially in light of union-friendly reforms.

One possible explanation for these trends is that increased trade hurts labor by escalating competition across states (Wood 1994). In Latin America, however, the countries with a greater degree of openness are not always the ones with the greatest decline in unionization. For example, in Ecuador, where imports and exports account for 55 percent of GDP, unionization declined by 6 percent; whereas in Peru, where trade as a share of GDP stands at 39 percent, unionization declined by 67 percent (see table 1).

What this study argues is that it is the international transformation of the production process that has been harmful to unionization, and that labor law reforms and systems of workplace inspection have not adequately addressed the problems presented by internationalization. The dismantling of ISI protections and the increase of cost-based global competition are not the only factors precipitating change; the segmentation and geographic dispersion of production and the resulting change in the production cost structure have also hurt labor.

Under the old ISI system, large, centralized firms purchased their production inputs, transformed the inputs into the final product, and then sold the final product. Under internationally segmented regimes, many firms in developing countries now produce under contract for multinational corporations (MNCs). These firms do not own the material used to make the product, nor do they control the final product. As a result, their cost structure is based heavily on labor costs, and thus their incentive to weaken or avoid unions and collective bargaining is augmented considerably. The dispersion of the production process also creates coordination and collective action problems for labor, especially in countries where labor laws do not favor industrial unions and bargaining.

One of the clearest examples of this new form of production is Export Processing Zones (EPZs). Over 2.5 million people work in EPZs in Latin America, with 1.2 million in Mexico, 700,000 in Central America, and 540,000 in the Caribbean (Singa Boyenge 2007). The unionization rate in Mexican EPZs is one-third the rate of large traditional enterprises (Bizberg 1996); it is even lower in EPZs in Central America (Anner 2004).

While EPZs represent perhaps the most dramatic example of industrial restructuring and union decline, other processes also have adversely affected unions. In the auto and other heavy industries, corporations have outsourced increasingly complex components of their products through systems of modular production (Frigant and Lung 2002; Salerno 2001; see also Salerno and Carneiro Dias 2002). Every major auto plant built in Brazil since 1996 uses modular production, as opposed to the traditional, centralized Fordist system. And while 65 percent of workers in the old traditional auto plants are unionized, only 37 percent of workers in new modular plants are union members (Anner 2003). These problems facing labor in these restructured economies were not adequately addressed by Latin American labor laws and state enforcement mechanisms.

THE LIMITATIONS OF THE REFORMS

National labor relations institutions mitigate the market economy's adverse impact on labor (Garrett and Lange 1996). Historically, the protections provided by national institutions facilitated the rise of national labor movements (Tilly 1995). When comparing states with relatively similar economies, those with more labor-friendly institutions tend to have much stronger union movements (Western 1997). This helps explain why Sweden has a 77 percent unionization rate compared to Norway's 51 percent, or why Britain's unionization rate is three times higher than that of the United States (ILO 1997). In Latin America, the rate of unionization varies from under 2 percent to over 25 percent (see table 1).

Thus, while economic globalization is creating new challenges for labor throughout the world, it is by no means engendering a convergence to common low levels of unionization. As the persistent discrepancies in unionization rates suggest, national labor relations regimes have the potential to mitigate the adverse impact of globalization. For this reason, reforms in labor relations regimes are crucial. Indeed, labor's future is partly tied to how labor institutions are reformed and the fit between the reforms and current economic challenges.

Labor's ability collectively to pursue its demands is based on three complementary rights: the right to form unions, the right to collective bargaining, and the right to strike. Without unions, collective bargaining and striking are very unlikely. Without effective bargaining, unions can become empty vessels. Without effective strike potential (most often expressed as a threat to strike, as opposed to an actual strike), labor's ability to leverage improvements in working conditions at the bargaining table is greatly curtailed.

These rights, moreover, cannot be evaluated in the abstract but in the historical, political, social, and economic context in which they are situated. The same laws that are used to empower labor by a populist government may be used to suppress labor by a military government (Drake 1996). Laws that assist workers effectively when factories are large and protected from foreign competition may not work as well when industry fragments and faces strong competititve pressures. For countries like Colombia, El Salvador, and Guatemala—where unionists faced decades of particularly violent anti-union repression—labor laws will most likely need added protections to help workers overcome their fear of organizing.

Most Latin American collective labor law reforms are considered union-friendly because they facilitated the unionization process by lowering the number of workers needed to form a union or facilitated the administrative process to legalize a union. For example, three countries lowered the threshold for enterprise union formation, while only one country raised the threshold (see table 2). At the same time, many reforms lessened the administrative burden of union formation and weakened (but did not eliminate) the state's capacity to reject requests to form or register labor unions (see table 2). As Teri Caraway found in her comparative study of Indonesia and Argentina, these policies promote the formation of small, weak, and fragmented unions (Caraway 2006).

While some countries expanded the right to bargain and strike to the public sector, these rights were not significantly altered in the private sector. In El Salvador and Guatemala, the existence of a union at the firm level does not mean that an employer has an obligation to bargain or even meet with the workers. Instead, the laws establish a much higher threshold for collective bargaining than for union formation, which results in many small unions with no collective bargaining ability. In an era when corporate operations are increasingly complex and globally integrated, understanding an enterprise's economic status is even more crucial for labor unions. Yet in 14 out of 17 countries in Latin America, unions are not guaranteed access to company financial information during bargaining (see table 2).

While several national labor laws allow industry or national-level bargaining, most legislation favors enterprise or municipal-level bargaining. When enterprises were large or concentrated in one geographic location, the restriction in the law did not create an enormous concern for labor unions. For example, the Brazilian labor law promotes union formation at the municipal level. When industry was concentrated in the industrial suburbs of São Paulo, this restriction did not prevent powerful new unions from developing. But when enterprises decentralized, outsourced, and dispersed production locations throughout national territories, the geographic and industry-level restrictions on bargaining became a debilitating factor for labor.

Strike leverage is another crucial source of union power. In most countries in Latin America, the percentage of workers needed to authorize a strike in an enterprise remains high. While, on average, 20 workers are needed to form a union, labor legislation in most countries requires the support of at least a majority of workers in an enterprise to

Table 2. Summary of Core Collective Labor Law Reforms

	Workers Needed to Form an Enterprise Union		Collective Bargaining: Right to Information		Percent of Workforce Needed to Authorize a Strike	
	Before	After	Before	After	Before	After
Argentina	NA	NC	No	Yes	NA	NC
Bolivia	20	NC	No	NC	75	NC
Brazil	30	NC	No	NC	NA	NC
Chile	25/40[a]	25/10[a]	No	NC	Majority	NC
Colombia	25	NC	No	NC	Majority	NC
Costa Rica	12	NC	No	NC	60	NC
Domin. Rep.	20	NC	No	NC	60 + 1	51
Ecuador	15	30	No	NC	Majority	NC
El Salvador	40/51[a]	35	No	NC	51	NC
Guatemala	20	NC	No	NC	67	NC
Honduras	30	NC	No	NC	67[b]	NC
Mexico	20	NC	No	NC	Majority	NC
Nicaragua	25	20	No	NC	60	Majority
Panama	50	40	Yes	NC	Majority	NC
Paraguay	20	NA	No	NC	75	NC
Peru	20	NC	No	Yes	75	Majority
Venezuela	20	NC	No	NC	Majority	NC

[a]Numerator is the number of workers needed to form a union. Denominator is the percentage of workers at an enterprise needed to form a union. Both conditions need to be met to form a union in these cases.
[b]Percent of union members.
NA = not available; NC = no change.
Source: Vega Ruiz 2005.

call a strike. Five countries require between 60 and 75 percent of the workforce to approve a strike action (see table 2). In addition, many countries have burdensome administrative steps that must be fulfilled before a strike can be legalized. For example, in Costa Rica, legal obstacles to strikes have resulted in only two legal strikes in the last 50 years (ICFTU 2001). These limitations on the right to strike weaken labor's bargaining power and thus lessen its ability to address issues facing workers at the negotiating table, because employers who are not concerned that workers can disrupt the production process have less of an incentive to bargain in good faith.

What this situation illustrates is that the favorability of reforms should be judged not simply in reference to the old laws, but instead in reference to the new economic context. While the same law in one context allowed for the development of strong unions, in another context, it may inhibit union development.

THE ENFORCEMENT GAP

While labor laws provide an important framework for policy, without an adequate system of enforcement, they run the risk of remaining declarations of good intentions. A crucial component of enforcement is labor inspection, the visit by state representatives (most often of the Ministry of Labor) to a worksite to determine if a violation has occurred and, if so, the actions needed to sanction the current violations or prevent future ones. As Francis Blanchard, director-general of the ILO from 1974 to 1989, noted, "Labour legislation without inspection is an exercise in ethics, but not a binding social discipline" (quoted in Von Richthofen 2002, 8).

The International Labor Organization's founding constitution in 1919 called on states to establish systems of labor inspection to ensure respect for national for national labor legislation. The ILO elaborated on what a system of labor inspection should entail in its 1947 Labour Inspection Convention (Convention 81). Convention 81 provides basic requirements that apply to all countries, regardless of their level of economic development. It states that inspectors should be responsible to a central authority, should be allowed to enter any workplace freely without prior notice, should apply adequate penalties for violations of legal provisions, and should provide advice regarding effective means for compliance. The ILO further recommends that states develop systems of collaboration among inspectors, workers, and employers.

Some states have favored certain ILO guidelines over others. For example, Scandinavian countries emphasize tripartite consultation. Britain and the United States have chosen to decentralize their inspection functions.[5] France, Portugal, Spain, and Latin American countries have more centralized structures, in which each workplace inspector is responsible for a much broader range of issues. Each system has its pros and cons. The decentralized system allows for a greater degree of specialization but lacks the power of a centralized authority, while a centralized system can more effectively coordinate enforcement procedures but often lacks the flexibility and agility of a decentralized system (Von Richthofen 2002).

Another area of difference applies to the use of penalties. Many countries rely principally on fines to ensure compliance with labor laws. Michael Piore and Andrew Schrank argue, however, that the French/Latin model emphasizes employer training and provides inspectors with significant discretion in deciding when to report violations. Discretion purportedly allows the inspector not to apply the law so strictly that the employer will be forced out of business. Instead, the Latin model favors employer training over fines (Piore and Schrank 2006). Of course, greater inspector "discretion" may also provide an opening for greater inspector corruption, particularly in a region known for a lack of business transparency and a tendency to pay inspectors relatively low salaries.

Employer training can also offer an effective tool, particularly when there are new laws for employers to learn; for example, new health and safety regulations. By contrast, firing workers who attempt to form a union—a collective labor law violation—is probably not the result of ignorance of the law, and therefore cannot simply be addressed through employer training. In such cases, fines may be a more effective resource of action.

Adalberto Cardoso and Telma Lage, who examine the Brazilian system of workplace inspection, argue, "the effectiveness of labor legislation depends . . . on the interaction between the overall sanctions and the probability of the employer getting caught breaking the law" (Cardoso and Lage 2005, 453). That is, to ensure compliance, the cost of paying the fine must be greater than the potential financial benefit of violating the law.

The probability of getting caught may not be only a function of the number of workplace inspectors. Active and well-informed labor unions are one of the best mechanisms to ensure vigilance of labor standards at the workplace (Weil 1999). These unionists can detect violations and then inform the appropriate government agency, which can then address the issues. Active unionism in the workplace coordinated with labor inspections is far more efficient than relying on spot inspections or hoping that an individual employee will have the courage and knowledge to report a violation.

What this dynamic suggests is that in countries with lower rates of unionization, there is a need for a proportionately higher number of inspectors relative to the size of the workforce. A system that works well in Sweden, where 77 percent of workers are unionized and vigilant for labor law violations, will not work as effectively in Guatemala, were less than 2 percent of workers are unionized and workers remain fearful of retaliation for reporting violations because of a long history of violent anti-union repression. Yet in Latin America, where the unionization rate is, on average, much lower than in Europe, resources dedicated to enforcement are notably lacking. Research by the Inter-American Development Bank indicates that "scarcity of resources and institutional deterioration [in Latin America] are two traits that characterize the institutions in charge of labor policies (mostly ministries of labor)" (IDB 2003, 277).

Labor law enforcement is not solely addressed by workplace inspection. This is especially true for violations of collective labor law. Indeed, the departments of workplace inspection in some Latin American countries are not specifically authorized to address collective rights violations, which is another serious limitation of Latin American systems (Jatoba 2002). Instead, many issues are ultimately resolved in labor courts, where lack of resources and excessive delays in resolving cases have frustrated union development.

In the case of a collective rights violation—most notably, the right to unionize—delays in proper adjudication of the law could prove fatal for the union. The single most common measure employers take to avoid unionization is to fire the group of workers identified with a unionization attempt. If the labor court system is unable to rectify this situation quickly, the fired union activists will be denied access to their coworkers; those who were not dismissed will become fearful of associating with the union; and the unionization campaign will most likely stagnate and fail. Yet limited numbers of judges and lack of support staff and other resources cause inordinate delays in the labor court systems. In some countries, a case can take five to ten years to be resolved.

The limitations of workplace inspection and labor courts have become more apparent in the current economic context. Labor market fragmentation, informalization, outsourcing, and global competitive pressures create new challenges for enforcement not envisioned in the original systems. Smaller and more dispersed workplaces require more inspectors relative to the size of the workforce than an economy characterized by large and geographically concentrated work centers. The rise of cost-based global competition may be conducive to a corresponding increase in anti-union practices, unless a vigilant state ensures that all enterprises respect fundamental workers' rights. The limitations of Latin American collective labor law reforms and enforcement mechanisms relative to the region's shifting economic structures help to explain the continued decline of union power.

LABOR LAW REFORM AND UNION POWER IN LATIN AMERICA

When collective labor law reforms have been union-averse, union decline can be expected. For example, the 1991 reforms in Ecuador doubled the number of workers needed to form a union, from 15 to 30. In response, companies found it possible to hire groups of 29 workers from temporary employment agencies and avoid unionization (Arcos 2004). In Peru, reforms decreed by the Fujimori government in 1992 imposed new restrictions on strike activity (Córdova 1996, 326).[6] Dramatic underfunding of the Ministry of Labor's enforcement activities further undermined unions. The vice minister of labor referred to the Labor Ministry as the "James Bond Ministry" because it received only 00.7 percent of the national budget, making it one of the most underfunded ministries in Peru.[7] Unionization in Peru has declined by 66.67 percent since the 1990s.

In Bolivia, minor protective reforms were enacted to the labor law in 1995 (Cook 1998), although most labor laws were not reformed, and remain obsolete.

Informalization, privatization, and declines in the mining sector have all hurt the labor movement. At the same time, in the context of growing cost pressures from international competition, the lack of effective enforcement also adversely affected labor unions. The Ministry of Labor has an annual budget of US$1.2 million, the smallest budget of all government ministries. In 2004, there were only 18 workplace inspectors for La Paz, which has a population of more than 1 million. Most other urban centers had only two workplace inspectors. Because the average salary of a labor inspector is US$165 per month, moreover, many inspectors work second jobs to meet their financial obligations (ILO 2006, 70). As noted by Rodolfo Aróstegui, then vice minister of labor, "the law is not protecting workers enough, and the mandate of the Ministry is to protect workers" (Eróstegui 2004). In the years following the 1995 reforms, the unionization rate declined by 46.93 percent.

In Paraguay, constitutional reforms in 1992 extended the right to strike to public sector workers, and the Labor Code reforms that followed in 1993 and 1995 facilitated union formation and union plurality (Bronstein 1997, 24; Cook 1998). Unionization initially increased following democratization. Yet from the early 1990s to the early 2000s, while the number of unions in the country increased from 402 to 1,600, the unionization rate dropped from 7.7 percent to 2.8 percent of the economically active population, a decline of 64 percent. Paraguay now has the lowest unionization rate in South America. The causes of the decline can be linked not only to the changing economic context but also to the systematic dismissals of union activists and the long delays in the labor courts to address these types of violations (Pilz 2005). Court cases involving fired union leaders have lingered for up to nine years, and the law does not mandate the rehiring of workers who have been dismissed for union activity (U.S. Department of State 2007b). The union crisis is notably much more significant in the private sector. While 60 percent of public sector employees are covered by collective bargaining agreements, only 10 percent of formal private sector employees are covered (U.S. Department of State 2007b).

In 1992 in Guatemala, in response to AFL-CIO petitions filed through the General System of Preferences (GSP), the congress ratified the first major revision of the labor code in 45 years.[8] According to Henry Frundt, the reforms "simplified union registrations, increased fines, and strengthened court procedures" (Frundt 1998, 150–51). Yet by 2004, the percentage of workers organized in labor unions had dropped below 2 percent, the lowest rate in Latin America. In EPZs, where the ILO Committee of Experts has found the violation of collective labor laws to be particularly severe (CEACR 2005), there are only 51 recognized union members, who represent 00.07 percent of the EPZ workforce. Labor courts take approximately four years to resolve labor disputes, with some cases lasting up to ten years (Inforpress 2007). The issue is not simply a lack of resources. In May 2004, President Oscar Berger resorted to decree to severely reduce the budget of the Ministry of Labor to a scant 00.18 percent of the national budget (Ministry of Public Finance 2005).

The 1992 Dominican labor law reforms were also the result of the threat to lose U.S. trade privileges via GSP petitions filed by the AFL-CIO (Murillo and Schrank 2005). The reforms improved protection of the freedom of association, updated the fines for labor code violations, and "sought to improve the efficiency of the procedure for punishing infringements of labor laws" (Bronstein 1997, 23). Here again, the problem was most severe in the export-oriented segment of the economy. David Jessup and Michael Gordon explain, "EPZ companies continued to fire union leaders with impunity, resulting in what Dominicans called 'headless unions.' Of the nearly one hundred new unions that were registered during the next two years, all but a handful were rendered nonfunctional, and none was allowed to negotiate a collective contract" (Jessup and Gordon 2000, 186)

While the new code made it easier to form a union, it required that an absolute majority of workers in an enterprise be union members in order for the union to have the right to bargain collectively (Labor Code, Article 109). The practice of facilitating union formation but maintaining high thresholds for collective bargaining and strikes has had particularly adverse effects on union power in the growing EPZ sector, where factories tend to be large.

CASE SELECTION: BRAZIL AND EL SALVADOR

Brazil and El Salvador represent important test cases for this study because, according to ILO experts, collective labor rights were significantly re-enforced following democratization in both countries. Brazil now has the most labor rights guarantees in its constitution of any country in Latin America, while El Salvador is considered to have the most substantial of all the collective labor law reforms (Bronstein 1995).[9] Assuming that the experts are correct, Brazil and El Salvador methodologically represent "hard cases" for the argument; if unions became weaker even in these countries with more substantial reforms, than it appears that labor reforms here and throughout Latin America did indeed suffer from important limitations.

Another reason for choosing these two cases is that Brazil and El Salvador represent two different paths to reform. In Brazil, the constitutional reforms of 1988 were largely the result of internal processes and local labor activism. In El Salvador, the labor reforms of 1994 were sharply influenced by external forces, most notably U.S. government pressure and the expert advice of ILO officials. Therefore, the selection of these two cases may provide some indication of the impact of different paths to reform.

Brazil

In 1988, after 21 years of dictatorial rule in Brazil, the administration of José Sarney enacted constitutional reforms that strengthened collective labor rights. Brazil's constitution now has 34 labor rights guarantees (Bronstein 1995; 170). While the reforms left intact many aspects of the corporatist system, they did limit state interference in union affairs, require employers to bargain collectively, prohibit dismissal of union members, and give public employees the right to form labor unions (Constitution of Brazil, Articles 8 and 37).[10]

These reforms in Brazilian collective labor rights were the result of internal political dynamics, in which the local labor movement played an important role. In the late 1970s and early 1980s, a group of labor unions began to challenge the corporatist system of union control as they also confronted the military dictatorship. This group formed a political party, the Workers' Party (PT), and a labor central, the Sole Workers' Central (CUT), which pressured for union-friendly constitutional reforms. As Maria Lorena Cook explains, "From an already protectionist and state intervention base, constitutional changes in Brazil extended protections and established greater autonomy for collective action" (Cook 1998, 329).[11]

At first blush, it appears that Brazilian unions did well following the reforms. Between 1991 and 2000, 1,964 new unions were formed, the largest number for a one-decade period in the history of Brazil. Moreover, the unionization rate faced only a minor decline over the 1990s and early 2000s, from 24.88 percent to 23.58 percent (IBGE 2002).[12] Yet a disaggregation of the national unionization rate reveals that the legalization of unions in the public sector and their subsequent growth hide an important decline in unionization in the industrial sector. Over the course of the 1990s, industrial sector unions only accounted for 19 percent of union formation, while public service unions accounted for 26 percent (IBGE 2002).

Brazilian labor scholar Adalberto Cardoso elaborates on the problem masked by national unionization figures.

> If one takes the global number of affiliates and the unionization rate, the most accomplished researcher would say, with complete confidence, that unions are doing very well, thank you. . . . If we look more closely at the distribution of affiliation by, for example, economic sector, things look very different. (Cardoso 2001, 69) . . . We are talking about the loss of one-fifth of the . . . affiliates in the transformative industrial sector [and 506,000 union members in the industry sector] over the last ten years. These are astronomical figures that let us appreciate that the industrial unions are living a moment of crisis without precedent. (Cardoso 2001, 72)

More worrisome still, Cardoso explains that the rate of unionization in the industrial sector has declined by 10 percent.

These are two distinct tendencies. First, deindustrialization is causing a loss in the total number of unionists in the industrial sector. Second, industrial restructuring is causing a decline in the unionization rate among the remaining workers in the industrial sector. Moreover, the union movement has also weakened through fragmentation. Over the course of the 1990s and early 2000s, the number of unions in Brazil increased from 7,612 to 11,354. Some 71 percent of Brazilian unions have fewer than 1,000 members. By 2001, the country had five national labor centers, and 62 percent of unions chose to remain unaffiliated with any of them (IBGE 2002).

The reason union-friendly collective labor reform did not provide for a stronger union movement in the industrial sector can be found in the nature of industrial restructuring, the substantive limitations of the reforms, and deficiencies in the labor law enforcement mechanisms. In Brazil, following the end of military rule in 1985 and most especially in the 1990s, civilian presidents began a process of market-oriented reforms that led to the dramatic restructuring of the country's industrial sector. For example, the average tariff on imported automobiles dropped from 85 percent in 1990 to 34.3 percent in 1994, and it continued to decline throughout the 1990s (Comin 1998).

Firms turned to outsourcing to reduce costs and increase competitiveness. During the 1980s, on average, up to 13 core workers were needed to produce 100 vehicles per year; by 2001, only 5 core workers were needed (Anner 2003). While some of this decline can be tied to technological improvements, much of this trend is the result of MNCs' outsourcing the production not only of parts but also of large components to independent firms. As one unionist commented on a similar process in Argentina, "We used to make cars from start to finish. . . . All that is gone. Now, with a much smaller workforce, we just assemble components that are shipped in" (Mercedes Benz Production Workers 2002).

The changes brought on by market liberalization and industrial restructuring dramatically affected the geography of industrial production in Brazil. Many new major plants built in the late 1990s and early 2000s were situated outside the core industrial district of greater São Paulo, in regions where unions were weaker and wages lower.[13] This fragmentation of the workforce was particularly detrimental to unions in Brazil because labor reform did not alter the requirement for union formation and collective bargaining at the subnational level.

During the period of import substitution, the subnational union formation law did not produce significantly adverse effects on unions, because industrial production was already concentrated at the subnational level in the greater São Paulo region. The problem emerged in the 1990s, when industry spread out across much of the national territory. The reforms did not take this dispersion of industry into consideration. Thus, while municipal-level restrictions on unionization were not a major concern for unions when industry was concentrated, they became a major concern in the context of industrial restructuring.

Limitations in the Brazilian system of labor law enforcement have further trammeled the union movement. A U.S. State Department report found,

> It was estimated that more than 3 million complaints languished in the labor court system at year's end [2002]. Although most complaints were resolved in the first hearing, the appeals process introduced many delays, and some cases remained unresolved for 5 to 10 years (U.S. Department of State 2003).

The situation is even more severe outside the large urban centers. The 2005 ILO Committee of Experts report noted, "local inspection offices. . . . are ill-equipped and inadequate and often lack computers, telephones, and even the most basic furniture (tables, chairs) needed by inspectors to carry out their duties" (CEACR 2005, 310).

At the same time, the government reduced the resources dedicated to enforcement. From 1990 to 2002, the number of workplaces inspected dropped from 414,875 to 304,254, while the number of inspectors per 100,000 workers declined from 5.61 to 3.63 (see figure 1). The number of fines placed on employers for labor rights violations dropped from 1.41 per 100,000 to 1.17 per 100,000 (IDB 2003, 278). According to the

Figure 1. Brazil, Workplace Inspection

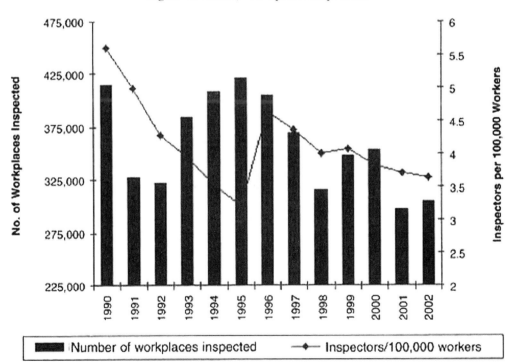

Source: Brazil, Ministry of Labor, IDB 2003.

Gaúcha Association of Labor Inspectors (AGITA), the labor inspectorate has suffered from "heavy political interference aimed at preventing inspection: political authorities, who are likewise landowners, have close links with the military police, which protects their interests, turning a blind eye to their actions" (cited in CEACR 2005, 309).

Labor relations reform remains a dynamic process in Brazil. In January 2003, ex-union leader Luiz Inácio Lula da Silva became president with the promise to move the country away from the extreme neoliberal policies of his predecessor. Under his presidency (which I discuss below), greater resources have been dedicated to enforcement, while plans to revise the labor laws further are pending.

El Salvador

ILO labor law expert Arturo Bronstein argues that of the collective labor law reforms in Latin America, "perhaps the most significant progress took place in El Salvador" (Bronstein 1995, 173). Although the 1992 Salvadoran Peace Accords and democratization opened the door for a discussion of labor reforms, international pressure via the U.S. General System of Preferences petitions and ILO expert delegations to El Salvador provided the specific mechanisms that allowed for the 1994 Labor Code reforms. The reforms were based on a 49-point program presented by ILO experts to Salvadoran business, labor, and government representatives (Davis 1995). Thus, unlike Brazil, El Salvador represents a case of reforms via external pressure and external ILO guidance.

The reforms simplified the procedures for union formation and strikes, restricted government interference in union affairs, and protected union leaders (Bronstein 1995, 173). Whereas previously the majority of laborers in a work center needed to join a union in order to form an enterprise union, following the reforms, only 35 workers were needed. One of the more innovative changes in the revised Labor Code was the establishment of two new categories of unions, one for "independent workers" and the other for workers in "neighboring enterprises." The first form of union is for self-employed workers, while the second is designed for enterprises with fewer than 35 workers. Both types of unions could potentially provide a means for organizing workers in the informal sector, where there might or might not be an employment relationship.

Given these reforms, one might conclude that if there were one country where unions should have grown in the 1990s, it would be El Salvador. Or at least, the rate of union decline might be less than in countries that did not enjoy such substantial labor law reforms. Indeed, on first examination, the rate of decline does not appear severe. Over the course of the 1990s, the unionization rate declined by 14 percent. Yet like Brazil, the national unionization rate in El Salvador hides more than it reveals. While industrial jobs grew via the boom in EPZs, the unionization rate in the industrial sector dropped precipitously.

The relatively small decline in the national unionization rate was a result of growing union membership in the construction sector. By 2004, less than 10 percent of all union members in El Salvador worked in industry, while an astounding 79 percent of union members were in the construction sector.[14] Indeed, unionization in El Salvador has largely been reduced to two construction workers' unions. From 1990 to 2004, while manufacturing employment increased due to the growth of EPZs, the number of unionists in the manufacturing sector dropped from 19,300 to 12,800. Over the course of the 1990s, the unionization rate in the manufacturing sector in El Salvador declined by a dramatic 68 percent (MTPS 2001, 2004).[15]

To understand this union decline following union-friendly reforms, once again the reforms must be examined in the context of shifting economic structures and the broader labor relations regimes. The low unionization level in the informal sector—despite the new provisions in the law—is largely related to the highly fragmented nature of that sector. Self-employed workers may not see the need to unionize when they have no employer counterpart with whom to negotiate income and benefits. In small informal enterprises where there is an employment relationship, changes to the ILO-proposed reforms made by the ARENA party government removed the right to collective bargaining from these unions, taking with it a major incentive for unionization (Davis 1995).[16]

The real hope for labor was to organize workers in the booming industrial sector. In 1992, following El Salvador's 12-year civil war, the government began promoting EPZs. Thirteen new EPZs were built in the 1990s. By 2002, total employment in the sector reached more than 75,000. The value-added generated in the sector reached US$475 million (BCR 2007), surpassing that of coffee, which had been the biggest Salvadoran export for more than a century.

The revised labor laws did not facilitate unionization in this emerging sector, however. While the reforms made it technically easier for workers to form unions, ensuring collective bargaining remained just as difficult. As before, the majority of employees needed to be union members in order to oblige an employer to negotiate at the enterprise level. Most EPZ factories have more than five hundred workers, and therefore over two-hundred and fifty workers would need to join the union in order for the union to gain the right to bargain collectively. In a country with a history of violent repression of unionists and a pattern of blacklisting and dismissing workers at the first sign of unionization, this was a prohibitively high threshold. To date, there have been no enterprise-level collective contracts in the EPZ sector.

Looking at the entire industrial sector (EPZs and domestic manufacturing), from the early 1990s to the early 2000s (the years following the "pro-union" reforms), the unionization rate in the manufacturing sector dropped from 29.95 percent to 7.92 percent.[17] At the same time, the percentage of workers in the manufacturing sector covered by collective contract agreements dropped dramatically from 37.03 percent to 2.71 percent (see table 3). The labor law reform that reduced the number of workers needed to form a union contributed to fragmentation, not a stronger union movement. Average union size in the manufacturing sector dropped from 334 workers to 283 workers. In sum, in the country with what had been classified as the most important union-friendly collective labor law reforms in Latin America, labor faced an important loss of organizational power.

State enforcement capacity and the political dynamics that influence enforcement played a role in this outcome. In the 1990s, there were 40 workplace inspectors for the entire country, or 3.19 inspectors for every 100,000 formal sector employees. Salaries of

Table 3. Union Representation in Manufacturing Sector, El Salvador

	1992 (Before Reforms)	2003 (After Reforms)
Number of unions	48	54
Number of unionized workers	16,036	15,269
Total manufacturing employment	55,398	192,774
Unionization rate (%)	28.95	7.92
Collective contracts	64	13
Workers covered by collective contract	20,512	5,225
Percentage of workers covered	37.03	2.71

Source: El Salvador, Ministry of Labor.

Table 4. El Salvador Labor Ministry and Central Government Budgets (US$millions)

	2000	2001	2002	2003	2004	2005
Total, Central Govt.	2,083.00	2,216.23	2,504.00	2,487.00	2,794.000	2,992.00
Ministry of Labor budget	6.85	6.85	6.06	5.70	5.54	7.03
Labor/Central Govt. (%)	0.33	0.31	0.24	0.23	0.20	0.23

Source: El Salvador, Treasury Ministry.

workplace inspectors ranged from US$70 to $75 per week, and were not enough to cover a family's basic needs. As Rolando Arévalo and Joaquín Arriola explain, "the precarious situation of human and financial resources is the best guarantee that not even those rights that are legally recognized are respected in the factories" (1996, 141).

To compensate for the low salaries, some staff at the Ministry of Labor compiled and sold lists of unionists' names so that enterprises could blacklist those unionists.[18] When inspectors did fine employers for labor law violations, the fines levied were often minimal. In 2003, the average fine in the apparel sector was US$286, and apparel sector employers paid a total of US$28,906 in fines. That same year, the apparel sector generated US$494 million in value-added. That is, fines paid by apparel export employers amounted to 00.0059 percent of the value of their production. At the same time, apparel sector violations constituted 81.45 percent of all violations in the manufacturing sector.[19]

The budget of the Ministry of Labor accounts for 00.23 percent of the total central government budget. Although the ministry's budget increased slightly from 2004 to 2005 due to pressure surrounding free trade negotiations with the United States, the overall share of the budget remains below the 2000–2002 level (see table 4). In a public opinion poll on the efficacy of government ministries conducted by the Public Opinion Institute of the Universidad Centroamericana (IUDOP), on a scale of 1 (unfavorable) to 10 (favorable), the Ministry of Labor received a 5.83. Among the 14 ministries in El Salvador, it was ranked second-to-last (IUDOP 2005, 4–5).

The Labor Ministry's poor performance is not simply from lack of resources. El Salvador has been ruled since 1989 by ARENA, a conservative political party that has vigorously pursued free-market policies. During the civil war, its founders were linked to death squads associated with the assassination of more than five thousand union activists. In the 1990s and 2000s, ARENA acted politically to weaken unions by limiting funding to the Ministry of Labor. It has also ensured probusiness court appointments. In 1998, 53.75 percent of labor court decisions favored workers; by 2001, only 24.51 percent of court decisions did so. A comparative study of Central America and the Dominican Republic written by the region's vice ministers of labor noted, "the labor courts in El Salvador need more resources, technical capacity, and training" (Viceministros de Comercio y de Trabajo 2005, 42). The report stated that only Nicaragua has fewer labor courts: the Dominican Republic has 23, El Salvador has 9, and Nicaragua has 3 (Viceministros de Comercio y de Trabajo 2005, 76).

Even when an employer is found guilty of illegally firing workers who attempt to establish a labor union, the law does not require the reinstatement of the fired workers. Instead, the employer is asked to pay a fine and severance pay. As a result, employers with enough money can rid themselves of any unionization attempt and be in complete compliance with the law. The ILO Committee of Experts repeatedly has criticized El Salvador's labor legislation on these grounds, but to date, no action has been taken to rectify this substantive limitation to the law.

While the ruling ARENA party was forced to accept certain changes in labor laws as a result of international pressure, the reforms did not respond to the exigencies of EPZ production; and meanwhile, the government was able to weaken respect for labor laws by undermining labor law enforcement. As in Brazil, however, the labor reforms remain a dynamic process. In the mid-2000s, international labor unions were once again able to apply external pressure. This time, the result was to increase resources dedicated to enforcement.

Second Round of Reforms in Brazil and El Salvador

The two paths highlighted by the cases of Brazil and El Salvador have led to further reforms. In Central America and the Dominican Republic, international labor movement pressure preceding the 2005 U.S. government approval of the Central American Free Trade Agreement (CAFTA) led to an increase in resources dedicated to enforcement. In several countries, inspectors received better salaries, better equipment, and more training (Viceministros de Comercio y de Trabajo 2005). El Salvador hired 69 more workplace inspectors as a result of that international pressure, more than double the number of workplace inspectors in place in the 1990s and early 2000s.[20]

In Brazil, once again, internal political dynamics provided the initial impetus for further labor relations transformations. Since President Lula da Silva took office, the state has increased the resources dedicated to enforcement. The number of workers covered by workplace inspection rose from 19.9 million in 2002 (the last year of the Cardoso administration) to 30.6 million in 2006. The Lula administration also established the National Labor Forum to discuss further changes to the labor legislation. The tripartite consultative process generated many important proposals. Labor reforms would allow for national unions and national collective bargaining. They would end the Brazilian craft union structure, which has fragmented the union movement. With the reforms, unioniza-tion by industry would allow temporary workers (which the union refers to as "internally subcontracted workers") to belong to the same union as permanent workers (Henrique da Silva 2005).

These developments are important, but some concerns remain. In El Salvador, where the number of workplace inspectors more than doubled, the ILO found that the law still does not ensure inspectors have adequate access to the workplace (ILO 2007, 351). The ILO report also notes that Salvadoran law does not provide for confidential employee reporting of violations. Thus, while hiring more inspectors is a critical step in improving government enforcement capacity, allowing inspectors free access to the workplace and allowing workers to provide inspectors with information without their employers present would further contribute to improved working conditions and empowering labor unions.

Two years after the passage of CAFTA, the U.S. government acknowledged, in its human rights report on El Salvador, "The [Salvadoran] government did not allocate suf-ficient resources for adequate inspection and oversight to ensure respect for association and collective bargaining rights in EPZs. There continued to be allegations of corruption among labor inspectors in the maquilas [EPZs]" (U.S. Department of State 2007a). This suggests that externally-imposed reforms have their limits. The election of Mauricio Funes of the left-oriented FMLN party in March 2009 offers the possibility that domestic political forces will deepen pro-labor reforms and improve enforcement. But, the left does not hold a majority in the legislature and can expect strong resistance from the opposition, which is led by the conservative ARENA party.

In Brazil, while the number of factory inspections has increased over the last ten years, they have not reached the level of 1995, the peak year for inspections. Moreover, differences in the government coalitions and a government corruption scandal delayed passage of the revised labor laws. At the same time, in Brazil and elsewhere, the growing informal sector continues to erode labor's power. While it is useful to modify labor laws to allow for unionization in the informal sector, the union movement's ability to take advantage of the new laws has been mixed, largely due to collective action problems associated with attempts to organize such a dispersed group of workers.

While there are limitations in the reforms in both El Salvador and Brazil, the present status of labor unions is much weaker in El Salvador relative to Brazil. The unionization rate in Brazil remains five times that of El Salvador. This suggests that reform processes in which labor has a strong voice are potentially more beneficial to labor than reforms imposed from the outside on a highly reluctant government.[21]

Yet for all countries, the real challenge is to ensure shifts in economic policies that allow for stable, productive formal sector employment. Ensuring respect for labor rights may be one step toward this economic upgrading, because appropriate labor laws and effective enforcement can push employers onto a high-road competitive model and thereby avoid the "race to the bottom" that is inimical to workers' rights.

TOWARD GLOBALIZATION-COMPATIBLE, UNION-FRIENDLY LABOR RELATIONS REGIMES?

When internal or external pressure might leverage deeper union-friendly reforms, what should those reforms entail? That is, what might more union-friendly, globalization-compatible labor relations regimes look like? In what ways could state transformation better equalize the relationship between labor and capital while also allowing international economic competition?

Attempting to suggest an ideal type of labor relations regime runs the risk of missing the important contextual variations across the region that requires special considerations. It also runs the risk of designing an "ideal system" without considering the political feasibility of achieving such a system. Therefore, rather than project some ideal type on the region, let us draw on the positive elements already present and suggest that a more systematic combination of these elements could provide an indication of what more union-friendly, globalization-compatible labor relations regimes would look like.

As Sebastián Etchemendy and Ruth Collier (2007) contend, labor legislation in Argentina continues to endorse strong national unions and collective bargaining. Not surprisingly, labor in Argentina proved able to regain some of its power once the economy rebounded. National bargaining does not mean "one size fits all" bargaining. Rather, while national bargaining can address big issues—including how to respond to global competition—it can be combined with sectoral, firm, and plant-level bargaining to ensure that agreements match the conditions at each level of economic activity while not dissipating workers' associational power. Thus, labor legislation that allows labor to coordinate its responses to economic changes will put labor in a more favorable position in regard to national and multinational enterprises.

Labor law reforms that begin to address outsourcing—like Article 81 of the Guatemala Labor Code and like those proposed by the union movement in Ecuador—are also steps in the right direction. Most important, more effective unionization is likely where workers have the ability to leverage firms that control the terms and conditions of the employment relationship, whether that control is exercised through direct employment or indirectly through outsourcing.

Reforms that lower the percentage of workers needed to strike—such as those in the Dominican Republic, Nicaragua, and Peru—are additional steps that can provide unions the ability to achieve meaningful agreements via collective bargaining. As industrial relations theory indicates, it is not striking itself that is so important, but the threat of a strike that forces employers to recalculate what they are willing to give at the bargaining table (Katz and Kochan 1992). At the same time, access to firm financial information relevant to bargaining—as allotted by labor legislation in Argentina, Panama, and Peru—ensures that labor goes to the bargaining table well informed and does not have to resort to labor unrest in order to test whether an employer is being truthful about its economic status.

The facilitation of collective bargaining provides unions with a means to achieve concrete improvements at the workplace. Honduras, unlike El Salvador, does not require that the majority of workers in an enterprise be union members. The result is that, although not one collective contract exists in the Salvadoran EPZ sector, unions have negotiated ten collective contracts in Honduras (Anner 2004). Stronger bargaining need not result in higher unemployment. Unions in Honduras did not use their bargaining power to push conditions beyond what enterprises could afford. Indeed, employment in Honduran EPZs remains higher than in El Salvador.

The increase of resources dedicated to enforcement—as reflected in steps recently taken by the governments of Central America and the Dominican Republic—is another sign of progress. While greater enforcement may lead to a reduction of extreme low-end forms of employment, it does not necessarily imply greater unemployment. Costa Rica, which maintains a higher minimum wage than the rest of Central America, managed to upgrade its EPZ capacity to attract firms like Intel. Greater training of workplace inspectors may also be conducive to greater investment in workers' skills and industrial upgrading (Schrank 2006). Thus, increasing respect for labor rights does not necessarily imply net job loss but instead a potential shift from very low-end sectors to relatively higher-end sectors, as has been seen in other regions of the world (Kuruvilla 1996).

Research shows that labor rights violations are less common in unionized workplaces because union members are often trained to detect such violations. It follows that countries with lower unionization rates will have a higher need for state enforcement mechanisms until the union movement grows and can carry out this function. Labor tribunals are also important, particularly in regard to violations of collective labor rights. Those inspectors and court magistrates, furthermore, need proper salaries, training, support services, and oversight.

While giving employers state training and advice instead of imposing fines may work in certain instances—such as a violation of new regulations for storing dangerous chemicals—employers that systematically fire workers who attempt to form labor unions are probably not ignorant of the law. In such cases, as Cardoso and Lage (2005) posit, fines and the risk of being caught must outweigh the benefits of union avoidance. For example, redress for a violation of the right to organize cannot be limited to a moderate fine. Otherwise, employers with the most resources will be able to remain legally union-free by paying fines.

CONCLUSIONS

Latin American labor scholars have established that collective labor law reform has been most often "union-friendly." In so doing, they have provided an important corrective to narrow "state decline" arguments. This article builds on that research by examining the fit between the collective labor law reforms, state enforcement capacity, and economic restructuring in Latin America. It argues that changes in labor relations practices did not adequately address changes in the structure of the economy.

Globally integrated production networks require unions with broad collective bargaining rights if labor is to share in the benefits of international economic integration. Reforms, however, have favored a proliferation of small unions with weak, decentralized bargaining rights. Moreover, highly competitive global markets require a vigilant state to ensure that enterprises do not compete through the systematic violation of labor rights. Yet in the years following the 1990s reforms, states cut resources dedicated to enforcement. Lack of effective enforcement was not simply the result of poor countries' lacking resources but often the result of political dynamics; government elites who enacted reforms in response to external or internal pressure often subsequently denied their labor ministries the necessary resources to enforce the reforms effectively.

The process of union decline is far from uniform. While in El Salvador and Guatemala less than 5 percent of the workforce is unionized, in Argentina and Brazil the rates remain above 20 percent. This variation is linked to levels of economic development, institutional factors, and historical legacies. Latin America's larger countries have had a history of strong economic development and corporatist labor relations regimes that allowed for stronger unions. Union movements that were stronger at the time of the reforms were better able to influence the reform process (either by proposing union-friendly changes or opposing changes to core labor rights) than countries with weaker union movements and externally imposed reforms.

Recent developments suggest that the process of labor relations reform in Latin America is far from finished. Union strategies, domestic politics, and international pressure continue to influence events. Following the path of an externally induced reform process, Central American countries and the Dominican Republic were pressured to dedicate more resources to enforcement in order to pass CAFTA. In an internally induced reform process, the Brazilian labor movement is working with the Lula government to enact deeper union-friendly reforms. Brazil maintains one of the stronger labor movements in Latin America, suggesting that internally induced reforms are perhaps deeper and more sustainable.

It is not clear whether recent reforms will be enough to reverse the decline of organized labor in Latin America. Yet whatever the future of regional labor unions might be, a fuller analysis of the dynamics of labor relations must look beyond labor laws to explore the fit between reforms and current economic exigencies, as well as state enforcement capacity and the political dynamics that shape it.

NOTES

The author thanks Teri Caraway, María Lorena Cook, Peter Evans, Kevin Middlebrook, María Victoria Murillo, Cathy Lisa Schneider, and Peter Winn for their insightful comments and helpful suggestions on earlier versions of this work. He also thanks the rigorous, thoughtful, and copious comments of four anonymous reviewers of *Latin American Politics and Society*.

1 On average, the unionization rate in the region dropped by 33.39 percent between the 1980s and early 2000s (see table 1). The weighted average real wage fell by 4.4 percent between 1990 and 2003 (ECLAC 2006).

2 On average, the unionization rates declined by 32.08 percent in the countries with "union-friendly" reforms, by 27.69 percent in the countries with predominately "union-averse" reforms, and by 40.93 percent in the countries with no or mixed reforms. It is important to keep in mind the limitations of these data, as noted at the bottom of table 1.

3 Etchemendy and Collier (2007) also found that in Argentina, highly unionized industrial sectors were able to maintain their union power. Yet Argentina, with its long history of centralized bargaining and industrial unionism, is an exception.

4 To illustrate this point, let us say that there are one million workers in an industry and half of them (500,000, or 50 percent) are unionized. Let us now say that half those jobs are lost. If the

unionization rate stayed the same, of the remaining 500,000 workers, 250,000 (50 percent) would be union members. But what we are seeing is that only 200,000 or 150,000 are union members (40 percent or less). Thus the drop in the number of jobs cannot explain the drop in the percentage of workers unionized.

5 For example, the U.S. system has one agency that deals with health and safety, another that addresses wage and overtime violations, and another that addresses discrimination.

6 The Administrative Labor Authority may call off a strike that it believes has lasted too long and impose a decision regarding the issues in dispute.

7 While the Ministry of Labor sought more state resources to improve its enforcement capacity, the Ministry of the Economy opposed these initiatives on the grounds that stronger unions would limit foreign direct investment and export-oriented economic growth (Villavicencio 2004).

8 The General System of Preferences requires beneficiary countries to respect internationally recognized labor rights in order to receive preferential trade benefits. The system also allows nongovernmental organizations (such as the AFL-CIO) to petition the U.S. Trade Representative when they believe countries are violating labor rights.

9 Following the constitutional reforms, several attempts were made to implement union-averse reforms, mostly notably by the Cardoso administration (1995–2002); yet all important efforts were defeated or stalled by labor or political opposition (Cook 2007).

10 Most notably, limitations on national union formation and union plurality were maintained, as was the union tax. Regulations restricted the exercise of the right to strike. It is also important to note that individual employment law reform in the 1990s moved in the direction of greater flexibility (Cook 2007). This may have undermined the effectiveness of the collective labor law reforms. (The author thanks an anonymous reviewer for these points.)

11 Not all the changes proposed by the labor movement were enacted (Cook 1998, 329). This is because the reforms were a result of a political process in which more conservative political parties also had a voice.

12 Brazilian unions grew significantly from the late 1970s through the 1980s due to effective union strategies, low unemployment rates, and strong industrial growth (Cardoso 2002).

13 Adding to the weakness of unions in new facilities was a concerted effort by employers to weaken a "worker" identity seen as conducive to unionization by engendering a "team" or "one family" attitude among employees and managers (Anner 2004).

14 In the building trades (construction sector), being a union member increased a worker's likelihood of working, because many construction firms used the unions as hiring halls to recruit new workers.

15 Only 1,703 workers were able to form unions in the informal sector, representing 00.11 percent of the estimated 1.5 million workers in that sector (MTPS 2004).

16 The prohibition on collective bargaining appears in Article 211 of the Labor Code.

17 The rate is calculated as a percentage of formal sector establishments with five or more workers.

18 One employer said that Ministry of Labor representatives came by on the weekends to attempt to sell him a computerized database of all workers with union experience in the EPZ (Anonymous interview 1995).

19 Calculations are based on data provided by the Salvadoran Ministry of Labor.

20 Author's communication with high-ranking officials in the Salvadoran Ministry of Labor.

21 It is also true, however, that what allowed labor to have a voice in the Brazilian reform process is that it started from a much stronger position of power than labor in El Salvador. As the recent round of reforms in the 2000s suggests, this dynamic is likely to continue, as the stronger Brazilian labor movement attempts to exert pressure and use its influence on the Lula administration to deepen collective labor reforms.

REFERENCES

Anner, Mark. 2003. Industrial Structure, the State, and Ideology: Shaping Labor Transnationalism in the Brazilian Auto Industry. *Social Science History* 27, 4: 603–34.

———. 2004. Between Solidarity and Fragmentation: Labor Responses to Globalization in the Americas. Ph.D. diss., Cornell University.

Arcos, Marcelo. 2004. Adviser, FENACLE/CEOSL. Author interview. Quito, July 15.

Arévalo, Rolando, and Joaquín Arriola. 1996. El caso de El Salvador. In *La situación sociolaboral en las zonas francas y empresas maquiladoras del istmo Centroamericano y República Dominicana*, ed. Organización Internacional de Trabajo. San José: Oficina de Actividades para los Trabajadores. 109–58.

BCR (Banco Central de Reserva de El Salvador). 2007. *Boletín.* <www.ber.gob.sv/boletin.htm>; Accessed October 3, 2007.

Bizberg, Ilan. 1996. Las relaciones industriales en México: cambio y permanencia. In *Transformación económica y trabajo en America Latina: proyecto comparativo internacional,* Avances de investigación, ed. Rainer Dombois and Ludger Pries. Bremen: Universitat Bremen. 6–57.

Bronstein, Arturo S. 1995. Societal Change and Industrial Relations in Latin America: Trends and Prospects. *International Labour Review* 134, 2: 163–86.

——. 1997. Labour Law Reform in Latin America: Between State Protection and Flexibility. *International Labour Review* 136, 1: 6–26.

Buchanan, Paul G., and Kate Nicholls. 2003. *Labour Politics in Small Open Democracies: Australia, Chile, Ireland, New Zealand, and Uruguay.* New-York: Palgrave Macmillan.

Caraway, Teri. 2006. Freedom of Association: Battering Ram or Trojan Horse? *Review of International Political Economy* 13, 2: 210–32.

Cardoso, Adalberto. 2001. Problemas de representação do sindicalismo brasileiro: o que aconteceu com a filiação sindical? In *Los sindicatos frente a los procesos de transición política,* ed. E. De La Garza. Buenos Aires: CLACSO.

——. 2002. Neoliberalism, Unions, and Socio-Economic Insecurity in Brazil. Labour, *Capital and Society* 35, 2: 282–316.

Cardoso, Adalberto, and Telma Lage. 2005. A inspeção do trabalho no Brasil. *Dados: Revista de Ciências Sociais* 48, 3: 451–90.

Cingranelli, David. 2003. Democracy, Globalization and Workers' Rights: A Comparative Analysis. Paper presented at the 99th annual meeting of the American Political Science Association, Philadelphia, August 28–31.

Collier, Ruth Berins, and David Collier. 1991. *Shaping the Political Arena: Critical Junctures, the Labor Movement, and Regime Dynamics in Latin America.* Princeton: Princeton University Press.

Comin, Alexandre. 1998. De volta para o futuro: política e reestruturação da indústria do complexo automobilístico nos anos 90. São Paulo: CEBRAP/Annablume/FAPESP.

Committee of Experts on the Application of Conventions and Recommendations (CEACR). 2005. Report, <www.ilo.org/public/english/standards/relm/ilc>; Accessed November 30, 2005.

Cook, María Lorena. 1998. Toward Flexible Industrial Relations? Neo-liberalism, Democracy, and Labor Reform in Latin America. *Industrial Relations* 37, 3: 311.

——. 2007. The Politics of Labor Reform in Latin America: Between Flexibility and Rights. University Park: Pennsylvania State University Press.

Córdova, Efrén. 1996. The Challenge of Flexibility in Latin America. *Comparative Labor Law Journal* 17, 2: 314–37.

Davis, Benjamin N. 1995. The Effects of Worker Rights Protections in United States Trade Laws: A Case Study of El Salvador. *American University Journal of International Law and Policy* 10, 3: 1167–1214.

Drake, Paul W. 1996. *Labor Movements and Dictatorships; The Southern Cone in Comparative Perspective.* Baltimore: Johns Hopkins University Press.

Dunlop, John Thomas. 1993 [1958]. Industrial Relations Systems. Boston: Harvard Business School Press.

ECLAC (Economic Commission on Latin America and the Caribbean). 2006. *Social Panorama of Latin America,* 2005. Santiago de Chile: ECLAC.

Eróstegui, Rodolfo. 2004. Vice Minister of Labor, Bolivia. Author interview. La Paz, July 13.

Etchemendy, Sebastián, and Ruth B. Collier. 2007. Down But Not Out: Union Resurgence and Segmented Neocorporatism in Argentina (2003–2007). *Politics & Society* 35 (3): 363–401.

Evans, Peter B. 1997. The Eclipse of the State? Reflections on Stateness in an Era of Globalization. *World Politics* 50, 1: 62–87.

Frigant, Vincent, and Yannick Lung. 2002. Geographical Proximity and Supplying Relationships in Modular Production. *International Journal of Urban and Regional Research* 26, 4: 742–55.

Frundt, Henry J. 1998. *Trade Conditions and Labor Rights: U.S. Initiatives, Dominican and Central American Responses*. Gainesville: University Press of Florida.

Garrett, Geoffrey, and Peter Lange. 1996. Internationalization, Institutions, and Political Change. In *Internationalization and Domestic Politics*, ed. Robert O. Keohane and H. V. Milner. Cambridge: Cambridge University Press. 48–79.

Henrique da Silva, Artur. 2005. General Secretary, CUT. Author interview. São Paulo, August 10.

Hyman, Richard. 1995. Industrial Relations in Europe: Theory and Practice. *European Journal of Industrial Relations* 1, 1: 17–46.

Inforpress. 2007. CAFTA and Labor Justice: A Long Struggle Ahead. *Central American Report* 34, 26 (June 8): 4–5.

Instituto Brasileiro de Geografia e Estatística (IBGE). 2002. *Sindicatos: indicadores sociais 2001* (primeiros resultados). Rio de Janeiro: IBGE.

Instituto Universitario de Opinión Pública (IUDOP). 2005. Los salvadoreños evalúan el primer año de gobierno de Antonio Saca. San Salvador: IUDOP, Universidad Centroamerieana "José Simeon Cartas."

Inter-American Development Bank (IDB). 2003. *Good Jobs Wanted: Labor Markets in Latin America*. Washington, DC: IDB.

International Confederation of Trade Unions (ICFTU). 2001. Report for the WTO General Council: Review of the Trade Policy of Costa Rica, 2001. <www.icftu.org>; Accessed July 3, 2007.

ILO (International Labor Organization). 1997. World Labour Report: Industrial Relations, Democracy and Social Stability, 1997–1998. Geneva: ILO.

——. 2005 *Paorama Laboral 2005. America Latina y el Caribe*. Lima: Oficina Regional para America Latina y el Caribe.

——. 2006. Labour Inspection: Report to the International Labour Conference, 95th Session. Geneva: ILO.

——. 2007. Report of the Committee of Experts on the Application of Conventions and Recommendations: International Labour Conference, 96th Session. Geneva: ILO.

Jatoba, Vera. 2002. Labour Inspection Within a Modernized Labour Administration. Lima: International Labour Office, Regional Office for the Americas (IACML-ILO Project).

Jessup, David, and Michael E. Gordon. 2000. Organizing in Export Processing Zones: The Bibong Experience in the Dominican Republic. In *Transnational Cooperation Among Labor Unions*, ed. M. E. Gordon and L. Turner. Ithaca: Cornell University Press. 179–201.

Katz, Harry C., and Thomas A. Kochan. 1992. *An Introduction to Collective Bargaining and Industrial Relations*. New York: McGraw Hill.

Kerr, Clark, John T. Dunlop, Frederick Harbison, and Charles A. Myers. 1960. *Industrialism and Industrial Man: The Problems of Labor and Management in Economic Growth*. Cambridge: Harvard University Press.

Kuruvilla, Sarosh. 1996. Linkages Between Industrialization Strategies and Industrial Relations/Human Resource Policies: Singapore, Malaysia, the Philippines, and India. *Industrial and Labor Relations Review* 49, 4: 635–57.

Lee, Cheol-Sung. 2005. International Migration, Deindustrialization and Union Decline in 16 Affluent OECD Countries, 1962–1997. *Social Forces* 84, 1: 71–88.

Lora, Eduardo. 2001. *Structural Reforms in Latin America: What Has Been Reformed and How to Measure It*. Washington, DC: Inter-American Development Bank.

Mercedes Benz Production Workers. 2002. Author interview. Virrey del Pino, Argentina, November 11.

Ministerio de Trabajo y Previsión Social. 1991. *Boletín Estadístico*. Guatemala City: Government of Guatemala. <http://www.mintrabajo.gob.gt/>.

——. 1995. *Estadísticas del Trabajo*. San Salvador: Government of El Salvador. <http://www.mtps.gob.sv/>.

——. 2000. *Estadísticas del Trabajo*. San Salvador: Government of El Salvador. <http://www.mtps.gob.sv/>.

——. 2005. *Boletín Estadístico.* Guatemala City: Government of Guatemala. <http://www.mintrabajo.gob.gt/>. Ministerio de Trabajo, Empleo y Seguridad Social. (various years). *Estadisticas de Trabajo* (unpublished mimeographs). Buenos Aires: Government of Argentina.

Ministry of Public Finance. 2005. Presupuesto 2005. <www.minfin.gob.gt/main.php?id_area=3>; Accessed August 5, 2007.

MTPS (Ministerio de Trabajo y Previsión Social) 2001. *Estadísticas del trabajo.* San Salvador: Government of El Salvador.

——. 2004. Estadísticas del trabajo. San Salvador: Government of El Salvador. Eróstegui, Rodolfo.2004. Vice Minister of Labor, Bolivia. Author interview. La Paz, July 13.

Murillo, María Victoria, and Andrew Schrank. 2005. With a Little Help from My Friends: Partisan Politics, Transnational Alliances, and Labor Rights in Latin America. *Comparative Political Studies* 38, 8: 971–99.

Ohmae, Kenichi. 1995. *The End of the Nation State: The Rise of Regional Economies.* New York: Free Press.

Pilz, Dania. 2005. Perdida de protagonismo del movimiento sindical y deterioro de las condiciones laborales marcan el final de una década. Asunción: Centro de Documentación y Estudios.

Piore, Michael J., and Andrew Schrank. 2006. Trading Up: An Embryonic Model for Easing the Human Costs of Free Markets. *Boston Review* 31: 1–22.

Portes, Alejandro, and Kelly Hoffman. 2003. Latin American Class Structures: Their Composition and Change During the Neoliberal Era. *Latin American Research Review* 38, 1: 41–82.

Rodrik, Dani. 1997. *Has Globalization Gone Too Far?* Washington, DC: Institute of International Economics.

Sabel, Charles F. 1982. *Work and Politics: The Division of Labor in Industry.* New York: Cambridge University Press.

Salerno, Mario Sergio. 2001. A indústria automobilística no Brasil. Paper prepared for the International Metalworkers' Federation and International Labour Organization project.

Salerno, Mário Sérgio, and Anna Valéria Carneiro Dias. 2002. Product Design Modularity, Modular Production, Modular Organization: The Evolution of Modular Concepts. *Actes du GERPISA* 33: 61–73.

Schrank, Andrew. 2006. Labor Inspectors in the CAFTA Region: Cosmetic, Costly, or Constructive? Paper presented at the workshop Multinational Production and Labor Rights, University of North Carolina, Chapel Hill, September 22–23.

Singa Boyenge, Jean-Pierre. 2007. ILO Database on Export Processing Zones. Geneva: ILO.

Tilly, Charles. 1995. Globalization Threatens Labour Rights. *International Labor and Working-Class History* 47: 1–23.

U.S. Department of State. 2003. Brazil: Country Reports on Human Rights Practices, 2002. Washington, DC: Bureau of Democracy, Human Rights, and Labor.

——. 2007a. El Salvador: Country Reports on Human Rights Practices, 2006. Washington, DC: Bureau of Democracy, Human Rights, and Labor.

——. 2007 b Paraguay: Country Reports on Human Rights Practices, 2006. Washington, DC: Bureau of Democracy, Human Rights, and Labor.

Vega Ruiz, María Luz. 2005. La reforma laboral en America Latina: 15 años después. Lima: Oficina International del Trabajo, Oficina Regional para America Latina y el Caribe.

Viceministros de Comercio y de Trabajo. 2005. La dimensión laboral en Centroamérica y la República Dominicana: construyendo sobre el progreso, reforzando el cumplimiento y potenciando las capacidades. Report. Washington, DC: Inter-American Development Bank. <www.iadb.org/trade/2_spanish/pub/trabajo-CARD.pdf>; Accessed March 19, 2008.

Villalba, Roberto. 1996. Derechos humanos en Paraguay: movimiento sindical. Asunción: Serpaj.

Villavicencio, Alfredo. 2004. Vice Minister of Labor, Peru. Author interview. Lima, July 21.

Von Richthofen, Wolfgang. 2002. *Labour Inspection: A Guide to the Profession.* Geneva: ILO.

Weil, David. 1999. Are Mandated Health and Safety Committees Substitutes for or Supplements to Labor Unions? *Industrial and Labor Relations Review* 52, 3: 339–60.

Western, Bruce. 1997. *Between Class and Market: Postwar Unionization in the Capitalist Democracies.* Princeton: Princeton University Press.

Wood, Adrian. 1994. *North-South Trade, Employment, and Inequality: Changing Fortunes in a Skill-Driven World.* New York: Clarendon Press.

Chapter 11

Welfare Regimes in Latin America: Capturing Constellations of Markets, Families, and Policies

Juliana Martínez Franzoni

Is it possible that empirical analysis truly honors the notion of welfare regimes, whether state or nonstate? Can it shed light on the role of labor markets and families, the sexual division of labor behind them, and the qualitatively different roles they play under specific welfare "mixes"? This article presents both a theoretical framework and a methodology that come closer than previous efforts to capturing the complex array of interactions among labor markets, families, and public policy in Latin America. Drawing on cluster analysis based on available data for 18 countries, a preliminary application of this theoretical framework and methodology confirms, refines, and complements previous studies that focused on public policy and, to a lesser extent, labor markets that disregard families and unpaid work. More specifically, the study identifies three welfare regimes. Two are state welfare regimes, one protectionist and one productivity; and one is nonstate familiarist.

In a region where people's well-being is deeply embedded in family relationships and is frequently more dependent on female unpaid labor than on public policy, closer attention to how social structures interact with public policy has not only academic interest but policy implications: policy changes could improve welfare regime "architectures" (Esping-Andersen 2002). Unlike policy prescriptions packaged under the Washington Consensus (Williamson 1990) as "one size fits all," those architectures are likely to be plural and path-dependent. This article demonstrates that an empirical typology of welfare regimes can be a useful tool, at the very least, to emphasize the need for a more selective emulation of policy lessons across welfare regimes (Martínez Franzoni 2006).

Because Latin America is considered one of the most disparate regions in the world, the notion of welfare regimes often raises skepticism among scholars. To a large degree, skepticism grows out of the deep-rooted notion of welfare states, conceived as those "in which organized power is deliberately used to modify the play of market forces in order to guarantee individuals a minimum income, narrow insecurity, and ensure that all citizens, regardless of status or class, are offered the best standards available in relation to a certain agreed range of social services" (Briggs, quoted in Rudra 2005, 6). Based on the preceding description, it is not surprising that scholars are often skeptical of welfare states in Latin America.

As established by the seminal work of Esping-Andersen (1990), welfare regimes could, but do not necessarily need to include welfare regimes could, but do not necessarily need to include welfare states. Understood as constellations of practices that reallocate resources, welfare regimes may or may not include well-developed public policy (Gough and Wood 2004). Consequently, the study of welfare regimes sheds light on the redistribution of resources, whether or not such redistribution is state led. If labor markets are well organized and able to absorb the labor force, the less the role of state redistribution, the more dependent on markets and primary distribution the population will become. Yet when labor markets are highly informal and lead to large inequalities in income, nonmarket-based practices, such as family and community ties, expectations, and obligations, become more significant. It is then necessary to use concepts, such as the notion of welfare regimes, to help describe the interaction of various practices for the reallocation of resources.

In addition, the notion of welfare regimes provides a much-needed normative criterion to assess whether countries depart from desirable practices for resource allocation. As Gough clearly describes it, "the idea of a welfare regime is grounded on some independent measure of human well-being with which to evaluate different socioeconomic systems. This can just as well embrace ill-being" (Gough and Wood 2004, 27). The notion of a welfare regime helps describe and explain various "welfare mixes" (Gough and Wood 2004) without giving up a normative criterion, namely that all market economies must, in some way, either free people from sheer economic power or condemn them to slavery imposed by need (Castel 2004 [1997]).

THEORETICAL BACKGROUND

In the world of advanced capitalism, welfare regimes do not necessarily differ as much in the amount of resources they invest as in the criteria used to allocate the resources, whether those criteria are needs, citizenship, or contributions (Esping-Andersen 1990). More specifically, public resources might be allocated to the poor (that is, liberal welfare regimes, as found in the United States), universally (social-democratic welfare regimes, as in Sweden), or according to occupation (corporate welfare regimes, as in Germany).

Fernando Filgueira (1998) was the first to adapt Esping-Andersen's work to the Latin American context. He claims that we should focus not only on the amount that countries invest in people's well-being but also the criteria with which the investments are made. Drawing from the study of social policy during the "golden era" (the 1970s), he identifies three regional patterns, conditioned to coverage, benefits, requirements, and stratification of services. The first pattern groups countries with "stratified universalism," such as Uruguay and Argentina, with extended policies but segmented along occupations. Costa Rica, he argues, could be considered part of this cluster, although it shows higher universalism and lower stratification than the other countries in the cluster.

The second group involves exclusionary countries with residual states and almost nonexistent public redistribution of resources, such as El Salvador and Nicaragua. Third, he groups "dual" countries, such as Brazil and Mexico, which combine stratified universalism in urban areas and exclusion in rural ones. Later, gradual or radical management of the economic crises in the 1980s led countries with stratified universalism down one of two roads, either state-oriented (Costa Rica and Uruguay) or market-oriented (Argentina and Chile) (Filgueira and Martínez Franzoni 2002).

Drawing from Filgueira's findings and distinguishing among types of public expenditures, Evelyne Huber and John Stephens (2005) identify social policies aimed at social protection (such as pensions) and the formation of human capital (such as health and education). Based on coverage, level of expenditures, and allocation of social investment, these authors identify four clusters in addition to Chile that show descending degrees of coverage and fiscal effort: Argentina, Uruguay, and Costa Rica; Brazil and Mexico; Bolivia, Ecuador, Peru, Colombia, and Venezuela; and Guatemala, El Salvador, Honduras, and Nicaragua.[1] Huber and Stephens argue that social policies in Chile, Argentina, Uruguay, and Costa Rica (clusters 1 and 2) can be considered successful. However, these countries do show key differences in the allocation of public resources, as we will see.

To this end, Nita Rudra (2005) makes an important contribution. She distinguishes developing countries in Africa, Asia, and Latin America according to whether they rely on public policies that predominantly promote access to the market (productivist regimes) or that predominantly protect people from the market (protectionist regimes).

> Protective welfare states have roots in a political economy that has eschewed emphasis on international markets and focused government efforts on decommodification. Productive welfare states, in contrast, place high priority on commodification and are located in systems where states have actively encouraged international participation . . . Put simply, in less developed countries the welfare state will either support a workforce that meets efficient production goals or it will prioritize the system of (re)distribution (although not necessarily from the rich to the poor). (Rudra 2005, 17–18)

This is a key distinction in differentiating countries in terms of how public policy allocates resources.

Unlike scholars who primarily focus on public policies, Ian Gough and Geof Wood (2004) develop a broader typology. Similarly to Rudra, they review Asian, African, and Latin American countries and argue that the regimes studied by Esping-Andersen are actually three variations of welfare state regimes. These can be found in countries that count on legitimate states and extended labor markets, where the majority of the population is, to a large extent, successfully protected by either of these institutions. In many parts of the world, including most Latin American countries, states are practically non-existent, labor markets often exclude the majority of the population, and a great deal of welfare production rests on families and social support networks (Gough and Wood 2004). The less the relative weight of public policies, the more relevant it is to widen the spectrum of the analysis. Indeed, in informal welfare regimes, as found in Asia and Latin America, most of the population relies on family or community ties (Gough and Wood 2004).[2] A primary limitation of this work, however, is the difficulty of establishing the role of families and communities in empirical and comparative terms.

Working under the same typology, Armando Barrientos (2004) argues that in the last two decades, Latin America has shifted from a "conservative-informal" to a "liberal-informal" welfare regime. The first type shared many traits with the corporate-conservative welfare state regimes identified by Esping-Andersen in continental Europe. The primary source of protection was stratified systems of social security, targeted at formal workers and linked to their occupations. Meanwhile, informal workers depended on their income and family strategies to confront risks such as disease and old age. The challenge now, however, is that in the last two decades, collectively shared risks have become few, public policies have diminished, and individuals are increasingly on their own. Thus, the region resembles the liberal regime in developed countries; but unlike them, most countries in the Latin American region lack solid targeted state programs (Barrientos 2004).

One of Barrientos's primary contributions is that he goes beyond the rhetoric of laws and policies and explores actual practices. This permits a more comprehensive focus than with Filgueira's initial typology. Barrientos's main limitation, however, is an over-generalization that positions all Latin American countries together under one single welfare regime. In this highly heterogeneous region, geographic proximity cannot be expected to account exclusively for welfare regimes. For example, the differences in social expenditure between countries are enormous. In Central America alone, in 2000–2001, social expenditures varied from US$61 in Nicaragua, US$77 in Honduras, and US$88 in El Salvador to US$689 in Costa Rica (ECLAC 2004). While we might find a prevailing liberal policy paradigm driving most public policy reforms during the past two decades, the reality of public policy appears to be more heterogeneous.

Overall, these various studies focus on class, but overlook the sexual division of labor; that is, the expectations, behaviors, and perceptions attached to people's gender. Jennifer Pribble (2004), however, does address the effects of social policy regimes on the sexual division of labor in Chile and Uruguay, based on three programs: family allowances, maternity leave, and child care. These two countries demonstrate a similar level of social investment but different degrees of the sexual division of labor, stronger in Chile and weaker in Uruguay.[3] Pribble's analysis demonstrates the empirical yield of using gender-sensitive theoretical lenses to specify not only the quantity but also the quality of social investment.

However, the sexual division of labor transcends social policy and shapes people's access to resources. Socioeconomic location varies according to whether unpaid work is available. For instance, if a male worker has a housewife, he will allocate less income to purchase food or hire domestic service partly or completely to replace his wife's work. Occupational stratification is therefore deeply entwined with gender. The sexual division of labor also allocates provider and caretaker roles to men and women, respectively. In its traditional form, women are excluded from the workforce, subordinate to their spouses or partners in the access to services, and in charge of unpaid work, including the care of people without the support of the state, economically independent or not (Lewis 1993).

For example, if a heterosexual couple has paid work and leaves their children in a public daycare facility, public policy is "defamilializing" (Orloff 1996) caretaking during a good part of the day. If, on the other hand, the same couple lacks public services or has access to the services but chooses to rely on the market, caretaking becomes commodified. Again, these examples demonstrate the profound connection between resources allocated by labor markets, families, and public policies. Each has its own practices for resource allocation: markets revolve around money, families around unpaid work grounded on the gender division of labor, and public policies around some form of "authorized" allocation of collective resources.

The examples also illustrate an important difference between studying welfare regimes in developed and developing countries. As Rudra aptly summarizes it, "it is premature to attach welfare functions solely to Esping-Andersen's notion of 'decommodification' in countries where governments are still focused on encouraging wage labor and developing market economies. Rather, less developed countries' welfare states have a dual role . . . commodification' and 'decommodification'" (Rudra 2005, 14–15). In understanding redistribution in Latin America, access to paid work cannot be taken for granted.

Thus the analysis of welfare regimes stands at the intersection of various fields and promises fertile ground for empirical research. How successful are labor markets in absorbing the labor force and paying for it appropriately? That is, how effective are labor markets in "commodifying" labor (Rudra 2005)? And once the commodification of labor is achieved, to what extent do people rely on public and collective goods? In other words, to what extent is welfare decommodification (Esping-Andersen 1990)? When welfare is decommodified, do people turn to families and, more specifically, to female unpaid labor or, on the contrary, do they defamilialize caretaking (Orloff 1996)? Furthermore, to what extent do people depend on community support networks and social ties (Gough and Wood 2004)?

For Latin America, a typology that simultaneously and empirically addresses the interactions between commodification, decommodification, and defamilialization is not yet available. This study begins the effort to develop such a typology to study the various welfare mixes in the region.

METHODOLOGY

Empirical research that adequately reflects conceptual matters concerning welfare regimes requires a comparative analysis. To date, much of what we know about Latin America draws from a sound knowledge of a narrower sample of Southern Cone countries, which, along with Brazil, led welfare state building during most of the twentieth century; somewhat less attention has been given to Central American, Andean, and other South American countries. It is therefore imperative that comparisons and analysis of welfare regimes in the region include the less studied nations, which have distinct types and constellations of labor markets, public policies, and families.

How to compare 18 countries while simultaneously addressing those interactions? To begin with, statistical analysis must be performed. In an attempt to explore the proposed conceptual framework, this study uses available statistics, rather than developing new ones. To determine available indicators, the strengths and weaknesses of previously used primary statistical indicators are outlined, "ideal" measures are discussed, and the actual indicators utilized are explained.

The review of indicators focuses on the four innovative efforts to study welfare regimes that have been referred to so far: the 1990 Esping-Andersen groundbreaking research, Filgueira's pioneer 1998 study on Latin American welfare states, and the studies by Gough and Wood (2004) and Rudra (2005) on welfare regimes and welfare states, respectively, in the global South. All four studies make an important empirical contribution but also struggle with limitations imposed by available data.

As table 1 demonstrates, the available indicators for decommodification are superior to those for the other dimensions. The indicators in this dimension include expenditures and diverse sector measures, such as coverage. Esping-Andersen uses the most ambitious indicators, which he himself elaborated based on primary data. Sainsbury (1996) also considers entitlements, whether individually or family based. Scholars reviewing large numbers of developing countries, however, use less ambitious available measures, such as coverage.

For the most part, studies of the welfare mix have not considered the commodification of the labor force. Exceptions are indicators for quality of access to the labor market, as measured by a very weak indicator; namely, ratified International Labor Organization (ILO) conventions; and remittances, a sound "proxy" measure used to capture the role of international labor markets. Since women's access to the labor market cannot be taken for granted, various feminist scholars, such as Sainsbury (1999), look at indicators that go beyond the number of people who enter the labor force and depict the labor force in more comprehensive terms (e.g., wage gaps along gender lines). Generally, indicators concerning the commodification of the labor force pose a particular challenge: how to avoid conflating commodification with decommodification. For instance, while formal employment stresses the former, the economically active populations with social insurance stress the latter.

Feminist researchers also have made important contributions in measuring defamilialization. For developed countries, O'Connor et al. (1999) consider female and male labor participation, controlled by family type (e.g., nuclear or extended). In addition to how many women enter the labor force, they take into account policies that, by defamiliarizing caretaking, create better conditions for women so that they can enter the labor market. Examples are maternity and paternity leaves and child care.

In terms of performance or welfare outcomes, relatively homogeneous living conditions can be assumed for developed countries. However, the same is not true for developing countries. In the latter, indicators tackle basic living conditions, such literacy, life

Table 1. Indicators Used to Cluster Welfare Regimes (selected scholars)

Commodification
  Occupational segregation and wage gaps by gender (O'Connor et al.)
  Cumulative number of ILO conventions ratified by countries (Rudra)
  Remittances as a percentage of GDP (Gough)

Decommodification
Social expenditures
  Social as percent of GNP (Filgueira, 1998)
  Public expenditures as percent of total government expenditures (Rudra)
  Public expenditures in primary and tertiary education, health care, housing, wages, and social
    security (Rudra)
  Per capita expenditures in education (Rudra)
  Expenditures as a percent of GNP for tertiary education (Rudra)
  Public expenditures as percent of GDP in education, health care and social security (Gough)
  International flows as a percent of GDP (Gough)
  Private expenditure on health care (Gough)
  Individual or family-based access to social services (overall and by sectors) (Sainsbury)

Health care services[a]
  Summary index based on:
  1) benefit replacement rates during the first 26 weeks of illness;
  2) number of employment weeks required to qualify;
  3) waiting weeks before benefits are paid; and
  4) number of weeks in which a benefit can be maintained (weighted by the population
    covered as a percent of the labor force) (Esping-Andersen)
  Percent of children under 12 months old vaccinated against measles (Filgueira)
  Percent of children 12 to 23 months old vaccinated against measles, diphtheria, pertussis, and
    tetanus (Rudra)

Pensions
  Additive qualities of 1) minimum pension benefits; 2) standard pension benefits; 3)
    contribution period; 4) individual's share of pension financing (Esping-Andersen)
  Coverage as prevent of the economically active and total population (Filgueira)

Education
  Coverage of primary and secondary education as percent of children over total (Filgueira)

Defamilialization
  Female labor participation (O'Connor et al.)
  Maternity and paternity leaves (O'Connor et al.)
  Public and private childcare (O'Connor et al.)

Performance
  Adult literacy rate (Rudra and Gough)
  Infant mortality (Rudra)
  Human Development Index (Gough)
  Human Poverty Index (Gough)
  Life expectancy (Gough)
  Poverty gap (Gough)
  Human rights (Freedom House scores for political and civil liberties) (Gough)

[a]Esping-Andersen uses the same indicators for unemployment programs.
Sources: Esping-Andersen 1990; Filgueira 1998; Gough and Wood 2004; O'Connor et al. 1999; Rudra
2005; Sainsbury 1996.

expectancy, infant mortality, and poverty; or indexes that comprise several of these indicators, such as the United Nations Development Program (UNDP) Human Development Index.

How adequate are these measures for the empirical analysis of various dimensions of welfare regimes? How do they compare to ideal indicators? For commodification, it would be best to establish overall access to labor markets (whether national or international, as reflected in remittances) according to wages and a characterization of whether jobs are formal or informal. Ideal measures for decommodification in developing countries would involve collective allocation of resources at the community, regional, and international levels, rather than merely the national level. Ideal measures for defamilialization would involve time use, such as hours devoted to unpaid work, both domestic chores and caretaking, by women and men (Martínez Franzoni 2005). Given that the countries being studied are extremely inequitable, it is necessary to rely on variances as well as averages for all three dimensions.

With regard to the empirical basis for cluster analysis, the contribution made is twofold: the set of indicators is more comprehensive and systematic for each of the three dimensions, yet it relies on sources that are public, readily available, and the most legitimate in each field.

To consider all relevant measurements, all available indicators for each of the three dimensions considered were consolidated and the availability of each of these was assessed according to year and country. To improve the probability of gathering data for all 18 Latin American countries, data from a six-year period, 1999–2004, were used. The initial database comprised 37 variables and 100 indicators drawn from specialized and prestigious institutions (see appendix, table 5). Redundancies were eliminated by selecting the best indicator for each of the 37 variables. Then the most recent years with the largest number of countries available were selected for the study. Finally, 32 indicators remained for use in the analysis.[4]

Relationships between indicators and dimensions are conceptual and hypothetical rather than empirical. For future studies, it would be prudent to test this theoretical model by conducting a factorial analysis that empirically demonstrates whether indicators effectively correspond to each of the three conceptual dimensions. For the purposes of this study, however, and in light of the primary goal of this article—namely, to reconstruct the constellation of labor markets, public policy, and families behind the allocation of resources—further methodological complexity was avoided. Indicators selected to measure each dimension are presented in table 2.

To measure commodification, 11 indicators that address the degree to which domestic labor markets absorb, provide salaried jobs, and remunerate the labor force were used. The first aspect was measured in terms of labor market participation (direct correlation), female labor market participation (direct correlation), child participation in the labor force (inverse correlation), and unemployment (direct correlation).[5] The capacity to provide salaried jobs was measured in terms of occupied salaried (direct correlation) and unqualified independent workers (inverse correlation). The proportion of unqualified informal workers provides a proxy measure of self-employment; that is, for the transformation of households into productive units to compensate for labor markets that fail to provide (formal) paid jobs. Wages were measured in terms of per capita gross national product (direct correlation), income inequality as measured by the Gini coefficient (inverse correlation), population below the poverty line (inverse correlation), and remittances (inverse correlation). Remittances are also a proxy measure for emigration and the domestic incapacity to absorb the labor force. In addition, rural households were considered as a control variable for the proportion of households that could produce nonmarket goods.

Table 2. Welfare Regimes in Latin America, 1999–2004: Dimensions, Indicators, Sources, and Years for Cluster Analysis

Dimension	Indicators	Source	Year
Commodification	Labor market participation (gross national, years 15–64)	IDB	1999
	Unemployment (national rate)	IDB	1999
	Female economically active population (years 15–64)	IDB	1999
	Children participating in the labor force (ages 10–14)	IDB	1999
	Occupied salaried EAP (%)	ECLAC	2002
	Unqualified independent workers (%)	ECLAC	1999
	GNP (per capita, US$ 1995)	ECLAC	2003
	Poverty (as % of population under poverty line)	ECLAC	1999
	Income inequality (as Gini coefficient)	ECLAC	1999
	Remittances (as % of the GNP)	WB	2003
	Rural population	ECLAC	2000
Decommodification	Private expenditures on health care (per capita US$)	PAHO	2001
	Enrollment in private education (%)	UNESCO	2001
	Private consumption (as % of total consumption)	ECLAC	2002
	Public servants (% urban occupied population)	ECLAC	2002
	Expenditures in health care (per capita US$ 1997)	ECLAC	1999–2001
	Expenditures in education (per capita US$ 1997)	ECLAC	1999–2001
	Overall social expenditure (per capita US$ 1997)	ECLAC	1999–2001
	Overall social expenditures (as % of GNP)	ECLAC	1999–2001
	Salaried workers with social insurance (%)	UNDP	1990s
Defamiliarization	Extended and compound families (%, urban)	Arriagada	1999
	Economically active women in reproductive years (15–34)	ILO	2003
	Female heads of households	ECLAC	2002
	Nuclear families, spouses with unpaid work (%)	Arriagada	2002
	Domestic servants (as % of urban employment)	ECLAC	2002
	Population under 12 yrs old (%)	CELADE	2000
	Population over 65 yrs old (%)	CELADE	2000
	Dependent population 12–64 yrs old (%)	CELADE	2000
Performance	Infant mortality (under 5 yrs old)	UNICEF	2003
	Homicides (per 100,000 people)	UNDP	2001
	Gender Human Development Index	UNDP	2002
	School life expectancy	UNESCO	2001

Source: Author's calculations, supported by Juan Diego Trejos and Luis Angel Oviedo.

To measure decommodification, nine indicators related to coverage and expenditures, whether public or private, were reviewed. For the role of private services, expenditures on health care, enrollment in private education, and overall private consumption were considered. For the role of public social services, the proportion of public servants among the economically active population (EAP), per capita social expenditures, social expenditures as a percentage of the GNP, per capita expenditures on education and health care, and salaried workers with social insurance were considered. Indicators of private expenditures and enrollment are inversely correlated to decommodification (i.e.,

Table 3. Welfare Regimes in Latin America: Dimensions, Indicators, and Direct or Indirect Relation Between Dimensions and Indicators

Dimension	Indicators	Relation to dimension
Commodification	Labor market participation (gross national, years 15–64)	+
	Unemployment (national rate)	−
	Female economically active population (years 15–64)	+
	Children participating in the labor force (ages 10–14)	−
	Occupied salaried EAP (%)	+
	Unqualified independent workers (%)	+
	GNP (per capita, US$ 1995)	+
	Poverty (as % of population under poverty line)	−
	Income inequality (as Gini coefficient)	−
	Remittances (as % of the GNP)	−
	Rural population	Control
Decommodification	Private expenditures in health care (per capita US$)	−
	Enrollment in private education (%)	−
	Private consumption (as % of total consumption)	−
	Public servants (% urban occupied population)	+
	Expenditures in health care (per capita US$ 1997)	+
	Expenditures in education (per capita US$ 1997)	+
	Overall social expenditure (per capita US$ 1997)	+
	Overall social expenditures (as % of GNP)	+
	Salaried workers with social insurance (%)	+
Defamiliarization	Extended and compound families (%, urban)	−
	Economically active women in reproductive years (15–34)	+
	Female heads of households	Control
	Nuclear families, spouses with unpaid work (%)	−
	Domestic servants (as % of urban employment)	+
	Population under 12 yrs old (%)	Control
	Population over 65 yrs old (%)	Control
	Dependent population 12–64 yrs old (%)	−

Source: Author's calculations.

the higher they are, the less decommodification there is), while indicators of public expenditures are directly correlated.

To measure defamilialization, eight indicators were considered: extended and compound families (inverse correlation), economically active women in reproductive years (direct correlation), nuclear families with spouses with unpaid work (inverse correlation), and domestic servants (direct correlation). In addition, children under 12, adults over 65, and the ratio between economically dependent and economically independent people, as control variables for the type and amount of caretaking required. were considered. Table 3 details these three dimensions of welfare regimes in Latin America.

For people's well-being (i.e., performance), which could be the outcome of various welfare mixes, four indicators were selected. Child mortality reflects education (particularly female); public infrastructure, such as sanitation and potable water, provides a summary measure for human development. In addition, school life expectancy was considered; that is, average years of education achieved. The Gender Human Development Index addresses the gender gap in terms of human development as measured by income, health, and education. Homicide rates provide a proxy measure of whether people's lives are at risk.

Once all the necessary indicators were gathered, cluster analysis was conducted. This technique identifies groups of countries that are relatively homogeneous when compared to other groups. If the classification is successful, the object will be very similar in each cluster, and the various clusters will be quite different. This statistical technique is ideal for the purpose of this article, as groupings are identified inductively, without imposing predetermined ideas on the data. Once the grouping is accomplished, theory and interpretation can be carried out and reintroduced to the study.[6]

After clusters were identified, the statistically significant variables were determined. Variables that were not statistically significant at 5 percent were not considered relevant to the identification and understanding of each group (with the exception of remittances, which were considered with a much lower statistical significance). The analysis was completed by reviewing average values of all significant variables.

FINDINGS

The next step is to determine the number of clusters that maximizes internal homogeneity and external heterogeneity.[7] To this end, a graphic representation (dendogram), as presented in figure 1, provides valuable input. The dendogram represents the three identified clusters. Cluster 1 is relatively homogeneous, and comprises two countries, Argentina and Chile. Cluster 2 is the most heterogeneous of the three, and includes Costa Rica, Brazil, Mexico, Panama, and Uruguay. The third cluster is highly homogeneous and consists of two subgroups of countries. Subgroup 3a includes seven countries, subgroup 3b consists of four.

Table 4 shows indicators that were statistically significant to cluster countries, followed first by an explanation of findings for each dimension, and then by an overall interpretation of each cluster.

Commodification

Five indicators were found to be statistically significant: occupied salaried EAP; unqualified independent workers; per capita GNP; people below the poverty line; and a control variable, the proportion of rural population. The first two indicators measure formalization of the labor force. Remittances were statistically significant at 11 percent, and four indicators were not found to be statistically significant: gross national participation in the labor market, unemployment, female EAP, and child participation in the labor force. Average values show that the effectiveness of labor markets to incorporate and remunerate the labor force is highest in cluster 1 and lowest in cluster 3.

Countries in the first cluster show the highest formalization of the labor force (occupied salaried workers reach 73.54 percent, while unqualified independent workers are 16.10 percent), as well as the highest income levels (more than US$6,000 per capita GNP with "only" 22.7 percent of the population below the poverty line). The reverse occurs in countries in the third cluster. On average, occupied salaried workers total at least 20 percent less than in cluster 1 (50.22 percent and 43.69 percent in subgroups 3a and 3b, respectively), while unqualified independent workers are less than half of those in cluster 1 (33.80 percent and 34.30 percent). Average per capita GNP in cluster 3 is at most a third of the average per capita GNP in cluster 1 (US$2,080.26 and $928.77 in subgroups a and b, respectively).

Figure 1. Welfare Regimes in 18 Latin American Countries

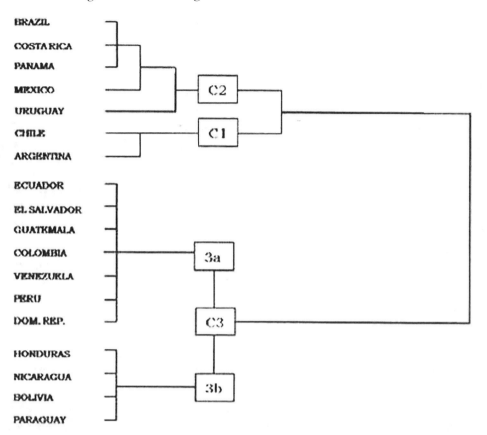

Dendogram with results from hierarchical cluster analysis (using average linkage between groups). Horizontal lines denote distance between countries in the same cluster. Vertical lines represent clusters that converge when progressively dissimilar countries are merged. The shorter the horizontal lines to the left of the vertical line that joins countries, the more homogeneous the cluster.

Source: Author's calculations.

Countries in cluster 2 have two-thirds of salaried workers among the economically active population and 21.34 percent of unqualified independent workers. Per capita GNP is twice as much as in cluster 3 yet a third less than in cluster 1. However, in cluster 2, people below the poverty line constitute 28.9 percent, only slightly above cluster 1 and about half of cluster 3.

Remittances, and thus the importance of transnational commodification of the labor force, are much less statistically significant (at .104 percent). However, they progressively increase from cluster 1 (.10 percent of GNP) and 2 (1.05 percent of GNP) to cluster 3 (more than 6 percent of GNP).

The first two clusters are predominantly urban (close to 90 percent and three-quarters, respectively), while cluster 3 is predominantly rural (one-third and more than 40 percent of the rural population, respectively).

Table 4. Welfare Regimes in Latin America, 1999–2004: Dimension, Statistically Significant Indicators, and Values

| | | | | | Welfare Regeme | |
| | | | | | Cluster 3 | |
Dimension	Indicators	Statistical Significance	Cluster 1 — Argentina, Chile	Cluster 2 — Brazil, Costa Rica, Mexico, Panama, Uruguay	3a. Colombia, Dominican Republic, Ecuador, El Salvador, Guatemala, Peru, Venezuela	3b. Bolivia, Honduras, Nicaragua, Paraguay
Commodification	Occupied salaried EAP (%)	0.000	73.54	66.04	50.22	43.69
	Unqualified independent workers (%)	0.001	16.10	21.34	33.83	34.30
	GNP (per capita, US$ 1995)	0.000	6,326.07	4,243.40	2,080.26	928.77
	Poverty (as % of population under poverty line)	0.000	22.70	28.86	53.46	67.70
	Remittances (as % of the GNP)	(0.104)[a]	0.10	1.05	6.63	6.52
	Rural population	0.000	0.031	11.45	26.50	34.47
Decommodification	Enrollment in private education (%)	0.011	36.10	13.46	25.66	28.49
	Public servants (% urban occupied population)	0.009	16.11	14.10	8.70	7.63
	Expenditures in health care (per capita US$ 1997)	0.000	272.00	177.00	43.43	25.75
	Expenditures in education (per capita US$ 1997)	0.000	311.50	195.20	77.43	52.25
	Overall social expenditures (per capita US$ 1997)	0.000	1,293.00	885.60	202.57	117.25
	Overall social expenditures (as % of GNP)	0.005	18.80	19.16	8.53	12.40
	Salaried workers with social insurance (%)	0.000	56.46	59.28	29.54	20.97
Defamiliarization	Extended and compound families (%, urban)	0.017	17.65	19.42	29.20	28.10
	Nuclear families, spouses with unpaid word (%)	0.001	51.55	46.54	40.59	38.50
	Population under 12 years old (%)	0.001	24.46	26.11	30.82	36.08
	Population over 65 years old (%)	0.029	8.43	6.68	4.53	3.50
	Dependent population 12 to 64yrs old (%)	0.007	49.05	48.87	55.02	65.58
Performance	Infant mortality (under 5 years old)	0.028	14.50	22.20	31.57	43.50
	Gender Human Development Index	0.000	0.84	0.80	0.72	0.68

[a]Indicator statistically significant at 10%. This and the following indicators showed a 0.80 correlation and were used alternatively but not simultaneously with similar results.

Source: Author's calculations, supported by Juan Diego Trejos and Luis Angel Oviedo.

Overall, countries in cluster 1 and 2 have higher domestic capacity to absorb their labor force and to do it in a salaried fashion. The primary difference has to do with levels of per capita GNP. Countries in cluster 3 have a higher reliance on self-employment and transnational labor markets. Nevertheless, with between 16 and 20 percent of independent unqualified workers, labor markets in clusters 1 and 2 are also unable to provide sufficient jobs and lead to self-employment. Therefore, although the clusters differ considerably in terms of commodification of the labor force, they are all, to some extent, informal.

Income distribution is not significant enough to differentiate clusters. There are countries with highly inequitable income distribution in all three clusters. The Gini coefficient was therefore not statistically significant. For instance, in cluster 2, Brazil has the greatest income inequality in the entire region. In the same cluster, Costa Rica and Uruguay show the least income inequality in the region. In the remaining clusters, the countries have medium to high income inequality.

Decommodification

In this category, seven indicators were found to be statistically significant: coverage of private education, salaried workers with social security, public servants, and all four indicators of social public investment (social expenditures; social expenditures as a percent of GNP, and expenditures on health care and education). Two indicators were not statistically significant: private expenditures on health care and overall private consumption, which are both fairly homogeneous.

The proportion of the EAP occupied in the public sector is highest in cluster 1 and somewhat lower in cluster 2, Public expenditures are consistently higher in cluster 1 than in cluster 2, whether considering overall social expenditures, on education, or on health care. However, the fiscal priority of public policy is slightly higher in cluster 2 than in cluster 1. The proportion of salaried workers with social insurance is higher in cluster 2 than in cluster 1.

In cluster 2, Mexico shows varied results: its values are consistent with other countries in the cluster in terms of the proportion of public servants (11.2 percent), salaried workers with social security (52.5 percent), and enrollment in private education (12.5 percent). However, values are much lower and lie between clusters 2 and 3 for social expenditures (US$456 devoted to social programs, in contrast to US$885.60 for cluster 2). Values are found to be even lower than some countries in cluster 3 for fiscal effort devoted to social policy (9.8 percent in comparison with an average of 19.16 percent in cluster 2).

Private educational enrollment varies widely between clusters 1 (36.10 percent) and 2 (13.46 percent). This proves to be the only indicator that places these two clusters on opposite ends of the spectrum. In this case, cluster 1 has the highest percentage of private enrollment and cluster 2 the lowest of all three clusters. This suggests that cluster 2 has more extended and universal educational services than cluster 1, where targeted services prevail and where a higher proportion of the population relies on private services.

In cluster 3, the proportion of the EAP occupied in the public sector is half or less than half of what is found in clusters 1 and 2 (8.7 percent and 7.63 percent in subgroups a and b, respectively). Moreover, percentages for salaried workers with social insurance are found to be quite low. Public expenditures are also consistently much lower than in clusters 1 and 2. When considered as a whole, social expenditures reach US$202 and $117 in each subgroup. Expenditures on education are US$77.43 and $52.25 and on health care, US$43.43 and $25.75. However, the fiscal effort on social expenditures is higher in subgroup 3b than in subgroup 3a (12.40 and 8.53 percent, respectively). Nicaragua and Bolivia individually show very high percentages of their small GNP devoted to social programs (13.2 percent in Nicaragua and 17.9 percent in Bolivia). With the exception of Colombia (13.6 percent), these percentages are considerably higher than all other countries in subgroup 3a, where most countries are found to devote less than 10 percent of their GNP to social programs. It is noteworthy that in cluster 3, where the population has much lower income levels, between 25.66 and 28.49 percent relies on private education.

Overall decommodification is higher in clusters 1 and 2, except for education and social insurance. Enrollment in private education indicates a higher role of targeted services in the former than in the latter. Interpretation of the somewhat higher proportion of salaried workers with social insurance in cluster 2 than in cluster 1 needs to consider the type of social insurance in each set of countries. With the exception of Mexico, all countries in cluster 2 have been "reluctant adjusters," particularly in terms of maintaining pension systems (and in some cases, such as Costa Rica, health care systems) organized around collective rather than individual accounts. It appears that countries in cluster 2 have a stronger presence of stratified labor-related social protection, while countries in cluster 1 have a stronger presence of individual labor-related social protection. Decommodification is therefore more pro-poor in countries in cluster 1 and pro-formal labor (and therefore more likely to reach middle-income groups) in countries in cluster 2. In either case, decommodification is limited by criteria used to allocate resources, whether by need or contributions made by salaried workers.

In cluster 3, decommodification is very low when compared with clusters 1 and 2. Access to private education is higher than in cluster 2 yet lower than in cluster 1. In addition, a small number of individuals in cluster 3 are salaried workers with social insurance. Since almost all countries have privatized their social security systems, there is a strong presence of individual labor-related social protection, yet without the level of coverage these systems reach in the countries in cluster 1.

Defamilialization

Five indicators were statistically significant here: extended and compound families, nuclear families in which spouses have unpaid work, and three control variables: population under 12 and over 65, and ratio between care-dependent and nondependent household members. Three indicators were not statistically significant: economically active women in reproductive years, female heads of households, and domestic servants.

Extended and compound families are lowest in clusters 1 and 2 and the highest in clusters 3a and 3b. Full-time female unpaid work plays a central role in all three clusters. However, nuclear families with spouses devoted to full-time unpaid work are higher in clusters 1 and 2 than in cluster 3. Here, the traditional "male breadwinner" family model is more prevalent in clusters 1 and 2 than in cluster 3.

The demographic transition is advanced in the first cluster, somewhat less in the second, and incipient in the third. There are two-and-a-half times as many individuals over 65 years old in cluster 1 than in cluster 3. The population of children under 12, by contrast, is 30 percent or more in cluster 3 and drops to one-quarter of the population or less in clusters 1 and 2. The dependency rate is therefore greater and constitutes a higher proportion of young people in cluster 3, and lower with a higher proportion of the elderly in cluster 1. This suggests a higher demand for unpaid work in cluster 3 than in clusters 1 and 2. There seems to be a higher demand for caretaking in a cluster where the nuclear family, which has a more traditional sexual division of labor with full-time female unpaid work, is lower, but the presence of extended families is higher.

Overall, we see high degrees of defamilialization in all three clusters. However, in clusters 1 and 2, nuclear families play a more important role, while in cluster 3, extended families do. While in clusters 1 and 2 families are less burdened by dependent family members, in cluster 3 there is a greater number of dependent people who need to rely on the commodification of fewer available people.

Performance

Two indicators are statistically significant: infant mortality and the Gender Human Development Index. Two indicators were not statistically significant: homicides and school life expectancy.

The variations for infant mortality are marked between clusters 1 and 2 and cluster 3. This indicator is very useful as a summary measure for human development, as it reflects education as well as public infrastructure, such as sanitation and drinking water. In terms of gender outcomes, the index shows a smaller gap between women and men in cluster 1 and 2 (.84 and .80, respectively) than in clusters 3a and 3b (.72 and .68, respectively).

INTERPRETATION

Based on available data, all three clusters show limitations in terms of commodification of their labor force and their ability to decommodify social risks. They are, to Some extent, informal, in that a large proportion of the population cannot reasonably expect to cope with social risks by accessing services from the state or participating in labor markets (Gough and Wood 2004). At the same time, variations across clusters are significant.

Various differences between clusters 1 and 2 were not found to be qualitative. For example, cluster 1 performs better in the supply of salaried work. Other differences, however, are indeed qualitative, and reflect the variations in social policy reforms carried out by countries in either cluster. Compared to the rest of the region, both sets of countries can be considered state welfare regimes. However, they do demonstrate variations in the allocation of social public expenditures. In cluster 1 there is more targeting to the poor (as reflected in the enrollment in private education) and more individually funded social security. In cluster 2 there is less targeting to the poor and more collectively funded social security that reaches formal salaried workers.

Cluster 3, by contrast, shows that low commodification of the labor force and transnational labor markets play a major role. Countries of this regime type demonstrate a worst case scenario: they are unable to succeed in commodifying labor, while social protection and the formation of human capital are minimally decommodified. For education, as an example, commodification is the second-highest after state welfare regimes, while wages are among the second lowest. This means that although the population relies significantly on wages, it has fewer opportunities to earn a living than in other regimes. Countries in this cluster have a largely informal labor market, and families play a central role. As Gough and Wood argue, the vast majority of the population depends on familial and communal strategies in the context of exclusive labor markets and residual public policy. Only a small part of the population successfully commodifies the labor force domestically; very few have access to public social services and transfers; and those who do access them confront scarce services and low transfers. Due to the nature of the residual social programs, nonstate agencies, such as civil society organizations and international agencies, play a significant role in the collective allocation of resources.

Labeling welfare regime types in order to capture constellations of variables is challenging. A comparison of clusters 1 and 2 with cluster 3 shows that most of the differences are qualitative in nature: the constellation of markets, states, and families is remarkably different. Therefore, when labeling each welfare regime type, for clusters 1 and 2 the role of social policy must be emphasized, and for cluster 3 the role of family strategies needs to be stressed. Cluster 1 will be referred to henceforth in this study as state-targeted, cluster 2 as state-stratified, and cluster 3 as informal-familialist welfare regimes.

With the exception of Mexico, countries with a state-stratified regime have been reluctant adjusters (Thorp 1998), whether they were early industrializers (such as Brazil and Uruguay) or not (Costa Rica) and whether they were initially socially homogeneous (such as Costa Rica and Uruguay) or not (Brazil). The confluence of Brazil and Mexico on the one hand and Uruguay and Costa Rica on the other corroborates that this regime is the most heterogeneous of the three. It combines countries that in the golden era showed stratified universalism (Costa Rica and Uruguay) and countries that during that time were dual (Brazil and Mexico) (Filgueira 1998). Income distribution is very unequal in the state-targeted regime and very heterogeneous in the state-stratified. The latter includes Brazil, which is the most inequitable country in the world. However, it also includes Uruguay and Costa Rica, which are the two most equitable countries in the region.

With a few exceptions, such as Ecuador and Venezuela, countries of the informal-familialist regime type were late industrializers and adjusted their economies radically. They were highly stratified at that time, and they continue to be so today. As one of the consequences, the proportion of spouses with paid work reflects family strategies that are deployed to compensate for low wages and weak or nonexistent public policy. To a larger degree than in state-stratified and state-targeted regimes, female paid work comes with longer hours of unpaid household chores. For these women, the simultaneous performance of income provision and caretaking reaches its peak.

RESEARCH AND POLICY IMPLICATIONS

This article has offered a conceptual and methodological approach to better understand welfare regimes in a region where states do not necessarily play the same central role in defining welfare regimes as they do in the global North. By drawing from available data, the article has demonstrated the empirical reward of this approach in the relevant distinctions among specific welfare mixes across Latin America.

Findings broadly confirm previous policy-based typologies elaborated by Filgueira (1998, 2004) and Huber and Stephens (2005). In addition, findings complement previous analyses by incorporating families and the sexual division of labor while drawing from available national statistics. As Gough (2004) previously has argued, Latin American countries are, to some extent, informal: most citizens are unable to cope with social risks by accessing state services or by participating in labor markets. Individuals therefore are required to rely heavily on family and communal arrangements.

Drawing from the combination of all three dimensions, relevant differences among countries are also demonstrated. Indeed, in two of the three clusters, informal arrangements interact with public policy that either emphasizes targeted policy or more universal yet stratified social protection. This demonstrates two variations of state regimes. In the third cluster, however, the population largely relies on family arrangements, as social public policies are inadequate or nonexistent. The latter is a true familialist welfare regime. As the regime becomes more informal, the need increases to investigate beyond public policy and consider defamilialization as a central dimension of the welfare mix.

The cluster analysis presented in this article strengthens comparative analysis and helps to overcome empirical limitations faced by previous studies. Progress has been made toward statistically capturing the role of families and the sexual division of labor. Several proxy measures were considered in order to overcome the lack of available indicators for this dimension. Specifically, the presence of extended and compound families, the absence of robust labor and state institutions, the relevance of international remittances, and the importance of female spouses with paid work were all used to establish the role of families. Incorporating additional and stronger data should not only improve empirical analysis but should also nourish a conceptualization that truly gives gender, unpaid work, and families a central role in the understanding of welfare regimes.

Methodologically, there is a trade-off between the number of countries considered and the data sources available. To achieve ideal measures of commodification, decommodification, and defamilialization, it is necessary to relinquish greater numbers of countries and rely on microdata. Microdata allow us to analyze in greater detail the various welfare mixes within each welfare regime. Drawing from national household surveys for selected countries, further research is looking at welfare "worlds" and explores the characteristics of the welfare mix when controlling by occupations and the sexual division of labor in the house-hold (Martínez Franzoni 2007). But regular household surveys, unfortunately, while relatively useful to explore commodification and somewhat less so for decommodification, do not provide substantial information for assessing the role of families and unpaid work. Proxy measures are equally important here as for the comparative analysis already described. Therefore, the study of welfare regimes, at least in selected countries, would be more effective if two types of surveys were utilized: income and expenditures, and time use.

From these identified welfare regimes, what can be determined in terms of policy implications and more equitable allocation of resources? Overall, each of the three welfare regimes identified in this article provides diverse scenarios to alter the current architecture of social policy. Far from settled, all welfare mixes are subject to controversy, as reflected in public policies that are in constant motion.

There are specific challenges, however, which vary depending on the type of welfare regime. For example, the state-targeted welfare regime does well among the poor, but the nonpoor largely rely on the market. Many individuals, particularly in middle-income sectors, fall between the cracks of targeted public policies and ineffective markets. In Chile, public discontent and changing political conditions have led, during the last center-left administrations, to policy reforms that re-establish solidarity and universal access to a minimum set of services, regardless of income level and contribution and regardless of whether people access private or public services. A good example is the AUGE Plan (Acceso Universal y Garantías Explícitas de Salud, Universal Access to Explicit Health Care Guarantees), approved during the Ricardo Lagos administration (2000–2006) (Castiglioni 2006).[8] Although in this case and others, several universal and solidarity-based policy tools were not approved, Chile (and also Argentina) is seeing a trend toward rectifying the most regressive and inequitable reforms that took place under the influence of the Washington Consensus.

The state-stratified welfare regime reaches the nonpoor but remains highly stratified between occupations and formal and informal jobs. Public social services have shown disparities in quality across the public-private divide in terms of both education and health care. Contrary to what occurs in state-targeted welfare regimes, in state-stratified regimes a large proportion of policy resources are not targeted to the poor, and the countries are therefore pressured toward further commodification of social risks. For example, in Costa Rica, public services still reach middle- and upper-middle-income sectors. During the past two administrations, individually defined contributions, along with benefits, have increased, and a higher proportion of middle-income groups have left public schools and health care in search of better-quality alternatives (Martínez Franzoni and Mesa-Lago 2003).

Although these changes are still relatively minor, strong movements have advocated increased commodification and retrenched public intervention (Martínez Franzoni and Castro 2007). Nevertheless, countries with a protectionist welfare regime are highly heterogeneous, and policy trends are currently influenced not only by path dependency linked to previous dualism or stratified universalism, as Filgueira (1998) points out, but also by the ideology of ruling political parties. This is seen in the clear distinction between Mexico and Uruguay or Brazil, for example.

In countries with an informal-familialist welfare regime, social programs are residual in terms of services, coverage, and functions, while most of the population falls below the poverty line and is in extreme need of sound social policies. In the context of the political transitions initiated in the 1990s, even right-wing governments have sought and usually managed to expand expenditures on targeted social assistance programs. El Salvador is a good example: from 2000 to 2004, social expenditures increased from US$108 to $150 (in constant dollars). However, social policy remains residual in terms of the services provided (very basic), their coverage (very limited), and the amount and source of resources programs receive (largely contingent on international cooperation or loans, unpaid work, and copayments by recipients).

In addition to establishing patterns in the region's welfare mix, the conceptual and methodological approach presented here also provides clues to understanding distinct environments for policy design and directions for policy change. If policy emulation takes place across welfare regimes, emulation would need to be highly selective to adapt policy tools to the actual constellation or welfare mix where those tools are to be used. Although this notion may appear commonsensical, up to now the welfare mix has not been present in policymaking or used as a relevant "filter" to adapt policies emulated from other countries, particularly across welfare regimes. As policymakers and policy advisers become more specialized, moreover, adaptation of a sound analysis of the welfare mix as a relevant conceptual notion to reconstruct policy environments is less likely to take place.

Conditioned cash transfers are a good example. The Guatemala Solidaria program inadequately attempts to imitate policy measures packaged under the Chile Solidario program. Whereas Guatemala has one of the lowest proportions of salaried and formal work in the region, Chile has among the highest; while Chile has a solid supply of public and private services, Guatemala struggles to build a basic network of schools and health care centers. While Chile has a large proportion of nuclear male-breadwinner families and women devoted full-time to unpaid work, Guatemala has a large proportion of extended families and dual earners. In short, Guatemala will need a great deal of creative adaptation to reproduce successfully the Chilean state productivist-welfare regime in its nonstate, familialistic welfare context. Beyond this example, bridges between analyzing and designing welfare regimes in the region are still fairly weak. The arguments presented in this article should have an impact on environments for policy design and analysis and place social policy and social programs in the context of welfare regimes.

APPENDIX: PRIMARY DATABASE FOR STATISTICAL ANALYSIS

Table 5. Welfare Regimes, Primary Database: Variables Indicators, Sources, Years, Number of Countries for which Data Available

Dimensions	Variables	Indicators (as percentages except coefficients)	Source	Recent Years	Countries w/data
Commodification	1. Economically active population (EAP)	Net urban participation	ILOa	2000–2003	17
		Gross national participation	IDB	1990–2001	18
		Occupied population (gross national, 5–64)	IDB	1990–2001	18
	2. Salaried EAP	Salaried occupied urban EAP	ECLAC	2000–2003	18
		Salaried occupied rural EAP	ECLAC	2002–2003	16
		Salaried occupied EAP weighted by rural/urban population	Own	2002	18
	3. Unemployment	National unemployment rate	IDB	1990–2001	18
		Urban unemployment rate	ECLAC	2000–2002	18
		Urban unemployment rate	ILOa	2000–2003	16
		Urban subutilization rate	ECLAC	1990–2003	18
		Urban subutilization rate	ILOa	1990–2003	18
	4. EAP with social insurance	Salaried urban workers contributing to social security	ILOa	2000–2003	14
		Employees with social security	IDB	1990–2001	15
		Salaried workers with social insurance	IDB	1990–2001	17
	5. Infant labor force	Employment rate ages 10–14	IDB	1999–2001	18
	6. EAP in the public sector	Public servants as % of urban occupied population	ECLAC	2000–2002	18
		Public servants as % rural occupied population	ECLAC	2000–2002	16
		Public employment as national rate (years 15–64)	IDB	1990–2003	13
	7. Flexibility in labor relations	Efficiency index	IDB	1990–2001	14
		Labor flexibility index (Lora)	LORA	1985–1999	18

Table 5. (*Continued*)

Dimensions	Variables	Indicators (as percentages except coefficients)	Source	Recent Years	Countrie w/data
	8. Informal EAP	Urban population occupied in low-productivity activities	ECLAC	2000–2002	17
		Urban population occupied in the informal sector	ILOa	2000–2003	17
		Unqualified independent workers (%)	ECLAC	1990–2003	18
		Independent workers in the informal sector	ILOa	1990–2003	17
	9. Per capita gross national product	Per Capita gross national income (US$ 1995)	ECLAC	2000–2003	18
		Per capita GNP (in PPP)	WB	2000–2001	18
		Per capita GNP (regular US$ 2000)	WB	2000–2001	18
		Per capita GNP (constant US$ 2000)	WB	1998–2003	18
	10. Income	Population under the poverty line	ECLAC	2000–2003	18
		Population under the poverty line	WB	1997–2000	10
	11. Income inequality	Gini coefficient	ECLAC	2000–2003	18
	12. International remittances	Remittances (as % of the GNP)	WB	2000–2003	17
	13. Self-consumption	Rural population	ECLAC		
Decommodification	14. Private expenditures in health care	Private expenditures in health care (per capita US$)	PAHO	1995–1999	18
		Private expenditures in health care as a percentage of GNP	WB	1997–2002	18
		Per capita expenditures in health care (US$)	WB	1997–2002	18
	15. Private expenditures in education	Private expenditures in education	OECD	2001	6
		Enrollment in pre-primary education	UNESCO	2000–2001	18
		Enrollment in primary education	UNESCO	2000–2001	18
		Enrollment in secondary education	UNESCO	2000–2001	18

Table 5. (*Continued*)

Dimensions	Variables	Indicators (as percentages except coefficients)	Source	Recent Years	Countries w/data
		Private enrollment in education (25% prim; 25% sec; 50% terc.)	Constructed	2001	18
	16. Private consumption	Private consumption as a percentage of total consumption	ECLAC	1990–2001	18
	17. Public expenditures in health care	Total expenditures	PAHO	1995–1999	18
		As proportion of the GNP	WB	1997–2002	18
		As proportion of the GNP	ECLAC	2000–2001	18
		As proportion of public expenditures	ECLAC	2000–2001	18
		Per capita (US$ 1997)	ECLAC	1990–2001	18
	18. Public expenditures in education	As proportion of GNP	ECLAC	2000–2001	17
		As proportion of public expenditures	ECLAC	2000–2001	18
		Per capita (US$ 1997)	ECLAC	1990–2001	18
		As proportion of GNP per student in primary, secondary, or tertiary education	WB	2000–2001	15
		As proportion of GNP per student in primary education	WB	2000–2001	16
		As proportion of GNP per student in secondary education	WB	2000–2001	16
		As proportion of GNP per student in tertiary education	WB	2000–2001	14
	19. Social consumption	As proportion of GNP	ECLAC	1990–2001	18
		As proportion of Public Expenditures	ECLAC	2000–2001	18
		Per capita income (US$ 1997)	ECLAC	2000–2001	18
	20. Allocation of social expenditures	Social expenditures targeted at human development	ECLAC	1990–2001	18
		Perception of corruption in heath care	TI	2004	10
		Perception of corruption in education	TI	2004	10
		Perception of corruption in public services	TI	2004	10

Table 5. (*Continued*)

Dimensions	Variables	Indicators (as percentages except coefficients)	Source	Recent Years	Countries w/data
		Knowledge of clientelistic networks	Latinobarometer	2004	18
	21. Economically active women in reproductive years	Net female urban participation (15 years old or more)	ECLAC	2000–2002	18
		Net female participation (years 15–64)	IDB	1990–2001	18
		Female EAP (years 15–64)	IDB	1990–2001	18
		Women unwillingly working less than 30 hours	IDB	1990–2001	15
Defamiliarization	22. Sexual division of labor	Rate female/male working hours	IDB	1990–2001	15
		Believe women must stay home and men go to work	Latinobarometer	2004	18
	23 Extended and compound families	Extended and compound families	Arriagada	1997–1999	17
	24. Domestic servants	Domestic servants as % of urban employment	ECLAC	2000–2002	18
		Domestic servants as % of urban employment	ILOa	2000–2003	16
Performance	25. Maternity leave	Length, target population, funding and wage replacement (index)	Laws	Current	18
	26. Child care	Target population, elegibility, coverage, and funding (index)	Laws	Current	18
	27. Female Partners without Paid Work	Nuclear families w/ spouses w/ unpaid work	Arriagada	1998–2002	18
	28. Part-time Female EAP	Women willingly working less than 30 hours	IDB	1999–2001	14
	29. Female EAP in Reproductive Stage	Economically active women ages 15–34	ILOb	1999–2003	18
		Urban female participation ages 15–34	ECLAC	2000–2002	18
	30. Female Heads of Households	Female head of households among total heads	ECLAC	1999–2004	18

Table 5. (*Continued*)

Dimensions	Variables	Indicators (as percentages except coefficients)	Source	Recent Years	Countries w/data
	31. Care demand	Children under 12 and elderly above 65 years old	CELADE	2000–2005	18
		Economic dependency	CELADE	2000–2005	18
	32. Health	Life expectancy at birth	WB	1997–2002	18
		Infant mortality rates children under 5 years old	UNICEF	2002–2003	18
		Infant mortality rates	WB	1997–2002	18
	33. Human capital	School life expectancy	UNESCO	2000–2001	17
		Iliteracy rates among adults	UNESCO	2000–2001	18
		Percentage youth 15–19 years old with complete primary education or more	ECLAC	2000–2001	18
		Average years education rural eap 15 years old or more	ECLAC	2000–2001	15
	34. Satisfaction of consumption needs	Population with unsatisfied basic needs	Countries	1998–2005	17
		Gender human development index	UNDP	2004	18
		Human development index	UNDP	2000–2003	18
	35. Citizen safety (*seguridad ciudadana*)	Homicides every 100,000 people	WHO	2001	14
		Homicides every 100,000 people	Interpol-UNODC-ONU	1994–2001	18
		Population that has experienced deliquency	Latinbarometer	2004	18
	36. Protection of rights	Jailed persons every 100,000	Carranza	2004	17
		Jailed persons every 100,000	CELS	1999–2002	18
		People on probation or in jail w/o charge	CELS	1999–2002	18
	37. Satisfaction with institutions	Satisfaction with market economies	Latinbarometer	2004	18
		Satisfaction with democracy	Latinbarometer	2004	18

Source: Author's calculations, supported by Juan Diego Trejos and Luis Angel Oviedo.

NOTES

This article is part of a larger research project on welfare regimes in Latin America, conducted at the Institute of Social Research at the University of Costa Rica and supported by the Center for Latin American Studies (CEALCI) at the Carolina Foundation. For contributions to previous drafts I am grateful to Merike Blofield, Michelle Dion, Christine Ewig, Fernando Filgueira, Evelyne Huber, Rubén Lo Vuolo, Juan Pablo Pérez Sainz, Jennifer Pribble, Isabel Roman, and Linda Stevenson. Jeremy Seekings and three anonymous reviewers for *Latin American Politics and Society* provided extremely valuable contributions to the article in its current form. All shortcomings obviously remain mine.

1 In their analysis a fifth cluster includes the English-speaking Caribbean.

2 In addition, when focusing on Africa, these authors also distinguish insecurity welfare regimes, wherein most of the population depends on highly personalized politico-military relationships.

3 Family allowances, for instance, have similar requirements for men and women in Uruguay, but Chile does not acknowledge men as dependent husbands or unemployed partners.

4 Indicators were eliminated for a number of reasons: data were missing for three variables for more than one country but also lacked criteria that allowed extrapolation for another country. Indicators on maternity leave and day care services were dropped because data were lacking on public expenditures that help control the gap between the legislation and its actual enforcement. In addition, data were extrapolated concerning four variables for which one country was missing. Public opinion data were eliminated, as there was a lack of previous studies that would facilitate the understanding of how public opinion relates to actual practices. When all these decisions were made, the database was ready for statistical analysis.

5 Notice that female and child participation in the EAP are considered directly and inversely correlated with commodification of the labor force, respectively. The assumption is that children enter the labor force after adult family members, yet wages are still insufficient and need to be complemented.

6 Various classification methods are available to incorporate all variables into the model. Following Rudra 2005, hierarchical conglomerates were used for the purposes of this study. The technique takes each single case and progressively aggregates dissimilar cases, as opposed to starting with predefined clusters and breaking them down until single cases are reached. In terms of allocating countries to groups, between-group linkages were utilized. Another option that the Statistical Package for the Social Sciences (SPSS) makes available was also attempted: the Ward method, based on variances. It estimates means for all variables in each cluster. Then, for each object, it estimates the squared Euclidian distance for the groups' means. Results obtained were very similar. The method of simple linkage relied on here is based on the minimal distance, or the rule of the closest neighbor. The first two objects clustered are those that have the least distance between them. The next shortest distance is identified, be it that the third object clusters with the other two or that it forms a new cluster of two objects. In each stage, the distance between two clusters is the distance between the two closest points. To identify the clusters, this study uses a conservative criterion: it requires that distances between countries and within each cluster be minimal.

7 SPSS does not provide a "stop rule" or coefficient that points to the optimal number of clusters. Instead, a combination of theoretical and empirical criteria is used.

8 This policy reform was launched in 2002 with 3 pathologies and was gradually extended until it reached 57 in 2007 (Castiglioni 2006).

REFERENCES

Barrientos, Armando. 2004. Latin America: Towards a Liberal-Informal Welfare Regime. In *Insecurity and Welfare Regimes in Asia, Africa and Latin America: Social Policy in Development Contexts*, ed. Ian Gough and Geof Wood. Cambridge: Cambridge University Press. 68–121.

Castel, Robert. 2004 [1997]. *La metamorfosis de la cuestión social. Una crónica del asalariado*. Buenos Aires: PAIDOS.

Castiglioni, Rossana. 2006. Cambios y continuidad en política social: educación, pensiones y salud. In *El gobierno de Ricardo Lagos. La nueva vía chilena hacia el socialismo*, ed. Robert L. Funk. Santiago: Universidad Diego Portales. 69–86.

ECLAC (Economic Commission for Latin America). 2004. *Panorama social de America Latina*. Santiago: ECLAC.

Esping-Andersen, Gosta. 1990. *The Three Worlds of Welfare Capitalism*. Princeton: Princeton University Press.

———. 2002. Towards the Good Society, Once Again? In *Why We Need a New Welfare State*, ed. Esping-Anderson. Oxford: Oxford University Press. 1–25.

Filgueira, Fernando. 1998. El nuevo modelo de prestaciones sociales en America Latina: residualismo y ciudadanía estratificada. In *Ciudadanía y política social*, ed. Brian Roberts. San Jose: FLACSO/SSRC. 71–116.

———. 2004. The Structural and Political Keys of the Reluctant Latin American Social State and Its Interplay with Democracy: The Development, Crises and Aftermath of Universal, Dual and Exclusionary Social States. Mss. São Paulo: UNRISD.

Filgueira, Fernando, and Juliana Martínez Franzoni. 2002. Paradigmas globales y filtros domésticos: las reformas administrativas de las políticas sociales en America Latina. *Revista de Ciencias Económicas* 18, 2: 191–215.

Gough, Ian, and Geoffrey Wood. 2004. Introduction. In *Insecurity and Welfare Regimes in Asia, Africa and Latin America*, ed. Gough and Wood. Cambridge: Cambridge University Press. 1–11.

Huber, Evelyne, and John Stephens. 2005. Successful Social Policy Regimes? Political Economy and the Structure of Social Policy in Argentina, Chile, Uruguay, and Costa Rica. Paper presented at the conference "Democratic Governability in Latin America," University of Notre Dame.

Lewis, Jane. 1993. Women *and Social Policies in Europe: Work, Family and the State*. Aldershot: Edward Elgar.

Martínez Franzoni, Juliana. 2005. La pieza que faltaba: uso del tiempo y regímenes de bienestar en America Latina. *Revista Nueva Sociedad* 199: 35–58.

———. 2006. Presión o legitimación: poder y alternativas en el diseño y adopción de la reforma de salud de Costa Rica, 1988–1999. *Historia, Ciencias, Saude-Manguinhos* 13, 3 (July–September): 591–622.

———. 2007. Regímenes de bienestar en America Latina: tipos, mundos y políticas. Working paper series no. 11. Madrid: Fundación Carolina.

Martínez Franzoni, Juliana, and Mauricio Castro. 2007. Régimen distributivo en Costa Rica: limites del desencuentro entre mercado laboral y política social. Prepared for the Project on Social Models in Latin America, Institute of Labor Studies, International Labor Organization, June. Draft version.

Martínez Franzoni, Juliana, and Carmelo Mesa Lago. 2003. *Las reformas inconclusas: pensiones y salud en Costa Rica, avances, problemas, recomendaciones*. San Jose: Fundación Friedrich Ebert.

O'Connor, Julia, Ann Shola Orloff, and Sheila Shaver. 1999. *States. Markets, Families: Gender, Liberalism and Social Policy in Australia, Great Britain and the United States*. Cambridge: Cambridge University Press.

Orloff, Anne. 1996. Gender in the Welfare State. *Annual Review of Sociology* 22: 51–78.

Pribble, Jennifer. 2004. Women and Welfare: The Politics of Coping with New Social Risks in Chile and Uruguay. Paper presented at the 25th International Congress of the Latin American Studies Association, Las Vegas, October 7–9.

Rudra, Nita. 2005, Welfare States in Developing Countries: Unique or Universal? Unpublished mss. Graduate School for Public and International Affairs, University of Pittsburgh.

Sainsbury, Diane. 1996. *Gender, Equality and Welfare States*. New York: Cambridge University Press.

———. 1999. Gender and Welfare State Regimes. Oxford: Oxford University Press.

Thorp, Rosemary. 1998. *Progreso, pobreza y exclusión: una historia económica de América Latina en el siglo 20*. Washington, DC: Inter-American Development Bank.

Williamson, John, ed. 1990. *Latin American Adjustment: How Much Has Happened?* Washington, DC: Institute for International Economics.

Chapter 12

Elections and Economic Turbulence in Brazil: Candidates, Voters, and Investors

Anthony P. Spanakos
Lúcio R. Renno

Political business cycle theories predict that inflation should increase in an electoral year and that the incoming president should begin his or her administration by tightening monetary policy to constrain inflation. Annualized inflation in the quarter following Brazil's 2002 presidential election was close to 40 percent, a significant increase from the previous year; and the incoming president, Luiz Inácio Lula da Silva, did indeed increase interest rates as a response. The rise in inflation occurred despite the historic anti-inflation policy stand of President Fernando Henrique Cardoso, Lula's predecessor; and Lula's support for higher interest rates went against his equally historic critiques of his predecessor's monetary policy as too constrictive. The immediate conclusion to be drawn is that both Cardoso and Silva behaved opportunistically—each abandoning his longstanding position in pursuit of political gain.

Less cynically, Lula's decision to increase interest rates may be seen as "responsible" policy, according to Karen Remmer's political capital model (1993). But closer analysis suggests that neither Cardoso's nor Lula's macroeconomic policies can be adequately understood in terms of either political business cycle or political capital models. Both arguments ignore the agency of candidates, "investors," and "voters," and the effects they can have irrespective of government policy stance.[1] A preference congruence model that examines elections as a dynamic negotiated process wherein candidates must address the preferences of both voters and investors can better explain the effect of elections on macroeconomic performance in Latin America's new democracies.

The policy preferences of these two groups are most likely to overlap before stabilization, when an increase in inflation is associated with a decrease in growth. With stabilization, however, particularly when it is accompanied by slow growth and moderate to high unemployment, voter and investor policy preferences are likely to diverge. That divergence creates incentives for candidates to court the former with proposals that frighten the latter. This can lead to capital flight, speculative attacks against a currency, rapid increases in inflation, and the deterioration of short- and medium-term debt profiles. Other political economy approaches focus on either the incumbent or the incoming government and do not pay enough attention to the effect that candidates, and their negotiation between pressures from popular actors and investors, can have on macroeconomic indicators. The preference congruence model aims to address this, offering a more comprehensive approach to the relationship between elections and macroeconomic policy in emerging market democracies. Furthermore, incongruence can bring about conditions that increase the likelihood of policy switches (see Stokes 2001b).

This chapter argues that the congruence between policy preferences of voters and investors produces good effects, while the lack of congruence can lead to very deleterious effects on key economic indicators.[2] After examining relevant literature on political business cycle and political capital models and the issue of voter investor congruence, the chapter analyzes the economic effects of Brazil's 1994, 1998, 2002, and 2006 presidential elections to explore why the 2002 contest differed so significantly from the earlier two. A more thorough analysis of the 2002 presidential campaign challenges expectations in the existing literature and makes the case for the importance of the agency of candidates and the preference congruence between voters and investors. Finally, the relevance of a preference congruence model is considered.

POLITICAL BUSINESS CYCLE AND POLITICAL CAPITAL MODELS

The political business cycle literature and its critics place great emphasis on the role of the incumbent and incoming administrations and ignore the impact of candidates' strategies and investors' preferences on elections. The main theoretical claim here is that the literature on elections and markets in Latin America also needs to pay attention to the growing role that investors play in elections as well as the importance of "bargaining" between candidates, voters, and investors.

William Nordhaus (1975) argues that politicians behave "opportunistically," loosening monetary policy before an election so as to reap the benefits of faster growth and increased employment before inflation becomes visible, only to tighten monetary policy once elected. In the process, they create a "political business cycle" (see also MacRae 1977; Fair 1978). Although most research on political business cycles has looked at the developed world (where the evidence appears to be mixed; see Alesina et al. 1997; Persson and Tabellini 2000), in the past decade, a number of studies have looked at political business cycles in emerging markets, particularly Latin America (Block and Vaaler 2004, Leblang 2002, Bernard and Leblang 2006).

Shifting the model to Latin America requires certain adjustments. Barry Ames finds that politicians do increase spending during an electoral year, but also that they continue to do so during the first year of their administration (Ames 1987). Additionally, where prices are not stabilized, there is less incentive for postelectoral constrictions in monetary policy. In Brazil, increases in spending, growth, and inflation often take place during the "honeymoon period," when traditional political business cycle approaches would expect rational actors to be more austere.

In a multicountry study of the political economy of democratizing countries in 1980s Latin America, Remmer finds little, if any, evidence of a traditional political business cycle (1993).[3] Challenging assumptions that increased demands encourage politicians to behave opportunistically, Remmer argues that democracy has not brought indiscipline to Latin American political economy. High levels of inflation before elections were accompanied by recession, not growth, contradicting the expectations of the political business cycle explanations. Inflation was a consequence not of expansionary policies but of incumbent mismanagement of the economy, policy failure, and political fatigue. Newly elected administrations, with bulky political muscle, would attempt to address longstanding problems in the economy and, in doing so, implemented stabilization plans immediately after elections (Remmer 1993, 405).

Remmer refers to this as the political capital model. The basic idea of this model is that a weak incumbent loses control of the economy, generating hyperinflation and recession. Newly elected politicians then galvanize their recent electoral success and popularity to enact dramatic, often draconian, economic stabilization plans, which are necessary to make fundamental long-term changes. Such plans are responsible reactions to the economic environment they encounter once in office. This reinforces Remmer's argument that elections breed fiscal responsibility.

Remmer takes her cases primarily from the 1980s, in the shadow of the debt crisis, a period she acknowledges as unique in Latin American history. In so doing, she can dismiss business cycle claims about reelection, because only two parties won reelection, and virtually all incumbent parties lost seats. During the 1980s, inflation was high enough that an inverted Philips curve existed, in which increases in inflation were linked to contractions in growth and employment. The situation was different in the 1990s, as presidents who stabilized prices were resoundingly reelected, producing incentives for opportunistic behavior.

In another multicountry study, Susan Stokes finds that once price stability exists, voters behave as though they are under a Philips curve (Stokes 2001a, 30), with a clear trade-off between inflation and employment. As the moment of stabilization becomes more distant, voters tend to privilege the latter over the former. The popular demands for growth in poststabilization Latin America differ from those that Remmer examines. Remmer's political capital model shows how politicians sought to redress "intractable economic problems" in prestabilization Latin America and, in doing so, chose economic orthodoxy, or at least fiscal constraint (Remmer 1993, 405). Constraining monetary growth under conditions of high inflation has positive short-term effects on economic growth, and therefore is both popular and "responsible." Once price stabilization is consolidated, however, a new government's choice of inflation-constraining policies is intended not to bring structural change but to attenuate an increase in short-term inflation. This has an immediately negative effect on growth, and can be achieved because of the "political capital" of a honeymoon period, as Remmer suggests.

Remmer's defense of democracy and the possibility that elections can lead to greater discipline leads her to contend that elections are not "disruptive events that interfere with otherwise rational patterns of macroeconomic management" (1993, 405). While she is correct in criticizing political business cycle research in this area, she overstates her case, because elections can indeed be "disruptive," not only because of macroeconomic man-agement, but because of investor responses to electoral campaigns. This is exactly where a broader definition of the actors involved in the electoral process becomes necessary to understand better how elections may generate economic turbulence.

THE PREFERENCE CONGRUENCE MODEL

Latin America, like the rest of the developing world, is capital dependent. The need for private financing—whether foreign or domestic—requires the inclusion of investor per-ception and behavior in the analysis of business cycles and policy choice in countries with emerging markets. The literature in political economy has long recognized the importance of investors in affecting domestic policy (Mahon 1996; Mosley 2003), but it has not yet incorporated the interaction between investors and elections (see Bernard and Leblang 2006). This is not surprising, considering that so many political economy models are tailored to suit the developed world, a world in which the space for the interference of financial actors is reduced and, thus, investor impact is limited (Mosley 2003). But the same cannot be said about investors and elections in emerging markets, where lack of confidence in one candidate can spur a run against a currency, leading to a rapid deterioration of the country's debt profile, which is exactly what happened in the 2002 presidential elections in Brazil.

Investor perception is critical because, as Juan Martinez and Javier Santiso write, "probably the most relevant definition of an emerging market is an economy whose political outcomes and uncertainties (such as a presidential election or a cabinet reshuffle)

tend to have high impacts on financial variables and therefore on stock markets"
(Martinez and Santiso 2003, 365). The increased perception of risk has serious potential
consequences. Nelson Barbosa Filho argues that 9 percent of Brazil's growth between
1966 and 2000 can be explained by changes in domestic liquidity, while as much as 40
percent is linked to international liquidity (Barbosa 2001). Liquidity is highest when there
is confidence in markets. When political events undermine confidence, markets become
less liquid. But all political events undermine confidence and, as Remmer (1993) proposes, elections can reinforce sound macroeconomic policies. This chapter argues that
electoral risk is neither random nor accidental; political risk is greater under conditions
with considerable divergence between investor and voter preferences.

Preference congruence between voters and investors regarding the need for inflation-
constraining policies is more likely to occur following periods of combined high inflation,
high enough that it is simultaneous with recession. This situation can be seen in prestabilization Latin America. Further, while preferences between voters and investors may
begin to drift after stabilization, they should still be close in the electoral period immediately following stabilization, when the experience of high inflation still looms in popular
memory. As price stability becomes normalized, a more traditional Philips curve emerges,
pushing inflation and unemployment in different directions, increasing the likelihood that
a political business cycle will occur and the likelihood of preference divergence. Voters
are more likely to feel reform fatigue and frustration with slower rates of growth, while
investors are more attentive to inflation creep and signals of possible loosening of reform
resolve. Presidential campaigns can highlight this difference, providing incentives for
candidates to propose expansionary policies, for voters to reward antiliberal policies,
and for investors to retreat, leading to downward pressure on exchange rates and growth
and upward pressure on inflation, stimulating an inverted Philips curve.

Elections, thus, can be minicrises. This recalls the basic proposition of political business cycle literature, in which elections weaken macroeconomic policy stands. Contrary
to traditional political business cycle literature, however, this article argues that elections
can worsen economic indicators even when incumbents do not behave opportunistically.
The openness of emerging markets and the perception of political risk therein allow
preelectoral runs on the currency or inflationary pressures that are linked not to current
but to possible future macroeconomic policy. In other words, agency cannot be limited
to incumbents but to candidates relevant enough to effect investor perception of risk.
Table 1 summarizes the differences between the political business cycle model, the political capital model, and the preference congruence model.

ECONOMIC CONSEQUENCES OF ELECTIONS IN BRAZIL

Inflation and foreign exchange rates are internal and external indicators of the value of
money. They are critical for Brazil, given that 80 percent of its public debt is linked
either to the exchange rate, inflation, or the interest rate. The deterioration of these
indicators produces a groundswell in public indebtedness. Because Brazil dabbled with
currencies in the 1980s and 1990s, the use of any long-term data on foreign exchange
is less than perfect. Nevertheless, the data used here come from the Brazilian government's Institute of Applied Economic Research (IPEA), the standard source in the field.
The institute has standardized the past 50 years of currency exchange by making historical rates for the exchange of reais and dollars.

The 1994 and 1998 elections show weakening of the exchange rate but control over
inflation from previous trends, whereas the 2002 election witnesses a rapid deterioration

Table 1. Summary of Models

	Political Business Cycle	Political Capital	Preference Congruence
Agent(s)	Incumbent president/ prime minister	Incoming president/ prime minister	Incumbent government, relevant candidates, voters, investors
Electoral effect on the economy	Incumbent loosens monetary policy, incoming government tightens policy, regardless of ideology	Incoming government implements structural reforms during honeymoon to address long-term problems	Candidates negotiate between voters and investors; divergence between the latter two increases economic risk
Methodological tools	Interest rates, inflation, growth and unemployment rates	Interest rates, inflation, growth and unemployment rates	Interest rates, inflation, growth, unemployment, exchange rates, cost of government borrowing
Explanatory effect	Cyclicality of growth rates, inflation, unemployment; nonimpact of partisan identity on macro-economic policymaking	How democracy gives incentive for responsible policymaking; how elections empower government to pursue reform	How elections affect value of money, government debt, growth; predicts policy switches of incoming government

Table 2. Inflation and Exchange Rate Movements Around the Brazilian Elections (averages)

	Inflation	Exchange Rate
1994 Election		
1991–April 1995	21.732	0.231
October 1993–October 1994	29.623	0.639
April 1994–April 1995	12.22	0.831
1998 Election		
1995–April 1999	0.755	1.106
October 1997–October 1998	0.249	1.145
April 1998–April 1999	0.329	1.385
2002 Election		
1995–April 2003	0.785	1.718
October 2001–October 2002	0.828	2.8
April 2002–April 2003	1.428	3.247

Source: IPEA.

in both. This study examines interest rates during the pre- and postelectoral period in each of the three elections to address whether the incumbent government behaved opportunistically. Because interest rates do not help explain the "electoral effect," or lack thereof, congruence is discussed.

Table 2 shows that the three elections produced significant deterioration in the real exchange rate. More specifically, of the 19 monthly data points used between October 1993 and April 1995, 14 show a decrease in value against the average value for the time period between 1991 and April 1995. Furthermore, all points from March 1994 until April 1995 are above the trend, with most falling between 0.8 and 0.95. This shows a progressive weakening of the currency, beginning during the campaign. Inflation, on the other hand, breaks its long-term upward trend. While average monthly inflation for the 12 months leading up to the 1994 elections is higher than the long-term trend, by July 1994, monthly inflation drops precipitously to 7.75 percent, and from August 1994 on, monthly inflation does not exceed 3 percent. Thus, while only 10 of the 19 points are below the average, these 10 points are continuous, and emerge during the campaign. The election of Fernando Henrique Cardoso thus coincided with a radical break from the previous trend of acceleration of inflation, producing a very positive net effect on the economy. At the same time, the election saw the real, the one-year-old currency, weaken throughout the period. Even at its weakest, in April 1995, however, it was still the equivalent 0.91 U.S. dollars.

The election of 1998 shows a similar weakening of the real exchange rate and a downward trend in inflation until early 1999, when the Brazilian government shifted its currency regime and allowed the real to float freely. Eighteen out of 19 data points show a real exchange rate that is weaker than the average of the period 1995 to April 1999.[4] At the same time, inflation is well below the long-term average at all but one point in the preelectoral period and two points in the postelectoral period. But the average for both of these periods, even considering the change in currency regime, is still well below the long-term trend.

The 2002 elections show a more accelerated deterioration of the real and a very significant negative effect on monthly inflation. Much as with the 1998 elections, the value of the real deteriorates over the course of the campaign, with all 19 points standing well above the long-term average; but the degree of this deterioration is more intense. Additionally, between July 2002 and April 2003, all but one of the points are above three *reais* to the U.S. dollar, and six more points have a rate of 3.5 or more to the dollar. Unlike 1994 and 1998, the 2002 electoral periods witness an average monthly inflation well above the long-term average. This is especially true of the second period, which gives more emphasis to the campaign itself and its immediate aftereffects. In this period, monthly inflation is nearly double its seven-year average, which suggests that the 2002 elections had a very powerful effect on inflation.

Literature examining the effect of elections on economic performance rightly begins by looking at the policies pursued by the government before and during the election, because government is the political institution most likely to have an effect on short-term rates and trends in terms of inflation, foreign exchange, growth, and unemployment. Political business cycle research assumes not only that government has the ability to manipulate these indicators, but because of reelection concerns, it has the incentive. Remmer's political capital model suggests that politicians will pursue contractionary policies following elections not because they are behaving opportunistically, but in order to deal with long-term macroeconomic problems. Interest rates are fundamental to both arguments. Figures 1 to 3 show monthly interest rates from October of the year preceding each election until April of year following the election.

As figure 1 clearly shows, interest rates increased consistently for the nine months preceding the 1994 elections. Not only is this contrary to political business cycle expectations, but monthly interest rates of 50 percent can hardly be considered pro-growth. The political capital model is more useful in explaining the increase in interest rates because the Finance Ministry, under candidate Cardoso's regents, saw inflation (inertial and otherwise) as the result of structural problems that had to be addressed. But the pursuit of high interest rates during a campaign is not expected by Remmer's model, which sees

Figure 1. Interest Rate Fluctuation Around the Presidential Election, 1994

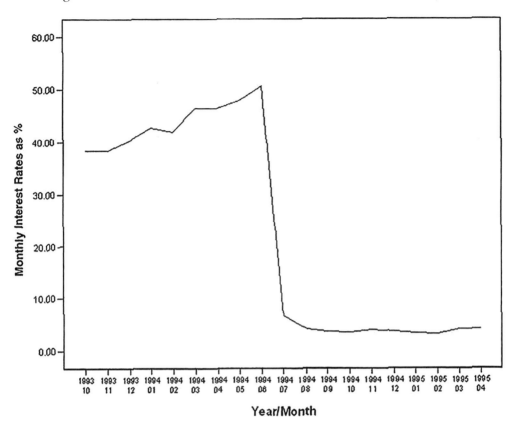

Source: Interest rates in figures 1, 2, and 3 based on the Taxa de juros—Over / Selic—Mensal—(% a.m.)—(BCB Boletim/M.Finan.—Bm12_TJOVER12 on IPEA website.

the election as conferring political capital. Instead, the deceleration in inflation gave the government tremendous political capital even before the election, explaining the pre-electoral increases in interest rates. The decrease in inflation eventually made it possible to reduce interest rates responsibly.

When inflation rates are very high, moreover, a policy aimed at short-term reduction can bring real, tangible benefits across society, and can therefore be employed by opportunistic politicians. Certainly, this was the case for the stabilization plans in Brazil before the Real Plan, all of which were short-term and ultimately unsuccessful. The Real Plan differs in that it dealt a permanent blow to inflation.

The 1998 elections, when President Cardoso ran for reelection, may look like a classic example of a political business cycle. Figure 2 shows how monthly interest rates sharply fell throughout the campaign until September 1998, when they began to rise. The political business cycle literature expects such a monetary loosening to spur growth before a postelectoral pullback. But the decrease in interest rates corresponded to a period in which inflation was decreasing, not increasing. Because of the overvaluation of the *real*, Brazil was facing certain deflationary pressures in 1998, which necessitated lowering interest rates. Clearly, Cardoso did not rush to devalue during the campaign, so as not to lose political support; but his use of interest rates was not what would traditionally be considered opportunistic. Following the election, both inflation and interest rates

Figure 2. Interest Rate Fluctuation Around the Presidential Election, 1998

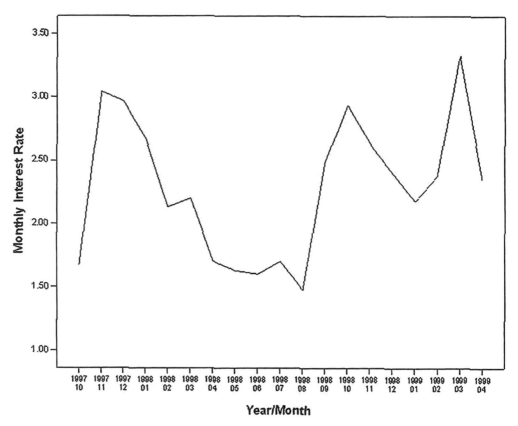

Source: Interest rates in figures 1, 2, and 3 based on the Taxa de juros—Over / Selic—Mensal—
(% a.m.)—(BCB Boletim/M.Finan.—Bm12_TJOVER12 on IPEA website.

increased.[5] This is not entirely incomprehensible to a political capital model, in which the politician recognizes a major problem—in this case, an overvalued exchange rate—and waits until the election is past to address it.

Cardoso behaved "opportunistically," but not the way political business cycle theories would predict, because he promoted policies that stunted growth and inflation before the election. Because political business cycle theories assume price stability, they do not envision such an activity—that is, constraining growth—can be potentially opportunistic. Returning to the political capital model and the need for a politician in a honeymoon period to address longstanding problems, the problems addressed following the 1998 election are considerably more shallow than those in the previous election. Whereas in 1994, wholesale changes were needed, the postelectoral change in 1998 was an important but much more specific reform: flexibilization of the exchange rate. Also, contrary to the political capital model, whereas the 1998 change was postelectoral, as the political capital model expects, the 1994 reforms began in the preelectoral period.

As already indicated, the 2002 elections produced significantly deeper effects on the exchange rate and a radically different direction in inflation. These results are expected by political business cycle theories. Though Cardoso was not a candidate himself, a member of his government, José Serra, was. But even the most casual glance at interest rates over the period leading up to the election challenges the idea that President Cardoso used monetary policy as a way to stimulate Serra's candidacy (see figure 3). The political

Figure 3. Interest Rate Fluctuation Around the Presidential Election, 2002

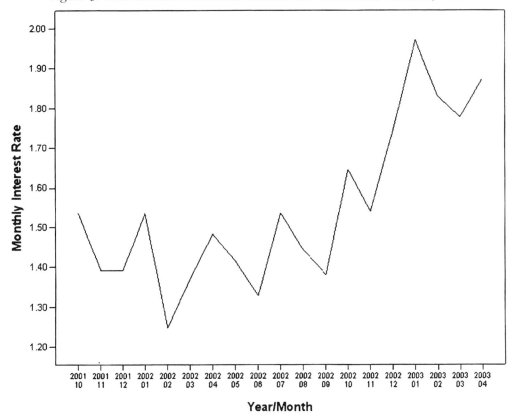

Year/Month

Source: Interest rates in figures 1, 2, and 3 based on the Taxa de juros—Over / Selic—Mensal—(% a.m.)—(BCB Boletim/M.Finan.—Bm12_TJOVER12 on IPEA website.

capital model helps explain the direction of the incoming Lula government, which raised interest rates (throughout 2002) in order to constrain inflation. But this decision was quite different from the high interest rates in 1994, intended to eliminate high inflation, or the slight increase in interest rates in 1999, which aimed to support the new floating currency. The constriction in monetary policy in 2003 aimed not to address "intractable problems" but to contain the pressures that had been allowed to develop during the 2002 campaign by all candidates, principal among them the incoming president.

A critical distinction can be made between the 1994, 1998, and 2002 elections. While the first two had positive effects on inflation, the last had quite the opposite, even though interest rates decreased in the first two cases and increased in the last. The effect was not produced solely by government macroeconomic policy, however, as the traditional political business cycle assumes. When policy proposals of the leading candidate were supported by both voters and investors—definitely the case in 1994 and slightly less so in 1998—future government policy was predictable, and the policy environment could be described as consistent and less risky. In 2002, voters, tired of slow growth and less concerned about inflation, demanded growth-oriented policies from their politicians, while investors were concerned about inflationary pressures. The divergence of interests led to greater perception of risk, a drying up of Brazilian markets, higher inflation rates, and deterioration of Brazil's debt profile.

In 1994, voters were concerned about inflation more than unemployment, as Cardoso's first-round victory and the massive volatility in vote intentions make clear (see

Figure 4. Vote Intention for Lula and Cardoso and Inflation Level, 1994

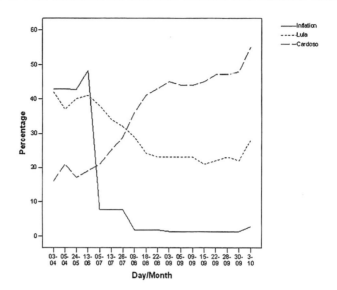

Source: Inflation based on INPC—Mensal—(% a.m.)—IBGE Outras/SNIPC—Precos 12_INPCBR12 available on the IPEA website. Data from Datafolha. IBOPE, IPEA.

figure 4). Voters clearly backed Cardoso mostly for the success of the Real Plan and quickly switched their vote intentions in favor of Cardoso in July, when the plan was implemented. According to Meneguello (1996) and Rua (1997), the Real Plan was the defining factor of the 1994 elections, and it was so successful because it spoke directly to voters' demands for curbing inflation. This is important because it shows that Latin American voters may place concerns about inflation above desires for growth and employment, especially when living under conditions that approximate hyperinflation.

Inflation, especially in emerging markets, is indicative of instability and risk for investors. While moderate levels of inflation can foster growth and can make for arbitrage opportunities, the uncertainty in a market characterized by extremely high inflation is very undesirable to most investment banks and pension funds, and certainly to rating agencies. Inflation deteriorates the value of money over time, discouraging investment and weakening long-term growth. It also increases the risk of policy volatility, particularly in terms of currency regimes, interest rates, and capital controls. Such effects are not encouraging, neither for potential investors in firms that operate in such an environment nor for potential purchasers of public or private debt. For this reason, financial analysts identified the stabilization of the economy as the most important task for the future president in 1994. Cardoso's tenure in the Finance Ministry, and his administration's team in the Central Bank and the Finance Ministry, reassured market analysts and investors that the antishock, exchange rate stabilization plan would continue and that inflation would be reduced to single digits.

Candidate Cardoso's pragmatism signaled that a future Cardoso presidency would be able to count on the support not only of his own party but also the parties of the center and right (the PMDB and PFL, respectively, in addition to his own PSDB).[6] The governability that such support ensured meant that Cardoso would be able to push through many of the liberalizing reforms that were favored by investors. Lula's oppositionist and antimarket stances appealed to more radical sectors of the population; but the vast majority of voters, to say nothing of investors, saw his policy proposals—such as defaulting on international obligations—as utopian criticism at best, and irresponsible populism at worst. Not surprisingly, Lula's decline in popularity and Cardoso's resultant rise reassured investors. Also, as Cardoso's proposed program represented a continuation and expansion of what was already government policy—which would be directed by known personalities, such as Pedro Malan, who had been renegotiating Brazilian debt with the IMF, and supported by a significant legislative majority—investors had a clear idea of what a Cardoso presidency might look like. This reduction of uncertainty is fundamental to risk management and cannot be overstated.

The election of Cardoso allowed for the continuation of the antishock stabilization program that was so popular among voters and investors. This continued growth was facilitated by the increase in capital inflows and privatization revenues, which reflected the considerable support the financial community gave to Cardoso and his government. Thus, the very significant overlap of preferences of voters and investors led to the electoral victory of a mutually acceptable candidate; and this explains the positive effects on the economy.

In 1998, the major candidates in the presidential elections were again Cardoso and Lula.[7] Cardoso, as a result of a controversial amendment passed during his mandate, was the first president who would campaign for reelection. Lula, for his part, had made his peace with Leonel Brizola, his competitor on the left, establishing his candidacy as the unified position of the opposition. Also, for the first time since the return of civilian rule in 1985, the incumbent administration had governed during a period of economic and policy stability. As a result, the government candidate had a very clear program with which he could be identified, and the opposition could more easily identify its objections. This situation should not be overlooked, because Brazilian political institutions, particularly parties, are often seen to have a minimal "brand" effect, giving only limited information to voters (Mainwaring 1995). This branding is equally important to investors, who, like voters, search for information to piece together possible future policy positions of different candidates.

Cardoso was in a fairly strong position in 1998. While the average rate of inflation from 1989 to 1998 was 861.87 percent, average annual inflation during Cardoso's government (1995–98) was only 9.7 percent. Growth was not especially impressive, but the average growth during the Cardoso government of 2.57 percent was virtually identical to that of the period 1989–98 (2.52 percent). The deep reduction in inflation without a simultaneous drastic recession was critical for Cardoso. While growth had slowed considerably in 1998 and the current account deficit had ballooned to 8 percent of GDP, inflation was only 0.13 percent, and the stability of the *real* was a powerful symbol. The emphasis on the currency was especially important following the Tequila crisis in 1995, the Asia crisis in 1997, and the Russian default in 1998. Each of these crises wore away investor risk tolerance, particularly for emerging market instruments. On the domestic side, however, all these crises were linked to exchange rate policies, and many to forced devaluations and the fear of a return of inflation.

The international crises led to increased pressure on the *real*. Cardoso's response was to protect the *real*, sacrificing growth for the sake of price stability. The protection of the *real* placed inflation at the forefront of the 1998 campaign. With low inflation that year, expectations might be that voters in such an environment might support growth-oriented policies (such as those supported by Lula). However, the recent memory of high inflation and the imminent threat of the return of inflation if policies of economic austerity were not maintained explain much of Cardoso's support in public opinion polls. Cardoso also blamed the international environment for the harsh but "necessary" measures implemented and for the slowing down of the economy. Indeed, voters thought that the incumbent administration, because of its experience and previous success in stabilizing the economy, was more capable of dealing with the international crisis than was the opposition.

Investors, at a moment of tremendous international turbulence, also preferred policies that favored the reduction of instability and the risk of inflation. Cardoso, the incumbent president, had given more than enough signs during his administration that he was in tune with the expectations of investors, both by pushing liberalizing economic reforms and by responsibly maintaining price stability. Therefore, 1998 saw a situation of minor instability, caused not by voter and investor preference disjunction but by turbulence in the international arena.

THE PRESIDENTIAL CAMPAIGN OF 2002

During the six months prior to the 2002 elections, the Brazilian economy reacted in a way that appears to be consistent with expectations generated by political business cycle research. Monetary supply (M1) increased consistently from R$45,981 million in March 2002 to R$55,690 million in October 2002, monthly inflation went from 0.62 percent in March of that year to 3.39 percent in November, and the real weakened from 2.35 per U.S. dollar on March 15 to 3.93 on October 17. All of this would suggest weakening monetary resolve as a means of priming the pump for electoral gain.

But neither growth nor unemployment bore the fruits that a loosening of monetary policy would imply or political economists might ordinarily expect. Notably, unemployment increased from 7.6 percent in March 2002 to 8.1 percent in October 2002 and growth sputtered. Moreover, monetary policy did not actually loosen during the electoral period. Monthly interest rates trended upward, from 1.37 percent in March 2002 to 1.65 percent in October 2002 (see figure 3). Additionally, monthly interest rates in 2002 were between 4 and 25 percent higher than for the same months in 2001, with the exception of only one month. This evidence is critical, because the political business cycle literature expects interest rate manipulation to be the primary proof of opportunistic behavior. In relation to the 2002 Brazilian elections, interest rates did not move in the expected direction, though inflation and monetary supply did.

Inflation and M1 increased and the *real* lost value not because of loose monetary policy, but because investors viewed the electoral ambit as full of ambiguity, and the demand for Brazilian assets decreased accordingly. As the clearest measure of investor willingness to invest in Brazilian bonds, Brazil risk increased from 686 basis points on March 18, 2002 to 2,296 bps on October 15, 2002.[8] The increase in the cost of borrowing and its effect on the exchange rate led to the increase in inflation. This result was a consequence of investor concerns about policies of potential future governments. The increased scarcity of capital forced high interest rates and negatively impacted growth and employment, while simultaneously contributing to the deterioration in the value of money (both internal and external, as attested by inflation and the foreign exchange rate). The role of investor perception, therefore, is critical to understanding the unexpectedly poor economic indicators of 2002. Additionally, investor perception of the risk of the Brazilian market was linked not to the policies of the Cardoso government but to those of its potential successor, shifting attention away from President Cardoso in favor of the various pretenders.

Lula was the frontrunner for the 2002 elections. He received only brief challenges from José Serra, the government's health minister, and, more briefly but intensely, from former Ceará governor Ciro Gomes. Lula had been the most vocal critic of the government for many years, but he had begun to moderate his rhetoric. He was challenged from the left by candidates who were also critical of the Cardoso government's liberal economic policies, and this competition prevented Lula from adopting a moderate position, such as the one he has adopted since being elected.

Lula's public relations team designed a new image, "Lula light" (or "diet Lula"), which had him abandon his Everyman outfits and his public style of bellowing into a microphone and blaming capitalism for Brazil's woes. The freshly manicured Lula now wore Armani suits, spoke softly, proposed a partnership between industry and labor, and even chose an industrialist from a right-wing party (the Liberal Party) as his running mate. This was to show that capitalists need not fear a Lula government, the PT was no longer a pure opposition party, and there was broad consensus that the government's economic strategies (e.g., high interest rates) were asphyxiating the Brazilian economy.

While many voters and investors welcomed the new vision of the PT and Lula, few could be sure whether this was simply electoral rhetoric, whether there had been a true shift within the PT and Lula's thinking, or some combination of both. Ambiguity was inherent in the campaign from the beginning. The man who, 13 years earlier, had spoken of a desire to establish a socialist government in Brazil now was courting the same investors he had lambasted for the "savage" capitalism they imposed on Brazil. While many argued that Lula, like all Brazilians, had changed since his first campaign for the presidency, his and the PT's antimarket rhetoric was not abandoned to the distant past. When asked about the riots in Argentina in December 2001, Lula said, "The people are robbing to eat, because for ten years, the IMF robbed Argentina" (*Veja* 2001). A PT document drafted a little earlier spoke of capping debt payments (*Economist* 2002).

At the same time, Lula was trying to distance himself from his previous criticism of the Real Plan, admitting that it had brought down inflation, which was certainly a gain for the Brazilian worker. However, he insisted, the Real Plan relied on high interest rates, which prevented growth. He proposed altering the country's "economic model" to permit robust growth with low inflation. The clues like these, given in speeches, suggested a state-oriented economy that would push growth and be more flexible with inflation. To highlight this, Lula insisted that, in contrast to the Cardoso government, the Ministry of Finance and the Ministry of Planning would be equally important. At the same time, he quoted growth for 2003 as potentially 7 percent, which he later reduced to 5 percent, and then spoke of an average growth of 5 percent per year for his term as president. When asked what an acceptable rate of inflation was, since such growth was likely to raise inflation, he responded zero. Not surprisingly, neither voters nor investors could be sure how a Lula government would change the "government economic model."

The Serra candidacy was confused from the beginning. Serra was an economist with UNECLAC[9] who, while a member of the Cardoso government, had criticized its economic policies. The internal criticism and his personal *jeito* (style) alienated many members of the Cardoso coalition, as well as most of the major leaders in his own PSDB party.[10] Serra's discourse was also marked by an essential ambiguity: it was unclear whether he was the candidate of the incumbent administration or its critic who vowed to create 8 million jobs. Though his proposals were less state-centered and based more on export-led growth than were those of Lula, his uncertain position in relation to the government he had been part of for eight years further contributed to the ambiguity of the electoral environment.

Ciro Gomes, for his part, was a smooth-talking Northeastern politician who could show the success of his administration in the state of Ceará, establishing his credentials as experienced in government (unlike Lula) but still part of the opposition (unlike Serra).

He proposed an alternative model, which would reduce dependence on international capital without threatening price stability, allowing for growth more consistent with the years of the Brazilian Miracle. As details became available, however, investors began to feel that a Ciro presidency would be less predictable than a Lula presidency. One of his chief reform proposals was that monetary policy should be determined by setting growth targets, though the economic adviser he chose, a University of Rochester-trained monetarist, Alexandre Scheinkman, disagreed and thought abandoning the inflation-targeting scheme would be a mistake. This further muddied the predictability of future policy and contributed to the increased perceived risk in Brazilian markets.

Candidates do not make criticisms and policy proposals in a vacuum, and the preferences of voters were critical in encouraging the discussion of changing the government "economic model." Voters had very clearly expressed their support for low inflation in the 1994 and particularly in the 1998 elections, when they overwhelmingly reelected a president during a year in which economic growth was statistically negligible. At the same time, with inflation apparently stabilized (inflation between 1999 and 2002 had averaged 8.68 percent), the electorate became increasingly preoccupied with growth (average growth during the same period was only 2.1 percent).

In a national public opinion poll published November 11, 2002, conducted by IBOPE (the Brazilian Institute of Public Opinion), 43 percent of Brazilian voters expected the new government to invest in growth and generating jobs, followed by 29 percent who said controlling inflation should be the main goal (IBOPE 2002). The same document states that, since 1999, more than two-thirds of all Brazilians have consistently mentioned unemployment as one of the worst problems facing the country. Though Brazilians ranked inflation as only the tenth most mentioned problem in 2001, it jumped to fifth position in 2002. This indicates that the acceleration of inflation in the election year increased popular concern about it, but not enough to displace unemployment as the main problem.

Accordingly, candidates—including the government candidate—criticized the Cardoso era as deficient in terms of economic growth and job creation, and all emphasized that growth under their watch would resume at much higher rates (most made comparisons with the Kubitschek era or the military government). Lula especially criticized the high interest rates, which served as a brake on growth. Brazilians, who in their daily lives saw the difficulty of getting credit and the very high cost thereof, sympathized with the argument and supported the idea of lowering interest rates.

Little discussion took place in public forums, however, regarding how interest rates would be lowered without inviting inflation. Not only was this a reasonable concern based on standard Philips curve expectations (Stokes 2001a, 30), but it was empirically critical, given the acceleration of inflation. Voters saw only the slightest signs that inflation was not totally removed from the economy, but investors witnessed increased inflationary pressures and, eventually, the effect of these on inflation. In many publicly released documents, investors asked all candidates, but especially the PT candidate, to be more explicit in their proposals for government (Schwartsman 2002, 1; Gustavo Loyola, in Alcântara 2002). PT emissaries were sent to Wall Street and Sao Paulo to meet with investment banks and to project the party's new, pragmatic vision of international finance; some went so far as to reassure analysts that the speeches about growth were "just electoral rhetoric" and that they would follow the path of the Cardoso government.[11]

There was nonetheless considerable reason to doubt this promise.[12] It was not simply that Lula was proposing two very different policies (increased social spending and growth; no change in inflation and reduction of indebtedness), but also that tremendous pressures within the PT and within any potential governing coalition might force the government to respond in a way inconsistent with its promises to the financial community. Moreover, only in private meetings was there discussion of maintaining the inflation-targeting policy fundamental to monetary policy. The few official public statements that addressed inflation spoke of broadening the range of "acceptable" inflation but gave no clear targets or ranges.

During 2002, the majority of voters clearly favored a discussion of economics that gave little attention and priority to inflation and that emphasized their frustration with the sluggish growth associated with the poststabilization Cardoso era. Investors saw things quite differently as they worried that inappropriate or ill-conceived growth strategies could reignite inflationary pressures. This fear led to the drying up of Brazilian capital markets, the deterioration of the value of the real, and a rise in inflation. Thus, the increase in inflation during the electoral period in Brazil resulted less from government monetary policy and more from voters' preference for candidates whose policy proposals were perceived by investors as ambiguous or misguided. The political business cycle model cannot explain this outcome because it does not devote appropriate agency to candidates, nor does it consider the potential fragility of stabilization and the importance of congruence of voter and investor perception thereof.

Similarly, while the political capital model allows for postelectoral constriction of monetary policy, it explains this as the result of a vision to address structural, long-term macroeconomics, not short-term, opportunistic behavior. The 2002 elections produced ambiguous results for this, however. Four years after his election, Lula continues to speak of social programs, but his government has produced higher primary surpluses than those of his predecessor and has raised interest rates to meet inflation targets. There has been little policy reform, which would suggest that the change in Lula's rhetoric was to address "intractable" or even long-term problems. Instead, however, all evidence suggests that Lula "switched" positions and that his policies represented small-scale adjustments within a political economy vision.

Lula's choice to pursue inflation-constraining policies was strongly influenced by the conditions that emerged from the divergence between voter and investor preferences during the presidential campaign, the response of the candidates, and the resulting economic wreckage. These conditions placed considerable constraints on Lula's administration, and he responded in a manner not inconsistent with that of his predecessor or of policy advisers from the same banks that were critical of his campaign. His policy switch could very well be the result of responsible behavior, as Remmer might suggest, though without the deep structural changes. It could just as well be a response to his not-so-responsible behavior—for example, sending mixed policy signals during the campaign.

THE PRESIDENTIAL CAMPAIGN OF 2006

The presidential campaign in 2006 had no identifiable negative effect on bondholder perception of risk and as Brazil risk continued the downward trend that it had been enjoying since the policy directions of the Lula government were clearly defined in 2003. In contrast to the 2002 elections, this time voters and investors knew exactly what policies they could expect if he were to be reelected.

Early into his first term, Lula gave important signals about macroeconomic policy. His selection of Antônio Palocci as Finance Minister and Henrique Meirelles as Central Bank president and his maintenance of the inflation-targeting, fiscal surplus, and floating exchange rate of the Cardoso government were well received by investors and corresponded to a sharp reduction in inflation and a return to growth (Sola 2006). By April 2003, investors "enthusiastically received" the bonds issued by the Brazilian government, in sharp contrast with the previous year (Colitt and Munter 2003, 1). The return of capital to Brazil coincided with a robust period of global growth and the first Lula government (2003–2006) saw improved growth. While the average growth performance in 2003 was weak, the average growth for his first mandate was almost 3.5%, a significant improvement over the Cardoso years. The return of growth and capping of inflation provided evidence for the competence of Lula's cabinet, adding to the perception of the Lula government's credibility.

Monthly inflation was 0.121% in April of 2006, negative for two months, and then increase slowly from June until the election. Political business cycle literature expects this. What it does not expect is the increase in interest rates in August to accommodate the slight increase in inflation. In other words, the Brazilian Central Bank followed its mandate rather than political incentives. Additionally, the monetary base expanded during the electoral period, but at no faster rater than it had for the same period in 2005. Finally, having paid off the Brady Bonds in 2005, the main instrument for analyzing "Brazil Risk" in 2006 was the global bond. These bonds were selling at roughly 200 basis points in April 2006, increased in May and June to roughly 257, and then came down in July. The sales price remained below 200 for most of September and the following months. Thus, during the most intense parts of the electoral campaign, perception of investor risk decreased.

This is important since, despite the relatively good economic performance, Lula was forced to compete in a second round of presidential elections, mostly due to the involvement of top government personal in recurring corruption scandals (Renno 2007). Geraldo Alckmin, a member of the more liberal wing of the PSDB ran against Lula in 2006. Rather than the second round exacerbate polarization and increase policy risk, support for Lula increased during the second round and this had no discernible negative effect on major economic indicators. As with any election, there was some policy uncertainty related to the inevitable differences between two different candidates and their coalitions. However, these differences were minimal and few structural changes were expected. Interestingly enough, in the second round, Alckmin's shifted away from a position that was sympathetic to privatization and tried to accuse Lula of favoring privatization. Despite this, there was no concern that either candidate would significantly effect the basic macroeconomic menu. The question that weighed most heavily on investors was whether Lula would pursue further reforms. Even if his motivation for reform dwindled, however, he was unlikely to reverse course in terms of policy, and domestic and global economic fundamentals were strong. As a result, in contrast to the electoral period of 2002, but similar to the elections of 1994, the Brazilian economy encountered no turbulence.

THE RELEVANCE OF THE CONGRUENCE MODEL

Analysis of the 1994, 1998, 2002, and 2006 presidential elections confirms the hypothesis that elections can act as "critical" moments that can significantly affect key economic indicators, such as inflation and the real exchange rate. On balance, there seems to be little evidence of opportunistic behavior, as measured by interest rate manipulation. Changes in economic indicators, furthermore, whether for better or worse, seem to be linked not only to current government policies but especially to the potential policies of candidates.

Neither of these results is expected by political business cycle research. Political business cycles also rely on Philips curve preference expectations of voters, which can be validated in Latin American public opinion data, but only after stabilization (Stokes 2001b). This latter point is critical, because prestabilization conditions can create incentives to produce shocks to inflation, not growth, during electoral periods, as seen in Brazil in the mid-1980s until the Real Plan.

Remmer's political capital model, in its shift away from unscrupulous, opportunistic politicians and its endorsement of the possibility of good macroeconomic management policies under democratic governance, offers improvements to the political business cycle model. But it was conceived during a period before stabilization, when incentives for business cycles were inverted and "intractable" structural problems needed to be addressed in order to bring back price stability.

With price stability, the concern has become sustainable growth. In such an environment, postelectoral inflation constraint appears to be responsible behavior, which works best when political capital is at its highest, during the honeymoon period. But this strategy makes no further attempt to impose severe changes or to address long-term problems in the economy. Instead, poststabilization macroeconomic policy seems conservative—to preserve price stability—rather than radical—aiming at wholly new policy.

The limitations of these approaches can be addressed by including candidates and investors as agents. As the Brazilian elections of 2002 make clear, candidates can increase investor perceptions of risk and can have a negative effect on inflation, even when an incumbent government increases interest rates. The 1994 and 2006 elections produced no such result, and the 1998 elections, given the "Asian flu" and the Russian default, had only a mildly negative effect on Brazilian economic indicators.

It is possible to argue that economic turbulence is linked not so much to preference congruence as to partisan attitudes, with market analysts preferring right-wing candidates (Block and Vaaler 2004, see Spanakos and Renno 2009). The elections of 2000 in Mexico, which produced the first president who was not a member of the PRI, did not have an appreciably negative effect on that country's macroeconomic indicators. Neither did the election of a Socialist, Ricardo Lagos, in Chile the same year. In both these cases, as well as the 1994 and 1998 presidential elections in Brazil, considerable overlap existed between the policy preferences of voters and investors; and politicians with predictable macroeconomic policies were elected, generating positive or only slightly negative effects on economic indicators.

The 2002 presidential elections in Brazil produced quite the opposite result. The 2006 elections, furthermore, involved virtually no political risk, as no viable candidate offered any challenge to the basis of Brazilian economic policy, primary fiscal surplus, floating exchange rate, and inflation targeting. Though questions persisted about Lula's appetite for further reform and the PMDB's reliability as a governing partner, there was little ambiguity about fundamental economic positions, and therefore little risk, from the perspective of investors. Voters, for their part, may have been disappointed with the corruption associated with the Lula government, but they overwhelmingly will vote for a candidate who brought moderate economic growth while maintaining low inflation.

The 2002 election is also interesting for political economy research because it is a very prominent example of what Stokes calls a "policy switch" (2001b). Stokes's groundbreaking study on the subject looks at how politicians, following elections, have imposed "neoliberalism by surprise." Examples abound in Latin America from the late 1980s and early 1990s: Alberto Fujimori in Peru, Carlos Menem in Argentina, Carlos Andrés Pérez in Venezuela. Policy switching is neither uncommon nor surprising in an arena in which information is asymmetrical and parties are clientelistic. This tendency increases under coalitional government (Stokes 2001b, 91). However, Stokes argues, strong parties "induced governments to reveal their policy intentions in campaigns, and once in office to follow through on these intentions"; therefore, strong parties were the most serious obstacle to switches (2001b, 21). This finding is expected, because such parties punish backbenchers who break ranks, and partisan voters are more likely to punish such parties if they do not do so, which provides substantial disincentives for party indiscipline.

This makes the PT government's macroeconomic policy stand even more surprising, given the party's high levels of discipline and clear ideological boundaries. That a party with a brand name (see Downs 1957) and a deep, participatory political base, a party that opposed liberalism and policies that generate "social exclusion," could switch policies offers a powerful challenge to Stokes's otherwise complete treatment of the subject. Analysis of policy switches would be improved by considering the congruence between investor and voter preferences during elections, because this could help explain why even such a disciplined party, with a consolidated brand name, might switch.

When investors and voters perceive a need to reduce inflation, it is easier for politicians to act consistently, and no policy switches are necessary, because candidates campaign on a policy agreeable to both groups. When growth is sluggish but warnings of increased inflation appear, investors and voters are likely to place very different demands on politicians and their respective parties. The need to win an election requires that politicians favor growth-oriented policies or remain noncommittal about their policy intentions. This ambiguity spooks investors, which leads to capital flight, downward pressure on exchange rates, and upward pressure on interest rates. By the time a growth-oriented politician is elected president, he or she may face short- and medium-term economic indicators that are considerably worse than those when the campaign began, increasing pressure to switch policy directions. A disciplined party might find itself with the unenviable choice between maintaining ideological consistency and risking higher inflation, or switching and losing ideological consistency. The post-2002 policy switch of Lula and the PT cannot be understood without looking at threats to price stabilization and the incongruence between voter and investor demands. When such considerations are added to policy switch literature, they can offer a more robust explanation for policy paths of politicians in emerging-market democracies.

What the four Brazilian elections analyzed in this article, and the other cases mentioned in this section, suggest is that extant political economy literature examining electoral politics, macroeconomic policy, and their effects on economic indicators in emerging markets could be strengthened by including analysis of candidate agency and of the preference congruence between voters and investors. Because the preference congruence model examines the negotiations between candidates, voters, investors, and the government, many frameworks can be used. One could be a revised version of Robert Putnam's 1988 two-level game, wherein candidates are theorized to play a two-level, two-stage game in which they must appeal to both voters and investors (levels I and II) but where the priority of each group differs depending on the stage of the game (voters take greater priority during stage I, the election, and investor preference becomes increasingly important especially in stage II, the postelectoral period).

NOTES

The authors would like to thank William C. Smith and the four anonymous reviewers of *Latin American Politics and Society* for their comments on earlier drafts of this paper. We also thank the following analysts for their participation in this study: Armínio Fraga, Ilan Goldfajn, Octavio de Barros, David Fleischen Michael Gavin, Lisa Schineller, Felipe Illanes, Alex Schwartsman, Emy Shayo, Morgan Harting, José Antonio Pena García, and Costa Alexandrakis. The authors would also like to recognize the support of the Fulbright Commission, the Departments of Political Science and International Relations at the University of Brasilia, Marco Antonio da Rocha, Paul Gootenberg, and the Latin American and Caribbean Studies Center of the State University of New York, Stony Brook. After the publication of the original article, the authors benefitted from comments from Chap Lawson, Kurt Weyland, Octavio Amorim Neto, David Samuels, Michael Coppedge, Taylor Boas, Carlos Pereira, and Marcelo Salomon. They would also like to thank Amit Khuram, JP Morgan Chase, Bernard Weis, and Photini Ten for their assistance with the data. The authors would like to recognize further support from the Instituto de Estudios Superiores de Administración in Caracas, Montclair State University, and the East Asia Institute at the National University of Singapore.

1 While investors are often identified as "foreign," extensive interviews with financial market analysts and consultants revealed no discernable difference in analysis that could be attributed to country of birth or residence. There is diversity among investors, as there is among voters, but it would be misleading to argue that foreign investors abandoned Brazilian capital markets in 2002, or any other year, and domestic investors did not. In this study, "investors" include all private individuals, institutions, and corporations that, through the purchase of property, license, title, bonds, or other assets, invest in Brazilian markets. The most important and visible of these investors participate in Brazilian capital markets; particularly, though not limited to, government bond issues.

2 An analogy with Putnam's two-level game (1988), wherein political actors in international arenas have to deal with both domestic and international pressures, helps explain the dilemma candidates face when dealing with investors' and voters' preferences. When the preferences of actors in domestic and international arenas are discrepant, it is much harder for policymakers to reach a consensus. Negative outcomes are more likely when there is preference dissonance. Similarly, when investors and voters disagree about what the country needs, economic turbulence, a clearly negative outcome for a developing country, is more likely to occur.

3 Two recent articles offer contradictory positions on this issue. Hallerberg and Marier (2004) do not find a negative relationship between elections and public deficits in Latin America; Amorim Neto and Borsani's 2004 statistical study finds that elections do have an effect on deficits in Latin America.

4 The starting date of 1995 is used for the 1998 and 2002 elections because of the very significant impact of stabilization. If this adjustment were not made, average monthly inflation between 1991 and April 1995 would be almost 5 percent, which is not representative of the trend that inflation took beginning in 1995.

5 This rise is linked not only to efforts to "protect" the real but also to speculation following crises in Indonesia and the Russian government's debt default, factors that were outside the power of the incumbent government.

6 The Party of the Brazilian Democratic Movement and the Liberal Front Party.

7 Ciro Gomes was also a candidate. While his support was impressive, given the resources available to him, his campaign in 1998 was clearly only a preparation for his candidacy in 2002. He ran as a candidate of the Popular Socialist Party.

8 One hundred basis points is the equivalent of one percentage point. The C bond is the primary instrument the Brazilian government uses for borrowing, and the price that investors are willing to pay for it represents their perception of the risk that the Brazilian government will renege on its commitments. "Brazil risk" is the spread of the effective coupon rate paid by the Brazilian C bond when compared to a bond issue of similar maturity issued by the U.S. Treasury. U.S. government bonds are used as a benchmark because the perceived probability that the U.S. government will not pay its obligations is considered to be zero. The spread entails subtracting the rate offered on U.S. government bond issues with similar maturity from that of the Brazilian C bond. This spread is calculated in basis points, with one hundred basis points equal to 1 percent.

9 The United Nations Economic Commission on Latin America and the Caribbean is associated with state-led growth and critical positions on economic liberalism.

10 Serra's own poor relations with the PFL (the government's main ally for two mandates) and his supposed involvement in the torpedoing of PFL precandidate Roseana Sarney led him to choose a running mate, Rita Camata, from the PMDB. This choice weakened the governing coalition and Serra's support among PFL politicians and their constituents, which was critical, given the complimentary nature of PSDB and PFL voting bases.

11 This was conveyed to one of the authors in a private conversation with the chief economist for Brazilian debt markets in a bulge bracket investment bank.

12 One analyst remarked, "We still do not know which PT will govern the country" (Grinbaum 2002).

REFERENCES

Alcântara, Eurípedes. 2002. O que eles temem em Lula: o nervosismo do mercado tem diversos motives, mas a indefinição sobre o que o PT realmente é o fator mais decisivo neste momento. *Veja*, May 22: 45.

Alesina, Alberto, and Nouriel Roubini, with Gerald D. Cohen. 1997. *Political Cycles and the Macroeconomy*. Cambridge: MIT Press.

Ames, Barry. 1987. *Political Survival: Politicians and Public Policy in Latin America*. Berkeley: University of California Press.

Amorim Neto, Octavio, and Hugo Borsani. 2004. Presidents and Cabinets: The Political Determinants of Fiscal Behavior in Latin America. *Studies in Comparative International Development* 39, 1: 3–27.

Barbosa Filho, Nelson H. 2001. *International Liquidity and Growth in Brazil*. Working Paper. New York: Center for Economic Policy Analysis.

Bernard, William, and David Leblang. 2006. *Democratic Processes and Financial Markets: Pricing Politics*. New York: Cambridge University Press.

Block, Stephen A, and Paul M. Vaaler. 2004. The Price of Democracy: Sovereign Risk Ratings, Bond Spreads and Political Business Cycles in Developing Countries. *Journal of International Money and Finance 23*, 6: 917–946.

Chaffee, Wilber Albert. 1998. *Desenvolvimento: Politics and Economy in Brazil*. Boulder: Lynne Rienner.

Colitt, Raymond, and Paivi Munter. 2003. Brazil's return to bond markets is well received. *Financial Times*. 30 April 2003. p. 1.

Datafolha Instituto de Pesquisa. Presidential election data sets. <www.datafolha.folha.uol.com.br>

Downs, Anthony. 1957 (republished 1997). *An Economic Theory of Democracy*. New York: Addison-Wesley.

Economist (The) 2002. Who's Afraid of Lula? May 18: 36.

Fair, R. 1978. The Effect of Economic Events on Votes for President. *Review of Economics and Statistics* 60, 2: 159–73.

Grinbaum, Ricardo. 2002. O PT em Wall Street. *Istoé Dinheiro*, July 24: 78.

Hallerberg, Mark, and Patrik Marier. 2004. Executive Authority, the Personal Vote, and Budget Discipline in Latin American and Caribbean Countries. *American Journal of Political Science* 48, 3: 571–87.

Instituto Brasileiro de Opinião Pública e Estatística (IBOPE). 2002. Pesquisa de opinião pública sobre assuntos políticos / administrativos OPP 570. Brazil, November-December. <www.ibope.com.br>

IPEA (Institute of Applied Economic Research). Economic data: daily series, historical series, and macroeconomic indicators. <www.ipeadata.gov.br>

Leblang, David. A. 2002. The Political Economy of Speculative Attacks in the Developing World. *International Studies Quarterly 46*, 1: 69–92.

MacRae, D.C. 1977. A Political Model of the Business Cycle. *Journal of Political Economy 85*, 2: 239–63.

Mahon, James E., Jr. 1996. *Mobile Capital and Latin American Development*. University Park: Pennsylvania State University Press.

Mainwaring, Scott P. 1995. Brazil: Weak Parties, Feckless Democracy. In *Building Democratic Institutions: Party Systems in Latin America*, ed. Mainwaring and Timothy Scully. Stanford: Stanford University Press. 354–98.

Martínez, Juan, and Javier Santiso. 2003. Financial Markets and Politics: The Confidence Game in Latin American Emerging Economies. *International Political Science Review* 24, 3: 363–95.

Meneguello, Rachel. 1996. Electoral Behavior in Brazil: The 1994 Presidential Elections. *International Social Science Journal* 146: 627–41.

Mosley, Layna. 2003. *Global Capital and National Governments*. New York: Cambridge University Press.

Nordhaus, William. 1975. The Political Business Cycle. *Review of Economic Studies* 42: 169–90.

Persson, Torsten, and Guido Tabellini. 2000. *Political Economics: Explaining Economic Policy*. Cambridge: MIT Press.

Putnam, Robert. 1988. Diplomacy and Domestic Politics: The Logic of Two-Level Games. *International Organization* 42, 2 (Summer): 427–60.

Remmer, Karen L. 1993. The Political Economy of Elections in Latin America. *American Political Science Review* 87, 2: 393–407.

Renno, Lúcio. 2007. "Escândalos e Voto: as eleições presidenciais brasileiras de 2006." *Opinião Pública*, 13: 260–82.

Rohter, Larry. 2005. Brazil's Opposition Shelters President from Scandal, for Now. *New York Times*, August 14.

Rua, Maria das Graças. 1997. Comportamento eleitoral em Brasília: a eleição presidencial de 1994. In Brasília: construção do cotidiano, ed. Brasilmar Nunes. Brasília: Paralelo 15.

Schwartsman, Alexandre. 2002. No Free Lunch: Lula in the Sky with Diamonds. BBA Economic Research on Brazil. May 13.

Sola, Lourdes. 2006. Financial credibility, legitimacy and political discretion: the Lula da Silva government. In *Statecrafting Monetary Authority: Domestic and Financial Order in Brazil*, ed. Lourdes Sola and Laurence Whitehead. Oxford: Centre for Brazilian Studies.

Spanakos, Anthony Peter, and Lúcio R. Renno 2009. Speak Clearly and Carry a Big Stock of Dollars: Sovereign Risk, Ideology and the Presidential Elections in Argentina, Brazil, Mexico, and Venezuela. *Comparative Political Studies*. 42, 10.

Stokes, Susan C. 2001a. Economic Reforms and Public Opinion in Fujimori's Peru. In *Public Support for Market Reforms in New Democracies*, ed. Stokes. Cambridge: Cambridge University Press. 160–88.

———. 2001b. *Mandates and Democracy: Neoliberalism by Surprise in Latin America*. Cambridge: Cambridge University Press.

Veja (São Paulo). 2001. *Ate aonde vai o risco do contagio*. December 26.

Vox Populi. Presidential election data sets. <www.voxpopuli.com.br>

Chapter 13

Institutional Weakness and the Puzzle of Argentina's Low Taxation

Marcus André Melo

L arge-N comparisons of taxation levels have advanced considerably our understanding of the factors influencing taxation worldwide. Nevertheless, the Argentine case defies standard explanations. It is one of the few upper-medium-income countries with very low taxation levels (Teera and Hudson 2004; Piancastelli 2001). In a group of 24 such countries, Argentina emerges as the country with the lowest tax effort (Teera and Hudson 2004). It ranks 24th, behind the oil exporters Oman (23rd) and Bahrain (22nd). Other countries in this category in Latin America, such as Mexico (21st) and Venezuela (17th), also have a very low tax effort; but standard arguments ("resource curse") provide convincing explanations for that.

Argentina, by contrast, has not "learned to tax" (Kaldor 1963). Why has the Argentine state been so unsuccessful in extracting resources from society? According to the literature on comparative taxation, the tax burden in Argentina should have been much higher than it has been at least since the 1960s. Current explanations of taxation levels have identified a host of economic factors, such as levels of economic development and GDP per capita, which are robust predictors of tax shares (i.e., total tax as a percentage of GDP). The economic literature on taxation takes the "residuals" of an economic-structural model containing standard variables—trade as a percentage of GDP, mineral resource availability, GDP per capita, share of agriculture in GDP, public debt burden, and so on (Tanzi 1992)—and treats them as ad hoc cultural, institutional, and political characteristics of a country. The standard procedure is to treat the difference between the predicted and actual tax ratio as the "tax effort" (Piancastelli 2001; Teera and Hudson 2004). Because Argentina has high per capita income levels—considerably higher than those of its counterparts in Latin America—the predicted tax level should be much higher than those observed in the last decades in the region, particularly in Brazil, Uruguay, and Chile.

The large-N studies of taxation have also identified dependence on mineral resources as a factor that depresses tax levels. But although this explanation might explain low taxation in Mexico, Russia, or Venezuela, which are important oil exporters, it does not apply to Argentina. Other explanations found in the literature that focus on the above-mentioned "residuals" stress the role of corruption and culture (and the related concept of "tax morale") as variables. When we make comparisons within Latin America, however, it is reasonably safe to assume that we are controlling for important dimensions of culture (with certain variations), such as Catholic religious affiliation and what has been commonly described as Iberian values, and therefore the puzzle remains. The same reasoning applies to corruption levels as a potential explanatory factor, despite some important variation within Latin America in that respect. These factors do not have good explanatory power, particularly if we seek to understand changes over time.

Other types of economic explanations include patterns of development strategy and the existence of tax handles; that is, sectors or products that are easily taxed by governments (Tanzi 1992). This can be part of the explanation but certainly is not the primary factor. Other potential explanations draw on political factors, such as type of political regimes (democracy and authoritarian regimes), form of government (separation of powers versus parliamentarism), and electoral rules. In line with existing literature, the analysis presented in this article concludes that political regimes do not help to explain the Argentine case of low taxation. The study of the effects of political institutions on taxation outcomes has also given rise to a burgeoning literature. Contributors to this literature have argued that fragmented party systems and coalition governments are correlated with larger governments. This, however, is not the case of Argentina, where a fairly robust party system has emerged since the postwar period and single-party majorities have predominated in democratic times. Likewise, presidentialism and electoral rules do not seem to provide solutions for our riddle.

This article argues that the key to explaining low taxation in Argentina lies in the nature of its political institutions, particularly federalism, and federalism's influence on instability. Along with other examples in the literature, it argues that the type of federalism adopted in that country has been an important source of instability. Other factors affecting the "discount rates" of political actors, such as political polarization (which increases discount rates) or power centralization (which lowers discount rates), can have the same effect on taxation outcomes. An effective tax system is a public good and can only be effectively created if actors have long time horizons. Argentina's federal institutions created wrong incentives for the actors involved, thereby contributing to the nation's systemic political instability (Levitsky and Murillo 2006a, b).

Federalism has sector-specific (i.e., tax) outcomes, including disincentives to taxation at the provincial level; incentives to provinces to grant tax exemptions, thereby reducing the tax base; a chronic pattern of central government interventions; and fiscal bailouts by central governments. Systemic instability, this article argues, also affects the tax behavior of governments. Facing a highly uncertain future, incumbent governments choose to extract resources from society through inflation rather than normal taxation. In addition, this study argues that even normal taxation is affected, because governments in these environments will tend to collect taxes that require less effort on the part of the state (e.g., customs taxes, bank debit and credit taxes), as opposed to income, property, and, to some extent, value-added taxes.

It is argued here that Argentine federal institutions—including not only fiscal matters but also the rules for electing senators and presidents and federal interventions in the states—have had two effects. First, the institutions of federalism (along with other factors) contributed to instability in the political system. Second, fiscal federalism created what the fiscal literature has called common pool problems. Political instability is certainly not the single factor that can universally explain taxation outcomes. Despite some controversy about the effect of some factors, large-N comparisons have provided relatively robust tests for the determinants of taxation levels, particularly the economic ones. The existing explanations, however, cannot accommodate the Argentine exception. Therefore, this article argues that the political instability explanation sheds light on why Argentina emerges as an outlier. To develop this argument, the case of Brazil is used for a systematic comparison.

The logic of case selection adopted here is partly similar to the "most similar systems" research design (Lijphart 1975) but could be more adequately labeled, following Lieberman (2005), a "nested analysis approach." In this approach, the point of departure is the large-N analyses, which are available in the comparative literature. This study does not attempt to validate the hypothesis in the large-N context, given the lack of historical data and the difficulty of operationalizing institutional instability across a large number of countries. The analysis provides two in-depth cases, one of which, Argentina, is an outlier in existing contributions. The main purpose is to show the plausibility of factors that have not been explored systematically in the current literature on taxation. Brazil is a good case for comparison because it shares with Argentina some common social, economic, and institutional features: the federal structure over a large territory, strong presidents, proportional representation, high levels of industrialization for a developing country, and a history of state-led development. Furthermore, both countries share the same cultural Iberian background and are comparable in terms of corruption levels. By controlling these potential sources of variation, this study can explore the analytically relevant aspects through in-depth analysis.

The analysis in this article discusses selected evidence for the last five decades. Throughout this period, Argentine rulers have been unable to reform the tax system. This was not because the opposition thwarted proposed reforms or because social actors were reluctant to pay taxes. Indeed, a distinctive pattern in the Argentine case is the absence of both reform initiatives and tax revolts. The very lack of significant reform initiatives is consistent with the argument of this study. The exception to the rule is the comprehensive tax reform implemented by President Carlos Menem (1989–99), which, however, was proposed because Menem faced no significant political uncertainties about the future, given the fiasco of his predecessors, the Radicals. Tax reform, moreover, was the only alternative available, because inflation financing had to be halted in response to hyperinflation.

To operationalize instability as an explanatory variable, this study uses a host of indicators of institutional instability, but the analysis is not univariate; it seeks to look at instability's microfoundations. Political instability is discussed with a transaction costs approach. It is argued that instability derives from the lack of institutions for credible commitment that guarantees intertemporal political transactions in a context of preference polarization.

The article is organized in three sections. The first section briefly reviews six types of explanations for tax capacity, which stress economic variables, political regimes, "quasivoluntary compliance," culture, corruption, and political institutions and political instability, respectively. The discussion shows that the first five types of explanation cannot fully account for the Argentine paradox. The analysis proceeds by making systematic comparisons between Argentina and Brazil. The second section considers the evolution of taxation in the two countries since the 1950s and explores how the political instability-political institutions type of explanation contributes to the understanding of the Argentine exception. The third section looks at recent tax reforms, advancing the hypothesis that the constitutional changes made shortly after the return to democracy, particularly in the workings of federalism—or in the political institutions that shape the way the federal government relates to subnational governments—explain to a large extent the distinct reform outcomes in Argentina and Brazil over roughly the last two decades.

EXPLAINING TAXATION OUTCOMES

The economic literature has made an important connection between levels of economic development, as measured by GDP per capita, and what is known as tax burden or share. Developing countries are often characterized by having a large share of agriculture in total output and employment, a small share of wages in total national income, and a large share of informal activities and occupations.[1] Lieberman (2003) has shown that income explains 40 percent of the tax burden in a large-N regression. Argentina is clearly an outlier in this respect. The contrasts between Argentina and Brazil are very significant (see figure 1). First, Argentina had a consistently higher per capita income than Brazil,

Figure 1. Tax Share in Argentina and Brazil, 1961–2003

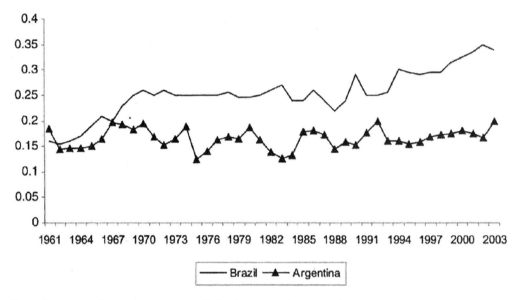

Note: Figures are for total tax revenue (federal, state, and municipal).
Sources: Brazil: Afonso 2004; Argentina: Secretaría de Hacientda 2004.

more than twice as high during the postwar period (Fausto and Devoto 2004, 151). One would expect Argentina therefore to have higher tax shares than Brazil and other Latin American countries.

Alternative arguments to explain taxation regimes stress politico-institutional factors. The first of these stresses differences in political regimes. Do regime types explain differences in taxation regimes? Authoritarian regimes are supposed to bring about a lower tax burden because of their incapacity to generate acquiescence to taxation. Conversely, democracies are expected to be associated with higher revenue extraction because citizens believe that they can influence government spending and therefore tend to comply with taxation (Levi 1989). This type of explanation rests on one important assumption: the importance of "quasivoluntary mechanisms." Torgler (2003), with data sets from the World Values Survey and Latinobarómetro, has tested this argument and found some evidence to validate it.[2] This is indeed surprising, considering that tax evasion is significantly higher in Argentina than in Brazil and, as indicated, the difference in income tax productivity is abysmal in both countries (Lora 2001).[3]

Admittedly, cross-country comparisons of perceptions are problematic. The argument that tax morale can account for Argentina's lower tax burden is inconclusive at best. Bergman (2003) argues that the ability of states to collect taxes depends on their ability to enhance voluntary compliance, which stems greatly from their deterrence capabilities. Argentina's low taxation, in his account, is caused by the state's weakness. Over time, the weak deterrence capability generates routine behavior and a tax culture. This argument is persuasive overall. However, it does not offer an account of the roots of this lack of deterrence capability. The question then becomes, what factors explain the lack of incentives to enforce compliance? More to the point, what are the determinants of the sustainability of deterrence practices? The argument here is that instability is the key determinant of bureaucratic capacity.

Alternative explanations based on political regimes and elites' resistance to taxation do not provide convincing accounts of the contrast between the two countries. Cheibub (1998) and Mahon (2004) have explored this hypothesis, and find regimes to be a relatively poor predictor of taxation. The Brazilian and Argentine cases show that these countries were governed by dictatorships for the same number of years (28) and in similar decades in the twentieth century, so political regimes per se cannot account for the differences observed.

What about elites' views of taxation? As mentioned, tax revolts have never occurred in Argentina (in contrast to Brazil in recent years). In Argentina, this can be explained by tax administrators' inability to enforce compliance. The evidence in the cases of Brazil and Argentina suggests that these different perceptions are important, and were particularly so during the heyday of developmentalism and in the period in which the two countries were governed by the military.[4] However different, the contrasting perceptions do not seem capable of explaining the vast contrast between the two countries during the postauthoritarian period.

A variant of the explanation based on elites' perception of taxation and that of the polity in general has been provided by Lieberman (2003). In his analysis of taxation in Brazil and South Africa, Lieberman argues that by defining the national political community in racial terms, as opposed to along regional lines, the South African elites created a sense of solidarity within the white polity. This solidarity and the perceived common threat from the black communities led to the introduction of a very progressive income tax system. Lieberman's elegant argument is persuasive and helps to explain what appears to be South Africa's exceptionalism. However, it is unable to explain differences in Latin America or Argentina's exceptionalism. Applied to Latin America, Lieberman's argument would predict that the definition of national political communities in Latin America is made difficult because of the region's social heterogeneity. In this context, Argentina is much more homogeneous than Brazil because the proportion of its indigenous and black population is much smaller. Thus, according to Lieberman's argument, we would expect Argentina to have a high extractive capacity, at least higher than Brazil's.[5]

Other rival explanations in the tax and fiscal sociology literature focus on cultural factors and corruption. Cultural factors are difficult to operationalize because culture is very difficult to measure and the causal mechanisms very difficult to specify. More significant is that accounts of "tax cultures" conflate cause and effect. As Lieberman (2003, 522) aptly argues, if patterns of taxation are described as tax cultures, then cultures cannot be said to explain patterns of variation. Nevertheless, religion and shared values can plausibly be expected to affect taxation and compliance. For the case of Argentina, however, it is difficult to pinpoint cultural specificities that might explain its exceptionalism. The same methodological caveats can be raised regarding corruption: it is difficult to measure and difficult to specify.[6]

Yet another alternative explanation for the Argentine puzzle and its stark contrast with Brazil focuses on political institutions. The general literature offers different claims about the influence of political institutions and tax burdens (Steinmo 1993; Gould and Baker 2002; Persson and Tabellini 2003). Mahon (2004) discusses a number of politico-institutional explanations for the causes of tax reform in Latin America and finds weak evidence for the role of political factors, such as institutionalization of party systems, number of parties, and presidential powers of presidents, in explaining tax reform outcomes. This finding contradicts the received wisdom that polities with a small number of disciplined parties and strong presidents and with fewer veto points would be more likely to reform. Argentina, in this literature, is not viewed as a fragmented polity; quite the opposite (despite recent changes).

Neo-institutional explanations have explored how the capacity to tax relates to solving the bargaining game between taxpayers and governments and between levels of government in federal systems. This issue has been approached from a transaction cost politics perspective, which views institutions as crucial for the establishment of inter-temporal political transactions (Dixit 1996; Alston 1996; Acemoglu et al. 2003). Weak and unstable institutions influence public finance in a number of ways. Cukierman et al. (1989) and Edwards and Tabellini (1991) focus on the incentives governments face when choosing alternatives for raising revenue: borrowing, taxation, and inflation tax. A government (or a legislative majority) may deliberately refrain from reforming a tax system for fear that a more efficient tax apparatus will be used in the future to carry out spending or redistributive programs that the current government disapproves of. Countries with more unstable and polarized political systems will tend to rely to a greater extent on inefficient taxes, such as tax inflation, tax seigniorage, and trade taxes, than will more stable and less polarized countries. The intuition behind this argument is that tax reforms are public goods, and a weak government is discouraged from pursuing them because they involve administrative as well as political costs. In addition, and more significant, future governments, as opposed to the governments that initiate reforms, can reap the benefits they produce.

Weak governments, which face the prospect of losing elections (or, in the case of dictatorships, of being toppled), have therefore an incentive to resort to inflation and other distortionary taxes, which generate revenue in the short term. Future governments must deal with the resulting fiscal problems. Weak governments have little to lose (as they are likely to be thrown out of office anyway). According to this argument, tax reforms are strategic choices made by governments. If there is political instability and political polarization, these strategic considerations may induce the current government to leave an inefficient tax system to its successor (Cukierman et al. 1989). However, the same logic can be applied to the choice of tax types. In this logic, the prediction is that governments will choose easy-to-collect taxes over difficult taxes.

The political instability argument provides an important clue for explaining the Argentine puzzle. The political instability/polarization argument, however, does not elaborate on the roots of political instability. Moreover, the argument is tested via large-N regressions without providing adequate microfoundations for the analysis. Recent contributions to the debate on political instability have used a transaction cost politics perspective. These typically are case studies, because credible commitments tend to be context-specific. The sources of political instability, in this view, come primarily from weak institutions and polarized politics (Spiller and Tommasi 2007). Weak institutions are those that encourage opportunistic behavior and do not promote gains from trade among those involved in political transactions. In turn, as demonstrated formally by Spiller and Tommasi (2003, 2007), polarization reduces the space for compromise and gains from trade between political actors.

Neo-institutional approaches have discussed federalism as a crucial institution in the explanation of taxation outcomes. Transaction cost politics approaches and principal-agent models have been used in analyzing taxation policies and fiscal behavior in federal democracies (Iaryczower et al. 1999; Filipov et al. 2004; Saiegh and Tommasi 1998). These contributions underscore that the quality of the federal governance structure, particularly its ability to overcome collective action and common pool problems, is the determining factor. Federal structures may create incentives for opportunistic behavior of provinces or states. They might lead to political instability if the central government depends on subnational actors, such as governors, for its political survival and if, at the same time, the latter depend on the financial support of the former for economic survival. In this case, there is great potential for fiscal disequilibrium.

The problems of collective action and common pool are crucial in federal systems because of the importance of tax share schemes among the levels of governments in federations, and also because of the distribution of tax competencies, which can potentially generate incentive compatibility problems. This might lead to recurring problems of bailouts to subnational governments. If there is a vertical fiscal imbalance between the federal government and the provinces, the result is a cycle of overspending, insufficient taxation, and institutional instability in province-central government relations (Rodden 2003). This neo-institutional literature predicts that the reform of fiscal and tax systems depends on the actors' ability to commit themselves in a credible way to refraining from opportunistic behavior. One way of solving the bargaining problem is for the actors to build institutions for credible commitments, such as independent tax administrations (Taliercio 2004).

The literature review in this section has identified a number of alternative explanations for the Argentine paradox. The arguments discussed—based on explanations that stress economic variables, political regime, cultural factors, or the elites' normative views and compliance toward taxation—cannot fully account for the widely observed variation between the cases of Argentina and Brazil. The political instability argument based on the transaction cost politics approach arguably offers a superior analytical lens.

DEVELOPMENT OF THE CAPACITY TO TAX IN ARGENTINA AND BRAZIL

Argentina's postwar history has been marked (until today) by political instability and political polarization. In contrast to Brazil, the state bureaucracy—including the tax, Foreign Service, and planning bureaucracies—is much weaker (Geddes 1990, 1994; Sikkink 1991). Political instability since the 1930s has played a crucial role in precluding the emergence of these bureaucracies. A sequence of military coups and short-term military governments underscores the great political instability and uncertainty in the period. It prompted the state to resort primarily to seigniorage to finance the increasing demand for public goods. Conflict-ridden federalism in Argentina was a key cause of institutional crises, known as the federal intervenciones.

As suggested by Gibson and Faletti (2004), the intervenciones in the provinces, the revenue-sharing schemes (coparticipación), and, in democratic times, the Electoral College were the mainstay of the Argentine political system for most of the twentieth century. The coparticipación scheme was set up in 1935 in Argentina. It was based on the centralization of revenue at the federal level and a semi-institutionalized, rule-based distribution to the provinces. The states delegated to the federal government the collection of their tax base in exchange for a larger volume of resources that would be generated. The law authorized the federal government to use the tax base of the provinces in return for a rebated share of the revenue raised. It should be noted that before coparticipación, the provinces and the federal government had their own sources of revenue (the former raising internal taxes and the latter raising taxes on foreign trade). "Thus, the federal and subnational governments did not have strong incentives or opportunities to cheat on each other" (Iaryczower et al. 1999, 16).

The coparticipación schemes proved to be an extremely unstable mechanism. In the 1940s and 1950s, the coparticipación laws were renewed almost yearly (Eaton 2001, 12;

Porto 2003).[7] But their importance was greatly enhanced—with important implications for political instability—in the 1970s, when the VAT was introduced in Argentina, and particularly in the 1980s.

The Electoral College, in turn, was the mechanism that ensured that central government control was not entirely hegemonic. Because the governors controlled the legislative assemblies at the provincial level, they played a key role in the president's survival in office. In addition, until the constitutional amendment of 1994 that introduced the direct election of senators, the governors controlled the senators who were elected by the provincial assemblies. Therefore the system rested on an unstable equilibrium between these three institutions. Although the federal government had the power to intervene in the provinces, and usually did, presidents (and senators) depended on provincial party bosses (usually the governors) for political survival (Jones and Hwang 2006). The other crucial element was the malaportionment of the Argentine Congress, which favored the smallest provinces.

Since 1930, Argentina has been characterized by the extreme volatility of its institutions and constitutional order, which explains its economic malaise (Gallo and Alston 2004; Acemoglu et al. 2003). The National Constitution was sanctioned in 1853 and reformed in 1860, 1866, 1898, 1949, 1956, 1957, 1972, and 1994. In turn, military dictatorships ruled the country in the periods 1930–32, 1943–46, 1955–58, 1962–63, 1966–73, and 1976–83 (Tommasi 2002, 3). During the years of Arturo Frondizi alone (1958–62), there were 35 failed attempts to topple the government. Between 1955 and 1983, Argentina was ruled by 16 different presidents. This is an average of less than two years for each term of office.

Volatility was also prevalent at the subnational level. The Province of Buenos Aires was governed by 74 different governors between 1900 and 1984. The average tenure in office was 13 months (Muni 2003, 5). Between 1853 and 1995, the federal government "intervened" in the provinces 131 times, with a yearly average of 1.36. Two-thirds of these interventions were implemented by decree and one-third by an approved law (Faletti 2001).

Instability became a crucial feature of Argentina's political system in the postwar period. As Della Paolera et al. (2003) show, the economy grew at high annual rates, but the cost was to create increasing fiscal imbalances. Political instability in Argentina has been indeed much higher than in Brazil. In a ranking of countries according to the volatility of the economic freedom index published by the Fraser Institute for the period 1970–99, Argentina comes up as the 7th most volatile case in a sample of 106 countries (compared to Brazil, ranked as the 31st most volatile) (cited in Stein and Tommasi 2005).

Chronic instability discouraged leaders from creating a robust bureaucratic machinery despite the country's highly qualified workforce (Fausto and Devoto 2004). Argentina never created a modern professional bureaucracy, and has shown low levels of institutionalization. On Evans and Rausch's (1999) "Weberianess scale," Argentina obtained a score of 3.8 percent compared to Brazil's much higher score of 7.6 percent, and below the Latin American average.

The establishment of a modern tax agency and the introduction of the VAT followed distinct paths. The Dirección General Impositiva (DGI) was introduced relatively early—it was set up in the 1930s—but it experienced gradual and sustained decay after the late 1950s. The VAT was finally introduced in 1975 to replace a sales tax on turnover, but in the mid-1980s it represented (excluding social security) only 18 percent of the then very low tax burden, which represented 14 percent of GDP (Schenone 1990, 115, table 10–1). The DGI's performance fluctuated dramatically over time. In the late 1950s and early 1960s, the government intervened and appointed *interventores* to its top management. The agency's personnel were qualified, but instability began to undermine its operations.[8] A remarkable trait in the evolution of Argentina's tax administration from 1950 on is the relative absence of comprehensive reform efforts, considering that its tax agencies are among the oldest in Latin America.

As a measure of institutional instability in tax administration, figure 2 shows tax administrators' tenure in Argentina. Between 1947 and 2002, the DGI had 49 directors, an average of 1.3 years on the job. In contrast, between 1968 and 2002, the corresponding figure for Brazil is 2.3 years (see figure 6, p. 131). Managerial turnover was compounded

Figure 2. DGI Directors' Terms, 1947–2002 (months)

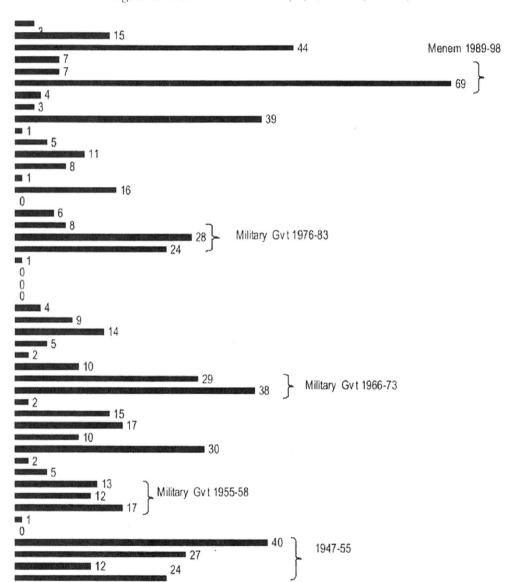

Source: Author's calculations on the basis of archival data from Museo Histórico de la AFIP, Buenos Aires.

Figure 3. Inflation Tax as Percentage of GDP, Brazil and Argentina, 1947–2001

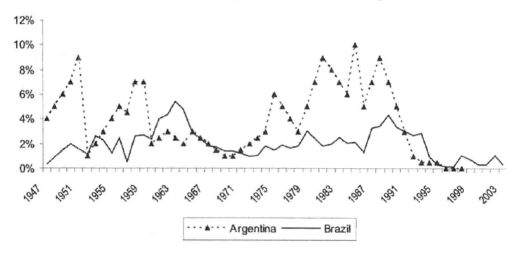

Sources: Della Paolera et al. 2003; Cysne and Coimbra Lisboa 2004.

in the 1980s because many technical staffers held two jobs to compensate for the low salaries (World Bank 1990).

Between 1950 and 1980, inflation was key to ensuring public revenue. Della Paolera et al. (2003) show the importance of the inflation tax as a source of deficit financing in Argentina throughout the postwar period until the convertibility regime in the 1990s, when it remained close to zero. In the 1940s and 1950s and again in the 1970s and 1980s, the inflation tax reached very high levels. In contrast, during the first half of the twentieth century, the inflation tax had been negligible.

Conversely, as shown in figure 3, the inflation tax created incentives for governments to extract resources from society using seigniorage rather than traditional taxation mechanisms. This is the key to understanding the underdevelopment of Argentina's public bureaucracy in the area of taxation. In her study of postwar Latin America, Geddes argues that the countries that made the least progress in building a few competent bureaucratic agencies in key economic sectors before the 1980s were Peru and Argentina, the same countries that had experienced the most political instability (Geddes 1994, 177).

The hypothesis advanced in this study is that in addition to its influence on the overall taxation pattern, political instability affects the type of taxes collected. Unstable governments will tend to collect taxes that require less effort on the state's part (i.e., customs taxes), as opposed to income and value-added taxes. Table 1 shows how the Brazilian and Argentine states relied on customs and income taxes. The significant cross-time variation in the patterns of taxation sheds more light on the extractive capacities of the two states. As shown in figures 4 and 5, furthermore, from 1950 on, the Brazilian state increased its reliance on the income tax; it virtually ceased to collect customs taxes after the 1970s. Since the 1950s, the income tax has come to represent more than a quarter of the country's tax revenue (although with the introduction of modern consumption taxes, the VAT became the most important type of tax).

By contrast, the Argentine state abandoned taxing income altogether in the 1980s, choosing instead to rely on customs taxes and, considering the extremely low tax burden, to resort to seigniorage. The Argentine state became increasingly specialized in collecting the easiest types of taxes and the VAT. The revenue collected with VAT, however—

Table 1. Customs and Income Taxes as Percent of Total Revenue, Argentina and Brazil, 1940–1988

	1940	1950	1960	1970	1980	1988
Customs taxes						
Argentina	23.4	5.8	2.8	17.1	9.0	9.1
Brazil	22.3	9.5	11.2	5.0	3.0	1.1
Income taxes						
Argentina	18.8	33.9	19.1	23.0	6.5	12.4
Brazil	9.2	28.4	27.8	24.7	28.6	22.8

Source: Thorp 1998, appendix tables VII.1, VII.2.

approximately 90 percent of total revenue—reached extremely low levels, equivalent to less than 10 percent of GDP, in the 1970s and 1980s. This is remarkable, considering the country's per capita income. Low revenue is also associated with tax amnesties; there were 12 in Argentina between 1970 and 1989. Other recent distortionary taxes that are easy to collect are the debt and credit tax on bank accounts (*impuesto sobre los créditos y débitos en cuentas bancarias*, ICDB) and export withholding (*retenciones*). Both show impressive growth in collection. The ICDB was introduced in 1983 and reintroduced in 1988 and again in 2001. In 2002, it accounted for over 10 percent of total tax revenue (CIPPEC 2002, 60). Similarly, the *retenciones* accounted for over 14 percent of tax revenue (CIPPEC 2002, 71).

The evolution of Brazil's fiscal federalism differed radically from that of Argentina. No revenue-sharing scheme through which the states delegate tax collection to the central government was set up. When taxes on consumption replaced taxes on foreign trade as the main form of taxation, the states did not delegate the power to collect consumption or sales taxes to the center. Instead, they retained important and exclusive tax powers. As elsewhere in Latin America, taxation in Brazil before the 1940s had been restricted to foreign trade, particularly import tariffs, which accounted for about 80 percent of federal tax revenue.

Like those in Argentina, Brazilian federal institutions provided incentives for the redistribution game between provincial elites and the center. Nevertheless, there are significant differences in the incentive structure of both countries. In Brazil, federal interventions occurred only in the first decades of the twentieth century; in Argentina, this became a permanent feature of the political landscape. Despite the malaportionment of the Brazilian Congress, which is comparable to that of Argentina, the federal center has been far less dependent on subnational governments than in Argentina. Presidents and senators are elected by direct vote; governors (or party bosses) do not control candidate selection for the legislature as they do in Argentina.

The Brazilian military proposed and implemented tax reforms in 1965 and 1967, in a sustained process of building the tax state in the country, unlike what occurred in Argentina. The reforms contained innovative aspects and had a strong fiscal impact (Shoup 1990). The reforms also included the revamping of the tax administration institutions and introduced, among other things, mechanisms to limit the Olivera-Tanzi effect (Rosenn 1968). In 1968 the Secretaría da Receita Federal (SRF), which came to represent, along with the Itamaraty and the Central Bank, the most professional sectoral bureaucracy in the country, was set up. The resulting increase in tax revenue was quite substantial. The tax burden as a percentage of GDP doubled in seven years, reaching 26 percent in 1971 (see figure 4). The already large gap in taxation ratios between Brazil and Argentina

Figure 4. Income Tax as Percent of GDP, Brazil and Argentina, 1940–2000

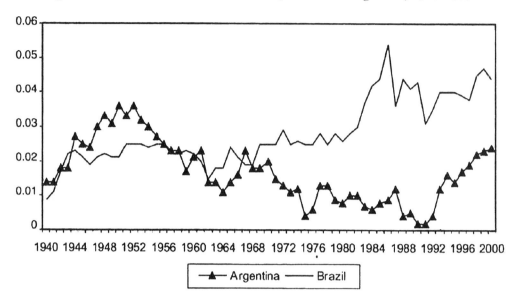

Source: Oxford Latin American History Database.

started to widen from the mid-1960s on. Unlike Argentina, the Brazilian institutions of federalism were more stable, and Brazil's high growth rates with import substitution industrialization helped legitimate state intervention and the deepening of the country's extractive capacity.

Growth does not explain the distinct taxation outcomes between the two countries because the Argentine economy also expanded at a very high rate in the postwar period (Veganzones and Winograd 1997). Growth and tax collection may be correlated. There is indeed some evidence of the relationship between economic growth and tax collection, but the causality is complex and highly conditional on current inflation (because of the Olivera-Tanzi effect). In the short run, the tax burden (tax revenue as a percentage of GDP) may actually increase. In the case of Argentina, several economic historians have argued that the problems of the economy have less to do with growth as such than to volatility (Della Paolera et al. 2003; Prados de la Escosura and Sanz-Villarroya 2004). Between 1947 and the mid-1970s, Argentina was one of the fastest-growing economies in the world; only Japan, Korea, and Brazil grew faster (Spiller and Tommasi 2007). Brazil's data are illuminating in this respect. Before 1976, Brazil's tax revenue grew at a rate twice that of the GDP; but then the two rates stayed approximately the same for two decades. Since then, this pattern has been reversed: tax revenue has been growing much faster than the GDP—more than 5 percent compared to a GDP growth rate of 2.5 percent (Afonso 2004).

With the advent of the SRF, meritocratic recruitment and low turnover marked both the tax and social security administrations at the federal level in Brazil (Kahn et al. 2001; Ferreira 1986). Between 1971, when the agency became fully operational, and 1985, the last year of the military period, the average tenure of the SRF director general was 4.5 years. Under Presidents José Sarney (1985–89) and Fernando Collor de Mello (1990–92), the SRF was politicized and saw its administrative and functional autonomy curtailed (Pires 1998–2000; Maciel 2000). Between 1986 and 1993, the SRF had eight directors

Figure 5. Customs Revenue as Percent of GDP, Brazil and Argentina, 1940–2000

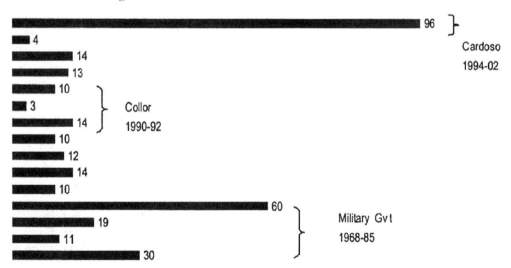

Source: Oxford Latin American History Database.

Figure 6. SRF Directors' Terms, 1968–2002 (months)

Source: Author's calculations of archival data from Secretaria da Receita Federal, Brasilia.

general, and the corresponding average tenure was less than 1 year (see figure 6). President Collor appointed the then-superintendent of the federal police to run the agency, alleging the need to combat corruption—a move that resembled many of Menem's moves. But Collor's impeachment reversed the trend. Throughout the tenure of his successor, Fernando Henrique Cardoso (8 years), the same person headed the SRF. The new Workers' Party administration led by Luiz Inácio Lula da Silva, elected in 2003—which had been the main opposition party during the Cardoso administration—continued the trend in low turnover by promoting the deputy head of the agency, Everardo Maciel, to director.

DEMOCRACY, STABILITY, AND TAX REFORM

The argument defended in this article is that rational rulers will embark on tax reforms only if they anticipate that they themselves will be able to reap the benefits from the reform; that is, the extra revenue generated. This argument is put forth because effective tax administrations are public goods that generate benefits in the medium term, and rulers have an alternative source of short-term funding; namely, inflation. Governments will favor inflation over normal taxation if the time horizon of their political calculus is short. If inflation turns into hyperinflation, however, the revenue losses from the so-called Olivera-Tanzi effect (resulting from the time lag between the tax-generating act and its actual collection), together with the systemic losses caused by hyperinflation, may close the option of inflationary financing.

Argentina's return to democracy was marked by the instability of the political environment. The immediate cause of the transition to democracy was the crisis associated with the military's defeat in the Malvinas War (1982). The government of Raúl Alfonsín (1983–89) also began and ended in the middle of crises. Hyperinflation and social unrest prompted the president to resign six months before the end of his term. Reflecting the instability that characterized his government, tax revenue reached an all-time low in 1989. Morisset and Izquierdo (1993, 6–8) estimate that an additional year of political stability (measured as the number of months between each change of finance minister) would have increased the tax effort by 6 percent for the period 1983–92. During the first years of the Austral Plan, there was some recovery in total tax revenue, 30 percent of which can be accounted for the reversal of the Olivera-Tanzi effect (Morisset and Izquierdo 1993, 4).

Menem's ascent to the presidency took place in circumstances that allowed him an enormous concentration of power. In terms of our main theoretical argument, this was equivalent to a drastic reduction in political uncertainties, because he faced no credible opposition following the debacle of his main rivals. This prompted him to embark on a reform agenda. It was under Menem that further crucial sources of instability—at least in the short term—were eliminated. These included the resistance mounted by the Peronist-controled Senate in a highly polarized environment, the fiscal crisis of the provinces, and hyperinflation. Menem had the support of an ample majority in the Senate and could secure the support of party bosses in the smaller provinces—"low-maintenance provinces"—for his broader reform strategy (Gibson et al. 2004). Subsequently, Menem's political reform involved eliminating the ban on the reelection of presidents, abolishing the Electoral College, and introducing direct election of senators and presidents.

According to the "instability leads governments to inflationary financing" argument, a stable environment would prompt rulers to embark on tax reforms ceteris paribus. The developments under Menem confirm these predictions. It is true that the first years of Menem's term were characterized by instability; the economic team proposed an array of measures in the area of taxation before the constitutional package of 1994, coinciding with the Convertibility Plan enacted in 1991. These measures were emergency responses to hyperinflation, but they also reflect the new administration's longer time horizons. The initial success of the plan proved to be crucial for guaranteeing fiscal and institutional stability, which was essential for Menem's "moderate populism" (Palermo and Novaro 1996).

With a longer time horizon, the Menem government consolidated a comprehensive tax reform initiative that helped to increase the tax share in the short term by 4 percent of GDP. As previously noted, this was the only option left when, in response to hyper-inflation, the Currency Board was introduced in 1991 and the alternative of inflationary financing by the Treasury was blocked. The regime of full convertibility, however, proved to be unsustainable because of increasing fiscal deficit, and it collapsed at the end of the 1990s. Its adoption represented the last step in a dramatic loss of credibility.

Unstable Fiscal Federalism

The key fiscal issue after the transition to civil rule was the collapse of the relatively stable scheme that the military had introduced, which had fixed a set of rules for revenue between the provinces and the federal government (coparticipation). Argentina is an extreme case of vertical fiscal imbalance.[9] The federal government accounts for about 60 percent of provincial spending (Gaggero and Sabaini 2002, 193). Provincial and municipal revenue represent 4.5 percent of GDP and receive coparticipation transfers equivalent to 8 percent of GDP. In Brazil, by contrast, the former raise the equivalent of 9 percent of GDP, and transfers account for 3 percent of GDP (Stein 1998). The Argentine provincial tax on gross receipts, which explores the same base as the national VAT, accounts for only 2 percent of GDP, or 9 percent of national revenue, whereas the Brazilian main state tax (ICMS) accounts for 8 percent of GDP and more than a quarter of total revenue. Under the Ley de coparticipación of the Argentine military government (Law 20.221 of 1973), 50 percent of the revenue was to be allocated to the federal government and 50 percent to be distributed to the provinces (with additional rules for further transfers to municipalities). This revenue-sharing scheme collapsed when the military government fell in 1983.

During the Alfonsín administration, the federal government distributed resources on the basis of bilateral deals with the governors (Tommasi et al. 2001; Eaton 2002). This arrangement degenerated into a system in which governors became predators of the central government. It involved an explicit arrangement for distributing the inflation tax (known as ATNs). It was only after the approval of the new coparticipación law in 1988, with the country on the brink of hyperinflation, that automatic transfers were restored (Nicolini et al. 2002). However, the fiscal crisis of the late 1980s led to a dramatic fiscal crisis at the provincial level, which prompted the government to nationalize the provincial pension systems. For this, the federal government was able to retain 15 percent of the coparticipation revenues but had to make very stringent concessions in the form of fixed transfers (unlike Brazil, where such retentions were simply imposed on the subnational governments. See Alston et al. 2005).

In addition to its impact on the spending side, federalism also contributed to depressing public revenue. Throughout the 1980s, by virtue of their control of the Senate, subnational interests managed to extend further the vast array of existing tax exemptions to encompass subsidies to nontraditional exports and the various regimes of industrial promotion that explicitly favored the small provinces. This was possible because the provinces had the power to decide over several types of tax exemptions from national taxes. These subsidies, which exceeded 6 percent of GDP in the late 1980s, contributed to the progressive paralysis of the tax administration (World Bank 1990, 21–26).

The national tax system was highly fragmented: it included at least 45 taxes, the majority of which were administered by the DGI. Of these, only 12 provided more than 1 percent of total national revenues, while 33 yielded in total less than 10 percent of revenues (approximately less than 2 percent of GDP). The system was extensively hard-wired. Seventeen of the 45 taxes were earmarked, either in part (5) or in full (12), for a variety of special funds (World Bank 1990, 23). Furthermore, the rules of the tax game were extremely volatile. An average of 3.4 "structural laws" were passed between 1973 and 1988; in the years 1976–80, 26 such laws were enacted (World Bank 1990, 36). Alfonsín's most important tax initiative, the December 1988 tax package, which produced the so-called Omnibus Law (Law 23548), was amended so much during the legislative process that it actually helped weaken the tax system rather than strengthen it.

The foundations of the federalist game were the institutions previously described (the coparticipation rules and the indirect election of presidents and senators), which prevailed until 1994. They represented centrifugal forces in the political system, and they were capable of offsetting the centripetal forces associated with the cohesion of Argentina's political parties. Presidents' dependence on state governments was compounded in that the small provinces controlled the Partido Justicialista, which was then overrepresented in the Senate. Governors' control of the local assemblies, in turn, was fostered by electoral legislation, which was based on closed-list proportional representation. The president's agenda and legislative powers were not strong enough to ensure the preponderance of the executive's preferences. Thus, the national government depended on the provinces' political elites for its legislative agenda, while the elites depended on the center for financial viability. This unstable equilibrium was fragile. Under Menem, there were four "federal interventions." Interventions implied change of leadership or withdrawal of fiscal or administrative autonomy.

The country's fiscal crisis was intensified by Argentina's inefficient and extremely narrow tax base, which remained from the import substitution period, and by high rates of tax evasion. In order to raise revenue, the Menem government proposed a tax reform, the centerpiece of which was a new VAT but which also included a reduction in tax brackets, a lowering of top marginal rates, and a simplified system.

Before 1988, the VAT had not been a very important tax. In the early 1990s, an overhaul of the VAT was proposed, which broadened the number of sectors covered and raised the rate. Menem managed to get approval for much of his reform package by engaging in a number of deals—a series of *pactos fiscales*—with provincial legislators, in which he exchanged support for concessions. Menem deployed a successful strategy of sequencing tax reform and tax sharing in such a way that approval of tax base broadening was achieved first, then rates were gradually increased, and only then, tax sharing was negotiated (Eaton 2002, 2006). In the subsequent pacts for provincial reform in the 1990s and under the government of Fernando De la Rúa (1999–2001), the federal government's inability to offer credible commitments led it to offer fixed values for transfers, which proved impossible to honor because of the growing fiscal deficit.

Recurrent government bailouts to provinces in this period further eroded the already poor credibility of fiscal institutions, and no credible commitments could be made by the actors involved to solve the severe coordination problems (Nicolini et al. 2002). The national revenue basis suffered from a "tragedy of commons" problem resulting from the absence of an enforcement mechanism (Tommasi 2002). The fiscal initiatives were marked by great volatility. The solution to the fiscal crisis that was finally adopted was an extreme one: the Convertibility Plan (2001), by which the Central Bank was divested of its capacity to finance the Treasury. By establishing a currency board arrangement, the Convertibility Law of March 1991 ended inflationary Central Bank financing of public sector deficits. Before this period, the federal government was able to accommodate the expansion in provincial expenditures through inflationary financing, but as of 1991 it could not. This radical enforcement mechanism, which solved the problem, proved to be unsustainable as well.

Menem's Tax Reform

The new government's response to the degradation of the tax system was initially proposed during Menem's honeymoon with Congress, as a result of the hyperinflationary crisis and general emergency in the country (inflation reached 112 percent for June 1989 alone). The reform focused on raising revenue in the short run and on the administrative aspects of tax collection (Morisset and Izquierdo 1993; see also Berensztein 1995; FIEL 1998, chap. 13). Some of the most important innovations included the increase in VAT rate and the extension of its coverage (the potential VAT base increased by more than 40 percent, from 52 percent of GDP to almost 80 percent). Other measures taken were the introduction and strict enforcement of a unified taxpayers' registration code, the simplification of many tax returns, the legislation of new penal statutes to prosecute tax evasion, massive computerization of all tax procedures and information, and the addition of more than one hundred thousand new names to a category of closely monitored major taxpayers (Morisset and Izquierdo 1993; Bergman 2003, 603). It should be noted that many of these measures had been contemplated in technical documents during the Alfonsín government (Silvani 1987; World Bank 1990). Only when the incentive structure changed as a result of the inauguration of Menem, however, were they implemented.

Before Menem, governments had resorted primarily to inflation tax as a source of funding. Figure 3 and table 2 show that in the 1970s and 1980s in Argentina, inflation tax measured as a percentage of GDP was consistently higher than in Brazil. Throughout this period, this share was at least equivalent to twice that observed in Brazil. It was only during Menem's administration that a number of important initiatives for revamping the tax system took place (of which, however, a significant number failed). In the words of one of the world's most prominent tax scholars, Richard Bird,

> In 1989 matters worsened steadily, so much so that when the Menem government unexpectedly came to power, the situation appeared to have become serious enough that even the longstanding preference of Argentines for paying "inflation taxes" rather than normal taxes seemed to have weakened enough to permit real tax reform. (Bird 1992, 20)

Table 2. Inflation Tax in Brazil and Argentina, 1963–1987

	1963–1973	1973–1978	1978–1983	1983–1987
Brazil				
Inflation rate	34.5	36.2	96.2	199.7
Inflation revenue as percent of GDP	5.20	4.42	6.66	8.24
Argentina				
Inflation rate	30.3	200.1	174.7	380.1
Inflation revenue as percent of GDP	—	25.03	12.04	22.0

Source: Edwards and Tabellini 1990, appendix table 1.

Figure 7. Productivity of VAT and Income Tax in Brazil and Argentina

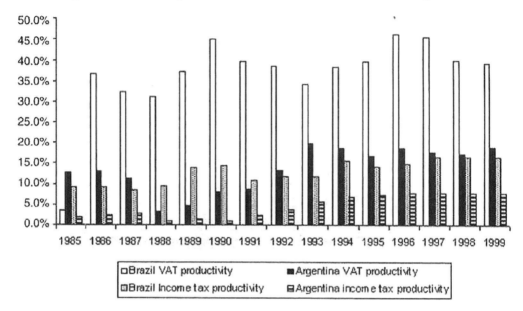

Sources: IMF financial statistics; Lora 2001, 42.

According to Lora's (2001) indicator of tax reform initiatives, Brazil's average score in the late 1980s was 0.37, and Argentina's corresponding score was 0.28. In the late 1990s, the gap widened: Brazil's score (0.52) was 71 percent greater than Argentina's (0.30).[10] In the first years of the Menem administration, the score rose from 0.20 to 0.37. It is important to note that these measures took place when Menem managed to stabilize the currency and started to negotiate the reelection amendment, thereby reducing the level of instability in the country. Significant changes occurred in the length of tenure of DGI's directors in this period. Menem appointed a former IMF director to head the agency (which in 1997 was fused with the social security tax office to form the AFIP). This director remained in his post for 44 months (figure 2). Menem's strategy can be explained by a combination of fiscal pressures and the constraints posed by the end of inflationary financing. His continued support to the agency, however, has to be understood in the context of his long-term strategy.

Tax administration was an area in which high volatility combined with dramatic measures had proved a short-term remedy for chronic problems. Although tax administration was historically characterized by weak deterrence and compliance capacity, at the end of the 1980s the situation became much worse.[11] The tax system was characterized by multiple tax rates for different activities, constant changes in the tax base, and the provision of tax credits that were rarely inspected. Argentina's VAT productivity in the 1980s was almost four times lower than Brazil's (see figure 7). Collection rates were much lower than the statutory rates due to the exclusion of many final goods and services from the tax bases and severe problems of administration and oversight. The problems affecting this area were further exacerbated as a result of the high turnover of top management and increased politicization in the 1980s.

Menem's comprehensive program to modernize the tax system, which included the revamping of the DGI in 1992, included a series of highly publicized populist measures to control corruption and tax evasion.[12] Yet this effort was short-lived (Bergman 2003, 603–4). As the unsustainability of the Convertibility Plan became apparent following the Tequila Crisis in 1994–95 and Cavallo's departure from the economic team, the government began to resort to tax handles and "easy" taxes, including ICDB and retenciones (see Gaggero and Sabaini 2002). The revenue from the VAT, which came to represent about 50 percent of total revenue in the mid-1990s, started to decline following the economic slowdown (Gaggero and Grasso 2005; Gaggero and Sabaini 2002, 92–93), and finally collapsed in 2000. The instability in tax administration continued during De la Rúa's administration. It is ironic that on his last day in office, De la Rue introduced changes in tax legislation. But overall, the performance of the system had improved during the 1990s.[13]

If the institutional changes implemented by Menem were prima facie enough to modify the initial (historical) conditions so as to initiate a process of tax reform, why was the effort short-lived? The answer may be divided into two parts. The first is the subjective incentives for initiating reform. The second is the objective reasons for failure.

It seems that the short-term incentives for reform came primarily from the hyperinflation crisis and from Menem's lack of significant opposition following the Radicales' debacle in office. Gradually, other incentives came to the fore, as a result of the elimination of a few sources of instability, particularly some of the institutional ones and the short-term success of the plan to combat hyperinflation. The reasons it was short-lived are distinct: the Convertibility Plan was too rigid as a measure to combat instability, and this rigidity was introduced to the detriment of adaptability (Spiller and Tommasi 2007).

Other sources of instability also played a role here. The conditions that determine reform initiation are not the same as those that explain reform failure or success. It is too early to reach broader conclusions regarding recent success in tax policy. Recent events indeed suggest path dependency, because preference polarization seems to have changed little, and many sources of instability continue. While some of Menem's arbitrary moves toward centralization of power—expanding the Corte Suprema and packing it with loyal members, intervening in the Tribunal de Cuentas and in the Fiscalia General—enhanced his ability to pass a reform agenda and ensure fiscal stability in the short run, they contributed to fueling political instability in the medium and long run. However, an important change occurred. In the context of financial globalization, inflation is no longer an option; and this may have long-term consequences, such as the recurrent use of opportunistic taxes.

The case of Argentina shows how political instability affects the strategic choices of governments for the tax system. It provides empirical backing for the central argument of this study. Systematically, governments "pass the buck" to future governments (Della Paolera et al. 2003). It also underscores how this combined with the difficulties in establishing a stable framework for intertemporal political transactions in the relations between the provinces and the federal government.

Again, the contrast with Brazil sheds light on the theoretical argument developed here. The Brazilian state faced a serious fiscal crisis in the 1980s, but it had a much better institutional and extractive capacity than did Argentina. Brazil had a highly trained federal tax administration and had managed to expand its tax base significantly with the tax reforms implemented by the military governments (figure 4). The return to democracy brought important changes to the fiscal landscape, particularly in terms of the structures of fiscal federalism in the two countries. After the transition to democracy in 1985, Brazil also experienced important institutional change, embodied in the Constitution of 1988. The most important effect of the new charter was a dramatic expansion in entitlement to social security and social assistance. Both the types and value of social benefits and transfers were extended significantly. In addition, Brazil granted civil servant status to about 250,000 federal employees, thereby creating a flow of future pension commitments at much higher levels than before. Furthermore, the constitution mandated the fiscal decentralization of the country by increasing the shares of municipalities and states in the total revenue. In addition to more resources, it allowed the states to set varying VAT rates. In a soft budget constraint, this produced a situation in which the states could engage in fiscal wars, thereby reducing total tax revenue.

As argued by Alston et al. (2004), the fiscal game in the 1990s reflected, to a great extent, the reactions of the federal government to this state of affairs. The federal government also reacted to the new fiscal federalism by resorting to a two-pronged strategy. The first step was to raise nonshared taxes (the so-called social contributions; a significant portion of the 10 percent increase in the tax-GDP ratio between 1992 and 2002 is due to rises in their rates). As in Argentina, this explains why these highly distortionary forms of taxation came to represent half the federal tax revenue. Social contributions are cascading taxes, which in many cases exploit similar tax bases.

The rigidity imposed by the Brazilian Constitution has caused the federal government to resort to an increasingly inefficient tax system. It should be stressed, however, that the institutions of fiscal federalism in Brazil do not lead to the extreme common pool problems found in Argentina. The second part of the strategy required changes in the constitution; it required withholding funds mandated for distribution to subnational governments. These changes were successful attempts by the executive to respond to the state of affairs created by the constitution and to rigidities associated with independent causal factors. Such an approach has also been taken in Argentina, but in Brazil it has involved major concessions by the federal executive.

Governors are powerful because the Brazilian Constitution vests the states with substantial tax powers. Brazil's version of VAT, the ICMS, is collected by the states and represents the single most important tax in the country. It accounts for one quarter of all the country's tax revenue. In addition, the institutional source of the states' power has to do with the states' prerogative to own banks and public enterprises. Although the pattern of negotiation between the federal government and governors presents some similarities (Treisman 2004; Eaton and Dickovick 2004), particularly the use of incentives for reforms, nothing like the succession of pactos fiscales in 1992, 1993, 1999, and 2000 and the concessions involved in Argentina has occurred in Brazil. The federal government was able to impose the privatization of state banks and public enterprises (thereby dramatically diminishing the power of governors) because of the fiscal problems facing the states following monetary stabilization.

The *Plano Real* brought inflation to zero and therefore represented an exogenous shock that undermined the states' ability to resist the federal executive's preferences. The federal government implemented a program aimed at renegotiating state debt. This included debt swap at favorable rates, which was linked to a number of conditions. Before 1994, several incentives in Brazilian fiscal federalism had encouraged states to behave fiscally irresponsibly. These can be seen in the history of opportunistic behavior by the states and associated federal bailouts. Although the institutions of federalism clearly served as important constraints and governors played an important role, the national executive, throughout most of the last decade, managed to get its agenda implemented by recentralizing the political game. This included passing legislation that adversely affected state governors (including the Fiscal Responsibility Law of 2000) and introducing measures that have led to a political recentralization of the country.

Although Cardoso did not pass a comprehensive tax reform, his government revamped small business regulations (the SIMPLES scheme, the Brazilian equivalent of the Argentine *monotributo*) and corporate taxation and implemented measures to close many loopholes in transfer pricing. Unlike Argentina, and in line with international trends, the government lowered (with oscillations) top personal marginal tax rates from 60 percent in 1985 to 50 percent in 1987, 25 percent in 1989, 35 percent in 1995, 25 percent in 1997, and 27.5 percent in 1999. For business, the corresponding rates were reduced from 40 percent in 1985 to 30 percent in 1990 and 25 percent in 1995. In addition, changes were introduced to broaden the tax base. VAT rates, in turn, rose marginally in the period 1985–95, but because of good tax management, VAT productivity was the highest in Latin America. However, not everything is rosy. Many distortionary tax handles have been introduced, such as taxes on financial transactions, but on a much smaller scale than in Argentina.

CONCLUSIONS

This article has discussed rival explanations for the puzzlingly low extractive capacity of the Argentine state. These explanations can be found in a host of large-N comparative studies but also in small-N analyses. Economic, cultural, and political regimes, elites' perceptions, corruption, and the definition of national political community have provided limited explanatory power for the underlying causes of this low extractive capacity.

The key finding of this analysis is that political instability and weak institutions (i.e., institutions that do not guarantee intertemporal political transactions, such those governing province-federal government relations) are ultimately the main explanatory factors. Preference polarization is a key factor fueling instability. It is not argued here that political instability produces unilaterally low taxation. In large-N comparisons, it would be necessary to control for the other variables that have proved to influence taxation levels. By examining these variables and investigating their applicability to the Argentine case and, where appropriate, the Brazilian case, this study has controlled for their explanatory power. A conclusive large-N validation is not feasible for this hypothesis because of data unavailability over the long run across a significant number of countries.

Instability in this study was examined through the lens of transaction costs politics. Instability is conceptualized as an outcome of strategic situations in which no commitment technology is available to guarantee intertemporal political transactions. It is argued that the incentives governments face to build state capacity are shaped in crucial ways by the level of instability in the political environment. In the area of taxation, political instability greatly influences the choices governments make about the instruments for extracting resources from society. In unstable environments, governments choose to extract resources from an inflation tax rather than by using normal taxation mechanisms. Because their time horizons are shortened, they are discouraged from building administrative capacities that yield long-term benefits that can be appropriated as public goods. Conversely, if the level of instability is low, governments have an incentive to modernize the tax administration and not to resort to inflationary financing, which causes long-term fiscal problems but short-term benefits. Political polarization also plays a key role because it reduces the space for accommodation, exacerbating the problems of instability. Thus instability and preference polarization reinforce each other.

The developments since Argentina's return to democracy seem to confirm the predictions of the argument. Menem faced no significant political uncertainties because Alfonsín's administration had failed, and therefore Menem had a long political horizon. As expected, this prospect, along with hyperinflation, prompted him to propose a comprehensive tax reform. When some of the sources of instability were removed by the Convertibility Plan and Menem's constitutional amendments (allowing for the reelection of presidents and calling for the direct election of presidents and senators), the reform could be consolidated. The amendments eliminated some of the sources of instability; and so did the convertibility regime, because it precluded inflation financing. However, the fiscal instability caused by recurrent provincial default has led the country back on an unstable track. The short-term stability was misleading, considering the systemic consequences of Menem's undercutting of Argentina's check-and-balance institutions.

In Latin America over roughly the last decade, governments have managed to keep inflation under control. The era of high inflation has come to an end (Treisman 2004). A key factor leading to this development is globalization. Unlike the 1950s and 1960s, international markets today promptly punish deviant behavior—sometimes overnight—producing pressures for immediate government intervention. Inflationary financing in this new context has become a nonoption. The trade-offs between taxation and inflation seem therefore to be a thing of the past. If this plausible argument is accepted, it follows that the hypothesis advanced in this article is applicable only to the postwar period. Other distortionary mechanisms of revenue extraction seem to be replacing ordinary taxation (for example, the boom in current account taxes). But the logic governing government's behavior has not changed: unstable governments would have more incentives to use such mechanisms than rulers in secure institutional environments.

NOTES

I thank the three reviewers for *Latin American Politics and Society* for suggestions and criticisms. I am grateful to many colleagues who also provided useful comments or suggestions: Lee Alston, Andrés Gallo, Mariano Tommasi, Tulia Faletti, Eduardo Lora, Alejandra Irigoin, Catalina Smulovitz, Oscar Oszlak, Mick Moore, Deborah Brautigam, and Odd-Helge Fjeldstad. Special thanks to Valeria Serafinoff for assistance during fieldwork and suggestions. Any errors or omissions are my own.

1 "Tax handles"—sectors that are by their very nature easier to tax, such as foreign trade or mineral resources—combined with other variables are also good predictors of tax burden (Teera and Hudson 2004; Piancastelli 2001; Tanzi 1992; Bird et al. 2004).

2 Torgler finds that the subjective perception of being caught is not statistically significant, whereas trust in the president is (see also Bird et al. 2004). However, the available data from the World Values Survey for Argentina and Brazil are very similar, 2.2 and 2.1 respectively, on a scale of 1 to 3. In the Latinobarómetro data set, in the period 1990–93, the tax morale indicator was higher for Argentina than for Brazil, and the gap increased between 1995 and 1997.

3 In 1990 it was 14.4 percent in Brazil, compared to 1 percent in Argentina, and it was at least twice as high in Brazil throughout the 1990s (Lora 2001).

4 This argument may help to explain a regional pattern. Indeed, Latin America is noted for its historical pattern of low taxation of income and assets, which some authors put forward as the basic cause of inequality in the region (Sokoloff and Zolt 2007).

5 In Argentina, the income tax/GDP ratio oscillated between 2.5 percent and 3 percent between 1946 and 1960, when it started to decline monotonically to reach the postwar lowest levels of 0.06 percent, in 1976, and 0.04, in 1991. In Brazil it stabilized between 2 percent and 2.5 percent between 1942 and 1982, then climbed to 5 percent in 2000 (see figure 4). There is therefore a fairly significant unexplained variation between the two countries.

6 Brazil ranks favorably in relation to Argentina in available ranks of perceived corruption. In the Transparency International Corruption Perception Index (CPI) of 1998 and 2004, Brazil ranked 36th and 59th, respectively, and Argentina ranked 42nd and 103rd. However, the most important caveat regarding corruption as an explanatory factor is that the divergence between the two countries began in the early 1960s. It is implausible and impossible to establish that Argentina has become increasingly corrupt since the 1960s and that Brazil has remained less corrupt or with similar levels of corruption over the same period. Explanations based on culture, which itself is supposed to change very gradually and over several generations, cannot account for divergence between decades.

7 When the last coparticipation law expired in 1983, it created an institutional vacuum that culminated in a crisis; more on this episode later.

8 Indeed, in the 1960s, members of the agency staff were trained in the United States, and participated in the Harvard International Tax Program. One of these was the agency's CPN (contador público nacional, certified public accountant), Oscar Oszlak, one of the country's premier political scientists (Oszlak 2004–2005).

9 The vertical imbalance is measured as the ratio of intergovernmental transfers from central government, including tax sharing, to total revenues (own plus transferred) of the subnational level. The problems associated with this are the result of tax assignment, of the incentives resulting from tax assignment and the overall federal fiscal game, and of the tax-raising efforts that provincial and national authorities exercise, given those incentives (Tommasi 2002, 8).

10 This score is normalized from zero to 1. It was built as an additive index of several dimensions, including reduction of top individual and corporate marginal rates, measures to broaden the tax base, and elimination of exemptions. It is interesting to note that Argentina's performance in other areas of market reform (privatization) was not bad (Etchmendy 2001).

11 According to a World Bank report, "The degradation of DGI as an institution has paralleled that of the erosion of the tax system. This degradation has simultaneously been the cause and effect of the vicious circle of poor legislation and poor administration that has brought about the collapse of the tax system" (World Bank 1990, 53).

12 One such measure was the requirement that any financial transaction in excess of ten thousand pesos had to made by check. Another was a tax on assets such as yachts (impuesto docente) (see Gaggero and Sabaini 2002).

13 Tax evasion declined between 1989 and 1999 from 66 percent to 32 percent (Gaggero and Sabaini 2002, 135).

REFERENCES

Acemoglu, Daron, Simon Johnson, James Robinson, and Yunyong Thaicharoen. 2003. Institutional Causes, Macroeconomic Symptoms: Volatility, Crises and Growth. *Journal of Monetary Economics* 50: 49–123.

Afonso, José Roberto. 2004. *Brasil: um caso a parte*. Paper presented at the 16th International Seminar on Fiscal Policy, Economic Commission for Latin America, Santiago, January 24–25.

Alston, Lee. 1996. Empirical Works in Institutional Economics: An Overview. In *Empirical Studies in Institutional Change*, ed. Alston, T. Eggertsson, and Douglas C. North. Cambridge: Cambridge University Press. 25–30.

Alston, Lee, Marcus Melo, Bernardo Mueller, and Carlos Pereira. 2004. *Political Institutions, Policy Making Processes, and Policy Outcomes in Brazil*. Washington, DC: Inter-American Development Bank.

———. 2005. *Who Decides On Public Expenditures: The Political Economy of the Budgetary Process in Brazil. Economic and Social Studies Series*, RE1-05-006. Washington, DC: Inter-American Development Bank.

Berensztein, Sergio. 1995. *Rebuilding State Capacities in Contemporary Latin America: The Politics of Taxation in Argentina and Mexico*. Working Paper no. 48. Buenos Aires: Universidad Torcuato Di Tella.

Bergman, Marcelo. 2003. Tax Reforms and Tax Compliance: The Divergent Paths of Chile and Argentina. *Journal of Latin American Studies* 35, 3: 593–624.

Bird, Richard. 1992. Tax Reform in Latin America: A Review of Some Recent Experience. *Latin American Research Review* 27, 1: 7–36.

Bird, Richard, J. Martinez-Vasquez, and Benno Torgler. 2004. *Societal Institutions and Tax Effort in Developing Countries*. ITP paper 04011. International Tax Program, University of Toronto.

Centro de Implementación de Políticas Públicas para la Equidad y el Crescimiento (CIPPEC). 2002. *Hacia un sistema tributario permanente para la Argentina*. Informe final. Buenos Aires: CIPPEC.

Cheibub, José Antônio. 1998. Political Regimes and the Extractive Capacity of Governments: Taxation in Democracies and Dictatorships. *World Politics* 50: 349–76.

Cukierman, Alex, Sebastian Edwards, and Guido Tabellini. 1989. *Seignoriage and Political Instability.* NBER Working Paper 3199. Cambridge, MA: National Bureau for Economic Research.

Cysne, Rubens Penha, and Paulo C. Lisboa. 2004. *mposto inflacionário e transferências inflacionárias no Brasil, 1947–2003.* Working Paper 539. São Paulo: Department of Economics, Getúlio Vargas Foundation.

Della Paolera, Gerardo, Alejandra Irigoin, and Carlos G. Bozzoli. 2003. Passing the Buck: Monetary and Fiscal Policies. In *Understanding Argentina: Essays on the New Economic History*, ed. Della Paolera and Bozzoli. Cambridge: Cambridge University Press. 28–68.

Dixit, Avinash. 1996. *The Making of Economic Policy: A Transaction Cost Politics Perspective.* Cambridge: MIT Press.

Eaton, Kent. 2001. Decentralization, Democratization and Liberalization: The History of Argentine Revenue Sharing, 1934–1999. *Journal of Latin American Studies* 33, 1: 1–28.

———. 2002. Fiscal Policy-Making in the Argentine Legislature. In *Legislative Politics in Latin America*, ed. Scott Morgenstern and Benito Nacif. Cambridge: Cambridge University Press. 287–313.

———. 2006. Menem and the Governors: Intergovernmental Relations in the 1990s. In Levitsky and Murillo 2006. 88–114.

Eaton, Kent, and J. Tyler Dickovick. 2004. The Politics of Re-Centralization in Argentina and Brazil. *Latin American Research Review* 39, 1: 90–122.

Edwards, Sebastián, and Guido Tabellini. 1990. *Explaining Fiscal Policies and Inflation in Developing Countries.* NBER Working Paper 3493. Cambridge, MA: National Bureau for Economic Research.

———. 1991. *Political Instability, Political Weakness, and Inflation: An Empirical Analysis.* Cambridge: NBER Working Paper 3721. Cambridge, MA: National Bureau for Economic Research.

Evans, Peter, and James E. Rauch. 1999. Bureaucracy and Growth: A Cross-National Analysis of the Effects of "Weberian" State Structures on Economic Growth. *American Sociological Review* 64: 748–65.

Faletti, Tulia. 2001. *Antecedentes históricos del proceso de centralización y escenario político institucional de la descentralización en Argentina.* Mimeograph. Washington, DC: Woodrow Wilson Center for Scholars.

Fausto, Boris, and Fernando J. Devoto. 2004. *Brasil e Argentina: um ensaio de historia comparada (1850–2002).* São Paulo: Editora 34.

Ferreira, Benedito. 1986. *História da tributação no Brasil: causas e efeitos.* Brasilia: Bazar do Livro.

FIEL (Fundación de Investigaciones Económicas Latinoamericanas). 1998. *La reforma tributaria en Argentina.* Buenos Aires: FIEL.

Filipov, Michael, Peter Ordershook, and Olga Shvetsova. 2004. *Designing Federalism: A Theory of Self-Sustainable Federal Institutions.* Cambridge: Cambridge University Press.

Gaggero, Jorge, and Federico Grasso. 2005. *La cuestión tributaria en Argentina. La historia, los desafíos del presente y una propuesta de reforma.* Documento de Trabajo no. 5. Buenos Aires: Centro de Economía y Finanzas para el Desarrollo de la Argentina.

Gaggero, Jorge, and J. C. Gómez Sabaini. 2002. *Cuestiones macrofiscales y reforma tributaria.* Buenos Aires: Fundación Osde/CIEPP.

Gallo, Andrés, and Lee Alston. 2004. *The Erosion of Rule of Law on Argentina, 1930–1947: An Explanation of Argentina's Economic Slide from the Top 10.* Mimeograph. University of Colorado.

Geddes, Barbara. 1990. Building State Autonomy in Brazil, 1930–1970. *Comparative Politics* 22, 2: 217–35.

———. 1994. *Politician's Dilemma: Building State Capacity in Latin America.* Berkeley: University of California Press.

Gibson, Edward, Ernesto Calvo, and Tulia Faletti. 2004. Reallocative Federalism: Legislative Overrepresentation and Public Spending in the Western Hemisphere. In *Federalism and Democracy in Latin America*, ed. Gibson. Baltimore: Johns Hopkins University Press.

Gibson, Edward, and Tulia Faletti. 2004. Unity by the Stick: Regional Conflict and the Origins of Argentine Federalism. In *Federalism and Democracy in Latin America*, ed. Gibson. Baltimore: Johns Hopkins University Press.

Gould, Andrew C., and Peter J. Baker. 2002. Democracy and Taxation. *Annual Review of Political Science* 5: 87–110.

Iaryczower, Matias, Sebastian Saiegh, and Mariano Tommasi. 1999. *Coming Together: The Industrial Organization of Federalism*. Working Paper 30. Buenos Aires: Centro de Estudios para el Desarrollo Institucional, Fundación Gobierno y Sociedad.

International Monetary Fund (IMF). International Financial Statistics. <www.imf.org> Accessed November 2005.

Jones, Mark P., and Wonjae Hwang. 2006. Party Bosses: Keystone of the Argentine Congress. In Levitsky and Murillo 2006a. 115–38.

Kahn, Charles M., Emilson Silva, and James Zyliack. 2001. Performance Based Wages in Tax Collection: The Brazilian Tax Collection Reform and Its Effects. *Economic Journal* 111: 188–205.

Kaldor, Nicholas. 1963. Will Underdeveloped Countries Learn to Tax? *Foreign Affairs* 41: 410–19.

Levi, Margaret. 1989. *Of Rule and Revenue*. Berkeley: University of California Press.

Levitsky, Steven, and Maria Victoria Murillo. 2006a. *Argentine Democracy: The Politics of Institutional Weakness*. University Park: Penn State University Press.

——. 2006b. Building Castles in the Sand? The Politics of Institutional Weakness in Argentina. In Levitsky and Murillo 2006a. 21–44.

Lieberman, Evan. 2003. *Race and Regionalism in the Politics of Taxation in Brazil and South Africa*. Cambridge: Cambridge University Press.

——. 2005. Nested Analysis as a Mixed-Method Strategy for Comparative Research. *American Political Science Review* 99, 3: 435–52.

Lijphart, Arend. 1975. The Comparable-Cases Strategy in Comparative Research. *Comparative Political Studies* 8: 158–77.

Lora, Eduardo. 2001. *Structural Reforms in Latin America: What Has Been Reformed and How to Measure It*. Working Paper no. 466. Washington, DC: Inter-American Development Bank.

Maciel, Everardo. 2000. Former director, Secretaria da Receita Federal (1994–2002). Author interviews. Brasília, various dates.

Mahon, James. 2004. Causes of Tax Reform in Latin America. *Latin American Research Review* 39, 1: 3–30.

Morisset, Jacques, and Alejandro Izquierdo. 1993. Effects of Tax Reforms on Argentina's Revenues. Policy Research Working Paper 1192. Washington, DC: World Bank.

Muni, Cecilia. 2003. *Determinantes políticos del desempeño fiscal para las provincias Argentinas*. Buenos Aires: Universidad Nacional de la Plata.

Nicolini, Juan. P., Josefina Posadas, Juan Sanguinetti, Pablo Sanguinetti, and Mariano Tommasi. 2002. *Decentralization, Fiscal Discipline in Subnational Governments, and the Bailout Problem: The Case of Argentina*. Washington, DC: Inter-American Development Bank.

Oszlak, Oscar. 2004–2005. Former Tax Auditor (1962–67), Dirección General Impositiva. Author interviews. Buenos Aires, various dates.

Oxford Latin American History Database. <oxlad.qeh.ox.ac.uk> Accessed November 2005.

Palermo, Vicente, and Marcos Novaro. 1996. *Política y poder en el gobierno de Menem*. Buenos Aires: Norma.

Persson, Torsten, and Guido Tabellini. 2003. *The Economic Effects of Constitutions*. Cambridge: MIT Press.

Piancastelli, Marcelo. 2001. *Measuring the Tax Effort of Developed and Developing Countries: Cross-Country Panel Data Analysis, 1985–1995*. Texto para Discussão 808. Brasília: Instituto de Pesquisa Econômica Aplicada.

Pires, Osires. 1998–2000. Former director (1993), Secretaria da Receita Federal. Author interviews. Brasília, various dates.

Porto, Alberto. 2003. *Etapas de la co-participación federal de impuestos*. Documento de Federalismo Fiscal no. 2. Buenos Aires: Universidad Nacional de la Plata.

Prados de la Escosura, Leandro, and Isabel Sanz-Villarroya. 2004. Institutional Instability and Growth in Argentina: A Long-Run View. Working Paper no. 04–67, *Economic History and Institutions series* 05. Madrid: Carlos III University.

Rodden, Jonathan. 2003. Reviving Leviathan: Fiscal Federalism and the Growth of Government. *International Organization* 57 (Fall): 695–729.

Rosenn, Keith. 1968. Adaptations of the Brazilian Income Tax to Inflation. *Stanford Law Review* 21, 1: 55–108.

Saiegh, Sebastian, and Mariano Tommasi. 1998. *Argentina's Federal Fiscal Institutions: A Case Study in the Transaction-Cost Theory of Politics.* Paper presented at the Modernization and Institutional Development in Argentina conference, United Nations Development Program. Buenos Aires, May.

Schenone, Osvaldo H. 1990. The VAT in Argentina. In *Value Added Taxation in Developing Countries*, ed. Malcolm Gillis, Carl S. Shoup, and Gerardo P. Sicat. Washington, DC: World Bank. 115–20.

Secretaría de Hacienda. 2004. *Sector público argentino no financiero: cuenta ahorro-inversión-financiamiento, 1961–2003.* Buenos Aires: Oficina Nacional de Presupuesto.

Shoup, Carl S. 1990. Choosing Among Types of VATS. In *Value Added Taxation in Developing Countries*, ed. Malcolm Gillis, Shoup, and Gerardo P. Sicat. Washington, DC: World Bank. 3–115.

Sikkink, Kathryn. 1991. *Ideas and Institutions: Developmentalism In Brazil and Argentina.* Ithaca: Cornell University Press.

Silvani, Carlos A. 1987. *Administración tributaria argentina: lineamientos generales para su estructura organizativa.* Washington, DC: International Monetary Fund.

Sokoloff, Kenneth, and Eric M. Zolt. 2007. Inequality and the Evolution of Institutions of Taxation in the Americas. In *New Perspectives on Latin American Economic History*, ed. Sebastian Edwards, Gerardo Esquivel, and Graciela Marquez. Chicago: University of Chicago Press. 83–138.

Spiller, Pablo, and Mariano Tommasi. 2003. The Institutional Foundations of Public Policy: A Transactions Approach with Application to Argentina. *Journal of Law, Economics and Organization* 19, 2: 291–306.

———. 2007. *The Institutional Determinants of Public Policy in Argentina: A Transaction Costs Approach.* New York: Cambridge University Press.

Stein, Ernesto. 1998. Fiscal Decentralization and Government Size in Latin America. In *Democracy, Decentralization and Deficits in Latin America*, ed. Kiichiro Fukasaku and Ricardo Haussman. Paris: OECD. 95–120.

Stein, Ernesto, and Mariano Tommasi. 2005. *Democratic Institutions, Policy-Making Powers, and the Quality of Policies in Latin America.* Washington, DC: Inter-American Development Bank.

Steinmo, Sven. 1993. *Taxation and Democracy: Swedish, British, and American Approaches to Financing the Modern State.* New Haven: Yale University Press.

Taliercio, Robert. 2004. Administrative Reform as Credible Commitment: The Impact of Autonomy on Revenue Authority Performance in Latin America. *World Development* 32 (February): 213–32.

Tanzi, Víctor. 1992. Structural Factors and Tax Revenue in Developing Countries: A Decade of Evidence. In *Open Economies: Structural Adjustment and Agriculture*, ed. Ian Goldin and Alan L. Winters. Cambridge: Cambridge University Press. 267–81.

Teera, Joweria M., and John Hudson. 2004. Tax Performance: A Comparative Study. *Journal of International Development* 16, 6: 785–802.

Thorp, Rosemary. 1998. *Progress, Poverty and Exclusion: An Economic History of Latin America in the 20th Century.* Baltimore: Johns Hopkins University Press.

Tommasi, Mariano. 2002. *Federalism and the Reforms of the 1990s.* Buenos Aires: University of San Andres.

Tommasi, Mariano, Sebastian Saiegh, and Pablo Sanguinetti. 2001. Fiscal Federalism in Argentina: Policies, Politics and Institutional Reform. *Journal of the Latin American and Caribbean Economic Association* 1, 2: 157–211.

Torgler, Benno. 2003. Tax Morale in Latin America. Paper presented at the Third International Research Conference on Responsive Regulation: International Perspectives on Taxation, Canberra, July 24–25.

Treisman, Daniel 2004. Stabilization Tactics in Latin America: Menem, Cardoso, and the Politics of Low Inflation. *Comparative Politics* 36, 4: 399–420.

Veganzones, Marie-Ange, and Carlos Winograd. 1997. *Argentina in the 20th Century: An Account of Long-Awaited Growth.* Paris: OECD.

World Bank. 1990. *Argentina: Tax Policy for Stabilization and Economic Recovery.* Washington, DC: World Bank.

Chapter 14

U.S. Power and the Politics of Economic Governance in the Americas

Nicola Phillips

A central dimension of the hemispheric project in the Americas during the 1990s and the first part of the 2000s was the construction of a regional economic regime, encapsulated primarily in the putative Free Trade Area of the Americas (FTAA) and defined in that context by a complex interaction of multilateral, hemispheric, subregional, and bilateral processes. From the time of the initiation of the negotiations in 1994, its construction remained tentative, its likely shape highly uncertain, and the process of its negotiation politically fraught. Indeed, the project for a comprehensive and encompassing FTAA gave way in late 2003 to an accelerating proliferation of bilateral trade negotiations as the primary avenue toward the realization of a trade and investment regime in the region, and by the end of the decade the relationship of these bilateral processes to subregional projects and the multilateral trade agenda was still taking shape. Yet in essence, whether pursued via the hemispheric or the bilateral route, the regional economic project aims to call forth a set of trade and investment structures as the cornerstone of a broader process of hemispheric cooperation, underpinned by the Summits of the Americas. That project, moreover, must be understood as aiming to foster the articulation of a system of economic governance in the Americas and the entrenchment of a particular approach to the governance of regional economic activity.

Understood in this way, the project alerts us immediately to the very specific nature of economic governance in the Americas. In the European Union, the principal laboratory and reference point for academic debates about regional economic governance, issues of economic "governance" are usually taken to refer to questions of supranational institutionalization, regional-level regulation, and the forms of "multilevel governance" that involve a significant degree of "decisional reallocation" to supranational and subnational governance structures (Hooghe and Marks 2001). The economic project in the Americas invites a rather different conceptualization of economic governance. It is not of a sort that envisages the construction of genuinely regional-level regulatory structures, or of supranational regulatory bodies comparable to those that are emerging, slowly and often contentiously, in the European arena. The challenges of economic governance in the Americas are also substantially different from those encountered in the EU, given that the scope and depth of integration in the latter, both projected and actual, significantly exceed those of the FTAA process or the Americas project more broadly conceived. The challenges of governance in the Americas relate instead to the construction of a regime of rules, associated at the most basic level with the negotiation and enforcement of the myriad dimensions of trade and investment agreements, and, furthermore, with the construction of appropriate institutional mechanisms for the governance of a regional economic regime of this nature.

They are also associated with the negotiation of the broader shape of the economic regime and the ways the various parts of the region will be gathered together within it. In this respect, the core governance challenges stem primarily from the huge diversity among the states and subregions in the Americas, the extent of which is unique among the regions of the world. Indeed, statistical calculations reveal that the differences in size and levels of development among the 34 countries participating in the FTAA negotiations (Cuba being excluded) were several times larger than those found among the member countries of the enlarged EU (Bustillo and Ocampo 2003, 4–5). Given the scale of the disparities in economic size and across the full gamut of development indicators, the construction of an economic regime in the Americas throws up a very particular set of economic governance challenges associated with the management of both national and subregional adjustment to the envisaged regime and the developmental consequences of participation in it. The key challenges thus lie most notably in the range of areas associated with special and differential (S&D) treatment for smaller and poorer econo-mies, along with the management of such issues as labor and environmental standards. The term *governance*, in this sense, is advanced here as referring broadly to the myriad processes and strategies associated with the construction of a viable economic regime in the Americas and the management of the various economic processes on which it rests.

The central concern of this article is to address the question of what sort of approach to economic governance has been emerging in the region, and what its implications are for the shape of the economic regime itself and the broader regional political economy. This essay argues that by far the dominant approach has been based on the assertion of U.S. power in the region, and has taken a form peculiarly in line with the distinctively U.S. interests served by that exercise of power. The political and economic projects associated with the hemispheric agenda must be recognized, in this respect, as being fundamentally of an ideological nature, and part and parcel of the neoliberal project that underpins the global hegemonic project of the United States. That is to say, the political and economic objectives encapsulated in the regional project are intrinsically informed and molded by the broader ideological—neoliberal—foundation of U.S. hegemony and the world order associated with it.

The ideological dimensions of the regional project are often overlooked in a focus on the technical details of trade negotiations and the political bargaining processes underway in the region, but they are crucial to an understanding of the nature and the politics of the emerging regional economic regime. More specifically, this article argues that the U.S.-led approach to governance in the Americas has been fostered by the systematic orientation of U.S. trade strategies to the construction of a distinctly "hub-and-spoke" set of regionalist arrangements, as a key means by which to capture control of the governance agenda and to ensure that the regional economic regime takes a form consistent with U.S. interests and preferences. The growing prioritization of bilateralism has become the predominant strategy to this end. The leverage afforded to the United States by the bilateral negotiation of trade agreements acts to situate primary influence over the shape of the rules that constitute the regime, and the primary functions associ-ated with the task of its governance, firmly in the agencies of the U.S. state.

This argument should not be taken to suggest, however, that the FTAA itself was a project that originated in or was sponsored predominantly by the United States. Indeed, the FTAA cannot be understood in any meaningful sense as a "U.S. project," when that is taken to refer to the roots of its impetus and momentum. Although the FTAA project arose from President George H. W. Bush's Enterprise for the Americas Initiative, announced in 1990, it was propelled predominantly by interest from Latin American and Caribbean governments, much as the North American Free Trade Agreement (NAFTA) was driven primarily by pressure from Mexico (Feinberg 1997, 2002). Indeed, over the 1990s, the FTAA process was characterized by a significant lack of political leadership or involvement from the U.S. government, as a consequence partly of the overall "benign neglect" of the region by the Clinton administration and partly of the disabling absence of fast-track negotiating authority. To this extent, it is important to recognize that the neoliberal project, while intrinsically associated with the nature and exercise of U.S. power, is one that is also driven and entrenched by governments across the region and an array of business interests. Yet a distinction must be drawn between the origins of the project and the particular form it has taken since its inception. The argument here is that U.S. agencies have pursued a distinctive set of strategies for orienting and molding the regional economic project, strategies that directly and specifically reflect U.S. interests and priorities. That is, while the FTAA itself cannot be understood entirely as a U.S. project foisted on a reluctant or recalcitrant hemisphere, the manner in which the project has unfolded and the particular form it has taken reflect nonetheless an articulation of the structural power of the United States in the process and the pursuit of a set of objectives that are distinctively, and in important ways uniquely, those of the United States.

To flesh out these arguments, this essay proceeds in two parts. The first looks at the sort of political economy envisaged and implied by the evolving regional economic project and the sets of negotiating interests, including those of the United States, that have been brought to bear on it. The second addresses the emerging U.S.-led approach to governance in the Americas and seeks to understand the significance of the hub-and-spoke form of regional negotiation for the tasks of governing the economic project.

THE UNITED STATES IN THE EMERGING REGIONAL ECONOMIC REGIME

The process of hemispheric integration represented a key dimension of the neoliberal project from its inception in the mid-1990s, both in the Americas and in the wider global political economy. It represented a device by which this global project was further embedded in the region and the region was further embedded in the globalizing world economy, reflecting "the triumph of economic liberalism, of faith in export-led growth and of belief in the centrality of the private sector to development processes" (Payne 1996, 106). Hemispheric regionalism thus represented a specific strategy on the part of its primary agents—various governments and business interests—to "lock in" a political economy and a mode of social organization that were ideologically and strategically hospitable to the rules of the neoliberal game. Of these agents, the U.S. government was the principal driving force, and the exercise of its hegemonic power since the early 1970s has been molded systematically to the purpose of disseminating the twin values of neoliberalism and democracy. The hemispheric project thus constituted not only an attempt further to reinforce the parameters of a neoliberal (and democratic) political economy in the Americas, but also to consolidate the foundations of U.S. hegemony itself in the global and regional contexts.

Within this broadest of structural frameworks, however, the roots of U.S. interest in the region, or specifically in a hemispheric FTAA arrangement, are not entirely self-explanatory. Outside the NAFTA area, the region of the Americas is only modestly significant in the overall profile of U.S. trade, and, indeed, this modest significance extends only to the parts of the region clustered geographically around the United States itself. U.S. interests in the region decline steadily as one moves south, in both the economic and the broader foreign policy and security spheres, becoming, on the whole, minimal by the time one reaches the Southern Cone economies. Moreover, given the widespread processes of unilateral trade liberalization that occurred across Latin America and the

Caribbean, particularly throughout the 1990s, market access—related benefits from a free trade agreement would have accrued predominantly to the Latin American region, for it is in the U.S. economy, not in Latin American and Caribbean economies, that barriers to trade and investment remained concentrated.

By the end of the 1990s, there remained some notable disparity between the low average tariff levels that prevailed in the United States and Canada (4.5 percent), the slightly higher levels in countries such as Chile, Bolivia, and most of Central America (under 10 percent), and the still higher levels across the rest of region, reaching over 14 percent in Brazil and over 16 percent in Mexico. The opportunities afforded by an FTAA for mitigating these barriers to U.S. trade were frequently been invoked by the trade policy establishment in Washington as one of the primary incentives for its successful negotiation, especially in view of their strong concentration in industrial sectors.

Yet simple tariff averages obscure the striking degree of sectoral variation in the U.S. tariff structure. Sectoral peaks reached 350 percent in the United States, 245 percent in Canada, and 260 percent in Mexico, compared with 35 percent in Brazil and 10 percent in Chile, for example, or a comparatively high 99 percent in Ecuador. Crucially, also, it is precisely in the sectors of most strategic interest to Latin American and Caribbean economies that market access has continued to be most impeded by high tariff and nontariff barriers in the United States (and, to an extent, in Canada). Agriculture is the most obvious case in point: the United States is responsible for about a fifth of total global agricultural subsidies (OECD 2003).[1] Textiles, steel, and, of particular interest in the Canada-U.S. relationship, softwood lumber are other instances of high levels of protection in the structures of U.S. trade policy. Even where tariff barriers are relatively low, moreover, U.S. trade strategies have been marked by frequent resort to particular ad valorem duties and contingency measures, such as the notorious Section 301 and its extensive armory of trade remedies (safeguards, antidumping measures, and countervailing duties). By comparison, the aggregate use of trade remedies in the rest of the region has remained fairly low, and their deployment has been confined almost exclusively to the five largest countries in the region, the United States, Canada, Argentina, Brazil, and Mexico (de Paiva Abreu 2002, 9–11; Tavares de Araujo 2002; Phillips 2004a).

While there were some market access benefits to be accrued by the United States from an FTAA, then, the structure of trade in the Americas is one in which the barriers to the U.S. market were significantly greater and more diverse than those encountered by U.S. exports to the rest of the region. Consequently, neither market access nor trade in goods was foremost among U.S. interests in the FTAA process. Rather, these interests clustered around a set of wider concerns with trade-related disciplines and the various facets of the so-called new trade agenda. These included, notably, trade in services as the focus of commercial activity, and extend to issues such as investment, intellectual property, government procurement, competition policy, environmental protection, and labor standards. The hemispheric agenda in the Americas was relevant to U.S. trade strategies inasmuch as it has been seen to offer significant opportunities for propelling this new trade agenda forward at a time when the dynamism of the multilateral process had slowed to the point of virtual paralysis. Indeed, the extent of disillusion among developing countries with the content, conduct, and implementation of WTO negotiations has become one of the principal obstacles to multilateral trade negotiations, including in the context of the so-called Doha Development Agenda that was launched in 2001 (Finger and Nogués 2002; Panagariya 2002; Narlikar 2003; Wilkinson and Narlikar 2004; Wilkinson 2006), and U.S. engagement and compliance with multilateral rules has steadily and significantly retracted (Tussie 1998; Bergsten 2002). In other words, U.S. interest in an FTAA has been derived in large part from the possibilities both for compensating the deficiencies of multilateral liberalization processes and for implanting in the region the range of trade disciplines that are central to contemporary U.S. trade policy.

The principal negotiating areas of the FTAA corresponded with those disciplines and translate directly into the architecture of nine technical working groups established at the 1998 San José ministerial meetings.[2] In this way, the working group structure reflected and facilitated a significant degree of U.S. leverage over the shape and substance of the hemispheric negotiating agenda. Moreover, it established in the negotiations an intrinsically uneven playing field, given the frequent absence of precedent in the relevant negotiating areas in Latin American and Caribbean countries (Phillips 2003, 272–23). This leverage was also reflected in the ways the U.S. negotiating positions were designed explicitly so as to bring the rest of the region into line with existing U.S. trade laws and strategies. This was notably the case, for example, in U.S. proposals on intellectual property rights, which effectively sought to extend commitments already agreed to under WTO provisions. The public summary of U.S. positions stated, "the United States is already in compliance with the requirements of the U.S. proposal. FTAA countries will need to make adjustments to their intellectual property rights regime in order to comply" [Office of the U.S. Trade Representative (USTR) 2001a].

In most of the negotiating areas, moreover, the template for U.S. proposals in the FTAA was derived from the commitments assumed under NAFTA. The notion of an FTAA as an extended NAFTA—or, as it eventually was dubbed, "NAFTA on steroids"—was vetoed early in the negotiations by the non–North American participants, in favor of an agreement that built on existing subregional arrangements. Nevertheless, the assertion of U.S. preferences in the negotiations and the shape of emerging provisions were based unequivocally on the NAFTA model. Thus, proposals in the areas of environmental protection, government procurement, rules of origin, safeguard mechanisms, and services, among others, were directly modeled on prevailing provisions in NAFTA, and indeed often sought substantially to expand these provisions.

The most obvious case is that of investment, in which the positions of successive U.S. trade representatives consistently favored an extension to a future FTAA agreement of the so-called investor-state provision contained in NAFTA's Chapter 11. This grants to corporations a legal status similar to that of states and expands their ability to use trade agreements to challenge local regulatory legislation. Other hallmarks of U.S. positions on investment included opposition to imposing performance requirements on corporations and a trenchant opposition to any sort of controls on capital flows, the aim being to eliminate governments' discretion in these matters through binding provisions in an FTAA. The commitment in the USTR to "investor-state" arrangements thus augured a permanent place for investors' rights at the heart of the hemispheric project, building on their prior incorporation into the existing bilateral investment treaties (BITs) between the United States and various countries of the region.

In a nutshell, trade was not only about trade. Indeed, for the United States in the FTAA, it was not even primarily about trade. Rather, U.S. interests in a hemispheric free trade area were dictated by the prospects of binding regional agreements across a range of other policy areas. These are "trade-related" inasmuch as trading arrangements necessitate, politically as well as economically, attention to a plethora of other policy areas. But these connections are secondary in importance to the point that trade was the mechanism by which the U.S. government chose to pursue its priorities in these other areas. This was clear in the debates surrounding attempts to link trade with environmental and labor standards, and equally clear in the ways the FTAA was articulated from the start as, so to speak, a "package deal": market access and trade benefits would come only with agreements on investment, intellectual property rights, government procurement, competition policy, and so on. Whether the negotiation of an FTAA had proceeded in accordance with the initial U.S. preference for allowing an "early harvest"—that is, to allow earlier agreements in those areas in which negotiations had advanced most rapidly—or, as agreed, as a comprehensive "single undertaking," trade itself was only a small (and, for the United States, minor) part of the much wider array of policy areas to be covered in a hemispheric "trade" agreement.

Notwithstanding the consequent commitment to a "comprehensive" FTAA on this basis, U.S. negotiating positions sought to limit the scope of this comprehensiveness. U.S. positions were marked by a refusal to permit inclusion on the negotiating agenda of its domestic trade remedy laws (particularly those relating to antidumping) and the system of agricultural subsidies—two areas of key interest to Latin American and Caribbean countries but also to Canada. Both trade remedies and agriculture had corresponding working groups in the FTAA structure, having been initially excluded but incorporated at the insistence of the majority of Latin American and Caribbean negotiators (Feinberg 1997; Svarzman 1998). Yet these two areas were consistently excluded from substantive negotiations, and U.S. trade officials insisted that these areas could be negotiated only at a multilateral level, given the possibility that FTAA provisions might easily have been undercut if European and other countries were not constrained to observe the same obligations (Schott 2002, 31; see also USTR 2001b). The U.S. Congress also established categorically that it would not countenance authorizing any agreement that calls for a modification of domestic laws on trade remedies.

This collection of priorities in the U.S. trade agenda gave rise to an overarching negotiating framework based on a notion of "WTO-plus," in which the FTAA negotiations would aim to exceed existing multilateral provisions in a range of key areas. The rationale was twofold. On the one hand, the negotiation of a range of trade disciplines in the hemispheric arena was seen to offer greater potential for success than in the multilateral arena. For instance, enactment of the post-Doha WTO agenda was widely judged unlikely to deliver comprehensive results on market access. The FTAA, conversely, did indeed aim for the complete elimination of tariff barriers to trade in goods, although the list of goods it would cover was somewhat smaller than that under negotiation in the WTO arena. An FTAA was similarly considered likely to make deeper inroads into such areas as the liberalization of trade in services, investment rules, and competition policy, which had not been incorporated fully into the WTO agenda (Salazar-Xirinachs 2000, 2002).

On the other hand, this vision was not only articulated as a means of advancing U.S. commercial and investment interests within the region itself, but also tied to an attempt by negotiators to establish "a spiral of precedents" (VanGrasstek 1998, 169–70; 2000), which would then be deployed as the baseline for subsequent multilateral and extraregional negotiations. This sequential strategy lay at the core of the "credo" of U.S. trade policy articulated by Robert Zoellick, the USTR in the Bush administration (Zoellick 2003a; also see Zoellick 2001). His strategy of achieving a "competition in liberalization" relied on ratcheting up, with each successive trade agreement, both the baseline requirements for agreement and the incentives for trading partners to negotiate with the United States *on U.S. terms*. The prioritization of regional negotiations was thus conceived as a direct means to advancing the process of multilateral liberalization.

Virtually without exception, Latin American and Caribbean negotiators initially adhered to the principle that an FTAA process should be merely "WTO-compatible," except in the area of market access, where, given that Uruguay Round commitments had been implemented only modestly, they advocated a substantially WTO-plus agenda (Bouzas 2000, 212). WTO-plus subsequently came to be accepted by Latin American and Caribbean negotiators, and was consecrated in the Ministerial Declaration of the Seventh

FTAA ministerials held in Quito in November 2002. Even so, the negotiators' central concern to ensure fuller implementation of the Uruguay Round market access provisions continued to inform the core of their negotiating strategies. In other words, the broad stance remained one based on WTO compatibility, seen as yet to be achieved, but at the same time it emphasized that a WTO-plus format must be genuinely WTO-plus and must reach across the full range of negotiating areas, including those areas excluded unilaterally from the negotiating agenda by the United States. The Brazilians, in particular, were adamant from the start of the negotiations that an FTAA would need to be "comprehensive" if it were to be either meaningful or acceptable (Barbosa 2001). Market access issues, furthermore, were seen as going hand in hand with issues of trade remedies, in that any concessions forthcoming from the United States on market access might easily be eroded by the discretionary use of these instruments (de Paiva Abreu 2002, 20).

In this context, it was predictable, but nonetheless notable, that the assumption of the joint presidency of the final stages of the negotiations by Brazil and the United States in 2002 would usher in a period marked by a hardening of negotiating positions, an increase in the skepticism or opposition of many governments to the conclusion of an agreement as originally projected, and an entrenchment of the divergences between the visions of the hemispheric project among the participating countries. The Southern Common Market (Mercosur) countries' interest in an FTAA was always rather less pronounced than that of many others because, of the countries of the region, they were the ones with the most at stake in the multilateral system, given their much more diversified trade structures and export destinations. The marked Brazilian reticence in the hemispheric process stemmed in important part from the trade-off an FTAA would represent with its more significant multilateral interests (de Paiva Abreu 2003, 23–24; Phillips 2004b, 116–19). The U.S.-Brazilian relationship in the FTAA context was consistently tense, crystallizing largely around resistance to a U.S.-dominated initiative and the consolidation of U.S. hegemony in the region. The government of Luiz Inácio Lula da Silva hardened the already hard line taken by the previous Cardoso administration.

Mexican interest in a putative hemispheric agreement was always among the most resolutely lukewarm, largely in view of the potential consequences of an FTAA for its existing (effectively) bilateral agreement with the United States (see Blanco and Zabludovsky 2003, 18–19). Conversely, the Canadian government, while enjoying the same preferential relationship with the United States, both through NAFTA and bilaterally, consistently advocated as comprehensive as possible an FTAA. To an extent, this can be attributed to a historical predisposition toward multilateralism that has long permeated Canadian foreign and regional policies. Canada also had an extensive investment relationship with many economies in Latin America and the Caribbean. Yet the primary reason for the Canadian commitment to a genuinely hemispheric undertaking was related—as in Mexico, but with different effects—to the implications for this preferential North American relationship of expanded access to the U.S. market for other countries under the terms of an FTAA. Interest in a comprehensive agreement stemmed from perceptions of the need to retain influence over the terms on which other countries of the region gained this access and the restructuring of hemispheric relationships that this process would presage. The only means of retaining this influence was considered to be a comprehensive and reciprocal FTAA agreement; conversely, the best way to lose it would be a descent into a patchwork of individual agreements into which interested Canadian parties would have no input. It is interesting that this same concern came to prevail in Mexico as progress in the FTAA negotiations began visibly to falter over 2002 and 2003 and the United States became much more proactive at a bilateral level with various countries in the region.

The result of these divergences in the negotiations was a steady loss of momentum in the FTAA process. In the first instance, this displayed itself in a questioning of the 2005 deadline, with support from Brazil and some Caribbean countries for extending the negotiation period. Over 2002 and 2003, it took the much more fundamental form of a fracturing of commitment to the single undertaking. A coalition emerged in favor of what came to be called an "FTAA lite," composed of the Mercosur countries, the Caribbean Community (CARICOM), and Venezuela. This was set out in the Brazilian government's announcement, some months before the pivotal ministerial meetings in Miami in November 2003, of its intentions to restructure Brazilian negotiating strategies in the FTAA context. It proposed to negotiate the key issues of market access, services, and investment in a bilateral 4+1 (Mercosur-U.S.) format, leaving only "basic elements," such as dispute settlement, trade facilitation, and S&D treatment on the hemispheric negotiating table (Amorim 2003). At the time, these proposals gained some (very guarded) support from some Mercosur partners and CARICOM, were rejected emphatically by the United States, and in any event were largely overshadowed by the broadly positive reception, at the September–October 2003 meetings of the FTAA Trade Negotiations Committee (TNC) in Port of Spain, of a Costa Rican paper on the importance of an encompassing agreement. Discussions at these meetings of the appropriate "level of ambition" for an FTAA clearly reflected this split between visions of the desirable shape and coverage of a hemispheric agreement.

The outcome of this fragmentation was an unlikely alliance between Brazil and the United States. It was formed on the basis of their agreement, brokered behind closed doors before the Miami meetings, to abandon the single undertaking in favor of a buffet-style arrangement in which countries could select the commitments they wished to make in an FTAA. The "Miami declaration," issued amid considerable rancor at the meetings, set out the new format of an FTAA that operated effectively at two levels, or speeds, the first comprising a "common and balanced set of rights and obligations applicable to all countries," the second "additional liberalization and disciplines" that countries may "choose to develop." Significantly also, the declaration reflected the abandonment of the WTO-plus format, referring merely to a commitment to make FTAA provisions "consistent" with multilateral provisions (FTAA 2003).

This new FTAA-lite format was opposed trenchantly by a grouping of 13 countries, led by Canada, Chile, and Mexico, each of which, for different reasons, saw its interests as being served only by a comprehensive and reciprocal agreement among all the countries of the region. Canadian reactions, in particular, revealed clearly the aforementioned concerns: Trade Minister Pierre Pettigrew stated, for example, that the consequences of an FTAA-lite would be a loss of "some of our place in the world" (quoted in Chase 2003). Canadian and Chilean officials sought together to respond by assembling a draft of an alternative plan. The principle of tailoring the pace of liberalization according to levels of development remained intact, but the text introduced the idea that benefits from an FTAA should be made conditional on the extent of obligations assumed under the agreement. While Zoellick accepted this in principle, he also indicated a likely "pragmatic" approach to dealing with the problem in future negotiations rather than a blanket sliding scale of access to U.S. markets depending on how much of the FTAA menu countries chose to adopt (De Jonquières 2003).

Governments opposed to scaling back the level of ambition in the FTAA in this way subsequently acquiesced as it became clear that this step was not, according to the USTR and Brazilian trade negotiators, open for discussion. As a result, the Miami meetings ended a day early, as negotiators declared that they had run out of topics. At the special Summit of the Americas held in Puebla in January 2004, however, recriminations persisted, and disputes over the foundation of an FTAA were still clearly in evidence. The Mercosur countries continued to press for a "gradual" FTAA and raised trenchant objections to U.S. aspirations to greater hemispheric-level liberalization in the areas of services and investment. They also rejected the creation of extranational tribunal systems, such as those established under the investor-state provisions of NAFTA, and demanded a system of compensation for the adverse competitive impact of government supports to U.S. farmers. No agreement was reached on the agriculture issue, and the talks were deemed largely to have failed, stymied by significant differences between the Mercosur countries and the group of other countries led by the United States. Virtually no activity or progress has occurred since that time, and a general perception has emerged across the region, including in the United States, that the FTAA project has become effectively moribund, at least in the short term.

THE NEW BILATERALIST IMPETUS

The counterpart of the move to an FTAA lite was the announcement of an acceleration of an existing predisposition in the Office of the USTR toward bilateral trade negotiations. Agreements with Chile and six Central American countries (the latter to form a Central American Free Trade Area (CAFTA-DR), were ratified by the U.S. Congress in July 2003 and July 2005 respectively. (The negotiations with Chile had been underway before the collapse of the FTAA negotiations in the same year of the agreement's ratification.) In April 2004, multiparty negotiations for Trade Promotion Agreements with a number of Andean countries were initiated, and around the same time for a Free Trade Area with Panama. Negotiations were concluded with Peru in December 2005 and Colombia in February 2006. Ecuador was also part of these negotiations for an Andean Trade Promotion Agreement. Bilateral Investment Treaties (BITs) also exist with Grenada (1989), Panama (1991), Argentina (1994), Ecuador (1997), Jamaica (1997), Bolivia (2001), and Honduras (2001), and negotiations were concluded with Uruguay in late 2005.

This shift to bilateralism in trade negotiations in the region has been mirrored in a rash of bilateral discussions, negotiations, and agreements elsewhere: with Singapore, Jordan, Bahrain, Thailand, Morocco, Australia, Oman, Israel, and Egypt, among others, and regional groupings, such as the Southern African Customs Union (SACU) and the Association of Southeast Asian Nations (ASEAN). A spate of bilateral trade and investment framework agreements has also been initiated with such countries as Saudi Arabia, Kuwait, Bahrain, and the United Arab Emirates. Turkey has been subject to sustained attention, and the prospect of a Middle East Free Trade Area (MEFTA) was advanced in mid-2003.

What explains this prioritization of bilateral negotiations? In the regional context, bilateralism represents, in essence, a political response by the U.S. government to the political difficulties encountered in realizing its *particular* vision of the FTAA and the regional economic governance agenda. As it became clear that U.S. preferences regarding the shape of an FTAA were unlikely to prosper in hemispheric negotiations, bilateralism became the strategy of choice for the pursuit of U.S. trade and economic policy priorities. In other words, the logic propelling a more robust pursuit of bilateral than of hemispheric arrangements rests on the apparently greater utility of bilateralism in serving key U.S. negotiating priorities; that is, of obtaining access to services markets in the region in exchange for concessions on market access for a range of goods, but equally the exclusion of significant concessions on agricultural liberalization or modification of domestic legislation on trade remedies. Crucially also, bilateralism offered a way of reviving the principle of WTO-plus in new trade agreements following the collapse of this aspiration as the foundation for an FTAA. Without exception, the bilateral agreements that trade officials in Washington referred to as "state of the art" trade deals conformed to a WTO-plus template. Notably, however, the terms of WTO-plus were the same as those that prevailed in the FTAA negotiations; that is, WTO-plus was not universally applied to the various areas of negotiation and, as in the hemispheric negotiations, did not encompass agreements on trade remedies, agricultural subsidies, or various strategic and politically sensitive sectors.

Yet the pursuit of bilateral agreements was also useful as a mechanism for increasing the incentives for other partners (notably Brazil) to engage in similar negotiations, or else for increasing their interest in the success of the FTAA negotiations and thus encouraging a softening of negotiating positions. The "incentive" was invoked consistently by U.S. trade officials in the FTAA process. In an article published in 2002, Zoellick stated, "we want to negotiate with all the democracies of the Americas through the FTAA, but we are also prepared to move step by step toward free trade if others turn back or simply are not ready" (Zoellick 2002). Similar pressures in the multilateral arena were brought to bear following the collapse of the WTO talks in Cancún in late 2003, when Zoellick declared his determination not to entertain or wait for the "won't-do" countries in the multilateral system and to undermine the emerging Brazil-led G-20+ coalition of developing countries (Zoellick 2003b). The echoes of U.S. tactics in dealing with opposition among members of the U.N. Security Council to the invasion of Iraq around the same time are hard to miss, leading one observer pithily to cast Zoellick as a "Donald Rumsfeld of trade policy" (Bhagwati 2004, 52). The early defection from this grouping of such countries as Colombia, El Salvador, Costa Rica, and Peru was directly a consequence of U.S. trade officials' rebukes and warnings that trade agreements with the United States could be threatened by participation in the G20+. Notably, all the countries in the Americas that defected from the G-20+ grouping have since been engaged in bilateral negotiations with the United States.

This form of "divide and rule" strategy in multilateral trade politics was also apparent earlier in the FTAA negotiations. In the process of presenting opening offers in the various negotiating groups in early 2003, the USTR chose to differentiate between the various subregional groupings in the Americas in a manner that explicitly disadvantaged Mercosur. It put forward four different sets of offers, in contrast with the single sets of offers put forward by all the other participants, ostensibly in recognition of the particular needs of smaller and poorer economies in the FTAA process. Even if this were the case, the opportunity thereby presented to put further pressure on the less-accommodating countries in the south of the region—particularly Brazil—would have gone neither unappreciated nor, indeed, lamented by U.S. trade officials.

It is thus through the progressive prioritization of bilateral negotiations, mirrored in and reinforced by U.S. strategies outside the Americas, that U.S. influence over the architecture of the region has been most easily asserted. Indeed, the bilateralist emphasis facilitates the construction of precisely the hub-and-spoke regional arrangements and the extension of NAFTA that the United States initially envisaged and desired in the FTAA context. Yet bilateralism also came to be favored by a number of other governments in the region as the best means of pursuing their strategic priorities in trade negotiations, given the height of the hurdles facing the successful agreement of a comprehensive FTAA.

The important point about bilateralism is that it found most robust expression in the particular area of market access, the defining pillar of Latin American and Caribbean interests in hemispheric trade negotiations. In this sense, the primarily U.S.-led drive to inject the most dynamism into bilateral negotiations was facilitated by an apparently greater resonance of bilateralism with the key negotiating priorities of Latin American and Caribbean governments than with an FTAA itself. Despite residual preferences for a more encompassing agreement in many parts of the region, the United States therefore encountered receptive responses to its overtures to "bilateral" agreements with subregional blocs as well as individual countries. At the same time, reactions to the U.S. bilateralist agenda have spurred other governments either to seek to pursue the same sorts of negotiations with trading partners, or else to expand their existing bilateral strategies in the region and outside it. Such a response has been clearly evident in Canada, Mexico, and Brazil, and indeed in a range of the smaller participating countries.

Of most relevance for our purposes here, however, are the implications of this form of U.S.-led bilateralism for the key governance issues associated with the economic regime in the Americas.

BILATERALISM AND U.S.-LED APPROACHES TO REGIONAL ECONOMIC GOVERNANCE

It is worth noting that many of these dimensions of U.S. bilateral approaches to key governance issues were embedded in the substance of the Trade Promotion Authority (TPA) legislation, which provided the framework for the negotiating strategy. The TPA legislation, which was passed under the Trade Act of 2002 and expired in 2007, granted Congress a much more significant input into the process than it enjoyed in the previous incarnation of fast-track authority in the early 1990s. The USTR was obliged to report more regularly and fully to Congress, and Congress retained the option of passing a "resolution of disapproval" on any given trade agreement—a provision described by House Ways and Means Committee Chairman Bill Thomas (R-Calif.) as "the old shotgun behind the door" (quoted in Eilperin and Dewar 2002).

Apart from diluting the principle of fast-track, the implication of this is that any concessions that U.S. negotiators might have felt inclined to make on market access face complicated prospects once they are transferred to the arena of domestic legislation, and that an FTAA and any other regional trade agreements would have needed to incorporate labor and environmental standards, given the political climate in Congress. The TPA bill also made significant concessions to certain protectionist groups—most notably producers of citrus fruits in Florida, sugar farmers, and the textile industry—to the manifest disadvantage of regional partners. In this way, concessions to domestic protectionist pressures were embedded firmly in the very framework of trade negotiations, as well as the substance of any agreements that might have emerged therefrom. Thus the TPA placed a very particular set of political demands on U.S. negotiators; consequently, the playing field in hemispheric and bilateral negotiations was distinctly uneven, and the framework for the negotiations infused with distinctively U.S. policy interests and political priorities.

This skewing of the negotiating terrain was manifested clearly in the pursuit of bilateral trade agreements. The Chile-U.S. agreement is a good case in point. It clearly represented a mechanism for circumventing the stalemate, dispute, or technical difficulty surrounding the various issue areas of key interest to the United States at the regional and multilateral levels. Certain concessions were made on market access for most agricultural goods, the commitment being to phase out duties and quotas on such goods over a 12-year period (a longer time frame than for other goods).[3] Yet this fairly minimal concession from the United States on agriculture was noteworthy for the absence of any related commitments on the reduction or elimination of subsidies, in many ways the much more pressing issue for Chile and the rest of the region's countries, including Canada. None of the U.S. bilateral agreements or NAFTA includes any disciplining measures on U.S. subsidies; indeed, the Chile-U.S. negotiations were complicated by the announcement, during the negotiating period itself, of substantial increases in the extent of subsidies and government support to U.S. farmers under the 2002 Farm Bill. Furthermore, the provisions on agricultural market access in the Chile-U.S. agreement, like those in NAFTA, were accompanied by a trade remedies chapter, which provided for the imposition of temporary safeguards by the U.S. government when increased imports were deemed, *by the U.S. government*, to represent a threat or injury to domestic producers. "Special" safeguards were put in place for a range of textiles and agricultural products, and no part of the agreement entailed any sort of alterations to U.S. laws on trade remedies.

In the meantime, the agreement called forth a number of fundamental changes to Chilean laws and policies and a significant circumscription of Chilean governments' policymaking and legal discretion, while further protecting and insulating U.S. domestic legislation and ensuring the U.S. government's room for maneuver in its trade and economic policies. The Chilean government committed itself to such measures as the elimination of a range of drawback and duty referral programs and its 85 percent "auto luxury tax," and to implementing the regulatory systems necessary for the enforcement of the U.S. meat inspection system. The agreement also went beyond direct trade issues to include provisions limiting Chilean governments' future ability to impose controls on capital flows, an important facet of the Chilean development strategy and, indeed, a central explanation for the Chilean economy's relative stability throughout the 1990s. The agreement stipulated that any such controls could be in place for a maximum of one year, and only in circumstances of demonstrable crisis. These provisions thus represented a crucial dimension of the strategy to mold the investment environment in the region in a manner consistent with the interests of U.S. investors.

The particularly distinctive dimensions of the Chile-U.S. agreement, however, were twofold. The first was that it and the Singapore-U.S. agreement were "the first FTAs anywhere in the world to have specific, concrete obligations to enhance transparency and efficiency of customs procedures" (Vargo 2003). These obligations permeated the provisions on such key areas as services, government procurement, and dispute settlement, and went along with extensive provisions relating to regulation in such areas of key interest in the U.S. "new trade agenda" as intellectual property, telecommunications, electronic commerce, and temporary entry for workers. The second dimension was that the agreement established what was claimed to be an "innovative approach" to labor and environmental issues. In this approach, the signatories to the agreement were obliged to enforce their own domestic laws on labor and environmental standards and to retain levels of protection that would divert the emergence of "races to the bottom."[4] The "innovative" content comes in the preference for the use of monetary penalties over trade sanctions for noncompliance with these constraints, with trade sanctions being available to the petitioning party should these monetary penalties not be paid.

The crucial point in this respect is that the United States operated explicitly with the intention of using the Chilean agreement as the template for a hemispheric agreement and a mechanism for establishing the baseline precedents for its trade negotiations in other areas. The system for dealing with labor and environmental standards in the Chile-U.S. agreement was, in this sense, envisioned explicitly as the benchmark for the treatment of these issues in the FTAA (Feinberg 2003, 1037). It represented in this sense a strategy for circumventing the entrenched opposition among Latin American and

Caribbean governments to the linkage of trade with labor and environmental standards—an opposition articulated most vociferously by Brazilian officials—and to some extent also for assuaging Canadian insistence that labor and environmental standards should be negotiated only as side agreements rather than integrated into the text of trade agreements. It was probably inconceivable that the U.S. Congress would ratify trade agreements that carried no provisions on these twin issues; nevertheless, the system of remedies (monetary fines rather than trade sanctions) represents a partial attempt to dilute the perceived trade—environment/labor linkage while, in effect, positioning the enforcement of labor and environmental standards at the heart of the regional economic regime.

The substance of the U.S.-Chile agreement thus augured the construction of a range of regulatory mechanisms designed to further a trade relationship peculiarly in line with the U.S. government's preferences regarding the mode of governance to be adopted in the Americas. The CAFTA agreement was similar in both substance and significance. It provided for the elimination of U.S. tariffs on most of its agricultural products within 15 years (slightly longer than in the Chilean agreement), and it excluded any concessions on subsidies and other nontariff barriers. It eliminated tariffs and quotas on textile products that complied with rules of origin provisions—that is, that they be made using cloth dyed and finished in the United States—and in this sense predicted an expansion of trade in textiles. It also amended the rule of origin to include some fabrics from Canada and Mexico, intended to foster the integration of North American textiles and apparel industries as "a step to prepare for an increasingly competitive global market" (USTR 2003a). Yet these provisions intersected with existing multilateral arrangements for the global liberalization of textiles and apparel quotas at the start of 2005. Taken together, this multilateral elimination of quotas and the terms of the CAFTA agreement were calculated to signify a 50 percent cut in the expansion of Central American textiles and clothing exports to the United States (Hilaire and Yang 2003, 15–16).

The CAFTA agreement further resembled the Chilean agreement in its explicit incorporation of a range of provisions that went beyond trade and impinge directly on domestic legal structures. In the agreement, the United States achieved its stated goal of "requir[ing] important reforms of the domestic legal and business environment that are key to encouraging business development and investment," which included fostering greater transparency, strengthening the rule of law, and enacting much more extensive protection and enforcement of intellectual property rights (USTR 2003a). What was most salient about the CAFTA agreement, however, is that in a number of areas it went beyond the equivalent provisions of the Chile-U.S. agreement, revealing clearly Zoellick's "competition in liberalization" strategy in action. Labor and environmental standards were the most striking examples. The again "innovative" environmental chapter provided for the benchmarking of environmental cooperation activities and input from international organizations.[5] The provisions on labor standards had three tiers, relating to the enforcement of domestic laws (as in the Chilean case), the establishment of cooperative schemes to improve these laws and their enforcement, and the elaboration of financial and technical assistance packages as part of a broader commitment to provide "trade capacity—building assistance" to developing countries. In the CAFTA context, a US $6.75 million, four-year grant was extended in 2003 to support "good labor conditions" in Central American trade partners, funded by the U.S. Department of Labor and channeled through the nongovernmental Foundation for Peace and Democracy (FUNDAPEM). It was oriented toward implantation of inspection systems, education of employers and workers on matters of labor laws, and construction of industrial dispute settlement systems (USTR 2003b).

Approaches to the broader governance challenges associated with special and differential treatment likewise bore the clear imprint of U.S. preferences. The place of S&D

treatment in the hemispheric negotiations reflected the U.S. vision of the regional economic regime (and specifically the FTAA) as one based fundamentally on the principle of reciprocity. In this view, and also that of the Canadian government, S&D treatment was not, in the words of Deputy USTR Peter Allgeier, "an end in and of itself." Rather, it was seen to represent a set of intrinsically transitional mechanisms to "foster economic development, adjustment and integration into the multilateral trading system" (Allgeier 2002). Accordingly, S&D treatment did not have a corresponding technical working group in the FTAA negotiations; instead, issues of pertinence to smaller and poorer economies were addressed in the Consultative Group on Small Economies and then filtered into the deliberations of the nine technical working groups. Certain hemispheric-level initiatives thereby emerged that purport to constitute viable means for addressing S&D treatment issues. One of the key innovations in the Quito ministerials was the announcement of, and U.S. support for, a hemispheric cooperation program designed to grant adjustment assistance, so as to enable all countries to participate "beneficially and equitably" in the negotiations. This remained a long way from constituting a comprehensive package on S&D treatment—certainly not one acceptable to the majority of smaller and poorer economies pushing for a rather different mode of governance in this area. Representatives of the smaller and poorer countries themselves—spearheaded by Caribbean participants—came to insist ever more strongly that the principle of reciprocity should give way to "special and differential treatment involving elements of extended or permanent nonreciprocity in obligations" (Girvan 2003).

The aforementioned "trade capacity—building assistance" program also reached beyond the elements of labor and environmental standards to include a range of institutional issues and policy concerns, but still did not constitute a comprehensive approach to S&D treatment issues in the region. Rather, it represented a move to supplement the existing technical assistance activities of the three formal regional institutions involved in supporting the hemispheric process—the Inter-American Development Bank (IDB), the UN Economic Commission for Latin America and the Caribbean (ECLAC), and the Organization of American States (OAS)—with a set of bilateral assistance packages coordinated and funded by the United States. Clearly, this new program fitted with an overall strategy of molding a bilateral approach to key governance challenges in the hemisphere, in the interests of increasing control and leverage over both the governance agenda and the sorts of policy and institutional structures—in this case related to capacity building—that were likely to emerge.

The U.S.-driven approach to economic governance over the 1990s and 2000s thus carried a range of structural and political consequences for both regional trade negotiations and the shape of the regional economic regime. It was facilitated by the absence from the hemispheric project of any aspirations to build regional institutions for the purposes of economic governance or regulation, which raised the question of where primary responsibility for the enforcement of the rules agreed in hemispheric and bilateral negotiations would reside. The substance of the bilateral agreements and negotiations in which the United States engaged during the 2000s, as well as the assertion of its influence over the shape of the hemispheric agenda, suggest a U.S. strategy to fashion a regional economic regime in which the U.S. government assumed a good part of this responsibility. This was clearest in the context of its "innovative" approach to labor and environmental standards, in which the enforcement of the system of monetary penalties resided directly with the U.S. government, on its assumption, of course, that it would invariably be the party petitioning against nonobservance of agreed standards in other countries. It was also clear in that its packages of financial and technical assistance for trade capacity building will be monitored by the U.S. Department of Labor and other state agencies.

CONCLUSIONS

The central contention in this chapter has been that the emerging mode of and approach to governance in the Americas came over the 1990s and 2000s to be dominated by a distinctly U.S.-driven agenda, reflective fundamentally of U.S. priorities and a strengthening of U.S. hegemony as the foundation of the new regional political economy. There was a second, parallel, subregional approach to governance, but this was, and remains, considerably weaker, patchier, and more brittle than the dominant U.S.-led approach. They have been limited by a raft of political and institutional obstacles to the deepening of integration in many of the subregional blocs themselves and the frequent absence, except perhaps in NAFTA, of significant progress on the internal coordination and implementation of rules in many of the key policy areas covered in the FTAA negotiations.

Those subregional initiatives, moreover, have been both undermined and molded by the active deployment of bilateral strategies by U.S. government agencies. Part of the rationale for the U.S. pursuit of bilateral agreements has been precisely to increase the incentives for other countries to negotiate similar deals, which has acted frequently to undermine the cohesion of subregional groupings. This has been particularly evident in Mercosur, in the impact of the bilateral agreement with Chile, the preliminary discussions with Uruguay, and the exacerbation of divisions between Mercosur countries as a result of U.S. pressure on Brazil after the Cancún WTO meetings.

On the other hand, the U.S.-led approach has also been oriented toward molding subregional approaches in a manner that brings them more closely into line with U.S. preferences, in that its bilateral negotiations with subregional blocs afford greater leverage for the USTR and other government agencies over the shape of the rules agreed on in internal bargaining processes. The prospect of agreements between the United States and subregional units, in this sense, is designed to increase the incentives for subregional blocs to accept a range of rules consistent with those that have come to define the hemispheric agenda, as a result of U.S. leverage over its shape, and to fashion internal governance mechanisms in a manner conducive to the successful agreement of bilateral trade deals with the United States.

What this chapter has sought most strenuously to do, however, is to direct attention back to the importance of politics and power in understanding the emerging economic regime and approaches to its governance. Issues of regional economic governance must be conceived as intrinsically political processes, which cannot be separated from discussions about the region's prevailing power structures and the ways power is exercised. By understanding how the hegemonic power of the United States manifests itself in the substance of the regional economic project, we can also see the roots of resistance to the U.S. vision of the hemispheric project.

Inasmuch as the FTAA process has been marked by the inability of the United States unilaterally to determine the terms or the outcomes of the negotiations—hence the USTR's turn to the apparently more conducive bilateral avenue with weaker partners—our attention is necessarily drawn to the contestation of the regional agenda that has been articulated both by governments and by the wide range of nonstate actors engaged in the process (Phillips 2008). This has been as much the case in the United States as across the rest of the region. The difficulties encountered in securing ratification of free trade agreements is surely the most salient indicator of the politics that have swirled, and continue to do so, around regional trade. The bilateral agreements with the Central American countries and the Andean countries have all been characterized by protracted ratification battles. The CAFTA agreement was ratified in 2005 by the US Congress by only the very slimmest of margins (217 votes to 215), and ratification in Costa Rica was long delayed and surrounded by intense social protest. In 2009, the agreement with

Colombia was stuck tight in the US Congress and the subject of a fraught political stand-off. Equally, Venezuela abandoned the Andean Community in 2006 in protest at Peru and Colombia's negotiations with the United States.

In one sense, this indicates clearly that neoliberalism is not the unified and monolithic entity it is frequently assumed to be; rather, a variety of visions of the neoliberal project have generated divergent and discordant positions in the range of trade negotiations, both in and outside the Americas. In another sense, it indicates the intrinsically contested, fragile, and complex nature of U.S. power. Unquestionably, the structurally hegemonic power of the United States molds the parameters of the regional political economy and defines, to a very significant extent, the contours of the regional agenda. Yet the myriad challenges to the particular U.S. vision of the regional project, and more broadly to the articulation of U.S. power in the region, are pivotal to an understanding of the evolution of U.S. strategies, both in the trade and economic arenas and in other areas of regional engagement.

NOTES

This chapter draws on and has benefited from extensive interviews and conversations, in various countries across the region, with government and trade officials, private sector and union representatives, and other interested parties. I have respected fully requests for confidentiality and anonymity. The article is based on an earlier paper delivered at the conference "Building the Americas," held at the Centre d'Etudes Internationales et Mondialisation, Université du Québec à Montréal, in November 2003. With all the usual disclaimers, I am grateful for thoughtful comments from several of the participants at this conference, Tony Payne, Wyn Grant, William C. Smith, the editor of *Latin American Politics and Society*, and three anonymous referees.

1 The EU leads the pack, accounting for around 40 percent of the global total, but in the regional context it should be noted that Canadian subsidies are also significant.

2 The nine areas were market access; agriculture; services; investment; government procurement; intellectual property rights; subsidies, antidumping, and CVDs; competition policy; and dispute settlement. Labor and environmental issues did not have separate forums in this structure, but instead were indirectly filtered into the activities of each of these working groups.

3 Sugar was notably excluded from the agreement. The U.S. government insisted that a surplus in sugar production needed to obtain in both countries for sugar to qualify for the tariff reduction scheme; it obtained in neither country. As it did obtain in countries like Brazil and Guatemala, however, the U.S. government would not have been able to use similar conditions in the FTAA negotiations (El Tratado de Libre Comercio 2003, 3).

4 This provision was criticized by the AFL-CIO, the largest labor union in the United States, because it did not "commit the signatories to have labor laws in place, or to ensure that their labor laws meet any international standard or floor." The union also voiced opposition to the implications of provisions in both the Chile and Singapore agreements concerning the temporary entry of professional workers to the United States. See Lee 2003. Members of Congress also voiced concern about both sets of provisions' potentially setting precedents for agreements with other countries, particularly those in Central America. See Levin 2003.

5 The Chile-U.S. and Singapore-U.S. agreements also carried these cooperation packages, but they were negotiated only after the original trade agreements.

REFERENCES

Allgeier, Peter. 2002. Deputy U.S. Trade Representative. Statement to the Trade Negotiations Committee of the World Trade Organization. Geneva, July 18.

Amorim, Celso. 2003. A ALCA possível. *Folha de São Paulo*, July 8.

Barbosa, Rubens. 2001. A View from Brazil. *Washington Quarterly* 24, 2 (Spring): 149–57.

Bergsten, C. Fred. 2002. A Renaissance for U.S. Trade Policy? *Foreign Affairs* 81, 6: 86–98.

Bhagwati, Jagdish. 2004. Don't Cry for Cancún. *Foreign Affairs* 83, 1: 52–74.

Blanco M., Herminio, and Jaime Zabludovsky K. 2003. Alcances y límites de la negociación del Acuerdo de Libre Comercio de las Américas. INTAL-ITD-STA Documento de Trabajo–IECI-01. Buenos Aires/Washington, DC: Inter-American Development Bank. April.

Bouzas, Roberto. 2000. Trade and Investment Issues in the Americas: A Look Ahead. In *The Future of Inter-American Relations*, ed. Jorge I. Domínguez. New York: Routledge. 197–214.

Bustillo, Inés, and José Antonio Ocampo. 2003. Asymmetries and Cooperation in the Free Trade Area of the Americas. Paper presented at the seminar "Confronting the Challenges of Regional Development in Latin America and the Caribbean," Milan, March 22.

Chase, Steven. 2003. Free-trade Zone Talks May Unravel. *Globe and Mail* (Toronto), November 17.

De Jonquières, Guy. 2003. The Divided Americas: Will the Talks on Creating a Common Market for the Region Become Another Cancún? *Financial Times*, November 17: 17.

De Paiva Abreu, Marcelo. 2002. The Political Economy of Economic Integration in the Americas. Paper prepared for the IDB/INTAL conference "Economic Integration in the Americas: Prospects and Policy Issues," Punta del Este, December 15–16.

——. 2003. Latin American and Caribbean Interests in the WTO. In *Trade Negotiations in Latin America: Problems and Prospects*, ed. Diana Tussie. Basingstoke: Palgrave. 19–31.

Eilperin, Judith, and Helen Dewar. 2002. Accord Reached on Trade Authority. *Washington Post*, July 26: A1.

Feinberg, Richard E. 1997. *Summitry in the Americas: A Progress Report*. Washington, DC: Institute of International Economics.

——. 2002. Regionalism and Domestic Politics: U.S.-Latin American Trade Policy in the Bush Era. *Latin American Politics and Society* 44, 4 (Winter): 127–52.

——. 2003. The Political Economy of United States Free Trade Arrangements. *The World Economy* 26, 7: 1019–40.

Finger, J. Michael, and Julio J. Nogués. 2002. The Unbalanced Uruguay Round Outcome: The New Areas in Future WTO Negotiations. *The World Economy* 25, 3: 321–40.

Free Trade Area of the Americas (FTAA). 2003. Eighth Ministerial Meeting. Miami, November 20. <www.ftaa-alca.org/Ministerials/Miami/Miami_e.asp>

Girvan, Norman. 2003. Trade Negotiating Committee Meeting: A Tale of Two FTAAs. *Caribbean Investor*, October 15. <www.CaribbeanInvestor.com>

Hilaire, Alvin, and Yongzheng Yang. 2003. The United States and the New Regionalism/ Bilateralism. IMF Working Paper WP/03/206. Washington DC: International Monetary Fund. October.

Hooghe, Liesbet, and Gary Marks. 2001. *Multi-level Governance and European Integration*. Oxford: Rowman and Littlefield.

Lee, Thea M. 2003. Chief International Economist, American Federation of Labor and Congress of Industrial Organizations (AFL-CIO). Statement before the Subcommittee on Trade of the Committee on Ways and Means, U.S. House of Representatives, Hearing on Implementation of U.S. Bilateral Free Trade Agreements with Chile and Singapore. 108th Congress, First Session. June 10. <waysandmeans.house.gov/hearings.asp?formmode=view&id=1162>

Levin, Sander M. 2003. Opening statement before the Subcommittee on Trade of the Committee on Ways and Means, U.S. House of Representatives, Hearing on Implementation of U.S. Bilateral Free Trade Agreements with Chile and Singapore. 108th Congress, First Session. June 10. <waysandmeans.house.gov/hearings.asp?formmode=view&id=1162>

Narlikar, Amrita. 2003. *International Trade and Developing Countries: Bargaining Coalitions in the GATT and WTO*. London: Routledge.

Office of the United States Trade Representative (USTR). 2001a. FTAA Negotiating Group on Intellectual Property. Public Summary of U.S. Position. January 17. <www.ustr.gov>

——. 2001b. FTAA Negotiating Group on Subsidies, Anti-Dumping and Countervailing Duties. Public Summary of U.S. Position. January 17. <www.ustr.gov>

——. 2003a. Free Trade with Central America: Summary of the U.S.-Central America Free Trade Agreement. *Trade Facts*, December 17.

——. 2003b. United States Provides $6.75 Million Grant to Support Good Labor Conditions in Central American FTA Partners. Press release 2003–63. October 1.

Organization for Economic Cooperation and Development (OECD). 2003. *Agricultural Policies in OECD Countries: Monitoring and Evaluation*. Paris: OECD.

Panagariya, Arvind. 2002. Developing Countries at Doha: A Political Economy Analysis. *The World Economy* 25, 9: 1205–33.

Payne, Anthony. 1996. The United States and Its Enterprise for the Americas. In *Regionalism and World Order*, ed. Andrew Gamble and Payne. Basingstoke: Macmillan. 93–129.

Phillips, Nicola. 2003. Hemispheric Integration and Subregionalism in the Americas. *International Affairs* 79, 2: 257–79.

——. 2004a. The Americas. In *The New Regional Politics of Development*, ed. Anthony Payne. Basingstoke: Palgrave. 29–58.

——. 2004b. *The Southern Cone Model: The Political Economy of Regional Capitalist Development in Latin America*. London: Routledge.

——. 2008. The Politics of Trade and the Limits to US Power in the Americas. In *Responding to Globalization: The Political Economy of Regional Integration in the Americas*, ed. Diego Sánchez-Ancochea and Ken Shadlen. Palgrave. 2008. 147–70.

Salazar-Xirinachs, José M. 2000. The Trade Agenda in the Context of the Inter-American System. Organization of American States, Trade Unit, March. <www.sice.oas.org/tunit/STAFF_ARTICLE/jmsx_Agda_e.asp>

——. 2002. Latin American Trade Policies in 2002 and Beyond: Diagnosis and Prognosis. Organization of American States, Trade Unit. January. <www.sice.oas.org/tunit/STAFF_ARTICLE/jmsx_diagnosis_e.asp>

Schott, Jeffrey J. 2002. Challenges to the Free Trade Area of the Americas. *Economic Perspectives: An Electronic Journal of the U.S. Department of State* 7, 3: 29–31. <usinfo.state.gov/journals>

Svarzman, Gustavo. 1998. La Argentina y el Mercosur ante el proceso de integración hemisférica. *Boletín Informativo Techint* 295 (July–September): 27–60.

Tavares de Araujo, José, Jr. 2002. Legal and Economic Interfaces Between Antidumping and Competition Policy. *World Competition* 25, 2: 159–72.

El Tratado de Libre Comercio Chile-EEUU: ¿un precedente para el ALCA? 2003. *Estudios sobre el ALCA* (Santiago de Chile) 15 (August).

Tussie, Diana. 1998. Multilateralism Revisited in a Globalizing World Economy. *Mershon International Studies Review* 42: 183–93.

VanGrasstek, Craig. 1998. What Is the FTAA's Role in the USA's Global Strategy? *Capítulos del SELA* 54: 163–73.

——. 2000. U.S. Plans for a New WTO Round: Negotiating More Agreements with Less Authority. *The World Economy* 23, 5: 673–700.

Vargo, Regina K. 2003. Assistant U.S. Trade Representative for the Americas. Statement before the U.S. Senate Committee on the Judiciary, Hearing on Proposed United States-Chile and United States-Singapore Free Trade Agreements. 108th Congress, First Session. July 14. <judiciary.senate.gov/hearing.cfm?id=854?>

Wilkinson, Rorden. 2006. The WTO in Hong Kong: What It Really Means for the Doha Development Agenda. *New Political Economy*, 11, 2: 291–303.

Wilkinson, Rorden and Amrita Narlikar. 2004. Collapse at the WTO: A Cancun post-mortem. *Third World Quarterly*, 25, 3: 447–60.

Zoellick, Robert B. 2001. American Trade Leadership: What Is at Stake? Speech to the Institute for International Economics, Washington, DC, September 24.

——. 2002. Trading in Freedom: The New Endeavor of the Americas. *Economic Perspectives: An Electronic Journal of the U.S. Department of State* 7, 3: 6–12. <usinfo.state.gov/journals/>

——. 2003a. Our Credo: Free Trade and Competition. *Wall Street Journal*, July 10.

——. 2003b. America Will Not Wait for the Won't-Do Countries. *Financial Times*, September 22: 23.

Chapter 15

Networks of Trade Protest in the Americas: Toward a New Labor Internationalism?

Marisa von Bülow

When labor organizations began to mobilize around the wave of free trade agreement negotiations that swept the Americas in the 1990s, their leaders realized how ill-prepared they were to deal with this new context. First, some of the key labor federations in the region did not speak to each other because of grievances inherited from the Cold War era.[1] Furthermore, there were few hemispheric or even subregional spaces to exchange ideas and information with other civil society actors. Even if the spaces existed, labor organizations that felt threatened by trade agreements were also struggling to elaborate common alternatives to the neoliberal model that came to dominate the hemisphere in the 1990s and that had free trade as one of its pillars.

Labor organizations were not the only civil society actors to face such organizational and ideological challenges. In fact, these have been at the core of a broader debate, held by scholars and activists alike, about the characteristics and potentiality of transnational civil society collective action. Since the publication of the pioneering studies on this issue more than four decades ago (see Kaiser 1969, 1971; Nye and Keohane 1971), the literature has analyzed the roles of an increasingly heterogeneous set of actors and has made an ambitious effort to understand the relationships between globalization and new coalitions. As Keck and Sikkink (1998, 15) argue, while many activists working transnationally today come out of the traditions of the past, they no longer tend to define themselves in terms of these traditions or the organizations that carried them.[2]

This article contributes to efforts to understand the novelty, variety, and dynamics of current transnational collective action by proposing a relational approach that bridges the gap between labor studies and the social movement literature and that is sensitive to the embeddedness of actors in dynamic political contexts. Such a relational approach assumes that behavior is explained best if analyzed from the perspective of the actors' relationships, rejecting "the notion that one can posit discrete, pre-given units such as the individual or society as ultimate starting points" (Emirbayer 1997, 287).[3] Furthermore, it "sees relations between terms or units as preeminently dynamic in nature, as unfolding, ongoing processes rather than as static ties among inert substances" (Emirbayer 1997, 289).

Thus, this article argues that in order to understand transnational collective action, it is not enough simply to reveal the specific interests of labor organizations, but it is necessary to identify the mechanisms by which actors are able (or unable) to overcome their differences and construct common purpose.[4] Some of the divisions among labor organizations are related to different ideological traditions that guide their perceptions about the world. However, these traditions are not tools that automatically provide instructions for behavior.[5] A relational approach seeks better to understand changes in prior beliefs that result from the interactions among actors.

The analysis focuses on the roles played by a key set of labor federations from Brazil, Chile, Mexico, and the United States in trade-related mobilizations from the beginning of the 1990s to 2004. The mapping of relationships among these federations and between them and other actors is based on the results of a social network questionnaire applied to 123 civil society organizations in the four countries. In-depth and semistructured interviews with key informants complement the network analysis by providing information on how relationships have evolved through time, the contents of ties mapped, and labor's reactions to changing political contexts.[6]

This is a relevant object of study because in the 1990s, for the first time in the history of the region, truly hemispherewide collaboration among labor organizations seemed to be feasible.[7] In fact, the converging positions of major actors in opposition to trade agreements such as the Free Trade Area of the Americas (FTAA) and their increased levels of collaboration with other civil society actors with respect to trade negotiations, at the domestic and transnational levels, would not have been imaginable as recently as the beginning of the 1980s. This broad consensus, however, hides key differences among actors and the persistence of obstacles to transnational collective action.

Recent agreements, as important as they are, have not led to an undisputed new era of labor internationalism. Instead, labor organizations can take—and indeed have taken—different paths to transnationality. While some actors have participated in trade debates mostly from within domestic borders, seeking to influence domestic institutions and processes, others have sought allies across national boundaries, have lobbied other government officials, and have spent scarce resources in building transnational coalitions. Furthermore, while some organizations have tended to focus primarily on labor's particularistic claims, others have attempted to broaden their agendas and have transformed their initial demands and visions.

These choices of paths are not fixed but are "contingently reconstructed by actors in ongoing dialogue with unfolding situations" (Emirbayer and Mische 1998, 966). More specifically, they can change because of lessons learned, and through negotiated interactions with other actors. Changes can also result from how actors interpret new political opportunities at the domestic level.[8] By bringing together a focus on relationships and on political contexts as sources of change, the approach advocated in this article can help to explain the variations in labor's paths to transnationality through time.

The first part of the article explains the profound shifts in how labor organizations and other civil society actors have discussed the contents and impacts of multilateral trade negotiations and have mobilized in order to influence them. It explains how, in the past 30 years, a global trade regime has emerged in parallel to the proliferation of new regional and bilateral trade agreements. It is in the Americas that this change in trade politics has been most clearly felt.

The second and third parts analyze the different paths to transnationality taken by a key group of labor federations in this new context. These paths are analyzed in terms of the various attempts at coalition building among allies and in terms of the different answers given by actors to the question, what should trade agreements look like? The last part of the article pays special attention to the proposal of inclusion of a social clause in free trade agreements The introduction of language in treaties that links access to trade agreement benefits to respect for labor rights has been the focus of contentious debates among labor organizations, business representatives, and governmental actors in the region at least since the beginning of the 1990s. What is more interesting is that this proposal also has been a matter of difference among labor organizations themselves, as well as between them and other civil society actors. This makes the issue a good example of the possibility of negotiating common ground within heterogeneous transnational coalitions. It also, however, indicates how fragile the new attempts at labor internationalism remain in the face of different interpretations and reactions to changing political contexts.

THE CREATION OF A GLOBAL TRADE REGIME

The trade policy arena has historically been a contentious one, and labor organizations have participated intermittently for many decades in debates about the potential impact of protectionist and liberal policies. It has also been a multifaceted arena. Although only recently have actors and scholars paid greater attention to the interfaces between trade and other policy arenas, such as the environment, food safety, or human rights, these were been completely ignored in the past (Aaronson 2001). Given the potential impact of trade negotiations on productive systems, the labor market, prices, and technological innovation, decisions about trade policies have always been a part of broader economic and political debates about development models and the role of the state. Furthermore, because gains and losses from trade are unevenly distributed, the moral implications of such decisions also have been an inseparable part of these debates (García 2003).

Governments officially acknowledged the link between international competitiveness and labor rights in the 1919 Preamble to the Constitution of the International Labor Organization (ILO), which states, "the failure of any nation to adopt humane conditions of labour is an obstacle in the way of other nations which desire to improve the conditions in their own countries" (ILO 2006). Although the ILO never had the necessary tools to enforce this principle effectively, it thus recognized the need to promote a balance between competitiveness and respect for labor rights, which was in fact one of the motivations behind its creation (ILO 2006).

At times, these early debates involved other civil society organizations. For example, negotiations on specific international regulations that linked trade and environmental issues included conservationists and naturalists, who lobbied state officials at the domestic as well as at the transnational level (Aaronson 2001, 45). However, perhaps the best-known instance of early transnational collective action related to trade did not deal with trade in goods but trade in persons: the transnational abolitionist movement that lasted from the end of the eighteenth century through the nineteenth century. It brought together activists in Europe and the Americas, who engaged in intensive dialogue and collaboration (Keck and Sikkink 1998, esp. chap. 2).

In spite of these precedents, however, as early as about 30 years ago, international trade was an issue of interest mostly to government officials (the executive powers and, in some countries, such as the United States, the legislative), to international organizations (in the twentieth century), and—unevenly through time—to farmers, producers of industrial goods, and workers. Civil society groups, such as the environmentalists, became interested in trade negotiations indirectly, through the filter of specific issues, such as the trade in furs or the protection of an animal species.

Indeed, for most of the history of the General Agreement on Tariffs and Trade (GATT), business organizations were almost the sole nonstate actors to follow negotiations closely.[9] This situation began to shift partly because of a progressive process of expanding the negotiating agenda. The Tokyo Round (1973–79) introduced debates about nontariff barriers, such as subsidies, national procurement, and health and regulatory standards, and the Uruguay Round (1986–94) subsequently deepened this trend.

This expansion of the scope of the negotiating agenda coincided with the transitions to democracy in Latin America and with a greater awareness by a broad variety of civil society organizations of the domestic impact of international negotiations. The new role of the GATT represented a wake-up call to many, whereby "what had been sort of an apathetic attitude towards trade agreements quickly became a central issue" (Dillon 2004) to civil society actors, such as nongovernmental organizations specializing in human rights, development, and consumer rights (see also Wallach 2004).

Thus, by the time the World Trade Organization (WTO) was created in 1995, a broad group of civil society actors from developed and developing countries alike had concluded that trade negotiations should be more closely followed, at the domestic as well as at the international level. The WTO's greater powers and expanded membership compared to the GATT helped further to justify this attention (Wallach and Woodall 2004; Williams 2005).[10] Not only did this new organization continue to expand the agenda to other policy areas, but it also gained new regulatory powers through the creation of a more efficient and stronger dispute settlement mechanism than the one that had existed under the GATT; the extension of the Trade Policy Review Mechanism, which, under the GATT, was limited to reviewing members' policies on goods trade, and under the WTO also reviews public policies on services and intellectual property; and the development of a set of mandatory codes.

The transition from the GATT to the WTO represents the culmination of the process of creation of a global trade regime. In this new context, the focus of much of the political economy literature on the interests of labor, capital, and states became too narrow to understand the coalition-building dynamics around trade.[11] Side-by-side with labor organizations, other civil society actors, such as environmental, human rights, faith-based, and consumer rights organizations, became part of the trade debates. Collaboration and conflict between labor and these newcomers became more relevant in explaining labor's choices of paths to transnationality from the 1990s on.

Free Trade and Labor in the Americas

At the dawn of the 1990s, the Americas became an important laboratory for this new chapter in the history of trade politics and transnational collective action. However, debates about trade agreements and regional integration were hardly a novelty in the region. The goal of free trade between the United States and Canada was more than a century old when the two countries finally signed an agreement (in 1989). Similarly, Latin America's history is punctuated by failed attempts to fulfill what many saw, at least rhetorically, as its "historical calling"; that is, to become integrated as only one country. The first round of attempts at integration in the nineteenth century—some of which included the United States—collapsed under the weight of geographical distances, the power of local caudillos, and the different interests of the subregions (see, e.g., Furtado 1976, esp. part 1; Lambert 1968; Bethell 1985).

Between the 1950s and the 1980s, the United States and Latin America pursued antagonistic trade policies. In the United States, the end of World War II inaugurated a period of trade liberalization. In Latin America, however, these were protectionist times. Both strategies were influenced by the Cold War. While in the United States free trade was perceived as an important part of the nation's anticommunist strategy, in Latin America, protectionist policies were considered a key tool in reaching autonomous economic development.[12]

Civil society participation varied considerably during these decades. According to Aaronson, "from 1945 to 1979, most Americans simply did not care about trade policy.... Trade policy was made in Washington and in Geneva by a relatively small circle of government officials, trade unionists, business leaders, and academics" (Aaronson 2001, 85). Even if most U.S. citizens remained oblivious to trade negotiations, labor and business organizations participated actively in the debates promoted by Congress, but not necessarily as opponents to free trade. Up to the 1960s, most affiliates of the American Federation of Labor-Congress of Industrial Organizations (AFL-CIO) were part of pro–free trade domestic coalitions (Destler 1998). In Latin America, though, trade policies remained a black box, accessed almost exclusively by a small circle of national bureaucrats.

At the beginning of the 1990s, a third round of trade liberalization and integration attempts began, in a very different context. Economic policies in the United States and Latin America converged, and a new wave of agreements was negotiated within an ideological framework provided by neoliberalism. Under U.S. leadership, this "new regionalism" consisted mainly of the negotiation of agreements aimed at creating free trade zones, while at the same time including a wide number of provisions in issue areas such as intellectual property and investors' rights.

In this context, the traditional understanding of free trade areas in regional integration theory as the first phase of trade liberalization in an ever-widening process that would lead to the formation of a customs union, a common market, and eventually an economic union (Balassa 1961) was not useful for understanding these negotiations. For example, the North American Free Trade Agreement (NAFTA) liberalized trade and, at the same time, introduced specific elements of domestic policy harmonization typical of the formation of a customs union or a common market.

On the other hand, freedom of movement of labor was excluded from the negotiating agenda, and the creation of supranational authorities was limited to those needed for dispute settlements.[13] At the same time, a few South-South initiatives, such as the Common Market of the Southern Cone (MERCOSUR) and the Andean Community, maintained the ambition to create common markets, once again justifying Latin American efforts at integration as a way of strengthening the region's autonomy and political power in the international system.[14]

Labor did not respond to these initiatives with one voice. In North America, the Mexican Confederation of Labor (CTM) supported NAFTA, unlike most U.S. and Canadian labor, as well as other Mexican organizations. In South America, the most important labor federations decided to give MERCOSUR their "critical support."[15] In both cases, however, these were disappointing experiences for labor. Although it is true that organizations from South America were able to participate in various decisionmaking and consultative forums, 15 years later this participation has had little impact on integration policies (Jakobsen 1999; von Bülow 2003).[16]

Similarly, NAFTA's labor side agreement has not led to concrete and measurable results in terms of better compliance with labor rights standards in North America. Some scholars argue that it has had an indirect impact because of the so-called "sunshine effect"; that is, the public nature of the agreement's complaint procedures and the public's adverse reaction have exerted pressure on governments and employers to follow the rule of law (see, e.g., Bognanno and Lu 2003). What is certain is that these experiences have helped generate important shifts in the alliances among labor organizations and between these and other civil society organizations in the region.

Debates about the impact of negotiations in these subregional tracks converged at the hemispheric level when governments launched the FTAA negotiations in the mid-1990s. Unlike both NAFTA and MERCOSUR, however, the FTAA talks never even incorporated a labor dimension (for a review, see Charnovitz 2005). The main arguments from those who opposed the agreement focused on the potentially negative impact of further trade liberalization on jobs, labor standards, and national sovereignty, all of which built on the critiques of NAFTA. Similarly, the diffusion to several countries of multisectoral domestic trade coalitions came out of the anti-NAFTA organizing experience in Canada, the United States, and Mexico. The creation of consensus-based transnational spaces and attempts to develop alternative proposals also built on labor's previous efforts to influence MERCOSUR (von Bülow 2003).

THE POWER OF LABOR ORGANIZATIONS, AND ITS LIMITS

The relevance of labor organizations emerges as a common pattern in the trade protest networks mapped in Brazil, Chile, Mexico, and the United States. This is, arguably, not surprising, because labor organizations enjoy more access to financial and human resources than many other civil society organizations, and their membership, in general terms, perceives itself as affected directly by trade agreements. Indeed, unions have participated in debates about international trade for many decades, and some of the most contentious disagreements over the benefits or dangers of trade liberalization have concerned the consequences for labor markets.

On the other hand, labor organizations in the Americas, a few notable exceptions notwithstanding, have traditionally had weak collaborative relationships with other types of organizations at the domestic as well as the transnational level.[17] International relations of labor movements, moreover, still are characterized by diplomatic relationships among labor federations, and their international relations secretariats are usually weak in comparison with those in charge of domestic affairs.[18] Sustained collaboration between workers' organizations from the North and South that compete for scarce jobs and investments is especially difficult to produce. Despite more than a century of internationalist rhetoric, labor organizations have retained deep national roots.[19]

To map the embeddedness of labor organizations in trade protest networks, this study asked key informants from 123 civil society organizations (CSOs) from Brazil, Chile, Mexico, and the United States various questions about their relationships at the domestic and transnational levels. Although this is not a representative sample, it does include the labor federations and the subset of CSOs that were most active in challenging trade negotiations until 2004.

Specifically, informants were asked to nominate their organization's closest allies in trade-related collective action.[20] Although labor organizations represented less than 20 percent of the total number of CSOs interviewed, they were among the most nominated in every country. In the Brazilian case, for example, 75 percent of the 29 CSOs interviewed nominated the Unified Workers' Central (CUT) as one of their closest allies; similarly, 65 percent of the 41 CSOs interviewed in the United States nominated the AFL-CIO. Although in Chile and Mexico labor organizations were less central, CUT-Chile and Mexico's Labor Authentic Front (FAT) still were among the three most nominated by informants (see table 1).

Still, not all informants nominated every labor organization as a close ally. Labor did not respond as a unified or homogeneous front to the challenges and opportunities created by trade negotiations. Labor organizations in the four countries studied took different paths in these debates in terms of the breadth of their alliances, the site of activism privileged (domestic or international), the amount of resources dedicated to trade-related mobilization, and the willingness to negotiate common agendas and frames with allies.

Labor in a New Relational Context

The scholarly literature on labor transnationalism has struggled to explain how and why labor organizations engage—or not—in transnational collaboration. Many authors use as independent variables the differences in industrial structure, state institutions, and practices or labor ideologies to explain the variety in form and frequency of labor transnationalism. Generally speaking, these authors have not explored the impact of labor organizations' relations with other actors. Transnational action is seen *ex post* as the

Table 1. Civil Society Organizations Most Nominated as Closest Allies in Trade Debates (by country, in-degree, and type of organization)

Country	Civil Society Organization	In-degree (%)[a]	Type of organization
Brazil	CUT (Unified Workers' Central)	75	Labor federation
	MST (Landless Workers' Movement)	68	Rural workers' movement
	FASE (Federation of Organisms for Social and Educational Assistance)	54	NGO
Chile	ACJR (Chilean Alliance for a Fair and Responsible Trade)	64	NGO
	ANAMURI (National Association of Rural and Indigenous Women)	41	Rural womens' organization
	CUT (Unified Workers' Central)	41	Labor federation
Mexico	DECA-EP (Equipo Pueblo)	60	NGO
	FAT (Authentic Labor Front)	57	Labor federation
	CILAS (Center for Labor Investigation and Consulting)	47	Labor NGO
United States	AFL-CIO	65	Labor federation
	Public Citizen	57	NGO
	IPS (Institute for Policy Studies)	50	NGO
	Friends of the Earth	50	Environmental organization

[a]In-degree counts the number of times each organization was nominated by the others as one of their closest allies in trade-related activities. In the table, in-degree is presented as a percentage of the total number of possible nominations.
Source: Author interviews.

product of a single, previously taken autonomous decision, as if organizations existed in bubbles and did not change their views through time as a result of interaction with others.

For example, Michael Dreiling and Ian Robinson can successfully explain the variation of union strategies on NAFTA on the basis of their differentiation of union types, defined "in terms of the inclusiveness of union collective identities and the degree to which union conceptions of a just political economy are at odds with the existing system" (Dreiling and Robinson 1998, 164). However, it is difficult to generalize this argument so that it can explain how organizations representing very different union types achieved a common position in regard to MERCOSUR, or how positions have converged in opposition to the FTAA. Past trajectories, political identities, and alliances are relevant, but in the 1990s, labor organizations became embedded in a new environment of relationships, which influenced the goals and strategies they pursued.

At the beginning of 1998, four years after NAFTA took effect, John Sweeney, the president of the AFL-CIO, made a historic trip to Mexico, the first by a U.S. labor federation president to that country in 74 years. During that visit, Sweeney talked to the whole spectrum of Mexican labor organizations, including independent ones, such as the FAT and the newly created National Union of Workers (UNT), thus officially ending the exclusive relationship it had nurtured with the CTM during the Cold War.

Contentious debates among labor organizations from both countries about NAFTA's potential impact are the key to understanding this change. As an AFL-CIO official explained,

> NAFTA was very significant in that the old Cold War definitions of trade union alliance—with whom we should work—were no longer viable. It put down a kind of practice dogma, if not an explicit dogma, that the only real partner in Mexico was the CTM, and that even that partnership, the only way it could be maintained, was on a very superficial diplomatic basis. The challenge of NAFTA completely overturned that premise. (AFL-CIO 2004)

The weakening of the AFL-CIO–CTM alliance helped, in turn, to change the role of the Inter-American Regional Workers' Organization (ORIT) in the debates about trade agreements in the Americas.[21] As table 2 shows, up to 2004, all of the labor centrals involved in trade protest networks in the four countries studied were affiliated with the ORIT at the regional level and with the International Confederation of Free Trade Unions (ICFTU) at the global level. Although the ICFTU was not the only global-level labor organization, it emerged as the strongest one in the post—Cold War era (Myconos 2005, esp. chap. 5). Similarly, ORIT was not the only regional labor organization, but in the 1990s it became by far the most representative and powerful, especially after several important, previously nonaligned labor organizations, such as the Brazilian CUT, decided to join.[22]

This revitalized ORIT contributed significantly to strengthening the view among labor leaders that sustained alliances with other civil society actors in the region were vital. Labor federations that had participated in efforts to build cross-sectoral trade coalitions at the domestic level, such as the Canadian Labour Congress, and organizations that had historical ties to other civil society actors, such as CUT-Brazil, were key advocates of the so-called social alliances within ORIT.

An important event exemplifies this trend clearly. During the Workers of the Americas Forum, held in parallel to the Belo Horizonte FTAA Ministerial Meeting in 1997, representatives of other kinds of CSOs were invited for the first time to participate in an ORIT-organized event of that size (CUT 1997). A final declaration signed jointly by ORIT, NGOs, and social movement organizations turned out to be the first step toward the creation of the Hemispheric Social Alliance (HSA), a broad transnational coalition that, between 2000 and 2004, mobilized against the FTAA negotiations.[23] At this point, the lack of negotiating channels strengthened a common identity among labor organizations that were most opposed to the agreement and weakened those in the AFL-CIO and ORIT that advocated a less critical position (Smith and Korzeniewicz 2007).

Reaching out to other civil society actors also meant formulating a broader agenda on trade negotiations. Until then, ORIT's demands, presented to negotiators in previous FTAA ministerial meetings, had been specifically labor-related: the creation of a Labor Forum (as a counterweight to the already existing Business Forum) and the creation of a working group on social and labor issues. But when ORIT formally declared its opposition to the FTAA negotiations, in April 2001, its arguments were based on a wider set of issues, including those that were considered relevant by NGOs and social movement organizations affiliated with the HSA (Anner and Evans 2004, 41).

However, not all of ORIT's affiliates accepted the argument that broader alliances and extended agendas were an imperative of new times. Their individual levels of engagement in the construction of the HSA varied widely, and several important labor federations were not active participants (Anner and Evans 2004, 42). For example, the Mexican CTM, the Brazilian Labor Force (*Força Sindical*, FS), and the Chilean CUT were

Table 2. Main Labor Central Participants in the Trade Debates in Brazil, Chile, Mexico, and the United States, 2004

	Brazil			Chile	Mexico			United States
Labor Central	CUT	CGT	FS	CUT	FAT	CTM	UNT	AFL-CIO
International labor organization membership	ICFTU-ORIT CCSCS	ICFTU-ORIT CCSCS	ICFTU-ORIT CCSCS	ICFTU-ORIT CCSCS	ICFTU-ORIT	ICFTU-ORIT	ICFTU-ORIT	ICFTU-ORIT
Position in trade debates (MERCOSUR, NAFTA, FTAA)	Critical supporter of MERCOSUR, participated in campaign against FTAA	Critical supporter of MERCOSUR but not active participant in campaign against FTAA	Critical supporter of MERCOSUR but with no clear position on FTAA	Internal division during U.S.-Chile FTA talks. Against the FTAA but not active participant in campaign against FTAA	Early challenger of NAFTA; participated in campaign against FTAA, joined UNT 1997	In favor of NAFTA, changed its position to oppose FTAA, but not active participant in campaign against FTAA	Created after NAFTA (1997); against FTAA but not active participant in campaign against FTAA	Early challenger of NAFTA; participated in campaign against FTAA
Active participant in domestic trade coalitions	Yes	No	No	No	Yes	No	No	Yes
Active participant in HSA	Yes	No	No	No	Yes	No	No	Yes

Source: Author interviews.

much less active than the CUT-Brazil, the FAT, and the AFL-CIO (see table 2). Debates about the scope of labor's "social alliances" were a key source of contention among organizations in the 1990s, and remained an unresolved issue in some cases, as ORIT's secretary-general explains.

> We had to overcome a lot of resistance. There was a lot of confusion about the defini-tion of civil society. Many argued that it was only NGOs, but there's also rural move-ments, etc. . . . One of the ICFTU officials argued, "what are social alliances worth if NGOs are only the dog and its owner?" We had to fight that. The second obstacle was the fear that labor unions would lose their identity. The third was the attitude that social alliances are all right, but the labor movement must lead them. In 1998 was when we had the most difficulties. Today, no ORIT affiliate questions the validity of social alliances. However, some do not put them in practice. (Báez 2005)

Báez mentions the difficulties faced in 1998 because of another key event: the Summit of the Americas, which was held in Chile that year. While ORIT affiliates, such as CUT-Brazil, the Canadian Labour Congress, and the AFL-CIO wanted to organize a People's Summit jointly with a group of Chilean NGOs and social movement organizations, the local affiliate (CUT-Chile) rejected the idea. In the end, two events were held simultane-ously, the Labor Summit and the People's Summit.

> It was very problematic for us in ORIT, because we were trying to forge a broader alliance, what became [known as] the "social alliance." We thought it was very impor-tant, very strategic . . . but it was difficult, because CUT was our main host. (AFL-CIO 2004)

According to the various coalition-building strategies chosen by actors up to 2004, it is possible to differentiate three groups among the major labor federations in the four countries studied. One type is those that participated systematically through time in domestic and transnational alliances and built a diverse array of trade-related ties with other types of organizations at both levels (CUT-Brazil, the AFL-CIO, and the FAT in Mexico). Second is those that had only a subregional presence and few trade-related ties with other types of organizations (the other two Brazilian federations, the General Workers' Confederation, CGT, and FS, along with the Chilean CUT and the Mexican UNT). Third is the Mexican CTM, which had a domestically oriented approach to trade debates while at the same time maintaining its regional and global diplomatic ties (see table 2).

Labor leaders from the first group justify their decision to seek sustained and strong links with other CSOs as a way of achieving better results in a context of diminished labor power.

> Many labor unions still think that they are the main actors of revolutionary change. This is false; labor unions have less and less power. We think that the specific labor agenda has to be converted into a public interest agenda, and we have not been able to do this conversion. (Villalba 2004)

Two active AFL-CIO participants in the trade debates at the time of the interviews went further in justifying the extension of labor unions' agenda and coalition-building practices as a way of changing other actors' perceptions about labor organizations' practices.

> The weakness of labor unions in the trade debates is that everybody assumes that it is entirely self-interest that motivates you, so they can dismiss that. When you are

working with religious organizations, the human rights organizations, it adds credibility. . . . The labor movement in the U.S. is too small and too weak to carry a lot of political debates if we are isolated, and we recognize that. . . . We want other people to understand that labor groups can play a progressive role in international trade discussions. (Lee 2004)

We have focused more and more of our work on issues like investment, services, intellectual property, all these things that may not have a huge impact on the U.S., but do have a huge impact on developing countries. . . . In Seattle [during the 1999 WTO meeting], the press reported that what we were for was only focused on workers' rights, and they characterized it as sort of the antidevelopmental agenda. We realized that we needed to be more aggressive and more public about the fact that our critique on trade is not just about labor standards. (Drake 2004)

The different views on the breadth of coalition building are reflected in the answers given by representatives of labor federations when asked how they would contact allies in order to plan parallel events to an FTAA ministerial meeting in another country.[24] Although all those who responded asserted that they would use labor's diplomatic channels (ORIT), the ones most committed to the creation of broader alliances—the AFL-CIO, CUT-Brazil, and FAT-Mexico—also said that they would coordinate their actions with other kinds of civil society organizations through multisectoral trade coalitions such as the HSA or its national chapters (see figure 1).

Accommodations like these, however, present labor with a dilemma. The extension of issues and agendas allows labor organizations to maintain relationships with many heterogeneous actors at once, but often at the cost of suppressed demands, diminished visibility of their own agendas, and greater complications in negotiating common actions.[25] As Sidney Tarrow has argued, activists often find themselves "divided between the global framing of transnational movement campaigns and the local needs of those whose claims they want to represent" (2005, 76). This problem is clearest when actors perceive that they have a new political opportunity to negotiate their demands. A good example of this dilemma is that faced by labor organizations that are active members of the Hemispheric Social Alliance.

THE SEARCH FOR ALTERNATIVES

Labor organizations involved in the trade policy debates often have confronted the question, if not this agreement, then what? The question may come from parliamentarians, government officials, the media, or other civil society organizations. Once again, responses have not been homogeneous. The different answers given by labor organizations also help to differentiate among the paths to transnationality those organizations take.

Indeed, it has been easier for labor organizations to find common ground simply by opposing negotiations such as the FTAA than by agreeing on an alternative that would be acceptable to all. Even in the context of the FTAA talks, however, there were attempts at building a common understanding of what such an alternative should look like, and these attempts went well beyond ORIT's boundaries. The initiative came mainly from the labor centrals that were most active in the HSA.

The document produced by HSA members, *Alternatives for the Americas*, represents a "unique effort" (Doucet 2005, 277) to craft a common platform among organizations from different countries and sectors. In its first edition, the authors defined it as "more than an economic doctrine. . . . It brings together proposals that were considered viable

Figure 1. Main Gateways Used by Selected Labor Federations to Contact Allies in Other Countries Before a Trade Summit

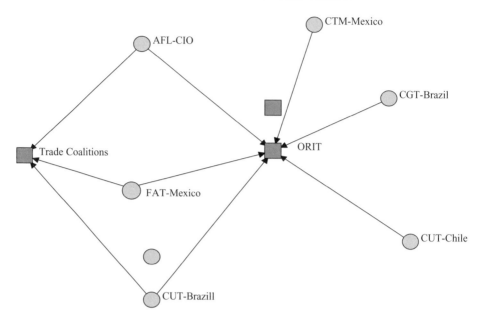

⬤ Labor federations

◼ Gateways used to contact allies in the other country to organize a trade-related event.

Source: Author interviews.

and on which there was a broad consensus. *The priority was the establishment of the basis of an inclusive alliance* (HSA 1998, 6, 10; emphasis added).

Thus, *Alternatives for the Americas* (henceforth *Alternatives*) was as much an attempt to foster the HSA's credibility with negotiators and other civil society actors as to build collective identity within the coalition.[26] The five editions produced between 1998 and 2005 illustrate three mechanisms by which members have attempted progressively to construct agreement: the extension of agendas, the suppression of divisive issues, and the transformation of initial demands.[27] The debates about the introduction of a social clause in free trade agreements is a good example of two of these mechanisms, the extension and transformation of demands.

The Debate over a Social Clause in *Alternatives for the Americas*

The section of *Alternatives* on labor rights presents two key demands: the incorporation of a social clause (or "labor clause") in trade agreements and the progressive upward harmonization of labor laws and conditions among signatories. While it would be hard to find any member of the HSA that would oppose these general demands, they presuppose a vision of global governance that is not shared by all, one that accepts international regulations that, in practice, would place limits on national sovereignty. The comparison

Table 3. *Alternatives for the Americas*: Main Proposals on Labor Standards
in Two Editions

1998 (1st Edition)	2005 (5th Edition)
Incorporation of a labor clause (the commitment to respect basic workers' rights with an enforcement mechanism delegated to the ILO with the possibility of trade sanctions targeted at governments or businesses), and a safety net for workers who lost their jobs	Incorporation of a labor clause (with the possibility of trade sanctions targeted primarily at businesses, and only initiated when expressly requested by organizations representing the workers whose rights have been violated), and a safety net for workers who lost their jobs
Progressive upward harmonization of working rights and conditions	Progressive upward harmonization of working rights and conditions; access of migrants, women, and informal workers to labor rights

Changes in italics.
Sources: HSA 1998, 2005.

of the proposals on the introduction of a labor clause in trade agreements in the first
and fifth editions of *Alternatives* (see table 3) exemplifies how actors have transformed
the initial version and extended their agenda to include migrants' and women's rights.

The introduction of labor clauses in trade agreements has been a perennial source
of contention among actors, not only in the Americas but worldwide.[28] Many in the South,
as well as some in the North, have seen labor clause proposals as safeguards and protectionist tools rather than as labor solidarity initiatives. Under the umbrella of the HSA,
nevertheless, some of the most important labor organizations in the Americas finally
reached a consensus on the issue.[29]

The 2005 edition of *Alternatives* differs from that of 1998 in several aspects. It puts
greater emphasis on a system that is based on incentives instead of coercion. It stipulates
that the perpetrators of labor rights violations (not the countries) should be the ones
made accountable. It asserts that the enforcement process must be transparent and public,
with the participation of civil society organizations and experts (see table 3). It accepts
the idea of supranational tribunals to investigate violations and decide on enforcement,
at the same time that it guarantees greater control of decisions by demanding the participation of representatives of those affected.

This agreement on the wording of a proposal became possible because advocates
of labor clauses transformed their initial demands. More specifically, it provides an
example of a negotiated outcome of differences between the AFL-CIO and Latin American
labor federations. The disciplinary focus on actors that violate laws, instead of on the
whole countries, was an early demand of the FAT and other Mexican actors during the
NAFTA debates about the labor side agreement. Similarly, the inclusion of those affected
by potential sanctions in the enforcement debates and the emphasis on incentives are
attempts to avoid using enforcement procedures as protectionist tools and to minimize
the potentially negative consequences of penalties on the development of the South.

By accepting these changes, actors in the North could downplay charges that their
defense of the social clause was motivated by "labor protectionism," because trade sanctions would only punish workers in developing countries by making goods produced in
those regions less competitive. This, however, remains a fragile consensus. Debates about
how labor rights and trade should be linked exemplify the tensions originating from the
extension and transformation of demands in order to accommodate different visions.

The fragility of this consensus relates to the dilemmas of the simultaneity of action
at multiple levels. More specifically, domestically rooted organizations, such as labor

unions, try to reach agreements with allies from other sectors and countries, while at the same time responding to local and national pressures from their constituencies and other actors. These pressures, however, are felt differently in each country, because of the various rules concerning trade policymaking and the changing domestic political contexts.

In Brazil, Chile, and Mexico, the negotiation of international trade agreements is under the exclusive jurisdiction of the executive branch. The proposed agreements are then submitted to the national congress for a yes or no vote, without the possibility of revisions or amendments.[30] The United States stands apart from the Latin American countries because its constitution grants Congress the primary power over trade policymaking. Since 1974, it has been Congress's responsibility periodically to approve a Trade Promotion Authority Act (TPA, best known as fast track legislation). This grants temporary authority to the President to negotiate trade agreements with other countries while limiting the role of Congress to approving or rejecting the treaties within 90 days, without the possibility of amendment. Although the restrictions on the role of Congress have sparked criticism by those who oppose trade negotiations, U.S. legislators still have considerably more power than their counterparts in Brazil, Chile, or Mexico. Through the TPA, they can specify objectives that they expect U.S. negotiators to pursue and can introduce criteria for labor standards that negotiations must meet for agreements to be subsequently approved. The President has to notify Congress before entering into an agreement, and is required to consult with congressional committees during the negotiations.

The different domestic policymaking rules and changing political contexts present various challenges to those who would contest trade agreements, including which decisionmakers to target, when to present alternatives, and the content of the alternatives. In the United States, efforts to influence trade policymaking are divided between lobbying Congress—especially during fast track and trade agreement votes—and executive agencies—especially during trade agreement negotiations. Thus, legislators ask U.S. labor representatives to present specific criteria that trade agreements would have to meet to become acceptable, especially when Democrats have held the majority in Congress (as they have since the 2006 legislative elections).

Although the AFL-CIO did extend its agenda on trade and thereby transform the contents of the labor clause proposal, if there had been the opportunity to negotiate what remains its key demand—the inclusion of enforceable provisions to protect core labor standards in future trade agreements—the strong ties built with allies would be in peril, as a Brazilian CUT representative admitted after the U.S. presidential elections of 2004.

> If [John] Kerry [the Democratic candidate] had won, with regard to the trade issue it would have been very complicated for us. . . . I think it could have created a conflict with the AFL-CIO on the social clause. Because even if CUT has agreed to a social clause, we have gone beyond that in our internal debate. . . . Today we are in favor of the contents of a social clause, but we think that introducing it in a trade agreement is not at all sufficient [to gain our support for it] (CUT-Brazil 2005).

The recent debates about the U.S.-Peru Free Trade Agreement in the U.S. Congress further illustrate the fragility of agreements established among members of the Hemispheric Social Alliance in the context of a new political opening to negotiate labor's agenda at the domestic level. Anchored in the changes that it was able to negotiate with the new Democratic majority, the AFL-CIO kept a neutral position with respect to this free trade agreement. It neither supported nor vocally opposed the FTA, an ambiguous and novel position by this federation in the period since the NAFTA vote. In a letter to congressional representatives signed by its legislative director, dated October 1, 2007, the AFL-CIO applauded the changes made by the new Democratic majority to the labor and environmental sections of the agreement; at the same time, however, it criticized the lack of response to its demands to change the contents of provisions on investment, procurement, and services (Samuel 2007).

Not all U.S. labor organizations reacted the same way, though. In fact, different interpretations of how best to deal with this new political opportunity led to a deepening of the recent split in U.S. labor. The newly created Change to Win Coalition opposed the U.S.-Peru FTA and criticized the AFL-CIO's position, siding with the majority of members of the national chapter of the Hemispheric Social Alliance. While also applauding the changes made by the new Democratic majority, it argued that they did not go far enough to gain its support (Burger 2006; Change to Win Coalition 2007).

CONCLUSIONS

Never before the mid-1990s were political conditions so favorable to labor internationalism in the Americas. Collaborative ties among labor organizations and other CSOs in the hemisphere have multiplied considerably in the past 15 years. Yet this new chapter is part of a process of arduous political negotiations, not only among labor organizations from different countries but also within countries and across social movement sectors. The multiple paths to transnationality taken by labor organizations in the context of trade mobilizations express not the birth of a homogeneous kind of labor internationalism, but the dilemmas that actors face in the search for ways to respond to a new and uncertain political context.

Some attempts at new forms of collaboration have succeeded. In the period studied, between the beginning of the 1990s and 2004, a common view was constructed among key ORIT affiliates in the hemisphere with respect to trade negotiations between Latin American countries and the United States. The opposition to agreements such as the FTAA was based on a broad set of complaints and demands that extended well beyond labor's particularistic demands. Through this expanded agenda, some of the region's most powerful labor organizations, such as the AFL-CIO, have tried to overcome the traditional difficulties in labor unions' relationships with NGOs and other civil society actors. Recent initiatives, such as *Labor's Platform for the Americas* (see Godio 2007), a document presented by ORIT affiliates to presidents during the Mar del Plata Summit of the Americas in 2005, support the argument that at least a group of key labor organizations has come to discuss trade negotiations and integration processes through broader frames.

Simultaneously, though, labor organizations maintain their roots at the domestic level, with agendas of their own and particular priorities. Thus, even among those that have struggled to build common paths to transnationality since the 1990s, the fragility of agreements is clearest when actors perceive that new windows of opportunity for negotiating concrete proposals have opened at the domestic level.

The various paths to transnationality taken by labor in the Americas in the period studied do not divide them or their allies neatly between an "internationalist" and a "nationalist" group. Different emphases are used ambiguously by the same actors, depending on the specific issue, the context, and the results of negotiated interactions at the domestic and transnational levels. The politics of scale, understood in terms of the paradox of the rise of transnationalism in parallel to the continued relevance of national-level claims and targets, represents a real source of challenges, both for scholars and for labor organizations.

In sum, there is no single type of labor internationalism waiting to be discovered. To understand the potential of and the obstacles to labor collective action across borders, it is crucial to consider the complex interactions between dynamic domestic political contexts and labor's embeddedness in new multiscale and cross-sectoral networks. A relational approach that is sensitive to domestic politics—domestic decisionmaking rules and perceptions of new political opportunities—helps to explain the different choices made by similar organizations across countries and through time.

ABBREVIATIONS

AFL-CIO	American Federation of Labor-Congress of Industrial Organizations
CCSCS	Coordination of Southern Cone Labor Centrals
CGT	General Workers' Confederation (Brazil)
CLAT	Latin American Workers' Confederation
CSOs	Civil society organizations
CTM	Mexican Confederation of Labor
CUT	Unified Workers' Central (Brazil, Chile)
ECLAC, CEPAL	Economic Commission on Latin America and the Caribbean
FAT	Labor Authentic Labor Front (Mexico)
FS	Labor Force (*Força Sindical*, Brazil)
FTAA	Free Trade Area of the Americas
GATT	General Agreement on Tariffs and Trade
HSA	Hemispheric Social Alliance
ICFTU	International Confederation of Free Trade Unions
MERCOSUR	Southern Cone Common Market
NAFTA	North American Free Trade Agreement
ORIT	Inter-American Regional Workers' Organization
RMALC	Mexican Action Network on Free Trade
TPA	Trade Promotion Authority Act
UNT	National Union of Workers (Mexico)
WTO	World Trade Organization

NOTES

This article is based mostly on the field research undertaken for the author's Ph.D. dissertation between 2004 and 2006 (von Bülow 2007). The doctoral research was made possible by grants from the Fulbright Commission, CAPES/Brazilian Ministry of Education, the National Council for Scientific and Technological Development (CNPq-Brazil), and the Political Science Department and the Latin American Program at Johns Hopkins University. I thank all the people who gave me the interviews that made this work possible, in Brazil, Chile, Peru, Mexico, and the United States, most especially Maria Sílvia Portella de Castro. A previous version of this article was presented at the 27th Latin American Studies Association Congress, Montréal, 2007. I thank Russell Smith, María Cook, and Marie-Josée Massicotte for their comments during our LASA panel, as well as the insightful critiques and suggestions made by three anonymous reviewers for *LAPS*.

    1 The first attempts at hemispheric collaboration date from the end of the nineteenth century, but they were short-lived. During the Cold War, previous initiatives fell under the ideological polarization between "free unionism," sponsored in the hemisphere mainly by the AFL-CIO, and unions that were linked to the Communist-led World Federation of Trade Unions. A third, non-aligned group existed, but its transnational activities were often limited to diplomatic exchanges. Unionism in Latin America was further stifled by the military dictatorships that dominated the region between the 1960s and the 1980s.

    2 Similarly, Tarrow (2005) speaks of "new transnational contention" and "new transnational activism"; and Waterman and his colleagues talk about "new labor internationalisms" (Waterman 1998; Waterman and Wills 2001).

3 Let it be noted that this is not a new approach, and many previous writers, such as Georg Simmel and Karl Marx, adopted a relational perspective in their writings.

4 For a call to shift from the search of general models to the study of mechanisms, processes, and episodes, see McAdam et al. 2001. These authors define mechanisms as "a delimited class of events that alter relations among specified sets of elements in identical or closely similar ways over a variety of situations" (24).

5 As Mark Blyth has put it, "structures do not come with an instruction sheet" (2002, 7).

6 Most of the interviews were conducted between May 2004 and September 2005. (For more details about the research, see the methodological appendix in von Bülow 2007) .

7 CUT-Brazil's former secretary of international affairs goes even farther to argue that in spite of previous instances of cross-border labor collaboration, it is only now, with the process of globalization and technological progress, that it is really possible to speak of labor internationalism. See Jakobsen 1999, 234.

8 The concept of political opportunities has been the focus of intense debate in the social movement theory literature in recent years. The definition used here is the one suggested by Tarrow in the second edition of *Power in Movement*: "consistent—but not necessarily formal or permanent—dimensions of the political environment that provide incentives for collective action by affecting people's expectations for success or failure" (1998, 76–77). In this chapter, however, the term emphasizes the relevance of considering how actors may differ in their interpretations of these opportunities, in agreement with the critique presented by authors such as Goodwin and Jasper. (For the debate about the often overly structural use of the concept of political opportunities, see Goodwin and Jasper 1999a, b; Tilly 1999; Tarrow 1999).

9 There are few but noteworthy exceptions, such as the Canadian coalition GATT-Fly, which gained an interest in negotiations through its work on development issues. See Laurie 1990.

10 The GATT was originally signed in 1947 by 23 countries; in its last meeting in 1994 it had 128 signatories. As of July 2007, the WTO had 151 members.

11 For example, Rogowski's model purports to explain domestic coalitions based on the different factor endowments across countries. The three factors he takes into consideration are labor, capital, and land (see Rogowski 1989). Midford argues that Rogowski's model fails to make adequate predictions; but Midford limits his critique to the way factors are measured and does not go beyond the basic model (see Midford 1993). Similarly, Hiscox contributes to the sophistication of the model by focusing on the impact of interindustry factor mobility to better understand variation in coalition building. In his analysis of the passage of NAFTA in the U.S. Congress, he does not even mention the participation in the debates of groups other than labor, farm, and business (see Hiscox 2002, esp. 69–70).

12 The technical justifications for Latin America's protectionism were provided by the Economic Commission on Latin America and the Caribbean (ECLAC, or CEPAL in its Spanish acronym), which, on the basis of a critique of classic trade theory inspired by Keynesianism, argued that the region's specialization in primary products was detrimental to its development because the terms of trade of these products (in relation to manufactured products from developed countries) tended to deteriorate over time. This critique led ECLAC to propose autonomous development policies based on a strong role of governments in promoting the industrialization of the countries of the region, through the extensive use of protectionist measures (see ECLAC 1949, 1959; Prebisch 1964; for a review of ECLAC's first 50 years, see Bielschowsky 1998). The proposed new development model, known as import substitution industrialization, became dominant in Latin America between the 1950s and 1970s. The many regional integration initiatives dating from this period were considered an essential part of the model, because greater regional integration would provide incipient industries with access to the larger markets they needed. In spite of the progress of some initiatives in liberalizing trade in the region, however, by the end of the 1970s, negotiations had stalled (Urquidi 1993).

13 For a comparison of old and new regionalisms in Latin America, see Devlin and Giordano 2004.

14 In December 2004, during the third Summit of Presidents of South America, the initiative for the creation of a South American Community of Nations was launched by the governments of

Argentina, Bolivia, Brazil, Chile, Colombia, Ecuador, Guiana, Paraguay, Peru, Surinam, Uruguay, and Venezuela.

15 For a comparison of labor's positions in both regions, see von Bülow 2003.

16 For an even more negative evaluation of labor's participation in the Andean integration see, e.g., Pardo 1998.

17 Perhaps the most important exception in the countries studied is CUT-Brazil, which, since its creation, has maintained strong ties to NGOs and other social movement organizations. Even in this case, however, throughout the 1990s, new ties were forged between CUT and other civil society organizations at the domestic and transnational levels.

18 See the analysis of the CUT-Brazil and the CGTP-Portugal in Costa 2005a.

19 For the historical debate on labor internationalism see, e.g., Hobsbawn 1988; Stillerman 2003.

20 A roster of organizations to be interviewed was created before data collection began, based on the analysis of documents such as membership lists in trade coalitions; lists of attendees at events; sign-ons, and so forth. During field research, this list was expanded by the interviewees themselves, based on the snowball procedure: actors were asked if there were organizations that should be added to the initial roster, and these were included if they were mentioned beyond a threshold of three times. In each case, the informant was the person in charge of following trade negotiations or in charge of legislative or international affairs. Most interviews were held between June 2004 and August 2005. Some of the interviews were anonymous at the respondents' request.

21 One consequence of these internal shifts in ORIT was to move its headquarters from the CTM building in Mexico City to Venezuela and, more recently, to São Paulo.

22 In March 2008, the members of the two most important regional labor organizations, ORIT and CLAT (Latin American Workers' Confederation), plus a few independent labor centrals, formed the new Labor Confederation of the Americas. After years of internal debate, in July 1992 CUT-Brazil finally decided to give up its international nonaligned position and became affiliated with the International Confederation of Free Labor Unions (ICFTU) and its regional arm, ORIT. For an official overview of the changes in CUT's international relations policies, see Unified Workers' Central 1992. For an analysis of the internal debates that preceded the decision to join the ICFTU and ORIT, see Costa 2005b, esp. 538–66.

23 The HSA comprises 18 "national chapters," which are domestic coalitions that bring together civil society organizations from various sectors, and 15 "regional members," among them the ORIT.

24 The question asked was, suppose the next ministerial meeting of the FTAA is held in Mexico (Chile, Brazil) and you need to discuss a strategy for participating in it with Mexican (Brazilian, Chilean) organizations. Do you (you can choose more than one): a) get in touch with organizations in this country directly; b) get in touch through domestic coalitions (which one); c) get in touch through transnational coalitions (which one); or d) other?

25 For the importance of this mechanism in coalition building among heterogeneous actors, see Mische 2003.

26 For example, during a meeting the author attended between civil society organizations and official negotiators held in Miami during the FTAA ministerial meeting of 2003, government officials criticized protestors for not presenting alternative proposals. In response, one of the members of the Mexican Action Network on Free Trade (RMALC) argued that ever since the NAFTA negotiations, civil society challengers of free trade agreements had been working on concrete and feasible proposals, which were consolidated in the *Alternatives*.

27 For a more detailed explanation of these mechanisms and how they work in the context of trade coalition building in the Americas, see von Bülow 2007.

28 For arguments critical of the idea of introducing a labor clause in Brazil, see Portella de Castro 1996; Pastore 1997. For a review of the debate in India, see Hensman 2001.

29 In its 14th Congress, in Santo Domingo in April 1997, ORIT's members decided to support the ICFTU's campaign for the inclusion of social clauses in trade treaties. See ORIT 1997.

30 In Brazil, the most important actor in the negotiations is the Ministry of Foreign Affairs, but others are also involved, especially the Ministry of Development, Industry, and Foreign Trade

and the Ministry of Agriculture. In Chile, the process is similarly centralized in the Ministry of Foreign Affairs, and especially in the General Direction of Economic International Relations (Direcon). In Mexico, the most important negotiating role is played by the Ministry of Economic Affairs.

REFERENCES

Aaronson, Susan Ariel. 2001. *Taking Trade to the Streets: The Lost History of Public Efforts to Shape Globalization.* Ann Arbor: University of Michigan Press.

American Federation of Labor-Congress of Industrial Organizations (AFL-CIO). 2004. Representative. Author interview. Washington, DC, July 10.

Anner, Mark, and Peter Evans. 2004. Building Bridges Across a Double Divide: Alliances Between U.S. and Latin American Labour and NGOs. *Development in Practice* 14, 1–2: 34–47.

Báez, Victor. 2005. Secretary-General, ORIT. Author interview. Belo Horizonte. December 16.

Balassa, Bela. 1961. *The Theory of Economic Integration.* Homewood, IL: Richard D. Irwin.

Bethell, Leslie, ed. 1985. *The Cambridge History of Latin America. Vol. 3: From Independence to c.1870.* Cambridge: Cambridge University Press.

Bielschowsky, Ricardo. 1998. Cincuenta años del pensamiento de la CEPAL: una reseña. In *Cincuenta años de pensamiento en la CEPAL: textos seleccionados.* Santiago: CEPAL/Fondo de Cultura Económica. 9–61.

Blyth, Mark. 2002. *Great Transformations: Economic Ideas and Political Change in the Twentieth Century.* Cambridge: Cambridge University Press.

Bognanno, Mario F., and Jiangfeng Lu. 2003. NAFTA's Labor Side Agreement: Withering as an Effective Labor Law Enforcement and MNC Compliance Strategy? In *Multinational Companies and Global Human Resource Strategies,* ed. William Cooke. Westport: Quorum Books. 369–99.

Burger, Anna. 2006. Change to Win Letter to the U.S. Senate Opposing the Oman and Peru Free Trade Agreements. June 15. <www.changetowin.org> Accessed October 15, 2007.

Change to Win Coalition. 2007. Restoring the American Dream Through Fair Trade, Not Free Trade. <www.changetowin.org/issues> Accessed October 13, 2007.

Charnovitz, Steve. 2005. The Labour Dimension of the Emerging Free Trade Area of the Americas. In *Labour Rights as Human Rights,* ed. Philip Alston. Oxford: Oxford University Press, 2005. Also available through Social Science Research Network, <http://ssrn.com/abstract=705301> Accessed October 1, 2007.

Costa, Hermes Augusto. 2005a. A política internacional da CGTP e da CUT: etapas, temas e desafios. *Revista Crítica de Ciências Sociais* no. 71: 141–61.

———. 2005b. Sindicalismo global ou metáfora adiada? Os discursos e as práticas transnacionais da CGTP e da CUT. Ph.D. diss., University of Coimbra.

Destler, I. Mac. 1998. Trade Politics and Labor Issues, 1953–95. In *Imports, Exports, and the American Worker,* ed. Susan M. Collins. Washington, DC: Brookings Institution Press. 389–422.

Devlin, Robert, and Paolo Giordano. 2004. The Old and New Regionalism: Benefits, Costs, and Implications for the FTAA. In *Integrating the Americas: FTAA and Beyond,* ed. Antoni Estevadeordal, Dani Rodrik, Alan M. Taylor, and Andrés Velasco. Cambridge: Harvard University Press/David Rockefeller Center for Latin American Studies. 143–86.

Dillon, John. 2004. Program Coordinator for Global Economic Justice, Global Justice Program at Kairos: Canadian Ecumenical Justice Initiatives. Author interview. Toronto, September 13.

Doucet, Marc G. 2005. Territoriality and the Democratic Paradox: The Hemispheric Social Alliance and Its Alternative for the Americas. *Contemporary Political Theory* 4, 3: 275–95.

Drake, Elisabeth. 2004. International Policy Analyst, AFL-CIO. Author interview. Washington, DC, August 4.

Dreiling, Michael, and Ian Robinson. 1998. Union Responses to NAFTA in the U.S. and Canada: Explaining Intra and International Variation. *Mobilization* 3, 2: 163–84.

Economic Commission for Latin America (ECLAC). 1949. *Estudio económico de América Latina.* Santiago: United Nations.

————. 1959. *El Mercado Común Latinoamericano.* Santiago: United Nations.

Emirbayer, Mustafa. 1997. Manifesto for a Relational Sociology. *American Journal of Sociology* 103, 2: 281–317.

Emirbayer, Mustafa, and Ann Mische. 1998. What Is Agency? *American Journal of Sociology* 103,. 4: 962–1023.

Furtado, Celso. 1976. *Economic Development of Latin America: Historical Background and Contemporary Problems.* Cambridge: Cambridge University Press.

García, Frank J. 2003. *Trade, Inequality, and Justice: Toward a Liberal Theory of Just Trade.* Ardsley: Transnational Publishers.

Godio, Julio. 2007. La importancia estratégica de la Plataforma Laboral de las Américas. *Nueva Sociedad* no. 211: 98–108.

Goodwin, Jeff, and James Jasper. 1999a. Caught in a Winding, Snarling Vine: The Structural Bias of Political Process Theory. *Sociological Forum* 14, 1: 27–54.

————. 1999b. Trouble in Paradigms. *Sociological Forum* 14, 1: 107–25.

Hemispheric Social Alliance (HSA). 1998. *Alternatives for the Americas.* HSA. <www.asc-hsa.org>

————. 2005. *Alternatives for the Americas.* 5th edition. HSA. <www.asc-hsa.org>

Hensman, Rohini. 2001. World Trade and Workers' Rights: In Search of a New Internationalism. In Waterman and Wills 2001. 123–46.

Hiscox, Michael J. 2002. *International Trade and Political Conflict: Commerce, Coalitions, and Mobility.* Princeton: Princeton University Press.

Hobsbawn, Eric J. 1988. Working-class Internationalism. In *Internationalism in the Labour Movement, 1830–1940,* ed. Frits van Holthoon and Marcel van der Linden. Leiden: E.J. Brill. 3–16.

Inter-American Regional Workers' Organization (ORIT). 1997. Síntesis de las Resoluciones Aprobadas por el XIV Congreso Continental de la CIOSL/ORIT. Santo Domingo: ORIT.

International Labour Organization (ILO). 2006. ILO History. <www.ilo.org/english/about/history.htm> Accessed October 17, 2007.

Jakobsen, Kjeld. 1999. Uma visão sindical em face da ALCA e de outros esquemas regionais. In *Mercosul, NAFTA e ALCA: a dimensão social,* ed. Yves Chaloult and Paulo Roberto de Almeida. São Paulo: LTr. 232–48.

Kaiser, Karl. 1971. Transnational Relations as a Threat to the Democratic Process. *International Organization* 25, 3: 706–20.

————. 1969. Transnationale Politik: zu einer Theorie der multinationale Politik. In *Die anachronistische Souveränität: zum Verhältnis von innen- und aussen-Politik,* ed. Erns-Otto Czempiel. Cologne: Westdeutscher Verlag. 80–109.

Keck, Margaret, and Kathryn Sikkink. 1998. *Activists Beyond Borders: Advocacy Networks in International Politics.* Ithaca: Cornell University Press.

Lambert, Jacques. 1968. *Latin America: Social Structure and Political Institutions.* Berkeley: University of California Press.

Laurie, Peter. 1990. Ah-hah! GATT-Fly. *New Internationalist* no. 204. <www.newint.org/issue204/raw.htm>

Lee, Thea. 2004. Assistant Director of Public Policy, AFL-CIO. Author interview. Washington, DC, August 6.

McAdam, Doug, Sidney Tarrow, and Charles Tilly. 2001. *Dynamics of Contention.* Cambridge: Cambridge University Press.

Midford, Paul. 1993. International Trade and Domestic Politics: Improving on Rogowski's Model of Political Alignments. *International Organization* 47: 535–64.

Mische, Ann. 2003. Cross-talk in Movements: Reconceiving the Culture-Network Link. In *Social Movements and Networks: Relational Approaches to Collective Action,* ed. Mario Diani and Doug McAdam. Oxford: Oxford University Press. 258–80.

Myconos, George. 2005. *The Globalization of Organized Labour, 1945–2005.* Hampshire: Palgrave Macmillan.

Nye, Joseph, and Robert O. Keohane. 1971. Transnational Relations and World Politics: An Introduction. *International Organizations* 25, 3: 329–49.

Pardo, Víctor. 1998. Trabajadores e integración: la experiencia andina. In *Comunidad Andina y Mercosur: desafíos pendientes de la integración en América Latina.* Bogotá: Ministerio de Relaciones Exteriores/Comunidad Andina de Fomento. 175–80.

Pastore, José. 1997. *A cláusula social e o comércio internacional.* Brasília: CNI.

Portella de Castro, Maria Sílvia. 1996. Considerações sobre o mercado de trabalho e o movimento sindical no âmbito do Mercosul. In *Processos de integração regional e a sociedade: o sindicalismo na Argentina, Brasil, México e Venezuela,* ed. Hélio Zylberstajn, Iram Jácome Rodrigues, Portella de Castro, and Tullo Vigevani. Rio de Janeiro: Paz e Terra. 44–71.

Prebisch, Raúl. 1964. *Hacia una política comercial en pro del desarrollo. Informe del Secretario General de la Conferencia de las Naciones Unidas sobre Comercio y Desarrollo.* New York: United Nations.

Rogowski, Ronald. 1989. *Commerce and Coalitions: How Trade Affects Domestic Political Alignments.* Princeton: Princeton University Press.

Samuel, William. 2007. Legislative Director, AFL-CIO. Letter to Congressional Representatives. Washington, October 1.

Smith, William C., and Roberto Patricio Korzeniewicz. 2007. Insiders, Outsiders, and the Politics of Civil Society. In *Governing the Americas: Assessing Multilateral Institutions,* ed. Jean-Phillipe Thérien, Gordon Mace, and Paul Haslam. Boulder: Lynne Rienner. 151–72.

Stillerman, Joel. 2003. Transnational Activist Networks and the Emergence of Labor Internationalism in the NAFTA Countries. *Social Science History* 27, 4: 577–61.

Tarrow, Sidney. 1998 [1994]. *Power in Movement: Social Movements and Contentious Politics.* 2nd edition. Cambridge: Cambridge University Press.

——. 1999. Paradigm Warriors: Regress and Progress in the Study of Contentious Politics. *Sociological Forum* 14, 1: 71–77.

——. 2005. *The New Transnational Activism.* Cambridge: Cambridge University Press.

Tilly, Charles. 1999. Wise Quacks. *Sociological Forum* 14, 1: 55–61.

Unified Workers' Central (CUT-Brazil). 1992. A CIOSL—Confederação Internacional de Organizações Sindicais Livres. São Paulo, International Relations Secretariat/CUT.

——. 1997. O sindicalismo continental e a ALCA. *Textos para Debate Internacional* no. 9: 2–8.

——. 2005. Director. Author interview. São Paulo, March 19.

Urquidi, Víctor L. 1993. Free Trade Experience in Latin America and the Caribbean. *Annals of the American Academy of Political and Social Science* 526: 58–67.

Villalba, Alejandro. 2004. Representative, FAT-Mexico. Author interview. Mexico City, August 17.

Von Bülow, Marisa. 2003. Labor Organizations in a Changed World: A Comparison of Labor Responses to NAFTA and MERCOSUL. Paper presented at the 24th International Congress of the Latin American Studies Association, Dallas, March 27–29.

——. 2007. Pathways to Transnationality: Networks, Collective Action, and Trade Debates in the Americas. Ph.D. diss., Johns Hopkins University.

Wallach, Lori. 2004. Introduction: It's Not About Trade. In Wallach and Woodall 2004. 1–17.

Wallach, Lori, and Patrick Woodall. 2004. *Whose Trade Organization? A Comprehensive Guide to the WTO.* Washington: Public Citizen.

Waterman, Peter. 1998. *Globalization, Social Movements and the New Internationalisms.* London: Mansell.

Waterman, Peter, and Jane Wills, eds. 2001. *Place, Space and the New Labour Internationalisms.* Oxford: Blackwell.

Williams, Marc. 2005. Civil Society and the World Trading System. In *The Politics of International Trade in the Twenty-first Century: Actors, Issues and Regional Dynamics,* ed. Dominic Kelly and Wyn Grant. Hampshire: Palgrave Macmillan. 30–46.

Chapter 16

Fading Green? Environmental Politics in the Mercosur Free Trade Agreement

Kathryn Hochstetler

The relationship between trade and the environment has become one of the central questions of recent research on the environment. Numerous studies have focused on the place of environmental concerns and actors in regional free trade areas, such as the North American Free Trade Agreement, NAFTA (Audley 1997; Deere 2004; Johnson and Beaulieu 1996); the European Union, EU (Barnes and Barnes 2000; Grant et al. 2001; McCormick 2001); or both (Beukel 1999, 126; Steinberg 1997; Stevis and Mumme 2000). Many of these studies highlight the difficulty of preventing the negative environmental impacts that result from increased trade in poorer countries in these areas.

We know comparatively little about the relationship between environmental politics and regional trade agreements in regions where all the participants are "developing," having economic statistics equal to or well below those of Mexico, Greece, and Portugal. Yet environmental choices in these less economically developed regions are likely to be important harbingers of what can be achieved for environmental protection in broader international trade agreements, such as the Free Trade Area of the Americas (FTAA). This chapter surveys the environmental provisions and actors of the Mercosur free trade agreement as a first step to assessing these relationships.[1]

The starting point of any discussion of the relationship between trade and environment in developing regions is the near-universal consensus that environmental issues are more conflictual for countries that still have significant development needs and aspirations. In Diana Tussie's summary,

> The main concerns of developing countries in this [trade-environment agenda] . . . relate, on the one hand, to how market access can be achieved and preserved without further degradation of the environment, and, on the other, to how the environment can be protected without affecting growth rates and the liberalization of trade. (Tussie 2000, 1)

With respect to the first concern, the increased economic production that is the promised benefit of free trade is considered more likely to lead to increased environmental degradation in developing countries, for two major reasons, First, the export structures of developing countries are more likely to be based on natural resources, which show a greater negative impact from trade compared to industrial production (Tussie 2000, 1–2). This holds true in Mercosur, where primary agriculture, mining, and energy products accounted for 56.6 percent of total exports in 1990 and 53.2 percent in 1998 (Schaper 2002, 251).

Second, developing countries as a group have lower levels of domestic environmental capacity and public environmental concern than do the postindustrial countries (Steel et al. 2003; Weidner and Janicke 2002). As a result, neither governmental capacity nor popular pressure is present on a sufficient scale to force mitigation of negative environmental impacts. If economies grow as a result of trade agreements, politicians in developing countries are actually likely to be rewarded politically, not chastised for the resulting environmental degradation. In a corresponding way, those politicians can normally assume that they can negotiate trade openings without needing to take steps to appease an environmentally based opposition coalition.

When countries with different levels of domestic environmental protection try to harmonize their environmental protections as they enter into free trade agreements, the second aspect of Tussie's summary is implicated, how to protect the environment without harming growth and trade rates. To developing countries, the effort to use trade agreements to promote higher common environmental standards often appears as a kind of protectionism in disguise. Because the higher environmental standards usually will require them to make changes in production processes, inputs, or equipment, developing countries worry that the resulting increased costs will hurt their ability to compete with countries that already meet the new standards. Because the comparative advantage of developing countries depends heavily on cost advantages, cost increases strike directly at their ability to compete. If the new standards appear arbitrary or unnecessary, as they often do when they are higher than national standards, those costs appear as wholly unwarranted and even intentionally designed to create new economic disadvantages for developing countries. A corollary is the expectation that countries facing the increased economic competition of a free trade area will be unlikely to strengthen their environmental protections, especially at the national level, because new environmental protections would make them less competitive.

This study takes up these claims about the relationship between trade and the environment in developing countries through a closer examination of Mercosur. Overall, the Mercosur experience broadly supports the consensus that developing countries are likely to be more conflicted about incorporating environmental concerns into their development efforts. However, the Mercosur experience also challenges important components of these arguments.

After a brief introduction to the Mercosur agreement itself, this study examines the domestic environmental capacities of the four member countries. While all four show significant gaps in environmental capacity—confirming the general claim about lower levels of environmental protection in developing areas—they also differ considerably in this respect. Brazil, in particular, has comparatively high environmental standards and capacity—especially on paper—in relation to Uruguay, Argentina, and Paraguay. The national differences became important at key points in the Mercosur negotiations over environmental issues, which would not be the case if domestic environmental capacity were as uniformly low as is commonly asserted.

Although Argentina, Paraguay, and Uruguay began the Mercosur integration process with very low levels of national environmental capacity, moreover, all three of them expanded that capacity considerably over the next decade, for reasons largely unrelated to Mercosur itself. This directly challenges the expectation that countries facing increased regional economic competition will not strengthen their national environmental protections.

This study also explores the regional level of Mercosur. Its overall empirical conclusion is that the collective environmental agreements of the Mercosur free trade area are weak and have declined over the course of the agreement.[2] These weaknesses stem partly from the weaknesses of the individual national policies, with little collective acceptance of any environmental provisions that are not already held by three of the four countries. Mercosur's environmental agency has a weak institutional status and a limited agenda, which reflects the intention of Mercosur's decisionmakers and supports the assertion that developing countries will try to minimize trade-limiting environmental provisions. Much of the activity of Mercosur's Working Subgroup on the Environment also supports the argument that fears about competitiveness lie at the root of developing countries' concerns about environmentalism, with Brazil's higher environmental expectations a common flashpoint.

Nevertheless, the actual decline in collective environmental provisions, illustrated through a case study of how a proposed environmental protocol was scaled back between 1995 and 2002, indicates a greater range in the possible environmental outcomes of a free trade agreement among developing countries than the conventional wisdom expects. It shows that some regional actors were interested in pursuing a more active regional environmental agenda, even though they ultimately were unable to do so. National environmental protections, after all, increased in all the countries under the Mercosur framework. The timing of the reversal is most clearly linked to the severe crisis of the entire Mercosur agreement and the Argentine economic crisis in the late 1990s in particular, which had little to do with the environmental protocol itself, but contributed to its decline.

The concluding section of the paper uses these observations about the Mercosur region to consider the likely role of environmental issues in moving from Mercosur toward a Free Trade Area of the Americas. Several recent studies argue that environmental issues will be fundamental in any efforts to negotiate broader free trade agreements. Audley and Sherwin (2002), Deere and Esty (2002, 5) and Gaines (2002) all agree that the domestic politics of trade agreements in industrialized regions preclude new trade agreements that do not include environmental provisions, and that civil society groups and their congressional allies in North America will block the FTAA and similar initiatives under such conditions. If the success of the FTAA depends on incorporating environmental provisions, does the Mercosur experience suggest that such an outcome is likely? What kinds of hemisphere-wide environmental provisions might be possible? This study suggests that the governments of the Mercosur countries might strongly resist adding a significant environmental component to a hemisphere-wide trade agreement. Recent interviews however, indicate that South American environmentalists will join their Northern counterparts in opposition to the FTAA despite low levels of mobilization around Mercosur. Thus the most important dividing line over the FTAA is likely to be the state-organized society split rather than the line between developed and developing countries.

THE COMMON MARKET OF THE SOUTH

The Mercosur agreement includes Argentina, Brazil, Paraguay, and Uruguay as full members, and Bolivia and Chile as associate members. Venezuela's full membership is still awaiting ratification by the Brazilian and Paraguayan congresses. The four member states signed the Treaty" of Asunción on March 26, 1991, agreeing to form a common market of the south, and a partial customs union began to function among them in January 1995. Table 1 summarizes basic economic and trade composition data about the Mercosur region and Mexico. It demonstrates both the comparative poverty of the region and the economic dominance of Brazil and, secondarily, Argentina in South America.

The country members of Mercosur have made a deliberate choice to keep the level of new institutionalization of Mercosur quite low. The predominant mode of organization is to give new regionalized areas of responsibility to existing actors and institutions. Thus,

Table 1. Basic Economic and Trade Data for Mercosur Countries and Mexico

	Argentina[a]	Brazil	Paraguay	Uruguay	Mexico
GDP/capita[b]	12,377	7,625	4,426	9,035	9,023
GDP[c]	458.3	1,299.4	24.3	30.1	884.0
Annual growth in GDP/capita, 1990–2000	3.0	1.5	−0.4	2.6	1.4
Primary exports (as % of merchandise exports)	1990: 71 2000: 66	1990: 47 2000: 40	1990: N.A. 2000: 81	1990: 61 2000: 58	1990: 56 2000: 16
Manufactured exports (as % of merchandise exports)	1990: 29 2000: 32	1990: 52 2000: 59	1990: 10 2000: 19	1990: 39 2000: 42	1990: 43 2000: 83
High technology exports (as % of merchandise exports)	1990: N.A. 2000: 9	1990: 7 2000: 19	1990: (.)[d] 2000: 3	1990: 0 2000: 2	1990: 8 2000: 22

[a]Because of the recent severe economic contraction in Argentina, the figures for that country are significantly more positive than is the current economic situation. Other countries in the region have also been negatively affected by the Argentine crisis.
[b]GDP per capita, as measured by purchasing power parity (PPP), in 2000 international dollars.
[c]GDP, as measured by PPP, in billions of 2000 international dollars.
[d]Less than half the unit shown.
Source: UNDP 2002, 190–91, 198–99.

the top decisionmakers of Mercosur are the four national presidents of the region. They preside over the agenda-setting meetings of the Common Market Council (Consejo del Mercado Común, or CMC), which is otherwise led by the national ministers of foreign affairs and economy. Primary responsibility for implementation is given to the Common Market Group (Grupo del Mercado Común, or GMC), which is made up of representatives from the national economic and foreign ministries and central banks. Even the joint parliament is simply made up of selected members of the four national congresses. The entire annual budget for Mercosur's administrative structure for 2002 was under US $1 million (GMC/Res No 1/02). The environmental institutions of Mercosur are not an exception to this general rule, but are simply a gathering of the four national environmental agencies.

Since 1991, Mercosur has survived a number of regional economic and political crises. A short list would include presidential impeachment processes in Brazil and Paraguay and Argentina's recent five-presidents-in-two-weeks political crisis. Economically, the countries have suffered hyperinflation in Brazil and Argentina, the region's economic powerhouses, followed by Brazil's deep currency crisis in 1998 and Argentina's debt default and currency crisis at the end of 2001. That Mercosur continues to exist at all is something of a miracle, especially given the near-complete absence of supranational institutions that might have helped stabilize it (Gómez-Mera 2005; Malamud 2005; Phillips 2001; Roett 1999). These characteristics of Mercosur form a backdrop for its specifically environmental negotiations, presenting significant challenges for consistent and effective environmental policies.

INSTITUTIONAL ENVIRONMENTAL POLITICS IN MERCOSUR

Despite the national and regional difficulties, environmental concerns are on the region's agenda. Mercosur documents regularly list regional quality of life and sustainable development as among the broader aims of an accord that was never meant to be narrowly economic. The original Treaty of Asunción cites preservation of the environment in its second paragraph as one of the overarching guidelines for regional integration. Since 1992, representatives from national environmental agencies have been meeting regularly, first as the Specialized Meeting on the Environment (Reunión Especializada de Medio Ambiente, REMA) and since 1995 as the Working Subcommittee No. 6 on the Environment (Subgrupo de Trabajo VI Medio Ambiente, SGT 6). Beginning in 2004, the Meeting of Environmental Ministers has met at least twice per year, with SGT 6 adopting a new role as its technical and coordinating agency.

In 2001, the governments of the region adopted the long-awaited Mercosur Environmental Framework Agreement (Acuerdo Marco sobre Medio Ambiente del Mercosur)—but in a form that was considerably less expansive than its original 1996 protocol version (Republic of Brazil 1997, Anexo 1; for the final document see Republic of Argentina). In addition, all four countries have signed and ratified a comprehensive set of the most important recent multilateral environmental agreements, on trade in endangered species, toxic waste, ozone depletion, climate change, bio-diversity, and wetlands preservation, as well as general documents like the Rio Declaration and Agenda 21 from the 1992 United Nations Conference on Environment and Development (compiled from Devia 1998b). All four member states also have put at least some national environmental protections in place and have active nongovernmental sectors concerned with environmental issues. The national environmental politics of Mercosur's four member countries are an important starting point for understanding the environmental politics of Mercosur.

NATIONAL ENVIRONMENTAL POLITICS

Institutionally, the primary participants in Mercosur's SGT 6 are members of the national environmental bureaucracies. It is significant that little has been achieved so far in regional environmental politics that was not already present at the national level in at least three of the four countries. This has generally meant that any regional harmonization of environmental standards occurs at low levels of protection, although national environmental protections have increased in all member states since the beginning of Mercosur.

Of the four countries, Brazil has the most extensive and usually the deepest environmental protections, despite well-publicized serious environmental problems. Characteristically, Uruguay occupies a position in the middle, with both its protections and its disasters usually on a smaller scale than Brazil's. Argentina and Paraguay lag for quite different reasons: Paraguay because of a more generalized lack of political institutionalization and Argentina because its environmental protections are comparatively undeveloped in a country where other political institutions are stronger.

With respect to its neighbors, Brazil's environmental politics have benefited from one irreplaceable element, time. While all four countries were under authoritarian rule in the 1970s and 1980s, only Brazil and its military government began the process of constructing environmental protections. Brazil has had a national environmental agency continuously since 1973; that agency reached ministerial status in 1985.

For nearly three decades, then, Brazil has regularly produced important environmental legislation and regulations. To cite several specific examples, in 1981 the military government gathered existing environmental legislation and institutions into a National System on the Environment (Sisnama), which was responsible for executing a national environmental policy (Republic of Brazil 1991). In 1985, collective actors, including environmental organizations and public defenders, were given legal standing to bring lawsuits in defense of "diffuse" or common interests. A year later, the national government began to require environmental impact evaluations and reports. These and other gains were consolidated—not introduced—in a special chapter on the environment in the 1988 Constitution (Fernandes 1998). In 1998, a new environmental crimes law significantly increased the penalties for environmental degradation.

Brazil is the only one of the four countries where the court system plays an increasing role in enforcing its large body of legislation (McAllister 2008). Recent decisions have at least slowed the introduction of genetically modified organisms, including seeds (Paarlberg 2001), and the construction of a water superhighway, one of Mercosur's large infrastructural projects (Hochstetler 2002a). Environmental organizations number in the thousands and exercise spirited oversight of government agencies, including sitting on standard-setting councils at all levels of government (Svirsky 2002).

The end result is comparatively extensive capacity for environmental policymaking in Brazil, although full use of that capacity has been a regular problem, especially in nonurban areas (Hochstetler 2002b; Hochstetler and Keck 2007). Brazil continues to suffer from numerous environmental problems, ranging from internationally known ones, such as deforestation in the Amazon and Atlantic forests and air pollution in Sao Paulo, to more mundane failures of basic sanitation and water services. These environmental problems are especially severe in the Northern (Amazon) and Northeastern regions. Brazil's federal system exacerbates these inequities, because those are also the regions with more limited environmental capacity (ABEMA 1993). A study of the actual practices of environmental impact assessment in Brazil, for example, stresses how much better the wealthier southern regions perform (Glassen and Salvador 2000). Despite these inequities, all of Brazil's states have had environmental agencies for more than a decade, and most of its municipalities have them, too.

Uruguay introduces the more typical pattern in regional environmental politics. Almost all developments in national environmental institutions and legislation there came only after the military government left power in the 1980s; and nongovernmental environmental actors emerged before the governmental ones. Nongovernmental actors continue to be an important source of information, analysis, and proposals for the environmental sector in Uruguay (CLAES 2001; Domínguez and Prieto 2000; REDES 2000). Uruguay created an environmental ministry in 1990, the Ministry of Housing, Territorial Ordering, and Environment (MVOTMA), but packaged environment with other issues that often take precedence. Other closely related issues, such as protected areas, remained with the Ministry of Agriculture until 2000. MVOTMA received financial assistance from the Interamerican Development Bank (IDB) for institutional and legislative development from 1996 to 1998, and used the loans to develop a basic set of environmental legislation. This included the comprehensive General Law on Environmental Protection and a new Law on Protected Areas, both passed by the National Congress in 2000. A national law requiring environmental impact assessment dates back to 1994.

The Uruguayan case is also fairly typical for the stage of development of the country's environmental institutions and legislation. It has the basic building blocks of effective environmental politics, and its priorities should now turn (and are actually turning) from creating legislation to building executive and societal capacity in ways that truly implement that legislation and improve environmental outcomes. The specific challenges in Uruguay include issues from inadequate environmental budgets to the need for special training to develop the expertise needed for effective studies of environmental impact (Panario 2001). As a small country that is literally downwind and downstream from its big neighbors, Uruguay is especially sensitive to cross-boundary environmental problems (Gudynas 1998, 135–36). Transboundary industrial pollution from both Brazil and Argentina and several national environmental scandals in 2001, including the discovery of widespread lead poisoning in the city of Montevideo, have drawn public and political attention to environmental issues and may provide an impetus for strengthening environmental protections (Gudynas 2001b).

Argentina represents an even more complex picture. Argentina created an environmental secretariat in the Ministry of the Economy in 1973, but it was dissolved in 1975. President Carlos Menem reconstructed a National Environmental Secretariat in 1991, after several lower-level attempts in the 1980s (Rodriguez 1998, 189). Two domestic environmental accidents, an oil spill and volcanic ash damage, spurred its formation (Hopkins 1995, 68). Menem's environmental secretariat did not have ministerial status but gained autonomy by reporting directly to him.[3] It is interesting that the early Environmental Secretariat was most active and effective under Menem's environmental secretary, María Julia Alsogaray—arrested in August 2003 on charges of misappropriating secretariat funds—who made no secret of her views that any environmental protections needed to be kept "profoundly coherent" with the demands of neoliberalism, including a small state role (Bugoni and Canas 1998, 9).

During the Menem-Alsogaray administration, environmental issues did gain constitutional status in the 1994 constitutional reforms, which ordered the national environmental agency to develop a set of basic environmental directives that would create a framework for additional provincial-level protections (Devia 1998a). Argentina received funds from the IDB for institutional and legal development, which resulted in some important pilot programs on water issues and supported the writing of a set of seven legal proposals that made up the basic directives, covering issues from national environmental impact assessments to solid waste disposal (Pigretti 1999; Republic of Argentina 1999). These laws were approved in the mid-2000s and Argentina now has a fairly complete legal framework for environmental protection.

The government of Fernando de la Rúa effectively lowered the status of the Environmental Secretariat in 1999, moving it into the Ministry of Social Development where environmental issues suffered from the severe congestion of that ministry's agenda and the general political and economic crises of 2001–2003. More recently, environmental issues gained unprecedented prominence in Argentina, thanks to the decision of several paper mills to set up operations in Uruguay, just across the river from Argentina. Argentine protesters (sometimes with Uruguayan environmentalists) kept the bridge between the two countries blocked for weeks at a time, as the two countries sought international legal mediation of their dispute (Vara 2007). In response, the Kirchner government placed a well-known environmental activist, Romina Picolotti, at the helm of the environmental agency, which had new resources and energy. Picoletti was asked to resign in December, 2008—and herself faces charges of inappropriate use of public funds, which she denies (*La Nación* 2 December 2008).

In Paraguay, the writing of a new constitution in 1992 laid out the first broad national environmental agenda as part of the country's efforts to build a post-Stroessner regime. Before 1992, environmental protections existed mostly in the form of a patchwork of municipal ordinances for Asunción and some national legislation, such as the 1931 Rural Code, most of which had been written for other purposes (Díaz Labrano 1998). The 1992 Constitution laid a solid legal framework in provisions that assert general rights to a "healthy and equilibrated environment" (Article 7), establish principles of regulation of potential environmental damage and compensation for actual damage (Article 8), and give citizens the constitutional capacity individually or collectively to challenge any authorities who are not protecting the environment (Article 7 and Chapter 2) (Diaz Labrano 1998, 114–25). It is not surprising, however, that the constitution promises quite a bit more than has actually been achieved, in both environmental and indigenous protections (Rodriguez 2002).

In the environmental area, legislators followed up quickly in 1993 with a law requiring environmental impact assessments, but other pieces of implementing legislation have taken longer. In 2000, Paraguay took an important step forward when it finally pulled a number of agencies and departments out of the Ministry of Agriculture and the Ministry of Public Health and Social Welfare to create a National Environmental Secretariat for the first time. Effective environmental protection will depend on this new agency's ability to secure the resources and political power it needs. International resources and agendas are likely to be especially important in Paraguay, where much of the sectoral environmental legislation is still generated through international conventions and treaties.[4] The IDB extended an $8 million loan in 2000 to "provide institutional support to better manage Paraguay's environment" (IDB 2001, 57).

As these descriptions suggest, the Brazilian case differs significantly from the other three, chiefly because Brazil has simply been engaged much longer in developing environmental protections. This longer time period has several implications. Brazil set up its institutions and legislation largely according to its own timetable and agenda and at its own cost, although it now receives significant international financing for its environmental programs. The first Brazilian national environmental agency, the Secretária do Meio Ambiente (SEMA), was inspired partly by the 1972 Stockholm Conference on the Human Environment, but also by more local developments (Guimarães 1995, 160–61). In the other three countries, international actors and resources have been much more central in setting up the basic institutional and legal structure for environmental protections. Perhaps as both a cause and a consequence of this difference, only Brazilians have made strong arguments about the endogenous (as opposed to imported) nature of environmental concerns in the region (Pádua 1992). Overall, Brazilian environmental politics and policies are consistently the most extensive in the region, and Brazil can be considered the regional environmental leader.

Still, the many gaps in Brazilian environmental protections despite their long history are a sobering lesson for Brazil's neighbors. It is obviously not enough simply to create the institutions and write the laws; effective implementation depends on much more, from tangible inputs like monetary resources to intangibles like political support. Brazil's partners in Mercosur are very conscious of these gaps, and have used them as a justification for not trying to match Brazil's levels of formal environmental protections.[5]

Although environmental protections are comparatively weak and new in Argentina, Paraguay, and Uruguay, they were initiated and developed there largely concurrently with the Mercosur integration process, although not because of it. Since the Treaty of Asunción was signed in 1991, all three countries have developed crucial new environmental legislation and consolidated national environmental agencies. As these summaries indicate, the Mercosur processes did not directly drive the timing of the environmental improvements; they were influenced by other factors, such as the end of authoritarian governments and the availability of international funding. Participants in the Mercosur negotiations were unable to cite specific examples of cross-country dissemination of proposals for environmental legislation or institutions, although they acknowledged that the practice of making regular reports on national advances might generally spur environmental developments (Breda 2001; Laciar 2001). In light of the general pessimism about the willingness of developing countries to limit trade with environmental restrictions, however, it is worth pointing out that the Mercosur experience shows that economic integration processes do not necessarily block environmental improvements, even if they do not cause them.

MERCOSUR'S WORKING SUBCOMMITTEE ON THE ENVIRONMENT

These national environmental actors are also the environmental actors of Mercosur. Their representatives met several times in 1993 and 1994 in specialized meetings. Despite their informal institutional status, they were quite productive in these meetings: they wrote 9 resolutions in the course of making recommendations for the treatment of environmental issues in Mercosur (Ollaik 2002, 6). They also reviewed existing national environmental legislation and made a list of 11 Basic Environmental Directives (Directrices básicas en materia de política ambiental) for the region, which the Common Market Group adopted as an official resolution (GMC/Res. No 10/94) (see Mercosur online). The GMC created a more permanent committee, SGT 6, to follow the agenda laid out by the specialized meetings.

Since 1995, representatives of the four national agencies have met as SGT 6 an average four times annually. Overall, despite their efforts to extend their agenda and activities, they have been unable to make environmental issues a significant component of the Mercosur process. Both by design and by the political development of Mercosur over time, the foreign and economic ministries dominate the Mercosur process, and they have regularly focused on other issues. Indeed, environmental issues have become less rather than more important in Mercosur.

As an institution, the Environmental Subcommittee has little formal power, in comparison both to environmental institutions in NAFTA and the European Union (Stevis and Mumme 2000) and to other institutions in Mercosur (Grandi and Bizzozero 1998). One of the limits of the working subcommittees of Mercosur as a group is that they have no permanent agenda or roles except the general admonition to achieve the objectives of the Treaty of Asunción.[6] Instead, the subcommittees' main role is to work on specific issues the GMC assigns to them and to propose resolutions and agreements to the GMC. The subcommittees can suggest additional agenda items, but they have limited capacity to be autonomous policy entrepreneurs. The GMC must also adopt any final proposals suggested by the subcommittees if they are to go on to become official and binding agreements for the Mercosur region. These provisions give the Ministries of Foreign Relations and Economy considerable control over SGT 6 (and the other subcommittees)—which they have not hesitated to exercise, often endorsing other goals over environmental protection. Participants in SGT 6 are quite aware of their secondary, technical role of assisting the real decisionmakers in the GMC (Breda 2001; Laciar 2001; Ollaik 2002).

The 2001 Environmental Framework Agreement expands and specifies the environmental aims of Mercosur. It does not, however, change the institutional status of SGT 6 and actually does not mention it directly anywhere. It also preserves longstanding weaknesses in contrast to the NAFTA and European Union environmental institutions. For example, the Framework Agreement affirms the absence of environmental dispute resolution mechanisms in Mercosur, saying simply that any Agreement-based controversies among the member states (and member states only, with no mention of other actors, such as citizens' groups) will be resolved through Mercosur's normal dispute resolution mechanisms (Article 8), which are themselves largely undeveloped. There is no regional court, and in practice, most conflicts are resolved through direct negotiations among the region's national presidents, a forum not especially open to broad social participation.

In addition, neither SGT 6 nor any other institutions in the region have the capacity collectively to evaluate environmental impact assessments, even for transboundary proposals. The environmental ministers of the region suggested in 1995 that the countries should develop harmonized procedures for such evaluation of potential impacts on shared ecosystems (Environment Ministers of the Member State of Mercosur 1995), but the GMC has never put this item on the agenda of SGT 6, and has deliberately avoided doing so. When an ad hoc committee was put together to discuss the Guaraní Aquifer that they all share, for example, there were no environmental representatives, even though the Meeting of Ministers asked three times in 2005–2006 to be included. Instead, transboundary environmental assessment appears in the Environmental Framework Agreement as just one of 14 areas in which the member states should "stimulate" further developments (Article 6.j).

SGT 6 was not involved in evaluating one of Mercosur's most substantial infrastructural projects, a proposed water superhighway, or hidrovia, to be built in the River Plate system. This project was blocked by the IDB's decision in 1997 to withdraw funding after regional NGOs provided alternative environmental and economic assessments, and then by legal actions by a broad coalition of opponents in Brazil and Argentina. Neither SGT 6 nor even the national environmental agencies individually have played a large role in these evaluations, although the Brazilian Ministry of the Environment did eventually support environmentalists in the court case there (Hochstetler 2002a). The GMC's institutional vision for SGT 6 continues to see it as a subsidiary committee to which the GMC can assign specific tasks that will enhance regional trade integration.

This limited view is matched by the limited content of the actual tasks the GMC has assigned. From the beginning, the agenda has leaned heavily toward trade promotion. Eliminating nontariff barriers and increasing global competitiveness (for example, through ecolabeling and ISO 14.000 compliance) were at the top of the first agenda of SGT 6 (GMC/Res No 38/95; SGT 6/Acta No 01/95. For minutes of the SGT 6 meetings, see Republic of Argentina; Republic of Brazil).

That agenda also included a few environmental issues less directly tied to trade, such as developing an environmental legal instrument and establishing a system for disseminating environmental information about the Mercosur countries via the Internet. SGT 6 has moved much more slowly on the nontrade issues, with the apparently straightforward Internet task still months from completion at the end of 2001, six years later. Even at that late date, one of the proposed solutions was just to provide new links from the official Mercosur website to the Brazilian and Argentine national agency web pages (which are quite good and informative, but obviously would not present new information) (Mercosur 2001). Indeed, the agenda for the 20th meeting of SGT 6 in 2001 was strikingly similar to that of its first meeting, indicating how slowly SGT 6 has moved through its small workload. The GMC has given SGT 6 a negotiating agenda only twice, in 1995 and 2002.

SGT 6 spent much of its first years—90 percent of its time from 1995 to 1998, by the estimate of one Brazilian participant (Ollaik 2002, 8)—reviewing the merits of claims that environmental regulations were being used as nontariff barriers in the region. Brazil's stricter environmental standards (or environmental protectionism, in its neighbors' view) were the most frequent target of such claims (Republic of Argentina n.d.). The group also spent considerable time debating the environmental protocol that forms the case study for this article. In its first eight years of existence, SGT 6 sent only that one significant resolution to the Common Market Group for approval; and the GMC turned down the environmental protocol in its first version before adopting the much less ambitious

Framework Agreement in 2001. This is a level of activity well below that of the other working subcommittees and below even that of the early specialized meetings on the environment. The pace picked up a bit with the creation of the Meeting of Environmental Ministers, with the CMC approving a joint action plan on environmental emergencies in 2004 (CMC/DEC N° 14/04) and one on sustainable production and consumption in 2007 (CMC/DEC N° 26/07).

The national delegations to SGT 6 have chafed under their limited agenda, asking to have it extended. They have added some agenda items on their own, such as regular discussion of joint administration of the Guarani Aquifer. They have used their regular meetings as a forum to share current projects, innovations, and problems, building considerable cross-regional social capital in the process. They also prepare collectively for international environmental gatherings, sharing schedules and observations and sometimes preparing common positions. In December 2000, SGT 6 delegates accepted an Argentine proposal to ask that SGT 6 be included in the broader process of "relaunching" Mercosur taking place at the time (Phillips 2001), with an agenda that addressed sustainable development more broadly rather than just trade aspects (SGT 6/Acta No 04/00). Despite the broad agenda proposal that emerged from this meeting, the 2001 priority agenda looked much like previous ones (SGT 6/Acta No 01/01).

Given the limited agenda and powers of the Environmental Subcommittee, it is not surprising that SGT 6 has not become a major focus for environmentalists in the region, even though it has tried to include nongovernmental sectors. Starting with its fourth meeting, in 1996, SGT 6 invited what it chose to call the private sector to participate in the opening day of its meetings, although nonstate actors were excluded from later decision-making sessions. As the private sector label suggests, the subcommittee has been especially interested in bringing in economic groups, inviting "those who have some direct interest in any of the stages of the process of production, distribution, and consumption" (SGT 6/Acta No 01/96). While this definition has been used to include environmentalists, it is obviously not a call specifically for their participation. A later meeting clarified that the subcommittee was looking for participants from each country who could represent the economic, social, and environmental sectors (SGT 6/Acta No 02/96).

Argentina and Brazil also hold broader national meetings before the Mercosur meetings to discuss the agenda. Governmental representatives, especially from Argentina, have presented written proposals and documents from national NGO networks in several of the closed decision-making sessions. Private sector actors can also ask to be put on the first-day agenda, to make their own proposals directly. Many meetings include such interventions, such as regular requests by the participating unions to take up issues of workplace safety. Despite these openings, there are also real limitations on nongovernmental participation. Documents are not routinely distributed to private sector representatives in advance, for example, so meetings can consist of observers sitting at the margins of a room while SGT 6 members sit at a central table and make cryptic comments about negotiating documents, without divulging their actual content (Mercosur 2001).

Nongovernmental participation (which was never high) has decreased over time. The lists of participants at SGT 6 meetings show clearly that the most consistent participants from the nongovernmental sector have been unions and business groups, especially those from Argentina and Brazil. After 2003, they stopped attending altogether, however. Environmentalist participants have included mostly groups from the hosting country, who attended meetings through the end of 2005, but now only attend occasionally.[7] Some of this attendance may have dropped because the Meeting of Ministers began to meet in 2004; it is a more prominent gathering that has no provisions for nongovernmental participation at all and requires prior approval for the attendance of *any* outside actors (CMC/DR/P.Dec, Article 22, Anexo 6 of RMMA/Acta N° 02/07).

In a series of interviews around the region in 2001, environmental organizations cited a variety of reasons for their increasing nonparticipation. These ranged from practical reasons, such as the lack of funds to travel to meetings and lack of knowledge about the meetings, to more critical stances asserting that either the agenda or the agreements of SGT 6 were too narrow and too protrade to warrant their continued interest.

The ECOS Foundation, the only regional environmental NGO specifically created to accompany Mercosur processes, had been the most consistent environmentalist participant in SGT 6 meetings. Even ECOS, however, insisted that the participatory openings must be increased and improved for SGT 6 to function well and to justify NGO expenses in attending meetings (Leichner Reynal 2002), and in fact, no longer attends.[8] Mercosur has no other forums that invite environmentalists' participation. The most likely alternative, the Economic and Social Consultative Forum (FCES), is only an advisory body and is even more heavily dominated by business and labor actors (Grandi and Bizzozero 1998; FCES 2001).

Regional environmentalists interested in the intersection of trade and the environment have begun to turn their attention much more to the proposed Free Trade Area of the Americas (FTAA) or to specific transboundary issues (see Hochstetler 2002a).

This rather bleak summary of the achievements of SGT 6 clearly extends from the group's very limited institutional role. As Stevis and Mumme (2000, 20–21) argue, however, the formal rules are just part of the story. Political contexts, structures, and conjunctures also work to create policy outcomes. Similar rules in two different contexts thus can have quite different outcomes, more or less favorable for environmental protection and development. SGT 6 was a much more dynamic organization in its early years, including its years as simply a specialized meeting rather than a permanent subcommittee, than in its more recent past. Historically, SGT 6's experience of negotiating a regional environmental legal instrument largely failed and left a distinctly negative impression, lowering environmentalists' expectations for the group (Leichner Reynal 2002; Luchiese 2001). Much of the downward movement stemmed from larger debates among Mercosur member states that were only partly related to the environment.

CASE STUDY: MERCOSUR'S ENVIRONMENTAL LEGAL INSTRUMENT

The effort to negotiate an environmental legal agreement for the Mercosur region took a decade, from 1991 to 2001. SGT 6 was unable to resist strong pressures from regional ministers of trade and foreign relations that abruptly scaled back this effort in 1997, eventually producing the joint Framework Agreement in 2001 rather than a full protocol to the Treaty of Asunción. While Argentina directly led the assault on the SGT's original protocol draft, the other countries acquiesced to the final result, showing their willingness to accept the "lowest common denominator" for environmental issues in the region. Although nothing in the Treaty of Asunción prohibits the possibility of "harmonization" that raises the region's collective environmental standards, the politics of Mercosur have meant harmonization downward in practice, especially after the Mercosur agreement itself nearly collapsed in 1999.

In the Treaty of Asunción, member countries agreed to harmonize national bodies of legislation that were related to the trade relations among them. The specialized meetings of regional environmental agencies received the task of reviewing existing national environmental legislation and laying out a future direction for that harmonization. From the start, the countries had different visions of their task. At this early stage, Brazil pushed to "harmonize up" regional environmental legislation to match its own legal framework. Brazilian economic actors supported the Environmental Ministry in this effort because they were concerned about Brazil's ability to compete with its neighbors. Its neighbors questioned whether Brazilian levels of environmental protection were necessary, noting that Brazil had problems enforcing its own advanced legislation (Environment Watch: Latin America 1994). The first basic directive produced by the specialized meetings in 1994 echoes these concerns about competitiveness in the context of Mercosur.

> 1. Assure the harmonization of environmental legislation among the Member States of the Treaty of Asunción, understanding that harmonization does not imply establishing a single legislation against which to compare the legislation. [For the comparison], actual implementation will be considered as well as the legislation itself. In the case of gaps in their environmental legislation, norms will be considered that both meet the environmental aims at stake as well as assuring equitable conditions of competitiveness in Mercosur. (GMC/Res. No 10/94)

When it created SGT 6 in 1995, the GMC included further work on the legal framework for environmental issues in Mercosur on the group's agenda; but it was already beginning to trim back the mandate that at least the Brazilians wanted. The 1995 agenda directive dropped any mention of harmonization and switched to the language of optimization, asking SGT 6 to

> elaborate a document that takes national legal orders as a point of departure, specifically those referring to environmental management, having as an objective the optimization of the levels of environmental quality in the Member States. (GMC\Res No 38/95, point 5).

SGT 6 discreetly challenged this rollback by returning to the basic directives as the principal point of departure for discussing the new legal instrument. The group's first meeting in 1996 included what it called an "interesting" debate over the Argentine proposal for how to proceed, which reflected different national opinions about the scope and content of the job it had been assigned. The procedures eventually adopted included both optimization and harmonization among the objectives for the legal instrument (SGT 6/Acta 01/96, point 4). SGT 6 members agreed that they would identify gaps in existing national legislation and try to fill them, thereby advancing the coverage of environmental issues in the region. They also agreed to wait to decide whether the scale of the proposed changes justified the designation "protocol" or "agreement," an issue not addressed in the GMC's directive. Environmentalists in the region supported the efforts at harmonization, producing their own analyses of existing national legislation and suggesting places for common improvement (FARN 1997; Grupo Y'Guazu 1995).

The initial small break with the GMC widened when Brazil's delegation to SGT 6, preparing to host the next meeting in August 1996, drafted the first version of what it called an "Additional Protocol to the Treaty of Asunción–Environment." Twenty-six articles in this first draft covered a broad array of topics and introduced numerous specific legal directives. The tone of the document's overall directives is captured well in a section introducing Article 4, on Quality Standards and Levels of Environmental Protection. It recognizes the right of each member state to establish its own levels of environmental protection but also demands that members put significant force behind efforts to achieve high levels of protection of the environment (Republic of Brazil 1997, Anexo 1, 41).

Other articles spell out specific instructions for environmental impact assessment, monitoring, environmental certification, internalization of environmental costs, biosafety, biological diversity, nontariff barriers, environmental information, environmental emergencies, natural resources, protected areas, species protection, water resources, solid wastes, and toxic products. In 1996, not even Brazil had developed legislation on all these issues, and the other countries had numerous gaps.

The draft certainly warranted the title of protocol for its scope and specificity. Overall, however, the document is best characterized as a collective rather than a supranational environmental agreement, because it is primarily about simultaneous national commitments for and implementation of environmental protections at home, and it gives little focus to transboundary or supranational agencies, procedures, or legislation.

The initial Brazilian draft, in its ambition and specificity, can be traced to Brazil's comparatively strong domestic environmental developments, On other issues, Brazilian negotiators have been the strongest voices in Mercosur for low levels of institutionalization and policy harmonization (Phillips 2001, 567), Thus the national environmental agency's draft of the initial project was an exception to the more general Brazilian vision of integration, and it more closely followed an expansive national vision of appropriate levels of environmental protection and coordination.

During the year following the August 1996 meeting, the delegations to SGT 6 sought comments on the draft document from other national committees and ministries, as well as from civil society organizations. In SGT 6 meetings, they presented comments they had received and suggestions for revisions. Just a month after the document was first presented, the Brazilian and Uruguayan delegations were able to report that other national actors had only minor suggestions for changes and encouraged rapid acceptance of the document. Argentina and Paraguay—the two countries with the lowest levels of national environmental protections—stressed the need to take the time to do full consultations and to examine possible contradictions with existing national legislation (SGT 6/Acta 03/96, point 3).

The document that emerged out of the year's worth of revisions was significantly different in its organization and somewhat different in tone. For example, the article on levels of environmental protection cited above (now number 6) retained the clause about national control over levels of environmental protection but adopted the GMC's language of optimization, rather than calling straightforwardly for high levels. The Environmental Protocol, however, remained a long and specific document. Reorganized, it now comprised 85 articles and covered an additional set of issues, such as soils, the atmosphere, and health (SGT 6/Acta 06/97, Anexo 10). In June 1997, SGT 6 formally raised it to the GMC for approval as an Additional Protocol to the Treaty of Asunción.

The GMC responded promptly but ambiguously. Citing concerns from the Argentine delegation, it asked for additional time to analyze the proposed protocol (GMC/Acta No 2/97). The Argentine delegation to SGT 6 was surprised by the position of Argentina's GMC delegation, as the Environmental Secretariat had consulted widely in Argentina before the SGT 6 negotiations. The environmental lawyer who had coordinated the Argentine consultations on the draft, Mirta Laciar, wrote a highly detailed report of her consultations that same month (Laciar 1997). In total, Laciar conducted 71 individual and collective consultations on the Environmental Protocol between April 1996 and June 1997 (1997, 30–31) and thought she had heard and addressed a wide variety of interests and opinions. The consulted parties were given advance copies of the proposed protocol and were asked for concrete suggestions for changes. The appendixes to the report detailed line by line the changes the Argentine delegation made in the proposed protocol, reflecting those consultations.

More broadly, Laciar argued in her report that the proposed protocol was more programmatic than regulatory. She also suggested that it could help establish the basic elements of a national (following the 1994 constitutional amendment) and regional environmental policy while still allowing Argentina further to develop its own specific policies (Laciar 1997, 34–35). She argued firmly that in writing the protocol, SGT 6 aimed "fundamentally not to alter the objective of the Treaty of Asunción, which is: the free circulation of goods, services, and productive factors" (36).

The Argentine delegation to the GMC was never nearly as explicit in laying out its objections to the proposed protocol, even to the SGT 6 delegation. The major sticking points were the treatment of biosafety issues, evaluations of environmental impact, and the precautionary principle (Laciar 1997, 9; Ollaik 2002, 10). The biosafety issues were especially intractable, as they highlighted the conflict between Brazil and Argentina over the use of genetically modified seeds in agriculture. Brazil, facing "resistance from adversarial NGOs, media critics, independent judges, opposition party leaders, . . . [and] defiant state governors" (Paarlberg 2001, 92), had placed restrictions on genetically modified organisms, while Argentine policymakers embraced them, opposition from groups like Greenpeace Argentina notwithstanding. The Argentine Foreign Ministry also objected in general to what it considered excessively high environmental standards and lack of consideration of the time Argentine industry would need to adapt to these standards (Gudynas 1998, 139). It is worth noting that even supportive environmental organizations criticized the document, citing inconsistencies in its treatment of issues, such as sovereignty over resources, and several places where it fell short of existing international agreements, such as the Rio Declaration (Leichner 2001, 10).

When the GMC finally elaborated its response to the SGT 6 a year later, in May 1998, it was no clearer, simply stating that it was returning the proposed protocol for "deepening of its technical analysis and for the presentation of new recommendations" (GMC/ Acta No 1/98). The SGT 6 delegations undertook new consultations at home, which resulted in no requests for changes from Brazil and Paraguay and some modifications from Argentina and Uruguay (SGT 6/Act No 10/98, point 4). With those made (and Argentina abstaining from the section on biosafety), SGT 6 sent a new version of the protocol back to the GMC in 1999 (SGT 6/Acta No 01/99, point 3).

In the meantime, however, unrelated developments in Mercosur sidelined all nonessential components of regional integration for what was to stretch into several years. The precipitating event was Brazil's massive currency devaluation in January 1999, which transformed the balance of economic competitiveness among the four neighbors overnight (Bulmer-Thomas 1999). As the member countries struggled to cope with various economic and political crises, they individually chose strategies that undercut regional integration rather than building it. For example, they partly abandoned the common external tariff, which had been one of Mercosur's most significant achievements. After nearly abandoning their coordination altogether, the member countries finally agreed to relaunch Mercosur in 2000. They did so on the foundation of a growth-oriented regional developmentalist strategy (Phillips 2001, 572), a vision that has never made much room for environmental considerations.

For almost two years, then, the revised Environmental Protocol languished in the GMC. Environmental NGOs made regular trips to the SGT 6 meetings to ask about its status, and even met independently to try to strategize ways to move the protocol forward (Leichner Reynal 2002; Luchiesi 2001; Ryan 2001; SGT 6/Actas No 02/99, 01/00, 03/00). SGT 6 also sent occasional queries to the GMC about the documents. The GMC also faced opposing pressures. Argentina's Foreign and Economic ministries had already expressed specifically environmental objections to the proposed protocol; now regional actors in the GMC were negotiating in the context of the economic developments that had transformed patterns of competitiveness in the region and left countries, especially Argentina, ambivalent about the integration process itself Finally, in the September 2000 GMC meeting, the Argentine delegation laid out what it would accept in an environmental agreement, and the GMC sent SGT 6 correspondingly more specific instructions about how to rework the environmental legal instrument.

The new instructions from the GMC directed SGT 6 to limit the document to reaffirming principles already in the Rio Declaration of the 1992 United Nations Conference on Environment and Development, which had been signed by all member states (GMC/ Acta No 03/00, point 6). It did allow commitments to cooperate to implement the Rio Declaration. Member states also could make a commitment to begin analyzing regional environmental problems. The Argentine delegation to SGT 6 followed the GMC's instructions to the letter and brought a new draft to SGT 6 in December 2000. This draft pulled together only the consensual definitions and principles and left specific sectoral issues to future negotiations (SGT 6/Acta No 04/00, point 4).

SGT 6 called an extraordinary meeting in March 2001 to discuss the new draft. The list of participants makes the politics of the process clear. Nonstate actors were not invited to attend even the first day, a measure allowed by treating the issue in an extraordinary rather than ordinary meeting. Paraguay and Uruguay sent just one representative apiece, while Brazil and Argentina brought full delegations, including representatives of their foreign ministries and environmental agencies—bringing with them competing texts. Three days later, they had a new document for the GMC, now an agreement rather than a protocol (SGT 6/Acta No 01/01). This new document was a mere fraction of the size of the earlier protocols, with just ten articles. All language of obligation and direct mandates disappeared, and was replaced with words like promote, stimulate, consider, provide incentives for, and so on. All the specific directives for different issues were cut, not just the controversial biosafety clause, and replaced with an appendix that simply listed them as thematic areas for future possible agreements.

SGT 6 sent the greatly simplified Environmental Framework Agreement not only to the GMC (composed largely of foreign and economic ministers), but also to the Common Market Council (over which the region's national presidents preside). Approval followed quickly this time: in April 2001, without comment, from the GMC (GCM/Acta No 08/01) and in June by the presidents (CMC/Acta No 02/01). After the years of negotiations, passage of the Environmental Framework Agreement has caused hardly a ripple.

The SGT 6 negotiators emerged from the process with a sense of caution and with few specific expectations. Just after final passage, Mirta Laciar stressed that there is no movement in Mercosur toward common or supranational environmental law and that the future was otherwise unknowable.

> Today's facts or starting points are that there is now this Agreement, that all participants in the SGT 6 plan to continue working [in SGT 6], that we are all oriented to trying to figure out how to develop sustainably in the context of globalization. The environmental coordinators are clear in wanting to move toward this. (Laciar 2001)

Given the recent economic and political meltdown in Argentina, Laciar seems prescient in retrospect. Raquel Breda of Brazil's Ministry of the Environment also stressed that SGT 6 was trying to work on issues within its members' own powers of implementation (Breda 2001). Regional environmentalists began nudging SGT 6 and the member states immediately to work on ratification and implementation of the agreement.

Even the most positive assessments stress that the Environmental Framework Agreement is only a first step toward sustainable development in the region—and simultaneously note gaps, like the absence of the precautionary principle, which was in the Rio Declaration (Leichner Reynal 2001). Because its scope is limited to principles already agreed on in the 1992 Rio Agreement, the Environmental Framework Agreement fails to establish a new environmental agenda but simply restates a vague commitment to work on environmental issues. No more was politically possible in Mercosur at the turn of the twenty-first century.

From the Region to the Hemisphere

The foregoing analysis demonstrates that environmental issues and actors have played only a minor—and decreasing—role in the Mercosur free trade area. The main environmental actor, the Working Subcommittee No. 6 on the Environment, has struggled with little institutional power and an agenda largely limited to trade promotion issues. The most significant regional environmental legal instrument, the Mercosur Environmental Agreement, was adopted in 2001, but is only a framework document that proclaims the intention of future action. These provisions fall far short of the strongest national-level legislation and institutions of the member countries, and some of the weaker ones as well. The weakness of environmental issues in Mercosur is partly structural, like other aspects of the trade agreement. Yet the weakness of collective environmental provisions is nonetheless the result of repeated explicit refusals by the region's trade and foreign ministers—and the presidents who orient them—to allow stronger regional environmental protections. Collective environmental protection also fell victim to regional uncertainties about the wisdom of continuing economic integration.

At the same time, the member states did generally increase their levels of domestic environmental protections during the years of economic integration through Mercosur. They consolidated national environmental agencies—or even created them—and wrote new environmental legislation. They did so to varying degrees, and all continue to have numerous gaps, especially in implementation. The final composite picture is one that confounds easy analysis of the relationship between trade and environment in developing countries. The best summary is that while trade integration does not evidently promote greater environmental protections in significant ways, especially in the form of collective environmental provisions, it also did not block environmental improvements at the national level when these occurred for unrelated reasons.

As the hemisphere contemplates additional trade negotiations and considers the role of environmental protections within them, Mercosur's positions in these debates are likely to be similarly complex. If the member governments accept environmental provisions, the Mercosur experiences suggest that they will insist on collective national commitments rather than allowing supranational agencies. Despite this expected resistance, recent interviews in the region belie the theoretical expectation of a sharp split between developing and developed countries on environmental issues.

Mercosur's environmental and social organizations are poised to take the side of their northern counterparts rather than that of their own governments, confounding the expectations of low public concern about the environment in developing areas.

The Mercosur experience itself suggests that the member governments are unlikely to initiate or support strong environmental institutions and provisions in other trade agreements. In their own regional agreement, they have kept their collective environmental commitments low, even if they independently raised national environmental protections. This is also the position that member governments have supported in various international negotiations to date. Brazil has taken some of the strongest positions against making the link between trade and other issues; lead Brazilian trade negotiator Jos6 Alfredo Graga Lima has insisted, "the inclusion of labor and environmental clauses does not need to be part of the negotiations for a free trade area" (cited in Audley and Sherwin 2002, 6). This despite Brazil's having the strongest history of national environmental institutions and legislation in the region. Along with others in Latin America, Brazilian officials fear that the United States, in particular, "already uses its domestic environmental laws to restrict imports in competitive industries and that it links trade and the environment for protectionist purposes" (Audley and Sherwin 2002, 7).

If Mercosur governments are eventually forced to include environmental provisions in a free trade agreement, they are likely to distinguish between collective national commitments and supranational arrangements. Supranational arrangements are outside the direct control of nation-states, establishing actors and processes that are at least partly independent of them. Mercosur's member states have strongly favored retaining national control over as many aspects of the integration process as possible, limiting their agreements (including their international ones) to collective coordination of national action within nation-state boundaries.

While the FTAA was being actively negotiated, two articles presented possible models for an environmental component of the FTAA that illustrated the supranational and collective alternatives. Gaines proposed an institution inspired by NAFTA's Commission for Environmental Cooperation with some weak supranational elements, including

> an independent, professional staff; defined mechanisms for private individuals or organizations to submit issues needing attention (and decision-making criteria for evaluating such submissions); and a citizen's advisory committee with specific powers and responsibilities to shape the agenda of the organization. (Gaines 2002, 206)

Mercosur's SGT 6 has none of these characteristics except the very informal provision that allows private sector groups to make presentations on the opening days of its meetings. Considering how little autonomy Mercosur decisionmakers grant their own national environmental agencies in a regional setting, they were unlikely to agree to grant such freedom of action to citizens across the hemisphere and an independent bureaucracy.

Audley and Sherwin (2002, 3) suggested a collective alternative: offer financial and technical assistance for strengthening national environmental protections as a strategy to gain regional acceptance of environmental provisions in the FTAA. This suggestion to handle the trade-environment link by building national environmental capacity would probably not have been proposed by Mercosur's member states, but they would have been considerably more likely to support it (versus Gaines' version) if they were convinced that some link were necessary to achieve a trade agreement they want. The four Mercosur member states and Chile repeated their commitment to both the Rio Declaration and to states' sovereign control over their environmental and development policies in their joint statement to the Latin American regional preparations for the UN's World Summit on Sustainable Development in 2002 (SGT 6/Acta No 03/01:Anexo 5A).

Part of the appeal of Audley and Sherwin's solution is that it respects this concern for national environmental sovereignty, while the Gaines proposal does not. When the environmental ministers of the Americas met in March 2001, they also endorsed strengthening environmental management systems at home as the solution to reconciling economic integration and environmental protection (Environment Ministers of the Americas 2001). A final point is that the Mercosur member states have all welcomed international financial assistance when it is offered for improving national environmental protections, whether it comes from the IDB, the Global Environmental Facility, or the USAID. In any event, the FTAA itself now appears to be dead, with the Mercosur countries leading the resistance to it (Carranza 2004).

How likely are Mercosur's governments to receive pressure to include environmental issues of whatever kind in future trade negotiations? Although none of the regional governments, developing or developed, has been promoting this agenda in the negotiations to date, they should expect significant political pressure at the point of ratification and in the streets beforehand. There was a broad consensus among observers that U.S. and Canadian activists would seek to block ratification of an FTAA without environmental provisions in the North (Audley and Sherwin 2002; Deere and Esty 2002, 5; Gaines 2002). Contrary to expectations, developing countries in Mercosur should also expect similar domestic pressures.

The member states of Mercosur are likely to get quite a bit more pressure from regional environmentalists about broader trade agreements than they have over Mercosur itself. Regional environmentalists have strong ties across the hemisphere on trade issues, ties that are often stronger than those among environmentalists in just the Mercosur countries. In addition, many of them have been willing to support Mercosur partly as a preferable outcome to a broader agreement like the FTAA, but are wholly opposed to the latter (Smith and Korzeniewicz 2007).

The regional networks date back at least to the Rio conference preparations, and have been multiplying since then (Friedman et al. 2001; Smith and Korzeniewicz 2007). In Uruguay, the environmental NGO CLAES coordinates a multinational effort called Sustainable South and maintains one of the best NGO websites and information centers on trade in the region (Gudynas 2001a; CLAES). The environmental group REDES, also in Uruguay, coordinates sustainable development discussions with Chile as well as the Mercosur countries in a project called Sustainable Southern Cone. REDES takes a very strong stance against free trade in general but less so against Mercosur, which it sees as a much more natural outgrowth of the history of the Southern Cone (Surroca 2001).

FARN in Argentina has carried out a number of discussions about the link between environment and trade with environmentalists in both Mercosur and the Andean Community. FARN had no specific position for or against the FTAA, but saw Mercosur as having more potential for making appropriate links between environment and trade (Ryan 2001). In Brazil, the Porto Alegre forums in January 2001 and 2002 brought together numerous activists from around the world, but especially the Americas, who are poised to fight trade agreements like the FTAA on a number of grounds, including environmental concerns (Korzeniewicz and Smith 2005). In short, many citizens' networks already exist that will make it difficult for Mercosur's member states to avoid some environmental commitments as part of broader trade agreements.

The needs and desires of development present an ongoing challenge for those who wish to integrate environmental concerns into trade agreements of any kind. The Southern Cone governments of Mercosur in particular have shown a strong collective resistance to incorporating such concerns into trade agreements they negotiate and join. On the other hand, some regional actors, such as environmental activists and agencies, would like additional attention to the environmental problems that may emerge with trade-pushed economic growth and integration projects. This is therefore not an issue that neatly divides developing and developed countries.

NOTES

The research for this paper was funded by an in-residence fellowship at the Instituto de Desarrollo Económico y Social, Buenos Aires, and by a research grant from the Fulbright

Commission. I would like to thank Dimitris Stevis and the anonymous reviewers for *Latin American Politics and Society* for their helpful comments.

1 Devia 1998b and Tussie and Vásquez 1997, 2000 cover some of the early arrangements in Mercosur regarding the environment.

2 The word collective is used rather than international to describe these environmental agreements because they continue to focus on the domestic situation and on national-level implementation. Thus, while a free trade agreement might potentially be an impetus for a region to consider and address its environmental problems holistically, Mercosur's environmental agreements remain essentially collectively agreed-on national commitments for action within the respective nation-state boundaries.

3 This agency's names have varied, including the Secretariat of Natural Resources and Sustainable Development (SRNyDS), the Secretariat of Sustainable Development and Environmental Policy (SDSyPA), and others.

4 Articles 14 and 15 of Law 1561 created the new National Environmental Secretariat. See Republic of Paraguay.

5 Nonimplementation of environmental legislation was also an issue for Mexico in the NAFTA negotiations, along with many other similarities with Brazil (compare Hochstetler 2002a; Mumme and Lybecker 2002). Mexico, in contrast, lags behind rather than leads its free trade area in environmental protections.

6 See Article 13 of the Treaty of Asunción, which created the subcommittee structure, and the GMC resolutions that created SGT 6 (GMC/Res No 20/95) and provided its first agenda (GMC/Res No 38/95), at Mercosur online.

7 The four member states of Mercosur rotate the presidency of Mercosurevery six months, with the president pro tempore hosting all Mercosur meetings and taking a leading role in preparing any Mercosur documents needed during that period. SGT 6 also follows this general pattern.

8 ECOS's participation was funded by the World Wildlife Federation and the Tinker Foundation; and ECOS, in turn, was able to fund some other regional NGOs to accompany SGT 6 and Mercosur. ECOS, however, no longer has funding specifically for Mercosur participation.

REFERENCES

Note: The texts of cited treaties, decisions, resolutions, and agreements of the CMC and the GMC are on Mercosur's website. Minutes of the SGT 6 meetings are available on the websites of the Brazilian and Argentine national environmental agencies. See entries below.

Associação Brasileira de Entidades de Meio Ambiente (ABEMA). 1993. Diagnóstico institucional dos órgãos estaduais de meio ambiente no Brasil. Espiritu Santo: ABEMA.

Audley, John J. 1997. *Green Politics and Global Trade: NAFTA and the Future of Environmental Politics.* Washington, DC: Georgetown University Press.

Audley, John, and Edward Sherwin. 2002. Politics and Parallel Negotiations: Environment and Trade in the Western Hemisphere. *Global Policy Program Working Paper* no. 25. Washington, DC: Carnegie Endowment for International Peace.

Barnes, Pamela M., and Ian G. Barnes. 2000. *Environmental Policy in the European Union.* Williston, VT: Edward Elgar.

Beukel, Erik. 1999. Trade Liberalization and Environmental Regulations: Regional Interests and Ideas in Europe and North America. In *Racing to Regionalize: Democracy, Capitalism, and Regional Political Economy*, ed. K. P. Thomas and M. A. Tetreault. Boulder: Lynne Rienner. 113–39.

Breda, Raquel. 2001, Technical Consultant on International Relations, Environment Ministry, Brazil. Author interview. Montevideo, December 6.

Bugoni, Mara, and Carlos Canas. 1998. Un modelo práctico: reportaje [interview] a María Julia Alsogaray. Aportes para el Estado) y la Administración Gubernamental 5, 12: 9–14.

Bulmer-Thomas, Victor. 1999. The Brazilian Devaluation: National Responses and International Consequences. *International Affairs* 75, 4: 729–41.

Carranza, Mario E. 2004. Mercosur and the End Game of the FTAA Negotiations: Challenges and Prospects after the Argentine Crisis. *Third World Quarterly* 25, 2: 319–337.

Centro Latino Americano de Ecología Social (CLAES). 2001. *Situación ambiental del Uruguay: informe sobre prioridades y urgencias.* Montevideo: CLAES (mimeograph).

———. Website. <www.ambiental.net/claes>

Deere, Carolyn L. 2004. Greening Trade in the Americas: An Agenda for Moving Beyond the North-South Impasse. *Journal of World Trade* 38, 1: 137–153.

Deere, Carolyn L., and Daniel C. Esty, eds. 2002. *Greening the Americas: NAFTA's Lessons for Hemispheric Trade.* Cambridge: MIT Press.

Devia, Leila. 1998a. *Legislación ambiental de la República Argentina.* In Devia 1998b. 81–107.

———. ed. 1998b. *Mercosur y medio ambiente.* 2d ed. Buenos Aires: Ediciones Ciudad Argentina.

Díaz Labrano, Roberto Ruiz. 1998. La defensa y preservación del medio ambiente en el ordenamiento jurídico del Paraguay. In *Devia* 1998b. 109–92.

Domínguez, Ana, and Rubén G. Prieto, eds. 2000. Perfil *ambiental del Uruguay 2000.* Montevideo: Editorial Nordan-Comunidad.

Environment Ministers of the Americas. 2001. Meeting of Environment Ministers of the Americas, March 29–30, 2001: Ministerial Communiqué. Point 7. <www.summit-americas.org/eng/documents.htm>

Environment Ministers of the Member States of Mercosur. 1995. *Declaración de Tarranco.* Montevideo, June 21.

Environment Watch: Latin America. 1994. *South America's Common Market Facing Environmental Roadblocks.* November: 7.

Estado de São Paulo. 2002. November 21: 1, A4.

Fundación Ambiente y Recursos Naturales (FARN). 1997. *Hacia regulaciones ambientales armonizadas para las inversiones privadas en grandes proyectos de infraestructura en el Mercosur.* Buenos Aires: FARN.

Fernandes, Edesio, ed. 1998. *Environmental Strategies for Sustainable Development in Urban Areas.* Brookfield, VT: Ashgate.

Folha de São Paulo. 2002. September 18: 1, A4, A5.

Foro Consultivo Económico-Social (FCES). 2001. Author's observation of FCES meeting. Montevideo, December 19.

Friedman, Elisabeth J., Kathryn Hochstetler, and Ann Marie Clark. 2001. Sovereign Limits and Regional Opportunities for Global Civil Society in Latin America. *Latin American Research Review* 35, 3: 7–35.

Gaines, Sanford E. 2002. The Free Trade Area of the Americas: Lessons from North America. In *The Greening of Trade Law: International Trade Organizations and Environmental Issues,* ed. R. H. Steinberg. Lanham: Rowman and Littlefield. 189–220.

Glassen, John, and Nemesio Neves B. Salvador. 2000. EIA in Brazil: A Procedures-Practice Gap. A Comparative Study with Reference to the European Union, and Especially the UK. *Environmental Impact Assessment Review* 20, 2: 191–225.

Gómez-Mera, Laura. 2005. Explaining Mercosur's Survival: Strategic Sources of Argentine-Brazilian Convergence. *Journal of Latin American Studies* 37: 109–140.

Grandi, Jorge, and Lincoln Bizzozero. 1998. Hacia una nueva sociedad civil del Mercosur. Viejos y nuevos actores en el tejido subregional. Paper presented at the seminar "Integración regional y participación de la sociedad civil," April 20–24, at CEFIR/ALOP/CLAEH, Montevideo.

Grant, Wyn, Duncan Matthews, and Peter Newell. 2001. *The Effectiveness of European Union Environmental Policy.* New York: Palgrave.

Grupo Y'Guazu. 1995. *Bases para la armonización de exigencias ambientales en el Mercosur.* Buenos Aires: FARN.

Gudynas, Eduardo. 1998. Mercosur y medio ambiente en Uruguay. In *Mercosur y medio ambiente,* ed. H. Blanco and N. Borregaard. Santiago, Chile: CIPMA. 130–42.

———. 2001a. Coordinator, CLAES. Author interview. Montevideo, November 19. Gudynas, Eduardo, ed. 2001b. Politicas ambientales en Uruguay. Montevideo: Coscoroba.

Guimaraes, Roberto P. 1995. *The Ecopolitics of Development in the Third World: Politics and Environment in Brazil.* Boulder: Lynne Rienner.

Hochstetler, Kathryn. 2002a. After the Boomerang: Environmental Movements and Politics in the La Plata River Basin. *Global Environmental Politics* 2, 4: 35–57.

——. 2002b. Brazil. In Weidner and Janicke 2002. 69–95.

Hochstetler, Kathryn, and Margaret E. Keck. 2007. *Greening Brazil: Environmental Activism in State and Society*. Durham: Duke University Press.

Hopkins, Jack W. 1995. *Policymaking for Conservation in Latin America: National Parks, Reserves, and the Environment*. Westport: Praeger.

Interamerican Development Bank (IDB). 2001. Lending by Country in 2000: The Year's Lending. <http://www.iadb.org/exr/pdf/lending.pdf>

Johnson, Pierre Marc, and Andre Beaulieu. 1996. *The Environment and NAFTA: Understanding and Implementing the New Continental Law*. Washington, DC: Island Press.

Keck, Margaret E. 1992. *The Workers' Party and Democratization in Brazil*. New Haven: Yale University Press.

Korzeniewicz, Roberto Patricio, and William C. Smith. Transnational Civil Society Actors and Regional Governance in the Americas: Elite Projects and Collective Action from Below. In *Regionalism and Governance in the Americas: Forms of a Continental Drift*, eds. Louise Fawcett and Móncia Serrano. London: Palgrave, 2005. 135–158.

Laciar, Mirta Elizabeth. 1997. *PRODIA subprograma a componente fortalecimiento institucional: "proyecto de protocolo adicional al tratado de Asunción sobre medio ambiente."* Buenos Aires: SRYNyDS.

——. 2001. Legal Consultant to Secretariat of Environment and Sustainable Development, Argentina; principal ministry representative to Mercosur. Author interview. Buenos Aires, July 12.

La Nación. 2008. El gobierno echó a Romina Picolotti y la reemplaza Homero Biblioni. 2 December.

Leichner, María. 2001a. Mercosur y su fantasma: el protocolo ambiental. Paper read at the Conferencia Internacional sobre Comercio, Ambiente y Desarrollo Sustentable: Perspectivas de América Latina y el Caribe. Mexico City, February 19–21.

Leichner Reynal, María. 2001b. *Mercosur firma el acuerdo marco sobre medio ambiente*. Website of ECOS Foundation. <www.fundacionecos.org>

——. 2002. Executive Director, Fundación ECOS. Author telephone interviews. February 1, 2.

Luchiesi Junior, Alvaro. 2001. Coordinator of Agriculture, Trade, and Environment, WWF-Brasil. Author interview. Brasilia, October 11.

Malamud, Andrés. 2005. Presidential Diplomacy and the Institutional Underpinnings of Mercosur: An Empirical Examination. *Latin American Research Review* 40, 1: 138–164.

McAllister, Lesley K. 2008. *Making Law Matter: Environmental Protection and Legal Institutions in Brazil*. Stanford: Stanford University Press, Stanford Law Books.

McCormick, John. 2001. *Environmental Policy in the European Union*. New York: Palgrave.

Mercosur. Official website. <www.mercosur.int>

——. Subgrupo de Trabajo VI Medio Ambiente (SGT 6). 2001. Author's observation of the 20th Meeting of SGT 6. Montevideo, December 6.

Mumme, Stephen, and Donna Lybecker. 2002. Environmental Capacity in Mexico: An Assessment. In Weidner and Janicke 2002. 311–27.

Ollaik, Leila. 2002. Mercosul Environment Group: Facts and Possibilities. Paper presented at the 6th meeting of the Brazilian Studies Association, Atlanta, April 4–6.

Paarlberg, Robert. 2001. *The Politics of Precaution: Genetically Modified Crops in Developing Countries*. Baltimore: Johns Hopkins University Press.

Padua, Jose Augusto. 1992. The Birth of Green Politics in Brazil: Exogenous and Endogenous Factors. In *Green Politics Two*, ed. W. Rudig. Edinburgh: Edinburgh University Press. 134–55.

Panario, Daniel. 2001. Director of UNCIEP; Professor, Universidad de la República de Uruguay. Author interview. Montevideo, November 27.

Phillips, Nicola. 2001. Regionalist Governance in the New Political Economy of Development: "Relaunching" the Mercosur. *Third World Quarterly* 22, 4: 565–83.

Pigretti, Graciela Berra Estrada de. 1999. *Proyectos de leyes de presupuestos mínimos ambientales: pautas de conciliación*. Buenos Aires: Presidencia de la Nación/SRNyDS.

Red de Ecología Social/Amigos de la Tierra (REDES), ed. 2000. *Uruguay sustentable: una propuesta ciudadana*. Montevideo: Impresora Editorial.

Republic of Argentina. Official environmental website. <www.medioambiente.gov.ar/mercosur>

Republic of Argentina. Secretaria de Recursos Hídricos y Ambiente Humana (SRNyAH). n.d. MERCOSUR: una decisión ambientalmente posible. Buenos Aires: SRNyAH.

Republic of Argentina. *Secretaria de Recursos Naturales y Desarrollo Sustentable (SRNyDS). 1999. Objetivos, ejecución y resultados del PRODIA 0994-1999)*. Buenos Aires: Presidencia de la Nación and SRNyDS.

Republic of Brazil. Senado Federal. 1991. Meio ambiente (legislação). [Compendium of current legislation.] Brasilia: Senado Federal.

Republic of Brazil. Secretaria do Meio Ambiente, Silo Paulo (SEMA-SP). 1997. O Mercosul e o meio ambiente. Silo Paulo: SEMA-SP.

———. Official website. <www.mma.gov.br>

Republic of Paraguay. Senate. Official website. <www.senado.gov.py/leyes/textos00/1561.html>

Rodríguez, Andrea Silvana. 1998. Marco jurídico-institucional ambiental aplicable a los humedales. In Los humedales de la Argentina: clasificación, situación actual, conservación y legislación, ed. P. Canevari, D. E. Blanco, E. H. Bucher, G. Castro, and I. Davidson. Buenos Aires: Wetlands International (Publication No. 46)/SRNyDS. 183–202.

Rodríguez, Rachel. 2002. Coordinator, Health Section, Sobrevivencia–Paraguay. Author interview. Campo Grande, Brazil, March 14.

Roett, Riordan, ed. 1999. *Mercosur: Regional Integration, World Markets*. Boulder: Lynne Rienner.

Ryan, Daniel. 2001. Assistant Executive Director, Foundation Ambiente y Recursos Naturales. Author interview. Buenos Aires, July 11.

Schaper, Marianne. 2002. *The Environmental Characteristics of South American Exports*. In Deere and Esty 2002. 247–58.

Smith, William C., and Roberto Patricio Korzeniewicz. 2007. Insiders, Outsiders, and the Politics of Civil Society. In *Governing the Americas: Assessing Multilateral Institutions*, ed. Jean-Phillipe Thérien, Gordon Mace, and Paul Haslam. Boulder: Lynne Rienner. 151–72.

Steel, Brent S., Richard L. Clinton, and Nicholas P. Lovrich, Jr. 2003. *Environmental Politics and Policy: A Comparative Approach*. Boston: McGraw-Hill.

Steinberg, Richard H. 1997. Trade-Environment Negotiations in the EU, NAFTA, and WTO: Regional Trajectories of Rule Development. *American Journal of International Law* 91, 2: 231–67.

Stevis, Dimitris, and Stephen Mumme. 2000. Rules and Politics in Regional Integration: Environmental Regulation in NAFTA and the EU. *Environmental Politics* 9, 4: 20–41.

Surroca, Carlos. 2001. Coordinator of International Programs, REDES/Amigos de la Tierra. Author interview. Montevideo, December 3.

Svirsky, Enrique, ed. 2002. *Entidades ambientalistas não-governamentais em conselhos do meio ambiente*. São Paulo: Secretaria de Estado do Meio Ambiente, Proaong.

Tussie, Diana. 2000. Introduction. In *The Environment and International Trade Negotiations: Developing Country Stakes*, ed. Tussie. New York: St. Martin's Press/International Development Research Centre. 1–9.

Tussie, Diana, and Patricia I. Vásquez. 1997. The FTAA, Mercosur, and the Environment. *International Environmental Affairs* 9, 3: 232–48.

———. 2000. Regional Integration and Building Blocks: The Case of Mercosur. In *The Environment and International Trade Negotiations: Developing Country Stakes*, ed. Tussie. New York: St. Martin's Press/International Development Research Centre. 187–203.

United Nations Development Program (UNDP). 2002. *Human Development Report 2002*. <http://www.undp.org/hdr2002>

Vara, Ana María. 2007. "Si a la Vida, No a las Papeleras". En Torno a una Controversia Ambiental Inédita en América Latina. *Redes* 12, 25: 15–49.

Weidner, Helmut, and Martin Janicke, eds. 2002. *Capacity Building in National Environmental Policy: A Comparative study of 17 Countries*. Berlin: Springer.